The Evolution
of Polo

ALSO BY HORACE A. LAFFAYE
AND FROM MCFARLAND

Profiles in Polo:
The Players Who Changed the Game (2007)

The Polo Encyclopedia (2004)

THE EVOLUTION OF POLO

Horace A. Laffaye

Foreword by Nigel à Brassard

McFarland & Company, Inc., Publishers
Jefferson, North Carolina, and London

Library of Congress Cataloguing-in-Publication Data

Laffaye, Horace A., 1935–
The evolution of polo / Horace A. Laffaye ;
foreword by Nigel à Brassard.
p.   cm.
Includes bibliographical references and index.

ISBN 978-0-7864-3814-3
softcover : 50# alkaline paper ∞

1. Polo — History.   2. Polo players — History.
I. À Brassard, Nigel   II. Title.
GV1011.L343   2009   796.353 — dc22   2009016337

British Library cataloguing data are available

Cover photograph: Billy and Bill Ylvisaker, Adie Von Gontard, Jr.,
and young Adie Von Gontard III before a practice game
in the 1970s (Museum of Polo and Hall of Fame)

Manufactured in the United States of America

*McFarland & Company, Inc., Publishers
Box 611, Jefferson, North Carolina 28640
www.mcfarlandpub.com*

To my wife, Martha

Table of Contents

***Between pages 126 and 127 are
eight color plates containing 17 photographs***

PART IV : THE PROFESSIONALS

Acknowledgments

Much of this book was written in the winter of 2008, at home in Wellington, Florida, the main center of polo in America, which provided a unique ambiance conducive to the arduous work of putting on paper thoughts and memories gathered during a lifetime of playing, watching and reading about the game.

This book has been a long journey. First of all, I wish to acknowledge the pioneer efforts of authorities like Maj. Gen. George Younghusband, who wrote the first book on the modern game, and Mr. James Moray Brown, the editor of the first genuine compendium of polo. After Mr. Moray Brown's premature death, the Rev. Thomas Dale carried on his work, both as editor of subsequent editions of the *Badminton Library* volume on polo and with his own writings, which culminated with the sumptuous *Polo at Home and Abroad*. Those early writers have marked the starting point for all subsequent polo historians.

I wish to thank in particular Mr. Nigel à Brassard, who went to considerable trouble on my behalf on several occasions and who kindly wrote the foreword for this book. Lady Susan Reeve was not only my most important link to South African polo, but she also became a friend and a constant source of support. Mr. James Ashton and Mrs. Rosemary Foot, Jim Ashton's children, kindly lent me photographs of their father and the Australian Goulburn polo team.

I am especially indebted to Mr. Chris Ashton for all the references from his magnificent *Geebung*. I could never hope to improve his prose; the only solution was to quote him if the chapters touching polo in Australia were to have more than a shade of authority. Mr. Roger Chatterton-Newman, once eminent editor of *Polo Quarterly International*, was ever willing to answer my multiple questions and to help when I sought assistance regarding fine points of the game in the British Isles.

I am greatly indebted to Mr. and Mrs. George DuPont for the freedom to use many photographs from the National Museum of Polo and Hall of Fame collection and for their invariably cordial welcome during my frequent visits to the museum. I would also add my gratitude to Alex Pacheco, a talented photographer, for taking some of the photographs for this book.

Dr. Alberto Pedro Heguy helped me understand a lot more about Argentine polo, especially the high-goal variety. A meeting with Alberto Pedro is on my agenda on every visit to Buenos Aires. Charles Llewellen Palmer was generous with time and effort, particularly so with regard to the 9th Lancers' and 10th Hussars' histories and his loan of photographs. Sinclair Hill shared his thoughts on contemporary polo through candid and extensive correspondence.

Miguel Novillo Astrada, polo player extraordinaire, voiced his opinions on the current polo scene in Argentina, England and the United States from a top professional player's point of view. During our long conversations, Miguel demonstrated a sharp intellect and a firm grasp of many issues confronting polo today. Fred Fortugno, wherever we met, was always a friend who went out of his way to help. I particularly remember him looking after Martha and me during our stay at Aiken.

To these names I must add my dear friend the late Thomas Burke Glynn. I was always amazed at his recall. His twinkling eyes and wonderful conversation are sorely missed.

Through the years, many personalities in the polo community have shared their thoughts on the game. All the outstanding players and observers of the game I met were remarkably patient with me, as well as providing entertaining and illuminating company. Thank you to: Mariano Aguerre, Dr. Enrique Braun Estrugamou, Dr. Alejandro Castro Almeyra, the late Carlos de la Serna, the late Heriberto Duggan, Norberto Fernández Moreno, the late Tommy Garrahan, Celestino Garrós, Juan Carlos Harriott, Jr., the late Horacio Heguy, Dr. Jorge MacDonough, David Miles, the late Dr. Emilio Montaña Cruz, John Nelson, Alfonso, Alvaro, Gonzalo and Paul Pieres, Dr. Ernesto Pinto, the late Dr. Eduardo Pondé, Jorge Torres Zavaleta and Marcos Uranga, in Argentina.

In Australia: Patrick and Jo Dawkins, Leonard Hamersley, and Nigel and Mollie Lacey. In England: Hugh and Margie Brett, Buff and Liza Crisp, Tony and Jill Emerson, Tony and Jean Lacey, Mrs. Lucy Lewis, the late Nigel Miskin, David and Mary Ann Wingfield and Col. David Woodd. In the United States: Santiago "Tato" Alvarez, Dennis Amato, Sebastián Amaya, Lester "Red" Armour, Bruce Balding, the late Alan Corey, Russell Corey, John Goodman, Carlos Gracida, Julian Hipwood, Skey and Gill Johnston, Nick Manifold, Peter Orthwein, Steve Orthwein, Peter Rizzo, Raúl Roldán, Frédéric Roy, the late Bob Skene, Charles Smith, Mike Teitelbaum, Alex Webbe, Bill Whitehead, and Paul and Sheldon Withers.

I hasten to add that I have had help from a large number of persons, including the staff at the Pequot Library in Southport and Fairfield University's DiMenna-Nyselius Library, both in Connecticut. Many others, not named, have assisted me; I hope they will not be offended if they are not in the list. I also wish to thank collectors of polo art who allowed items in their collections to serve as illustrations in this work, many of which have not been published before. I must respect their wish to remain anonymous. My appreciation to Sonja Norgaard for allowing me to use one of her photographs.

A word of appreciation to my habitual companions in watching games at Palm Beach: Peter and Elisabeth Grace, Robert and Mary Ann Mountford, John and Marilyn Perakos, and Frank and Trude Vlahovic. They always offer interesting conversation and thoughtful insights about the game. My long-time coworker, Mrs. Marge Hickey, was once more recalled to editing duties. Thanks to her for a superior job, as always.

Finally, a word of thanks to my father, one of those among the polo-playing band of *estancieros* of an age gone by, who taught me, among a host of other things, how to appreciate this great game.

The support and encouragement of my family were essential. I am especially indebted to our son, Patrick, who prepared the photographs and illustrations and helped with the production of the final manuscript, and to our daughter, Gisèle, for her search of books and other printed material. I am deeply grateful to my wife, Martha, for her patience and help in providing a household atmosphere conducive to creative writing. Without her help, this or any other book I have written would not have been completed.

Foreword

by Nigel à Brassard

This book, which I warmly commend to all lovers of the game of polo, tells the story of how the game has evolved over the centuries. The tale is a magisterial account of the game sweeping down the centuries and criss-crossing continents.

Dr. Horace A. Laffaye is arguably the greatest ever authority on the history of polo and is also an acute commentator on the modern game. I will never forget when I recommended a researcher at the Public Record Office in London to Dr. Laffaye. The researcher, with a mixture of admiration and gentle despair, remarked to me on Dr. Laffaye's tireless pursuit of accuracy. This attention to accuracy and detail is one of the hallmarks of this scholarly work.

This book is the fifth that Dr. Laffaye has written about polo. Each is distinguished by being authoritative and comprehensive and by demonstrating the incisive insights of someone who has a deep love and knowledge of the game.

In some ways this book shows that no sport has changed so much as polo. Yet it might also be said that no game has seemed to change so little. Certain aspects of the game — a mounted player trying to hit a ball through a pair of goal posts — have remained constant. And yet, as Dr. Laffaye chronicles, so many aspects of the game have changed, often reflecting the community in which the game was played. The contrasts between the army officers who first brought polo to Britain, the amateurs of the inter-war years, and the modern day professionals could not be more marked. I detect who I think Dr. Laffaye's heroes might be.

Most sports and games have writers that are indelibly associated with their character and essence. One thinks of Bernard Darwin on golf, George Plimpton and Norman Mailer on boxing, John Updike and Roger Angell on baseball and C.L.R. James and Neville Cardus on cricket. I believe that polo has now found its own distinctive voice: a voice that combines an encyclopedic knowledge of the game's development and its characters, and the lucid examination of the vagaries of the modern game. Polo is truly lucky to have found someone with the knowledge, understanding and passion that Dr. Laffaye has for this the greatest of games.

London, June 2009

Nigel à Brassard plays polo at Cirencester Park and is patron of the Courtenay and Band of Gypsies polo teams. He is captain of the Bucks Club Polo Team and a member of the Hurlingham Club, a member of the Finance and Grants Committee of the Hurlingham Polo Association, an ambassador of the Federation of International Polo and a director of Cirencester Park Polo Club.

1

Preface

This book traces the development of polo from its origins as a folk game played by tribesmen in Asia to the current crop of professional players. It was with a mixture of relish and reverence that I approached writing this work. Relish because of the enjoyment that research gives me; reverence because the chronicle of polo abounds with human elements that reflect the best in mankind: honor, competition, achievement, friendship. I hasten to add that in spite of occasional bouts of hero worship, the overall attitude is more analytical than reverential. Based upon newly found documentation, several episodes in the game's history that over the years have been taken at face value are vigorously challenged.

This book is intended to evoke a certain classical tradition and respect for the game's heritage. Polo is a game that started centuries ago in the rugged landscape of central Asia and now has spread throughout the world. It is played by men, women and children, mounted on true ponies and thoroughbred racehorses, on dusty paddocks and green fields, on bare grounds and in large stadiums. The competition might be for a priceless trophy or just to enjoy the pleasure of play, but the intensity and the will to win are equal.

At its most basic, polo is a simple game, and that is one of its attractions. A group of players of any age, strength and degree of skill can have fun scrambling around on a ground, occasionally bumping into each other, just trying to hit a ball through a pair of goal posts. No sporting pastime could be so elemental and so easy to enjoy. Therefore, it is inconceivable that a single individual invented such a game as polo. There is, however, a huge difference when comparing polo to other games: the horse. What separates polo from other ball games is the equine component.

Another of the game's allurements is that its art and skills can take a lifetime to learn and appreciate. How and when to turn on the ball; the multiple angles that come into play in a knock-in; the right time to leave the ball and take the player, the lovely arc of the ball when a powerful hitter smacks a penalty shot: every one of these requires time to absorb and enjoy. It is time well spent.

Much polo history that concentrates on matches won and lost most likely shows only a limited sense of how the game was developed, particularly within a sociological context. This book consists of much more than games lost and won. While not stingy on the detail of which teams played, who won, who lost and why, it is also a social narrative as seen through the filter of time. It intends to provide a sense of the varied and fascinating human environment in which polo developed through centuries of ups and downs. It is a story of hills and valleys about a game played on a surface as flat as a billiard table. It is less history, more of an evocative essay. This portrait of polo perhaps has extra passion because the game was a giant in my childhood memories. Polo literature and art reflects the way the game has changed. Thus, several mentions are devoted to the written word and the plastic arts to examine the game's evolution through the passage of time as seen by gifted writers and artists.

Evolution means change, but people — especially older gentlemen — are by nature reluctant to change, with the notable exception of those who are endeavoring to modify and improve things. The ruling hierarchies of polo have always been conservative in their approach to new ideas. In spite of such attitude, probably the only thing that has not changed in centuries is the width of the goal, which still is 24 feet, or 7.30 meters between the goal posts. Another thing that is still the same is a player's emotions when he misses the ball.

The game of polo has changed significantly in many aspects. Just as Americans were prepared to use sports as a metaphor for life and Britons took games along another path, treating simple pastimes not as games but as a sort of moral improvement, the current reality in many games, including polo, is the massive investment of money. Sports and games have become more entertainment than pastime, at least at the top level.

This work is not a history of the game. The definitive history of polo remains to be written and it will probably be a massive, multi-authored work. This book tries to be analytical, often judgmental, in looking at how powerful men and institutions tended to modify things, but more often remained immobile in the quagmire of tradition and fear of change. In spite of that conservative attitude, or perhaps because of it, change has occurred. However, it was usually individuals who spearheaded revolution, not institutions.

Special attention is given to the changes that have occurred in the last century, in tactics developed by thoughtful thinkers and applied by outstanding teams in their quest for success, mostly through trial and error. The evolution of the laws, from mobs engaged in a free-for-all melee to the current free flowing and largely open, speedy game, is also a subject of curious attention. Folk games were subject to a sort of common law, a *lex non scripta*. Nowadays, most rules read like a legal treatise.

Finally, the development of that imprescriptible companion, the polo pony, merits a description in some detail. *Equus caballus* is the animal force that nicely complements the graceful rider and classic striker of the ball. The symbiosis of man and mount contributes to make the ancient pastime of polo the most elegant of games. It always was, and it shall remain so forever.

PART I : THE TRIBESMEN

1. Folk Games: From the Silk Road to the Manipuri Valleys

Polo has continued its ceaseless gallop into the future. From the dim, impenetrable recesses of time, the mounted figure of this sport came cantering into the pages of our first histories and has gone swinging along ever since, side by side with the march of man, oblivious to changing fashions and changing nations, remaining always the calm patrician of sport. — Robert F. Kelley[1]

The origins of the game of polo are shrouded in the mist of history. China, Iran, Manipur, Mongolia, Pakistan, and Tibet all claim to be the birthplace of polo. It can be safely assumed that it began as a simple folk game played by the nomadic tribes in central Asia. Westward and eastward expansion followed, to Byzantium and China, most likely along the trail of the legendary Silk Road. Southwards, the game moved into Tibet, India, Assam, Manipur and Burma, now Myanmar. As to the word *polo*, it derives from the Tibetan po-lo or po-long, in reference to a ball made of willow, but also applied to the playing field or the game itself.

Ancient folk games, precursors of many modern sports, were characterized by several different factors, regardless of whether the mode was equestrian or pedestrian. There was wide variation regarding the number of participants, the ground's size and shape, the amusement's time span, and its regulations. Folk games were a deeply ingrained custom in most communities. A form of lacrosse among Native Americans, knappan in Pembrokeshire, Shrovetide football in Ashbourne, hurling in southwest England and Ireland, golfing precursors such as pall-mall and kolf in Europe, mounted games in Asia and, more recently, the game of pato in South America had a large following, either as spectators or participants. It was usual for most of a village's inhabitants to show up for the game.

Dunning and Sheard in their *Barbarians, Gentlemen and Players*, a seminal work on rugby football's sociology, quote Sir Richard Carew: "There was also a rudimentary division of labour within each team into which Carew, using a contemporary military analogy, called a 'fore-ward,' a 'rere-ward,' and two 'wings.'"[2] Sir Richard also mentioned a division into players on horseback and players on foot. This is interesting sociologically since it suggests that in these folk pastimes, elements of what were later to become separate games — in this case, hurling and polo — were rolled together in a single whole.[3]

The rules of folk games were unwritten and quite simple; they were consuetudinary or common law, legitimized by oral tradition and enforced by the participants themselves. They were also characterized by numerous variations based upon regional structures, such as the ball's size and shape, or in the case of more gruesome games, the animal carcass used as the token, be it a duck, or a headless goat or calf.

There was wide variation regarding the field of play. The existing polo ground at Shardu, in Baluchistan — a state between Afghanistan and Pakistan — that dates back several centuries is quite narrow and its four sides are bordered by stone walls. At the other end of the spectrum, if two villages competed, the grounds would be the land between the two towns; the winners were the ones who took the ball — or goat — to the opposing village.

Folk games were firmly entrenched in many societies. Proficiency in these primitive games was rewarded with a higher social status and perhaps even an early form of hero-worship. Throughout the game's early stages, the important thing was participation, either in active form, or vicariously as passive players or just interested spectators. Only two aspects seem to have been relatively constant: one was the manner of starting a game, usually the ball being thrown up in the air by a strong individual, and the second was related to a goal and, therefore, a determination of a winner.

In the case of polo's predecessors, the humble folk game eventually enjoyed royal patronage. The earliest written mention of the game in a 7th century work[4] appears to confirm that the first patrons of polo were the rulers of the Parthian dynasty, who were in power from 247 B.C.E. until 224 C.E. The royal support of polo was continued in Persia by the Turkic and Mongol rulers in the 11th century. Members of the Safanid dynasty, who ruled Persia after the Mongols, were reported by the English traveler Sir Anthony Shirley as superior polo players.[5] The game then went into a decline until the waning years of the 19th century, when two other Englishmen, Sir Horace Rumbold and Maj. Percy Molesworth Sykes, later Brig. Gen. Sir Percy Sykes, brought the modern version of the game to Persia.

From central Asia, the game of polo initially spread both eastward and westward. To the west, it was carried through the empire of Byzantium to Constantinople, now Istanbul, where it was played during the 4th century. Emperor Theodosius II, who ruled from 408 to 450, had a stadium — *tzykanistérion* — constructed within the Constantinople Grand Palace's walls for better enjoyment of the game, a plan of which is illustrated in Carl Diem's book.[6]

Emperor Manuel I Comnenos (ruled 1143–1180) was an ardent supporter of polo. A description of a game is given by Johannes Cinnamus, who wrote about it in 1190.[7] Two teams played with a leather ball the size of an apple. The sticks ended with a hoop, to which was attached a net of strings, resembling a racket. Interestingly enough, a similar instrument was used in Japan, which is difficult to explain because of the long distance involved. In no other Asiatic region was the game played with such equipment.

From Persia the ancient game was imported into Baghdad, Damascus and Egypt around 800 C.E., while Saladin (r. 1169–1193), the Crusaders' feared adversary, was known to be a polo enthusiast. In the Arabian work *History of the Mameluke Sultans in Egypt* by Take-Eddin-Ahmed-Makrizi, there is a lengthy note about those rulers and their involvement with polo.[8] It is intriguing that the Arabs who invaded Spain did not bring the game along with their magnificent horses.

These early forms of polo only had a remote resemblance to the modern game. In a variation known as Buzkashi, there were hundreds of participants, the winner being the horseman who had the courage to get hold of a headless goat by a leg and carry the carcass away from the pack. In another form similar to the modern game, the teams could be formed by up to 1,000 horsemen each, and the round ball, the *gui*, was the size of a man's head. At both ends of the ground, there were stone pillars as goals. The ball was hit at with a wooden stick, called *chowgān*—the game's name in Persian language—and the game continued until the ball was destroyed. The oldest existing goal posts, dating from the 17th century, which are located in the central square—Naghsh-é-Jahan—in Isfahan, Iran, are 24 feet wide, precisely the distance formulated in the current laws of the game. They are made of stone, seven feet high, topped by a design resembling a bishop's miter.

The second oldest goals are located in India, near the city of Bidar, some 80 miles northwest of Hyderabad. It has been estimated that they are at least 380 years old. The two sets of stone goal posts are seven and a half feet high with a circular base five feet, six inches in diameter, from which pillars rise. The distance between the bases is 11 feet, and between the sides of the pillars, 13 feet. They are, then, approximately half the width of Isfahan's goalposts. The ground's length between the posts is about 500 yards, precisely 407 paces as measured by Leslie M. Crump, an official at The Residency in Hyderabad, who reported his findings in *The Polo Monthly*.[9] They are set in an east-west direction, which was the goals' traditional setting. The ground's width was estimated to be less than 200 yards, based upon the location of some buildings. This disproportion is not surprising, because it mirrors the smaller grounds in northern India and Pakistan, where the narrow valleys mandated such configuration.

Local tradition is that this is the polo ground of the Bahmani kings. The tradition is that when Kasim Barid, who was the Barid dynasty's first ruler succeeding the Bahmanis (he did not take the title shah), began to look for a site for his tomb, he chose a place overlooking the polo ground so that even in death he might watch the game he loved so well. This appears to be the reason why his tomb, and that of his successor, Ali Barid Shah, are not enclosed by a wall like those of the Bahmanis, but were constructed with open arches. Mr. Crump wrote: "The names of Kasim Barid and Ali Barid Shah, who were both buried so as to overlook their polo ground, deserve enshrining in the roll of polo enthusiasts."[10]

The exact date of the polo field and posts cannot be determined. The Barid kings ruled Bidar from 1487 until 1619. The game was taken with the Mohammedan invasion that captured the city of Gulburga in 1323 and in 1347 established the Bahmanis, who later transferred the capital to Bidar. If this is an accurate assumption, the goalposts date back 650 years, and if constructed by the latest Barids, they are 380 years old.

The game's progress eastwards, towards the Celestial Empire, Indochina, Korea and Japan, was most likely along the Silk Road. According to Edward Parker, polo was introduced into China by the Tartars. Professor Parker states that the earliest specific mention of polo dates to the year 710, when the emperor assembled his courtiers at a retreat known as the Pear Orchard.[11, 12] Under the T'ang dynasty (618–907), polo benefited from imperial benevolence and several rulers were practitioners of the game, especially Ming Huan, who was mentioned as infatuated with the sport. The artist Li Kung-lin depicted him playing polo with his notorious consort Yang Kuei-fei. His devotion to polo is also remembered in a poem, which disloyally also mentions his return to the palace from a game under the influence of drink.

An article in the October 1903 issue of the *Asiatic Quarterly Review* mentions moon sticks or clubs used in the game, an obvious reference to the early polo mallets illustrated in the *Badminton Library* volume on polo.[13] By then the game was more organized. The teams aligned about 16 players each, while the targets were named east and west goals. Gongs were sounded to signal that a goal had been scored.

Besides the dangers inherent in a vigorous pastime, polo carried other unexpected risks. Emperor T'ai Tsu of the Posterior Liang dynasty (907–921) became rather upset after one of his relatives had a fall and was killed. The enraged ruler had all participants in the game, friend and foe alike, executed without further ado. During the Song dynasty (960–1279), Confucian scholars articulated their doubts about the game of polo: "Polo is akin to heavy drinking, gambling, popular music, licentious conduct, and other forms of immoral activities."[14] *Plus ça change, plus c'est la même chose.*

The Juche or Nüchên (early Manchus) emperors who succeeded the Cathayans and who are mentioned by Marco Polo under the name Chorené are frequently described in Chinese history as players of polo. The Mongols, who were great falconers and archers, are not mentioned as polo players; neither is the Ming Chinese dynasty (1368–1644) that in turn deposed the Mongols.

The rules of the game demanded that the ball should be struck only when galloping—beware current proponents of tapping the ball at a walk—and the game was subject to a certain unspoken etiquette rather than a written code. Etiquette is a much more controlling power in Eastern culture than all regulations in Western societies. Breakage of the unwritten but customary laws was met by scorn. At times, it was customary to allow one player, unimpeded, to throw the ball in the air in the middle of the field and to hit it towards the opposing goal. A witness relates a case in which one player disobeyed the code of conduct, hustling the hitter, only to be met by verbal abuse from other players and the spectators' jeers.[15]

In 727, a match was played at the court of Japan's emperor. It was a different version, with seven-a-side players, each team distinguished by red or white badges. However, the difference was that each player had a similar colored ball in his racket; the object was to throw each ball into a net. When one side netted seven balls, the game's second phase began. A paper ball covered with bamboo fiber was thrown into the ground and both teams endeavored to place the ball through a one foot, two inch hole in a board, five feet from the ground, thus winning the game, which was restricted to no more than half an hour. A modern version is still played in the city of Hachino-he.[16] Mika Mori has recorded in her book on Japanese polo that Persian ponies were imported to Japan by Shogun Tokugawa Yoshimune, who ruled from 1716 until 1745.[17]

Polo arrived in India from Persia with the Mughal conquerors in the 13th century and became quite fashionable at the court of the emperors. Akbar the Great (1542–1605) was considered to be an outstanding polo player; whether this is true or just a form of flattery, it will never be known. It is also reported that Akbar enjoyed playing polo at night, with a ball made of *Butea frondosa* (Flame of the Forest) wood, which is very light and burns slowly for a long period of time. No mention is made of any damage to the mallets.[18] Akbar's principal polo ground was located at Gharíwálí, some four miles from Agra—the Taj Mahal's site—and later at Nagarchin, also located close to Agra. There is an often-reproduced scene of Akbar playing with his courtiers.[19] Moray Brown notes that the artist must have been a conscientious Muslim because he strictly followed the Koran's precepts, which forbid the depiction of features; in the drawing, the faces of both men and horses are left blank.

It is a worrisome fact that polo is a dangerous game. In a back lane in Lahore's Anarkalli bazaar there is a small monument, the grave of Sultan Kutub-ud-Din Aibak, better known as the builder of the Kutub Tower at Delhi, who in 1206 died as the result of a polo accident. History says he received fatal injuries from violent contact with his saddle. Sultan Kutub's death was one of earliest recorded fatalities on a polo grounds.

The game gradually disappeared from the main Indian scene. By the mid–19th century, it was played in two widely distant locations: in the upper Indus valley, in remote areas such as Baltistan, Chitral, Gilgit and Ladakh, and in Manipur, a small state tucked between Assam and Burma. It is to Manipur that our story will move on later.

There are many mentions of the game of polo in ancient literature. Firdusi,[20] in his epic poem *Shâhnámah*, as well as Mahmoud Arifi in his *Book of Ecstasy*, also known as *The Ball and the Polo Stick*, repeatedly used metaphors to emphasize their writing. Abul Fazl, Emperor Akbar's court historiographer, extolled polo's virtues as a means of learning promptitude and decision, as well as a test of a man's value and courage. In the celebrated *Arabian Nights*, polo is the subject of two stories. Nizami, a Persian poet, describes how the beautiful Shirin, wife of Khusrau Parviz, together with her ladies-in-waiting, played a game against the king and his courtiers: "Seventy maidens like lionesses presented themselves before Shirin, all blazing with ardor. The maidens were seated in their saddles like cypresses. They all had moonlike faces veiled, and thus proceeded into the Shah's presence. The king of kings was overcome at seeing them."

There are many examples of early polo depicted in Oriental paintings and sculptures. Some of the best known is a series of murals in the tomb of Li Sieng of the T'ang dynasty.[21] There are twenty-two murals, of which five are depictions of the game of polo. These murals are cultural relics that provide contemporary evidence of the life and customs of the time. Li Sieng was the son of Emperor Kao Tsung and his wife Empress Wu Tse-tien, and was named crown prince. Described as licentious and depraved, he was stripped of all rank and status for plotting to seize power. Li Sieng died a commoner in 684. In 706, his remains were interred in an attendant tomb in his parents' mausoleum and posthumously he was given the title Crown Prince Chang Huai.

Both the British Museum and the Field Museum in Chicago have in exhibition sculptures of Chinese women indulging in polo, and several terra cottas have been found of women players in China. Most of them carry no mallet, perhaps because its use was explicitly understood. There is a bas-relief of two polo players in a temple in Indochina, illustrated in Carl Diem's book.

Firdusi was the pen name of Abul Kasim Mansur[22]; his work *Shâhnámah* (Epic of Kings) was illustrated with a rendition of Síawusch, the story's hero, who astonishes Afrásiáb, a semi-mythical king of Scythia, with his skills at polo. The manuscript in the British Museum depicts Afrásiáb in the left top corner, with an attendant carrying an umbrella for royal protection from the sun. Síawusch, his son-in-law, wearing the royal plume in his turban, appears in the right top. He is mounted on a bay pony, while his opponent is on a white and orange horse with a red mane and tail. The goalposts are also pictured, as well as the mallets. These must have been rather fragile, for there are mallet-carrying attendants on foot. The horses are shown with small heads, tapering muzzles, round quarters and high tails that betray their Eastern origin.

2. An Ancient Pastime Discovered by Western Eyes

The evolution and development of polo is the work of able men who have risen up from time to time in the history of the game. Dimly across the long expanse of centuries, we see the form of Siawusch, half-mythical, half-historical, yet the first of the series of great polo captains and makers of the game. —The Rev. Thomas F. Dale[1]

The tiny eastern Indian state of Manipur is located between Cachar to the west and Myanmar to the east. It enjoyed a semi-independent status until 1949, when it became part of the newly independent India. During the mid-nineteenth century, because of a tense political situation, numerous Manipuris settled in the border region of Cachar and in Cachar proper. It was in this remote area that Lieutenant Joseph Ford Sherer, adjutant of the Sylhet Light Infantry, first witnessed a game named *sagol kanjai* (*sagol*, horse; *kanjai*, hockey stick) played by the local people. It was a popular and rough pastime: usually seven players, mounted on 12-hand or so ponies (one hand equals four inches) strove to hit a wooden ball past the backlines of a rectangular field of play. The barefooted players wore turbans, secured by a strap, dhotis (a long cotton loincloth), leg-guards, and sleeveless jackets, always either yellow or red. There were no officials, with the single exception of a fellow on foot known as Huntre-Hunba, wearing a white dhoti, kurta costume and a light turban. His only function was to throw the ball in the air between the players in a line-up while shouting "huntre." After that, it was a chaotic situation. It was permissible for the players to pick up the ball with the hand, toss it in the air unimpeded, and smack it forwards, a practice reminiscent of the game of hurling, already in vogue in Ireland. There was another custom, which has remained as part of the laws of the game until these days: after a goal was scored, the teams changed ends.

Lieutenant Sherer, just like hundreds of thousands ever since, was smitten. Along the chain of command, Sherer reported to Capt. Robert Stewart, who was the deputy commissioner in Silchar, Cachar's capital. These two officers joined some of the tea planters in the district, who had seen the game as far back as 1854, in some impromptu matches. They are the first recorded Englishmen to play the game, which they called hockey on ponies. In typical British fashion, these pioneers decided to start a polo club and accordingly, the Silchar Kangjai Club was started in March 1859 at a meeting that took place in Stewart's bungalow. On the occasion, the following were elected to membership in addition to Captain Stewart

10

and Lieutenant Sherer: James Abernethy of Hailakandi, Arthur Brownlow of Hailakandi Valley, James Davidson of Soubong, Ernest Eckhardt of Silkuri, Julius Sandeman of Chutla Bheel, J.P. Stuart of Larsingah and W. Walker of Bograhagt. Thus, unhonored and unsung — indeed, almost unknown — as one writer has it, the first club to play the game of polo was organized in a remote outpost of the British Empire.[2] Four years later, an unknown hand drafted the first written rules of the game for the Silchar Club. (See Appendix 1.)

Two years later, Captain Eustace Hill, 3rd Native Infantry, saw the game in Cachar, got the details from Sherer, and started the game in Dacca, where his unit, the Lahore Light Horse — a regiment of East Indians, disbanded in 1865 — was stationed. In the meantime, some merchants traveling to Cachar from Calcutta (now Kolkata) saw the game and decided to give it a go. In September 1862, Lt. George Stewart (later major general) visited his brother Robert, now Cachar's commissioner, and saw the game as played by British planters and Manipuris.[3] Taking with him some sticks and balls, Lt. Stewart

Maj. Gen. Joseph Sherer earned his sobriquet "Father of English Polo" for his pioneer efforts in Cachar, Calcutta and Manipur. To quote Gilbert and Sullivan, Joe Sherer was the very model of a major general, as far as polo is concerned (Museum of Polo and Hall of Fame).

returned to Barrackpore, where he was stationed, and founded a club where practice games had taken place for a few months, when the game was picked up by some residents from Calcutta under the leadership of Mr. C.B. Stewart, a well-known local sportsman. Practice games were also held on the parade ground in Ballygunge, one of Calcutta's suburbs.

The first formal match was played on the Calcutta Maidan early in 1863, between the Barrackpore Club and the Calcutta Club. Maj. Gen. George Stewart wrote: "The only members of the Barrackpore Club I remember were, besides myself, Colonel Arthur Broome, Bengal Cavalry; the late Colonel J. [John Howard] Broome, 2nd Punjab Cavalry; the Hon. R. [Robert] Napier (the present Lord Napier); Colonel [William Wynne] Apperley, late 15th Bengal Cavalry; a veterinary surgeon of the name of Farrell, and a Captain King, since deceased. The Calcutta players were chiefly merchants, one of whom went by the name of 'Bobby Hills,' a little fellow, I think a relation of the General [Sir James] Hills who was in Kabul with Roberts."[4]

There is also a report that in 1862, during the Christmas Race Week in Calcutta, polo was played in public for the first time.[5] Rapidly, the game became popular, and in April 1863, another club was founded, the Calcutta Hockey Club, still extant as the oldest polo club, its colors red with a white sash. Among the initial members were C.B. Stewart, R.S. Hills (the Bobby Hills of the Rugby School cricket eleven of 1855), John Thomas, Elliott Angelo, and Col. Richard Beadon.[6]

Then, in March 1864, Lt. Sherer brought over to Calcutta a team of Manipuris known as the Band of Brothers, along with their nifty ponies. The players were Tullain Sing, Chowba Sing, Anon Sing, Omah Sing, Tubal, Attomba and Monge Pa. The Manipuris created a grand sensation with their high saddles, leg guards, bridles ornamented with shells, rope reins, and diminutive ponies. There is no record of the Calcutta team; however, there is a photograph of the original members in 1863, identified as Colin Smith, Duncan Stewart, R.E. Goolden, D.G. Landale, R.S. Hills, Elliott Angelo, John Thomas, W. Blandford, Montague Champneys, Lewis Pugh Evans, Capt. Cross and Capt. Howe Frederick Showers.[7] After the game was over, the cagey Manipuris sold their ponies, presumably for good prices. Some of the ponies were still played on Edward, Prince of Wales's visit in 1875.

As it was, during the match the small Manipuri ponies ran circles around the bigger Indian mounts; the final score is not recorded. When later on Sherer took his team to Imphal, Manipur's capital, to play against local teams, the visitors were unable to win a single match. While in Calcutta, Sherer was given a dinner at the Indigo Club, during which he was presented a silver tankard and salver, as well as the title by which he was hence known, "Joe Sherer, The Father of English Polo." His portrait, bearing that inscription, hung in the Retreat Club in Silchar.

More than 100 years later, the portrait was re-discovered by Captain John Tessier-Yandell while on a temporary posting in Silchar. In the Retreat Club's bar, an old picture caught his attention. A tarnished silver plaque informed that was presented by Lt. J.E. [sic] Madden in 1898, and further examination of the frame and printed matter below disclosed the subject's name.[8] The captain's musings were interrupted by his wife's return from the club's store, an old polo ball in her hand. It was made of bamboo root, the last polo ball from the first polo club. The ball was eventually presented to Prince Philip of Edinburgh, mounted on a plinth, and in turn presented by him to the Calcutta Polo Club as the Sherer Trophy, first played for on 22 December 1973. This is how Capt. Tessier-Yandell began his quest for more information on Lt. Sherer; he eventually became the authority on this polo pioneer. The profile that follows is largely taken from his thorough research. Poignantly, Capt. Tessier-Yandell relates how, standing in that dusty and ghost-ridden club in Cachar, he lifted his glass to Joseph Sherer, now rescued from oblivion.[9]

Joseph Ford Sherer was born at sea on 12 April 1829, the son of Lt. George Moyle Sherer — later Maj. Gen. Sir George Sherer, K.C.S.I.[10] — and Jane Baillie, daughter of Maj. Gen. Sir Joseph O'Halloran, Bengal Army. Young Joe was nominated to a cadetship in the East India Company and was commissioned on 10 December 1847. Soon after, he sailed for India and was posted to the 49th Bengal Native Infantry Regiment. Shortly after joining, he was involved in the Second Sikh War, being rewarded with a medal and campaign clasp. Promoted to lieutenant in 1851, Sherer became qualified in Hindustani, Assamese and Bengali; obviously, the young officer had a facility for languages. Three years later Lt. Sherer was posted to the Sylhet Light Infantry and was appointed as the regiment's adjutant eleven months later. Sherer saw duty during the Indian Mutiny, receiving another medal. His aptitude for skirmish warfare came to his superiors' attention and he returned to Assam's Cachar District as commandant of the Kookee Levy, in addition to the post of assistant superintendent of the district. It was then, in 1859, that Sherer was one of the founders of the first polo club, Silchar. Sherer was responsible for the new game's organization and promotion in both Cachar and Calcutta. Joseph Sherer had married at Simla, on 10 October 1853, Charlotte Catherine Goldney, seven years younger than the groom.

In 1858, the British Crown had assumed responsibility for all the territories previously administered by the East India Company, popularly referred to as "John's Company," and a large number of officers were left without an appointment. Sherer then joined the non-regimental Staff Corps in 1865 with the rank of captain. He continued to serve mainly in Assam, steadily rising through the ranks: major in 1867, lieutenant colonel in 1873, and colonel in 1879, retiring in 1883 with the rank of major general. His last mention in the *London Gazette* appears in 1899 with the official announcement of his appointment as additional commissioner for land taxes "for the Town and Port of Hastings and the liberties thereof." The name Joseph F. Sherer then sinks back into the obscurity of a life serving Crown and country, but it remains a bright star on polo's firmament.[11] Robert Stewart, arguably the first English polo player, died in retirement in 1885.

An unsigned article was published in *Baily's Magazine* in 1875 stating, "Polo has been played in India by both European officers and native irregular cavalry for the last thirty years, and General Outram, Brigadier Mayne, Colonel Skinner, Major Nightingale, and the Scinde Horse, Hodson's Irregulars, and Fane's Seikhs [*sic*] were all adepts in the game."[12]

Skinner's Horse, Central India Horse, Scinde Horse, and the 19th Lancers—originally Fane's Horse—achieved fame and glory as polo playing regiments. However, there is no record of Gen. George Outram, Brig. Henry Mayne, Col. James "Old Sekunder" Skinner or Maj. Arthur Nightingale, all distinguished soldiers during the Indian Mutiny, ever playing polo, certainly not in 1845.

Returning to the game's unabated growth in India, in 1862 polo was brought to Punjab and the Northwest Provinces by the previously mentioned Lt. George Stewart of the Guide's Corps. Stewart not only started the game in Barrackpore, but also in Cawnpore, Lahore and later, in Peshawar, where a variation of Manipuri origin was already in vogue under the name *kàn-jai bazèè* (*kàn-jai*, hockey stick; *bazèè*, game). By 1863, polo had been started in Burma at Tonzang by British officers stationed in that remote outpost, located just south of Manipur.

The game was also introduced at Hazaribagh, India, about 1862, as a side effect of an unusual occurrence. Kaifa Singh and Konai Singh, two princes of the blood, had been deported to Hazaribagh because of their intrigues against the rajah of Manipur. Some of his attendants followed the princes, and as most Manipuris look upon their ponies and their sticks as precious possessions, they took them in their exile. Their pastime soon caught the Europeans' attention and polo took off. The Manipuris' attachment to ponies is supported by a record of a player pawning his wife in order to purchase an expensive pony.[13]

During the summer of 1864, Captain Alexander Kinloch, Rifle Brigade,[14] saw the game in Srinagar, where the Rajah of Kashmir had constructed a field 350 yards long by 60 yards in width, and took polo to his garrison city of Meerut, where both the Rifle Brigade and the 19th Hussars took it up. Shortly after, the 54th Foot (Devonshire) Regiment was reckoned to be on top of the heap at the time. In 1868, a big leap took the game from Calcutta across the subcontinent to Bombay (now Mumbai). The messenger was Mr. Walter Crum and the first members were John G. Anderson, Stephen E. "Spider" Atkinson, C. Gaddum, Donald Graham, a Mr. Peel and T. Taylor.[15] Thus, by 1870, the game had spread all over India. Indigo planters in Behar and Tirhoot gave impetus to polo in those areas. It was also played in Madras and Lower Bengal.

However, the real push was given by the cavalry regiments, both British and those from the Army-in-India. The 10th Hussars, about which more anon, were deployed to India in the

"Mean Meer" March 1875.

" Tommy - Atkins "
"Rock"

An unidentified early polo player in India, his pony Tommy Atkins and his dog Rock. The photograph was taken in Meean Meer, a small cantonment near Lahore, in March 1875. The player is wearing white long pants, a common attire for polo in tropical climates. Potted plants, the stone pillar, and a dog allowed to rest in the middle of the drive are reminders of faraway England (private collection).

winter of 1872. Having been the pioneers of the game in England, they took polo into India with gusto. The 10th showed for the first time that bigger ponies were better that the small Arabs or country-bred ponies. On their way south, the 54th Devonshires, who had defeated all their opponents, passed through Muttra, where the 10th Hussars were quartered, and proceeded to challenge them to a polo game. The 54th were mounted on small ponies, 12.3 hands, and when Thomas St. Quintin pointed out to their captain that it was unfair that 10th had big ponies, measuring 13.2 hands, he laughed and stated that the big ponies could not turn as quickly as the small ones, as had been the case in Calcutta almost a decade before.[16] In the event, the big ponies held the advantage, galloping faster and riding off the smaller ones. The game became so one-sided that they mixed players from both teams to make it an even and enjoyable contest.

A turning point in the game's evolution had been reached: in polo, larger ponies were faster and stronger than their smaller brethren. In spite of such obvious fact, it took more than 30 years for the ruling bodies in Britain and India to abolish height restrictions, although the limit was 13.3 hands and was later increased to 14.2 hands. It is difficult to say how strictly the measurement rule was applied in India. There are many references to the fact that the rule was observed more in its breakage than in its compliance. In some tournaments, there were some attempts to measure ponies, but mounts of any size were ridden. A wag observed that some ponies would put a cavalry charger to shame.[17]

The ponies themselves knew the truth. A keen observer of the game, Rudyard Kipling wrote, "They're chargers — cavalry chargers!' said Kittiwynk indignantly, 'They'll never see thirteen three again.' 'They've all been fairly measured and they've all got their certificates,' said the Maltese Cat, 'or they wouldn't be here. We must take things as they come along, and keep our eyes on the ball.'"[18]

In another tournament all the ponies were measured, with four of the largest excluded, but on second try they were allowed to play. Somehow, they became smaller. Some ponies were taught to splay their forelegs, so a few centimeters were saved when under the official measurer's bar. The height limit was mentioned in both the United States and Argentina's rules of the game, but it was totally ignored in practice.

The 10th Hussars' great adversaries in England, the 9th Lancers, were posted to India in 1875, and their rivalry continued. Both regiments would account for the first seven Indian Inter-Regimental Tournaments. The first two were taken by the 9th Lancers, in 1877 and 1878.[19] It is of note that the great John Watson was the umpire in the final game. Before the finals at Meerut, Tim Butson,[20] the Lancers' captain, stated that the rule forbidding crossing was all nonsense, and he would not pull up for any man living. Shortly after the start of the game, Thomas St. Quintin came out of the bully hitting the ball and Butson crossed him; a tremendous collision ensued, but luckily, neither players nor mounts were seriously injured.[21] This was the first tournament played under the new rules and everyone realized the danger of crossing the line of the ball. Unfortunately, many injuries and even deaths still occur because of disregard for the capital rule of polo.

The year 1875 was a watermark for the game of polo in India. Because of the visit by Edward, Prince of Wales and later King Edward VII, a grand gathering took place in Delhi. Representatives from all regiments met, rules were drawn up, four-a-side was adopted, and an annual Inter-Regimental Tournament was instituted.

Col. Thomas St. Quintin, who had participated in the first game in England and would take polo to Australia in due time, was unanimously elected honorary secretary of the Inter-Regimental Tournament. The 10th Hussars presented in 1883 a trophy for the Indian Cavalry Inter-Regimental, which was taken by the 12th Bengal Cavalry at Ambala (at times spelled Umballa).[22] The 12th was not particularly well mounted, one of the reasons being that they were stationed in Jhansi, a rather out of the way location. According to Lt. Col. Denzil Holder, Jhansi was a poor station, with a very indifferent polo ground.[23] Nevertheless, young Ulick Browne of the 12th Bengal Cavalry had drilled his team to play as a unit, at the time in which either the game was characterized as a melee or some runs of individual effort. They took the cup, to everybody's surprise, except the 4th Battalion of the Rifle Brigade, with whom they had been practicing for the past twelve months. Browne was a pioneer in the game's development, because no other team had perfected teamwork as had the 12th Bengal Cavalry. This was Hiri (Heera) Singh's debut in tournament polo. The brilliant Hiri would go on to be considered the best Indian player of his generation, showing his skills at back on the Maharajah of Patiala's celebrated teams, and, perhaps in no small measure because of his polo prowess, reaching the rank of colonel in the Patiala Cavalry. The 12th Bengal Cavalry went on to take the Punjab Polo Cup five consecutive years, but another Inter-Regimental victory eluded the team. Ulick Browne married, gave up polo and divided his time between Surrey in England and County Mayo in Ireland, devoting himself to country pursuits. Browne inherited the title Marquess of Sligo and became something of an authority in antiquities. At his behest, his father donated to the British Museum some columns that had been damaged by a fire in their ancestral home. The columns came from the treasury of Atreus in Mycenae, circa 1200 B.C., and had been excavated, acquired, and taken to Ireland by his grandfather. Buried in the debris, they had been forgotten.

The infantry regiments, more noted for their prowess at hockey, started their own polo competition in 1884 for a cup presented by the Earl of Airlie; the King's Own Scottish Borderers took the trophy.[24] While stationed in India, the K.O.S.B. won the Infantry Tournament several times. Bombay started its own Open Cup in 1883, the Calcutta Turf Club gave a cup for all comers — natives were excluded from the Inter-Regimental — and the Maharajah of Mysore presented a trophy to be played for at Bangalore. Ornate silver trophies became tangible evidence of the spread of polo throughout India.

Until 1880, the game of polo in India was a leisurely affair. To quote "An Elderly Gentleman": "We did not have any foolishness, such as hustling, and riding off and galloping about like maniacs. Not at all; we took our pleasures calmly."[25] Nevertheless, the challenge provided by competition at tournaments brushed aside the thoughts of playing polo as it were croquet at times, and rugby football at other occasions. The main changes were about the number of players, the ground's size, the increase in the height of the ponies, the standardization of the rules and the feeble attempts to play it as a team game.

A letter to the editor of *The Pioneer* in Allahabad, published on 4 September 1878, gives an idea of what the games were. Signed by "Hoolvi," who had played with the Manipuris in the Northwest Province and the Punjab, it says: "This [off-side rule] and the height of the ponies are the two worst rules they could institute, and causes all the mischief in addition to their present play motto, which seems to be — 'every one for himself and devil take the foremost,' or as you remarked, 'mad dog like' regardless as to the position of their sides or the direction the ball is struck."[26]

The number of players in each team was usually, but not always, eight, sometimes with two goalkeepers. It was soon realized that goalkeepers had a small role in an open game, and this led to their abolition. At the team's other end, the number 1 player, also known as the flying man, was hampered by the offside rule that gave the opposing back great advantage. Nevertheless, the number of players was reduced to five, and then four-a-side. The field of play became larger, especially in its width, which allowed more lateral movements in launching an attack and causing further problems for the defensive players, who had to cover more ground closer to the goals. The net result was higher scores than hitherto. The game was played under numerous local rules, which became confusing. Order was restored when the code of rules then in vogue in Bombay was adopted as the matrix for the inter-regimental tournament.

Rudimentary tactics began to develop. The usual line-up placed the heaviest man on the team at back, and the number 1 was most of the time a lightweight mounted on the fastest ponies. As the game evolved from trot to gallop, the notion of a stationary, burly back quickly became obsolete. Even with different degrees of ability, and beyond a rudimentary division of labor, every member of the team had to contribute in both attack and defense.

There was a certain ethos in the soldier's games. In the course of a match at Meerut, where General Sir George Richards Greaves was in command, he enjoyed playing on different regimental teams. On one occasion, while playing on the 8th Hussars team, one of his opponents urged another player to "ride the general." Sir George shouted back, "Ride the general! Ride the general! By heaven, and what next?"[27] He explained later that the man on the ball should be left alone until he missed it. Lt. Col. Edward Miller notes that although his ideas on polo were sketchy and his execution poor, Sir George Greaves was personally very popular.

The game had been revived in the main by the cavalry regiments. For the Indians, polo — the game of sahibs and rajahs — had been dormant for some 200 years, but the game's new popularity in the military stations stirred up the princely classes from their slumber. The Maharajas of Cooch Behar, Patiala and Dholepore, and the Nawab Vikar-ul-Oomra started their own teams, usually made up from officers and subalterns from their own states' armies.[28] In 1886, Sir Pratap Singh invited Col. Stuart Brownlow Beatson, 11th Bengal Cavalry, to help him organize a regiment of Jodhpur Lancers. Col. Beatson also brought polo to Jodhpur and trained a team, composed of Sir Patrap Singh, Col. Stuart Beatson, Thakur Hurji Singh and Thakur Donkhal Singh. That team won their first competition in 1893, the Rajputana Challenge Cup. On Queen Victoria's Diamond Jubilee in 1897, a team representing Jodhpur traveled to England and played at Hurlingham and Ranelagh.

By 1891, it was clear that there was a need for an organization to govern the game of polo in India, similar to the Marylebone Cricket Club and the Hurlingham Polo Committee in England.[29] Preliminary meetings were held at Ambala and Simla, Lt. Henry Spencer Follett, 7th Dragoon Guards, being appointed honorary secretary. The first official meeting of the Indian Polo Association took place in March 1892, and the inaugural Open Championship in 1898. The Indian game had reached maturity.

PART II: THE ARISTOCRATS

3. The European Journey

Ireland

It may be that the first game of polo in Europe took place in Ireland in the summer of 1868. A detachment from the 10th Hussars was diverted to the Emerald Isle and somehow the officers arranged a game against a team of locals at Rathbane, near Limerick.[1] Col. Henry Russell so stated in a letter to *The Polo Monthly*.[2] This event happened a year before Lt. Edward Hartopp's impromptu game at Aldershot in England, to be described later. It also precedes the traditional inaugural game in Ireland, held at Gormanstown Strand in 1870, between a team representing County Meath and the 9th Lancers. "Chicken" Hartopp was Meath's captain and they were able to defeat the Lancers, at the time serving duty in Dublin. It is not surprising at all that Ireland claims priority in this endeavor, given the special affinity between horse and man in that country.

There is another claim for primacy on Irish soil. In the *Stonyhurst Magazine,* there is a notice informing that a polo stick and a ball from Tibet has been donated to the Society of Jesus school in Lancashire.[3] This reminded the notice's unknown writer that polo was introduced in the British Isles by Valentine Irwin, a former pupil. Irwin entered the Indian Civil Service and in due time was appointed commissioner in Manipur — perhaps succeeding Robert Stewart — where he played polo. Valentine Irwin returned to Ireland on leave around 1865, and at that time introduced the game in Roscommon. According to the note, many accidents occurred; therefore, the new game found no acceptance. Norman Cinnamond's tutor at Stonyhurst College, Father Frank Irwin, S.J., who was Valentine's nephew, confirmed the story to Cinnamond, who in turn mentioned it in his book *El Polo*.[4] Valentine Irwin's contribution to polo in Ireland is also noted in Stonyhurst College's website.

The All Ireland Polo Club was founded in 1873, mainly through the efforts of Horace Rochfort, who had established the County Carlow Polo Club, and two years later a set of rules was promulgated by the club. In 1886, the Irish followed the great majority of British clubs when the Hurlingham rules were adopted. The issue of a polo field in Dublin was put before the Board of Works, which allowed a parcel of Phoenix Park, known as the Nine Acres, to be used for polo. Some difficulties occurred because, although the board could grant permission to play polo, there was no body, earthly, heavenly, or otherwise — as Thomas Levins Moore quaintly put it — that could grant exclusive rights, because Phoenix Park had been given to the Dubliners as their playground.[5] Moreover, the citizens of Dublin had made full use of the park, enjoying their football, hurling and wrestling. The All Ireland Polo Club was granted leave to erect a small pavilion and a boundary fence; however, anyone had the right to use the field. The pavilion was burnt to the ground in 1987, but a new structure, along the original lines, was then constructed and play on the old ground continues to this day. This makes Nine Acres the oldest recognizable polo ground in Europe. It is not possible to accurately identify its predecessors: a pasture in Rathbane, a paddock at Aldershot Garrison, a common in Hounslow. Perhaps even the isle of Malta may claim priority for its dusty field at Marsa.

The rest of Ireland took to polo with alacrity. County Kilkenny held games at Prior Wandesford's property in Castle Comer. County Sligo and County Westmeath soon followed suit. The game was played five-a-side, all players lining up behind each goalposts; when the umpire tossed the ball in the middle of the field, a mad race ensued as ten men converged on the ball. Given this dangerous situation, it came to as no surprise that the first recorded modern polo fatality was on Irish soil. Robert Darley, a cousin of the famous Miller brothers, suffered a broken skull when his pony crossed his forelegs, tripped and fell.[6] The venue was Phoenix Park, and the year, 1877. In those early days, no player wore head protection except for a cloth forage cap.

The All Ireland Open was instituted the following year; the 7th Royal Fusiliers became the first holders of this challenge cup.[7] That same year, 1878, Capt. John Watson returned from service in India with the 13th Hussars to become the most formidable figure in polo for the next two decades.[8] Watson's contributions to the game were many and varied. Technically, he developed the backhand stroke, which was revolutionary at the time. It put an end to the customary practice of turning around in a wide circle while tapping the ball, thus speeding up the game's pace. Curiously enough, he never used the nearside backhander stroke; he always hit the ball on the offside. As far as tactics is concerned, Watson organized his players as a team, insisting — perhaps a bit too rigidly — that each one remain in his place, in the manner of the straight line or "column" game later advocated by Cameron Forbes, first in the Philippines and later in America.[9, 10]

Under Watson's theory the main task of the number 1 was to neutralize the opposing back — also called number 4 — thereby allowing the two middle players, the number 2 and the number 3, then called half-back, to obtain control of the ball, and ergo, of the game. The back's responsibility was mainly defensive because his only attacking role was to feed the ball forward. The players were supposed to stay in their allotted positions, with no interchange contemplated or — under Watson's strong leadership — permitted. The rotational tactics would have to wait before their development by the Peat brothers' Sussex team, and the concept of an attacking back would be brought on to perfection by the Patiala team in support of their outstanding back, Hira Singh. Currently this tactic is the staple of many teams led by Adolfo Cambiaso, who nominally is listed as number 1, but in practice roams through the entire field.

As to the number 1, his role was so minimal that he might as well have ridden without a mallet. The offside rule handcuffed his mobility and scope of action, giving tremendous advantage to the adversary's back, in those days the strongest player and usually team captain as well. Number 1, traditionally the weakest player on a team, had to wait until 1911, when the offside rule was abrogated, to claim his place in the sun and the opportunity to shine in the most difficult position to excel at in the game.

John Watson, player, was a superstar. His winning record speaks for itself: Hurlingham's Champion Cup, the County Cup, Ranelagh's Open Cup and the International Cup — later known as the Westchester Cup — against America. He also drafted the rules of the game. In Chatterton-Newman's felicitous phrase, "He found it [polo] a virtual free-for-all, and gave it pace, order and science."[11]

Other important trophies were put up for competition in Ireland: the All Military Challenge Cup in 1886, first taken by that remarkable polo-playing regiment, the 10th (Prince of Wales' Own Royal) Hussars,[12] and the Irish County Cup in 1890. The latter trophy was presented by the All Ireland Polo Club with the idea of promoting the game in the country clubs and providing for a reunion of all clubs in Dublin City. County Fermanagh produced the first winner,[13] a feat that was repeated the following two years, thereby obtaining permanent possession of the Cup; a new trophy was then donated, but the character was changed to that of a perpetual trophy. This trophy was won by County Dublin in 1909; regrettably, it was stolen from John Leonard's home, never to be recovered. Some sixty years later, a similar fate would befall the original Cowdray Park Gold Cup. The Dublin fortnight included the Horse Show, the County Cup and the All Ireland Open. After its initial successes, the County Fermanagh Polo Club unfortunately became dormant.

Ireland was a fertile ground for polo in its early years. An abundance of good horseflesh combined with a relative decrease in expenditure, compared to the game's cost in England, contributed to its popularity. Several good teams from England made the crossing in order to compete in the All Ireland Open Cup to challenge local teams imbued with *furor hibernicus*, which played hard, but always within the rules. They were rewarded with some success, like the ones achieved by several regiments in the early years, when most of the players were army officers, and later by civilian teams such as Eaton, the Old Cantabs, and the Miller brothers' Rugby — who were Irish anyhow — and also with the appreciation of Dublin's crowds. The locals were a knowledgeable bunch, having had the opportunity to watch the game free of charge for years, and having a congenital, well-educated eye for a horse.

England

In his often-quoted passage from *Chances of Sports of Sorts*, Col. Thomas St. Quintin relates how some officers in the 10th Hussars started polo in England.[14] The regiment was in Aldershot Garrison for the 1869 summer drills; one afternoon following lunch, Lt. Edward Hartopp read in *The Field* an account of polo on horseback as it was played in India (see Appendix 2). Without further ado, some half a dozen officers had their chargers saddled, procured a few walking sticks and tried — without too much success — to hit a cricket ball.

Colonel Robert S. Liddell, in his book *The Memoirs of the Tenth Royal Hussars*, gives a slightly different version: "Lord Valentia, Mr. E. Hartopp and Mr. George Cheape of the 11th Hussars, attached to the regiment, were the originators. The first game that was ever played took place at Aldershot on a piece of ground below Caesar's Camp. Amongst those who took part in it on this day were Lieutenant Hartopp, the Hon. Thomas Fitzwilliam, Lieutenant Edward Watson & c. The officers rode their chargers and golf sticks and billiard balls were used; later on it was found that a cricket ball, whitened, was more suitable for the purpose. The 9th Lancers adopted the game the following year, and assisted materially by introducing an improved stick."[15]

Regardless of which version was closest to the truth, the seeds of polo were planted in England.

The next step was to improve the equipment. Long-handed sticks were fashioned, as well as wooden balls the size of a cricket ball, painted white. As to mounts, Capt. William Chaine was deputized to cross the Irish Sea and purchase ponies. Captain Chaine was instructed to find ponies about 14 hands high, docile, and handy; it did not matter if they were a bit slow. The concept of pace was not in their minds; that would change soon enough. Captain Chaine returned with some 17 ponies; the 10th Hussars, having returned to their quarters in Hounslow, near Heathrow Airport, marked out a polo field on the Heath, had it rolled, and began practicing in earnest. The 9th Lancers were then stationed at Aldershot, and duly they received a challenge from the 10th Hussars. The first formal game in England thus was held on Hounslow Heath. The polo game was preceded by a cricket match between the two regiments, which was left unfinished. A great number of people came down from London to witness the novel sight of a polo match, and Hounslow Heath was crowded with spectators.

They played eight-a-side, with basically no rules. St. Quintin tells that they tried some sort of organization, placing four men on the bully, two halfbacks, one back and one goal-keeper. Nevertheless, after a few minutes, all players, with the exception of the two goalkeepers, became entangled in a hopeless melee where no one could see the ball, let alone take a shot at it.[16]

The year is not exactly known; estimates vary from 1869 to 1871. A celebration of the game's centennial took place in 1970 with a match at Windsor Park, the players and umpires — the Duke of Edinburgh and Earl Mountbatten of Burma — attired in period costumes. Some contemporary evidence points out to 1871. A detailed description of the match at Hounslow Heath was published by *The Morning Post* in July of that year, according to a reprint in *Chances of Sports of Sorts*. The report's initial paragraph reads: "Nearly all fashionable London journeyed from Town to Hounslow on Tuesday to witness a new game called 'Hockey on Horseback,' between the Officers of the 10th (Prince of Wales's Own) Hussars from Hounslow Barracks and the officers of the 9th (Queen's) Lancers, who had come from Aldershot."[17]

The game was watched by the Prince and the Princess of Wales, Prince Arthur, and the Duke of Cambridge. Royal patronage of the game of kings was evident at its very beginning. Final score was three goals for the Hussars against two goals by the Lancers. Despite some rather caustic words by the unnamed reporter, polo quickly expanded in England: "It was admitted by all who were looking that [the game] was more remarkable for the strength of the language used by the players than anything else."[18]

Early matches included the Household Cavalry versus the Light Cavalry at Lillie Bridge ground on 27 June 1871. Then there would be a reasonable priority claim for this match. Assuming that the "Tuesday" mentioned in *The Morning Post* refers to the month of June, in 1871, it was precisely the 27th. The last Tuesday in June 1870 was the 28th. Common sense would dictate that the encounter at Hounslow Heath took place in 1870. The summer of 1869 would have been too soon because Captain Chaine had to travel to Ireland to purchase ponies; the 9th Lancers had to start their practice games from scratch, secure their own ponies and manufacture some mallets. The 10th Hussars were dedicated to level and mark out the grounds at Hounslow Heath. All that would take time, but perhaps not as long as two years. In the face of the available evidence, it is reasonable to assume that the proto-game in England was held on 28 June 1870.

There is corroborating artistic evidence. The artist Terence Cuneo was commissioned to paint a work commemorating that historic event.[19] It is signed and dated December 1970. A plaque on the frame reads:

Centenary Commemoration Polo Game
Windsor 28th June 1970
To commemorate the introduction of Polo into England by a Match played between
The 9th Lancers and The 10th Hussars in 1870.
9th/12th Lancers v The Royal Hussars
3 goals   nil
Presented by Lt. Colonel R.S.G. Perry, D.S.O.—Joined 9th L 1929—Commanded Reg.
March 1944—March 1946

A reproduction of the painting adorns the cover of the recently published book *Smith's Lawn—The History of Guards Polo Club 1955–2005*, by Maj. John N.P. Watson, and is also illustrated in *Polo Quarterly International*, in the Winter 1992 issue.

The two pioneer polo regiments suffered the indignation of being amalgamated with other regiments, first, the 9th Lancers with the 12th Lancers in 1960; nine years later the same fate befell the 10th Hussars and the 11th Hussars, which formed a unit that was designated the Royal Hussars. Tradition had to give way to modern army methods.

Erstwhile opponents 9th Lancers and 10th Hussars—light cavalry regiments—joined forces in a game against the 1st Life Guards and the Royal Horse Guards at Richmond Park in 1870, the Heavies emerging as victors.

Polo in the Greater London area was concentrated on the Lillie Bridge ground in West Brompton, better known as a cricket and athletics field. It was a small ground, only 200 yards long; however, it had to do until better grounds were made available to the growing polo population. Capt. Edward Hartopp, Capt. Macqueen and the Hon. Debonnaire Monson were the prime movers in the enterprise, which was launched under the highest patronage. Edward, Prince of Wales, allowed his name to appear as patron, Earl Spencer became president and Viscount Valentia vice-president. The Committee of Election consisted of Lord Sholto Aberdour, Captain William Clayton, Viscount Lowry Cole, E.M. Dunsey, Col. David Ewart, the Hon. Charles FitzWilliam, Captain Hartopp, Reginald Herbert, Dermot, Earl of Mayo, Cristóbal de Murrieta, Captain Macqueen, John, Marquess of Queensbery, Lord Arthur Somerset, and Henry, Marquess of Worcester. Under their auspices the number of playing members, initially limited to 100, soon enrolled, and the club was formally established.[20]

On Tuesday, 2 June 1873, the first grand meet at polo took place at Lillie Bridge before a very large assemblage of London's fashionable *élite* world, the match being between the Lords and the Commons. On this occasion, the weather was beautiful, and the recent rains had made the ground on good playing order. The sides were fairly even, and, after some brilliant play, the Commons ultimately succeeded in winning four games (goals) to their opponents' two. The Spanish player Adrián de Murrieta made two goals, while his pony, a wiry bay with black points, appeared to enjoy the sport as much as his rider. Since what may be called the opening day, polo constantly increased in popularity. *Baily's Magazine* noted that "the club being as select as possible, admission to the members inclosure is only obtainable by vouchers."[21]

What attracted the society's interest were the players. When two years later the Hurlingham Club organized a tent-pegging contest featuring the 5th Lancers, "everybody was there, or meant to be; and if everybody had not looked cold and cross it would have been a pretty sight. As to the tent pegging, there was some disappointment, mainly among the female members of the country-cousin brigade, as to the actors on the scene. When it was discovered that the performers were not what a dear old Irish lady used to call 'the horse officers,' but that the 'pegging' was relegated to the troopers, all interest in it died out. The east wind might have been encountered cheerfully if the 'captains' had been to the fore, but there was no enthusiasm about the sergeants."[22]

The Hurlingham Club in Fulham, started as a pigeon-shooting endeavor in 1867, by 1874 began to cater to polo players and quickly became polo's guiding light under the Hon. Debonnaire John Monson's astute management, ably supported by Capt. John Walter Smyth — later Sir Walter — as polo manager. Hurlingham's history and profound influence on the game will be examined later.

At the time, the vast majority of polo players were cavalry officers, but in 1872, Capt. Francis "Tip" Herbert, having left the service, founded with his older brother Reginald the first civilian club on the British Isles, the Monmouthshire Polo Club, with grounds at Clytha, near Usk.[23] The first match was held on 23 September, followed by a dinner at the Angel Hotel in Abergavenny.[24] Monmouthshire had a significant impact upon English polo, being the winner, runner-up and joint-winner in the only final tied game in the history of polo's major tournament, the Hurlingham Club Championship Cup. When Tip Herbert became manager of the Ranelagh Club, Monmouthshire went into decline and finally closed its doors around 1897.

The Beaufort Polo Club was established in a corner of Gloucestershire around 1872 by Capt. Francis Henry, formerly of the 9th Lancers, and at the time in the Royal Gloucestershire Yeomanry. Captain Henry is mentioned as a participant in the first match between the 9th Lancers and the 10th Hussars in 1870.[25] This statement is incorrect, because the then-lieutenant Henry had retired from the 9th Lancers in 1866. Furthermore, he is not listed in the roster of players that participated in the celebrated game at Hounslow Heath.[26] All the original members hunted with the Duke of Beaufort Hunt. There is no mention of the Beaufort Polo Club in the 1895 edition of J. Moray Brown's *Polo*. The grounds were in Norton, between Malmesbury and Hullavington. In 1929, the Beaufort Club was revived by Herbert C. Cox, a Canadian player who developed seven playing fields at his Down Farm in Westonbirt, near Cirencester, to supplement the original grounds. Down Farm was purchased in 1977 by Capt. and Mrs. G. Simon Tomlinson of team Los Locos fame. Twelve years later, they formally established the new Beaufort Polo Club, which is now thriving as a venue for country polo.

A peculiar entity was the International Gun and Polo Club in the seaside resort town of Brighton. The club was formed for the purpose of holding meetings in England and on the Continent for pigeon shooting, polo, archery, tilting in the ring, fashionable fêtes and other rural amusements. The club's headquarters was the Bedford Hotel in Brighton, while the polo ground was in Preston, Sussex. Reviewing the scarce annuals issued by the club, it appears that only prizes for polo, polo ponies racing, tent pegging and shooting were given. The club's founder was George Marshall, who held proprietary rights. The total membership was a little over 300; it reads like a list of European high society.

Nevertheless, polo played a prominent part. Among the prizewinners were good players such as Edward Baldock, John Scott Chisholme, Capt. Frank Grissell, the Herbert brothers, James Mellor, Richard St. Leger Moore, Adrián de Murrieta, Hugh Owen, the Peat brothers, the Marquis of Queensberry and Sir Charles Wolseley. The continental meetings were held in Baden-Baden, Berlin, Brussels, Hamburg, Paris and Spa. The club's rules are printed in English, German, French, Italian, Spanish, Flemish, Russian and Arabic, in that order. Admission tickets to events were only issued with a member's voucher. Members were firmly advised, "Should any Member furnish Vouchers to Ladies not received in general society he will be expelled from the club."[27] In keeping with the club's policy of holding meetings else-where, polo matches took place not only on their home ground near Brighton, but also in Cheltenham and in London's Richmond Park.

Other early provincial clubs included Derbyshire, established in 1880 by that grand old supporter of the game, the Earl of Harrington, who built grounds at his seat, Elvaston Cas-tle, and at Trent Bridge. Then we have Barton-under-Needwood in Staffordshire, which had some battles with Monmouthshire. Manchester Polo Club, founded by Colin Ross, Ashton Radcliffe, Bailey Worthington and others in the same year as the more celebrated Mon-mouthshire, had a short time span, for it closed in 1877. It was restarted as Manchester Gar-rison by the 18th Hussars five years later and reorganized as Manchester Polo Club by Sir Humphrey de Trafford, who played with officers of the Queen's Bays stationed there. The venue was Old Trafford, now better known as the home of the Manchester United football team. The ghosts of Busby's Babes must surely mix with yellow and chocolate clad poloists on many a foggy night.[28]

The Cheshire Polo Club, with grounds in Little Budworth, just north of Tarpoley, claims its antiquity to 1872.[29] In fact, the club is the result of a merge among three other clubs: Man-chester, founded in that year, Wirral, which dates back to 1885, and Bowdon, where play had started in 1891. Manchester and Bowdon joined in 1906 with grounds at Ashley, retaining the name Manchester as the senior club. In 1939, just before the outbreak of World War II, the club moved to Little Budworth and took the name Mid-Cheshire Polo Club, retaining the traditional scarlet and white colors. Cheshire Polo Club was established in 1951 and remains a powerful force in the area, being the home of the Junior County Cup, a provincial trophy dating back to 1905. Another old trophy is the Cheshire Champion Cup, presented to the Liverpool Polo Club in 1911 by its women members.

Nearby, Chester Polo Club, started in 1881 by Lord Arthur Grosvenor, played their matches at the Rodee, the public grounds in the walled city of Chester, where there is a race course. The club was revived by Alfred Tyrer in 1895, but fell into abeyance. A new Chester club was formed in 2005. Most appropriately, the home ground is on the Rodee track.

The universities also had polo clubs: Oxford, founded in 1874 by Walter Hume Long, later Viscount Long of Wrexhall, and Cambridge a year earlier, established by the Hon. John Fitzwilliam. The Inter-University polo match first took place in 1878, the Dark Blues taking the honors.

Between 1870 and 1890, the game made slow progress. Balls and sticks of every conceiv-able pattern were used, with balls ranging from inflated India rubber to tennis balls. At the beginning, it was no more than a scrum or a maul — to use rugby terms — which slowly evolved into a slow, dribbling game. It was the time of five-a-side players, snaffle bridles and blink-ers, docked tails and no martingales. The increased use of the backhander stroke, as devised by John Watson, changed it into a faster galloping game, in which the celebrated Sussex County team of the brothers Arthur, James Earnest "Johnnie" and Alfred "The Boy" Peat reigned supreme from 1879 until 1893. Along their many years of almost unbroken success, the Peat brothers were helped by players such as James Babington, Edward Baldock, Henry Ashton Case, Gerald Hardy, Thomas Pinchard Kempson, Thomas Kennedy, the Earl of Lewes, Sir Francis Mildmay, Sir Algernon Peyton, Geoffrey Phipps-Hornby, Sr., and their brother-in-law, Edward Kenyon Stow. In 1894, playing with the Earl of Harrington, then in his fifti-eth year, Sussex was defeated 4–3 in the Hurlingham Champion Cup final. The Peats' ponies had been trained to be changed every time the ball went out of play, when time out was called for one minute. When the rule was modified that year, their ponies could not keep up the pace and Sussex lost in overtime to the Freebooters, among whom was their old teammate Gerald Hardy, who scored the seventh and winning tally. The Peat brothers then sold their ponies and did not appear on a polo ground again.[30]

The Peats' influence upon the game was most significant. Up to their time, most players considered the pony just a conveyance to get near the ball. The brothers three from Wimbledon were the first to pay special attention to training their ponies for polo and purchased the best available mounts. Johnnie Peat, at number 1, became the best striker and goal scorer of the day. Not only that, but instead of going after the opposing back, he made the back go after him. Edward Miller wrote that Arthur Peat at back was as good as, if not better than, John Watson, which is saying a lot, while "The Boy," not as brilliant as his siblings, was as good as any number 3 of the day.[31] But what made the Sussex County team almost unbeatable — eleven Champion Cups in thirteen years — was their combination play. For all their individual brilliance, it was combination play that made the team so successful. Their merit was that they assimilated and applied John Watson's teachings better than any others, and complemented their tactical prowess with superb ponies.

Further improvements were achieved by the celebrated Rugby team led by Capt. Edward Miller, who — with his younger brothers Charles and George, ably assisted at various times by Walter Jones and the Earl of Shrewsbury at the number 1 position, and W.J. "Jack" Drybrough at back — were the Sussex County successors as the most dominant force in English polo. The Miller brothers were experts in the selection and training of polo ponies, which they put to good use on the polo grounds. The times of slow, dribbling polo were gone forever.

Another change that contributed to speeding up the game was limiting the teams to four-a-side. Although this practice was formally adopted in 1883 by the Hurlingham Polo Committee, in 1880 the Royal Scots Greys had taken the All Ireland Open with only four men on the team.[32] The goalkeeper's lonely position had previously been abandoned.

In early English polo, the honor of victory had to be its own reward. That would soon change. The conditions for the International Gun and Polo Club stated, "The Polo Prizes consist of Silver Cups and Medals specially manufactured for the occasion."[33] The Prince of Wales, always an interested spectator, donated a trophy for the match between military and civilians at Hurlingham on 12 June 1889.

During this entire period, polo was dominated by army officers. Almost every cavalry regiment in Britain and in India had a polo club. As previously described, there were several civilian clubs and many good players, of whom the vast majority were military men. It was a peculiar army, in a transitional stage from the Crimean war — saddled with its Wellingtonian legacy — to the rude awakening of the Anglo-Boer conflict at the turn of the century. The army's central core was the regiment, each one with its own traditions, mottos, battle honors and strict hierarchical order: cavalry first, then the infantry guards, then the regiments of the line. The officers obtained their commissions by purchase, a quaint and ingrained custom. When Edward Cardwell, later Viscount Cardwell of Ellerbeck — appointed Secretary for War in Gladstone's Liberal Party cabinet — tried to implement a modicum of reform, the establishment closed ranks in bitter opposition, led by no other than the commander-in-chief, the Duke of Cambridge and a cousin of Queen Victoria. Even the queen herself was said to have reservations about doing away with the old practice of purchasing commissions.

Some of these reforms, which included the abolition of flogging — but only during peacetime — had been resisted mainly by the cavalry, which represented the army of "the good old days before the confounded meddler, who knew nothing about these things, had got his way with the Queen."[34] Two things that did not change were pay and leave: in the first case, there was too little, in the latter, far too much. In some regiments, officers would take up to a six-month leave in a year. In the 1930s, Lt. Col. Humphrey Guinness, Royal Scots Greys, several times an international player, used to say about leave: "at any time," which meant plenty and often.[35]

No social event was ever considered too small to justify escape from duty. There were notorious escapades, in which the 5th Lancers, a great polo regiment, were prominent. It got to such a degree that the Duke of Cambridge had to handle the situation. Col. Valentine Baker, a respected soldier who was commanding the elite 10th Hussars, was convicted of attempting to assault a woman on a railroad carriage. The printed reference states, "His sad story needs no comment."[36] After serving time, Colonel Baker joined the Egyptian Army, and as Baker Pasha, rose to high command.

Nevertheless, the peacetime high jinks did not deter the officers from duty in battle. Philip Mason recalls the story of a Prussian officer admonishing his colleagues never to underestimate the foxhunting, polo-playing British officers' conduct in war.[37]

The progress of polo in England was hampered by the continuing use of the offside rule and, to a lesser extent, by the lack of individual handicaps. Both were set aside almost simultaneously in 1911. The catalyst was the unexpected and overwhelming triumph of the American team in the 1909 Westchester Cup matches at Hurlingham. The cup's rules indicated that the competition must be carried out under the host association's rules and regulations. The British challenge in 1911 would then be played under American rules, which had abolished the concept of offside many years before because it was quite evident that it did not favor the smooth flow of the game. For the Hurlingham Defense Committee, if they harbored any hope of bringing back the trophy to English shores, there was no alternative but to practice games under the no-offside concept. The majority of players, after a few games, were in favor of the new rule.

As to individual handicaps, the problem had been recognized by astute observers of the game around the turn of the century. A halfway solution was implemented in February 1903 with the institution of the Recent Form List. This rule established that in some selected tournaments no more than two players on the list could play on the same team. It was not enough. Lopsided scores in many important matches — in 1902, the Freebooters beat the Black and Tan by 12 goals to one in the finals of the Champion Cup — continued to plague the landscape. Yet, there was no change until July 1910, when the Recent Form List was abolished and the Hurlingham Polo Committee issued the first handicap list. Four Americans, the Big Four team players, were joined by a lonely Briton, Walter Buckmaster, a stockbroker who was the leader of the Old Cantabs team — Cambridge University's former students — as the first 10-goaler in Britain.[38]

Scotland

According to the well-known polo writer James Moray Brown, the game was played in Scotland in 1872. He ought to know because his own regiment, the 79th Cameronian Highlanders, was garrisoned in Edinburgh, together with the 7th Hussars, which counted the Duke of Connaught among its officers. Play was on a field near Duddington. Moray Brown reminisced that those were the days of the dribbling game and charging for the ball. It was during the latter, at the beginning of a match, when he had the misfortune of colliding with Queen Victoria's son, both riders going head over heels.[39]

The game received a big boost when 17 acres were leased at Murrayfield — now the site of the Scottish Rugby Union stadium — backed by the Murrayfield Woods, where a ground was laid out by Tom Drybrough, one of the players and author of a book on the game. The ground measured 260 by 175 yards and had sideboards. The Edinburgh Club was formally established in 1880. The team of William Younger, Captain Gordon Mackenzie, and Tom and Jack Drybrough took the County Cup in 1893 and 1894, a remarkable achievement for a remote and isolated club in the northern reaches. The next Scottish club to be affiliated with the County Polo Association was Ayrshire, started in 1908.

France

The city of Pau, located in the Basses-Pyrénées — now Pyrénées Atlantiques — presents a strong claim to be the first place where polo was played in Continental Europe. A large foreign colony, in which the British were predominant, started polo together with racing, foxhunting, rugby, steeple chasing, tennis, pigeon shooting and cricket. Pau was the first of many continental resorts, such as Brioni, Cannes, Deauville and Ostend, where polo was brought over for the enjoyment of mainly English vacationers, with a sprinkle of North and South Americans.

British sporting influence upon the town goes back a long time. In his history of golf, Robert Browning writes: "It is said that after Wellington's victory at Orthez in 1814, two officers of Scottish regiments who were billeted at Pau and who had optimistically included their golf clubs in their kit, played a rough and ready game on the Plain of Billère."[40]

Polo was played on that same Billère Plain, adjacent to the golf course where the royal and ancient game has been played since 1856; the Pau Golf Club is the oldest in Continental Europe. The game of polo was started by two Americans, the publisher James Gordon Bennett, who is credited with bringing the game to New York, and William Knapp Thorn, who played for America in the first Westchester Cup in Newport. William Thorn, Jr., Commodore Cornelius Vanderbilt's grandson, was one of the best-known sportsmen in both France and America; he hunted, played polo, rode races and was a fine equestrian. He died in 1910, of a brain hemorrhage, at home in his beloved Pau.

Other early players included the Comte de Madré, later patron of the Tigers team, the Scots Jack and Tom Drybrough; the former a mighty back who met his end during a match at Rugby, the latter a well-known author of a treatise on polo. Charles Carroll, the American Henry Ridgeway, who was also Master of the Pau Hunt, James Mellor, of the famous Monmouthshire Club, the international Walter McCreery, a winner of steeplechases, and the American Alfred Torrance also played. Torrance was killed during a steeplechase at Croix-de-Berny.[41] Later players included the Russian Prince Sergey Belosselski, Sir Victor Brooke (Field Marshal Alan Brooke's grandfather) Eustace Jameson, J. Morris Post, Robert Stewart-Savile (donor of New Zealand's Savile Cup), and Mexican Olympic player Guillermo Hayden Wright.

The "upper ten thousand" English or Parisians, who spend six months of the year in Pau, did not have an entirely happy relationship with the local townsfolk because the visitors did not mix well with the Palois. In 1876, Bertall wrote, "Pau is not a French town; Pau, obviously and clearly is part of England."[42] The foreigners felt that they were scalped by the local merchants on every possible situation; a letter to *The Times* suggested that the Palois' only interest was emptying the visitors' purses.[43] It is not at all remarkable that reproaches from both sides were about money. On their part, the locals objected to the isolation and the conspicuous consumption by the visitors. An unnamed observer pointed out in 1886: "The arriving Peerage, the Gentry, and the rich merchant class, live in a different world. Wealth is everything. Whoever has the most money is first in Pau. From princes whose destiny is to wear the most beautiful crowns in the world, to newcomers like Gordon Bennett, who throws away gold at his parties...."[44]

Instead of town and gown, it was town versus vacationers. Let us remember that Pau was a provincial town in the Bearn, the proud birthplace of Henri IV, one of the great rulers of France. The author's father grew up in Pau in the 1890s and the children were educated at the local *lycée* and at the Ursuline Sisters' school. The family's *petit hotel* was on the Place Albert Premier, in the heart of the Quartier Anglais. In spite of having a French-born father and the family's verbal facility with the local *patois*, they were considered foreigners. When the five children were out for a ride aboard a carriage or mounted on small ponies, the usual comment they heard was, "There they go: *les Americains*."[45]

Polo continued at Pau through the early 20th century; after 1902, there was another ground in Jurançon, across the river on the Bourda field. Nevertheless, polo was not resumed after the Kaiser's War. Other sports continued to thrive in Pau. The Stade Palois rugby team was for many years a top national team in rugby-mad southwest France. The beautiful golf course remains a top attraction for tourists and locals alike; steeplechase races are part of the French racing season. The motorcar racing fraternity meets yearly at the Parc Beaumont circuit, which traditionally signaled the start of the European season featuring the Grand Prix de Pau. The Pau Hunt remains active; Frederick Prince, of the polo-playing family from Boston's North Shore, was master until the 1930s.

There is another British heritage in town: the gardens. The English brought with them their hobby of gardening. Private gardens are everywhere, because the Palois readily adopted the pastime. The public parks, of which Parc Beaumont is the prime example, displays British gardening ideas and practice. The poet Alphonse de Lamartine said Pau had the most beautiful land-sight on earth (Naples received the same accolade for its sea-view). It remains a quiet, low-key provincial town. The game of polo is totally forgotten.

Early French provincial polo also took roots in Compiègne, Deauville, Dieppe and Lille.[46] The game was revived in the early 1930s by an Englishman, Lt. Col. Harold St. Clair Smallwood, who had ten ponies shipped from the National School of Equitation at Kingston. Play was carried on at Pourville Sporting Club in Pourville-Sur-Mer, near Dieppe. The players were of both sexes and different nations. Some ladies who showed promise were the Hon. Stella Winn, the Hon. Eileen Wood and a Miss Osborne. The British who summered in this part of France and indulged in polo were Lord Victor Paget, Mr. Maurice Neill, Col. Frederick C.S. Samborne-Palmer, Capt. Palmer and Comm. Crosse, while Prince Sturdza of Rumania and Lt. de Bovet, French Army, were two of the Continental players.

While the game at Lille, close to the Belgian border, did not take great strides, polo in Compiègne was thriving until 1911. Play was carried on at the Prince Ferdinand de Fancigny-Lucinge's ground in the Oise Department. Polo at Deauville was played sporadically, but took full force in 1893. The Société du Polo de Deauville was founded in 1894; the grounds were located, as they are now, in the center of the local racetrack. The International Tournament was first played in 1895, and in 1950 M. François André, whose effigy in bronze surveys the scene in the town's center, created the Coupe d'Or, an important event in the continental polo calendar in the month of August, which has been played without interruption into our days.

In Paris, the first matches took place at the Jardin d'Aclimatation, and on land between the lake and l'avenue des Acacias, in 1891. It was at Bagatelle, in the Bois de Boulogne, that the first formal installations for polo were erected, near the Tir-aux-Pigeons. The Vicomte de la Rochefoucauld and the Duc de Doudeville were the originators, quickly joined by the Duc Decazes, Maurice Ephrussi, Luis de Errazu, the three Escandón brothers, Eustaquio, Mauricio and Pablo, the Duc Honoré Charles de Luynes, the Comte Jean de Madré, the Marquis de Podenas, the Prince de Poix and the brothers Maurice and René Raoul-Duval. René, who had been with the 7th Hussars in India, brought with him the latest ideas on the game.

In April 1892, the Cercle du Polo was formed by high-placed aristocrats, who had no difficulty in obtaining from the Ville de Paris a parcel of land previously used by the garrison's officers as a training ground for jumping and equestrian shows. A pavilion was promptly constructed, in Normandy style, based upon a design by the Spanish Conde de Urribarren. Admission to the Cercle du Polo was severely restricted; only males were allowed to be members. As to the distaff side, the rules were conformed to avoid *les intrusions suspectes.* Entry passes were only allowed to mothers, wives, unmarried sisters and daughters of *Messieurs les poloistes.*[47]

In 1894, the 4th Hussars and the 17th Lancers teams visited Bagatelle and played a match. The 17th Lancers, known as the "Death's Head and Glory Boys," won the match and are credited as the first winners of the Paris International Open. They presented a trophy to be kept by the first team to win the tournament two years in a row. This was accomplished by the American Freebooters; a new cup was then donated by the Polo Club de Paris in 1908.

There is conflicting data about this tournament. Edward Miller, in the third edition of *Modern Polo*, usually a reliable source, is the authority for the above. The club's annual lists the tournament as the Paris Open, stating it was presented[48] by the Hurlingham Club on the occasion of the match between the 4th Hussars and the 17th Lancers.[49] The listed winners do not match with Miller's list; most likely, they are different tournaments. Adding to the confusion, *The Polo Annual* lists the Comte de Madré's Tigers as the 1912 Paris Open winners.[50] Among several gaps in the *Polo de Paris Annual,* there is one between 1908 and 1920. Norman Cinnamond gives this tournament's results as those of the Challenge Cup de Paris.[51]

Two significant developments took place at Bagatelle at the end of the 19th century. One was the establishment of goal judges, whose assistance was invaluable to the umpires; the second was the implementation of a numerical handicap system, the first in Europe.

Bagatelle remains the most aristocratic and charming venue for polo in France. The ground is rather small, located in a picture-perfect setting within the Bois de Boulogne. The overall feeling is that of a mini Palermo: it is the gathering of the polo clans in a beautiful metropolis.

Spain

Don Pedro González, later created Marqués de Torre-Soto, was the first Spaniard to play polo. According to Norman Cinnamond, González had learned the game in England, and upon his return to Spain in 1870, started polo in Jerez de la Frontera, Andalucía.[52] This date, 1870, is suspect. The game had barely begun in England and it was totally confined to cavalry officers. Perhaps Don Pedro had witnessed a game or two, but it is highly unlikely that a civilian, and a foreigner at that, would have participated in the earliest matches. Cinnamond goes on to say that Pedro González as a young man learned how to play polo at Wadhurst Park, Kent, the property of his uncle, Cristóbal Pascual de Murrieta from the banking family.[53] His cousins Adriano and Cristóbal de Murrieta became interested in polo after visiting Hurlingham Club with their father; polo at Hurlingham had been started in 1874.

Nevertheless, there is no question that the first game of polo in Spain was played in Andalucía, at the Club de Polo de Jerez, whose colors were red and green hoops. Of the eight founding members, four have English surnames, perhaps because of the large British interest in sherry production.[54] Thanks to the benign climate, play was carried on year round, in winter on the plain of Melgarejo and in summer on dried-out marshes near Puerto Real and La Tapa del Puerto. It was more like a friends' reunion than a club proper; Don Pedro González provided ponies and equipment, so the group had no other choice than to join the game. They started by using the local saddles, the "jerezanas," but soon enough hard-gained experience taught them to stick to the more practical English saddle. The initial headgear was a cap in the style of Goya, latter replaced by the pillbox, then in vogue in England. A new polo ground was constructed by Don Pedro on one of his vineyards at El Pinar. Matches against members of the Gibraltar garrison and community followed and continued until the Spanish events of 1931.

Polo in Madrid began in 1876 at the Royal Casa de Campo, one of the many residences of King Alfonso XII. Although his interest in the game did not reach that of his posthumous son, Alfonso XIII, his wish that polo be played at Casa de Campo gave impulse to the game in the Spanish capital. Play stopped in 1884, when the monarch died prematurely. The Polo Club de Madrid was then established, later to be named Real Puerta de Hierro Polo Club, thanks to Alfonso XIII's patronage. Another ground was laid out in the center of the Castellana racetrack; it turned out to be a rather poor field, quite sandy, which in dry weather allowed the players to canter about in a cloud of dust and in the wet season to slide in the mud.

Polo spread around Spain: to Barcelona in 1896, promoted by Don Enrique de Ibarrola; to Valencia one year later, on a park near the Grao road. On 21 July 1897, Granada hosted on the Aramilla grounds the first international match versus the Gibraltar Garrison Polo Club, which had been founded in 1881. The Spanish team was led by the Marqués de Larios and was completed by his brothers Ernesto and Leopoldo and the Duque de Arión. As to the team from Gibraltar, it was made up by officers of the Cameronian Highlanders; their names are not known.

The game in 19th century Spain remained mainly regional: Catalonia, Andalucía, Granada and Madrid were the principal centers. The best years of Spanish polo were in the future, in the 1920s.

Other European Countries

Polo in Russia was started around 1893 by Prince Sergey Belosselski-Belozerski, colonel of the 2nd Dragoons, whose father presented the club with a beautiful ground on Krestovsky

Island near St. Petersburg.[55] A British resident, Mr. R.W. Tamplin, well known with the Brighton Harriers, gave sound advice as a player and a manager. Other members of the British Embassy, such as the Hon. Charles Hardinge, Col. Guy Percy Wyndham and Henry Hamond Dawson Beaumont, joined the fray. Sir Nicholas O'Conor, the British ambassador, presented the Queen Victoria Cup in commemoration of the sovereign's 1897 Jubilee. Other players participated, among them the Grand Duke Boris Wladimirovitch, Prince Napoleon Murat, Prince Kantacojène and Baron Graevenitz. The club itself was founded in 1896.[56] A tournament took place in 1901 among a visiting team from Hamburg, the British Embassy's staff and the St. Petersburg Club, the St. Petersburg team winning the prize.

Polo in St. Petersburg was a very expensive pastime, even for the diplomats. Sir Neville Henderson, later ambassador to Argentina and Germany, was a junior diplomat in the British Embassy. Henderson was able to afford the exorbitant cost through his winnings at bridge; as costs escalated, his pony string was changed to less expensive ponies from the Caucasus. Polo was a vehicle for social mixing with after-game parties starting at midnight and lasting until dawn.[57] Even during the Russian aristocracy's boycott of the British Embassy in the years of the Russo-Japanese War, polo players led by Prince Belosselski kept up their regular attendance to the embassy to meet with the English equestrians.

In Turkey, the Therapia Polo Club was formed in 1896, with grounds in Buyukdere, Therapia, some eleven miles from Constantinople. The nearest polo clubs were in Budapest, two days by train, and in Cairo, just three days by steamer. There is no record of inter-club matches between team from the Ottoman Empire and Hungary or Egypt.[58]

The first club in Germany was the Hamburger Polo Club, which was started in 1898 at Bahrenfeld by Heinrich Hasperg, Baron von Heintze-Weissenrode and Eduard Eggers. It remained the most important club until the advent of the Second World War. The Hamburger Club provided all the players that represented Germany in the 1936 Olympic Games. Play in Hamburg was eventually resumed in 1958; Miles Reincke, who was on the Olympic team, was one of the prime movers in bringing polo back to Germany.[59]

By 1910, there were other clubs in Berlin, Bremen, Frankfurt, Hanover and Munich, which compares favorably with single clubs in the Netherlands, Hungary and Turkey. Gibraltar and Malta also had polo clubs that drew most of their members from the garrison's officers as well as some civilian members and the occasional diplomat.[60]

4. The British Carry the Flag

To Argentina—1872

Argentina is a far better country for the British drive that pushed through it, from gale swept Patagonia to the tropics, and from the dirty shores of the River Plate to the magnificent Andean peaks. From pirates to polo players, they were always pioneers. — Andrew Graham-Yooll[1]

A letter to the editor of London's *The Field* from a reader in Buenos Aires started the ball rolling for polo in Argentina. "Hockey on Horseback: Could any of your readers oblige me by informing me, through the columns of *The Field*, the rules of hockey as played on horseback in India? Also as to what kind of sticks and balls are employed. I saw an account in *The Field* about a twelve-month ago, and then thought it a very suitable game to introduce into this country. A Gaucho. Buenos Ayres, Jan 12 [1870]."[2]

Regrettably, "A Gaucho's" identity is unknown. Whoever this British colonist was, without any doubt he was a visionary as well as a prophet of the eventual domination of polo by the land of the gauchos. This is the first mention of the game of polo in Argentina by the world press.

Obviously, "A Gaucho" had read the same article signed by "N.S.S." that caught Lt. Hartopp's eye and convinced him and his fellow 10th Hussars' officers to start the game in England. The article had been published by *The Field* in its edition of 20 March 1869.

The letter to the editor from "A Gaucho" was neither forgotten nor consigned to the dustbin. *The Field*'s edition of 16 April 1870 contains two pertinent letters. The first one is signed "Bhal" and explains the game as played in Hazaribagh, in the state of Behar, India. The letter includes a diagram of the field of play and shows the players' positions on the field, including the goalkeeper. The second letter, signed "Musafir," briefly describes the game and mentions that it has Persian origins. This correspondence provoked a missive from F. D'Acosta—a real name at last—who played at Barrackpore, north of Calcutta. D'Acosta mentions that the writers will confuse "A Gaucho" because "Bhal" states that the grounds dimensions are 120 yards by 50 yards. "Musafir" mentions 400 yards in length by 120 yards in width. Following a long discussion on the game, including an explanation of the "charge" or bumping, D'Acosta mentions that such practice, although dangerous, is also inevitable. Therefore, his recommendation is that, if charge you must, do not do it at a 90-degree angle.

D'Acosta ends his letter wishing "A Gaucho" good luck in his endeavor to launch the game in Buenos Aires and suggests as an essential ingredient for the players an ample stock of brandy and soda.

After these salvos of correspondence, there is not a word about polo in Argentina until a notice appears in the 19 September 1872 issue of *The Standard*, the British community newspaper. Perhaps the yellow fever epidemic in Buenos Aires, which caused some 26,000 deaths in 1871, was the reason for the parentheses in the news. On that date, there is an announcement that a polo match would take place in Cañada de Gómez, Santa Fe Province, in conjunction with an equestrian festival that included races, to be held on 3 November 1872. Although it was six weeks before the match, both players and umpire were announced. The teams were "Consul Joel, Mr. Lane, Mr. Dana, Mr. Schnack and Mr. Hope vs. Mr. Weldom, Mr. Krell, Mr. Soppe, Mr. James and Mr. Markworth. Mr. [Joseph] Greenwood was designated as umpire."[3]

Little is known about the selected participants, with the exceptions of Lewis Joel, who was the British consul in Rosario (also mentioned as American consul in Cobija, Bolivia), and Paul C.L.E. Krell, the first settler in Cañada de Gómez. Peter Adolf Schnack is mentioned in Mulhall's book[4] as proprietor of a model establishment in Cañada de Gómez, and a Mr. E. Soppe is found in the St. Bartholomew's Church, Rosario, contemporary records. The Hope family were settlers in the area, and their descendants appear almost uninterruptedly in the Argentine Polo Association handicap lists until the 1980s. Mr. Greenwood owned estancia Irwell, named for a river in his native Lancashire.

Although a report on the races appeared on November 9, no mention of the polo game is made. Similarly, it is ignored in a letter written by *The Standard*'s Rosario correspondent on 14 November, which contains a description of the races held at Cañada de Gómez. Did the announced polo game ever take place? Historian Víctor Raffo is of the opinion that although no written confirmation exists, the report is a clear indication that the game of polo was played at some estancias in the vicinity of Cañada de Gómez.[5]

The next mention of polo in the Argentine press appears, once more, in the Editor's Table section of *The Standard*: "We hear that some fashionable young Britishers are brooding over the idea of starting a Polo Club here, as soon as political matters settle down. We consider the thought a happy one: the horses of the country can easily be trained to it, and we have no doubt many young Argentines would gladly join the Club. 'London Society' for September has an interesting article on this now popular sport."[6]

The 20 January 1875 edition of *The Standard* reported the fact that three polo games were held at estancia La Buena Suerte, located in Azul, Buenos Aires Province, on January 4.[7] Nevertheless, it is well known that polo was played in Argentina before that year.

The Buenos Aires neighborhoods of Belgrano and San José de Flores were sites of summer rest for Argentine and foreign families. Near Flores on the corner of the current Rivadavia Avenue and Emilio Mitre Street stood a country store belonging to Nicolás Vila that had a weathervane of a galloping pony. The neighborhood was known as Caballito (little horse), after the artifact. Nearby, an English resident, William Leslie, manager of the Maua Bank, was the owner of a quinta on Morelos Street, previously known as Savarese, and also de la Riestra, after the former owners. On Leslie's quinta there was a flat tract, Eizaguirre's paddock, where polo was played in the 1870s. However, it was on a close-by uncultivated piece of land — whose boundaries were the Western Railway's (now Sarmiento) tracks and the Avellaneda, Fragata Sarmiento and Seguí streets — where the first matches in Argentina took place.

In the summer of 1943, one of those pioneer players, Walter Ford, already in his 90s, took Francisco Ceballos, a former president of the Argentine Polo Association, on a tour of the neighborhood.[8] This parcel of land was later the Buenos Aires Polo Club's grounds — the first polo club in Argentina — and later still, of the Flores Athletic Club, whose players, led by the famous Hugh Scott Robson, were good enough to take the Open Championship in 1894.

There is also a strong oral tradition that the game of polo began in Entre Ríos Province. Juan Manuel Puente, a respected reporter for the magazine *El Gráfico*, repeatedly mentioned the story in his column. The only supporting written source is a paragraph in Elvira Ocampo de Shaw's *Hurlingham*, in which she in turn quotes an interview with an unnamed individual, probably Frank Balfour.[9]

There was indeed a polo match played in Concordia, Entre Ríos; however, the date is unknown. It is known that the contest was interrupted by the sudden appearance of the local mounted police, which felt that they had to stop the proceedings before the participating Englishmen killed each other. Perhaps this is the origin of an Argentine phrase about early British sportsmen — *ingleses locos* — translated as mad Englishmen.

This was not the only police intervention during the dawn of sports in the country. Eduardo Olivera writes: "Everywhere football was played, there were funny episodes; at Empedrado, Corrientes, the chief of police placed under arrest all the British players because he thought they had gone mad. Contacted by telegraph, Señor Fitzsimón [*sic*] secured the players' freedom. The chief of police obeyed the order, under the condition that the players would not appear naked."[10] Without doubt, the usual football attire was considered unbecoming in a far away province.

Setting aside the Entre Ríos constabulary's apparent good intentions, obviously surprised and bewildered by a pastime carried out with total ignorance of the rules of play, it would be far fetched to postulate that any sport began in the hinterland. All the games imported by the British — cricket, football, golf, rowing, rugby, swimming, tennis, and others — began near the port of Buenos Aires. It would be a stretch of imagination to give the Concordia pioneers priority in polo matters. Lacking any other documentation, perhaps unpublished or hidden in a family attic, Caballito's primacy remains credible.

The first polo game in Argentina to receive extensive printed coverage took place at estancia Negrete, located in Villanueva, Buenos Aires Province, some 100 miles southwest of Buenos Aires as the bird flies. Although the matches at Negrete were not the first to be played in Argentina as reported in *The Standard* on 4 September 1875, the primacy of games played at Negrete has become ingrained in Argentine polo lore as dogma.

The estancia's history is long. It was established around 1776 by Ciriaco Negrete, who named it El Carmen to honor the Virgen del Carmen. His heirs sold the property to Paulino Lagosta, who kept the original Catholic name; however, the name Negrete remained indelible in popular lore. In those days, it was customary to identify properties by the owner's name and the woods planted by Don Ciriaco Negrete became a certain reference point for travelers and militia crossing the desolate pampas. It also came to the attention of some Indians, who burned the dwelling in the early 1820s in retribution for a punitive raid conducted by the Prussian Colonel Federico Rauch.

Lagosta's heirs contracted John Hannah, an experienced sheep master, to run the estancia. Hannah's improvements were immense, including importing the Merino breed and, later on, the Rambouillets. In 1845, John Hannah, administrator, became John Hannah, proprietor.

Estancia Negrete hosted some of the earliest polo matches in Argentina. Part of the cypress planted by the British princes in 1881 is at left (private collection).

Hannah continued purchasing adjacent land, and by 1863 he owned some four square miles and proceeded to build the house that still stands today.

Enter David Anderson Shennan. Another Scot attracted to the margins of the River Plate as a land of opportunity, Shennan became an associate of Carlos Krabbé, whose commercial firm, Krabbé, Higgin and Co., is still in existence. Hannah, now septuagenarian and a veteran of almost half a century of hard work and anxieties brought about by civil, international, and Indian wars, longed for his native Scotland. John Hannah, endowed with a well-earned fortune, his brother Robert laying in Negrete's cemetery, a victim of cholera, in 1870 sold to Krabbé and Shennan the magnificent estancia. Near the manor house there is a plaque placed by the Círculo Tradición Nacional. It reads: "It was here at Negrete where the eminent agrarian Mr. John Hannah developed the Argentine wool industry."

There is another memorable landmark at Negrete. In front of the dwelling there stands a cypress planted in 1881 by the princes Albert Victor, Duke of Clarence, and his younger brother George, Duke of York. Eventually, the Duke of York would become King George V in 1910, succeeding his father, Edward VII, the *bon vivant* eldest son of Queen Victoria. A fading plaque near the tree, the only survivor of the two specimens planted, commemorates the event.

On Monday, 30 August 1875, the first documented polo game took place at Negrete. The guests from Buenos Aires had arrived on Saturday, and after Sunday's repose, six matches were held on Monday. The preparation had been minutely precise. The gardens, designed by a French architect, were emblazoned with flags, and the United Kingdom's emblem flew over Negrete's cupola. A polo ground 300 yards in length by 200 yards wide was marked — the chronicle states it looked like a billiard table — Argentine flags on each corner, and the goals, eight yards apart, were marked by Geneva flags.

The first match pitted Camp, wearing blue jerseys, versus City, wearing white. The Camp players were the host: David Shennan; Charles Krabbé, his partner's son; Arthur King, from estancia La Corona; Charles Dashwood, employed at Negrete; and Edward Hawes. City, some of whom had little knowledge of the game, was captained by Hamilton Langley, who owned an estancia in Pergamino. The already mentioned Walter Ford, a veteran from the games at Caballito; David Methvin, John Wanklyn, a Mr. Thompson and Earle Welby, who was the British Legation's secretary, completed the team's roster. It was five men against six, in what was an early attempt to establish some sort of handicap. Each player had a spare horse, and the game lasted less than one hour, Camp winning by 3 goals to nil.

Five other matches were held, with several different players. At the day's end, David Shennan and Arthur King were considered the best players. This may be the earliest recognition of the modern Most Valuable Player award. The injury list included a banged elbow, cuts to a finger and a nose, plus a broken mallet. The reporter noted that four players on each team appeared to be the best number to assure a flowing game. It took several years before that prescient observation came into being.

Estancia or camp polo in Buenos Aires Province first took place at Henry Wilson's La Buena Suerte, as mentioned earlier. Many other estancias located in Buenos Aires Province took up the game. Among those was La Caledonia, home of the famous Tarquino, who was the first Shorthorn bull imported from Britain. In Cañuelas — now Adolfito Cambiaso's country — near La Caledonia, William and James White's La Campana, later owned by John Brown, was the site for many polo games. South from Buenos Aires, in 1824 the Gibson family purchased Los Yngleses, curious not only for the archaic spelling — with a Y — but also because the new owners were Scots. Nevertheless, the local custom was to call *inglés* everything and everyone that was British. The estancia, initially settled by Esteban Márquez, had several names; one was Rincón de Tuyú. The Gibson brothers formed a polo club, Tuyú, which entered in the initial championship of the Polo Association of the River Plate. The current owners are the Boote family, who inherited the land through Lorna Boote, neé Gibson. A scion from that family, Juan José Boote, a 7-goal player winner of the World Cup with White Birch, is also a top-notch polo pony trainer.

Other early polo games took place at La Castaña, owned by Charles Daniel, a great sportsman. Later on, polo was played at San Anselmo, in La Colina; Alban Woodroffe's El Mirador, in Carlos Casares; El Jabalí, owned by the Campbells, also in Carlos Casares and La Norumbega, property of Arthur Richard Yeomans, in the bordering 9 de Julio district.

The next center of polo was Santa Fe Province. The first recorded game took place in Rosario on 9 June 1887, in celebration of Queen Victoria's Jubilee. Other matches took place in Rosario, such as the inevitable Camp v. City and English v. Argentines. However, the strength of polo in Santa Fe was, once more, at the estancias: Edmund Traill's Chirú, located at Traill railroad station[11]; Las Limpias, in Carlos Pellegrini, another property of the prolific Traill family; Las Lomas, also of the Traills and Alfred Dickinson, in Las Rosas; and Magnus Fea's La Victoria, in Los Cardos.[12] The oldest Argentine polo club in activity is Venado Tuerto Athletic and Polo Club, founded on 16 July 1888 by many local estancieros.[13]

In Córdoba Province, the Santa Eufemia Polo Club was formed at estancia El Montecito. Later, John Edward Benitz, one of the famous Benitz family, founded Los Algarrobos Polo Club at the similarly named estancia in Woodgate, now Monte Buey. In Santiago del Estero the Gramilla Polo Club was started in 1892 and in the northernmost province, Jujuy, polo had begun by 1883, promoted by the Leach brothers, Walter, Stephen and Norman.

The Buenos Aires Polo Club was founded on 20 October 1882; play was carried on at the old Caballito grounds. There is also notice of a match between Buenos Aires Polo Club and a team from Bahía Blanca, some 600 miles from Buenos Aires. The Southern Railway transported the ponies to and from, free of charge. Perhaps the fact that Walter Ford was employed by the railway and Herbert Gibson was the president, both polo players, had something to do with such generosity. In the event, Buenos Aires took the first match and the second ended in a tie. *The Buenos Aires Herald* mentioned that the Bahía Blanca ponies were at some disadvantage, because they had been trained on sandy soil and experienced some difficulty adapting to Caballito's green grass.[14]

The matches at Buenos Aires were all among the club's members for the simple reason that there were no other clubs. For instance, matches were Scottish v. English, Argentines — meaning British born in Argentina — v. The World, or Married vs. Bachelors. The game's continuing expansion was reflected by the appearance of new clubs: Belgrano, second oldest in Argentina, founded prior to 1886 (the exact year is not known because the minute book was lost); Lomas Academy, later formally organized and renamed Lomas Polo Club; and neighboring Quilmes Polo Club. The Belgrano Polo Club organized the first handicap tournament in 1892, some 20 years before individual handicaps were implemented in Argentine. The handicaps were awarded to each team — not to individual players — in this tournament, which was won by Santa Fe Polo Club.[15] The foundation of the Hurlingham Club in 1888 changed the face of polo in Argentina. Its history and tremendous influence on the development of polo in the Argentine Republic are described in a later chapter.

All the pioneer players were of British origins. The majority were estancieros and their employees — administrators, clerks and youngsters learning the ropes — but among the players there were also bankers, diplomats, insurers, merchants, railway executives, shippers and stockbrokers.

Andrew Graham-Yooll has painted a rather sad canvas of one group in particular: "Many were 'remittance' men, the unwanted or disgraced relatives sent away with a small allowance to avoid embarrassment to their families. Not a few had titles; Eton, Harrow and Oxbridge educations; some became teachers, others alcoholics; still others redeemed themselves by a discreet and respectable existence and a few discredited themselves for all time by marrying a 'native' girl. Some made fortunes; other lost what they had including their identity and their language in remote parts of the country."[16]

Just as in North America, their reception and reputation were mixed. Some were good riders, which automatically enhanced their standing with the gauchos, many of whom were peons who worked cattle at the estancias; agriculture only blossomed years later with the boom of European immigration. Others could barely ride, but they had no other option than to learn the basics of the art of equitation. These young men were given tame or old horses, easy to ride. The natives would refer to these horses as *"mansito, como para un inglés"* (quite tame, just for an Englishman to ride).

The British influence on polo in Argentina was overwhelming and unchallenged. An examination of the list of the winning teams of the Polo Association of the River Plate Championship reveals that the first non Anglo-Saxon names appear in 1895. They were the *capataz* (foreman) Sixto Martínez and two peons, his brother José and Francisco Benítez, from estancia Las Petacas, who joined their mentor, the burly Irishman Francis Edmund Kinchant, the estancia's administrator, as members of a top team. In 1901, two peons, Juan Carrizo and Roque Fredes, joined Percy Talbot from Rosario and a nobleman, Baron Gastón Peers de Nieuw-

The Casuals team that took the 1894 P.A. of the River Plate Championship. Mounted on Criollo ponies are (from the left) Arthur Follett Holt, later Sir Follett Holt, Robert "Johnny" Smyth, Francis Robinson and Percy Talbot. In the match at Cañada de Gómez, Santa Fe Province, Percy Talbot scored the only goal in the final game against Quilmes (private collection).

burg, who would represent Belgium in the 1920 Olympic Games, on the San Carlos team. Gastón Peers married an Argentine society lady — Ernestina Costa Oliveira Cézar — and was administrator of estancia La Barrancosa near Venado Tuerto. José "Tincho" González, a foreman, joined three Traills on the 1906 North Santa Fe team. The 1907 and 1909 Western Camps teams included Eduardo Lucero, the foreman at John Campbell's estancia El Jabalí. The following year, the Italian Count Enrico de Galleani, was on the winning Las Rosas team.

It was not until 1915 that an Argentine team, El Palomar, took the Open. Army Captain Samuel Alfredo "Toto" Casares, Lindsay Holway, a bespectacled lawyer, and the brothers Charles and Lewis Lacey were the team members. Years later, Julio Negrón, a multi-talented sportsman from across the River Plate in Uruguay, took the Open four times playing for Hurlingham, the quintessential British club in South America.

In the 33 championships played under the aegis of the Polo Association of the River Plate, all but eleven out of the 61 winning players were of British origins. This trend started to change during the 1920s because the First World War had

An unidentified early player wearing a striped jersey and a pillbox cap. Watercolor and gouache over photographic print, dated 1882, signed Schreiber (Museum of Polo and Hall of Fame, previously in the Stephen Sanford collection).

depleted the ranks of British polo players in Argentina. It also marked the beginning of the slow but inexorable decline of the United Kingdom's economic influence upon Argentina.

To Australia — 1874

Historian Chris Ashton described the establishment of polo in Australia:

"The story that follows is about individuals and teams and families which have shaped polo in Australia for the past 120 years; it is a story of epic and comic and tragic moments on and off the field which have become polo folklore; it is a portrait of a sport and a people who play it which has evolved from the paddock polo of farmers and station managers to a surrogate battlefield for urban entrepreneurs seeking conquests in new arenas."[17]

The man credited with the introduction of polo to Australia is Colonel Thomas St. Quintin.[18] In 1874, St. Quintin, then a captain who as an officer in the 10th Hussars had participated in the first polo match in England, was seconded to accompany Col. James Thacker, the Indian government remount agent, on a visit to Australia. The first port of call was Sydney, where the first polo match took place in Moore Park on 23 July 1874. Captain St. Quintin marked out the ground, and the players included the governor, Sir Hercules Robinson, later Lord Rosemead, his A.D.C., Capt. Edward Beauchamp St. John, Sussex Regiment, and other officers, of whom W. Maxwell, Morrisset and G.F. Want are known. The Sydney Polo Club became the first such club in the southern hemisphere.[19] Among the early players, and a good one at that, was Andrew Barton Paterson, the immortal "Banjo," lawyer, farmer and war correspondent who became famous for his poetry. His poem *The Geebung Polo Club* is one of the gems of polo literature.

NEW SOUTH WALES

Inland, Muswellbrook was the first polo club to be organized, in 1890, with Donald Macintyre, who had witnessed games at Hurlingham in 1887, as president. The first games seem to have been played in March 1888 at Moreduval, the property of the brothers Robert and W.B. Simson and a friend, T.J. Finlay. The Simsons had learned polo from the Chirnside family in the Western District of Victoria. Also in 1888, practice games took place at Kayuga, Donald Macintyre's property. There were only four players: Jack Campbell, Reginald White, the host, and one of Kayuga's hands, Donald Cracknell.[20] Other clubs followed Muswellbrook's lead: Tamarang, Scone, Narromine, Quirindi, Gunnedah and Tamworth.

On its way to polo supremacy in Australia, New South Wales' progress was steady and slow. Polo grounds were developed, height limits imposed on ponies, and tournaments organized, some lasting one week and including pony races, gymkhanas and stick and ball races. It was a social opportunity to meet friends and maybe future wives, to enjoy competition and trade stories, to purchase and sell ponies. It was called a carnival, a term that lasted for years. In 1898, the Northern Challenge Cup was instituted as the main prize in New South Wales until the governor, William Humble Ward, Earl of Dudley, donated the Countess of Dudley Cup in 1910 as emblematic of the state's polo championship.[21]

Victoria

Along his journey through Australia, Capt. St. Quintin moved on to Victoria in order to visit his brothers John and Henry, who were farming at Dwarroon Station in Victoria's Western District. A game was played at Jetty Flat, near Warrnambool, on 20 August 1874. Players were the three St. Quintin brothers, Tom Brown, A. Mackenzie, Oliver Palmer, A. Urquhart and C. Woodward. Shortly after that event William Hood, Tave Palmer and George Ware started Warrnambool, the first polo club in Victoria.

An early match took place at Melbourne's Albert Park on 10 December 1875. Players included Andrew Chirnside, William Hood, J.B. Lombard, F. Mack, Francis Murphy, Herbert Powers, James Robertson, Alexander Sullivan, George Ware, George Watson and Frederick York Wolsely.[22] The early matches against New Zealand are described elsewhere in this work, as well as the 1899 international game versus England. In contrast with New South Wales, there was no support for the game from the governor, Sir George Bowen.

The long sea voyage did not deter some polo players from testing their skill in Europe. As an example, Camperdown's captain, William Manifold, and Allan Strang from New Zealand are on record as winners of the 1906 Prix International at Ostende. The team was appropriately named Globetrotters, because it was completed with Frank Barbour from West Meath, Ireland, and Hugh Scott Robson from Argentina.

An early system of handicapping was devised in Victoria. This consisted of putting the best team at scratch, the other teams then receiving a number of goals proportioned to their estimated worth. Apparently, the plan worked well.[23] A criticism arose because some people thought that too much depended on the single handicapper's judgment. However, is that not true of the current handicap committees? Another early Australian invention was that of a stick for picking up balls, which umpires find so useful in every game of polo. It is unknown who had such a brilliant idea.

The Western District polo teams were the cream of the crop in Australian polo during that era. Clubs such as Camperdown, Caramut, Colac and Warrnambool became the talk of the town, while the Affleck, Hood, De Little, Manifold, Robertson and Urquhart families are enshrined forever in Australian polo lore. Chris Ashton vividly described the golden years: "Victoria's Western District speaks of faded grandeur. Its bluestone mansions are memorial to the mother country, as are its gardens with their walkways and shrubs, their flower-beds and trees, each a corner of a foreign field that is forever England."[24]

South Australia

According to Charles De L'Isle, the first game in South Australia was played in 1874 by R.N. Colley, William Austin Horn, A.R. Malcom and John L. Stirling, later Sir Lancelot Stirling. If that statement were correct, then South Australia would challenge New South Wales as the place that started polo in Australia, because Capt. Thomas St. Quintin had also arrived in 1874. Sir Lancelot Stirling, who stated that when he returned to Adelaide from England in that year he brought some polo sticks, bases the above affirmation upon some personal notes. In his notes, Sir Lancelot also gives credit to Mr. William A. Horn for taking the initiative to form the Adelaide Polo Club.[25]

The year 1874 is suspect. The *Australian Dictionary of Biography* indicates that Stirling returned to Australia in 1876 after receiving his education at Trinity College, Cambridge, and being called to the bar at the Inner Temple.[26] However, there is no question that Sir Lancelot was the pioneer of polo in South Australia.

An article in the South Australian newspaper *Register* of 4 April 1896 reports that a match was played at Montefiore Park: "We believe it [polo] was first played in Adelaide in 1876. Messrs. R. [Robert] Barr Smith, W. [William] Gilbert, E.C. [Edward Charles] Stirling, Hart, Horn, and Maj. Goodwin taking part in the opening match at Montefiore Hill: but it was not until three years later that the present Adelaide Club was formed."[27]

Along those lines, an early polo player from Adelaide, Mr. Edmund Bowman, wrote some notes on polo in South Australia: "It was in 1876 that I returned from England and early that season some games were played, the first I remember being at a garden party given by the Hon. Alex Hay at Linden. Another game followed shortly afterwards at another garden party given by Mr. C.D. Hardy at Mitcham."[28]

The next report of a polo game in South Australia occurred in 1880, when the *Register* commented on a match between the Western Districts of Victoria and South Australia at Albert Park, Melbourne, with South Australia ending up the winners. The Melbourne periodical *Argus* reported this match.[29] It mentioned that the game lasted two and a half hours, the visitors using the same ponies for the entire match, while the Victorians changed mounts at halftime. The unknown scribe noticed that the "cattle" mounted by the locals were much larger than those ridden by the Adelaide men, and that their mallets were about a foot longer. The concept of "behinds" (missed shots at goal, which only counted in the case of a tie) was already in vogue. The match was won by South Australia by four goals to two.[30]

Two return matches were played at the Old Racecourse in Adelaide, one being drawn and the other taken by South Australia. During the 1880s and 1890s there were many matches between South Australian teams and others such as Camperdown, Caramut, Colac, Mortlake and Warrnambool.

In 1892, W.T. Morlick started the Burra club and Sir Lancelot Stirling, the Strathalbyn club. These clubs and Adelaide, plus Mount Crawford and Broken Hill, comprised all the South Australian polo clubs up to the start of the Great War.[31]

QUEENSLAND

The Eagle Farm Racecourse in Brisbane was the site of the initial polo game in Queensland. A notice in *The Brisbane Courier* of 20 March 1877 indicates that a match was held between teams named Bush and Town on 16 March. The Bush players were Ron B. Bingham, W. Scott, R. Newton and C. Garbutt, while Town aligned Capt. Henry Locock Berkley, R.J. Warburton, Donkie and Power.[32] The match ended in a draw at four-all, even though the goal posts had been moved farther apart than their original setting at 20 meters.[33]

The next mention of the game is a report indicating that William W. Hood, a relative of the Hoods of Victoria, had started polo while managing Burenda Station in Augathella. Mr. Hood had learned the game in India, and upon moving to Australia, had brought mallets and polo balls in his equipage. Then he moved to Westbrook Station and founded the Toowoomba Polo Club, which in 1887 played a match versus Brisbane.

Other early clubs in Queensland were Allora, Gatton, Half-Holiday and Ipswich, which amalgamated to form the Queensland Polo Association in 1894. Adolph Feez, a Brisbane lawyer and polo player, was elected president. The following year a Queensland team made the long journey by train to New South Wales, where they defeated Camden, Sydney and a combined team. Next year, their southern neighbors returned the visit and, once more, Queensland emerged victors at Eagle Farm.

To the south, interest in the game was generated in the dairy farming area around Clifton. This culminated with the formation of the Downs Polo Association in 1905. The center of polo had moved south, and the result was that the Queensland Polo Association became dormant in 1907, not to be revived until 1920. In spite of this setback, until the Great War, Queensland boasted the second largest number of polo clubs in Australia, after New South Wales.

TASMANIA

The Hobart Polo Club in Tasmania was founded in 1889 by Mr. W.H.B. Robinson, who was private secretary to the governor, Sir Robert Hamilton. The polo ground was located in the center of the Risdon Racetrack. Players included Alex Boyes, Herbert Hill, R. Horsfall, the Lewis brothers, R. Roope-Reeve, L.L. Smith and Charles E. Webster.

The intrepid sailors on board HMS *Curacoa*, described in the section on New Zealand, also visited Tasmania and played games there in 1892 and 1893. According to Viscount Kelburne — later Earl of Glasgow — the game was played up country, not in Hobart, against some tough Tasmanian farmers. In a letter to Keith Little, the Earl of Glasgow reminisced, "With eyes like hawks they seldom missed the ball but their knowledge of the rules was rudimentary! Wherever the ball went they made for it and crosses were frequent. I don't want to exaggerate but certainly one arm was broken as the result of a collision between ponies. I remember seeing, as the result of another collision between ponies, the pony of Lieut. Vivian de Crespigny going round in circles with de Crespigny dismounted, being dragged over the ground, holding on to the bridle. It was the most dangerous game I have ever seen played."[34]

Play was also carried on in the Launceston area, where a German landowner, Rudolph von Stieglitz, had three polo grounds on his property, Andorra.[35] Col. Cyril St. Clair Cameron, formerly of the 9th Lancers, was a leading light in Tasmanian polo. The colonel's daughter, Vera Gwen Cameron, was prominent in women's polo in the inter-war period.

WESTERN AUSTRALIA

It seems that polo was first played in Western Australia in 1892 when the Fremantle Hunt Club was established and some of the members — among whom Captain Cairns Candy, A.D.C. to the governor, was prominent — took up the game. The matches were held at Orgy's Field (one must wonder its origins), a racecourse close to Preston Point Road, and in Richmond Park, at the time better known as Pearse's Paddock. Frank Bluett, Hendy Henderson and the brothers Bill and Jim La-Hoar were identified as players in a letter from George Evans to William Garnsworthy Bennett.[36]

The Perth Polo Club was founded in 1896 with Mr. Neil McNeil as president, and enjoyed the patronage of the governor of Western Australia, Sir Gerard Smith. It preceded the foundation of the Western Australia Polo Association, an event that occurred in 1903. Clubs established around the turn of the century included Goldfields, Victoria District, Geraldton (later changed to Moonyonooka) and Cue. Another Northern District team was Mingenew Polo Club, formed in 1906 when Gordon Law-Smith came from South Australia to gain working experience on Nangetty Station and became instrumental in forming the club.

In 1912 a team from Eaglehawk in Victoria played in Mingenew, as told by Mr. Harry Pass to Mr. Leonard H. Hamersley. The late Harry Pass participated in that tournament, playing on the Geraldton team.[37]

In his opus magnus, *Geebung—The Story of Australian Polo*, historian Chris Ashton has pointed out that Western Australia has suffered more than the other states from what Geoffrey Blaney referred to as "the tyranny of distance."[38] This accident of nature was also observed by Col. St. Quintin in his autobiography; he noted that the long distances between clubs would be detrimental to the game's improvement because, of necessity, competition would be limited. A modern celebrated player, Bob Skene, made the following observation while visiting Len Hamersley's remote Walkaway Club on Wells Station: "This must be the loneliest polo club in the world."[39]

The oldest trophy in Western Australia was the Alcock Cup, presented in 1902 by Alcock Sports and misplaced for many years, finally surfacing in 1975. As it was customary in the rest of the British Empire, the game of polo enjoyed the trappings of privilege and displayed social graces. After an 1899 match at Lotens Paddock between Coolgardie and Perth, it was announced that the Hon. Mrs. Cairns Candy would give afternoon tea, and, while describing dress at the polo match, it was noted that Lady Smith was in fawn canvas with brown trimmings, black bonnet and pink roses. The elegance continues.

The Geebung Polo Club

There is no question that Rudyard Kipling's *The Maltese Cat* is the crown jewel of the literature of polo. *The Geebung Polo Club* by Australian poet Andrew Barton Paterson, better known as "Banjo," comes a close second. In five stanzas, it describes a match—we cannot call it a game—between the city boys of the Collar and Cuff team and the Outback's Geebung boys. Its popularity is world-wide, and teams in Argentina and Canada have taken Geebungs as their name.

It has been a matter of debate among polo scholars as to the place where the mythical contest was held. The Earl of Glasgow thought that it was a match in the Tasmanian upcountry between sailors on HMS *Curacoa* and local farmers. Lord Glasgow wrote: "With regard to the poem 'The Geebung Polo Club,' A.B. Paterson was our guest on HMS *Curacoa* and came with us from Sydney to Hobart. Lieut. A.C. Lowry played intermittently, but he did play in 'The Geebung Polo Club' game. A.B. Patterson was there and myself. Maybe I was the spectator who Paterson said had his leg broken 'just from looking on.'"[40]

Mr. W.E. FitzHenry states that in 1939, Banjo Paterson wrote to *The Sydney Morning Herald*, "When a cavalry officer came out from England and started a polo club, we took to the game like ducks to water. We played a match against a Cooma team, real wild men with cabbage-tree hats and skin-tight pants, their hats held on by a strap under their noses. 'The Geebung Polo Club' was written just after the Cox brothers came down from Wagga Wagga and played in Sydney."[41]

Only one geographical feature is mentioned by name in the poem, the Campaspe River. This river is in the state of Victoria. The state of Queensland has a population named Geebung, and also a Campaspe River. A few polo clubs claim to have been the club of the mythical contest, among them Tamarang and Cooma, the latter also claiming that Goulburn was the team described as Cuff and Collar. Paterson himself said it was just a story. The last word belongs to Chris Ashton:

Who or what inspired the poem does not matter. What matters is the ring of truth it evokes of the sound and fury of Australian polo. It has become the unofficial anthem because in its black comedy, in the maniac will-to-win regardless of risk to life and limb that it describes, players a century on recognize something of themselves. The 40-odd polo clubs of Australia today can all be classified in varying degrees as battlers or silvertails. As a rule of thumb, the further south, the more Cuff and Collar they become and the further north, the more Geebung. But as the climax of the poem shows, regardless of rank or wealth, the game is the great leveller.[42]

To South Africa — 1875

> *How much better a lot of teams in South Africa would have been if they only had the motto "A ship is greater than any member of her crew."*—Tommy Pope[43]

Although polo was initially the province of British cavalry regiments, the infantry started the game in South Africa. The 75th Infantry of the Line Regiment, also known as the Gordon Highlanders, after service in Hong Kong and Singapore, was sent to the Cape Province, where it was employed in minor operations in the Lower Drakensberg. Around the same time the 1st Battalion, the Duke of Cornwall's Light Infantry, was deployed in South Africa from the island of Mauritius. Both regiments were garrisoned in King William's Town, near East London. Also quartered there was the Cape Mounted Rifles, a South African unit. The first recorded game took place in October 1874 at the Parade Ground between the Gordon Highlanders and the Cape Mounted Rifles.[44]

The Gordons returned to England from Natal in 1875 and the Light Infantry two years later, but because of the Zulu War in 1879, several regiments came from India and the game took renewed strength after that conflict's end. Polo was played in Cape Town in 1885 at a club formed by army officers within the Kenilworth course and at a pasture on Observatory Road, and in Natal by the officers stationed at Fort Napier, in Pietermariztburg; a year later, they formed the Garrison Polo Club. The Military Ninth Division played during the 1880s at Harrismith, Orange Free State, while play in Transvaal began in Johannesburg in 1894, when the owner of the Goldfields Hotel founded a polo club. The game was dominated by the military, but civilian clubs sprouted in several places. The Dargle Polo Club was the first civilian club in South Africa, a claim disputed by Mooi River Polo Club. The 1902 edition of the *South African Polo Calendar* gives the foundation years 1886 for Dargle and 1889 for Mooi River.[45] Another early civilian polo club was Tintern, which was formed on the Carter brothers' farm about 1893.

Mallets were manufactured by the players themselves or by a carpenter, a Mr. Hill at Cotswold. The heads were made out of local bush timber such as bitter almond. Gordon McKenzie compared those mallets to a fishing rod with a sledgehammer as the head.[46] The Dargle players agreed to play under a local code, that of the Garrison Club. These included a 14-hand pony restriction; breaking the rule was punishable by a one-pound fine. There are a few recorded matches: away at Mooi River and against the Garrison at Fort Napier are two of those. It appears that their first match was against the 6th Inniskilling Dragoons, who had a crack team; the final score, 22–0 in favor of the Inniskillings, tells the story without comments.

Another team that was also mauled by the military was Durban, which would dominate

South African polo in the late 1920s and early 1930s. A challenge was received from the 3rd Dragoon Guards stationed in Natal; they had well-trained ponies and their captain was Robert H. McCorquodale, who carried the reputation of being a fine player. Against such odds, the Durban players, with little experience, mounted on Natal ponies, did well to stay in the game. The final score is not recorded.

Other civilian clubs of the 1890s were Greytown; the Shaw's Karkloof; Kokstad, where Lt. Henry Chase Damant became a legend in South African polo; Matatiele; Merino Walk; Nottingham Road and Underberg. Polo at the Port Elizabeth club was started around 1888 by Arthur Hands. The North End and Uitenhage teams played on ponies brought over from Colesburg. Polo went into recession because of the Rand's gold fields rush in the 1890s.[47]

A momentous event happened on 12 May 1906 when the South African Polo Association was established at a meeting at the Officers' Club in Pretoria. At the same meeting, it was resolved that the Rand Polo Club be invited to establish the Beresford Cup as the open championship cup to be played for annually. This came to fruition and the Beresford Cup became the symbol of the South African Championship. It had been presented by Capt. John H.G.H. de la Poer Beresford, later Lord Decies, 7th Hussars, who would go on to take the Olympic gold medal and the Westchester Cup in 1900. The first contest for the Champion Cup, as the Beresford Cup was then known, was in 1899, when the 5th Lancers were the winners over the 18th Hussars, by 5 goals to nil.[48] The South African Inter-Regimental Cup was first played for in 1902 and was taken by the 18th Hussars.[49]

The concept of individual handicaps was adopted by the South African Polo Association on 24 April 1911; the top rated players were the Hon. John Denis Yelverton Bingham and Maurice Nicholl Kennard. Wing Commander Bingham took the bronze medal at the 1924 Paris Olympic Games. Lt. Col. Kennard was killed on the first day of the battle of the Somme in France; he was one of "the first over the top" in command of a battalion of the West Yorkshire regiment.[50]

Restrictions on the ponies' height were finally abolished in 1924, after the measure proposing abolition took heavy defeats in the two previous annual general meetings, following spirited discussion. Thus, South Africa joined the great majority of polo-playing countries in allowing ponies of any height to participate in the game.

To America — 1876

Was the flamboyant James Gordon Bennett the originator of polo in America? Ongoing research is trying to determine if the strong oral tradition that polo was first played in Texas is indeed valid.

Current dogma is that after witnessing polo matches at Hurlingham, James Gordon Bennett procured mallets and balls, took them with him to America, and the first polo match took place at Dickel's Riding Academy in New York City. It was, of course, the indoor version of the game. The first outdoor game was played at Jerome Park racetrack in Westchester County. The Westchester Polo Club was founded on 6 March 1876 and in 1880 Henry L. Herbert, backed by August Belmont, Jr., and James Gordon Bennett, leased land in Manhattan on 110th Street and 6th Avenue. A clubhouse and stables were built; this was the Manhattan Polo Association. Constant use of the field made grass difficult to grow; play was carried out in clouds of dust, so after two seasons, polo was abandoned and the lease transferred. During the summer, the Westchester players took the game to Newport, Rhode Island, while the Meadow Brook Club on Long Island began play at the Mineola racetrack, later moving to their own property in Westbury. Henry L. Herbert started the Brighton club in Long Branch, New Jersey, and the Buffalo Club took off in upstate New York.[51]

In 1878, a polo field was marked out on the Military Parade Ground in Prospect Park, Brooklyn, where a match between Westchester Polo Club and Queens County Hunt drew 10,000 spectators. In reality, all the players were Westchester members. Polo in New England was centered in two clubs near Boston: Myopia and Dedham, while The Country Club, more celebrated as a golf venue, played a lesser part. Harvard was the first college to take up the game, playing on a rough field near Waltham. Connecticut had clubs in New Haven and Hartford, while Vermont saw the game at Norwich University and military polo at Fort Ethan Allen in Burlington. In Rhode Island, the Rumford Club, near Providence, was also significant, but it was eclipsed by the grand gatherings at Newport, Point Judith and Narragansett, just across the water.

The initial rules of the game were those of the Hurlingham Polo Committee. However, the independent Americans soon enough made significant changes: they abolished the offside rule, did away with the hooking of mallets, and banned the backhander stroke. These changes opened up the game and favored the individual players because, once in control of the ball, it was easier to keep possession. On the other hand, although the number 1 achieved great freedom once liberated from the shackles of the offside rule, it caused a deterioration of team play. In the first international game against the British, John Watson gave a lesson that the Americans took to heart: combination play would usually win when matched against individual brilliancy. The Americans returned to use the backhander stroke after that series, when they realized that it represented a tactic that could turn defense into attack much quicker than turning with the ball in a circle.

The early game of polo in the vast United States dispersed its players far and wide; however, the best polo was played in the northeast, from Boston to Philadelphia; in California, from Burlingame to San Diego, and in the plains, in Iowa and Texas. Each one presented different characteristics and social differences. In the East, it was the province of the aristocracy and the wealthy classes, from undergraduates at college to railroad barons. Californian polo was

Newspaper publisher James Gordon Bennett is credited with bringing polo to the United States. Here he is next to a true pony, perhaps his own Sultan, circa 1880 (Museum of Polo and Hall of Fame).

tinged with a strong British influence, especially in Southern California, with titled players dominating the scene until World War I. The same British influence was briefly noted in Texas; more so in Iowa and Wyoming. South Carolina became the winter polo capital of the Eastern establishment, especially at resorts such as Aiken and Camden. Cowboy polo in Texas developed into a game of its own; it had to wait many years before it was given the chance to prove its worth in the East-West series, which changed the face of American polo.

EARLY POLO IN TEXAS

There is an oral tradition that polo was first played in Boerne, Texas, a town near San Antonio, on property owned by an Englishman, Capt. Glynn Torquand.[52] Captain Torquand had purchased land in Boerne in 1872 and retired from the army in January 1875. If he was a serving officer until 1875, it is unlikely that he had played polo in Texas three years earlier. In those days, extended leave from British regiments was common; it is possible that he traveled to Texas planning his retirement. At the time, polo in England was the province of cavalry regiments; his own unit was the Coldstream Guards, which was an infantry regiment. There is no record of the Coldstreams playing in 1872, just three years after the game was introduced in England. Most likely, Torquand witnessed a game, and like many others, was smitten and brought it to Texas. Precisely when that happened is still an unsolved matter. Some of his companions were Capt. Egremont Shearburn from the 9th Lancers, John Molesworth, Mr. Mitchell and Mr. Stanley. What is certain is that in 1883 the local *Express News* described the first game played in San Antonio.[53] There is also a report of Englishmen playing polo in Vanrob, near San Antonio, in 1877.[54]

THE BRITISH IN IOWA

A fascinating saga is that of polo in Le Mars, Iowa. The story of the British colony in and around Le Mars starts in Philadelphia in 1876, where William Brooks Close, a former Cambridge University student, and Daniel Paullin, a land agent who was hawking real property sales in Illinois and Iowa, began discussions on purchasing large tracts of land in Iowa.

William Close had three brothers, John B., James B. and Frederick B., who all shared the middle name Brooks, after their mother's maiden surname. Frederick Close arrived in America in 1872, living in the Allegheny Mountains in Virginia, eschewing his brothers' Cambridge educations. Following discussion with Paullin, the Close brothers established the Iowa Land Company. By 1882, the company was offering 500,000 acres for sale.[55]

The Close family was well connected socially and financially in England and managed to obtain financial backing for their venture. Upper-class Englishmen, the already mentioned remittance men, were encouraged to travel to the Midwest to first learn the basics of farm and ranch management, to then move forward running the properties on behalf of their wealthy families, just like many others who had performed similar tasks in Canada and Argentina. Locally, they became known as "pups." One pup named Jack Wakefield was known for riding his horse into the House of Lords tavern, demanding to be served on horseback. Quite often pups got into scrambles with young American males. Pups did not seem to take farm management very seriously and were known to have unhitched plow horses for informal racing.

Polo, golf, steeple chasing, toboggan sledding and riding to the hounds were other popular sporting events enjoyed by the Le Mars British settlers. Fred Close introduced polo at Le

Mars and established the Northwestern Polo League in 1885, which promptly organized a tournament for a Challenge Cup. Other polo clubs were formed at Blair and Omaha, Nebraska; at Sioux Falls and Yankton, South Dakota; and Cherokee, Council Bluffs, Onawa, Salix, Sioux City and Sloan in Iowa.

The polo match for the championship of the Northwest afforded lots of excitement: Captain Julian W. Orde, F. Carmichael, Willie Gaskell, and Fred Close for Sibley, played Captain Maclagan, Jack Watson, Henry Moreton and O. T. Pardoe for Le Mars, the latter team winning by three goals to one.[56] As far as mounts, the standard cow ponies proved sufficient for the players' needs.

A noteworthy match was held in June 1890 at Crescent Park, Sioux City, between the local team, led by Fred Close, and Le Mars. Alfred Currie Colledge, Capt. G.C. Maclagan — who had played at the Calcutta Polo Club — Count von Muller and Jack Watson formed the Le Mars team. Henry Drake also played for Sioux City. The report continues: "There was a collision or rather an attempt by one pony to hurdle another which cut across its path, resulting in the death of the Sioux City captain, Fred B. Close. The unfortunate man had but recently returned from England with a shoulder badly bruised in hunting — with upper arm strapped to his body and only the hand free to drive, he was unable to manage his mount well enough to avoid the accident which led to his death before the eyes of Mrs. Close."[57]

The game in this area lasted until 1898, by which time the polo-playing British colonists had been replaced by younger American players whom they had tutored. When Le Mars played St. Louis, Capt. Maclagan's American teammates were Ed Dalton and the Sammis brothers.[58] This is a fitting conclusion of the account of the British polo developments on the playgrounds of northwestern Iowa.

SOUTH CAROLINA

The polo club at Aiken, South Carolina, affiliated with the Polo Association in 1895; however, by that time the sleepy town became a winter destination for equestrians from the Northeast and polo had been played for many years on a ground donated by the Whitney family. Colonel Clarence Wallace, a New Yorker prominent in social circles, started polo, and Mr. Davis, the town's mayor, became one of the players. Other polo pioneers in the winter colony were Captain R.B. Barber, from Englewood, New Jersey, Mr. Peterkin, of the Manhattan Club, Mr. W.R. Lincoln from Baltimore, Mr. Edward Tuttle from Boston, and Mr. Custis from Aiken.[59] Northern families such as Bostwick, Corey, Hitchcock, Knox, Milburn, Stoddard and Von Stade brought their children and entourage, along with their horses, whether polo ponies, jumpers, hacks or hunters.

Aiken remains a horse town. Many streets are still unpaved, for the benefit of horses that perform their daily exercise on the way to Hitchcock Woods, a reserve donated by the family. Aiken polo celebrated its 50-year jubilee in 1932 with a polo match in which both players and spectators donned period costumes.

There was polo also at Camden, where a club joined the Polo Association in 1890. The major players were Roger L. Bartow, Jr., Clem Brown, Alexander D. Kennedy, William C. Salmond and K. Gerald Whistler. The Camden Polo Club was for many years on a par with their better known neighbor, Aiken. Its story is told by polo player and sporting book collector John H. Daniels[60] under the charming title *Nothing Could be Finer*, after the lines in the song "Carolina in the Morning."[61]

THE GAME IN WYOMING

The British also took the game to Wyoming. It was Malcolm Moncreiffe who laid out the first polo grounds in Wyoming on land later owned by Charles Whiton.[62] Moncreiffe also built another field on his Polo Ranch, which was known as Moncreiffe Field for more than sixty years, until the land was purchased by Mr. and Mrs. Charles Pollard in 1984.[63] Malcolm Moncreiffe was born in Perth, Scotland, and immigrated to America, settling first in Miles City, Montana — where he probably saw polo — and later in the area near Gillette, where he went into cattle ranching. When his older brother William came to visit, they purchased large tracts of land around Big Horn. After a wedding journey to Europe, Malcolm and his wife, Amy, built their home at the Polo Ranch.

Another polo player that settled in the area was Captain Frank Grissell, who had participated in the first polo game on English soil in 1869 as a member of the 9th Lancers team. After leaving the service, in 1891 Capt. Grissell became the original homesteader on a tract of land in Dayton, which he named IXL Ranch, after his regiment. Bucky King notes that his brand was purchased by the Milward brothers, who later operated the dude ranch IXL.[64]

There was also a small group of players in Miles City, Montana, under the leadership of William Lindsay. It is possible that Montana and Wyoming players connected to engage in some games.

CALIFORNIA, HERE COMES POLO

According to historian Dennis J. Amato, polo in California took off in 1876 when the California Polo Club was established.[65] One of the local worthies involved in the club was Captain Nell Mowry, who was a long-distance rider in the San Francisco Bay area. Mr. Amato raises the question that perhaps James Gordon Bennett was somehow involved in the enterprise, because his research indicates that Capt. Mowry appears in reports related to James Gordon Bennett. Nevertheless, Dennis Amato's evaluation is that it "was as best a fad that lasted several months and then quickly died out."[66]

After the feeble attempt by Capt. Mowry to get polo going in California, it fell upon the English to revive the game in the 1880s, when Mr. C.A. Summers and Captain Hutcheson established polo in Los Angeles. Once more, the efforts were unsuccessful. Nevertheless, persistence paid off and, in 1888, Dr. J.A. Edmonds, who had learned the game in Long Island, spearheaded the foundation of the Santa Monica Polo Club. Another of the founders, Senator John Jones, had a polo ground built, as well as a racetrack. In 1891, Robert Lee Bettner joined a group of Englishmen to establish the Riverside Polo Club.[67]

Eventually, California had its own governing body, the Pacific Coast Polo and Pony Racing Association, which folded in 1909. It was started by British residents, and its rules of play were those promulgated by the Hurlingham Polo Committee, which included the concept of the offside position. The affiliated clubs were Burlingame, Los Angeles, San Mateo, Santa Barbara, Santa Monica and Coronado, the latter being the first one to join the Polo Association in 1909.[68]

EARLY POLO IN COLORADO

An undated etching by Max F. Klepper appeared in the 11 June 1892 issue of *Harper's Weekly*. The pertinent caption reads, "Polo above the snow-line at Colorado Springs." The etching depicts four players just cantering about on a flat field, with a background of snow-capped mountains. This is the first reference about the game in the state of Colorado.[69] The article mentions that polo was one of the most fascinating features of Colorado Springs. Ruth Olson Kahn goes on to mention that references to the game of polo abound around Colorado Springs.

The Cheyenne Mountain Country Club near Colorado Springs was founded on 23 February 1891 and claims to be the second country club in America, after The Country Club in Brookline.[70] Within months, polo was started on a field in front of the clubhouse. When Foxhall Keene became a member in 1896, he insisted that the polo ground be enlarged to 900 by 450 feet, which impinged upon the 9-hole golf course. It is not easy to have a 10-goaler around. Nevertheless, polo at Cheyenne Mountain was a going concern in the mid–1890s, although the club did not affiliate with the Polo Association until 1913.

One of the founders was Count James Pourtales, who came to Pike's Peak from Silesia to restore the fortunes of his estate, Glumbowitz. As it were, Count Pourtales went broke in the panic of 1893. The club's delegate was Charles A. Baldwin, who with his wife, Virginia, built Claremont, a magnificent house designed after the Petit Trianon in Versailles. Other polo players were William Sanford, the club's first president, Jay Lippincott from Philadelphia, the artist Robert Lewis Reid, who presented a polo painting that hangs in the polo bar, and Capt. Ashton Potterand. Celebrity visitors included personalities such as Harry Payne Whitney, the Moncrieffes from Wyoming, Teddy Roosevelt (the only U.S. president to play the game), Hervey Lyle and Lawrence C. Phipps.

When the Devereux brothers, Horace, James and Walter, and their sons moved to Colorado in the mid 1880s, they settled in Aspen. Close by, Irishman Hervey Lyle was the manager of a coal mine owned by Jerome B. Wheeler, who also was the proprietor of a smelter that was managed by Walter Devereux, Sr. Hervey Lyle had played polo in India and taught the rudiments of the game to the Devereux family. Play started in Glenwood Springs, at the time a frontier town; in the mid 1890s, the Glenwood Polo and Racing Association participated in its first game: Glenwood against Colorado Springs.[71] The club enlisted local cowboys and pack-trip guides, whose tough ponies were already proficient in cutting, so they became excellent polo ponies. Hervey Lyle went on to take to take the Polo Association Senior Championship on the Gould's Lakewood team. Walter Bourchier Devereux, Jr., became a successful coach at Princeton University and wrote *Position and Team Play in Polo*, published in 1924 and translated into Spanish by the Marqués de Viana.

The Denver Polo Club, one of the first polo clubs of the West, affiliated in 1912; however, it closed in 1917 because of the World War. The club briefly rejoined the Polo Association (U.S.P.A.) in 1921. Spencer Penrose, one of the partners in the plush Broadmoor Hotel, started the Broadmoor Club at Colorado Springs, which joined the U.S. Polo Association in 1923. It boasted three polo grounds and two practice fields, and the season, which extended from May until November, attracted players from all over the United States. Penrose, who had made his fortune in the nearby Cripple Creek gold mines, and later an even larger one in Utah copper, presented the Spencer Penrose Polo Park Gold Cup, a two-foot high trophy that was played without handicap.

To Canada — 1878

The first game of polo on Canadian land was played in July 1878 by British officers in Halifax, Nova Scotia, on Mr. G. Hoskins' property named Brucefields. No other mention of the game is made until September 1889, when the *Halifax Recorder* informed that polo games had been played twice a week during the summer on the Halifax Riding Grounds.[72]

Polo in Western Canada started in Calgary, Alberta, in 1886. It was fueled by the cattle boom resulting from lucrative investments by British and Eastern Canadian corporations. Along with the investments came many remittance men, the younger scions of wealthy English families. On their journey west, many stopped to be educated on the prairie's ways at the Agricultural College in Guelph, Ontario. Regardless of the training curriculum and the youths' commitment, their arrival was viewed with suspicious eyes. The local settlers considered many as too lazy to plough and too shiftless to own cattle.[73] But it was mainly that the game of polo was brought to Alberta's increasing number of cattle ranches by the remittance men.

In 1889, Capt. Edmund Mead Wilmot, having resigned his commission in the Derbyshire Rifle Corps, returned from England bringing to his Pincher Creek Ranch new sticks and balls, as well as a new bride, Agatha Jessopp. Then the game took on in earnest in southern Alberta. Calgary had a polo club in 1890, formed by Henry Bruen "Harry" Alexander;

The Fort Macleod polo team in 1890 included, from left, Insp. Montague Baker on the celebrated Canadian pony Bendigo, Stanley Pinhorn, Capt. Edmund Wilmot and Albert Browning. Bendigo was exported to England and became one of Walter Buckmaster's two best ponies (Museum of Polo and Hall of Fame).

High River boasted another club one year later, started by Maj. Colin George Ross. From the main populated centers, it spread to Fort Macleod and Pincher Creek. Later on, it was played in Pekisko, Millarville and Fish Creek in Alberta; then it progressed eastwards to Brandon and Winnipeg in Manitoba and Indian Head in Saskatchewan.

Nevertheless, just as it happened in Argentina, it was at the cattle ranches where polo prospered in Western Canada. John Varty's research indicates that although remittance men started the game, it promptly became the province of many and varied individuals. The players were the ranch owners and store clerks, retired military men and cowhands, farmers and lawyers.[74] That was not the situation in Victoria, neither in Vancouver, nor down east in Montreal or Toronto.

Another force in Western polo was the Canadian Mounted Police, even though the game was neither endorsed nor officially supported. The Mounties had been sent to the territory to close the whiskey fort that had sprung north of the international limit with the United States along the 49th parallel. The main post was Fort Macleod; others were Fort Calgary and Lethbridge. The first meeting of the Fort Macleod Polo Club took place at the garrison, and the police fielded a strong polo team.

Millarville first appeared on the scene at the Calgary Challenge Cup under the name Sheep Creek, after a nearby creek. The tournament was taken by the host team, High River Polo Club. The Calgary Challenge Cup probably is the oldest active polo tournament in the Americas, predating the Argentine Open, first played in 1893, and the U.S.P.A. Junior Championship, established in 1900, later renamed the 20-Goal Championship, and now the Silver Cup.

By 1889, matches were played on Victoria Island between Royal Navy officers from the Esquimalt Station and a civilian team from Victoria. The civilians were H.A. Barton, M.G. Drummond, H.F. Newton and Cecil W. Ward, while the navy was represented by Capt. the Hon. Hedworth Lambton, Lt. Thomas Ulric Thynne, Lt. George John Scott Warrenton, and Staff-Surgeon Christopher Pearson. The next documented match was held at Beacon Hill in 1891 between Victoria and a team from HMS *Warspite*, the latter winning 7–5.

In 1893, there was also a polo team in the Cowichan area north of the city of Victoria, clustered in the British settlement at Duncan. Two years later, they joined four Victoria players in a match against a combined Army-Navy team, which was held at Beacon Hill Park, located on Victoria's waterfront.

A High River team led by Maj. Colin G. Ross — who would later be a staunch supporter of polo in Southern California — and completed by Marston Sexsmith, Harry Robertson and R. Knowlton, traveled east to meet teams from Montreal, Toronto, Buffalo and Rochester. This was an outstanding accomplishment, not only for the self-taught ranchers, but also for the cow ponies of Western Canada. Two of the team's members, Robertson and Sexsmith, were selected to play for Canada against the visiting British team from Ranelagh.

In Montreal, the game began around 1899 on George A. Simard's farm. Other early players were Archibald Allan, P.A. Beaudin, Emile Daoust, Gen. Frank Meighan and Dr. A. Migneault. The Montreal Polo Club was organized by members of the Canadian Hunt Club; however, the two clubs remained separate. Mr. Simard bought a carload of Western ponies, some saddle broken, most not. The first game reflected the importance of trained ponies; after half an hour, no goals had been scored. The ball was missed much more than it was hit.[75] The Toronto Polo Club was founded in 1899 and matches against Montreal began in 1901 for a trophy presented by Mr. Alfred Beardmore. The following year there was a tournament in Toronto: in addition to the host club, Montreal, High River, and Rochester from New York

State participated. The Western team from High River took the cup with ease; the standard of play by the westerners was much superior. In 1904, the Eastern Canadian Polo Association was founded with Lt. Col. Williams as its president; Montreal and Toronto were the only member clubs. They were soon joined by Back River and Kingston polo clubs.

An important event occurred in 1910 when a British team, the first one to do so, visited Canada. The same team had taken the U.S. Open Championship at Narragansett Pier in Rhode Island. Two of the players were the Grenfell twins, Francis and Rivy, who were destined to be killed in World War I. They played against a Canadian team of Marston Sexsmith, Maj. Hartland Bridges MacDougall, Harry F. Robertson and Captain MacBrien. After the match, a trophy was presented to the Canadians on behalf of Arthur Grenfell, the twins' elder brother, who was in Western Canada with a view to invest capital. The trophy was to be played annually and became symbolic of the Canadian Championship until 1939, when the Second World War put a stop to polo in Canada. The trophy itself is a copy of the Warwick Vase, which dates back to the fourth century B.C.[76] The Grenfell Cup is now in the Canadian Sports Hall of Fame in Toronto.

In spite of its rich tradition, the origins of polo in Canada have been largely ignored by historians of the game, with the sterling exception of Tony Rees, whose splendidly researched *The Galloping Game*, subtitled *An Illustrated History of Polo in the Canadian West*, is an indispensable source. Iris Clendenning has also done her bit for eastern polo in *The History of the Montreal Polo Club*.

A huge country, Canada suffered just like Australia from the tyranny of distance, which prevented a consolidation of resources for the creation of a truly national polo association. The style of the game in the West was totally different from its Eastern counterpart, which developed along the lines of the New England and New York's style of polo. The Western provinces, Victoria in its long ago heydays, British Columbia, the checkered polo-wise Manitoba and Saskatchewan, and the powerhouse Alberta developed a kind of game characterized by skillful horsemanship on home-bred ponies and a mixture of raw individualism tempered by discipline on the polo ground.

To New Zealand — 1885

> *By an oddity, seamen or, more accurately, officers of the Royal Navy, that guardian shield of the great Victorian Empire upon which the sun never set, were the first to acquaint New Zealanders — principally citizens of Auckland and Christchurch — with the glories of the game.* — Sir Terence McLean[77]

Contrary to established dogma, polo in New Zealand began on the South Island. Arthur Rhodes was the founder of the Christchurch Polo Club in 1885.[78] Arthur Edgar Gravenor Rhodes had recently returned to New Zealand after graduating from Cambridge University and being called to the bar at the Inner Temple. It is possible that he learned the game while at university. What is certain is that polo was played in Christchurch in the summer of 1885–86, and each summer thereafter.[79]

While most of the published accounts on the beginnings of polo in New Zealand report that Edward Dennis "Teddy" O'Rorke, a local worthy from Auckland, brought the game from the North Island to Christchurch, it is more likely that he learned polo in Christchurch. His father, Sir Maurice O'Rorke, speaker of the House of Representatives, was a close friend of

Robert Rhodes, Sr. The O'Rorkes had visited Christchurch many times in the 1880s. As a dedicated horseman, it is almost certain that Teddy had met cousins Arthur and Heaton Rhodes and played polo with them. He would eventually marry Amy, Heaton Rhodes' sister.

The Royal Navy was instrumental in developing the game of polo in New Zealand. The opening in 1888 of the graving dock Calliope gathered several British ships in Auckland's Waitemata Harbor; serving on board were several polo-playing officers. Among them were Seymour Elphinstone Erskine, Lt. Maurice Fenwick, Francis E.M. Garforth, William Story and the Hon. Reginald Tyrwhitt.[80] They met with Edward O'Rorke and some practice games were arranged. The Auckland Polo Club was formed shortly after. A momentous event occurred in 1889 when Lt. Robert Stewart-Savile,[81] aide-de-camp to the governor of New Zealand, William Hillier, Earl of Onslow, presented a trophy bearing his name. It was to be played for by New Zealand teams only, with the exception of the Imperial Services, who could enter one team yearly. The first competition took place in Auckland on the Ellerslie racecourse in February 1890, which makes the Savile Cup the oldest national sporting trophy in the islands. It was a three-cornered affair, in which Christchurch took the honors, defeating both Auckland and a Royal Navy team.[82] The reasons why Christchurch emerged the victors were twofold: they had much better ponies and the team as a whole seemed to have grasped the game's fundamentals very quickly. The Christchurch team, anchored by the Rhodes cousins, would go on to take the Savile Cup four years in a row.

Edward O'Rorke also carried the gospel to Wellington and the Waikato.[83] The event for the Savile Cup provided extra impetus for the establishment of a ruling body; therefore, the New Zealand Polo Association was founded in 1891 by the following clubs: Amuri, Auckland, Christchurch, Dunedin, North Canterbury, Rangitikei and Waikari. The Earl of Onslow was elected president.[84]

In Wellington, once more the Senior Service contributed to New Zealand polo's growth when HMS *Curacoa* paid the city a visit. The officers on board showed great keenness to play polo because they owned nine ponies purchased in Australia, which they sent ahead by steamer to the ports of call and played as often as possible. The team was made up of Lt. Commander Arthur Edward Harford, Lt. Vivian Champion de Crespigny, Lt. A.C. Warren and Midshipman Viscount Patrick James Kelburn, later Earl of Glasgow. Lt. Arthur Cole Lowry, Midshipman John Kenneth Crawley and Chaplain Hugh K. Moore played some matches as well.[85]

The first tour was to New South Wales and Victoria, Australia, in 1899. It was reciprocated two years later when in February a team from Victoria returned the visit. The players were R. Albert Affleck, Robert Alec D. Hood, Edward Manifold, and George and Colin Robertson. The initial game was at Hagley Park, the home of the Christchurch club, which presented Edward O'Rorke, Heaton Rhodes (captain), W.H.P. Woodroffe and J.D. Hall. Victoria was represented by George and Colin Robertson, Alec Hood (captain) and Albert Affleck. The visitors won 5–4, because of better combination play, the bane of New Zealand polo for years to come. The local newspaper, the *Press*, published a detailed report of the game, in which it referred to the periods as "spells." Two days later another game took place against a side called South Island, where Alister Clark replaced J.D. Hall at back. Victoria won again, 6–4. They also played matches against Manawatu, Oroua, Rangitikei and Hawke's Bay. The Victorians also played two games versus New Zealand, at North Palmerston and, in the tour's last match, at Miramar in Wellington. The honors were evenly divided, Victoria taking the first game 8–5 and losing the second 4–3.

The final game was described as a "Test" match, the teams being J. Octy Robinson and the Strang brothers for New Zealand, and the Robertsons, Edward Manifold and Alec Hood for the visitors. The umpires were Albert Affleck and Sydney Williamson. On the team's return to Australia, Mr. Manifold praised the New Zealand ponies and the ground at Christchurch. New Zealand's reputation as producer of top polo ponies had early recognition and continues into our days.

There was another international game at Hagley Park in March 1901, when a team of officers from the Indian Imperial Contingent played against Christchurch Polo Club in front of a crowd of 8,000. The local team was the winner, four goals to nil. The visiting players observed that the ground was very soft; there is no doubt that they missed the hard polo grounds of India.[86]

Following the Victorian team's tour, Jack and Walter Strang left for England with some ponies. They participated in a few tournaments at Crystal Palace, where the London Polo Club held its matches. On one occasion, they faced Winston Churchill, of whom Jack Strang wrote: "I think he is a better at politics than polo!"[87]

The game in New Zealand was affected by the Anglo-Boer War, 1899–1902, during which many New Zealanders and their horses departed for the South African veldt. It then experienced a rebound, up to the beginning of World War I, which event once more brought polo in the isles to a full stop.

5. Polo in India:
Conflicts and Harmonies

When you go to a country you must conform to the habits of that country if you wish to be successful.—Lord Roberts of Kandahar[1]

During the 1870s and 1880s, the game of polo rose to predominance in India. Eventually, almost every cavalry regiment, both Army-in-India and Native Cavalry, boasted a polo club. An important source of concern was the custom that every officer support the expenses of a regiment's polo, whether he played or not. Matters came to a head when in 1899, non-playing officers at the Naini Tal station presented a petition stating that the practice of expecting all officers to contribute to the regimental polo team fund, regardless of rank or interest in the game, was despotic.

For the British officers polo became an ideal pastime to combat the idleness and boredom of service in far away, isolated stations. It was also thought that in tropical climates, hard exercise, preferably twice a day, was a good way to keep healthy. Together with hunting and pig sticking — a cult unto itself — polo became nothing short of a craze. This obsession raised concerns both in India and at home. The high military authorities were concerned that the officers were paying more attention to polo and their polo ponies than to garrison matters such as continuing military training and the care of the regiments' chargers. At home, irate parents paid visits to high-ranking officers at the War Office, with the complaint that their sons had exhausted their allowances because they were spending it all in purchasing and keeping polo ponies.[2] In his *Letters on Polo in India*, Maj. Roland Grimshaw, writing under the nom de plume "A Lover of the Game," sternly advises his reader: "The game makes sufficiently stringent demands on the pocket ... you must be prepared to forego many of the flesh-pots of this life."[3]

Sir Winston Churchill in letters to his mother regularly complained about the necessity of procuring better ponies, which, needless to say, placed a strain upon his allowance. In spite of that, it was the ability of his regiment's officers to buy a string of no less than 25 mounts from the Poona Light Horse that enabled the 4th Hussars to run away with the Inter-Regimental Tournament in 1899.[4] The 4th was not fancied by the experts to do well in the tournament, but then, as always, better mounts made the difference. The 34th Poona Light Horse Native Cavalry had gained a reputation of making a profitable business by purchasing unmade ponies, training them to good standards, and then offering the mounts for sale at much increased prices.

Polo at the Indian stations was usually played on Mondays, Wednesdays and Fridays; therefore, the game assumed a central position in the officers' daily routine.[5] Thus the game of polo became an accepted part of cavalry training, a central point of the daily life at the regiment stations, and offered a semblance of social interaction between Indian and British Army officers.

The Native Cavalry regiments shared Indian and British officers; therefore, there was more social contact between the two nationalities. "Hindu Horse" was the appellation given to the Native Cavalry by their British Army counterparts. The British officers who served in the Native regiments were considered more intellectual than their counterparts in the regular army regiments, many of whom prided themselves in their ignorance of world affairs, concentrating most of their energies on women, liquor and sports.[6] Interest in military proficiency came in a distant fourth, and, at times, was thought of as "bad form" by fellow officers. This attitude of gifted amateurs in the business of war remained a constant in many cavalry regiments. Lt. Col. Denzil Holder, Skinner's Horse, wrote in the preface to his memoirs, "I asked the compiler of our family tree what had happened to the family money and he replied, 'I think it went mainly on expensive cavalry regiments and riotous living.'"[7]

This lackadaisical attitude ended when shots were fired in anger. The British officers' leadership in many conflicts, from the Victorian "little wars" to the world conflicts, was beyond reproach. The number of Victoria Crosses awarded to polo-playing officers bears witness to the bravery of these men, who sometime battled insurmountable odds.[8] The military weaknesses shown in Word War I were not the fault of the more junior officers, but of some generals ensconced in chateaux miles away from the trenches.

The relationship between Indians and British was a most complicated one. Following the Crown's takeover of the military duties previously held by the East India Company, a sizable part of the country was under princely rule, supported by treaty with the United Kingdom government. These large states, of which Hyderabad was the most extensive, were ruled by the maharajas in the style of medieval times. Most had immense fortunes, which they dissipated in pursuit of worldly pleasures, one of them being polo. Many became very adept at the game, especially in the 20th century. The names of the maharajas of Jaipur, Kashmir, Kisangarth, Patiala and Bhopal loom large in the panorama of polo. Their teams, staffed by relatives and their own army officers, were frequent winners of the Indian Open Championship.

The maharajas' private armies supported what were really professional polo players. Skill at polo meant for both officers and noncommissioned officers nothing less than a wonderful opportunity for promotion and extra privileges. Hira Singh, who was a corporal in the Bengal Cavalry, moved on to the Patiala forces, where he reputedly rose to colonel "chiefly due to his skill as a polo player."[9]

Polo became a vehicle for social contact between Indians and British. While the game of cricket, at which many Indians became outstanding players, was the province of less prominent local leaders, polo enjoyed the patronage of the top-level Indian potentates. For the princes, their teams' success at polo usually brought along British interest and support for their home state, besides honors and decorations for the individual ruler, such as the Star of India and the Order of the Indian Empire.

Manly virtues were at the root of both British and Indian ambitions. They entered the game with utmost dedication to fair play, trust in each other, and sportsmanship: every one a time-honored rule of civilized conduct. Breakage of this unwritten code had dire consequences. The Maharaja of Alwar, an 8-goal handicap player whose team dominated Indian polo in the early 1900s, not satisfied with one of his ponies' performance, ordered it doused with gasoline and set on fire. The British Resident witnessed the barbaric spectacle, and soon enough the petty tyrant was in exile in Paris. To ease the pain of banishment, a large entourage accompanied the deposed ruler to the city of lights.[10]

Patrick McDevitt made the point that for both the ruling classes of the princely states and the British military establishment in India, the game of polo developed into a "central marker of the masculine ethos thought to be necessary to defend the imperial status quo in the face of increasingly strident calls for reform and independence."[11] However, rather than viewing the Indian aristocracy as a parallel and equal hierarchy to the British aristocracy, it would be more accurate to characterize it as mimetic but inferior.[12] The Indian potentates indulged in polo because it was a way to emphasize their power and eminently aristocratic social standing, not because it might be a path to becoming more British. Although this fraternity could not overcome deeply entrenched British racism and attitudes of cultural superiority, at least within the polo community, there was an equality of opportunity and fair

The Queen's Royal West Surrey Regiment polo team took the Infantry Inter-regimental Tournament in India three times. This is the 1903 squad (left to right): Capt. Herbert Engledue, Lt. Brownlow Mathew-Lannowe, Maj. William Glasgow and Lt. Robert Creek. Only "Bunny" Mathew-Lannowe achieved further fame in polo when he took the Warwickshire Cup, among many others, and was a reserve on the 1924 bronze medal Olympic team (From Capt. Engledue's family album, now in a private collection).

competition. Nevertheless, the camaraderie usually ended with the game's last bell. Indians, including some who had been received by royalty, were not allowed in most of the British Army regimental messes.

The caste system and centuries-honored rules of conduct did not permit Indian women, especially Muslims, to mix socially with other races. The custom known as purdah (curtain), which confined females to certain areas of homes and palaces, virtually made impossible any meaningful social contact with foreigners and other Indians. Strict purdah was also observed overseas. There is a photograph of the Maharani of Jodhpur watching a polo game at Roehampton Club from her automobile in the 1920s. The maharani cannot be seen, because she is behind curtains. The car's chauffer is a woman, and the Rolls Royce's Spirit of Ecstasy mascot on the radiator has been replaced by Jodhpur's eagle.[13]

British regiments serving their tour of duty in India were not immune to some problems. In 1902, two troopers in the 9th Lancers beat to death an Indian cook. When a court of inquiry failed to identify the culprits, one of the victim's relatives appealed directly to the viceroy, Lord Curzon. The viceroy, appalled at the regiment's callousness, mandated an extensive investigation that, again, was unable to identify the murderers. Lord Curzon punished the whole regiment. Officers on leave were recalled to duty. Other ranks on furlough were called back and extra sentry duties were mandated. Furthermore, regimental leave was denied for six months.[14] Curzon's courageous action provoked wide consternation among the Army and the British community in India. The waves reached England. In the House of Commons the Hon. Heneage Legge, a former 9th Lancers commanding officer, rose to protest the collective punishment. Nevertheless, at the 1902 Delhi Durbar honoring Edward's VII coronation, the British spectators, including some in the viceregal staff, cheered as the regiment paraded in the course of the celebrations.[15]

The most egregious single episode of British rule in India, the Amritsar massacre, evoked different reactions, reflecting deeply ingrained prejudice by a large segment of the ruling class on one side, the wish for independence on the other, and an attempt at objective evaluation by distant observers. On 13 April 1919, Brig. Reginald Dyer ordered his Indian and Gurkha troops to fire on a crowd of men, women and children who had gathered at the Jallianwalla Garden in Amritsar for a religious ceremony. The garden was a wall-enclosed place with entrances so narrow that two armored cars equipped with machine guns could not enter the enclosure. The fire lasted for about ten minutes; casualties were reported officially at 379 but less biased estimates put the number at over 1,000. The wounded were left unattended because a curfew had been put into effect. To add insult to injury, Punjab's governor, Sir Michael O'Dwyer, send a telegram to Brig. Dyer signaling his approval of the action.

In the massacre's aftermath, Dyer was cashiered and sent home, while Governor O'Dwyer was relieved of his post. Nevertheless, the *Morning Post* collected 26,000 pounds sterling, a huge amount of money in those days, destined to a fund for Brigadier Dyer. In England, the House of Lords commended Dyer, but the House of Commons censured him. During the debate, Winston Churchill said, "It was a monstrous event, an event which stands in singular and sinister isolation."[16]

Polo in India was vastly different from the game practiced on the lush green British grounds. On the firm and slippery Indian grounds, turning around in a circle was tantamount to risking a heavy fall; it was mandatory to pull up on a straight line before making a turn. On a field in England, sod with a rich, holding turf made it possible to turn without losing too much speed, or taking the risk of a fall. Ponies in India were trained with a rather severe single-rein bit, which had to be used with a slack rein. British players, accustomed to milder bits and shorter reins, could not easily adapt to the change. This is perhaps the reason for the charge leveled at British players newly arrived to India: as soon as they disembarked and played on Indian grounds, they instantly became "has-beens" to the locals, although they were high up on Hurlingham's handicap list.

The science of biting is all-important in polo. The introduction of polo was immediately followed by a demand, fostered by trial and error, for many new types of bits. Lt. Col. Roland Grimshaw wrote: "Indeed, there are so many bits these days that to enter into each and every kind is a big task."[17]

The preferred bit in India was the one used by the 9th Lancers, which had a straight, thick, steel bar mouthpiece. Some were fitted with a port, with the purpose of discouraging the pony from putting his tongue above the bar. Another popular bit was the half-moon Ramsey-Pelham, a rather severe one. The best bit was the double bridle, a combination of a Weymouth and a bridoon; however, very few ponies could be handled with such combination.

Military polo in India benefited greatly from the support given by the commander-in-chief, Sir Frederick Roberts,[18] who was well aware of the advantages of polo as both a pastime and a school of horsemanship. Sir Frederick issued an order making compulsory the wearing of protective headgear at a time when there were many fatal accidents on the polo field. General Roberts also insisted on strict umpiring, more severe penalties for fouling, and, furthermore, club captains were made responsible for warning off ponies showing vice.[19]

The smart players wore white long pants, ties and cloth caps. This attire most likely would elicit sardonic smiles today. It is of note that in Argentina, ties, and sometimes bow-ties, were quite common in camp polo, especially on Sundays or on national holidays. Needless to say, umpires wore sports jackets and hats well into the 1950s.

Cloth forage caps were almost useless as a protection in case of a fall or being hit by a mallet. They were only of value in shading the sun. Therefore, many players discarded caps and went bareheaded. However, it did not take long to find out that with the increased speed at which the game was being played and with the stronger hitting, it was dangerous to ride on the field without protective headgear.

In the matter of tactics, Indian polo was at the forefront. John Watson, while serving in the 13th Hussars in the 1870s, started the regular practice of hitting backhanders as a way of quickly turning defense into attack, while at the same time coaching his teammates to keep their positions in a straight line ahead. It was said that some players paid so much attention to keeping their position on the field and riding off their opponents that at times they forgot the ball and the importance of scoring goals.[20] Watson took his system to Britain in the 1880s, after leaving the service, and low scoring games became the rule rather than the exception in the British Isles. John Watson's disciples exaggerated his precepts and defense became more important than goal scoring.

Another player who had significant influence upon the game in India was a subaltern in the 17th Lancers, Gordon Renton. Into his regimental style of play, Renton introduced a less rigid system, stressing combination play between forwards and defensive players. His teachings were behind the success achieved by the 17th Lancers in the Indian Inter-Regimental Tournament in 1888 and 1889.[21] Playing on those teams was a young lieutenant who would absorb and expand Renton's ideas into one of the most successful polo teams ever. Lt. Col. Edward Darley Miller would rise to the top as a player, organizer, horse expert and writer on the game of polo, and his Rugby teams would dominate the polo scene in England for several years.

In the early 1890s, the Queen's Bays enjoyed a good run in the Inter-Regimental Tournament, which it won from 1892 to 1894.[22] Led by Capt. William Kirk, their team set a standard of play well above the one displayed by their contemporaries. Their successful run was cut short in 1894 as the result of their deployment to Egypt. Credit for the Bays' success was, firstly, the fact that the team remained intact and they practiced assiduously, and, most important, they kept on improving their pony string.

The Maharaja of Patiala's team developed to the highest degree the tactic of blocking the opposing players in order to give their back, the talented Hira Singh, space for his patented runs toward goal. Hira Singh was the outstanding player of his generation, and his teammates, no mean players, were only happy to punch holes in their adversary's defense for Hira to score goals. These developments were partially imitated by great Jodhpur teams under Sir Patrap Singh. Their star player was Dhonkal Singh, who was thought by many to be as good as, or better than, Hira Singh. As far as ponies go, both teams had such riches that the number of ponies allowed to each team in some tournaments had to be limited to 18 or 24.

The next improvement was developed by Capt. Henry De Lisle of the Durham Light Infantry.[23] In his own words: "Our first success was in the Infantry Cup of 1894 at Lucknow. We met the Gordon Highlanders in the finals. Their best player, Freddie Ker [*sic*], pinned his faith to the dribbling game. At this he was most skillful. On the other hand we had trained on the principle that pace will always defeat the slow game, and dribbling tends to slow down the game. Our success confirmed the theory of pace, and from thence forward we continued to practice and play fast."[24]

De Lisle implemented a regime of intensive training for both man and mount that had not been applied before. Upon this solid foundation, he devised a pattern of play based on team discipline, a policy of passing the ball to a better-positioned teammate, and pace. Their practice chukkers were as fast as a regular game. This careful preparation and the sound game tactics permitted the Durham Light Infantry to take the Indian Inter-Regimental Tournament three consecutive years, 1896–1898. In the entire tournament's history, only one other infantry unit won the cup, the 3rd Rifle Brigade in 1900. The Durham L.I. also took the first Indian Polo Association Championship in 1898.

It was thought at the time that both Jodhpur and Patiala would have defeated the Durham Light Infantry three times out of four, because of their abundant string of superlative ponies and a number of players for selection far greater than those available to Captain De Lisle. The Durhams owed their success to pre-game preparation, strong leadership, sound field tactics and team play. In their glory years, only five players played on the team. Capt. De Lisle played at number 3; the team captain was always the best-mounted player on the team and he was a hard hitter, able to score goals from the field's centerline. At back, he was supported by Capt. Charles Carmac Luard, a very good cricketer who was a beautiful striker, although not as good a rider as the forwards were. Capt. Henry Benfield Des Vœux Wilkinson at number 2 was reckoned to be the team's best player; according to De Lisle, should handicaps had been in force at the time, Wilkinson would have been handicapped at nine goals. William John Ainsworth played at number 1 in most of the tournaments. He was a good cricketer, played at center forward on the regiment's football team and was a certain scorer in both polo and soccer. In their last season, Ainsworth and Lionel Forbes Ashburner tossed for the position, and Lt. Ashburner won. It was no loss to the team, because Capt. De Lisle was of the opinion that Ashburner would be worth an 8-goal handicap.

De Lisle's three principles of polo can be summarized as: first, possession; that is, keep the ball among one's own players. Second is pace. It is virtually impossible to win polo matches unless you can play fast polo. The third is accuracy in shooting at goal. Possession, pace and scoring comprise the trinity that Captain De Lisle, the first real thinker on polo since John Watson, preached and practiced at the end of the 19th century.

The next foursome to come to the front in India was the Alwar (sometimes spelled Ulwar) team. The mastermind was Capt. Robert Lumsden Ricketts, of the Native Cavalry regiment Hodson's Horse. Ricketts, the dominant personality and tactical innovator of Indian polo in the 1890s, made the case for applying brains to the game in his *First Class Polo*.[25] He is a leading contender — along with America's William Cameron Forbes and Canada-born Lewis Lacey — for the title of sharpest intellect ever applied to the game.

Robert Ricketts kept up to date with the development of other games played in England, such as rackets, where an aggressive offensive approach became the norm. Capt. Ricketts increased the conditioning scheme practiced by De Lisle by making the team members play other games, mainly rackets. He also paid attention to the manufacture of mallets, trying to achieve balance without sacrificing strength. The result was a significant improvement in hitting, both in accuracy and in length. With the backing of the Maharaja of Alwar, who filled the number 2 position with ease, a good string of ponies was secured. The game's fast pace was now a given, but they raised the speed to something not seen before on Indian grounds. The Alwar team, completed with Moti Lal at number 1, Ricketts at number 3 and Rao Raja Amar Singh at back, was never beaten nor even seriously extended in a tournament during its three-year existence. Captain Ricketts even wore a turban instead of the typical polo pith helmet worn by British officers.

Ricketts expanded De Lisle's simple three precepts into six fundamental tactics, which he summarized as "the direct approach to the goal." According to Ricketts, they were:

1. Hitting the ball early to start it on its journey as soon as possible.
2. Sending the ball by the most direct route.
3. Sending the ball up the field to be sent on by players ahead, instead of one player taking the ball up the field.
4. Early positioning, which not only facilitated the quick accomplishment of # 3, but also forced opponents to gallop fast in order not to be left at a disadvantage.
5. Hitting the ball hard to make it travel fast.
6. Fast galloping and quick turning, which tended to reduce the time between successive incidents in the game.

It was all about pace. Ricketts was adamant that practice games must be conducted at full speed; therefore, the desired result was that tournament play lost all its terror for the team. Capt. Ricketts wrote:

Pace will upset the play of a man

1. who does not like hitting a fast moving ball;
2. who is not quick enough on moving to the proper position;
3. who has not the quick grasp of the situation to realize what is about to happen;
4. who has not got the match-playing temperament which prevent him from getting bustled.[26]

Putting into practice the above precepts, the Alwar team took three Indian Polo Association Open Championships, from 1901 to 1903. Even though Ricketts advised his players to hit the ball hard, he added the caveat that the stroke should be an easy swing, more like a golf drive than a cricket hit. Compare this to Sinclair Hill's repeated admonition to Charles, Prince of Wales: "The faster you go, the slower the swing!"[27]

Regrettably, the Alwar team was dissolved and the lessons imparted by Captain Ricketts were not widely followed. Only the Poona Light Horse among the military teams and the Indian Pilgrims, the latter winners of the Indian Polo Association Open Championship in 1906 and 1907, absorbed to some extent Ricketts' teachings. The 1907 Pilgrims team included the Maharaja Jay Singh of Alwar and Moti Lal, two of the original Alwar team members. Perhaps Ricketts' theories, although now considered relatively simplistic, were ahead of the times. His tactics were never endorsed in England until the American victory in the 1909 Westchester Cup impressed upon the British polo hierarchy the necessity of reviewing their training practices and game strategy. Brigadier Ricketts himself has ventured the opinion that the tac-

tics were "not understood by a community whose games-playing education was elementary ... the essentials of which British polo players seem to find very difficult to grasp, or at any rate to practice."[28]

In India, the 10th Hussars under Lt. Col. John Vaughn learned the novel tactics and had a sensational run in the Inter-Regimental Tournament, in addition to taking the 1910 Indian Polo Association Open Championship. Their strongest players were Bill Palmes at number 3 and William "Pedlar" Llewellen Palmer at back. In a military environment with strict divisions between officers and noncommissioned officers, there was also a polo club for the noncommissioned officers and privates of the 10th Hussars, established in Muttra through the energy of Lt. the Hon. Charles Cavendish, and afterwards supported by the officers generally and Lord Airlie in particular.[29] Prior to the departure of the regiment from Lucknow, David Ogilvy, 6th Earl of Air-

This 10th Hussars team dominated Indian polo in the 1910s. The Hon. Arthur Annesley, Bill Palmes, William Llewellen Palmer and William Gibbs (left to right) are pictured with the Inter-regimental Tournament trophy. It was a time of transition in the development of the polo mallet. Capt. Annesley has a modern cigar head, while Capt. Palmes and Capt. Gibbs hold the almost obsolete curved head, probably the Le Gallais model (courtesy Charles Llewellen Palmer, Esq.).

lie, a generous man, had a well sunk close to the Divisional Polo Ground for the benefit of future players, and it was named David's Well after his lordship.[30]

The famous Golconda team sponsored by the Nizam of Hyderabad had a long time of preeminence in Southern India. Led by Capt. Shah Mirza Beg — whose capacity for pure ball control was not equaled by his contemporaries — based his team's tactics upon a development of the dribbling methods of early polo. Their list of successes was a very long one, as was the terrible toll of those opponents over whom they established early ascendancy. However, they were apt to collapse when forced beyond the comparatively moderate pace to which their system was adapted.[31] Pace, once more, would tell.

The Indian Polo Association adopted the handicap system in 1911. The first 10-goalers were Capt. Leslie St. Clair Cheape, Kings's Dragoon Guards, Capt. Vyvyan (known as Vivian) Noverre Lockett, 17th Lancers, and Capt. Ralph Gerald Ritson, Inniskilling Dragoons. Capt. Shah Mirza Beg, perhaps the best Indian player of his time, was rated at 8 goals. In 1912, Captains Frederick "Rattle" Barrett, 15th Hussars, and Edward W.E. "Bill" Palmes, 10th Hussars, joined the elite fellowship of ten goalers. India would not have any native 10-goalers until 1923, when Gen. Joginder Singh and Col. Jaswant Singh of the Patiala team were elevated to that lofty position. However, England's Hurlingham Polo Committee was the official body that recognized their skills while playing for Comte Jean de Madré's Tigers team. The Indian Polo Association never conferred the maximum handicap on a native Indian player. The most egregious omission was that imposed upon Rao Raja Hanut Singh, perhaps the best Indian player ever. It has been ventured that a Rao Raja could not be rated in handicap above a maharaja, but this is only speculation.

It was another time, another country. However, even half a century after independence and partition, there is nostalgia. A letter from Brigadier Denis Ormerod to the author briefly touches the memories: "In passing, it may interest you that during the war, the great polo player Bob Skene served in the same Regiment as me (2nd King Edward VII's Own Gurkha Rifles), so for a short time, I had the privilege of playing polo with him at our Regimental depot in Dehra Dun, India. Great days!"[32]

6. The Beginning of
the Internationals

"And so the lure of the International continues, and the lure becomes a magnet."—James C. Cooley[1]

Although it is difficult to ascertain what was and what was not an international contest, several matches in the early development of polo were held that can reasonably be considered to fulfill international characteristics. Other so-called internationals took place; one example is the Patriotic Cup between England and Ireland, instituted in 1903, some nineteen years before the Irish Free State achieved independence from Great Britain.

The issue of nationalities has always bedeviled sporting contests. An early example was the 1900 Olympic Games in Paris, in which players of different nationalities were members on medal-winning teams. The situation is more complicated in our day, because of the ease in obtaining European Union passports by individuals with Old World ancestry. The most blatant example was set by Italy, whose team took the European Polo Championship with three Argentine-born members. In spite of informal protests by other participants, the same attitude prevailed at the 2007 qualifier for the 14-Goal World Championship held in Spain. Once more, three Argentine natives sporting European Union passports played for Italy during its unsuccessful bid for a place among the final eight nations in Mexico 2008.

England—France at Dieppe, 1880

Little is known about the first international game of polo. It has always been reported as the first international match, although perhaps some purists might feel that the visit of a team of Manipuris to Calcutta in the 1860s qualifies as to primacy. It should be pointed out that the team was indeed formed by Manipuris; however, they were living in Cachar, part of India. The match between Englishmen and Frenchmen, ably supported by two Americans, took place in Dieppe, a port on the English Channel coast that holds bitter memories in Canadian minds because of the 1942 raid, a bloody rehearsal for the Normandy invasion.

There has been some dispute as to the exact year when the match took place, 1880 or ten years later; contemporary information points out to the early date. The precise site where the contest was held has not been identified. The teams were composed as follows:

English Team	*French Team*
Reginald Herbert	Duc Antoine de Guiche
Arthur Peat	Vicomte Leon de Janzé
James E. Peat	Raoul de Brinquant
William Ince Anderton	Marion Story
Edward H. Baldock	Henry Ridgeway

According to James Moray Brown in his *Polo*, a volume in the *Badminton Library* set of books covering many sports and games, "There was an enormous crowd present. The ground was kept by a regiment of infantry and enthusiasm ran high. Occasionally some gallant Gaul would rush in and pick up the ball when the game was going against his countrymen, while sacres! Parbleus! and other French expletives flew about thickly, accompanied by much shouting and gesticulation. In spite of all, however, the English team won by the crushing majority of eleven goals to none!"[2]

The Anglo team was composed of fine players. Reginald Herbert, "Tip" Herbert's older brother, was an all-around sportsman with two Hurlingham Champion Cups to his credit. Arthur and James Peat were among the top players in England; as previously described, their record in Hurlingham's Champion Cup remains unsurpassed because only Walter Buckmaster has been equal to their eleven wins. William Ince Anderton was a useful player and Edward Baldock carried the reputation of being a solid forward.

The Franco-American team is less known. Antoine Agénor Armand, Duc de Guiche, was probably team captain by virtue of rank, if not ability. He was still listed as an active player in 1912.[3] Less is known about the polo abilities of the Vicomte de Janzé, although there a cartoon of him by the artist Charles-Fernand de Condamy.[4] M. Raoul de Brinquant's polo career is also a mystery. Mr. Marion Story played at the Country Club of Westchester; his handicap was 2 goals, and his name is not listed in the American Polo Blue Books after 1904. Of Mr. Henry Ridgway, it is known that he played at Bagatelle. Perhaps he was an archetypal American in Paris.

There is no further significant mention in the literature about this game in Dieppe.

America — England at Newport, 1886

John Elliott Cowdin, the 10-goal player and Hall of Fame inductee from the Rockaway Club, has called this game the most important in the history of American polo.[5] The superior knowledge of the game and better teamwork won the day for the British, and the play of John Watson, team captain and back, was a revelation to the Americans. Cowdin wrote that Watson "would direct his men and back the ball to them in such a way that the ball always came to the man to whom he shouted, and he would then carry the ball down the field and make the goal. These matches taught us more about polo than we could have learned by ourselves in a great many years."[6]

Thus, John Watson, the "founding father of polo," in Roger Chatterton-Newman's words, exerted his influence upon the game on three continents, Asia, Europe and North America.[7] It must be pointed out that the rules of the game as played in the United States had done away with the off-side, and allowed neither the backhander stroke nor the hooking of sticks. The game obviously was played under Hurlingham rules, because the backhander stroke, John Watson's concoction, played a capital role in the series.

The International Polo Cup, later known as the Westchester Cup, came about at a dinner in the spring of 1886 at the Hurlingham Club in Fulham, which was attended by Griswold Lorillard. Mr. Lorillard proposed that a Hurlingham team should visit America to play matches against the Westchester Polo Club in Newport, to which his hosts agreed, provided the travel expenses for players and ponies were taken care of. This small matter was resolved and Tiffany and Co. was commissioned to manufacture an appropriate trophy.

This presented a minor problem for Frank Gray Griswold, who, as secretary of the Westchester Polo Club, was in charge of all the arrangements. Mr. Griswold wished the trophy to be emblematic of the game of polo, but the designer at Tiffany's had never seen a match, and there was no opportunity for him to do so. Obviously, the designer had access to one of the most famous polo prints, "Polo Match at Hurlingham between the Royal Horse Guards (The Blues) and the Monmouthshire Team, July 7th, 1977," by the

The Westchester Cup, the oldest international polo trophy, manufactured by Tiffany and Co. in 1887, some six months after the first contest for the cup in Morton Park, Newport (Museum of Polo and Hall of Fame).

hand of George Earl.[8] Examination of the polo players' figures represented on the cup leaves little doubt that they are Capt. John Brocklehurst and Francis "Tip" Herbert; they are depicted in the same attitudes as the central figures in George Earl's painting.

The first game was played on 25 August 1886 at Morton Park, just a few blocks away from Newport's Bellevue Avenue, the site of some of America's most spectacular mansions.[9] Although right from the start Foxhall Keene quickly scored the first goal, the visitors ended up on top 10–4.[10] The second game took place on Saturday the 28th. The final score, 14–2, amply tells of the difference between the two teams.[11]

The Americans lacked the power of the backhander shot and did not possess a player endowed with the genius of John Watson; however, they planted on the polo grounds the seed of an international rivalry on the polo grounds that was to fructify many hundred-folds. The matches caused little stir in the press. Capt. Edward Miller, who was to become the doyen of British polo, was playing cricket in America at the time, and he did not find out about the matches until his return to England. The British team returned home without the ornate trophy because the work had not been finished. Tiffany's records reveal that the date of manufacture was 17 January 1887.[12]

Although both the U.S. Polo Association and the Hurlingham Polo Association rightly consider this series as the first international event between the two countries, it should be pointed out that there were games between representatives of the Hurlingham Club and the Westchester Polo Club. The Polo Association was still to be born in America.

Argentina — Chile at Valparaíso, 1893

The Buenos Aires newspaper *La Nación* printed in its 14 November 1893 edition a report on the departure of a cricket team with destination Chile. Titled "Sport: International Cricket — The Chile vs. Argentina Match and the Departure of Players and Companions," the report said:

> Thanks to the courtesy of our colleague The Times of Argentina we are able to publish the following about international cricket. It is quite possible that in the future the lasting reconciliation between Argentina and Chile will be attributed to a famous expedition undertaken by a few cricketers, accompanied in this endeavor by beautiful ladies, who departed from Buenos Aires on Monday, 13 November 1893. The team that left Central Station at 9 o'clock in the evening bound for Valparaíso was the following: Messrs. J.R. Garrod, E.R. Gifford, R.E.H. Anderson, H.B. Anderson, P.M. Rath, G.A. Thompson, C.W. Thompson, H.M. Mills, E.J. [Denny] Stockes, A. Lace, P.L.G. Bridger, B.B. Syer and F.W. Clunie as umpire. They were joined by Mr. and Mrs. Percy Clark, Mr. and Mrs. W. Samson, Miss Pakenham, Mr. and Mrs. H.C. Thompson, Mr. and Mrs. Miles, and The Times of Argentina special correspondent, Mr. R.H. Morgan. [Mrs. Henry Mills was also in the traveling party.]
>
> The party's attire and traveling implements was the subject of much hilarity and jokes. The extravagant headgear, the goggles to protect the eyes from dust, the baggage, truly Noah's Arks, in which toothbrushes were dancing among flannel trousers, books and cigarettes, the entire proverbial luggage of English travelers, invaded the wagons and overflowed the platforms. When the locomotive's whistle signaled departure, three cheers gave a farewell to the expeditionaries.[13]

They traveled by train to Mendoza, at the foot of the Andes Mountains, which they crossed mounted on mules. Somehow, the party managed to cross the Andes without loss of men, women, mules or baggage. It must have been quite a journey.

Incidentally, the team won all three cricket matches, as well as a football match, a doubles tennis match and a billiards contest. The newspaper *The Standard* published a sports supplement in the 17 August 1925 issue. The section dedicated to cricket has a photograph of the international team.[14] The next notice pertaining to polo is a brief addendum:

> Cricket News.
> By The Times Special Correspondent.
> Valparaíso, Nov. 22, 6:45 PM.
>
> This afternoon a polo game was held on a very unsuitable ground. Valparaíso was represented by Lyon, Edmonson, Raby and Scott. The Buenos Aires team was formed by Preston, Clunie, Clarke and Anderson. Valparaíso won comfortably by 9 goals to 3.[15]

A few days later, *River Plate Sport and Pastime*'s "Boots," most likely its editor Frank Balfour, published a short note: "The Buenos Aires team, which was a weak one, played on any ponies they could borrow, and were beaten by six goals to three."[16]

In the 6 December 1893 issue, a member of the touring party who chose to hide his identity under the pseudonym "Cleek" — must have been a golfer — wrote for the *River Plate Sport and Pastime* a more complete report, repeating the discrepancy in the final tally:

> There was a game of polo in the afternoon between Edmonson, Raby, Lyon and Scott for Valparaíso, and Clunie, Harry Anderson, Percy Clarke and Preston for Buenos Aires. The ground was very short and very narrow, and, unfortunately the ball was always, in the umpire's opinion, in touch, which made the game very sticky and slow. Individually the Valparaiso team are all good men, but they have yet to learn their places, which they will soon do when they get a full size ground to play upon. As it was they beat our men six goals to three, they were very good about giving our players the best ponies they could find for them. Their ponies are not as good, or as fast, as ours, but the game is young there yet and it is hardly fair to judge them; no doubt we shall see a great improvement when they come over here next year.[17]

What is the historical significance of this match, played outside of the tour's main purpose as a cricket series? Without any doubt whatsoever, it was the first international polo match played in South America. However, was it really a test between Argentina and Chile? That opinion was ventured in *El polo internacional argentino*[18] and Francisco Ceballos in his *El polo en la Argentina*[19] seems to agree with such stance. On the other hand, historian Dr. Eduardo Bautista Pondé expressed the view that it was only a match played between British players who lived east and west of the Andes.[20]

Every visiting player was a member of either Hurlingham Club or the Buenos Aires Cricket Club. Richard Evan Hughes "Harry" Anderson played at Hurlingham and was the owner of Kitty, one of the best polo ponies around. In championship matches, Kitty was played by Fred Bennett, winner of the Open with Flores and Hurlingham. Joseph Percival "Percy" Clarke, born in Twickeham, England, played for Belgrano Polo Club and years later was president of the Hurlingham Club. Frank Clunie, who was the umpire for the cricket eleven, started playing at John Brown's estancia La Campana, participated in the Open Championship and was secretary of the Hurlingham Club. Tom Preston had learned the game in India; he arrived in Argentina in 1879 and was one of the pioneers who started polo on the Caballito ground.

As to the players from Chile, Victor Raby was related to the famous American players Philip and Stewart Iglehart, whose mother was a Raby. Andrew William Scott was on the Valparaíso Polo Club's Committee. Horacio Lyon belonged to that well-known polo family, one of whom, Jorge, was president of the Chilean Polo Federation and was an international player in Argentina in 1949. No information has been uncovered about E.W. Edmonson; it is possible that he was part of Edmonson and Co., shipping agents in Valparaíso.

The final point is that an improvised polo game among cricket players merits strong consideration as the first international match played by Argentina and Chile.

America—Argentina at Ranelagh, 1896

Encouraged by the performance of a team representing Buenos Aires in 1895, whose results were 17 wins, three losses and three ties, the following year five players from Argentina made the long sea voyage to England to play some games and sell their criollo ponies at the season's end. The trailblazers were the Furber brothers, Frank and Stanley, Hugh Scott Robson, Dr. Newman Smith and Robert McClintock Smyth, better known as Johnny. All were good players. The ambidextrous Hugh Scott Robson, Argentine-born, was polo's first star in South America. Frank Furber was a two-time winner of the Polo Association of the River Plate Open Championship, while his brother Stanley carried the reputation of a heavy hitter. Dr. Smith was a physician who made it to the Open Championship's finals, and Johnny Smyth, a Championship Cup winner, was considered one of the better players in the Venado Tuerto area. Later in life, Johnny Smyth moved to Jujuy, in northernmost Argentina, to administer Finca San Lorenzo, a sugar cane plantation. He became a pioneer fruit culturist in that remote area and the rose and tropical gardens he created still stand.[21] While ranching in the Venado Tuerto area, Smyth had five top polo ponies. In the course of a political revolution, an armed party arrived at the estancia to requisition horses; forewarned, Johnny took the ponies into the dining room. The soldiers took all the other horses, but as they did not venture near the house, the precious polo ponies were saved.[22]

The Ranelagh Club had organized an International Tournament in which teams from

America, England and France took part. There is a brief paragraph about the tournament in *Baily's* magazine: "Saturday, the 18th ultimo, saw the final struggle at Ranelagh of the International Tournament between an American side and a Buenos Aires team. Although in the first period the Americans had much the best of it the Buenos Aires men pulled themselves together in the second 20 minutes, and were declared the winners by six goals to five. Playing for America were Mr. McCreery, Mr. Mackey, Mr. Wright and Mr. Wheeler (back), and for Buenos Aires were Mr. F. Furber, Mr. Smyth, Mr. Newman Smith, and Mr. Scott Robson (back)."[23]

Frank Jay Mackey had a strong international career: gold medalist in the Paris 1900 Olympic Games, winner of the Paris International Tournament, the Warwickshire Hunt, Social Clubs, Cirencester Challenge and County Cups in England. He lived a charmed life. Mackey was the donor of trophies in far-flung places such as California and Paris.

Walter Adolph McCreery was an American born in Zurich who spent most of his life in England. He represented America in the 1900 Westchester Cup and took the silver medal in the Olympic Games. His sons Richard and Walter Selby became prominent players in the 1920s. Walter was a habitué on the California polo scene, while his brother pursued a military career in which he rose to be Sir Richard Loudon McCreery, commander-in-chief, British Army of the Rhine. Both brothers joined the 12th Lancers and became good players.

William Hayden Wright was another globetrotting player. He played on the U.S.A.–Mexico squad that won the bronze medal in the Paris Olympic Games and took the Paris Tournament twice. Charles Wheeler was also a familiar figure in American and European polo circles.

This International Tournament at Ranelagh in July 1986 was the first one in which a team from Argentina emerged winners, a portent of things to come.

Australia — England at Melbourne, 1899

The first match between Australian and British teams took place in Victoria during Melbourne's Thoroughbred Racing Cup Week. Three Manifold brothers (probably James Chester, William Thompson and Edward) from the Camperdown Club and Ernest De Little, a Cambridge-educated man who had tried polo in India on his journey home, represented Australia. De Little carried the reputation of being the best Australian player of his time. For many years, the four Manifold brothers made the Camperdown team one of the most feared in Australia. Generous, horsy and conservative, the Manifolds adapted the role and duties of English country gentlemen to Australian conditions and gave back to the country much of the wealth acquired by their pioneering predecessors.[24]

The English team was Maj. the Hon. George Bryan at number 1, Bertie Hill at number 2, Capt. the Hon. Thomas Brand at number 3 and Capt. Neil Wolseley Haig at back. Tom Brand, later Lord Hampden, was on the staff of his father, Henry Robert Brand, the 2nd viscount Hampden, in New South Wales, while his fellow officer George Bryan, later Lord Bellew, was staying with him. Both were former 10th Hussars. Neil Haig, 6th Inniskilling Dragoons, was on the staff of Lt. Col. Sir Gerard Smith, Western Australia's governor.

Australia won the first match, England the second, both games being decided by just one goal. Col. St. Quintin was umpire for the English team; his observations on the Australian team bear repeating: "The Australians were undoubtedly as fine players as you could wish to see, but, fortunately for us, they did not understand the science of the game and playing together, and each man played his own game. They were also a very rough lot in their play, and as they became more and more excited the element of danger was strong and the whistle more and more in demand."[25]

This was the last series featuring Australian versus British teams until 1928, when officers representing the Army-in-India polo team visited New South Wales for six weeks.[26]

Australia—New Zealand at Australia, 1899

In response to an invitation from Australia, the Strang brothers and Octy Robinson from the Oroua Polo Club joined Arthur Southey Baker from nearby Manawatu Polo Club to cross the Tasman Sea on their way to Sydney. All were past winners of the Savile Cup and took their own ponies on the journey. Allan, J.A.P. "Jack" and Walter Strang were farmers.

It appears that the only written record is a note from Walter Strang in 1954: "I only played twice and one game was against the Manifold brothers and R.A.D. Hood. We lost that game and the one against Victoria. New Zealand won all the other games."[27]

There is no mention of this tour in Chris Ashton's comprehensive *Geebung—The Story of Australian Polo*; therefore, given the encyclopedic character of Mr. Ashton's work, it is more than likely that the visit failed to attract the attention of the local newspapers.

Argentina—England at Hurlingham (Buenos Aires), 1908

A scarcely known match may be considered the first international polo game in Argentina. Four British officers who traveled to Buenos Aires in connection with the International Horse Show and Sports in Buenos Aires played against a team of Argentine Army officers. The venue was the Hurlingham Club, on the outskirts of Buenos Aires, situated close to a large garrison, Campo de Mayo. The game was held on 30 November 1908.[28] The English officers were Lt. Geoffry F.H. Brooke, 16th Lancers; Maj. the Hon. John G. Beresford, 7th Hussars; Capt. Edmund H. Bayford, 18th Hussars, and Col. Alexander J. Godley, Aldershot Staff. The Argentine officers were Lt. Alberto de Oliveira Cézar; Lt. Samuel A. Casares; Lt. Alfredo M. Quiroga, and Col. Isaac J. de Oliveira Cézar.[29] The match was umpired by Mr. Harold Schwind, a well-known player; the final score was 4–1 in favor of the visitors.[30]

Maj. Gen Geoffry Francis Heremon Brooke was a prolific writer on military and equine matters. His treatise *Horse Sense and Horsemanship of Today—Economy and Method of Training Hunters and Polo Ponies* is a classic in equine literature and went through several editions. Brooke was painted by Sir Alfred Munnings when attached to the Canadian Cavalry Brigade on the Western Front. Although his name is usually spelled Geoffrey, the *London Gazette*'s consistent spelling is Geoffry.

John Graham Hope Horsley de la Poer Beresford, later Lord Decies, had played in the 1900 Westchester Cup and in the same year took the gold medal in the Paris Games. He won the Ranelagh Open Cup, the Irish Open Cup and the Inter-Regimental Tournament in both India and England. The then Captain Beresford presented the cup that bears his name, now emblematic of the South African Polo Championship.

Not much is known about Capt. Edmund Heseltine Bayford, 18th Hussars, who was the recipient of the Distinguished Service Order. General Sir Alexander John Godley was a master of fox hounds and was keen on all equestrian sports. He played cricket and became a good yachtsman. Gen. Godley was instrumental in the training of the New Zealand army before the First World War. His organizational ability was not matched by his performance on the field of battle. In addition to many articles of a professional character, he published his autobiography, *Life of an Irish Soldier*, and *British Military History in South America*.

As to the Argentine officers, Col. Isaac José de Oliveira Cézar was one of the pioneers of military polo, which he introduced to the army after watching a match of what he called "a game of crazy gringos." Oliveira Cézar was one of the founders and the main supporter of the ill-fated Asociación de Polo Nacional, an organization that tried to cut the shackles placed by the Polo Association of the River Plate on the development of the game. His son, Alberto, took the Copa Anchorena — now the Tortugas Open Championship — and the Military Championship; years later, he was elected vice-president of the Argentine Polo Association. Lt. Samuel Alfredo Casares was a member of the first committee of the Argentine Polo Association and was military attaché in the 1920s in London, where he had many successful seasons on La Pampa team. In the Argentine, Lt. Col. Casares took the 1915 open and the Copa Anchorena; he was rated at 5 goals in the first handicap list. Lt. Alfredo Mauricio Quiroga, a cavalry officer, was also rated at 5 goals.

7. Polo Myths: Billiard Ball, Walking Sticks, and All That

Myth: a traditional or legendary story, usually concerning some being or hero or event, with or without a determinable basis of fact or a natural explanation. — Webster's Encyclopedic Unabridged Dictionary of the English Language[1]

The oldest myth about the modern game is that polo was brought to England by regiments that had learned the game in India. As related earlier, polo as known by the Europeans was confined to the district of Cachar in Assam until 1862, when the game began in Calcutta. The 9th Lancers returned to England from India in September 1859 and went back to India again in 1875.[2] The 10th Hussars were deployed to Crimea from India in 1856 via the Red Sea, across the desert to Alexandria, and thence to Crimea, where pipe clay and red tape had destroyed the Light Brigade. On the evacuation from Crimea, the regiment returned home to England, where they started the game at Aldershot Garrison, following Lt. Edward Hartopp reading about the game in The *Field*. The 10th Hussars returned to India in 1873.[3]

Another myth related to the above is that the first scramble at Aldershot — it is difficult to call it a match — was played with a billiard ball and heavy walking sticks. The usually accurate Rev. Thomas Dale, a respected historian of the early days of polo, states that hockey sticks and a billiard ball were the implements used by those adventurous players.[4] The Rev. Dale cites Shorncliffe, a military camp near Folkestone in Kent, as the game's venue. The 10th Hussars were quartered at Shorncliffe; however, they went to Aldershot in Hampshire for the summer drills. Col. Robert S. Liddell indicates that golf clubs and a billiard ball were the implements used in the scramble. Col. Thomas St. Quintin, in his autobiography, is quite precise on these points. In *Chances of Sports of Sorts*, he states, "When the 10th Hussars were under canvas at Aldershot ... routed up some old heavy walking-sticks and a cricket ball, and began to try to knock the ball about."[5] Since Colonel St. Quintin was a participant in that event, it is rather difficult to challenge his assertion.

The First Game of Polo in Europe

It has been argued that polo on the European continent was first played in Malta, where the port of Valetta was an occasional scale on the maritime voyage from India to the British

Isles, via the Suez Canal and Gibraltar. However, there is no written documentation in support of such an assumption. The opening of the Suez Canal was performed by French Empress Eugenie on 17 November 1869 in the imperial yacht *Aigle*, followed by the Peninsular and Oriental Steam Navigation Company vessel *Delta*.

Chicken Hartopp and his fellow 10th Hussars officers played "hockey on horseback" in the summer of 1869, thereby setting a clear claim to priority over the Maltese grounds.

The 1957 *Year Book* of the Hurlingham Polo Association states, "Polo is rumored to have started in Malta, having possibly come there from India, even before it began in England in the early '70s."[6] In the 1962 *Year Book*, the rumor became fact in the eyes of the Hurlingham Polo Association: "Polo started in Malta in 1868 having come there from India before it began in England in 1869."[7] The same sentence has been printed in the Hurlingham Polo Association's year books until 2006. This erroneous statement was reproduced in *The Polo Encyclopedia*.[8] Research for this work revealed the earliest mention of a game on the island in a history of the 9th Lancers.[9] On its way to India in 1874, the regiment defeated the Malta Polo Club by 5 goals to nil.

The island of Malta did become a center of polo, especially for Royal Navy officers, because it was the home base for the Mediterranean Fleet. British royalty took its first tentative steps on Malta's polo grounds in the persons of the Duke of York, who would be King George V, and Prince Louis of Battenberg — later changed to Mountbatten — and First Marquis of Milford Haven, when both were officers in the Royal Navy.

The Numbering of the Argentine Open Championship

Not a myth but an unexplained omission is that the 2007 edition of the famed "Abierto de Palermo" was labeled by the Argentine Polo Association as the 114th Open Championship. Actually, it was the 116th edition. The Argentine Open Championship, started in 1923, is the successor to the Polo Association of the River Plate Championship, which dates back to 1893. After its founding in 1892, the P.A. of the River Plate held two yearly championships of equal hierarchy from 1893 to 1895.

Official and semi-official sources have discredited the first 1893 championship. One source — *Centauros*, the Argentine Polo Association's publication — claims that the April 1893 competition was a qualifier for the October tournament.[10] This assertion is based upon an article by Dr. Armando Braun Estrugamou in *Polo*, an official publication of the Asociación Argentina de Polo in 1960.[11]

In January 2008, the Argentine Polo Association's website went even further; it claims that all three spring tournaments in 1893–1895 were held at Hurlingham and that all were qualifiers for the Cañada de Gómez championships. The fact is that in March 1894, the third open championship was played in Cañada de Gómez, and the fourth was played at Hurlingham in October of the same year. The fifth championship took place in Cañada de Gómez in April 1895, and the sixth at Hurlingham in October. It is hard to understand the rationale behind such egregious manipulation of printed historical data by the Argentine Polo Association.

Polo Around the World, edited by Javier Bustinza and with text by Carlos Beer, states that the April 1893 tournament was the first Hurlingham Club Open and the one held in October, the first Argentine Open.[12] There is no documentation in print supporting such claim.

The case is quite clear. The pertinent minutes of the Polo Association of the River Plate state: "That two championship tournaments be held each year, one on a ground of one of the Buenos Aires clubs, and one in Santa Fe, the grounds in every case to be approved by the Committee of the Association."[13]

The final match of the first Open Championship was held at the Hurlingham Club on 8 April 1893. The host team defeated Quilmes "A" by 4 goals to 1. The winning team was Frank J. Balfour, John Ravenscroft (replaced during the match by Tom Parry), Robert W. Isherwood and Hugh Scott Robson.

The final game of the second Open Championship took place in Cañada de Gómez on 15 October 1893. A different Hurlingham team beat Santa Fe by one goal to nil. Hurlingham's line-up was Frank J. Balfour, John Ravenscroft, Cadwallader J. Tetley and Frank Furber. Tetley scored the goal in the third chukker of the match.

The contemporary magazine *River Plate Sport and Pastime* was explicit in its comments. Under "Sporting Notes," "Boots" (probably Frank Balfour, one of the Hurlingham team players) informs us, "We publish this week a phototype of the winners of the Polo Association's Championship Cup at the Cañada de Gomez tournament. It will be remembered that Hurlingham won the first tournament held under the auspices of the Polo Association, at Hurlingham in April, and by winning the next, that held at Cañada de Gomez in October, they took possession for good of the Cup, which had to be won twice by an affiliated club. The Cup, which is supplied by Mr. Black, will make a fitting decoration for the dinner table of the new club house at Hurlingham."[14]

River Plate Sport and Pastime covered the 1894 tournament in Cañada de Gomez in the 28 March edition. The final paragraph read, "So ended the third and one of the most enjoyable championship polo tournaments."[15]

The first official publication released by the Asociación Argentina de Polo is a 1923 booklet that includes tournament results, officers, names, colors and locations of affiliated clubs, and players' handicaps. The results for the open championship indicate Hurlingham as the winner of both championships in 1893.

When all the contemporary data is taken into account, the inescapable conclusion is that in 1893, just as is in 1894 and 1895, there were two championships of equal significance. The Hurlingham Club must be credited with another championship, and the names Robert W. Isherwood, Thomas Parry and John Ravenscroft must be added to the long list of winners of the most prestigious open tournament in the world.

Oldest Open Tournament

Another myth is Hurlingham Club's claim that its own championship runs concurrent with the Argentine Open Championship. How can the Hurlingham Club appropriate as its own tournaments played 200 miles away at another club, Cañada de Gómez? It is nothing short of amazing that at the official launching of the 2006 Hurlingham Open Championship, the claim was made that it is "the oldest Open tournament in the world."[16] The British Inter-Regimental Tournament (1878), the All Ireland Open (1878), as well as the County Cup (1885) in England, New Zealand's Savile Cup (1890) and the Calgary Challenge Cup (1892) in Canada have all been cheerfully set aside by the Argentine Hurlingham Club. None of those tournaments were played on handicap, because at the time, individual handicaps were not awarded in those countries.

The cold fact is that the Hurlingham Open was inaugurated in 1929 as the club's senior championship. Some three years later, the name was changed to the Hurlingham Club Open Championship. In the November 1929 issue of *Polo & Equitación* the tournament report is titled "The First Annual Tournament of the Hurlingham Club was an Extraordinary Success."[17] Extensive research in the polo literature has failed to uncover any mention of a Hurlingham Open Championship prior to 1929. It is just another case of instant antiquity. *Caveat emptor.*

The Tortugas Open Championship and the Anchorena Cup

The Hurlingham Club is not the only institution in Argentina in quest of ancient lineage for its open championship. The Tortugas Country Club, organizer of one of the open championships that make up the unofficial Triple Crown of Polo, lists the winners of the Copa Anchorena from 1930 on as previous holders of the Tortugas Open.[18]

Tortugas, together with Hurlingham and Los Indios, are the "Big Three" of Argentine polo. The facts are as follows: Tortugas Country Club was founded in 1926 and affiliated in 1927.[19] The Copa Emilio de Anchorena was instituted in 1907,[20] and was awarded by the Argentine Polo Association as the trophy for the Tortugas Open Championship, when it was started in 1958.[21]

10-Goal Handicap for 25 Consecutive Years

Cecil Smith, the cowboy from Texas, was one of the all-time polo greats. Spirited discussions took place regarding his polo handicap throughout his career. Smith reached the 10-goal plateau in 1934, was lowered to 9 goals the following year, and to 8 goals in 1936, regaining the top handicap in 1938. In 1942, he went down again to 9 goals. Handicaps were not issued again by the U.S. Polo Association until 1946 because of World War II. In that year, Cecil Smith went back to 10 goals, a rating that he maintained until 1962. The record is well documented in the U.S.P.A. year books.[22] Nevertheless, when editor Gwen Rizzo wrote an article mentioning that fact in *Polo Players Edition* magazine,[23] letters to the editor poured in, including a few demanding an apology to Mr. Smith's family. The year-by-year changes in Cecil Smith's handicap were elaborated by Sherry Browne, executive secretary of the U.S.P.A., in a letter to Rizzo.[24]

The Coronation Cup Resumes in 1951

The 1957 *Hurlingham Polo Association Year Book* and subsequent yearbooks indicate that the Coronation Cup was first played after World War II in 1951, in a series of matches between an Argentine club, La Espadaña, and a Hurlingham team, the eventual winners of the three games played.[25]

Brigadier Jack Gannon, the Hurlingham Polo Association's long-time honorary secretary, wrote the chapter "Polo in 1951" for *The Horseman's Year.*[26] The chapter contains a careful description of that year's polo events held in England. Brig. Gannon states that the series was played for the Festival Cup, perhaps so named because it was the time of the Festival of Britain.

The first match was played on 7 July at Cowdray Park's River Ground. It should have been held at the Duke of Sutherland's Sutton Place, in Surrey; however, the field was not up to par due to winter flooding. The second game was played at Roehampton Club on 25 July in front of a large crowd. At the conclusion of the match, Princess Elizabeth — later Queen Elizabeth II — presented the Festival Cup to the winning Hurlingham team. The series already decided, the third match was played at Cowdray Park on August Bank Holiday. In spite of continuous rain, it was a game that featured open polo, watched by about one thousand car-loads of spectators.

No mention of the Coronation Cup is made in Brig. Gannon's article in *The Horseman's Year*. There is, however, a Roehampton Club's program for the "Special Match for the Festival Cup: La Espadaña (Argentine) v. Hurlingham (England) on 25th July at 3.0 P.M."[27]

Perhaps the Coronation Cup was the trophy for the Festival Cup; however, until photographic proof of the prize-giving or other contemporary documentation is made available, it should be safe to assume that the Coronation Cup was resumed in 1953 at Cowdray Park, as part of the celebrations on Queen Elizabeth II's coronation at Westminster Abbey.

8. The British Clubs

I would like once more to remind members that their duty to a club like this need not end with their mere membership and the enjoyment of what a house agent would describe as the amenities of the club. They could help us a lot with a little casual propaganda. — Sir Harold Snagge, K.B.E.[1]

The game has departed forever from the big three London clubs, Hurlingham, Ranelagh and Roehampton. For a while, it would be pleasant to think that all could begin again, or that one of the two survivors — Hurlingham and Roehampton — could be the home to a national museum of polo. But then, you think that perhaps it is just as well that polo is gone. The game as played in those years belonged to a different era, a time that will never return. These days, the ancient pastime is surrounded by loud publicity, a small dose of vulgarity and plenty of financial haggling.

The elegant spectators that flocked to Fulham, Barnes and Roehampton a century ago, many in horse-drawn carriages, to watch regimental and civilian teams battle on hallowed turf were from a different world. Hurlingham and its confreres were part of that era. The mighty citadels of polo and its mounted heroes have fallen. Let them rest.

The Hurlingham Club

The Hurlingham Club in Fulham has exerted more influence worldwide on the game than any other polo club. The rules of the game that were drafted by its Polo Committee were initially religiously followed by all countries where polo was played. Only America and India, in later years, implemented some modifications to suit local conditions. Nevertheless, during the formative years, the few changes put forward by Hurlingham were given careful attention in both New York and Lucknow. John Watson, the committee's most influential member, strongly felt that polo should be left alone rather than be overburdened with too many rules. Certainly, the game flourished when its rules were relatively simple, and the committee was therefore reluctant to make changes. The most egregious example was the persistence of the offside rule, which discriminated against the number 1 player and made the game slower and untidy.

The Polo Committee itself was strongly weighted by Hurlingham Club members, who controlled the voting. Initially, that committee was composed of Hurlingham's members only. Even in 1903, when three members from the County Polo Association were added, as well as two from the Army Polo Committee and one from the newly created Roehampton Club, Hurlingham's representatives exceeded the total of all other appointed members. The Ranelagh Club refused to accept the single offered seat, given the fact that it had more polo players than Hurlingham. Many years passed before Ranelagh accepted representation on the Hurlingham Polo Committee.

The Hurlingham Club started as a pigeon-shooting club.[2] Even today, when polo at Fulham is but a distant memory, the club's badge carries an image of a pigeon. The site's history goes back to 1628, but the original Hurlingham House, still standing on the club's grounds, was built in 1760 by a London physician, Dr. William Cadogan. In 1797, it was purchased by John Ellis, who added a neo-classical mansion, which is part of the main house today. In 1808, the house was sold to George, Earl of Egremont, who let the property to his mentor, Euseby Cleaver, Archbishop of Dublin, known locally as "the Mad Archbishop." In 1820, Lord Egremont sold Hurlingham House to John Horsley Palmer, governor of the Bank of England, who lived there until his death in 1857. Another banker, Richard Christopher Naylor, purchased the property from Mr. Palmer's estate. A ten-year lease was granted by Mr. Naylor to Francis Heathcote, a promoter of live pigeon shooting. Heavy betting took place at the meetings, which were also attended by a large number of women and patronized by Edward, the Prince of Wales. Four hundred to five hundred birds would be "grassed" in an afternoon.

In March 1870, Capt. Debonnaire John Monson, later Lord Monson, was appointed manager. It was an important decision for the game of polo, because soon enough Capt. Monson concluded that for the club to prosper, it must offer attractions other than pigeon shooting, a pastime many people considered barbaric. At a meeting on 6 July 1872, Lord De L'Isle put to the General Committee whether part of the grounds could be used for "the game of Paulo" [*sic*]. In November of that year, it was agreed to ask Mr. R.C. Naylor if he would consider leasing the orchard for "a Palo" field.[3] This proposal was extended to an offer to purchase the entire property, a bold and expensive proposition that bore fruit on 22 May 1874 when the land and buildings were purchased for £27,500.

The first polo game was played on 6 June 1874 between the 1st Life Guards and the Royal Horse Guards. It fell to Henry Adelbert, Marquess of Worcester, later Duke of Beaufort, the honor of scoring the first goal of the match.

The initial Hurlingham Club Polo Committee was composed of Viscount Charles Castlereagh, Viscount Arthur Valentia, Lord John Churston, Mr. Reginald Herbert, Hon. Hugh Boscawen, Sir Charles Wolseley, Capt. Francis Herbert, Capt. Charles Needham, Sir Bache Cunard, Mr. Adrian de Murrieta and Mr. John G.F. Brocklehurst. This committee approved the first Hurlingham Club rules, which were elastic, but embodied the usual and customary etiquette of the game as played in those early days. The first code of rules was issued on 1 May 1875.[4]

A certain amount of antagonism remained between the pigeon-shooting members and the increasing number of polo players and social members. Pigeon shooting was a continuing source of troublesome issues, not the least several rows about settling betting debts. However, more importantly, social perception regarding pigeon shooting was changing. The matter was put to the annual general meeting, where a resolution was passed abolishing pigeon shooting. This resulted in a lawsuit started by the pigeon-shooting members, which failed to change the majority's decision. Finally, in 1906, pigeon shooting ceased at the club and the enclosure was transformed into a tea ground.

Reflecting the Victorian age's unwritten codes of behavior, no person was eligible for membership unless they were "received in general society." Just as in the contemporary International Gun and Polo Club, there was an absolute prohibition on any member bringing to the premises any "unsuitable women." For many years, there were no women members. When finally, in 1913, women were accepted as full members, they were required to pay the same annual subscription — eight guineas — as the men and were permitted to enjoy all the club's privileges. However, they were not allowed to attend the annual general meeting or to vote. Besides, they were subject to annual re-election. Things progressively improved and, in 1934, there was a women's polo match, Oddments taking on the Valkyries.

Slowly but surely, polo became the dominant pursuit. A great deal was due to the untiring efforts of Capt. John Walter Smyth, later Sir Walter Smyth, the polo manager. Within five years of his appointment, the balance was shifting down on the side of polo, and first the Champion Cup, established in 1876, and then the Inter-Regimental Tournament in 1878, were offered for competition. These new tournaments caught the attention of all army officers and the less numerous civilian players on the Hurlingham Club and went far to place it in its preeminent position. However, not everything was rosy. In 1897, a formal petition was presented by social members who complained about the excessive charges levied to subsidize polo, to the enormous amount of £4,000 per year.

As mentioned earlier, the club was represented by a team led by John Watson in the 1886 Westchester Cup. Hurlingham also hosted the 1900 and 1902 Westchester contests. These were important to the club, not only for the prestige attached to international events, but also from the financial point of view. The receipts for the 1902 were £4,440 — in terms of today's currency it should be multiplied times forty. The club also was the host for the polo matches in the 1908 London Olympic Games. The 1909 Westchester Cup series was held at Hurlingham, when the American team known as the Big Four carried away the trophy. Not all was lost for the club, because Harry Payne Whitney presented to the Hurlingham Club an example of the most famous polo bronze: *The Meadow Brook Club*, sculpted by Herbert Haseltine, polo player and the most prominent *animalier* of the 20th century. This beautiful sculpture adorns the club, along with other works of art, such as a beautiful watercolor by the hand of Gilbert Holiday depicting the 1936 Westchester Cup, which was also held at Hurlingham's Number One field. Another painting that hangs in the club is the monumental oil *The Hurlingham Team in Front of the Pavilion*, by Henry Jamyn Brooks, dated 1890, and accompanied with a key identifying the team members and all but one of the fifty-three portrayed polo personalities. There is also a polo print, after an oil painting by M.F. Nutting, showing a mounted player on the pony lines near the "chestnuts goal," with the pavilion floating a blue flag — Hurlingham Club's colors — far away in the background.[5]

The Hurlingham Committee did not take criticisms lightly. *The Times* published some articles on polo at Hurlingham to which the committee took strong exception. It passed a resolution that "personal allusions to polo teams and regiments and criticism of the official umpire should not be allowed and that the free pass for the reporter should be withdrawn."[6] Lord Shrewsbury, polo player and committee member, was asked to see the editor, George Earle Buckle, which he did. Mr. Buckle stated that he must reserve his right of criticism, but promised to talk to the reporter. A letter was then sent to *The Times* requesting Mr. Buckle not to allow the reporter the use of the annual pass granted to the newspaper.

The Hurlingham Team in Front of the Pavilion. The mounted players, from the left, are Johnnie Peat, Lord Francis Mildmay (leaning on his pony), Alfred Peat, the Earl of Harrington (wearing a blue cap), Capt. Julian Spicer (behind Lord Harrington), John Watson, Capt. Thomas Hone, Edward Kenyon Stow and Arthur Peat. Print after the painting by Henry Jamyn Brooks (private collection, Alex Pacheco photograph).

Perhaps the committee was in this sour mood when they told the Duke of Westminster, patron of the Old Etonians team that was going to America in quest of recovering the Westchester Cup, words to the effect that the Hurlingham Club would contribute to the expenses, but only if they won back the trophy.

Social discrimination continued when the committee informed the County Polo Association that "no one was to take part in any polo match or game on the Hurlingham ground unless a member of a recognized Social Club or specially invited by the committee."[7] The blow was softened in 1906, when Hurlingham announced that the rule would not be enforced during County Polo Week.

There were increasing signs of dissatisfaction in the polo world in regards to Hurlingham's exclusive control of the game's destiny. The main objectors were the Ranelagh Club Committee and the County Polo Association; the latter went so far as to ask that a national association be instituted, with a central office and information bureau to be located in London. The Hurlingham Club haughtily disagreed, claiming that it had made the game of polo what it was in England. Furthermore, a bureau of information would encourage professionalism and pony dealing, which should never be allowed to enter into the management and direction of the game. This was in 1913.

The Great War changed Britain's social fabric. When the conflict was over, hundreds of polo players had paid the ultimate price; several years would pass by before the game showed signs of recovery. It came as no surprise that the American challenge for the Westchester Cup came early and was successful from the American viewpoint.[8]

The interwar years saw the club prosper after a shaky period in the late 1910s. The Westchester Cup series was again a financial bonanza for the club's treasury. So much polo was played and so many tournaments were staged that the club had to lease grounds near London in order to accommodate the great increase in demand for matches and cups. The Hurlingham Club leased the Worcester Park Polo Club's fields and Maj. Cecil Wyburn Peters, a committee member, lent the club 25 acres in Sunbury. A large covered stand was built in 1934 with a view to hosting the Westchester Cup matches two years hence. The stand, with its signature clock on the roof, is depicted in Charles Walter Simpson's painting *The Duke of Windsor, When Prince of Wales, Playing Polo*, illustrated in Mary Ann Wingfield's *Sport and the Artist*.[9]

Hurlingham survived World War II on better terms than it did the Great War. However, the ancient game of polo had not yet returned to England when, in October 1946, nothing less than a thunderbolt fell upon the club. The London County Council was to serve a compulsory purchase order on the clubhouse and the rest of the grounds, with the exception of the number two polo field, as a public open space. However, the number two ground was not spared the axe; it was to be compulsorily purchased by the Fulham Borough Council for development into a housing complex. After much negotiation and hearings, both polo grounds were lost, but the club survived its worst crisis. The last remnant of polo at Hurlingham was the old covered stand, from which more than 8,000 spectators had watched the glorious 1936 Westchester Cup matches and innumerable Champion Cup finals. The polo ground was now converted into a running track. The large stand, by then disfigured with graffiti and largely abandoned, underwent demolition in 2003. *Sic transit gloria mundi.*

The Ranelagh Club

In 1878 the Herbert brothers, Reginald and Francis, and Edward Kenyon Stow, perhaps frustrated by the pigeon shooters' strong influence at Hurlingham, started looking for alternative venues for polo. They were able to form a strong committee, as usual peppered with blue bloods, and secured a handsome Georgian house, formerly the property of Lord Ranelagh, which had been already used as a club. The founders' idea was to establish a social club along the lines set by Hurlingham; to this, they added lawn tennis and pony racing, a special attraction dear to the Herberts. The scheme prospered. The Prince of Wales gave his patronage and attended the first match of note at Ranelagh: a night game played under the lights provided by electric Chinese lanterns. As to the ball, it was specially manufactured for the occasion, large and light; shades of Akbar the Great and his Flame of the Forest wood ball.

Both teams were formed by strong players. One side, named Hurlingham, was Lord Charles Petersham, later Earl of Harrington; Johnnie Peat; Windham Wyndham-Quin, Lord Dunraven; and Earnest Peat. Their opponents bore the Ranelagh name; they were Alfred Peat, Lord William Lewes, Ince Anderton and Edward Baldock. The game attracted great attention, undoubtedly drawn by the presence of the Prince of Wales and the King of Greece.

Ranelagh, almost a next-door neighbor to Hurlingham, was not a rival in those early days; it was more an expansion than an alternative. Many players belonged to both clubs. A problem soon arose because the lease was a short one and the land had been secured by a speculative builder. Fortunately, a much better location was found across the River Thames, separated from the river by a towing path and bounded by Barnes Common and the waterworks reservoir. It had historical associations with the Kit-Kat Club; actually, the club's programs sported that name. Barns Elms, a one-hundred acre property of the Chapter of St.

Hugh Scott Robson was the initial name in a long list of Argentine superstars. Mounted on the mare Queen, Robson is wearing Ranelagh's red and white jersey, at the club's Old Ground (Museum of Polo and Hall of Fame).

Paul's, was vacant, and Sir George Hastings was able to secure a long-term lease from the Ecclesiastical Commission. The Rev. Thomas Dale, a former Ranelagh polo manager and prolific author on the game, described the stately dark red brick Georgian house, the gardens and park as of "a delightful old-world character."[10] Near the house there was a lake a quarter of a mile long, fed by the Beverly Brook.

The beginnings were small. The clubhouse was fitted, one polo ground was laid out and a pony racecourse constructed. The Herberts decided to give up the club's management in 1894. A committee chaired by Lord Dudley took over the reins, the club becoming a proprietary one. Dr. George Hastings, later Sir George, was the prime mover, for nothing less than perfection would satisfy him. The club prospered widely, with golf being a strong part of the membership; croquet and lawn tennis were also added. At one time, Ranelagh was the largest polo club in the world, based upon the number of polo players.

In contrast with the occasional acrimony that marked the relationship between poloists and pigeon shooters at Hurlingham, golfers and polo players enjoyed a peaceful co-existence at Ranelagh. There was even a golf tournament for polo players. Like most golfers around the world, the Ranelagh players took themselves a bit too seriously. On the first day polo was played, one concerned golfer sat in the middle of a green to protect the hallowed turf from sacrilegious hooves, the green in question being close to the polo ground. Lest we be too critical of the unknown golfer's protective watch, the 14th green at the Hurlingham Club in Argentina is located right behind the east goal and there have been a few instances of polo ponies running onto the green and causing some damage. The verbal abuse heaped upon the culprits by the golfing community had to be heard to be believed.

Eventually, three full-size polo grounds and one practice ground were available. A beautiful pavilion was built on the Old Polo Ground, which was considered the best in London for watching a game. A painting by Henry Lucas-Lucas depicting some of Sir Humphrey de Trafford's polo ponies shows Ranelagh's wooden pavilion in the background.[11]

Another innovation put forward by the club was the formation of a club team. While Monmouthshire had pioneered the concept of a polo club and its attendant team, most team entrants in London tournaments bore names unrelated to each polo club. Ranelagh fielded its red and white quartered jerseys in many contests.

Since its beginnings, the game of polo has shown a predilection to allow a relatively few players to control the club games, to the detriment of less skilled players and beginners. The Ranelagh Polo Committee took a strong stance against this current by allowing every member an equal share of playing time for home games. This proved so successful that, with the exception of open tournaments, play on the club's grounds had to be restricted to members only.

The Ranelagh Open Cup was established in 1897 as a challenge cup presented by the club's golf-playing members. In was taken in June by the Rugby team of the three Miller brothers and Walter Jones; they were subsequently challenged in July and beaten by a Ranelagh team composed of Alfred "Toby" Rawlinson, Donkhal Singh, Walter Buckmaster and Jack Drybrough. This was the first instance of an Indian player being on the winning team of a major championship in England. Ted Miller thought highly of Donkhal Singh, writing that he was as good at number 1 as Johnnie Peat, Larry Waterbury and Leslie Cheape.[12] After that challenge, the Ranelagh Open was modified to be an annual event, with the peculiarity

Lt. Col. Edward Miller was the world's polo authority for some three decades. Founder of the Rugby and Roehampton polo clubs, Col. Miller, 17th Lancers, also had a significant impact upon polo in Continental Europe (Museum of Polo and Hall of Fame).

that the winning team automatically qualified for next year's final game. This anomalous practice ended in 1907.

Ranelagh was a strong supporter of military polo. The Aldershot Cup, the Aldershot Infantry Cup, the Army Cup and the Subalterns' Cup were established between 1896 and 1907. Other competitions of note were the Hunt Tournament and the Novices' Cup.

The glory of Ranelagh was the King's Coronation Cup, presented in 1911 in celebration of King George V's coronation. Initially it was contested for among the winners of the London season's three most important tournaments: Hurlingham's Champion Cup, the Inter-Regimental Tournament and Ranelagh's Open Cup. Occasionally, a visiting team from overseas would be invited to participate in the contest. Therefore, the first winner was the team representing the Indian Polo Association: Leslie Cheape, Shah Mirza Beg, Gerald Ritson and Vivian Lockett.

When the Roehampton Open Cup was created in 1914, it was added to the Coronation Cup's roster. After the Second World War, the Coronation Cup was played for as a tournament in 1953, the year Elizabeth II was crowned at Westminster Abbey. Seven teams participated: Argentina, Chile, Cowdray Park, England, Meadow Brook (representing the United States), Spain and Woolmers Park. Argentina defeated England by the odd goal at Cowdray Park. Following this tournament, the Coronation Cup was not played for until 1971, when a single match against the United States was held at Cowdray Park. The following year the venue was moved to Smith's Lawn in Windsor Park, where it has been held ever since without interruptions, exceptions being the 1992 and 1997 Westchester Cup matches, and the 2001 hoof and mouth disease outbreak, which forced the cancellation of polo for the season at Guards Polo Club. The Coronation Cup returned to Cowdray Park for that year only. The Coronation Cup Day at Guards in Windsor Park is the largest single-day event in the world of polo.

The times prior to the Great War were halcyon days for polo in England. The number of players had dramatically increased since the turn of the century during the Edwardian era. The wealthy classes did not suffer the inconvenience of property and death taxation, while the Household and cavalry officers, who made up a significant part of the polo-playing population, had experienced the leisurely pace rendered by conflict-free time since the end of Anglo-Boer war. While the machine gun was being perfected in other countries, the conservative War Office established a special commission to study and report on the best type of sword for the British cavalry, the 1908 pattern.[13]

Although many polo players were members of both Hurlingham and Ranelagh, the respective polo committees did not see eye-to-eye. The issue was that of representation in the Hurlingham Polo Committee, the sole arbiter of polo in the United Kingdom and most of the world.

In May 1939, the famous and beautiful Ranelagh Club ceased to exist and, on Lord Mountbatten's initiative, the Hurlingham Club leased its stables and three of the four polo grounds. Polo matches were held all summer, but now under the aegis of Ranelagh's old adversary. No one knew it at the time, but it was also Hurlingham's golden afternoon.

The Rugby Polo Club

"During the winter of 1891–2 my brother [George] and I began to make a polo ground at Spring Hill Farm, and formed a club during the summer, but very few games took place there till 1893."[14] Those words by Capt. Edward Miller tell about the club's origins. The Rugby Polo Club August Open Cup was inaugurated that year and was played for until the onset of World War II. The local team, Ronald Chaplin, 8th Bengal Cavalry, John Reid Walker, of thoroughbred racing fame, and the brothers Edward and George Miller were the winners over a 14th Hussars team. This match was painted by Henry Lucas-Lucas, a prolific artist that made Rugby his base.[15]

The first important win for Rugby was the 1895 County Cup. Then the full Rugby team took off, being unbeaten from 1897 until 1903. The three Miller brothers, Edward, George and Charles, were joined at times by Jack Drybrough, Walter Jones, Capt. Gordon Renton and the Earl of Shrewsbury. They were a formidable combination. Their first endeavor was the selection and training of their mounts, because they quickly realized that however important tactics were, they became useless if their ponies could not take them to the ball.

For a decade, the Rugby team had brought the "off-side" tactics to a fine art. The main principles of those tactics were: marking your opponent; hitting to the boards when in your 50 yards zone; hitting to the center on all other occasions; playing backhanders from the boards; turning in anticipation of a backhander from one of your side; not meeting the ball; not taking the ball round the ground, and not shooting at goal from long range, but playing an approach shot first.[16]

The only team that came close to Rugby was the Old Cantabs, made up from former students at Cambridge University, which under Walter Buckmaster's guidance secured no less than six champion cups before the war. Both teams were evenly matched; contemporary writers felt that Rugby's supremacy came about because of their faultless teamwork. While the Old Cantabs were superior strikers of the ball and had a superstar in the person of Walter Buckmaster, those qualities were nullified by the close marking permitted by superior ponies and the outstanding accuracy of Rugby's short passing game.

In 1920, the Rugby Polo Club was handed over as a gift to the Rugby School and a long lease was secured. The club counted more that one hundred playing members and was the preeminent provincial polo club. Many foreign members stayed at Rugby for the late summer and early spring season. It was a hub of polo pony trading, which the Miller brothers had started early on.

All that changed in years to follow. Capt. Edward Miller passed away in 1931 and his brother George four years later. Charles Miller devoted most of his time to the Roehampton Club, another creation of the brothers three. An attempt was made to get polo going on at the club in 1947; however, it was not successful. Britain was still straining to recover from the post-conflict economic chaos and it fell upon Lord Cowdray's broad shoulders the enormous task of bringing back the game in England.

Another Rugby Polo Club was established in 2001. The old grounds once more were the scene of the successors of Ted Miller loudly exhorting his younger siblings to further efforts, Lord Harrington and his flowing bear riding with the impetuosity of a youngster, which he was not; of Walter Jones and his superb string of ponies, reckoned to be the best in the world; of Sir Humphrey de Trafford, whose ponies were on a par with Jones'; and of the tremendous backhanders from Jack Drybrough, a mighty back that met his untimely end on those grounds.

Cirencester

The Cirencester Club was founded on 9 June 1894 after a meeting at the 4th Gloucester Militia camp.[17] *The Wilts and Gloucestershire Standard* reported that the Earl of Bathurst, who was present at the creation, said that it would give him great pleasure to place his park for playing polo.[18] This generous offering by the Bathurst family has continued to this day. That same afternoon a match was played between the Gloucestershires and a Cirencester Park civilian team, the latter winning.[19] The venue was the Ivy Lodge field, which is still in use, making it one of the oldest polo grounds in Britain.

In 1895, an annual tournament that drew six teams was established. Capt. Henry Charles Talbot-Rice, the Gloucestershire Regiment, presented a handsome cup. The Royal Scots Greys — Capt. Charles James Maxwell, Capt. Pringle, Capt. Arthur Richards and Lt. John Collinson Harrison — were the winners.

Cirencester obtained some good results in national tournaments: the County Cup, the Roehampton Cup, the Junior County Cup and the Whitney Cup were added to the club's cupboard. However, the economic depression, which caused so many polo clubs worldwide to close their doors, many of them forever, also made its mark upon Cirencester. Sadly, after members determined that the club could not carry on, they sold its assets at auction in 1933. A few of the trophies went to neighboring clubs, such as Cheltenham and Beaufort.

During World War II, the Bathurst estate contributed to the war cause in many ways. The magnificent Ivy Lodge turf was ploughed up to grow crops; many trees were brought down, and Deer Park, the club's foundation place, was the site of an American army base and a hospital. When the war was over, it took several years to bring back polo in England. The game returned in 1952 to the club, now renamed Cirencester Park, thanks to the exertions and support of Henry, the 8th Earl Bathurst, and his brother, the Hon. George Bathurst, a keen polo player himself. The Ivy Lodge ground was re-seeded and has regained its reputation as the best all-weather polo field in England.

Cirencester Park has been the home base for some of the best teams in post-war Britain. Most prominent was Lord Samuel Vestey's Stowell Park, a team that achieved a brilliant record in high-goal polo, including the big three of British polo: Cowdray Park's Gold Cup, the Queen's Cup at Guards and the Warwickshire Cup at Cirencester. Lord Vestey's brother, the Hon. Mark Vestey's Foxcote team, also achieved the same triple crown. Capt. and Mrs. Tomlinson's Los Locos, a terror for opposing teams in medium and low-handicap polo, as well as being successful in high-handicap tournaments; the Buccaneers of Capt. John MacDonald-Buchanan's early days, and currently Urs Schwarzenbach's Black Bears are included in some of those best postwar teams.

The club is the host for a few national tournaments, such as the County Cup and the Warwickshire Cup, the oldest high-goal tournament in England, dating back to 1894. This trophy shows a checkered history. It was presented to the Warwickshire Polo Club by the townspeople of Leamington Spa; when the Warwickshire club folded, the tournament was in abeyance until 1932, when the winning captain in 1913, Mr. Frank Hargreaves, presented the cup to the Roehampton Club to be played between Roehampton and Hurlingham, or a visiting team from overseas. It was then temporarily known as the Hargreaves Cup. Competition for the Warwickshire Cup was resumed in 1959, first as a prize for a quarterfinal tie in the Gold Cup and later as a tournament on its own.

Cirencester Park remains as it always was: friendly, low-key, offering excellent polo in a magnificent setting. It is the embodiment of country polo at its best.

The Roehampton Club

The tremendous popularity of polo around the turn of the 19th century strained the capacity of the London clubs to accommodate all the prospective players. Ranelagh had eased the tension, but the other clubs around the metropolitan area lacked one or more facilities, preventing them from achieving great success. The Kingsbury Club season only lasted from August to mid–September; the near-by Wembley Park catered mostly to players who hired ponies to play. The ground saw a great amount of matches and was rather small. However, it was the non-renewal of the lease that brought the club to its knees. First purchased for an aerodrome, it proved to be unsuitable and the site is now Wembley Stadium.

The Eden Park Club was a great favorite with visiting teams and featured an excellent ground. It was situated near Beckenham Junction and it was rather difficult to get to the ground. Worcester Park had a ground at New Malden, Surrey, but its proximity to Hurlingham resulted in being leased by the bigger club to accommodate its surplus of players. The Crystal Palace Club carried the disadvantage of a small field, for it was used as a soccer pitch and the surface left a lot to be desired. Finally, the Hutton Polo Club, in Shenfield, Essex, which had been started as the Priory Polo Club in 1887, was far away from the main centers of polo.

The Wimbledon Polo Club seemed to fit the need and was successful for some two years. Its ground was well laid out and the quality of polo was excellent. The great disadvantage was the relatively long distance from town. Society would not travel in crowded trains or drive the extra distance on a Saturday afternoon.[20] Thus, the need for more room for polo remained unanswered.

Enter the Miller brothers. Edward Miller left his regiment, the 17th Lancers, in 1893 and started the Rugby Polo Club at his home, Spring Hill Farm in Warwickshire. Because of his Irish connections, he always had a ready supply of polo ponies, which he trained and sold. In addition to being an outstanding player — he was rated at 8 goals when well past his prime — Ted Miller was a perceptive judge of horses. With his brothers, they developed the largest pony supply enterprise, trading both at home and on the Continent, a highly profitable business. With his younger brothers Charles, who had been an indigo planter in India, and George, they met with other interested parties: the Earl of Shrewsbury, Walter Jones — both members of the celebrated Rugby team — Sir Humphrey de Trafford, Capt. Neil Haig, Inniskilling Dragoons, and an American, Frank Jay Mackey, who spent most of the year playing polo in Europe. They established a limited liability company, rather than a syndicate as the Ranelagh Club had elected to form. Lord Shewsbury was elected chairman and the president was H.S.H. Adolphus, Duke of Teck, a former 17th Lancers officer who would eventually be King George V's brother-in-law. The initial shareholders were mostly aristocrats and military officers.[21]

Although not as pretentious as either Hurlingham or Ranelagh, it nevertheless occupied a distinguished place as a younger brother and completed the Big Three of London polo. It was almost mandatory to have a sprinkle of royalty and some more of nobility in the committees in order to maintain a sense of respectability. This, all three major clubs achieved with advantage.

Charles Miller found a suitable piece of land to house the club. A banker, William Gosling, had been the original owner, and on his death Charles Lyne Stephens, a politician, purchased the site. The next owner was his son, Stephen, who leased 57 acres to the club. The village's name, Roehampton, derives from the Old English words for rook or rough. Nothing to do with the roe deer that appears on the club's badge.[22] The property was close to both Ranelagh and Hurlingham, which facilitated the movement of polo ponies among the three clubs. Three polo grounds were laid out, in addition to a race course for ponies, a horse show ground, stables, and a ground reserved for women to practice driving, tilting and jumping. Additional attractions were archery and croquet, and in 1904, a 9-hole golf course was constructed, later expanded to 18 holes when additional land was leased.

The club was opened on 1 April 1902, Charles Miller being secretary and manager. Grace Miller, Charles' wife, was a member of the social set that was centered by the reigning monarch, Edward VII. The first 400 members paid no entrance fees. Seventy-one of the first 248 members were army officers, either retired or on active duty, practically all from cavalry regiments. A good number of titled members reflects not only the financial freedom required — not only for indulging in polo — but also the high social circles to which the membership at large belonged.

After cavalry officers, the largest membership group was stockbrokers. Many applicants filled in the question "Occupation" with the words "None," or "Landowner," or more arrogantly, just left the space blank. Waldorf Astor simply wrote "undergraduate." Among the new members there was only one artist, one doctor, one engineer, a churchman and someone who described himself as "various miscellaneous duties paid and unpaid."[23] In contrast to most contemporary social clubs, twelve women were among the original members, starting the tradition of strong female membership that continues to this day. On the other hand, there was a provision in the rules prohibiting membership to people living in the club's vicinity. Obviously, an exception was made with Johnny Traill, whose property, La Esterlina, was located across the street from the club. Perhaps his 10-goal handicap accounted for this lenient treatment.

As far as polo tournaments are concerned, the Roehampton Cup was instituted in 1902 for a trophy donated by Mrs. Alison Cunninghame of Craigends. After serving for some years as a golf trophy, it now resides at the Ham Polo Club, the last polo club in London, located in nearby Richmond Park. The Roehampton Junior Championship was instituted in 1903 for a challenge cup donated by William Ayrault Hazard, long-time secretary of the Polo Association in America and its chairman in 1921. The Roehampton Open Cup, the last of the "big" open competitions, was offered by the club in 1913. An interesting tournament was the Ladies Nomination Cup, in which every player on a team was nominated by a woman. The individual trophies awarded to the winning team were given to the nominating lady, presumably as a reward to their prescience in selecting a good player.

Although Roehampton was considered a bit of a poor relation in comparison to its older neighbors, in reality it was not so. The social standing of the players' roster was as blueblooded as their congeners. Admiral Lord David Beatty, of Battle of Jutland fame, was a frequent polo player. So was Sir Winston Churchill, who had met Edward Miller at the Indian Inter-Regimental Tournament. Lord Hugh Salisbury was also a habitué on the grounds, as well as the Duke of Westminster. Foreign dignitaries felt at ease in Roehampton. King Alfonso XIII of Spain enjoyed playing golf left-handed and polo right-handed. The Miller brothers taught him polo and George Miller spent part of the polo season in Spain. The Spanish monarch enjoyed watching polo so much at Roehampton that he underwrote the cost of a special grandstand on top of the polo pavilion for the use of his entourage and his guests. The Marqués de Villavieja, one of the pioneers of polo in Spain, moved his ponies to Roehampton after a row with a supercilious Ranelagh committee member, Dr. Charles Lewinger. News of the incident reached King Edward VII's ears and the Ranelagh Committee had to beat an apologetic retreat.[24]

The Grand Duke Mikhail Mihailovitch, a member of Russia's Romanov dynasty, was an honorary member.[25] Confirming the strong female presence at Roehampton, the Duchess of Constance Westminster, Lady Edith Castlereagh and Lady Dorothy Dalmeny all enjoyed pony racing and carriage driving at the club.

Polo at Roehampton quickly recovered after the war under a new polo manager, Maj. Clement Charles Lister, 21st Lancers, who was one of the original club members. In spite of limping as the result of a wound, Maj. Lister showed concern for youngsters and newcomers to the game, an endeavor in which he was joined by Johnny Traill and the three Miller brothers. The wooden horse in Roehampton saw plenty of practice in the years between the wars. Would-be polo players could easily be duped by unscrupulous horse dealers and be considered to be in the way by more advanced players. Either way, then and now, it was not a comfortable situation for tyros. Roehampton's management went a long way in alleviating these faults in the system, which regrettably still exists.

The depression's onset was marked at Roehampton by long lines of men in front of the club seeking daily labor. The lucky ones selected by Col. Charles Miller, "you, you and you," were paid two shillings and two pennies for a day's menial work.[26]

In spite of hard times, polo continued to thrive. Many outstanding players graced the polo fields, such as Capt. Charles T.I. "Pat" Roark, the great Irishman who was widely considered the best British player of the inter-war period. Other prominent figures were Eric Tyrrell-Martin, a 9-goal international, Dudley Frost, Maj. Philip Magor, who owned estancia La Estrella in Argentina; and several members of the Traill family. Johnny made up a team which he called the Traillers, with his two sons, John Basil "Jack," James, and nephew Anthony, who was the son of 9-goaler Joseph Edmund Traill. The white-shirted Traillers were quite successful in mid and low-handicap polo. It is sad to note that Jim Traill's Sunderland aircraft was shot down by friendly fire while escorting a convoy in the Atlantic, while Tony Traill was killed in Burma in command of 45 Squadron, Royal Air Force. Jim and Tony Traill had taken the 1939 National Handicap Tournament in Argentina, on a San Jorge team with Rodolfo Boero and Thomas Willans. Tom Willans, a pilot in the R.A.F. Transport Auxiliary, was also killed in the war.[27]

After World War II, polo returned to Roehampton in July 1947. It was, however, on a diminished scale, but it was polo at last. By 1950 the club realized that the number two ground would not see much use and the space was allotted to the golfing community, an event that The Times bitterly reported as a sacrifice to provide a few extra bunkers for the golfers. The newspaper also commented upon the dissolution of Ranelagh and the mutilation of Hurlingham.[28] By 1952, although several tournaments were played at Roehampton, including the County Cup and an international match against an Argentine team for the Festival Cup, which was witnessed by Princess Elizabeth, who presented the trophies, polo was being played for only ten days during the summer season. The end for polo came in July 1956, when the last game took place on the old number one ground.

Cowdray Park

The most picturesque setting for a polo game in Britain is the one at the River Ground at Cowdray Park. With the background provided by the ruins of Cowdray House — it was never a castle — and further away the Sussex Downs, it provides an unforgettable image. It is also the venue for England's premier high-goal handicap tournament, the Cowdray Park Gold Cup, established in 1956.

The club is approaching its centenary, as it was established in 1910 by Weetman Harold Pearson, 2nd Viscount Cowdray.[29] The property's origins are ancient. The Lords of Midhurst were the Bohun family from the reign of Henri Beauclerc (1100–1135), son of William the Conqueror and better known as Henry I, until the Genovese explorer Christopher Columbus first set foot in America in 1492, Spanish flag in one hand and sword in the other. The Bohuns' lodgings were named La Coudraye, bearing in mind their Norman ancestry; it was replaced by the now ruined house. The heiress, Lady Mary Bohun, married Sir David Owen, whose son Henry sold the estate in 1529 to Sir William FitzWilliam, Henry VIII's sometime whipping boy. Sir William was later created Earl of Southampton by a perhaps remorseful monarch. Upon his death, the earldom became extinct, and his half-brother, Sir Anthony Browne, inherited the property.[30] It stayed in the family until 1843, when it was purchased by George Perceval, Earl of Eglinton. By then, Cowdray House had been destroyed by a fire in 1793.

Sir Weetman Pearson, head of a large civil engineering firm, purchased the estate in 1909. What had started as a construction enterprise in Yorkshire was expanded to a global conglomerate that built harbors, tunnels, dams and railways worldwide. To cap it all, Pearson's workers discovered large oil reserves in Mexico. Friendship with Mexican president and dictator Porfirio Díaz was not hurtful to the company's interests in that country. When Díaz was deposed by a revolution, Sir Weetman, by then 1st Viscount Cowdray, offered his Scottish estate in Aberdeenshire as a place for exile. Instead, Porfirio chose Paris.

Lord Cowdray's eldest son, Harold, started playing polo while at Oxford, being the team captain. At Cowdray Park, Harold Pearson laid out the House Ground and later on added the Lawns and River Grounds, the latter so named for the Rother River. His team he called Capron House, after their home near the ruins. When Lord Cowdray transferred the property to his son, Harold Pearson changed the team's name to Cowdray. Up to the onset of the Second World War, polo at Cowdray was essentially a family affair. The big occasion was Goodwood Week in August, the thoroughbred racing festival held at the nearby domain of the Earl of March. The main trophy was the venerable Cowdray Park Challenge Cup, presented by the 1st Lord Cowdray. It was first played for in 1911 and appropriately taken by the host team.[31]

Harold Pearson, 2nd Viscount Cowdray, a 6-goal handicap player, became chairman of the Hurlingham Polo Committee. Regrettably, he passed away in 1933, aged 52, and his only son, John, inherited the title. Lord John Cowdray would go on to be chairman of the Hurlingham Polo Association, the committee's successor, for no less than 20 years. Much more important, he saved the day for England by virtue of his support of the game during the dismal post war years.

Polo at Cowdray Park changed after the war. Lord Cowdray managed to salvage a dozen polo ponies and three-a-side practice games were played in the summer of 1947. Three of John Cowdray's sisters — his twin Angela, Yoskyl and Daphne — had played before the war and were only too happy to join the fray. One of the best players was John Lakin, married to the Hon. Daphne Pearson. Lakin, who had played for Oxford and reached a 7-goal rating, was one of the best English players at the time. Alistair Gibbs, a player from Gloucestershire now married to Yoskyl, also played, as well as the diminutive Archie David, a veteran player who was a constant figure in English polo for many years. Lord Cowdray, in spite of being handicapped with an artificial arm — he had lost his left upper extremity in Dunkirk — also played regularly, and was on the winning team in the revival of the Cowdray Park Challenge Cup in 1948. His teammates were Maj. Colin Davenport, R.A.V.C., Daphne Lakin and John Lakin. Fortuitously, two celebrated players from Argentina, Lewis Lacey and Jack Nelson, witnessed the games and suggested that a Cowdray Park team visit their country the following year.

Cowdray Park is the only British club team to play in the Argentine Open.[32] The 1949 season featured teams from Chile, Mexico and the United States, in addition to England. The opening match of the inaugural tournament, a 24-goal handicap event, pitted Chile versus England at the number one field at Palermo. The English team had to recur to the services of John Basil Traill, Johnny Traill's son, because Eric Tyrrell-Martin broke his ankle on the day he was to depart from Cairo to join the team. John Lakin, Australian Bob Skene and Lt. Col. Humphrey Guinness, Royal Scots Greys, completed the squad that defeated Chile by three goals. Handicapping the players presented a problem for the organizers, but the three visitors were arbitrarily assigned a 6-goal rating. After the tournament, Skene's handicap was raised to 8 goals and he was launched on his way to a brilliant career in California, a 10-goal rating and a place among the game's immortals.

Cowdray Park also participated in the Argentine Open Championship, with reserve player Lt. Col. Peter Dollar, 4th Hussars, replacing Jack Traill at number 1.[33] Local team Los Indios defeated Cowdray in an early round.

The 1953 revival of the Coronation Cup was celebrated with a seven-team tournament; the final game took place at Cowdray Park and the recently crowned Queen Elizabeth II presented the massive trophy. Argentina defeated England by one goal in a closely contested match. The Coronation Cup resumed in 1971, also at Cowdray Park, with a single match against America. It has been played yearly ever since at Windsor Park with one exception due to the outbreak of hoof and mouth disease and twice because of the Westchester Cup contests. The epidemic forced the Guards Polo Club to cancel the season, and the match against Brazil was played at Cowdray Park.

Polo in Britain took a big step forward in 1956, when Lord Cowdray presented the Gold Cup, emblematic of the British Open Championship. In the inaugural tournament the Argentine club Los Indios once more became Cowdray Park's nemesis. On a bright and sunny afternoon, on a heavy field due to an early drenching rain, Dr. Jorge Marín Moreno, Pablo Pedro Nagore, Antonio Heguy and Juan Carlos Echeverz, a 20-goal team, defeated Cowdray Park's Lt. Col. Alec Harper, Charles Smith-Ryland, Rao Rajah Hanut Singh and John Lakin. The Gold Cup, successor to the Hurlingham's Champion Cup as the most prestigious British tournament, has taken place without interruption, drawing in recent years about 20 high-goal teams.

The advent of the Gold Cup changed the atmosphere at Cowdray Park from a family pastime watched by friends and relatives to fierce competition witnessed by thousands of spectators, a large number of commercial sponsors and the inevitable coterie of beautiful people, mixed in recent days with the occasional streaker.

9. Fashionable Chic: Polo on the Continent

In our imagination, we are used to seeing the French Riviera as a place where the rich and beautiful people go to play. In reality only a handful places along the coast cater to the jet set. There is another face to the French Riviera, one of easygoing charm and personality. — Dagmar Van Tiel and Wouter Van Tiel[1]

Inevitably, polo has been associated with a cachet of glamour ever since the ruling classes and the aristocracy were attracted to the game and took a prominent part in its development. Luxury spas and seaside resorts were the favored habitats for wealthy vacationers, who enjoyed the advantages of plenty of leisure time and the wherewithal to make full use of the facilities offered by plush establishments.

Ostende in Belgium, Biarritz, Cannes and Deauville in France, Baden-Baden in Germany, Brioni in Italy and San Sebastián in Spain became symbols of conspicuous spending, Meccas of frivolity, refuges of kings and princes — quite often incognito under assumed names — and sites of high-stakes gambling and amorous rendezvous. Polo was an important attraction in the afternoon, as were the gaming tables at the casino, from evening to daybreak. It was a time and place where gentlemen tipped their hats when meeting each other and took their hats off for a lady.

Deauville

Deauville on the English Channel coast became the first center of holiday polo. It remains so, and the month of August makes the charming Normandy town one of the main polo centers in Continental Europe. The Société du Polo de Deauville dates its foundation to 1894, and play began the next summer with a competition for the International Tournament.[2] Quickly, Deauville became the place to see and be seen, following the completion of the polo season at Bagatelle. The club proper was founded in 1907 by Baron Robert de Rothschild, Capt. J. Jaubert — who often hid himself under the pseudonym "Nemor" — and Duc Armand de Guiche, who would later inherit the title Duc de Gramont. The Duc de Gramont would be president for half a century. Play started in the center of the Hippodrome de la Touques, located just outside the town.

During the First World War, Deauville and its hotels were converted into a huge convalescent area for wounded soldiers. The resort was to serve the identical purpose in the next war. Play resumed in 1919, when Baron Eduard de Rothschild and three British Army captains, Francis Penn-Curzon, Life Guards, Teignmouth Melvill, 17th Lancers, and Jack Harrison, Royal Horse Guards, took the Continental Championship.

King Alfonso XIII of Spain went to Deauville in 1922, playing incognito under the name Duque de Toledo; he and the Duque de Peñaranda, Marqués de Villabrágima and Conde de La Maza were the victors in the Continental Championship. Later that season, the royal personage joined Tommy Hitchcock, Lord Rocksavage and the Marqués de San Miguel in winning the Coupe Gramont.

Like in any other playgrounds of the rich, "at Deauville, society was a public performance, displaying itself brazenly on the broad promenades in the late morning, in the enormous dining rooms in the evening, in the casino all night long."[3]

Polo and fun continued throughout the golden years of the period between the wars, the heyday of the Roaring Twenties in America and the Lost Generation in continental Europe, so vividly described in the literary works of Ernest Hemingway and William Somerset Maugham, among many others. As a grim reminder of how dangerous sport polo can be, the American Colonel Henry Herman Harjes, a well-known polo personality residing in Paris, was killed in 1926 when his pony collided with another ridden by Martínez de Hoz, a player from Argentina, while competing for the Coupe Pulitzer.

Play was resumed after World War II and in 1950 M. François André—proprietor of the Hotel Royal and the Casino de Deauville — presented the Coupe d'Or, which remains one of the most important tournaments on the Continent.[4] Many of the top European teams have their names engraved on the trophy: From England, Arthur Lucas' Woolmers Park, Alex Ebeid's Falcons and teams bearing traditional names like Cirencester Park and Hurlingham. The Americas are represented by São Silvestre from Brazil, Cibao La Pampa from the Dominican Republic and Hurricanes and Santa Barbara from the United States. Hanut Singh led a team from India and Mariano Olazábal, his own Rancho Portales, from Mexico. San Miguel came from Argentina, and Cabañeros and Puerta de Hierro from Spain. Africa had Anadariya and Songhai-Chopendoz. Of course, the ubiquitous Kerry Packer had his success with Ellerston. Winning French teams included Guy de Monbrison's Pointe-Noire, Baron Elie de Rothschild's Laversine, Robert de Balkany's Sainte Mesme, Guy Wildenstein's Diables Bleus, Hubert Perrodo's Labergorce, André Fabre's Royal Barriére, Edouard Carmignac's Talandracas and Patrick Guerrand-Hermès' La Palmerai.

Years later, it was added to the Coupe d'Or the sonorous adjective of "Championnat du Monde," which led to spurious claims of world champions when the team Indies took the cup in 1957.[5, 6]

A familiar and elegant figure at Deauville for many years was Anne, Comtesse d'Ornano, who was also Lady Mayor of the town and never failed to attend the polo games. Deauville basks in the sun because of its upper class exclusivity and remains one of the last citadels of exquisite good taste. Perhaps to call Deauville in the twenty-first century a resort is a misnomer; it is more an experience. The three polo weeks in August have to be experienced. It is the only manner to understand and fully appreciate Deauville's unique charm.

Polo at Deauville has always been one of the highlights of the French social season. As part of the festivities, the mounted polo teams parade through the streets of the fashionable town on the Channel coast. The Park Lane team is in the foreground (Museum of Polo and Hall of Fame, courtesy Sebastian Amaya).

Ostende

When visiting Deauville in 1902, King Leopold II of Belgium watched polo games at that seaside resort and decided that there should be polo in his own beautiful seaside resort, Ostende, by the next summer. Manuel de Escandón, Marqués de Villavieja, was summoned before the royal person and was commanded to arrange for the construction of a field and secure the best players, never mind the cost. As sole proprietor of the Belgian Congo, the monarch could well afford any wish that came to his mind.[7]

Thanks to unlimited funds, a wonderful looking ground was available by the next June. Available and attractive, but it was not ready for polo. After the first chukker, the ponies' legs sank into the soft ground and the season was given up. The Miller brothers were called from Rugby as consultants and, in 1904, all enjoyed a full season of polo. Leopold II, although ensconced in his villa next to the polo ground, seldom attended the games.

Capt. Edward Miller managed what became the Ostende fortnight, from mid–July to early August. Just as in Deauville, the scene was frantic, especially after sundown. Miller relates how a keen polo player went to bed far too early because he had a big match the next day. This sound practice was considered unfair play by his opponents — and by his own side — so one of his team dressed as a Parisian cocotte, entered his room at the Palace Hotel, turned on the lights and sat on his bed. All hell broke loose, to the great amusement of all the many polo players who had gathered in the corridor.[8] Fun always took priority over serious play at Ostende.

The players were a mixed crowd. The main supporters in number were the Hungarians, with figures such as Count Géza Andrassy, Count Ludwig Karolyi, Count Anton Sigray, Count Laszlo Széchényi and several others. A few Germans — such as Edgar Flinsch and Georg Helfft — also joined the fray, with Heinrich Hasperg, Jr., from Hamburg. The Spaniard nobles were also in force, led by the Marqués de Villavieja and his brothers Eustaquio and Pablo de Escandón, the Duke of Santona and the brothers Joaquín and José Santos Suárez, and the Duke of Alba and his younger brother the Duke of Peñaranda, who was executed by the Republicans during the Spanish civil war. The local Belgian players were led by Alfred Grisar, and included Commandant L. Crockaert, Maurice Lysen, the Baron Gastón Peers and Clement van der Straaten.

A story that made big news in 1904 happened when Sir Ernest Horlick accidentally hit the Marqués de Villavieja behind his ear, just below the helmet's rim. Villavieja fell from his mount and remained unconscious for about fifteen minutes. Rumor about the player being killed quickly spread. Mr. Bishop, a reporter for the *New York Herald*, was leaving to catch the Dover boat and in his eagerness to be the first to report the news, telegraphed a writeup of the event to London and Paris before boarding. There was great consternation all around because the Marqués de Villavieja was a respected figure in social and polo circles. Sometime afterwards, the Belgian police turned up, quite indignant that the fatality had not been reported. One of the Englishmen pointed to a bare spot and told the constabulary that as he was only a foreigner, it did not matter much, so they had buried him on the spot. Officialdom does not like that sort of thing, and there was hell to pay. Luckily, King Leopold II was on the side of the fun-loving English. The Marqués de Villavieja confirms the weird story in his memoirs.[9]

Expenses for ponies and players alike were rather high, although most of the cost was borne by M. Georges Marquet, director general of the Société des Bains de Mer and of the Kursaal, where the baccarat rooms and casino were located. The single polo ground, although much improved from the early days, remained barely adequate for the short season because of heavy usage. In spite of those drawbacks, Ostende was one of the prime locations for summer polo on the Continent. The final blow occurred when the Clerical Party came into power in Belgium; gambling was abolished, and that ended the game of polo at Ostende. M. Georges Marquet was sentenced to three months in jail.[10]

Cannes

The idea of polo on the French Riviera originated in 1906 with four polo players who thought that the Paris season was too short. The four players were the Duc Antoine de Guiche, French Army Captain J. Jaubert, Baron Jacques de Meyronnet Saint-Marc and Prince Jan Ghika of Romania. The quartette secured the cooperation of M. André Capron, the mayor of Cannes, who was able to place the municipal resources of the town at their disposal. By the summer of 1907, a beautiful full-sized polo field was laid out on the road winding up to the Golf Club at Mandelieu, about three miles from Cannes. Captain Edward D. Miller, the celebrated player, polo pony dealer and organizer from the Rugby Club, was appointed as polo manager with the understanding that he was to bring a number of ponies for players using the club's facilities who had none or not enough of their own.

Armand, Duc de Guiche — who had a private polo ground on his estate at Vallière, near

Chantilly — was the club's president. Social success was assured when Prince Louis d'Orleans-Bragança, the Grand Dukes Boris Wladimirovitch and Mikhail Mihailovitch, the Conte Alfonso di Caserta, Dom Miguel Maximiliano de Bragança, Duque de Vizeu and the Hon. Robert Bacon, American Ambassador in Paris, were announced as honorary members of the Polo Committee.[11]

The first season at Le Polo de la Côte d'Azur was an unqualified success. The string of twenty ponies shipped by Capt. Miller could not meet the demand and he was asked to bring at least thirty for the next season. Every player, moreover, went away enthusiastic and with a determination to return. Of the players who participated in the inaugural season at Cannes, eleven were French, sixteen were British and five were American. Polo players from Austria-Hungary, Belgium, Germany and Romania also made their mark. The club's list of players is sprinkled with princes, dukes, margraves, earls, barons and lords, perhaps more than any other polo club at the time. There were also good polo players, such as Tom Drybrough, the American in England Charles T. Garland, Frederick Gill, Alfred Grisar, Capt. Harry Romer Lee, Goadby Lowe from Meadow Brook, the Miller brothers, Stewart Shipton (from Argentina but listed as British), Louis Stoddard from New Haven, Connecticut, and Lord Wodehouse, who became a 10-goal player.[12]

The polo club suddenly was the fashionable meeting spot of the smartest society in Cannes. "Quo vadis?" became beyond a doubt the *mot du jour* in sophisticated circles. "Au polo" was the smart response.

Brioni

One of the most charming Continental polo grounds was on the beautiful island of Brioni in the Adriatic Sea, near Pola. It was a full-size sand ground, magnificently situated near the sea, the white village of Istria just opposite overlooking the field of play. Nearby, there was another smaller ground of turf, used for practice. The island's proprietor was Carlo Kupelweiser, who had a fancy for the game and started polo in 1926. The favorable location gave polo players in Central Europe the convenience of year round play, which was not possible anywhere else in Europe. The climate was such that, with the exception of the months of December and January, the two grounds were in excellent condition.

Carlo Kupelwieser purchased some 40 ponies and handed over the running of the polo operation to the experienced Colonel Edward Miller, while Captain Charles Campbell and Rittmeister Hans Fischer were in charge of the pony string and participated in the tournaments as useful players. Capt. Campbell was a 6-handicap player, and Captain James Pierce, another good horseman and player, was on Baron Louis de Rothschild's team from Vienna.

Many Continental players, as for instance the Princes Hugo Windisch-Graetz, Adolf de Schaumburg-Lippe, Albert Dietrichstein, Karl Egon Fürstenberg, Baron Franz Mayr-Melnhof, Dr. Hans Fries from Vienna, and Messrs. A. Drach and Richard Weininger, stabled their ponies at Brioni. They traveled from Vienna, Munich and Berlin for the polo on the island's beauty spot. From Hungary, Hubert von Aich, Baron Andreas Hatvany and Count Joseph Wenckheim joined the polo crowd at Brioni, as well as Count Ludwig Karoly, a veteran from the Ostende days.

Quite a number of English players visited Brioni in spring and autumn, among them Sir Ian Walker, Capt. Gwynne Reid Walker and Capt. Desmond Miller, Col. Miller's son.

The British Mediterranean Fleet, based on the island of Malta, paid its annual visits in July to this lovely island and gave sailor polo players such as Sir Roger Keyes, Commander Edward G.G. Hastings, Lt. Comm. Lord Louis Mountbatten and Lt. Michael W. Ewart-Wentworth the chance to enjoy polo while the fleet was at anchor. Lady Mountbatten presented the Brioni-Malta Challenge Cup, one of the highlights of the summer polo season at Brioni.

In 1930, Mr. Carlo Kupelweiser died as the result of an accidental gunshot wound while hunting. Then the Marcheses Gaetano and Gian Franco Litta Modignani, enthusiastic Italian polo players, became the club's presidents, and Commander the Hon. Valentine Wyndham Quin, Royal Navy, succeeded Capt. Campbell as polo manager. Later players included the Duke of Spoleto, who was honorary president, Prince Karl Hohenlohe-Langenburg, Prince Otto Windisch-Graetz, and Counts Emanuele Castelbarco, Parodi Delfino and Lanfranco di Campello.

Brioni, one of the playgrounds of Central European high society, always maintained its aristocratic connections until Austria's annexation by Germany caused the game of polo to end, just before the onset of the Second World War.

10. American Polo Comes of Age

No first class American player ever hits a backhander if he can get the ball to the same position by hitting it under pony's neck. — Capt. Edward D. Miller[1]

Two years before the foundation of the Polo Association, Henry Lloyd Herbert had the brilliant idea of assigning individual handicaps to polo players who were to compete for the Turnure Cups and the Herbert Trophies. Initially, the maximum value was five goals; Thomas Hitchcock and Foxhall Parker Keene were at the top of the list, which comprised 42 players. When the association was formally organized, the top limit was raised to ten goals and Foxie Keene was the first player in the world to sport the magical "10," the much dreamed of summit for all polo players. To date, fewer than 100 players worldwide have achieved such rating.

The genesis of the Polo Association occurred at a dinner given on 21 March 1890 by John Elliot Cowdin to a number of men interested in polo. The founding fathers set up a committee of five to formulate a plan, which would harmonize and advance the interests of the several polo clubs. The committee members were Henry L. Herbert as chairman; Oliver W. Bird, Meadow Brook; John E. Cowdin, Rockaway; Thomas Hitchcock, Jr., Westchester Polo Club; Edward C. Potter, Country Club of Westchester, and Douglas Robinson, Jr., Essex County.

At a formative meeting, Mr. Hitchcock proposed that the Westchester Polo Club be the Central Organization of the new entity. This motion was along the precedent set by the Hurlingham Club in England. However, a more democratic solution was found. After careful consideration, it was deemed for the best interest of the game, and all concerned, to form an association to be called the Polo Association, with a constitution and rules to govern all polo clubs that should be elected to membership.[2]

The first regular meeting was held on 6 June 1890 at the Equitable Building in New York City. At that meeting, the following clubs were elected to membership, and therefore can be considered the founding members: Country Club of Westchester, New York; Essex County, Orange, New Jersey; Meadow Brook, New York; Morris County, Morristown, New Jersey; Philadelphia Polo Club, Philadelphia; Rockaway, Cedarhurst, New York; and Westchester Polo Club, Newport, Rhode Island. Henry Herbert was elected chairman, and Douglas Robinson, Jr., a member of the Essex County Country Club, was elected treasurer. Mr. Henry L. Herbert would remain at his post until his demise in 1921.

Oyster Bay Polo Club in Long Island — of which future president Theodore Roosevelt was a member — joined the association later in 1890. Three clubs in Massachusetts — Harvard, Hingham and Myopia — followed suit in 1891; they were joined in the association's ranks by Tuxedo in New York State. In the Midwest, the Country Club of St. Louis was affiliated in 1893 and the Chicago Polo Club in 1895.

The earliest trophy is the Polo Association Cups, started in 1890 in Newport; the winners being Meadow Brook with August Belmont, Thomas Hitchcock, Oliver Bird and Robert Winthrop. The Championship and Added Cups, the equivalent of the modern Open Championship, were established in 1895. Playing at Prospect Park in Brooklyn, the Myopia team of Augustus Peabody Gardner, Robert Gould Shaw II, Rodolphe Agassiz and Frank Blackwood Fay took the silver cups to Boston's North Shore.

Polo at the racing center and spa town Saratoga, in upstate New York, was started in the late 1890s by John A. Manning, John Sanford, E.L. Smith and R.W. Smith. Play was on a field donated by William Collins Whitney, Harry Payne's father. The polo season coincided

Lawrence Waterbury on Cinderella. A proper polo player, Larry is wearing a tie. Waterbury is noted for being the only poloist to represent his country in all four team positions. Cinderella, a brown mare played by Englishman Riversdale Grenfell, was purchased by August Belmont, who lent her to the American team (private collection).

with the thoroughbred racing calendar in the month of August. The club, affiliated in 1899, went into abeyance in 1930.

The Westchester Cup was revived in 1900 with a single, unofficial match at Hurlingham, the hosts being the winners. A formal challenge was issued two years later, and America obtained its first taste of victory against England, winning the opening match by just one tally, two goals to one. At the game's conclusion, the British complained about a legal tactic employed by the Americans. In those days, the rules allowed a knock-in when the defending side had hit the ball behind its own backline. During the game, every time there was pressure near the American goalposts, the defenders would hit the ball behind the back line; then, they would be allowed to bring the ball back into play. Actually, the British were hoisted by their own petard, because that practice was legal according to the Hurlingham rules. In America, one-quarter goal was deducted from the total, for what was then called a safety knockout. In England, it was "bad form" to hit the ball behind your own back line in order to save a goal. After the Westchester matches the rule was changed; a penalty shot was exacted upon the offending side.[3]

England changed its lineup for the second and third games of the series, which they took with comfort. In those games, the Waterbury brothers showed the possibilities of playing across the field, as a variation of the then prevalent theory of playing up and down the ground. They also exploited the forehand shot under the pony's neck, from the boards to the center of the field, and the cut shot from the left side of the ground towards the middle. Larry and Monty Waterbury displayed a style of combination play that hitherto had not been the staple of play in America, and most certainly never in England.

In each of the last two matches, the American team scored only one goal. These were missionary efforts from the American point of view; nevertheless, its gospel would bear fruit a few years later with the challenge led by Harry Payne Whitney.

Seven years would go by before the Americans, once more, challenged the Hurlingham Club for the Westchester Cup. This was a different story. Under Harry P. Whitney's leadership, the American squad was able to collect the best pony string seen on a polo ground up to that time. Many were the stuff of legends: Balada, Bendigo, Cinderella, Cinders, Cobnut, Cottontail, Little Mary, Mohawk and Ralla; names that even today are spoken of with due reverence. Of those, only Cottontail is enshrined in the Polo Hall of Fame. Cobnut, Cottontail, Little Mary and the Roan Mare were immortalized in bronze by Herbert Haseltine in *The Meadow Brook Team*, while the Irish-bred mare Ralla merited her own sculpture by the same gifted animalier.[4]

The 1909 Westchester Cup series irrevocably changed the balance of power in the world of polo. Up to then, Britain had dominated, although players in India might have raised a few questions about such judgment. The success of the American expedition to Hurlingham meant that a new power was now on top of the heap. This accomplishment was the result of several factors: meticulous preparation, strong leadership, sound tactics, good chemistry among the players and superb pony power. The Americans were seriously handicapped by the ground, which was heavy and cut up badly. Even more, they had to play under Hurlingham's Rules of the Game and they were unaccustomed to the offside rule. However, the team came through with excellence and, more importantly, modified the way the game was played.

Henry (Harry) Payne Whitney absolutely changed the tactics of contemporary polo and proved himself a worthy successor to the leadership qualities first shown by John Watson with his Freebooters team, a quality that in England was continued in practice by Edward Miller with his own Rugby team, and Walter Buckmaster with the Old Cantabs.

James "Monty" Waterbury on Conover, a pony from Texas owned by Harry P. Whitney. The pony has polo boots on the front legs and bandages on the hind legs. With his brother Larry, Waterbury revolutionized combination play (private collection).

The effect of America's victory was no less than a revolution in polo, for revolution it was. Tactically, the Big Four pressed attacks continuously, even sending up field the back, Dev Milburn, who would temporarily find himself in the number 1 position. Larry Waterbury, or more often Whitney, would then cover the rearguard. Technically, their hitting was a revelation to the British players. It was dogma that the back should never meet the ball; the American Devereux Milburn took such risk, repeatedly, and with spectacular results.

The exceptional pony string collected by Whitney included several of the best ponies in Britain. For two years prior to the challenge, Whitney had given Capt. Miller, the premier polo pony dealer in the British Isles, a blank check to purchase the best ponies. In Edward Miller's own words, "It was, to say the least, a shock to me when every pony I had sold turned up to play against us."[5]

The following year Louis Stoddard invited an English team to visit Lakewood in New Jersey. Walter Buckmaster, George Belville, Capt. Claude Champion de Crespigny and Capt. Edward Miller were so impressed with the advantages of the American code, especially the abolition of the offside rule and the system of individual handicaps, that upon their return to the Mother Country they lobbied hard to institute those changes. The offside rule was

An American player-patron at the turn of the 19th century, financier George J. Gould was one of the owners of the Georgian Court estate in Lakewood, New Jersey, later made famous by George Bellows as the site for his trilogy of polo paintings (private collection).

immediately discarded; in reality, the Hurlingham Committee had no choice because, according to the terms of the deed of gift, the Westchester Cup had to be played in the holder's country and under its rules. The handicap system was changed early in 1911; India, Argentina and South Africa followed suit within months. On the other hand, the pony height restrictions, practically in abeyance although still in the books, were not abolished until after the war.

A throw-in is captured during a match at Georgian Court between the local team Lakewood, in yellow with black sleeves, and Devon, in white. From the left, Charles Wheeler, Robert Collier, Monty Waterbury, George Kendrick III, Charles Snowden and George Gould mark each other. The ball is a white blur between the legs of Kendrick's pony (Museum of Polo and Hall of Fame).

The Big Four's handicap history is interesting. Larry Waterbury reached the 10-goal pinnacle in 1900 and his younger brother Monty, two years later. All four players were handicapped at 10 goals by the Hurlingham Polo Committee following the 1909 Westchester series; in America, they were 9-goalers and remained so until 1917, when the quartette was raised to 10 goals. By that time, all but Devereux Milburn were past their prime. Whitney had retired from international play

Harrison Tweed, a winner of the Junior Championship, is depicted in bronze by 8-goal player and sculptor Charles Cary Rumsey. This is a representation of a typical player in the early 1900s. Mr. Tweed, sleeves rolled up, wears neither knee-guards nor a helmet. The pony lacks leg bandages as well as a martingale, and his tail is untied. Another example of this sculpture is in the Metropolitan Museum of Art, New York (Museum of Polo and Hall of Fame).

in 1913 but kept on playing club games at Meadow Brook. It appears that the general eleva-
tion in handicaps in 1917 was a way to honor their achievements. It is of note that Foxhall
Keene, who was rated 10 goals in 1891, was also raised to that same handicap in 1917.

Mr. Dennis Amato, a reputable American historian, is of the opinion that, following the
1902 Westchester Cup series, the Polo Association raised its standard in awarding the top rating.[6] Thus, Foxie Keene and Monty Waterbury lost their 10-goal handicap. What followed
was a virtual moratorium for 10-goalers in America, which lasted until 1917.

By the early 1920s, the old lions were giving way to the new generation of top players,
best personified by Tommy Hitchcock, a 10-goaler at age 21. Malcolm Stevenson, Louis Stoddard and James Watson Webb — the only left-handed player to reach that summit — were the
younger players that, together with Dev Milburn, would fill in the slots on the American international team. They would eventually be called "The Second Big Four," because they were,
like their predecessors, unbeaten in international play.

The span between the two world wars was the golden age of American polo. The record
is most impressive. Starting with the 1909 victory in the Westchester Cup, and ending with
the 1939 series at Meadow Brook, American teams took nine out of ten international series,
winning eighteen out of the twenty matches. The only blemish was in 1914, when an English
team took two closely contested games and the Westchester Cup therewith.

The full story of American intervention in the Olympic Games is described in the pertinent chapter. In short, Foxie Keene took the gold medal in Paris in 1900 as part of an Anglo-
American team. A creditable performance by a weak American Army team won the bronze
medal in Belgium in 1920. At Paris in 1924, the supreme skills of Tommy Hitchcock were not
sufficient to contain a balanced and superbly mounted Argentine squad. For some unexplained
reason, there was no polo in the 1932 Olympiad at Los Angeles. The official statement explaining the decision said it was entirely "due to the practical difficulties of organizing polo, expense,
etc., in the countries who would enter these events, with which polo associations are well
acquainted."[7]

However, there are contemporary reports indicating that while Great Britain was luke-
warm to the idea of participating, and that India needed more time to make a decision, both
South Africa and Argentina were enthusiastic about playing in the Olympics.[8] It is safe to
assume that if it had been so, the gold medal would have been taken by the United States,
because in that same year, an American team retained the Cup of the Americas as visitors in
Buenos Aires. Argentina was growing fast as a power to be reckoned with in world polo; however, it had not yet reached full maturity. Whether or not it was reached in 1936, it is impossible to tell. American polo declined to enter the Olympic competition in Berlin and an
ill-advised selection process did not allow some of the best American players to participate in
the Cup of the Americas at Meadow Brook. The Argentines won that series fairly, because it
was not their fault that the United States Polo Association selected a weaker team than the
full international squad.

Polo in the United States Army

The game of polo in the American Army was started at Fort Riley, Kansas, in 1896 by
lieutenants Henry Terry de la Mesa Allen, Charles G. Treat, Sterling Price Adams and Samuel
D. Sturgis. All participated actively in the development of Army polo and some reached high

rank. Army officers had significant roles in polo overseas. In Cuba, a local team representing the Rural Guards mixed with the American forces; in the Philippines, army polo was popular, and in China, the game brought together British and American soldiers on the polo field.

An outstanding team in the 1900s was the 10th Cavalry squad, based at Fort Robinson, Nebraska. The team played in the Midwest and at Colorado Springs. When the unit was deployed to Fort Ethan Allen, Vermont — where the polo field still stands — the 10th Cavalry held its own against good civilian teams. Among those who played for the Cavalry were Lts. Hank R. Adair, "Biddy" Cook, Ephraim H. Graham and Bruce Palmer.

The Sixth Field Artillery succeeded the Tenth Cavalry as the best team in the United States Army. Lts. Louis Beard, René DeRussy Hoyle, Corlandt Parker and Alfred L.P. Sands carried over all opposition in the years 1910–1912. The American Army of the Occupation of the Rhine polo team's participation in the 1920 Olympic Games and at Ranelagh Club in Barnes, a London suburb, has been described elsewhere in this book.

In 1922, "Polo at the Pier," a phrase meaning polo at Point Judith Club, in Narragansett Pier, saw the first victory of an Army team in the Junior Championship, defeating a good Meadow Brook foursome in the finals.[9] Army teams would be very successful in this tournament during the 1920s.

There were two contests between American and British army squads, in 1923 and 1925. Polo player William Waldorf Astor presented a cup to be played for in the International Military Tournament. Maj. Arthur H. Wilson, Maj. John K. Herr — the last commander of the U.S. Army Cavalry — Lt. Col. Lewis Brown, Jr., and Maj. Louis A. Beard represented the U.S. Army. In a three-match series, the U.S. Army team emerged victorious at Meadow Brook. Two years later, a return series took place at Hurlingham that was witnessed by King George V. The American team — Capt. Arthur "Jingle" Wilson, Capt. Charles H. Gerhardt, Capt. Peter P. Rodes and Maj. Louie Beard — won the trophy in two straight matches.

Because of cost restrictions, most officers lived in genteel poverty on Army bases; furthermore, promotion in rank was slow. The U.S. cavalry had many advantages: it was ideal for the practicing poloist, it was socially remunerative and it was the branch from which officers frequently moved to the top of the heap in the army at large. During these lean years, many Regular Army officers went to seed. A few burned themselves out, and others annoyed their colleagues with pioneering studies in tactics and occasional rude espousal of modern forms of war. There were several examples. The most notorious was Colonel William Lendrum Mitchell of the Signal Corps, forerunner of the Army Air Corps, who was court-martialed for insubordination, found guilty and suspended from the Army without pay. Thereupon, Col. Mitchell resigned from the service. Others were General Adna R. Chaffee, Jr., 15th Cavalry, one of the fathers of the Armored Corps, and the controversial General George Smith Patton, Jr., also listed as a player in the 15th Cavalry, in 1912. All three officers, incidentally, were polo players. Lt. Mitchell was a member of the Jacksonville Polo Club in 1899, while his unit, the Wisconsin Volunteers, was stationed in Florida during the American-Spanish War in Cuba. Later on, Billy Mitchell is listed on the Signal Corps polo roster.

Nevertheless, the best was yet to come. In 1930, an Army team traveled to Argentina to compete in a series versus the Argentine Army team and participate in the Argentine Open Championship. Under the leadership of Col. Wyllis Virlan Morris, the United States Army delegation was constituted by Maj. Chandler Wilkinson, Maj. Charles C. Smith, Capt. Peter Rodes, and Lt. Morton McDonald Jones and, as alternate, Lt. Homer W. Kiefer. In the Open Championship, the U.S. Army team defeated Los Pingüinos, the Braun Menéndez family team, and then Las Rosas, anchored by the Miles brothers, the international players David and John. In the final match on the number one ground at Palermo, they faced the famous Santa Paula, which had taken the Pacific Open Championship earlier that year. The Army team almost produced an upset. Santa Paula was trailing 5–8 after the fifth of seven chukkers. Very slowly, Santa Paula started chipping at the score, and in the last period Manuel Andrada galloped the length of the field to make the winning goal, putting the final tally at 9 to 8 goals.

Captain Wesley White, who was one of the umpires, wrote: "During the nineteen years that I have played and watched polo, I have never seen such an enthusiastic crowd. They seemed to lose all control of themselves and there was so much noise it was impossible for the umpires to hear the final bell. When it became evident that the bell had rung, a crowd of about five thousand swarmed onto the field, lifted the Santa Paula players from their ponies, and carried them to the center of the grand stand for the presentation of the trophies."[10]

To put the Army team accomplishment in perspective, only three other foreign teams have reached the final game of the Argentine Open: Meadow Brook in 1932, which they won, the South African Springboks in the following year, and Bostwick Field in 1950.

After the Open, the military national teams squared off for the Inter-Armies Cup, presented by the American ambassador to Argentina, Mr. Robert W. Bliss.[11] It was not much of a contest, because the American team, perhaps smarting from that tough loss in the Open Championship, overwhelmed the Argentine Army team in both games, 10–7 and 16–1. It should be pointed out that the games were played with no handicap given; the American team totaled 21 goals, while the Argentina squad was rated at 10 goals aggregate.

No story of American military polo can be complete without the mention of Capt. Wesley J. White, Field Artillery. A good player — rated at five goals — a severe injury to his wrist ended his active career as a player. Nevertheless, Capt. Smith took up umpiring with such brilliant results that he was universally recognized as the best umpire ever. Wesley White authored *Guide for Polo Umpires*, first published by the U.S. Polo Association in 1929, a work that went through six editions. When asked about his philosophy on umpiring polo games, Capt. White said, "The best players like to know that the game is going to be played as it was intended to be played. If the rules are wrong, enforce them as they are written, and it will not take long to change them."[12]

11. The Anglo-Argentines: Squires or Gauchos?

It is a well-known fact that by 1914 Argentina, as a place of British investment and trade was comparable with Australia and Canada, and exceeded only by the United States and India. — Henry Stanley Ferns[1]

The overwhelming preponderance of British polo players in Argentina began to fade following the end of the Kaiser's War. When a state of war between the United Kingdom and the German Empire was declared on 4 August 1914, volunteers, both British and Argentine-born, flocked to the recruiting offices. They included railroad and bank employees, businessmen, office clerks, engineers, lawyers, physicians, teachers, mechanics, farm owners and their hands; in short, representatives of almost every profession and trade.

As described in *The Forgotten Colony*, "From the far off regions of the Southern Andes, from Patagonia, from the sugar plantations of Tucumán, from the forest zones of the Chaco, from the estancia establishments in the plains of the province of Buenos Aires and the Pampa, from the hilly districts of Cordoba, and the province of Santa Fe, from the low-lying districts of Entre Ríos and Corrientes, in a word from north to south and east to west, they wended their way to Buenos Aires to take the first ship homeward bound."[2]

The number of British citizens residing in Argentina was small when compared to other European immigrants. In percentages, the contribution to the war by the British living in Argentina was significant. Total population in Argentina according to the May 1914 census was 7,885,237 inhabitants; of these, 2,357,954 were foreign nationals, the British comprising 28,300, of which 19,519 were males. In the census figures, British born in Argentina were recorded as Argentines. In terms of numbers, the small percentage of British people had an economic and educational influence in Argentina that was totally out of proportion to the net population. The same consideration applies to all sports and games, especially up to the start of the world conflict.

The recorded number of volunteers from Argentina is 4,852, of which 528 gave their lives. The percentage of casualties in the British and colonial forces was between ten and eleven percent; the Argentine volunteers suffered exactly the same percentage of deaths. Interestingly enough, more than half the volunteers were officers, in a two to one proportion to non-commissioned officers and other ranks. About eleven percent received decorations, including one Victoria Cross, Britain's highest award for valor.[3]

Approximately one-quarter of all volunteers did not return to Argentina. Many polo players were killed; thousands others elected to remain in what they considered their home, the British Isles. This was expected. While most of the European immigrants stayed in Argentina to take advantage of the tempting opportunities in the new world, the British refused to be considered, or even called, immigrants, because, in their own eyes, they were visitors.

The influence of the British-owned railroads was strong. Several high-placed executives were polo players of note. Herbert Gibson, from the family-owned Los Yngleses, was president of the Southern Railway, the largest in Argentina. Oliver R.H. "Harry" Bury — whose brother J. Luard Bury took the Open Championship — was general manager of the Rosario and Entre Ríos Railways and an enthusiastic polo player, reaching the finals in the 1893 Open. Arthur Follett Holt, later Sir Follet Holt, three-time winner of the Open, was chairman of the Rosario and Entre Ríos Railways.[4] The Buenos Aires & Rosario Railway had in 1892 its own polo club, almost unique in the world of polo. The only other railway polo club was the Bengal-Nagpur Railway in India, active in the 1920s.

The Polo Association of the River Plate, which true to its name included clubs located in Uruguay, across the wide River Plate, governed Argentine polo. In practice, there was little competition between Argentine and Uruguayan clubs. A committee, in which the principal figure seems to have been the honorary secretary, ran the Polo Association of the River Plate. Frank Balfour, a towering personality in organized polo as player, breeder, publicist and administrator, filled this important post for many years until he returned to his native England in 1912.[5] Balfour, a 7-goal player, besides taking five Open Championships between 1893 and 1903, was the editor of the *River Plate Sport and Pastime*, a most valuable source for sports in Argentina from 1890 until shortly after the turn of the century, when it merged with *The Review of the River Plate*. According to Argentine Polo Association officials, there are no minute books from the Polo Association of the River Plate.[6] Furthermore, no individual has been identified as president or chairman of the organization and the only known secretary was Frank Balfour. This is a dark hole in the history of polo in Argentina.

The Polo Association of the River Plate was reluctant to make waves. Its main function seems to be the organizing body for the Open Championship, which it did well, and to follow and implement the modifications to the rules of the game as emanated from the Hurlingham Polo Committee in England. Pony height restrictions were in the books; however, they were ignored widely and there is no record of an official measurer ever being appointed. In the matter of overseas tours, the association washed off its collective hands. It fell to individual players to initiate the profitable journeys to Europe in search of buyers for their criollo polo ponies. England, and to a lesser extent, Belgium, France, Germany and Spain, became purchasers of Argentine-bred ponies. From 1896 on, teams and individual players from Argentina participated in the principal European tournaments, achieving significant successes. The London 1912 season showed to great advantage the quality of Harold Schwind's El Bagual team and the individual brilliance of its players: the cousins Joe and Johnny Traill, Leonard Lynch-Staunton and John Argentine Campbell, the latter being the sole Argentine-born. Their success convinced many others that there was a large market for ponies in Europe and that Argentine players could compete on equal terms with the top English teams. In spite of the changing times, the P.A. of the River Plate remained immutable in its isolation policy.

Col. Isaac de Oliveira Cézar, a cavalry officer, was the prime mover behind the creation of a competing governing body, the Asociación Nacional de Polo, which was founded on 11 March 1913. This entity sponsored a strong team to participate in the London polo season:

La Victoria, the winning team of the 1900 Polo Association of the River Plate Championship, included (from the left) Chamberlain "Jumbo" Hinchliffe, Luard Bury, Magnus Fea and Francis Kinchant. This faded photograph is one of the few recording a championship team in 19th century Argentina (private collection).

the three Traill cousins, Bob, Joe and Johnny; and Leonard Lynch-Staunton. Ironically, they were the holders of the Polo Association of the River Plate Open Championship Cup. Misfortune followed the visitors when Joe Traill sustained a severe injury and was unable to play. The team had no reserve players and English clubs promptly recruited the other members of the touring party.

In October of that year, the Asociación Nacional de Polo sponsored two tournaments in Las Rosas, Santa Fe Province. John Raymond, Charles "Bunny" Land, Edward "Toby" Grahame Paul and Charles Rutherford took the open competition, and Jack Brooker, Ernest Peel, and the brothers Stephen and Eustace Cox, the handicap tournament. All eight players would go to war in two-year time. Maj. Eustace Cox, Devonshire Regiment, already decorated with the Military Cross, died of wounds received in France in April 1917. On the other hand, Capt. C.D. Rutherford, Royal Regiment of Artillery, was subject to a court-martial and dismissed from the service.[7]

The new Asociación Nacional de Polo failed to thrive. Although some civilian teams had supported the new enterprise, it was not enough to challenge the establishment. In order to obtain financial help from military sources, the entity's goals were extremely broad and included an ambitious horse-breeding program for cavalry use. With most of the resources going towards achieving such objective, polo petered out and the association folded.

It was a wake-up call that the Polo Association of the River Plate failed to hear. The world conflict intervened and not much happened until 1921, when Jack Nelson, just returned from a tour to Chile financed with private means, proposed a visit to England featuring the best available players. Once more, the governing body adopted a negative attitude. Again faced with refusal, on 15 November 1921, Francisco Ceballos, Jack Nelson, Col. Isaac de Oliveira Cézar, Alfredo Peña Unzué and Dr. Carlos Rodríguez Egaña signed a document creating the Federación Argentina de Polo. This institution then sent a team to England with the financial support of the Buenos Aires Jockey Club, which carried the reputation of being the wealthiest club in the world. Lewis Lacey, Jack Nelson, David and John Miles formed the top team, while Luis Nelson (Jack's brother), Toby Paul, Alfredo Peña and Carlos Uranga were the reserves. The pony string was carefully selected and represented the best quality that had left the shores of the River Plate up to that date.

This year of 1922 rang a bell in world polo. At full strength, the team was unbeaten in England. With other various formations, the federation's team took the Whitney Cup, the

Ladies Nomination Cup, the Roehampton Junior Tournament, the Roehampton Open Cup and Hurlingham's Championship Cup. This extraordinary performance merited some attention from the other side of the North Atlantic when the U.S. Polo Association invited the team to participate in the American Open. This they did, and proceeded to defeated a powerful Meadow Brook foursome that included Tommy Hitchcock and Devereux Milburn.

Back home, things were moving along the organizational front, no doubt encouraged by the federation's team successes. The majority of the polo clubs supported the new governing entity but a minority supported the old guard, personified by the Hurlingham Club. The probability of secession was raised in everybody's mind. Fortunately, cool heads prevailed and several meetings took place between Francisco Ceballos and Miguel Alfredo Martínez de Hoz representing the Federación Argentina de Polo, and Ernest Jewell — Hurlingham's president — and J. A. Monroe Hinds on behalf of the Polo Association of the River Plate.

The federation's representatives made it clear that were ready to accept a compromise, if the new entity would have its name and the rules and regulations in Spanish language. Another requirement was that representatives from all affiliated clubs must elect the committee. With the benefit of hindsight, it seems ridiculous that something so basic as the rules of the game being written in the national language should be a point of discussion; however, the Polo Association of the River Plate's grip on the game admitted of no changes in the status quo. Only the specter of secession brought the P.A. of the River Plate to the table. Finally, at a general assembly held at the Hurlingham Club on 14 September 1922, the Asociación Argentina de Polo was born.

Joseph Albert Monroe Hinds was elected president and Francisco Ceballos, vice-president. On reading the minutes and the election results, it appears that the decision to nominate Hinds without opposition had been reached beforehand. Monroe Hinds got all 28 votes from the delegates. The rest of the electoral process went along institutional party lines: for vice-president, Ceballos got 17 votes and his opponent, William Agar Benitz, 11 votes. Nevertheless, Willy Benitz got his way into the committee, because he was elected as a member at large, together with Charles Lacey and José Alfredo Martínez de Hoz.

Therefore, peace was reached between the two factions and the new Asociación Argentina de Polo began its deliberations on a positive note. After Monroe Hinds finished his mandate in 1923, every succeeding president belonged to the federation's cause. The chain was broken in 1941 when Gen. Carlos Kelso, an officer of Australian descent, became president. By that time, the Polo Association of the River Plate had faded into memories.

Hurlingham Club's influence began to decrease in the 1920s. Although it remained the Open Championship's home field, in 1928, the new grounds at Palermo were opened to the public and the tournament became popularly known as the Campeonato Abierto de Palermo. The Hurlingham Club maintained its influence within the British community, but the balance of power in polo had definitely tilted towards the Argentine players. The first yearbook issued by the Argentine Polo Association in 1923, a slim volume comprising 24 pages, lists 248 players with official handicaps. Of those, 139 were British and 109 were Argentines. Reflecting the growth of polo, the 1930 handicap list included 974 players; of those, only 288 had British surnames.[8]

Out of 19 polo clubs listed in 1923, eleven could be considered British or at least with a strong British constituency. By 1933, there were 58 affiliated clubs, of which 13 had British roots. Hurlingham was the only "English" club in a metropolitan area and all the others were based at estancias. The Benitzs' Los Algarrobos was an example, as were small towns like

Venado Tuerto, where there was a large Irish contingent, or sugar cane plantations such as the Leach brothers' in Jujuy and the Shipton family's La Corona in Tucumán. Many of the players out in "the camp" maintained membership at Hurlingham and stabled their ponies at the club for the big spring tournaments; it was their home base in town.

The Hurlingham Club was the last fortress of the Forsyths in Argentina and the symbol of the British establishment in South America. How perceptive was Philip Guedalla's observation in 1932: "Seventeen miles out of Buenos Aires a charming suburb clusters around an admirable club. It has its games, its dances and its life and its contacts with Buenos Aires are almost confined to the successful efforts to catch the morning train to town or lunch on Saturdays at Harrods. One begins to wonder whether the prim British instinct of keeping oneself to oneself dictated this retreat. Was Hurlingham the cause of the surprising segregation of the races? Or was it just a consequence?"[9]

There was, however, some infiltration by English-speaking Argentine families into the small town of Hurlingham. Surnames such as Beláustegui, Casares, Finochietto, Mosquera, Nevares, Ocampo, Parodi and Quirno began to make their appearance in the club members' roster.[10]

In spite of the changes, the aura of Englishness remained strong at the club. Andrew Graham-Yooll wrote: "Hurlingham Club still stands, as exclusive as ever since its foundation in 1888 exclusive to wealth if not always to nationality — with immaculate golf course, a splendid polo field, a cricket green for the summer and an Argentine military garrison and a rubbish tip for neighbors. A terrorist's bomb destroyed one of the club's older store sheds in 1975 but it hardly moved a hair in the stiff upper lip."[11] Not all settlers from the British Isles shared the same characteristics and experienced similar receptions in Argentina. For instance, the Welsh were different. They settled in northern Patagonia and kept pretty much to themselves, maintaining their religion and their language — into the 1960s the only newspaper outside of Wales printed in Welsh was in Chubut — and did not contribute, not even in their beloved Rugby football, to sport in Argentina.

The Scots, who first arrived to Argentine shores in numbers in 1825 on board the good ship *Symmetry*— with a copy of the bible in one hand and a bottle of strong spirit in the other, as Andrew Graham-Yooll quaintly put it —first settled in the Scottish Colony some 20 miles southwest of Buenos Aires. Although the grand design of the colony did not bear fruit, they and their descendants became a formidable force in Argentine ranching and mercantile circles. Many became celebrated polo players and one Scottish family, the Drysdales, were among the richest merchants in the capital and owned large extensions of prime grazing land in western Buenos Aires Province. The family club, Santa Inés, named after one of their estancias, took three Open Championships in the 1920s. John Drysdale was one of the earliest presidents of the Hurlingham Club and Alexander Drysdale donated the first boards on a polo field in Argentina. The Drysdale Cup was a coveted trophy played on handicap by teams competing in the Hurlingham Open.

Other Drysdale estancias were Nueva Escocia, where Eduardo Roberto "Gordo" Moore — together with his brother Juan Reginaldo "Sonny"— learned the game from their father, Don Roberto, a winner of the National Handicap tournament. Eduardo Moore brought a new dimension to polo with his massive polo pony export business. As a player, he made a mark on British polo for his marvelous stick work and superior tournament record with the Vestey organization. His prowess as a player obtained recognition by the Hurlingham Polo Association when Moore became the first 10-goaler in England since the legendary Gerald Balding achieved such rating just before World War II. With the support of his pal Héctor Barrantes, a superb master of the horse, Stowell Park was the dominant force in high-goal polo in the 1970s. When Lord Samuel Vestey gave up polo, Gloucestershire remained a force to be reckoned with under the Foxcote emblem, the Hon. Mark Vestey's team. Foxcote still is a presence in British polo featuring Mark's children, Ben, a Brigade of Guards officer, Tamara, and Nina, the third now Mrs. John Paul Clarkin.

Mention has been made of estancia Negrete, owned by David Shennan, a Scot who organized the first polo matches reported in the local press. Hugh Robson, an immigrant born in Dumfriesshire, progressed from ploughman in Scotland to large landowner in Argentina. The Robsons merit serious consideration as the first polo family in Argentina. Hugh Scott Robson, Hugh's grandson, became the first star of Argentine polo. An ambidextrous player in an epoch during which it was legal to hit the ball with either hand and a superb horseman to boot, Robson — often mistakenly referred to as Scott-Robson — won six Open Championships in Argentina, as well as the Anchorena Cup, now the Tortugas Open. A frequent traveler to Europe, he was on teams that took the Warwickshire Cup, the International Cup at Ranelagh and the Rubgy Open Cup. In the Continent, Robson took the German Open in Hamburg and the International Cup at Ostende. A measure of his worth as a player is the fact that he was on England's Recent Form List every year it was published, until its abolition in 1911. Three of his five brothers were also good players. Tom Robson took five open championships; the younger siblings, Edward and Peter, also have their names engraved on the championship silver cup. Hugh Noel, Robson's only son, was educated in England, joined the Royal Scot Greys and became an 8-goal international player. Several of the Robson girls married into polo families, such as Auld, Campbell, Gebbie, Livingston, Mallet and Mohr-Bell.

The Irish immigrants were different. Pushed out of their native island by the tragic famine, they immigrated to Argentina in large numbers and, as opposed to the other settlers from the British Isles, they were assimilated into Argentine society with much ease. The reason was religion. Almost all Hibernians were from the south; there are very few Irish in Argentina with Ulster ancestry. Fr. Anthony Fahy, a legend in his own time, was in fact the leader of the Irish community in Argentina.[12] The overwhelming majority of Irish immigrants were Roman Catholics, which made assimilation through marriage into Argentine society much easier. Protestants had much difficulty marrying in Argentina because of bureaucratic barriers and nationalistic suspicions. Many loyal British subjects were suspected of being spies, or of being involved in contraband, especially in the mid-nineteenth century.

The Irish were liked in Argentina. *The Southern Cross*, the voice of the local Hibernian community — still published as a monthly — wrote in 1875, "In no part of the world is the Irishman more respected and esteemed that in the Province of Buenos Aires; and in no part of the world, in the same space of time, have Irish settlers made such large fortunes."[13]

The Irish also climbed the social ladder. Among the founders of the Argentine Jockey Club in 1882 were many Irish surnames, such as Casey, Dowling, Duggan, Gahan, Garrahan, Ham, Lawrey and Murphy, alongside those of the aristocracy, Alvear, Casares, Elía, Ortiz Basualdo, Lanús and Ramos Mejía.[14]

If the Scots boasted of good polo players, the Irish claimed many more. Surnames such as Cavanagh, Duggan, Garrahan, Ham, Harrington, Kearney, Kenny, Lawler (Lalor), Mac-Donough, Moore, Nelson and O'Farrell became prominent as large landholders and polo players around the turn of the century, and remain so into present times.

A typical Irish polo family were the Traills, whose ancestors, the brothers Robert and Edmund, immigrated to Argentina in the 1860s and settled in Santa Fe Province, where their descendants still farm.[15] Neither Robert nor Edmund shone as polo players; thoroughbred racing was their amusement. As a group, sons Edward "Ned," John and Robert William — Robert's progeny — and Joseph Edmund took 26 individual Open Championship trophies. Their teams, North Santa Fe and Las Rosas, won 13 Open titles between 1898 and 1923. The secrets of their success were good equitation and better horsepower. They had imported from England the thoroughbred stallions Forrester and Springjack, which were sires of important bloodlines in Argentina. At one time, they had over 2,000 horses in their several estancias; many were taken to Britain to be sold during their frequent trips to their mother country.

The Traills, especially Johnny in his generation, became the example of the ambivalence of being British in what Professor Archetti calls the process of hybridization in the world of Argentine polo.[16] When the team El Bagual (Wild Horse) visited England in 1912, the players were described by the London press as "good Argentinian sportsmen." The fact was that the team patron — there were already patrons in those long ago days — Harold Schwind, was born in Edinburgh and Johnnie Traill in the London suburb of Penge, while Joe Traill and Leonard Lynch-Staunton were born in Ireland. The only Argentine-born was the appropriately named John Argentine Campbell — educated at Fettes College in Edinburgh and Cambridge University — who considered himself British and died for his country in the First World War. John Campbell was school captain at Fettes, was a Blue in athletics, cricket and rugby at Cambridge, played international rugby for Scotland and cricket for Argentina. A 9-goal player, Campbell led his own team, Western Camps, to two Open Championships in 1907 and 1909. John Campbell was a 41-year-old lieutenant in the Inniskilling Dragoons when he was killed in France in 1917.

It is a bit ironic that all five players were thought to be British in Argentina and Argentines in Britain. Johnny Traill did not join the army during the war because of indifferent health. Traill stayed in England, upset at being so useless. When the army decided to send two officers to Argentina with the purpose of purchasing mounts for the cavalry, Johnny Traill — one the foremost horse experts in Argentina — volunteered to join the party, but his services were rejected. In his own words: "An English vet and a Major went over and I later heard that they had gone to a big estancia and bought thirty or forty very nice looking horses as riding horses. What they probably did not realize was that the animals had been tamed from below by the Argentine gauchos who had handled them well, riding them bareback with only a head-collar and lead rein; none of them had ever had a saddle on or a bit in their mouths. I can just imagine what they had been like with a bit of English corn in them and a saddle on for the first time. I knew only too well how a five-year-old colt could buck!"[17]

Prof. Eduardo Archetti concluded, "Traill, a real gaucho, speaks to the ignorant British."[18] Archetti takes the concept of hybridization even further. One year, in 1906, Edward Traill was unable to play because of injury and José "Tincho" González, the estancia's foreman and one of the *petiseros* (grooms), took his place on the North Santa Fe team. In the championship game, North Santa Fe defeated Hurlingham and *The Standard*'s reporter wrote that the petisero performed just as well as Ned Traill would have, "up to a point which compelled the admiration of every polo lover."[19] Prof. Archetti's evaluation of this situation is that the idea of symbiosis of the Argentinean style of polo as a hybrid is very important; his conclusion is that González was Traill and Traill was González.

This may very well have been the case on the polo ground and in the spectators' eyes;

however, the social and cultural gap was much too wide to be bridged. This gap was mostly due to lack of education and was certainly not the gauchos' fault, because the opportunities for their education were almost non-existent at the time.[20] The only chance for advancement available to the workers in the pampas was to excel at polo or at football. Only in the late 1920s did the concept of playing for pay in soccer became established; the professional Asociación del Fútbol Argentino held its first championship in 1931. As to polo, promising players who earned minimal wages at estancias would slowly find their way into teams.

The prime example of a gaucho rising to be a celebrity was Manuel Angel Andrada, who grew up in Coronel Suárez, about 550 miles from Buenos Aires and rose to be a national hero after his successes in the U.S. Open, the Cup of the Americas and the Olympic Games. "Paisano" Andrada was one of the best backs of his generation; he played and taught polo until shortly before his death in 1962. His skills as a polo player took him to the top. He had a 9-goal rating — it was said that he was not given a 10-goal handicap because his command of the English language left a lot be desired. He took six Argentine Open Championships and earned the unquestioned respect of his fellow polo players and the admiration of polo-savvy aficionados. It could be said that he arrived when he was named captain of polo at the prestigious Tortugas Country Club.

One of the stories of the Argentines' pluck in playing polo has Manuel Andrada as the hero. In 1931, following their victory in the Pacific Coast Open the previous year, the famous Santa Paula team — Alfredo Harrington, the brothers Juan and José Reynal and Manuel Andrada — entered the United States Open at Meadow Brook. With their success on the West Coast, critics were favorably impressed, but not overly so. They were a good team, undoubtedly, but they did not hit the ball far enough. When facing sluggers like Guest, Hitchcock and Hopping, they would be beaten, said the experts. Nevertheless, they kept on winning, in spite of an injury to Andrada's right thumb during a practice match at Mitchel Field. On the eve of their debut in the open, it was announced that Andrada would play against Harold Talbott's Roslyn. It was a strong foursome, with Mike Phipps, Cecil Smith and Cocie Rathborne. In the fifth chukker, Andrada went down again; however, he was able to finish the match, which was won by Santa Paula.

In the semifinal game versus Greentree — led by Tommy Hitchcock — Andrada was on the pony lines, his right arm in a sling. Andrés Gazzotti replaced him and Santa Paula managed to squeeze another win. Still the critics were not convinced. The final game pitted the defending champions, Hurricanes, against the South Americans, for whom more trouble lay ahead. The Polo Pony Show was held on the day before the match; Alfredo Harrington, showing Huracán, had his leg smashed into a gate. Back into the lineup came Andrada that evening. Two physicians advised Andrada not to play. The burly back leaned over to Tommy Nelson, the team manager, and asked him, "What pony shall I play in the first chukker?"

The next day, Andrada was at back, as well as Gazzotti, this time around at number 1. In spite of his swollen thumb, "Old Man Andrada simply picked up his team and hurled it at the Hurricane goal."[21] Santa Paula took the U.S. Open Championship away from Stephen Sanford's Hurricanes, the holders.

The Argentine style of polo, based upon anticipation and speed, developed during the 1920s. Initially the creation of Anglos such as the Laceys, the Lands, the Mileses, the Nelsons and the Traills, soon enough those qualities became part of the polo education of teenagers and young adults who lived at the estancias. "Camp" polo became the game's university, and playing at Palermo the graduation ceremony. Many young players began polo during the long

summer vacations at the estancias, Argentina's polo nurseries. Just as other kids started playing soccer on any uncultivated piece of land in the cities, the *potreros*, those with the benefit
of a better economic status, would amuse themselves practicing for hours hitting a polo ball,
mounted on tireless ponies or, as they grew up, on any kind of horse. They were the recipients of incalculable benefits. More often than not, they were scions of families where polo
had been played for a generation or more, so advanced schooling and training were at hand;
usually horses were readily available and with them came along *petiseros* who were experts in
their taming and schooling.

For a long time, it was dogma that a polo pony had not completed its training until it
had worked among cattle. Only after such apprenticeship, they were introduced to mallet work.
The same was with the children. First, they learned how to ride, afterwards how to hit the
ball, and later on, how to play the game. That is why the young players who make their debut
at Palermo never fail to impress with their polo equitation, their timing at hitting the ball,
and the speed and anticipation they show getting to every play. It was like that in 1929, when
an unknown 6-goal team, Dorrego, took the first National Handicap Tournament for the Copa
República Argentina. Dorrego was an unusual team, made up of Danish colonists in southern Buenos Aires province.[22] At Palermo, they were to face the winners of all the other circuits in Argentina. The final match was between Dorrego and Washington, which numbered
Manuel Andrada at 7 goals, two Anglos, Hesketh Hughes (who in 1936 would represent
England in the Westchester Cup) and Pedro Chisholm, plus an Argentine, Juan Echaide.
Receiving seven goals on handicap, Dorrego emerged from the severe test the winners by
eleven goals to seven. The phrase so often said, "They played much better than their handicap" was, once more, heard at Palermo. Oddly enough, the chronicle mentions that the Danes
had "inferior ponies," an almost certain recipe for defeat.[23] Dorrego made up the difference
in horsepower by their long hitting and a firm commitment to an attacking game rather than
trying to defend the goals they received on handicap. Their strategy paid off with a handsome victory.

12. Olympic Interlude

The Olympic Games are the largest peacetime gathering of humanity in the history of the world. — Jim McKay[1]

The ancient Olympic Games were revived in 1896 mainly through the efforts of Pierre de Fredí, Baron de Coubertin, a French national who at the Sorbonne Congress in 1894 proposed that the revival should take place in Paris. The delegates felt that Greece, as the cradle of the Olympic Games, should be site. Thus, the first Olympiad of the modern era was held in Athens.

An International Universal Exposition was scheduled to be held in Paris in 1900. Nothing better than to stage the second Olympic Games simultaneously. Baron de Coubertin, secretary-general of the French Union of Sporting Societies, appointed the Vicomte Charles de la Rochefoucauld as president of the organizing committee and Robert Fournier-Sarlovèze, a cavalry officer, as secretary. Both were polo players. Political clashes resulted in the Vicomte de la Rochefoucauld's resignation and chaotic conditions regarding the number and qualifications for each Olympic event. In reality, the new committee organized a great number of events in conjunction with the exposition, which lasted from April until November. The words "Olympic event" seldom appear in the contemporary press.

Regrettably, Pierre de Coubertin played no role in the 1900 Olympic Games. The games themselves were a shamble; many years later, winners of gold medals had no idea that they had participated in an Olympic event. Venues were changed, facilities were inadequate and the issue of what was an Olympic event is still unsettled.

Dr. Bill Mallon is of the opinion that four criteria must be in place for any sport to be considered worthy of Olympic event recognition.[2] First, the event should be international, accepting entries from all countries. Second, no handicap events should be allowed. Third, the entries must be open to all competitors, with no limitations because of ability, age, competency, or national origin. Fourth, no motorized events to be permitted. As far back as 1900, the International Olympic Committee delegates had adopted as its motto *"Citius, Altus, Fortius"* (swifter, higher, stronger), and they certainly desired that the Olympic events be a competition among the best in the world.[3]

Take heed, Federation of International Polo!

Paris 1900

Historians of the second Olympiad held in Paris have encountered many obstacles in their quest to ascertain the true characteristic of the polo competitions that took place in 1900 in the City of Lights. Olympic Games authority Dr. Bill Mallon writes: "It is difficult to make sense of what was and was not the 'Olympic' polo tournament in 1900. Many different match scores, tournaments results, and team rosters have been seen in the varying sources. The 1900 Olympic polo tournament also appears to have been a bit of a lark, with the players changing teams and representing various nations with no real rhyme or reason."[4]

The polo season in Paris extended from May through July. There were seven principal tournaments; in chronological order they were the Grand Prix International d'Exposition, Prix de Longchamps, Grand Prix International de Paris, Coupe de Bagatelle, Grand Prix de Suresnes, Challenge Cup Match, and Grand Prix de Dames. All the matches had the polo ground at Bagatelle as the venue.

The first one, the Grand Prix International d'Exposition, is regarded as the "Olympic event" by most authorities, in the absence of any official designation by the International Olympic Committee. Five teams took part in this competition: Bagatelle, Compiègne, Foxhunters, Mexico, and Rugby. It was a straight elimination contest. In the first match Foxhunters (Alfred Rawlinson, Frank Mackey, Foxhall Keene and Denis Daly) defeated Compiègne (Duc de Bisaccia, Auguste Fauquet-Lemaître, Jean Boussoud and Maurice Raoul-Duval) 10–0, and in the semi-finals, Bagatelle (Baron Edouard de Rothschild, Robert Fournier-Sarlovèze, Frederick Gill and Maurice Raoul-Duval). In this match, Capt. John Beresford replaced Foxhall Keene.

The second semi-final matched Mexico (Manuel de Escandón, Marqués de Villavieja, his brothers Eustaquio and Pablo de Escandón, and Guillermo Hayden Wright) versus Rugby (Walter McCreery, Frederick Freake, Walter Buckmaster, Comte Jean de Madré). Rugby vanquished Mexico by eight goals to nil. In the final game, played on 2 June 1900, Foxhunters — in which Keene replaced Beresford — defeated Rugby by three goals to one.

A report on the tournament appeared in *Baily's Magazine*:

> It was generally felt that the two teams from England would pass into the final, and Rugby looked on paper as a very difficult team to beat. The Paris Bagatelle and North American teams were easily disposed of with hardly the semblance of a struggle and Rugby and the Foxhunters were left to contest the final for the Grand Prix International de l'Exposition — a fine trophy.
>
> The ground, unluckily, was cut up after the heavy rain, and not all Mr. Gill's efforts could make it good. This state of things just suited the Foxhunters, who were a very strong team of hard hitters. To make matters worse for Rugby, Mr. Buckmaster had a nasty fall. Eventually the Foxhunters won by three to one.[5]

An examination of the rosters reveals some anomalies. Maurice Raoul-Duval appears on both Bagatelle and Compiègne teams. Perhaps his brother René was one of the players? Only Compiègne and Mexico have four true nationals on their teams. On the Foxhunters team, Keene and Mackey were Americans; Beresford, Daly and Rawlinson were British. Although John Beresford and Daly were Irishmen, Ireland was still part of the United Kingdom in 1900. The Rugby team had the Frenchman, Comte Jean de Madré, in its line-up. All this goes along with the lackadaisical character of these Olympic Games.

London 1908

At the International Olympic Committee in London in 1904, Rome was selected as the site for the 1908 games. However, an unexpected event occurred on Italian soil on 4 April 1906. Mount Vesuvius, overlooking the Bay of Naples, erupted with considerable material loss. Italy withdrew as a host nation because of the national catastrophe. The Eternal City would have to wait until 1960 for the opportunity to stage the Olympic Games. In reality, the reasons were both political and financial. The prime minister, Giovanni Gioletti, had embarked on far-reaching construction projects, such as the Simplon Tunnel connecting Italy with Switzerland, a large aqueduct in Puglia and extensive land-reclamation endeavors in different parts of the peninsula. Simply stated, there was no governmental money available to stage the Olympic Games.

England, at the time the richest nation in the world, picked up the gauntlet. The man in charge of organizing the games on short notice was William Grenfell, Lord Desborough. A superior athlete, Grenfell was on the Olympic fencing team, represented Oxford University in both athletics and rowing, stroked an eight across the English Channel and swam across the Niagara. Lord Desborough was known as a big game hunter and deep-sea fisherman; he also climbed the Matterhorn by three different routes. He was one of those phenomenally gifted all-round sportsmen — like Reginald Herbert — typical of the Victorian age.

Under such an energetic chairman, the 1908 London Games were on schedule. The games were also known as the "Battle of Shepherd's Bush" because of the acrimony between Americans and British regarding disqualifications and issues on athletics and ... tug-of-war! Shepherd's Bush was later known as White City Stadium.

The 1908 polo Olympic competition consisted of two games only. All participants were British because Ireland was still part of the United Kingdom. The teams entered bearing their clubs' names; All Ireland drew a bye into the final game.

The Hurlingham Club presented a cup and four gold medals to be given to the winners. All Ireland was represented by Maj. Auston Rotheram, a well-traveled player and winner of the Irish Open Cup and the Mackey Cup in California. He was joined by John Paul McCann, an icon in Irish polo, Capt. John Hardress Lloyd, who would be a 10-goaler and captain of the 1911 Westchester Cup team, and Percy Philip O'Reilly, also a winner of the Irish Open Cup.

The host team, Hurlingham, presented Walter Jones, from the Rugby team, the future international Sir Frederick Freake, Walter Buckmaster and Lord John Wodehouse, later Earl of Kimberley and a prominent figure in English polo. Roehampton aligned the younger Miller brothers, Charles and George, Capt. Herbert Wilson, a Westchester Cup winner, and Patteson Nickalls.[6]

Both games were held at the Hurlingham Club in Fulham; Capt. Edward Fagan and Maj. Kenneth MacLaren were the umpires. On 18 June, Roehampton beat Hurlingham by four goals to one and on 21 June defeated All Ireland by the comfortable score of eight to one. Hurlingham and All Ireland were declared joint runners-up.[7]

Therefore, a purely inter-club competition achieved Olympic distinction.

Antwerp 1920

The selection of Antwerp to be the host city for the 1920 Olympic Games came almost by default. Berlin had been selected as the site for the 1916 Games, which never took place because of World War I. The war ended in 1918 and Baron Pierre de Coubertin began the quest for a host city able to put on the show on short notice. The original candidates were Amsterdam, Antwerp, Budapest and Lyon. Surprisingly, Havana made a cable bid; however, nothing more was heard afterwards. Amsterdam withdrew its candidacy, it is said, out of respect to the Belgians, who through no fault of their own had suffered much during the war. Budapest was out of the running because Hungary had fought on Germany's side during the war and the International Olympic Committee had the Central Powers banned from competing in the games.

Therefore, it came down to Belgium, a country that had been an innocent victim of Germany's invasion in the war, to host the games. The small country was ill-prepared to conduct an event of such magnitude on a tight schedule, with only a little over one year to finish all preparations. The games went on, but barely. There were numerous complaints as to the venues, the facilities and the living accommodations. However, the 1920 Olympic Games contributed towards recovery after World War I and many innovations that are still in practice at this writing saw their debut at the games. For example, in the opening ceremony the Olympic flag, five intertwined rings — black, blue, green, red and yellow — on a white background, was first flown. One athlete took the Olympic oath on behalf of his fellow competitors, and a large number of pigeons — the doves of peace — were released at the end of the ceremony. More important, live pigeon shooting was not included as part of the games; it was replaced by clay pigeon shooting.

The polo tournament was played on a field within the Wellington Hippodrome at Ostende, on the English Channel coast. Polo had been a feature of Ostende's social calendar for many years. There was a polo club, Antwerpen, in Brasschaat; however, to avoid some of the congestion near Antwerp, the venue was moved eastwards to the resort town where polo had been played since 1904.

The host team was Maurice Lysen, Clément van der Straaten, Alfred Grisar and Baron Gastón Peers de Niewburgh. Gastón Peers had lived and played in Argentina, where he had married a high-society lady; Baron Peers was a winner of the Polo Association of the River Plate Open Championship in 1900. Alfred Grisar remains the foremost Belgian player. A gifted athlete, Grisar played for Belgium in polo and football, and in national competitions in cycling and tennis. A left-handed player, he reached a 6-goal handicap and among his many trophies took the Coronation Cup in 1924.

Great Britain was represented by three serving army officers and Lord Wodehouse, a 10-goal player who was killed during the London Blitz. The other players were the international Lt. Col. Teignmouth Melvill, who was the commanding officer of the 17th/21st Lancers, Maj. Frederick Barrett and Maj. Vyvyan Lockett, both winners of the Westchester Cup at Meadow Brook.

The Spaniards were the Marqués Alvaro de Villabrágima, the Duque Hernando de Peñaranda, the Conde Leopoldo de La Maza and the Duque Santiago de Alba. Villabrágima is considered the best Spanish player ever. The Duke of Peñaranda was an 8-goal player and his older brother "Jimmy" Alba was a four-goaler.[8]

The United States was meagerly represented by a team formed by officers from the Army of the Occupation of the Rhine. Capt. Arthur Harris, Capt. Terry Allen and Capt. John Montgomery were led by Col. Nelson Margetts.[9] Brig. Gen. Terry de la Mesa Allen had a distinguished career in two world wars, being wounded twice at St. Mihiel in the first and commanding the 1st Infantry Division, the "Big Red One," in the second. Allen was described as having the bowed stride of a horseman saddle-hardened as a child. Gen. Terry Allen made *Time* magazine's cover on 9 August 1943.

Capt. John Carter Montgomery was a previous winner of an Olympic bronze medal, in his case in the equestrian competition in Stockholm in 1912, with his horse Deceive. Col. Margetts led his American Army team when they took the Novices' Tournament at Ranelagh, and later on had a long career in America and the Far East.

The competition started with the match between Spain and the United States. The strong Spanish team was well mounted, so they easily defeated the Americans 13–3. The following day it rained intermittently; however, the show went on and England beat Belgium 8–3. Two days later, the American team vanquished the host country 11–3 to take the bronze medal. On 31 July, in the best match of the tournament, Great Britain beat Spain 13–11. The chronicle records that the Spaniards were much better mounted than the British. In fact, the Spanish Grandees had brought over their best mounts, while the British officers had to rely upon their regimental ponies. Thus, Great Britain retained the Olympic crown they had conquered in London twelve years earlier. Lord Wodehouse was the squad's only member who had participated in the 1908 games.

In 1920 at the Antwerp games, there was a considerable amount of mismanagement and confusion; rules were not clearly defined; certain officials were incompetent or prejudiced. Gross injustice seemed at times to prevail. Yet, in its official report, the American Olympic Committee, recalling those incidents, stated, "In the days of a generation back, bloody war would have been fought over less, but there at Antwerp, while they stormed and swore, thousands who offended learned — and some for the first time — that you can compete without hate, lose and yet smile, win and still be gracious; that to cheer for the other team is better sportsmanship than to cheer for your own, and that to hiss or boo your opponents because you are beaten is to be held up to ridicule and contempt in the eyes of sportsmen."[10]

Paris 1924

The main polo venue for the Paris Olympic Games in 1924 was the polo ground at Garches–St. Cloud, while two games took place at Bagatelle, in the Bois de Boulogne. Five countries sent representatives for the polo competition. The holder of the last two Olympic events, Great Britain, sent a team composed of army officers. Britain had to face two important international events that year, because it had challenged the Americans for the Westchester Cup in the month of September. The team selected to participate in the Olympics was Capt. the Hon. Frederick Guest, Lt. Col. John Bingham, Wing Commander Percival Wise, who had transferred to the Royal Air Force from the Army, and the Irish veteran Maj. Frederick "Rattle" Barrett.

Spain, the silver medalist in Belgium, called upon the experienced Duque Hernando de Peñaranda and the Marqués Luis de San Miguel as forwards, and Marqués Alvaro de Villabrágima and Conde Leopoldo de La Maza in the defense.

The pre-tournament favorites were the Americans, led by 10-goaler Thomas Hitchcock,

Tommy Hitchcock's charming smile disappeared when play began. Almost single-handedly, Hitchcock won the silver medal for America in the 1924 Olympic Games in Paris. Few other players have had as much influence on the game as the celebrated Tommy did in his time (Museum of Polo and Hall of Fame).

Jr., ably supported by Elmer Julius Boeseke, Jr., from Santa Barbara at number 1, Texan Frederick Roe at number 3 and Philadelphia's Rodman Wanamaker II at back.

Argentina sent Arturo Kenny, Jack Nelson, Capt. Enrique Padilla and Juan Miles. Completing the competing squads, the French hosts aligned the Comte Pierre de Jumilhac, Jules Macaire, the Comte Charles de Polignac and Hubert de Monbrison.

The tournament began on 28 June at St. Cloud, where America overwhelmed France 13–1, and three days later did the same against Spain by a 15–2 score. On 2 July, Argentina easily disposed of France at Bagatelle, 15–2. Then the Americans rather easily defeated Great Britain by 10 goals to two, and the following day, Argentina beat Spain 10–1, on a heavy field because of rain. On 5 July (one match took place every day) Britain defeated France at Bagatelle by 15 to 2.

What was essentially the final match took place on 6 July between Argentina and America, the two undefeated teams. In his reminiscences, Jack Nelson relates that on the morning of the match he went to Notre Dame Cathedral to attend mass. Nelson lit some candles to ask for divine help and while doing so, to his surprise, he saw Hitchcock — his mother, the celebrated Mrs. Louise Eustis Hitchcock, was a Catholic — engaged in the same endeavor. Philosophically, Jack Nelson felt that the odds were even with the Almighty's favor.[11]

During the entire match the Americans were ahead, but in the last chukker the South Americans were able to level the score, and with only seconds left, Jack Nelson scored the winning goal, perhaps with some help from above. Nelson retrieved the ball, which is proudly exhibited in the Argentine Polo Association's office in Palermo.

Unknown to Hitchcock, his future wife was at the game. The former Peggy Mellon was on her honeymoon with her husband, Army Capt. Alexander Laughlin, a businessperson in Pittsburgh. They attended the match on a whim, because neither was interested in polo. Less than two years later, Alexander Laughlin died while having a tooth removed under general anesthesia. Tommy Hitchcock and Peggy Mellon Laughlin were married in New York City in 1928.[12]

The gold medal won by the polo team was the first one ever for Argentina. It had enormous repercussion in the home country. The team left Buenos Aires without fanfare; upon their return, the players were received as national heroes. Three aristocratic Anglo-Argentines and an Army artillery officer achieved a historic victory over the favored Americans. The foursome was hailed as champions of the world, because lacking any world championships, the Olympics were considered the top of the world in sporting events. Of course, it was not so. The best possible team did not represent America; one can image what the result would have been if the "Big Four" had competed in the Olympic Games. Only Tommy Hitchcock was a first stringer, because Boeseke's years of glory were in the 1930s and both Fred Roe — a Texas banker — and Roddy Wanamaker were just above average players at six and seven-goal handicaps. The 1925 U.S.P.A. *Year Book* only mentions the Olympic tournament in two pages, in comparison to the fourteen pages dedicated to the Westchester Cup held at Meadow Brook.[13]

For the Argentines, taking the Olympic gold medal was a dream come true. Polo became a popular game, at least among the middle class in Buenos Aires.[14] Upon arrival at the port of Buenos Aires, the entire Olympic delegation was greeted by thousands of people. The modest harvest of medals — this was the first Olympiad that had official representation — was seen by many as the emergence of a national power in world's sports. It was not to be; however, in the euphoria created by a respectable showing in various sports, it was understandable.

Miguel Martínez de Hoz, president of the Argentine Polo Association, was in an overwhelming mood; he felt that it represented the golden harvest of an Argentine style of polo: "The Argentines have established in Europe a style of speed and precise passes; the thought that slow polo and short passes is being abandoned to benefit the sport, which acquires beautiful characteristics based on upon pace and lightning speed."[15]

Talk began to abound referring to this perceived new style of polo, the Argentine style. Maj. José Pedro Sierra, a 4-goal handicap cavalry officer, had an article published in *El Gráfico*, a popular magazine devoted to sports and games: "This superiority is related to three factors: the stamina of the rider, the Argentinean way of riding and the quality of the horses. The habit of equilibrium has been acquired — through neither advice nor acceptance of the rules of riding-schools — in the usual and natural practice of riding in the countryside."[16]

In Maj. Sierra's opinion, the national players of British origin who played in France were typically Argentinean or, better still, criollos, because they rode in a distinctive manner. Sierra's evaluation may be summarized as a transformation of the immigrants from foreigners into hybrids, following contact with the gaucho equestrian culture.

Francisco Ceballos takes a slightly different tack. According to Paco Ceballos, the British's descendants are perceived as being between two cultures; they are hybrids in the sense of combining the best of both traditions. It should be noted that both Kenny and Nelson were gentlemen-riders of great repute in racing circles. Nevertheless, when playing polo, their equitation was more akin to the accepted riding in polo contests. As skilled riders, they easily accommodated to varied requirements. Another example of a rider changing his style to adapt to different needs was that of Australian Ken Mackay, who, after finishing a polo game at the Sidney Show grounds riding a flat polo saddle with a loose rein and short stirrups, changed into moleskins and, in a stock saddle with long stirrups, won the open cattle draft competition.[17]

In the final analysis, the Olympic Gold medal gave supreme confidence within the polo community to those who felt that the Argentine style of polo, relying on a relentless attack, based upon speed at the expense of conservative defense, was the way to go in international contests.

Berlin 1936

Twenty years after the Olympic Games were to have taken place in 1916, they were held in Berlin at the height of the Nazis' power. The main venue was the new Olympic Stadium; adjacent to the stadium a polo ground, the Maifeld, was laid out.[18] The expectation was that seven countries would participate in polo; however, India and the United States declined. America's absenteeism took much out of the Olympic competition. The national side — Eric Pedley, Mike Phipps, Stewart Iglehart and Winston Guest — had successfully defended the Westchester Cup at Hurlingham in June 1936. It was a team truly representative of America's polo prowess, and their clash with the Argentines was eagerly anticipated. It was not to be; neither in Berlin in August nor at Meadow Brook in September.

Argentina, the defending gold medalists, sent a strong team and an even stronger pony string: Luis Duggan, Roberto Cavanagh, Andrés Gazzotti and Manuel Andrada, a 27-goal combination, played in the two matches. The host team, Germany, had four players from the Hamburg Club: Heinrich Amsinck, Walter Bartram, Miles Reincke and Arthur Köser.

Great Britain had originally selected the foursome that had played so well versus the Americans in the Westchester Cup: Hesketh Hughes, Gerald Balding, Eric Tyrrell-Martin and Capt. Humphrey Guinness. However, on short notice three of the team found themselves unable to travel. Three officers, Capt. Bryan Fowler, Capt. William Robert Hinde and Capt. David Dawnay, joined Captain Guinness on the British team.

Hungary selected Lt. Tivadar Dienes-ohem, Capt. Imre Szentpály, Kálmán von Bartalis

The 1936 Olympic Games final match, Argentina versus England at Maifeld, was held next to the Olympic Stadium in Berlin. Roberto Cavanagh, from Argentina, is about to hit an under-the-neck, near side shot. Bandages applied over cotton pads were common in that epoch (private collection).

and Graf István Bethlen. The last team to enter, Mexico, had Maj. Juan Gracia Zazueta, Capt. Antonio Nava Castillo, the civilian player Julio Muller Luján and Capt. Alberto Ramos Sesma.

The tournament took place from Monday, 3 August, through Saturday, one match being played every day. The tremendous discrepancy among the teams was solved by having Argentina, Britain and Mexico play a round robin to decide the gold and silver medalists, while Germany and Hungary would play one match, the winner to play the third place team in the round robin for the bronze medal.

On Monday, Great Britain defeated Mexico 13–11, after being comfortably ahead during the entire match. On the next day, Germany and Hungary played to an 8-all tie, and on Wednesday, Argentina defeated Mexico 15–5. After watching this game, Brig. Jack Gannon wrote: "Andrada was playing very steady game, for a fellow of his age, but they were all hitting well, and so superbly mounted that it made me tremble to think what would happen when England met them."[19]

On Thursday, the Hungarians dashed Germany's hope for a shot at the bronze medal, winning by 16 goals to six. In turn, Mexico routed Hungary on Saturday, 16–2, to take third place in the competition. The final match, played on Friday, was no contest. It was a confirmation that Brig. Gannon's concerns were well founded. The British officers were mounted on their own regimental ponies, which when matched against the top of the cream of Argentina's polo ponies could not stay at their speed. Pony-power won again. It was seldom during the game that the British players hit the ball twice in succession, such was the difference in velocity. Britain was, unluckily, not to score, because twice or thrice the ball hit a goal post, only to bounce out through the back line. The final score, 11–0, tells the story of what will happen in a polo game when thoroughbreds or nearly thoroughbreds are matched against inferior mounts.

The Argentine squad then crossed the Atlantic to face the United States international team at Meadow Brook. On those historic grounds, the four players that had taken the Gold Medal in Berlin conclusively defeated the American team. Argentina's subsequent polo history has been one of rarely broken success.

The Olympic Oaks

A cutting from a Black Forest oak was presented to the Argentine polo team, as well as to all the Olympic champions. Following Jack Nelson's suggestion, the cutting was planted between the two grounds at Palermo, behind the number one field's central stands. It is still there. In 1986, fifty years after the Olympic Games, two cuttings taken from the Palermo oak tree were presented by Marcos Uranga, the Argentine Polo Association's president, to Roberto Cavanagh and Luis Duggan, the last two survivors from the 1936 Olympic polo team. There are a few oaks in Argentina rising from acorns picked by polo enthusiasts who planted them on their properties.

One hundred and thirty oak saplings were presented during the 1936 Olympics. They were some 18 inches tall, in terra cotta pots. The United States had 24 oaks, four of those going to sprinter Jesse Owens. One was planted at his mother's home in Cleveland; another at his high school, James Ford Rhodes High School in Cleveland; and another at Ohio State University, his college. The exact identity of the fourth oak is in doubt; however, an Olympic oak was planted at All American Row.[20]

An oak at Connellsville High School in Connellsville, Pennsylvania, commemorates John Woodruff's win in the 800-meter race. Originally planted on the grounds of the Carnegie Library, it was transplanted to where it now proudly stands, near one end of the school's stadium. Another Olympic oak is the one won by high hurdles winner Forrest Towns; it is at the University of Georgia campus.

Two seedlings were donated to the University of Southern California. One was given by Ken Carpenter, who won the gold medal in discus throwing and the other by Foy Draper and Frank Wykoff, two members of the 400-meter relay team. They were planted in Associates Park, near the Physical Education building. The two trees were practically unknown at the U.S.C. campus until one died of root rot in 2005. A replacement oak tree, with an appropriate plaque at its base, was planted. There is another tree near Los Angeles, on Hobart Street in Korea town. It is at a private home and is the tree given to Cornelius Johnson for his victory in the high jump.

Gold medal wrestler Frank Lewis' tree was planted near the Sigma Chi fraternity house at Oklahoma State University. In later years, his son wrote, "The tree suffered from a number of problems, not the least being poor care and maintenance. When my father heard the tree was noticed by a Jewish student who was offended by its presence, my father did not hesitate; he instructed the fraternity and Oklahoma State University to cut it down."[21]

The only known oak in England was the sapling presented to Harold Whitlock, who won the 50-kilometer walk. Whitlock decided not to plant the tree in his garden in case he had to move. Therefore, he presented the sapling to his former school, Hendon Grammar School. The tree was taken down in 2007 because it developed rot and was considered a hazard to the schoolchildren.[22]

Out of 33 oaks won by Germany, 14 are known to exist. There is one Olympic Oak in New Zealand, at Timaru Boys' High School. Jack Lovecock, later Dr. John Edward Lovelock, won it in the 1,500 meter race. Another Olympic oak is on the grounds of Kyoto University in Japan. It was given to Naoto Tajima for winning the triple jump.

The search for more surviving Olympic oak trees goes on.

Afrásiáb, a semi-mythical king of Scythia, is shown in the left upper corner of this Chinese painting on a scroll with an attendant carrying an umbrella for royal protection from the sun. Síawusch, his son-in-law, appears in the right upper corner (Museum of Polo and Hall of Fame).

Polo at Rugby — August 1893. Rugby v. 14th Hussars. From left, the Rugby players, in blue, are George Miller, attempting a hook, Ronald Chaplin, wearing a vest, Edward Miller and John Reid Walker. The 14th Hussars, white with blue sash, are Lt. Robert Stephens, Lt. Willian Eley, Capt. Cyril Stacey and Capt. James Richardson. The final game of the August Open Tournament, won by Rugby, was captured by Henry Lucas-Lucas, oil on canvas, signed and dated (private collection).

Javier Novillo Astrada (left) and Ignacio "Nachi" Heguy battle for the ball at Palermo in one of several clashes for the Argentine Open Championship. Scions of famous polo families, both reached the top level in the game (Museum of Polo and Hall of Fame).

Detail of a Chinese scroll depicting a game of polo during the T'ang Dynasty, which lasted from 618 until 907. The seals identify the artist as Qiu Ying (Museum of Polo and Hall of Fame).

Kaliman, owned by Guy Wildenstein and played by Memo Gracida, its subsequent owner. Kaliman was Best Playing Pony in the 1987 and 1989 U.S. Open Championships. Oil by Larry Dodds Wheeler, painted at La Herradura, in Wellington (private collection).

The 5th Lancers 1907, watercolor by "Snaffles," signed and dated 1907. Charlie Johnson Payne is one of the most important sporting artists of the 20th century. The subjects are Capt. James Jardine (upper left), Capt. Maxwell McTaggart (top right), the Hon. Robert Browne-Clayton (B.C.) in the center, Lt. William Sebag-Montefiore (lower left), Capt. Onslow Chance and the inevitable dog Sandy, carrying a polo ball (private collection).

The most elegant polo club in London, Ranelagh Club, in its heyday. The drawing was made by T. Raffles Davidson after architect Alfred Burr had completed additions to the Georgian building (private collection).

Crab Orchard versus Las Monjitas. This photograph illustrates a facet of the current style of polo: players close together fighting for possession of the ball. From the left are Jeff Blake, Ignacio Novillo Astrada, Eduardo Novillo Astrada, Adolfo Cambiaso and Javier Novillo Astrada. The ball is in front of Ignacio's pony. The final game of the 2008 U.S. Open Championship at International Polo Club Palm Beach was won by Crab Orchard (Museum of Polo and Hall of Fame, Alex Pacheco photograph).

One of the most famous polo prints, *Devereux Milburn, the American Polo Player, Changing Ponies*, after an oil painting by Sir Alfred Munnings. The pony is Gargantilla, the property of Alfredo Peña Unzué, later purchased by Harry Payne Whitney. Gargantilla ("necklace," after the white spot on her neck) came to America as part of the 1922 Argentine pony string (private collection).

Local favorite Isla Carroll took the 2004 U.S. Open. From left, Guillermo "Memo" Gracida, Argentine Francisco "Pancho" Bensadón, South African Stuart "Sugar" Erskine and patron John Goodman, plus assorted children, celebrate the win at International Polo Club Palm Beach (Museum of Polo and Hall of Fame).

Left: Cathy Stewart Brown from Nashville, patron of the Wildwood team. All eyes are on the airborne ball. Cathy's pony, Flash, wears extra protection over the front leg tendons and coronets. Gulfstream Polo Club (private collection, Dan Burns photograph). *Above:* Lester "Red" Armour III, who, together with Joe Barry and Tommy Wayman, formed the backbone of American polo in the 1970s and 1980s (Museum of Polo and Hall of Fame).

A game of polo in England before the end of the 19th century. Helmets were not yet in vogue, only cloth caps. Oil painting by George Rowlandson (private collection).

Charmer, a bay mare, the property of Walter Jones. Bred in Ireland, by Talisman, a winner on the flat. Charmer never missed a match in 14 years while playing for the Rugby team and in the international matches of 1902 and 1909. Oil by Henry Lucas-Lucas (the author is grateful to Mr. Dennis J. Amato for providing information about Charmer; private collection, Alex Pacheco photograph).

Top left: The power of Memo Gracida's off-side forehand at full speed. Mexican-born Guillermo "Memo" Gracida held a 10-goal rating for the longest time. His organizational skill and tactical prowess set a new standard in the game (Museum of Polo and Hall of Fame, photograph by Alex Pacheco). *Top right:* The standard of polo elegance in the 1890s is exemplified by Walter Jones, number 1 on the Rugby team that had such an enormous influence on polo in England. Oil by Ernest-Gustave Girardot (private collection, Alex Pacheco photograph). *Bottom:* Patron George Haas, Jr., and his gray mare Feather in an oil on canvas by Sam Savitt (private collection, on permanent loan to the Museum of Polo and Hall of Fame, Alex Pacheco photograph).

PART III: THE AMATEURS

13. The Mighty Americans

It was Hitchcock who changed over the old game of polo from passing to power. The passing act still remains, but the hard riding, smashing game now gets the call. — Grantland Rice[1]

The period between the two world wars was to be known as "the Golden Era" of polo. It was certainly so in the United States. The American international team was unbeaten during those years, with the exception of a few hiccups at the hands of the Argentines, most notably at the 1924 Olympic Games and the 1936 Cup of the Americas.

This time-span of almost total dominance began in 1921 at Hurlingham, when the American team recovered the Westchester Cup.[2] It marked the international debut of Thomas Hitchcock, Jr., James Watson Webb and Louis Stoddard, who joined team captain Devereux Milburn on a squad that in some observers' opinion merited the sobriquet of "the Second Big Four." They were all 10-goal players. When in 1924, Malcolm Stevenson made the team as a defensive number 3, Watson Webb moved up to the forward position in Stoddard's slot. This same team vanquished the Army-in-India squad in the 1927 series, which was Milburn's swan song in international contests.

In these two post-war series with the British, there was not too much doubt as to which team would be the winner; in particular, the 1924 event was a rout. The tradition of superb play started by the Waterbury brothers, Whitney and Milburn, in 1909 continued through the 1920s and 1930s.

After two defeats in a row, the Hurlingham Polo Committee, which alone was vested with the right to challenge for the trophy, tried a different approach in making a thorough attempt to lift the International Challenge Polo Cup, as the Westchester was officially called, from American hands. Breaking with tradition, the Hurlingham Committee entrusted the Army-in-India to handle the attempt at recovering the trophy. In doing so, the Army-in-India selection body followed a winning formula. The team was picked far in advance of the matches. It consisted of fellow serving officers who liked each other, understood each other, and liked to play with each other.[3] They were well mounted, were allowed to proceed without interference, and practiced with earnest concentration. Such unity of purpose usually wins rewards and may win games.

It was wise for the Army-in-India team not to play in England en route to America. The team went directly from the very fast grounds of India to the fast fields in America without disturbing its pace of play on the slow English grounds. The Hurlingham Committee did not achieve its purpose without sacrifices. Players who had proven their ability to play the American brand of polo were left on the sidelines. There was no more brilliant hitter in the world than Lewis Lacey, the player from Argentina who was a member of the last British team on the strength of his Canadian nationality; however, he was omitted from the British group of challengers. Lord Wodehouse and Wing Commander Percival Wise, who played extraordinarily well in America the previous year, were ignored. On the other hand, Capt. Pat Roark, the sterling Irish player whose polo was little short of sensational at Meadow Brook in 1926, was eligible for the British squad because he was formerly an officer in the Poona Light Horse.

As expected, the selection of an Army-in-India team to represent Hurlingham and British polo aroused harsh and acerbic criticism in England. In addition, in order to give the experiment a better chance, control was passed entirely into the hands of the selection committee of the Army-in-India, to the open skepticism of many Londoners. That was done, to the delight of admirers of Indian polo and critics of London's polo ways and means, as put by a writer in India, "before whom, the intrigues of an Eastern Court pale into insignificance."[4]

William Goadby Loew wears the Meadow Brook Magpies shirt, depicted by Sir Alfred Munnings. In his autobiography, Munnings, who was not too happy with the sitter, noted that as he worked along, the painting was getting better and better in spite of his mood (private collection).

Robert Strawbridge, Jr., and Devereux Milburn, prominent players and administrators of the game for decades, engaged in conversation. Milburn wears a bulky, old-fashioned knee guard on his right leg. The car appears to be a proletarian Model T Ford (Museum of Polo and Hall of Fame).

What appeared to be on paper an even contest, resulted in a comfortable victory for the Americans. In the first match, the American foursome gave as fine an exhibition of coordinated team play as the famous Big Four ever offered. Yet, in the second match, the British, with a new line up, gave the United States team a good match; however, three goals scored in the first chukker were the difference when the final bell tolled.[5]

The American Maj. Anson Rudd, Signal Corps, presented a friendly if critical view of the Army-in-India team's defeat.[6] In Major Rudd's view, the visitors were on even terms with the Americans in regard to pony power and riding ability. Where they failed was in hitting ability and positional play, one following the other. The main cause was their obsolete practice of hitting from the saddle, rather than rising on the stirrups for the strike at the ball. This developed into faulty teamwork when opposed by long hitters such as Hitchcock and Milburn. Major Rudd felt that the problem arose because of the army training methods: their cavalry soldiers were taught to use a close seat, because a cavalryman without a good seat could be unhorsed. It involved long training days riding without stirrups, jumping without reins and all other requirement of military equitation schools. A close seat is no good for polo.

On the other hand, the civilian American players adopted the custom of rising on the stirrup while hitting. This practice gives the hitter a "stance," balanced by inward pressure of

James Watson Webb, the only left-handed player to reach a 10-goal handicap. No other than Lewis Lacey considered Watson Webb the toughest number 1 to mark. Mr. Webb and his wife, Electra Havemeyer, from another polo family, started what is now the Museum of American Folk Art in Shelburne, Vermont. While Electra assembled her huge collection, Watson was master of foxhounds of the Shelburne Hunt (Museum of Polo and Hall of Fame).

the knees against the saddle. In turn, it increases the player's reach and flexibility, allowing him to hit the ball harder. This concept was years later neatly expanded by Lord Mountbatten in his description of "brace."[7] A player hitting the ball while sitting on the saddle cannot achieve length and accuracy when compared to the brace stance.

Major Rudd thought that this weakness in hitting led to poor position play. He felt that the essence of superior teamwork is the anticipation of the next stroke and being in position to receive the ball. The consequence of short hitting is that teammates tend to get close together, because if not, they will lose possession of the ball.

The American players, knowing that they could expect long passes, were spaced among themselves at longer distances than the British were, and time after time booming shots would go over everyone's heads to land clear in front.

These new tactics had started to take form since the end of the war, when the American team regained the Westchester Cup at Hurlingham.[8] It reached its zenith in the last match of the 1928 Cup of the Americas, when Devereux Milburn, who had inherited the captaincy from Harry Payne Whitney — with a brief interlude by Lawrence Waterbury — in turn handed over the conductor's baton to Tommy Hitchcock. The greatness of the first Big Four was based upon its balance between attack and defense. Much has been made by commentators of polo as to their devastating offense; little mention was made of its impregnable defensive methods. Milburn was an exceptional defender, a master of the backstroke and a clever positional player. Nevertheless, this true back was able, when the opportunity arose, to come through and regale the spectators with astounding offensive plays. Milburn had the advantage of having Whitney, a selfless number 3, who was always alert to cover the back door during his down field forays. Upon Whitney's retirement from international polo, Malcolm Stevenson performed the same function on behalf of the team captain. Devereux Milburn was the prototype of the modern back; when he was moved up to the number 3 position in the 1913 Westchester series, his effectiveness was markedly reduced.

The concept of a balanced game was a staple of American international teams throughout the 1920s and 1930s. However, the tactics, or at least the style of play, changed during Hitchcock's years of captaincy and became prevalent at the Cup of the Americas matches. The fine Argentine pony string was affected with an epidemic and did not fully recover its form in time, in spite of a postponement. A sporting offer by the U.S. Polo Association to lend ponies was politely rejected by the visitors. Hitchcock correctly assumed that the Argentine ponies would not stand the strain of a long series; therefore, his plan stressed pace. He was proven right. Shortly after the start of the third and decisive match, it was obvious that the visitors' ponies were not into the game. Three hard-fought games in the space of seven days had exhausted the Argentine ponies' physical reserves.

The American style of play then evolved into hitting the ball as hard as possible with every stroke and then running as fast as your pony would carry to the next stroke. Needless to say, the most influential player was Tommy Hitchcock. His terrific hitting power was the most spectacular facet of his play. However, Hitchcock was a master of every stroke of the game. An incredibly precise dribble would be the prelude to a booming shot, but it was the set-up that allowed him to hit the ball in the open. Tommy Hitchcock had power, but it was controlled power.

Some commentators voiced reservations about the influence of Thomas Hitchcock, Jr.'s style upon American polo. One stated: "Sometimes this fetish of hard-hitting is harmful to American play. Mr. Hitchcock's method of scoring goals has seeped down into American play. Even our low goal players scorned the time-honored (and generally sensible) method of placing the ball in scoring position first."[9]

Just as it happens with Adolfo Cambiaso's tactics today, many less talented players tried to imitate Hitchcock's play. More often than not, the outcome was a long shot that would land on an open space, the ball to be fought over by players from either team. There was, however, a sterling exception. It was the Old Aiken team, which was composed of young players whose rudiments of the game had been coached by another Hitchcock, the famous Louise Eustis Hitchcock, Tommy's mother. Early in their polo education, these future cracks were imbued with the importance of the passing game, short shots at goal, the basic positional game and combination play. There sprung the backbone of American polo in the 1930s. Players like Pete Bostwick, Gerald Dempsey, Ebby Gerry, Raymond and Winston Guest, Frank Hitchcock, young Earle Hopping, the Iglehart brothers, Philip and Stewart, Jimmy Mills, Billy Post, and Cocie Rathbone cut their teeth with the Meadow Larks and some went on to achieve fame and glory with Old Aiken.

Tommy Hitchcock himself preached the gospel of long hitting. In his special instructions to the United States polo squad in 1930, he wrote: "Do not dribble the ball. Take a full swing at it every chance you get. There are few exceptions to this rule: (a) When shooting at goal, it is better to miss the ball altogether and leave it in front of the goal, than to hit it over the backline. Therefore, a dribble or short shot to place the ball in order to make a surer shot at goal is often justifiable; (b) In passing the ball to one of your own side, a short pass wide is often better than a long pass, as it reduces the hazard of an opponent getting the ball."[10]

Hitting the ball as hard as you can became the staple of American polo. The championship gained by the Argentine club Santa Paula in the 1931 U.S. Open was based upon a tac-

The two best American players of the 1930s, Cecil Smith for Old Westbury and Tommy Hitchcock for Greentree, in action at the U.S. Open. Cecil Smith is on Bonnie J, one of his top ponies, now enshrined in the Hall of Fame (Museum of Polo and Hall of Fame).

tical game of short, safe passes. The American hierarchy remained unconvinced. In an interview granted by Louis E. Stoddard, the U.S. Polo Association's chairman, he said,

> I am not sure that the victory of Santa Paula meant a clear-cut vindication of a short and safe passing game rather than the long, hard-hitting one of the modern type favored by so many in this country. Certainly, Santa Paula's victory showed that it is not absolutely necessary to hit hard in order to win. In fact, I am somewhat of the opinion that it may be altogether necessary to hit short shots in order to perfect the type of team play which carried Santa Paula through. A team of long-hitters, who had been together as long as Santa Paula and who were governed by the same spirit and idea of play, might readily develop into a stronger team than Santa Paula solely because of their longer hitting.[11]

Five years later, the Argentine national team, which counted two of Santa Paula's members in its ranks, decisively defeated the Americans in the Cup of the Americas. Their style of play was precisely a pattern of short passes, but carried on at unremitting high speed. American observers were surprised and amused by the manner in which the Argentines carried their mallets long before their Olympic victory in Paris. Accepted dogma was that the mallet was to be carried straight up; the Argentines carried their mallets downwards in a swinging action in rhythm with the beat of galloping hooves. No one had taught them how to carry a mallet according to form.

The American team that retained the Cup of the Americas in Buenos Aires was under Carleton F. Burke's management. Burke instructed his team on the tactical concept of forwards blocking the opponents away from the center of the field and making way for the number 3 and the back to come through. It was a successful concept that allowed Mike Phipps, Elmer Boeseke, Winston Guest and Billy Post to take the Argentine Open under the name Meadow Brook — the only foreign team to achieve that feat — and the Cup of the Americas.

Burke's tactical ideas also prospered in the celebrated East-West series of 1933. It was a rough series; with Cecil Smith first, and Tommy Hitchcock later, knocked unconscious. Rube Williams' leg was broken following a crash with Hitchcock and young Earle Hopping, and Boeseke's ankle and foot were badly sprained. One commentator called the series "lusty mayhem,"[12] while the polo community at large expressed serious concern regarding the pattern of heavy bumps and intimidating riding, which bordered, and occasionally passed, the limits of safe play.

The dismal economic situation extended worldwide. England was unable to mount a challenge in 1933 and the only possible way to continue the series was for the United States team to travel to England. This was accomplished in 1936, perhaps at the expense of an American presence in the Olympic Games. The Americans, riding on the crest of success, were the overwhelming favorites to retain the Westchester Cup in two games. One year prior to the series, an English team, presumably the one selected to represent Hurlingham in due time, entered the U.S. Open Championship. They were defeated in the first round by Laddie Sanford's Hurricanes, a team that failed to reach the final match. This raised concerns on both sides of the Atlantic Ocean. The Americans, although eager to continue their supremacy, were looking for more of a challenge, while the British were worried as to their potential dismal showing in front of the home crowd. As it were, the English side, after wholesale changes, acquitted itself nobly. Both games were lost, but only by one goal in the first match and by two goals in the second.

The last challenge for the Westchester Cup before World War II took place at Meadow Brook in 1939, when the clouds of war were gathering in Europe. Hurlingham sent a strong, well-mounted team to America. They arrived with plenty of time to get accustomed to American grounds and style of play. Under the third Viscount Cowdray's non-playing captaincy, the British team, Gerald Balding, Aidan Roark, Eric Tyrrell-Martin and Australian Bob Skene practiced for months in California. An unexpected omission from the Hurlingham contingent was that of Capt. Charles T.I. Roark, Aidan's older brother and better known as Pat. Captain Roark was universally considered the best British player in the span between the two world wars. A recent loss of form was offered as the reason why he was not selected as part of the squad. However, his play in California was reminiscent of his former glory, and some questions were raised which were never answered. Tragically, Captain Pat Roark died as the result of head injuries sustained when his exhausted pony fell as play continued for several minutes after the bell had sounded. This accident was the main reason for a change in the United States rules limiting to 30 seconds the playing time after the bell.

The series at Meadow Brook was, once more, taken by the American team with relative ease in the two matches played. Mike Phipps, Stewart Iglehart, Tommy Hitchcock and Winston Guest were a formidable combination, perhaps the best team in the world at the time. The contest for the Westchester Cup would not be renewed until 1992 at Windsor Park, when the American team, John Gobin, Adam Snow, Owen Rinehart and Rob Walton, defeated the local team. However, the British team, Julian Daniels, Henry Brett, Will Lucas and Andrew Hine, returned the favor five years later at the same venue. Therefore, the historic trophy resides in England, sadly, within a vault's dark confines.

The Cup of the Americas has not been played for since 1980, and the Avila Camacho

Cup, between Mexico and the United States, remains in abeyance since 1988. The last competition for the Westchester Cup, now relegated to a single game, was in 1997. International polo is certainly not what it used to be. However, at the time of writing, negotiations are being conducted between America and England for a renewal of competition in 2009, the centenary of the first American victory in the series.

Throughout this time span the Meadow Brook Club kept its primacy among the principal American polo clubs. It can be safely said that it was a bastion of the Wasps, the white Anglo-Saxon Protestants that dominated politics, finance, education and myriad of other endeavors in the Northeast. Membership at Meadow Brook was restricted, as was at their erstwhile rivals, Rockaway. There was no polo on Sundays at the puritan clubs. In order to provide an outlet for those poloists not able to gain membership at Meadow Brook, the Sands Point Club was started on Cow's Neck, Long Island. The club was on property initially owned by the brothers Walter and William Cornwell, then by George E. Reynolds of the Reynolds tobacco family, and later by Julius Fleischman, polo player and yeast magnate. It was purchased by a syndicate headed by W. Averell Harriman, the club's first president. The initial board of governors was a mixed bag; Vincent Astor, Walter Camp, J. Cheever Cowdin, Max Fleischman and Thomas Hitchcock, Jr., were some of the governors. Among other early members were Bernard Baruch, Irving R. Berlin, Walter P. Chrysler, Marshall Field, James V. Forrestal, Harry Guggenheim, Mrs. William Randolph Hearst, Edward F. Hutton, Robert Lehman, William S. Paley, John and Stephen Sanford, John M. Schiff, Alexander Charles Schwartz, Cornelius Vanderbilt and John Hay Whitney.

The game of golf was also offered to the membership; the original 9-hole course designed by George E. Reynolds was extensively remodeled and enlarged by the celebrated architect Albert Warren Tillinghast.[13] A polo team took the 1927 U.S. Open; however, financial difficulties in the 1930s were only met with Mr. Harriman's personal commitment. Polo was not resumed and World War II; the old Fleischman Field was demoted to golf range status.

American polo in the Golden Age was characterized by the impact produced by two forceful and remarkable personalities: Tommy Hitchcock and Devereux Milburn; one, the last survivor of the immortal Big Four, and the other, the undisputed leader of international teams after Dev Milbun's retirement.[14]

Tommy Hitchcock was always a dominant personality at Meadow Brook's International Field. The crowd cherished him because of his fighting qualities and for that mixture of dash and dexterity which characterized his play. Nevertheless, he was recognized among his peers as a tactician of the first class, able to appraise his opponent's weapons with an instinct that was sound and sagacious; a player, moreover, who in pleasing others, obviously pleased himself.

It is sad to note that Hitchcock only twice played high goal polo beyond the United States' shores, at Hurlingham for the Westchester Cup and in Paris at the Olympic Games. Pressure of business — it was said — did not allow him to travel overseas to play polo. It is hard to believe that his employer, Wall Street's Lehman Brothers, could not spare Hitchcock from his work at the firm. Therefore, both the Cup of the Americas in 1932 and the Westchester Cup in London in 1936 missed the presence of the player who was considered the best in the world. His biography does not mention the 1932 series, and the 1936 events — the Westchester Cup and the Cup of the Americas — only merit two paragraphs.[15] Meadow Brook was Thomas Hitchcock, Jr.'s home court. Perhaps the American idol had lost his zeal for international travel.

Devereux Milburn's *The Science of Hitting* brought a startling new technical discussion to the game. Initially published in *The Spur*, later reprinted in Newell Bent's *American Polo*, the article is both significant and instructive.[16] Dev Milburn clearly describes the three most important things in striking the ball: the grip, the brace and the action of the body in making the different strokes.

To Milburn, the grip is of the first importance. He divides the polo strokes into forehands and backhands. Forehand strokes are the offside fore shot and the nearside back shot. The correct grip for those two shots is the finger grip, as opposed to the palm grip. Milburn's rationale is that if the handle is gripped by and in the fingers, the mallet's shaft becomes almost an exact prolongation of the wrist and forearm, which is conducive to ease and facility in hitting. If the handle is in the hand's palm, the stick comes out of the hand at a right angle to the wrist and forearm, which results in an awkward stroke.

The backhand strokes are the nearside forward shot and the offside back shot. In these shots, the handle should be slightly shifted to allow the thumb to be extended down the back of the shaft to act as a rear support. Milburn found this of great help in making what he considers the most difficult shots in polo.

Dev Milburn compares the brace to the stance in golf. It consists of hitting from the feet in the stirrups, braced by the knees and the inside of the thighs against the saddle, and the feeling should be that of hitting from the stirrup irons, rather than from the seat. Milburn observes that players trained in India seemed to hit the ball from the seat, the result being that they hit mainly with the arm, with very little body motion added to the stroke.

The third and last element of good hitting is the body's action in making the different strokes. Devereux Milburn recommends that in every stroke the player should lean out and get well over the ball when he is about to hit. This is done by pivoting the body from the knees and the waist. Milburn stresses the importance of getting the right shoulder well back at the start of the offside shot — the most used during a game — and to follow through in every stroke.

Although previous writers on the game had described in detail most of Milburn's concepts, *The Science of Hitting* explained succinctly and with great clarity the basics of hitting the ball. As far back as 1896, Captain Edward Miller had illustrated the idea of the thumb being along the mallet's shaft rather than around it when hitting a backhander.[17] On the other hand, Miller advised that the player should sit on the saddle when hitting the ball.[18] The evolution of the game of polo continues without interruption.

14. Of Lords and Ladies

Polo is a social game and some of its most serious hazards are encountered at the parties and entertainments which are such inevitable features of all tournaments. — H.R.H. Prince Philip, Duke of Edinburgh[1]

From the very early days of polo in England, the game enjoyed the patronage of royalty and nobility. As far back as 1872, the Court Circular reported

> Their Royal Highnesses the Prince and Princess of Wales went down to Windsor yesterday and witnessed a match at Polo between the officers of the Royal Horse Guards and the 9th Lancers. It may be said to have been introduced to society under the highest auspices on that afternoon at Windsor. It was on the 16th, and the gathering was a brilliant one, the Paddington officials being much astonished at the influx of a lot of pretty, well-dressed women, attended by equally well-dressed men, who all wanted to go to Windsor by the 2 o'clock train. The Prince and Princess, the Duke and Duchess of Teck, and a circle of friends and intimates, witnessed the game from a tent, and when a trumpeter gave the signal, and the ball was flung into the center of the ground, then began an exciting scene. Such dashing charges, such confused melees, a waving of hockey sticks in the air, a clever struggle between three or four of the combatants for a stroke at the white ball that lay under their ponies' feet, a struggle from which one horseman emerges triumphantly, his hockey stick, it is true broken, but with the ball flying before him to the goal, another charge and rally, and dense mingling of ponies' heads and a coming to grief of some human ones, another outcome of the ball, and a goal has been won. Though the match was a drawn game when the trumpet sounded, the 9th Lancers appeared to be the better men. The game was pronounced, emphatically, "very good" and is, we think, sure to be popular. There is something very exciting about it. A man must be able to ride, and handle his horse well; he must stand the racket of sore shins or a bloody coxcomb, be quick of eye and nimble of hand. It is a game, too, that ladies will enjoy to look at, a sort of tournament in which they can back their knights, and much better fun than seeing pigeons killed at Hurlingham, or a cricket ball knocked about at Prince's or Lord's.[2]

This royal patronage and support of the game has continued without interruption to the present time. Although there is no notice of Queen Victoria attending a game, her son, the future King Edward VII, and his wife, Princess Alexandra of Denmark, were frequent spectators at Hurlingham and Ranelagh. King George V played polo in Malta while a serving naval officer and in later years witnessed many matches, most notably the Westchester Cup series in 1921.[3] Three of his sons, David, Prince of Wales, later Edward VIII, the Duke of York, later George VI, and the Duke of Gloucester, were polo players. The Duke of York was an excellent lawn tennis player, reaching the quarterfinal round in men's doubles at the All-England Championships at Wimbledon.

Top: A quintessential English tradition, the country house party. This one is at Watermoor House, near Cheltenham in Gloucestershire. Standing, from the left, are Capt. Edward Metcalf, the Earl of Bathurst, Maj. Edric Kingscote, Maj. Philip Magor (in back), the Hon. Aubrey Hastings, Maj. Frederick Barrett, Capt. Lewis Dunbar, Alfred Grisar, Edward, Prince of Wales, leaning against a column, Thomas Kingscote and Richard Reginald "Rex" Smart. Seated are the Countess of Bathurst, Joyce Kingscote, the Hon. Mrs. Thomas Kingscote, the Duke of Beaufort, Mrs. Violet Kingscote and Mrs. Frederick Barrett (private collection). *Above:* Aristocrats in action for the Harrington Cup, House of Lords versus House of Commons, on the Number 1 ground at Ranelagh. Capt. the Hon. Frederick Guest is about to score a goal for the Commons. Lord Digby, in a white shirt, is to the left and Capt. Geoffrey Shaw is behind Capt. Guest. The Ranelagh Club polo pavilion is in the background (private collection).

The polo clubs' preoccupation with securing appropriate patrons, chairmen and committee members has been described in several paragraphs throughout this book and the trend continues to the present time, at least in tradition-bound Britain. Titled gentlemen, field marshals — or at the very least, generals or admirals — and prominent social figures intermingled with the occasional wealthy American or Continental worthy were a *sine qua non* in any self-respecting polo club's committee.

Nevertheless, many were good polo players. For instance, the Irish family de la Poer Beresford has been prominent in many avocations as political leaders, soldiers, sailors, clergymen and sportsmen. Indeed, it would be difficult to mention one of them who had not a marked taste for sport. Henry de la Poer, third Marquess of Waterford (1811–1859), was perhaps the most famous Irish sportsman who ever lived. He was one of the parties of wild sportsmen at Melton Mowbray who painted the tollgate and other houses red, as they are shown in the well-known Henry Alken print. This is one of the legends of the origin of the phrase "painting the town red."[4]

Several Beresfords were, and are, good polo players. Lord William Leslie Beresford was one of the pioneers who took his place in the first game in England at Heathrow Heath between the 9th Lancers and the 10th Hussars. Colonel Beresford, 9th Lancers, was awarded the Victoria Cross for gallantry in the Zulu War. An interesting character was Lord Charles William de la Poer Beresford, first Baron Beresford, A.D.C. to Queen Victoria, member of parliament, and admiral of the Navy, popularly known as "Charlie B."[5] Lord Charles Beresford was Sir John Fisher, the First Sea Lord's great adversary in matters of naval strategic goals; he is listed in the Hurlingham handicap list as late as 1912.[6]

Major John Graham Hope Beresford, 7th Hussars, played for Hurlingham in the 1900 Westchester Cup and took the Olympic Gold medal in Paris that same year. He was the donor of the Beresford Cup, emblematic of the South African Open Championship. Maj. Beresford was later created Lord Decies. Brig. Gen. George de la Poer Beresford, an expert in the selection and training of polo ponies, was in charge of the pony string for the 1927 challenge for the Westchester Cup. Brigadier Beresford was the author of a chapter in *Polo*, a treatise edited by the Earl of Kimberley for the Lonsdale Library of Sports, Games and Pastimes.[7]

Lord Patrick Tristam de la Poer Beresford earned the Sword of Honor as the top cadet at Royal Military Academy Sandhurst and took Cowdray Park's Gold Cup, among many other trophies. Lord Patrick Beresford was a member of the Commonwealth team that traveled to Buenos Aires in 1966 to compete in the 30-goal championship with Argentina and the United States, and in a match against the Argentine Army team at Palermo. His older brother John, eighth Marquis of Waterford, also was on the Commonwealth squad. Lord Waterford won the Gold Cup at Cowdray with a Guards team that included Prince Philip, his brother Patrick and Paul Withers. The Marquis of Waterford's son Lord Charles Beresford, a 7-goal player — married to Teresa Donoso, of the Chilean polo family — represented England several times in international test matches. The latest addition to this polo dynasty is Lord Richard Le Poer, who is now climbing the Hurlingham Polo Association handicap list.

Many other families achieved prominence in polo circles. The tragic story of the Grenfell brothers deserves a brief account.[8] The nine Grenfell brothers served their country well and four were killed in active service. Pascoe Grenfell, the eldest, was killed in the Matabele War; Robert, in the cavalry charge of the 21st Lancers against the Mahdi's Dervishes at Omdurman. It was while trying to save Robert Grenfell that Capt. Paul Kenna and Lt. the Hon. Raymond de Montmorency, both polo players, earned the Victoria Cross. Reginald, 17th

Lancers, died in India from the effect of the tropical climate. The twins, Francis Octavius and Riversdale Nonus, were killed in World War I, Francis being awarded the Victoria Cross. Francis and Riversdale Grenfell took the Hurlingham Champion Club with the Freebooters team, aided by Captain Leopold Jenner, the manager at Ranelagh Club, and the Duke of Roxburghe. When handicaps were instituted in England, Rivy was rated at nine goals and Francis at eight goals. They also were on the Ranelagh team that won the Open Championship in America. Lt. Col. Arthur Grenfell, Buckinghamshire Yeomanry, the donor of the Grenfell Cup in Canada, was twice wounded and earned the Distinguished Service Order.[9] Harold Grenfell was in command of the 3rd Dragoon Guards and became a brigadier general. Another brother, Cecil, was described by Col. Miller, who was a friend of the family, as a keen polo player but never in the same class as his younger brothers Francis and Rivy. John Grenfell served in the South African War with the Imperial Yeomanry Brigade.

The Nickalls brothers, Pat, Cecil and Morres, all three educated at Rugby School and then at New College in Oxford University, showed early promise when they took the County Cup at an early age, accompanied by Henry Savill, on their own Chislehurst, County of Kent, team. They went on to win the Ranelagh Open Cup four years in a row, with Capt. Bertie Wilson and Capt. John Hardress Lloyd occasionally filling some slots in the team. They were the sons of Sir Patteson Nickalls, a member of the London Stock Exchange and president of the Polo and Riding Pony Society.

Young Patteson Nickalls played for Oxford, just as his brothers did. Pat, a fine horseman, was a strong back and the best player of the three brothers. However, an excitable temperament sometimes marred his play. Morres Nickalls, known as Bobby, was described as a clever number 2, and an excellent horseman with good hands. All three played for England against Ireland for the Patriotic Cup, while Cecil and Pat also represented their country in the Westchester Cup.

Cecil Nickalls was a great all-around athlete who excelled at rugby and cricket during his schooldays at Rugby. Cecil went on to Oxford, where he surely would have been a Blue in both games, had he not devoted most of his time to foxhunting and polo. Lt. Col. Edward Miller considered Cecil the best number 1 in England. During the war, Lt. Col. Nickalls was in command of an artillery battery when the ammunition dump exploded; Nickalls was blown up, gassed and wounded, never fully recovering his health and being afflicted with bouts of depression. After the war, while performing as a popular and efficient manager of the Rugby Club, Cecil Nickalls took his own life, to the sorrow of all those who knew him.

One family that has been prominent in British polo is the Mountbattens. Prince Louis of Battenberg — married to Princess Victoria of Hesse and the Rhine, granddaughter of Queen Victoria — was one of the early players on the island of Malta while on duty with the Mediterranean Fleet during the 1870s. The Prince Louis Cup, presented by his younger son, Lord Louis Mountbatten, remains a coveted prize for Maltese polo players. When the Great War, as World War I was then known, broke out, English popular sentiment ran strongly against Imperial Germany and German surnames. King George V prudently thought it would be appropriate to anglicize the family name; therefore, in 1917 the Royal House of Saxe-Coburg became the Royal House of Windsor. The monarch also asked his blood relatives to modify their surnames; thus, Battenberg was changed to Mountbatten, a literal translation. The marquisate of Milford Haven came his way in 1917. His German heritage may have cost Prince Louis the post of first sea lord of the Admiralty, the highest professional seaman in the Royal Navy. This was an event that his son Louis never forgot nor forgave; in due time, Lord Louis Mountbatten would be named first sea lord.

The polo links continue. Princess Alice, the now Marquis of Milford Haven's eldest daughter, had married into the Greek royal family and her only son, Prince Philip of Greece and Denmark, adopted the surname Mountbatten when he became a British citizen in 1947, the year he married the then Princess Elizabeth. Prince Philip would go on to reach a 5-goal handicap and is deservedly credited with giving the game a tremendous boost with his charismatic personality and good sportsmanship.

Lord Louis Mountbatten, later Earl Mountbatten of Burma, was a prominent personality in the world of polo.[10] Lord Louis discovered the game while on a visit to India while accompanying his second cousin David, Prince of Wales, in 1922. A serving naval officer, somehow he managed to play quite a bit of polo around the globe. Mountbatten started the Bluejackets, a team composed of Royal Navy officers that acquitted itself rather nicely during the London season. Another of his teams was Asdean, based on a country house in Sussex, not far from Cowdray Park, and also from Portsmouth, the naval base where Mountbatten discharged some of his duties. While serving on the Mediterranean Fleet, the dashing officer was a fixture in Cannes, Brioni and other fashionable ports of call. His wife, the wealthy Edwina Ashley, was an easily recognizable figure in the smart set of the 1920s and 1930s.

Lord Mountbatten's naval and military career was meteoric. At the start of the war, he was commanding officer, 5th Destroyer Flotilla, with the rank of captain. The war's end saw him presiding over the Japanese surrender ceremony in Singapore, as supreme allied commander, Southeast Asia. Further honors were to come. In 1947, Mountbatten was appointed by the Labour government as viceroy of India. After the partition of India and Pakistan, Mountbatten was the first governor-general of the Republic of India. Both his naval and governmental records have given rise to serious criticism. As chief of combined operations, Lord Mountbatten bears a heavy responsibility for the disastrous raid on Dieppe, on the Channel coast, during which more than half of the men involved — the overwhelming majority Canadians — became either casualties or prisoners of war. As viceroy of India, Mountbatten oversaw the division of Punjab and East Bengal during the partition between Pakistan and India that resulted in chaos among Hindus and Moslem civilians in the course of one of the largest population shifts in history. Richard Symonds estimated that, at a minimum, half a million people died and 12 million were homeless.[11]

Nevertheless, Lord Mountbatten's greatest contribution to the game was his *Introduction to Polo*, written under the pen-name "Marco" with editorial assistance from his friend Peter Murphy. The book was published in 1931 to benefit the Royal Navy Polo Association, to which Mountbatten assigned the royalties. It is a lucid treatise, aimed mostly at beginners of the game, that reached seven editions. It is safe to assume that *Introduction to Polo* is the most widely read book on the subject and forms the cornerstone of any polo library. The six chapters, "Horsemanship," "Equipment," "Striking," "The Game," "Team Play" and "Specimen Organization" are complemented by appendices on "Stable Management," "History of the Rules," and others covering the rules of the Hurlingham Polo Association and its Notes, the United States Polo Association Rules and Guide for Umpires, a comparison of the Hurlingham and U.S.P.A. penalties, and finally, a reprint of *Rules and Tactics* by Tommy Hitchcock. Subsequent to that publication, Lord Mountbatten wrote *An Introduction to Umpiring*, giving much needed advice on the art of refereeing polo games.[12] Although somewhat dated, it should be mandatory for both aspiring as well as active umpires and referees.

Earl Louis Mountbatten of Burma was assassinated by terrorists while vacationing in Ireland. On 27 August 1979, a fifty-pound bomb placed in his sailboat was detonated by remote control. The 79-year-old earl was killed, together with his grandson Nicholas Knatchbull, age 14, and a local lad, 15-year old Paul Maxwell, who was acting as a crewmember. On the following day, the 83-year-old Lady Brabourne, Nicholas' paternal grandmother, succumbed from her grievous injuries. It was a senseless multiple murder. John Knatchbull, 7th Baron Brabourne, his wife — the former Patricia Mountbatten — and their son Timothy were injured but survived. One of the perpetrators was caught and convicted to life imprisonment, but was released nine years later.

George Mountbatten, fourth Marquis of Milford Haven, whose Cowdray Park–based Broncos team has been quite successful in English polo and in the occasional foray onto Florida grounds during the Palm Beach season, now carries on the polo family tradition. His wife Clare is an active participant in tournaments, both in ladies' and mixed teams.

During the 1890s, many polo clubs came into being in different parts of the kingdom, and the Hurlingham Club offered a trophy, the County Cup, for competition among the provincial clubs. The arrangement was that the tournament should be held at Hurlingham during the latter part of July, and, as at the time the club had only one ground, a certain amount of mild friction and occasional disappointment arose between Hurlingham members who could not always get games when they wanted one, and country players who now and then felt aggrieved. Fortunately, in 1898, an arrangement was made with the Eden Park Polo Club to the effect that it should be the scene of the County Cup tournament. The provincial club members welcomed this solution. A special governing body was formed for watching over the interests of provincial polo players, and the County Polo Association saw the light of day. A strong committee was appointed with Mr. Tresham Gilbey as president, rules were adopted, and the new body started with powerful support. The Hurlingham Club eventually recognized the wisdom of establishing amicable relations with the County Polo Association, and it was mutually agreed that the final tie for the County Cup be played for on the Hurlingham ground. The County Cup is still being played today — lately at Cirencester Park — being the third oldest polo tournament in the world.

By the turn of the nineteenth century, polo in the British Isles was plagued by individual brilliancy at the expense of combination play. The lessons taught by the Peat brothers and their phenomenally successful Sussex team appear to have been soon forgotten, with the notable exceptions of the Miller brothers' Rugby Club and Walter Buckmaster's Old Cantabs. It was not until much later that the Americans, by developing gradually their scheme of play along orthodox lines, and assisted considerably by the abolition of the offside rule, converged towards a similar conclusion as the Peats had done years before: the game of polo is based upon teamwork, accurate hitting and good ponies. These three essentials, which most British polo players seemed to find very difficult to grasp, or at any rate to practice, retarded the development of polo in Britain. The tactics of the Meadow Brook team were never fully accepted in England, where polo continued on the same lines as before with fluctuating development of detail. The rude awakening of 1909 at Hurlingham and the surprising defeat of the Americans by the four British Army officers at Meadow Brook in 1914 did not change the basic tactical structure of English polo.

This failure to adapt to change became painfully evident in 1921 at Hurlingham. Led by Devereux Milburn, the Americans ran away with the Westchester Cup, not to be seriously challenged by England until the advent of the Second World War. In London the system of heavy succession of tournaments with little or no intervals for pony training was very detrimental to the production of any thought-out, tactical developments. There were so many cups and tournaments in the crowded summer calendar that the polo managers at the big clubs — Hurlingham, Ranelagh and Roehampton — were practically overwhelmed by the sheer numbers of teams and players clamoring for a shot at the silver. The grounds suffered, and combination play, as the result of new tactical thinking and practices, became stagnant.

The practice of obtaining the services of one of the star players for a side led to purely individual ball-chasing on the part of the star, accompanied by its inevitable corollary, ignorance of the best type of combination by the remainder of the team. Thus the wrong ideal was often envisaged even in the best teams, namely, that of a side carried by and playing up to a commanding performer. Capt. Pat Roark in the Hurricanes, Lewis Lacey and Johnny Traill in El Gordo, Maj. Vivian Lockett for the 17th Lancers, Lord Wodehouse and Maj. "Rattle" Barrett, the latter two in the twilight of their high-goal careers, repeatedly are noted for their sterling performances, but nothing is mentioned about great teams and new developments in the realm of tactics.

It is very true that the First World War robbed the British of some of their top and most promising players: Geoffrey Bowlby, Harold Brassey, Leslie Cheape, Noel Edwards, Francis and Rivy Grenfell, Lord Hugh Grosvenor, Brian Osborne, Bertie Wilson. The list is interminable.

Therefore, it fell to visiting teams to provide the matrix of polo in England during the inter-war years. First, it was the American squad in the 1921 Westchester Cup, and a year later the Argentine Polo Federation team. Then it was teams from India such as Jodhpur with a young Hanut Singh, and Count Jean de Madré's Tigers, who enlisted the 10-goalers Jaswant Singh and Jagindar Singh, and finally, perhaps the greatest of them all, Jaipur, formed by the Maharajah of Jaipur, with Abhey Singh, Prithi Singh and once more, the one and only Hanut Singh. The Jaipur team took all the tournaments they entered in the 1933 London season, a feat that can perhaps be equaled but never surpassed.[13]

The London polo season extended from the first week in May to the last week in July; very little serious polo was played in the rest of England because all the good players were in London. Largely, spring polo was limited to getting the ponies ready for the London summer season. The game of polo was an important part of a varied social and sporting calendar which offered thoroughbred racing at Epsom and Royal Ascot, tennis at Wimbledon, cricket at Lord's, coming-out parties and court functions.

Such an extremely crowded season placed a tremendous burden upon the three principal clubs. A review of the 1930 clubs' programs indicates that there were forty tournaments scheduled in less than twelve weeks: fifteen at Ranelagh, fourteen at Hurlingham and eleven at Roehampton.[14] Each of these clubs was a small country club in itself, and the game of polo was not always the prime attraction because it had to share space and membership with golfers, except at Hurlingham, along with tennis players and bowlers. There were six tournament polo grounds, all of which had little run-off or security areas at each end, which tended to slow down the game because of the danger of running out of space. Usually, there were three weekly tournaments in every club; these were arranged to be of different handicap in order to avoid scheduling conflicts. Rain, a constant in the equation of British polo, could wreak havoc in the tight schedules. Many tournaments were not completed unless some teams scratched out. Quite often, two tournament games had to be played on each field every afternoon, almost every week.

The grounds, after a month or so of hard play, became so cut up and bumpy that was difficult for even good players to hit the ball with confidence and control. Perhaps this is one of the reasons why so few English players developed into strong hitters during this time. The

Ball over the boards at Roehampton. The 1939 Junior Championship final game pitted the Hon. Keith Rous' Jaguars versus Lord Mountbatten's Asdean. Both team captains were Royal Navy officers. Edward Nutting (Jaguars) is second from left, Keith Rous (Jaguars) left, wearing ribbed knee guards, and Lord Mountbatten is to our right (private collection).

grounds had excellent turf; however, the constant play made heavy rolling a necessity, and this in turn made them firm and slippery towards the end of the season, which was very hard on the ponies.

When the London season ended, the provincial clubs started their tournaments, which continued through September. Rugby Polo Club and Moreton Morrell in Warwickshire continued strong until the outbreak of war in September 1939. So did Beaufort and Cheltenham in Gloucestershire, Cowdray in Sussex, Kirtlington in Oxfordshire, newcomer Rhinefield in Hampshire, and Toulston in Yorkshire. Military polo thrived at Aldershot, Colchester, Shorncliffe and Tidworth, while the Royal Air Force had a club on Halton Aerodrome. In the southwest, Taunton Vale had two grounds at Orchard Portman, while West Gloster's ground was in Filton, next to the Bristol Aircraft works. The West Somerset Club carried the reputation of being the best place in England to train a team, with two good grounds and a fine practice field. A great asset was its wonderful stretch of sand on the beach, which formed a perfect schooling ground and practice field. The main ground, overlooked by Dunster Castle, was a favorite spot for polo artists, including Cecil Aldin and Vincent Haddelsey.[15, 16]

Polo in England was thriving in spite of the economic situation. It was not cream of the crop polo, as the international matches demonstrated, but it was good polo and great fun. It is of interest to record Gerald Balding's opinion of British polo in the 1930s: "Polo is not taken so seriously as in America or Argentina."[17] Perhaps it is significant that Gerald Balding is the last Englishman to reach the 10-goal handicap plateau.

15. The Game in the Former Dominions

Where but in Kenya can a man whose grandfather was a cannibal watch a really good game of polo?—Marina Tatiana Sulzberger[1]

Australia

Polo in the isolation of Western Australia was resumed shortly after the end of World War I. Trophies donated in that era were the Warrener Cup presented by Mr. R. Warrener in 1921, the Charles Cup in 1923 presented by Mr. Joseph Charles and the Gooch Cup, the gift of Mr. Gordon G. Gooch of Wandagee Station, Carnavon, in 1926. Leonard Hamersley observed, "These cups are still in circulation to this day, and it is said by many players that the Gooch Cup is the most difficult to win. This is probably borne out by the fact that it is played off handicap. Mingenew beat the then invincible Broomehill team in the inaugural game final played at South Perth, 1926."[2]

The Broomehill team was so dominant that after winning the Joseph Charles Cup three years in a row, Mr. Charles donated another trophy, which Broomehill proceeded to win for three consecutive years. Joseph Charles, now wiser, was generous enough to donate yet another cup; however, it was now for perpetual competition.[3] The Broomehill foursome, wearing their red jerseys in the billowing dusty field, was once described as burning embers in the smoke of a bushfire.[4]

In 1929, the centenary of Western Australia, two teams from South Australia, Adelaide and Clare, traveled to Perth to compete in the Western Australia Centenary Polo Cup, presented by Mr. Nelson Pearse. Adelaide won both the Joseph Charles Cup and the Centenary Cup, the latter after defeating a combined Western Australia side.

The 1930s depression hit polo in Western Australia hard and all the clubs north of Perth closed their doors. There was a minor revival after 1935; however, almost no polo was played until after the Second World War had ended.

On the opposite side of Australia, the game of polo was dominated by teams made up of family members. The names Ashton, Bray, Munro, Nivisen, Ross and Skene are the stuff of legend in New South Wales polo history. No quarter was expected or given during those matches that pitted against each other teams of fathers, sons, cousins and the occasional

Goulburn dominated Australian polo in the 1930s. This team took Hurlingham's Champion Cup in 1937. From the left are Bob Skene, Geoffrey Ashton, Jim Ashton and Bob Ashton (courtesy James Ashton and Rosemary Foot).

brother in-law. The Vychan team was established by Tom "The Boss" Bray at the Corriedale sheep station, on the Lachan River. With his sons Angus, Dougal and Tom, Jr., and at times Tom Skene, they achieved considerable success, including the Countess of Dudley Cup, wearing their red with gold V stripe jerseys. The Munro cousins appropriately wore the Munro tartan colors; their contests against the Nivisens bordered the limits of violence, which, however, did not last after the final whistle, with one notable exception. Commanded by his brother Rowland to mark his opponent, Roy Munro took one of the Nivisens off the field onto an adjacent paddock through an open gate, which he proceeded to lock. Years later, Wallace Munro told Chris Ashton that neither players, nor wives nor grooms in the Nivisen camp ever forgot or forgave the incident.[5]

The 1928 Countess of Dudley Cup in New South Wales was significant for Australian polo because of two novelties. The first one was the visit of an Army-in-India team and the second the defeat of Harden by a Goulburn team in an extra chukker. Harden had won the tournament three years running, which in effect had disheartened many teams. Archie McLaurin, Knox, William and Tommy Ross had achieved an aura of invincibility that the four brothers Ashton from Goulburn were determined to do away with. Their plans received a jolt when Geoffrey Ashton, Goulburn's number 2, injured during a practice game, was unable to play in the tournament. Alfred Pitty took his place on the team, playing at number 1, while Bob Ashton moved back to the number 2 position. Goulburn and the Ashton brothers were on their way to preeminence in the Australian game and to a spot in the sun in world polo.

The Army-in-India team participated in the Countess of Dudley Cup. Under Lt. Col.

Teignmouth Melvill's management, the team was made up of Lt. Charles Keightley, 5th/6th Dragoons, Capt. Charles P.J. Prioleau, the Guides, Lt. Peter Dollar, 4th Hussars, and Lt. George Prior-Palmer, 9th Lancers. Reserve was Capt. Robert H. Wordsworth, 6th Lancers, who already was in Australia; they added up to a total of 22 goals in handicap. Fiercely independent Australia had not yet assigned individual handicaps; therefore, it is rather difficult to assess the teams' relative strengths. The Army team met Harden — in which Irwin Maple-Brown had replaced Archie McLaurin — in the semifinal match and was narrowly defeated 4–3. After the Dudley Cup, the Army-in-India team met a foursome from Victoria and went down 5–4. Harden had beaten Victoria 12–3 in a previous game.[6]

The most important observations made by the Australians were that the Army players hit longer forward passes than was customary in Australia and, secondly, used curb bits. The visitors brought with them their own saddles and bits, mostly Pelhams and double bridles. At the time, snaffle bits were the standard in Australia because it was felt that ponies in snaffles could be stopped quickly and turned better than those in curbs. Col. T.P. Melvill, an international player of great repute, stressed the point that the use of a curb takes a lot less out of a rider when handling anything but a very tractable pony. Another perceived advantage of the curb bit is that it allows the rider to play with a longer rein, giving him more freedom in hitting.

Colonel Melvill witnessed a match at the Goulburn Carnival, as tournaments were called in Australia, in which all eight players were using snaffles. Melvill wrote: "Practically, no attempt was made to stop, as we understand it. The ponies were pulled 'round on their forehand with both hands, practically at full speed, almost like a bicycle. To pull them 'round like this in India, where the footing is not so secure, would, in my opinion, be suicidal."[7]

The example set by the visitors regarding bits was by-and-large disregarded by Australian polo players, with the notable exception of the Ashton brothers.[8] It was to serve them well a few years later, during Goulburn's successful polo tour around the world.

The game in South Australia was the province of the Mount Crawford team. Its members were Cyril and Eric Murray, with their cousin Elliot Murray and brother-in-law Ron Angas. With Cyril Murray as team captain, the white, yellow and black team won the Barr Smith Cup, emblematic of South Australia's championship, every year they participated but one, 1923, when Caramut, a visiting team from Victoria, took the palm. The Murrays left the running of their properties to managers so they could devote most of their energies to the game they loved so well.

South Australian polo was looked down by the eastern powers that, because of the long distance involved, had not been able to witness Mount Crawford's prowess. However, in 1925 Anthony Hordern from Sydney and Robert Melrose[9] from South Australia donated the Australasian Gold Cup, to be played for by teams representing each state, as well as a team from New Zealand. The Hawke's Bay club from New Zealand, Victoria, Queensland and three squads from New South Wales converged on the Kensington Racecourse in Sydney to decide the best team in Australasia. The favorite was the Ross family Harden team from New South Wales. However, the N.S.W. Polo Association decided to combine players from different club teams to represent the state. Therefore, a depleted Harden team did battle against Mount Crawford in the first round. Rather surprisingly, Harden was defeated by eight goals by a Mount Crawford team that was also lacking one regular player, Elliot Murray, who was replaced by Gordon Law-Smith from Adelaide. The South Australians went on to capture the Gold Cup against all comers.

In Victoria the traditional clubs from the Western District remained as the teams to beat. A team from the Garden State took the Australasian Gold Cup in 1926, a feat not repeated until 1955. The team members were bearers of distinguished names in Victorian polo circles: Jamie Affleck, Ronald Cumming, Charles Kelly and Keith Urquhart. With John Manifold in place of Kelly, Caramut took the Barr Smith Cup, while Camperdown, of the celebrated Manifolds, Melbourne Hunt of the Creswicks, and Caramut of the Urquharts were winners of the Stradbroke Cup, South Australia's second most prestigious tournament. The family teams, so characteristic of Australian pastoral families, are also in evidence in Victoria.

Although success in the Australasian Gold Cup continued to elude Queensland teams until 1952, a Cressbrook team formed by Greenmount and Cressbrook players, Bert and Roy Bell and Jack and Tom Allen, took the 1923 Countess of Dudley Cup. The Darling Downs was the busy center of polo in the state. Like elsewhere in Australia, family clubs and teams constituted the backbone of the game. The rivalry between Pilton and Greenmount assumed epic proportions. Both teams had brothers on their lineup, Tom and Jack Allen for Greenmount, and Bob and Frank Armstrong for Pilton. The level of antagonism was increased by relatives and supporters sitting on the sidelines. The mother of one of Pilton's players, Bill Feez, gave the local children a few pennies to cheer for the team. Jack Allen, Sr., one of the wild men of polo from before the war, would scream, "Kill the buggers! Ride them into the ground!"[10] However, it was not carried any further and all was forgotten after the match.

The Australian "tyranny of distance" affected Queensland polo as well. Most of the interstate travel was limited to their southern neighbor, New South Wales. The journey to Sydney involved a land trip to Brisbane and then travel by freighter to Sydney, or a two-day trip by train. The 1920s was a good time for Queensland polo, and competitive visits to New South Wales followed with some success. Polo in Queensland was by no means a rich man's game and the long journey southwards meant that business had be left to family members or temporary caretakers. Sometimes, selling the ponies at the end of a tournament helped to defray the costs involved.

The Queensland Gold Cup was instituted in 1926 and taken by Toowoomba. A Handicap or Silver Cup was also donated by the same group of donors, to be competed for by teams beaten in the first rounds.[11] After the 1930 contest, won by the "A" team from Spring Creek, the economic depression dictated the temporary suspension of the Gold Cup until 1937, the last time it was played in Australia before the onset of the Second World War.

It is fitting to close this section on Australian polo with a mention of the pioneering voyage around the world undertaken by the Ashton brothers in 1930.[12] They arrived to the port of Hull in England after a six-week sea voyage and proceeded to Gloucestershire to acclimatize the ponies. The Hurlingham Polo Association rated Geoffrey and Robert at 7 goals, Jim at 6 goals and Philip at 4 goals; as a 24-goal aggregate team, they were under-handicapped. The proof was in their performance during the London season. Goulburn took the Whitney Cup, defeating Laddie Sanford's Hurricanes in the semifinals. Then they reached the finals of Hurlingham's Champion Cup and, playing as Australia, they beat India on the Indian Empire Day at Hurlingham. At season's end, both James and Phil Ashton's handicaps went up one point. However, the real winners were the Australian ponies.

In the finals of the Champion Cup, they lost 7–9 to the Hurricanes, a 31-goal team. *The Polo Monthly* commented, "The game was a genuine triumph for the Australian ponies. It has to be remembered that they were pitted against a team which could produce a large number of the finest ponies in the world. Taken on the whole, the Australian ponies were giving away size and weight. But this did not prevent them from making a remarkably good show, and the Messrs. Ashton are entitled to the warmest congratulations on the way in which they had managed their stud since its arrival in England after travelling all the way from Sidney."[13]

The Ashton brothers then proceeded to New York; however, they did not participate in the American season. They sold their ponies to great advantage and returned home to find out that the wool market had crashed. The dollars earned from the pony sale were left in America; when the Australian currency dropped against the U.S. dollar, the Ashtons more than recovered the cost of their journey around the world.

In 1937, with up-and-coming star Bob Skene as a reserve player, Goulburn once more traveled to England to compete in the Champion Cup. As Chris Ashton recounts, "For the first time in the Ashton camp, merit took precedence over ties of blood. Jim decided that Skene, on six-goals, would replace Phil, on five goals, for Hurlingham."[14] Jim Ashton's wisdom as team captain was rewarded when the Goulburn team took Hurlingham's Champion Cup over the anointed favorites, the Hon. W. Keith Rous' (later Earl of Stradbroke) Jaguars. Bob Skene scored six of nine goals for the Australians.

Canada

The scattering of players from Canada's western provinces and the wane of ranching due to the ceaseless inroads of agricultural pursuits contributed to the decline of polo in the region. World War I effectively closed polo for years. Most of the players joined the armed forces and the artillery and the cavalry branches took many of the horses, never to return to the range. The game was revived under different circumstances, because it was the development of the polo pony breeding industry that brought the game back to the area. Prior to the war, the ranchers did not give much thought to exporting their polo ponies; their only interest was playing the game. The horse used by the ranchers was a cow pony, taken straight from the range to the field of play. They were hardened by their life outdoors and wiry from working with cattle, a good education for polo ponies.

The good economic climate in the United States gave impulse to polo and therefore, the need for more ponies. Breeders in Western Canada were alert to take advantage of the situation and an excellent export market was created. Polo was revived because it could be played inexpensively on the prairies. The Western Canada Polo Association was created and gave the resurgent game a sound foundation.

The game in the rest of Canada struggled through the lean years of the depression. Toronto was able to maintain the indoors version of the game at the Eglinton Hunt Club. The Toronto Polo Club played games against Montreal Polo Club and other clubs south of the border, such as Buffalo Country Club, Rochester and Lake Shore Hunt in Derby, New York. Montreal managed to keep the game going, with support from members such as Thomas MacDougall, Blair and Howard Gordon, and Gavin Ogilvie. There was also an annual low-goal tournament in Quebec.[15]

The only polo club in the Province of Manitoba was in Winnipeg, in association with the St. Charles Golf Club. In British Columbia, there were clubs in Vancouver and Douglas Lake, while in the cradle of Western Canadian polo, the Province of Alberta, Calgary, Cochrane, High River and Lord Strathcona's Horse kept the flag flying.[16]

Frederick Mannix with his team in England. Fred is one of the Canadians who shaped the game in his own country, as well as being influential in the United States. From left, the Prince of Wales, Mannix, New Zealander Tony Devcich and Charlie Graham, May 1986 (Museum of Polo and Hall of Fame).

India

Following the best Indian teams such as Alwar, Golconda, Jodhpur and Patiala, and regimental clubs like the Queen's Bays and the Durham Light Infantry, the 10th Hussars (the Prince of Wales's Own) compiled an outstanding record as a polo playing regiment in both Britain and India. They took the Indian Polo Association Open Championship in 1910 and the Indian Inter-Regimental Tournament from 1907 until 1912. There is a team photograph in Cirencester player Charles Llewellen Palmer's collection showing the four captains, Gibbs on Redoubt, Annesley on Rajah, Palmes on Surprise and Llewellen Palmer on Simple Simon. Palmer's pony was by the undefeated St. Simon, one of the best racehorses ever, and was considered the best pony in all of India. One of his hooves, set in silver, is in Llewellen Palmer's collection.[17]

There is a story that all the 10th Hussars team players were 10-goalers. If the story were correct, that team would be the first 40-goal team in history. However, polo handicaps in India were not established until 1911, when three players—Capt. Leslie St. Clair Cheape, Capt. Vyvyan Lockett and Capt. Gerald Ritson—none of whom were 10th Hussars—were given the 10-goal handicap. The next year, Capt. Edward William Eustace "Bill" Palmes, the team's number 3, was elevated to the maximum rating. Capt. William "Pedlar" Llewellen Palmer, at back, was handicapped at nine goals. Capt. the Hon. Arthur "Pic" Annesley and Capt. William Otter "Giblet" Gibbs were both 6-goal players. Players involved in previous wins were Col. John Vaughn, at 8 goals, and Lt. Maurice Arthur De Tuyll, who was handicapped at 4 goals.[18, 19] Regardless of the 40-goal controversy, the 10th Hussars team is secure in its place as one of the best formations in the history of the game.

In regards to other reputed and actual 40-goal teams, the four members of the 1909 Meadow Brook team were handicapped at 10 goals by the Hurlingham Polo Committee in 1911; however, they never played as a 40-goal team because in America all four players were handicapped at 9 goals. The first 40-goal team to play as such was an American team that played a friendly match—on handicap—against a British team in 1939. Mike Phipps, Cecil Smith, Tommy Hitchcock and Stewart Iglehart formed the team that lost 14–16 to the British squad, after giving 10 goals on handicap. In 1974 Coronel Suárez became the first 40-goal team to participate in an official tournament in Argentina.[20] This was followed by La Espadaña, with Carlos Gracida, Alfonso Pieres, Gonzalo Pieres and Ernesto Trotz, later by Indios-Chapaleufú I, that of the four Heguy brothers, and the current holders of the Argentine Open Championship, Adolfo Cambiaso, Lucas Monteverde, Mariano Aguerre and Bartolomé Castagnola.

Polo in India between the wars saw two periods of supremacy. Following the end of World War I, military polo was the dominant force; after 1930, native Indian polo, supported by the ruling princes, took the upper hand. The division between Army-in-India — the regular British Army units on rotation in the sub-continent — and the Native Cavalry regiments staffed by British and Indian officers remained a constant in their respective inter-regimental tournaments. The only common grounds for competition were the Indian Polo Association Championship, open to any team, and the innumerable tournaments held at stations and clubs throughout India. During the 1920s, only Jodhpur and Bhopal were able to break the Army's hold on the Open Championship trophy. However, from 1930 until the outbreak of war, Jaipur became the overwhelming champion, Jodhpur being the only team to put a dent in Jaipur's string of victories, in 1931. This Jaipur team, led by Maharaja Jai Singh and propelled by Rao Rajah Hanut Singh, was practically invincible; when they traveled to England in 1933, they took every major tournament in the London season. Asked about this formidable stretch, Hanut Singh said with sublime self-confidence, "We were the best strikers; we had the best ponies, we were the best horsemen. What could the others do?"[21]

Few people in the world other than the Indian princes and Thakurs (nobles) were able to set off on a privileged career in polo. Members of the ruling class could start the game at an early age under good tuition by past masters. They could afford to purchase the best horseflesh available and depend on a veritable army of grooms to train, keep and travel with the magnificent ponies. At a time in which the global economic situation was in a crisis, the Indian oligarchy was able to afford any luxury, including the game of polo, without apparent damage to their privy purses.

As a comparison, the 1921 American team in England took 30 grooms to take care of 50 horses,[22] while the 1936 Argentine Olympic team had seventeen petiseros and one veterinarian to handle 42 ponies.[23] In 1925, the Jodhpur team took 60 horses to England, each one with its own syce.[24] The Maharaja of Jaipur's team took 51 syces to provide care for 39 horses during the 1933 London season.[25]

Denzil Holder stated that his regiment, Skinner's Horse, the famous Yellow Jackets so named because it was the only Native Cavalry regiment wearing yellow, never had more than a two-gun polo team, meaning two top class players. To win the Indian Cavalry or the Indian Inter-Regimental tournaments, Maj. Holder was of the opinion that a club had to have a four, or at least a three-gun team.[26]

In the 1920s, the 15th Lancers, the P.A.V.O. (Prince Albert Victor's Own) cavalry and the Central India Horse all fielded four-gun sides. Therefore, one or the other dominated Indian regimental polo for two decades, with only occasional intrusions by the 10th Hussars and the 17th/21st Lancers, the best two teams of soldiers in England.[27]

The social isolation prevalent in the 19th century did not undergo any changes during the remaining days of the Raj in British-ruled India. Lt. Col. Denzil Holder's candid reminiscences paint a picture of soldiers — mainly the cavalry — in military stations having few comings and goings with the civilians who, outside the big towns, were all in government service. If they did not meet at some sport or game, civil servants, army officers, and their

Maharaja Jai Singh of Jaipur, the Indian prince who led his own team on a clean sweep of all the major English trophies in 1933 (Museum of Polo and Hall of Fame).

families did not meet at all. The administrators lived quite distant from the garrisons in the civil lines, the habitat of the "heaven born," as usually called by the soldiers. The army officers were far away from their homes and relations; naturally, they clung together.

Rhetorically, Lt. Col. Holder questions himself, "What were the highlights of my time in India? First of all, of course, polo: the thunder of galloping hooves, the dash for the ball, the thrill of those few feet clearing or avoiding an opponent. Then our ponies — our capital, their performance on the ground, the price we paid for them, usually raw and unbroken, the way they were trained and what we sold them for, to other buyers."[28]

New Zealand

It was extraordinary, surely an indication of the spirit inherent in the game, that, despite the rigours of the Great Depression in the New Zealand community, not least on the farming front, men both old and young somehow contrived to play polo. — Sir Terence McLean[29]

It was in 1920 that Mr. Robert L. Levin — later to be president of the New Zealand Polo Association — began his quest for a national polo grounds. This search crystallized when the Fielding Jockey Club allowed the making of a polo ground inside the racing track. Play began in 1923 and the new ground was the best in New Zealand. There was no doubt that the availability of this field, as level as a billiard table, contributed enormously to the improvement of polo on the isles. In spite of the difficult economic situation, the number of polo clubs in New Zealand grew from nine in 1921 to sixteen in 1929. The Fielding polo ground became the venue for the Savile Cup, the oldest sporting trophy in New Zealand. The question of the Savile Cup being played alternatively on the South Island was pragmatically solved by holding two tournaments in the North Island, where most of the polo activity was carried out, and one in Christchurch every third year. The main ground in the South Island was on Hagley Park, the scene of the first international matches against the Australians. This scheme was in force until 1938, when, unfortunately, polo became dormant in the South Isle.[30]

There was no individual handicapping system in New Zealand until 1926, except for a team total handicap. This arrangement was not at all satisfactory because it produced many lopsided scores. Once more, Robert Levin came to the fore and arranged a committee to look at players on an individual basis. It was, however, a local national handicap, thus the several 10-goal players in pre-war New Zealand polo.[31] In international competitions, New Zealand handicaps were reduced by three goals.

Members of the Hawke's Bay Polo Club organized a team for participation in the newly created Australasian Gold Cup in Sidney. The team was Jack Lyons, Oswald Nelson, Fred and Willie Mackenzie, with Neil Campbell as a spare. During the first game, Nelson had a fall and was replaced by Campbell. Nevertheless, they were beaten in the first round by New South Wales. In 1934, the Christchurch Polo Club sent a team to compete in the Gold Cup in a tournament held in conjunction with the Melbourne Centennial. Gilbert H. Grigg, Richard M.D. "Peter" Johnson, Capt. George Hennessy and Derrick Gould were accompanied by Dan Riddiford and Peter D. Hall as alternates. Johnson and Hennessy were retired British Army officers. In the first round, the New Zealanders defeated Victoria by the exorbitant score of twenty to one. The good play of the visitors was maintained for the first three chukkers of the semifinals against Queensland, in which Johnson was the dominant player. Then a Queensland player galloped with determination at Johnson, shattering his right leg. Fifty years later, Mrs. Grigg had no doubt that the incident was intentional.[32] Dan Riddiford, one of the alternates, had returned to New Zealand because of his father's death; therefore, Peter Hall, a weaker player, replaced Johnson. Queensland won the match, only to be defeated in the finals by New South Wales — Phil, Geoffrey and Jim Ashton, plus 20-year-old Bob Skene. The Ashtons and, it seemed, all Australians, did their best to assure the Christchurch players of their sympathy.

Was this incident the result of an exaggerated display of Geebung polo? Someone with the pen-name "Barracker" wrote in Queensland's *Toowoomba Chronicle* the following line in doggerel: "Unless you'll lightly risk your neck you're not a polo man."[33] The incident is briefly mentioned in Keith Little's *Polo in New Zealand*, and not at all in Gene Makin's *History of Polo in Queensland*. Perhaps Mrs. Makin herself provides the answer. Specifically referring to the 1934 Australasian Gold Cup, she writes, "All the ponies had interchangeable saddles made by the same saddler. Each saddle weighted 20 pounds, and was heavily stuffed, with extremely long saddle flaps and knee rolls. The surcingle went through the saddle, while the long saddle flaps protected the rider's trousers from sweat. Woe betide anyone who, when riding off, got his knee against one of these Queensland knee rolls!"[34]

On the same page, Gene Makin mentions that Frank Armstrong broke his collarbone in a practice match against New Zealand and had to be replaced by Michael "Mick" MacGinley, the father of Jim and Pat MacGinley of post World War II polo fame.[35] To place things into perspective, Kiwi polo had a reputation for hard riding. Paul Withers, a tough competitor, had this to say in an interview many years on: "But I do feel that U.S. polo is less rough than the New Zealand game — there it's like rugby on horse back."[36]

New Zealand took another shot at the Australasian Gold Cup in 1938, when the New Zealand Polo Association sent to Sydney a team of Bob Nolan, George Peake, Bob Mackenzie and Ken Peake, with Gordon Vosper and Lyall Kay as reserves. The tournament was played on the Kyeemagh Polo Ground — now part of Sydney's airport — as part of Australia's 150th Anniversary celebrations. The team from New Zealand defeated Victoria's Hunt Club in the first round and the Hunter River team from New South Wales in the second round. The final match pitted New Zealand against, once more, the Ashton brothers, two of whom were on the Town and Country Club. Accurate hitting and the speed of their ponies accounted for the first victory for New Zealand in the Australasian Gold Cup. Bob and Geoffrey Ashton, together with J.D. MacLeod and W.W. Horsley, played for Town and Country. Their best ponies had been left in England following their conquest of the Hurlingham Champion Cup in the previous year.

There were great expectations in New Zealand for a visit of a full Australian team to challenge for the Gold Cup in 1939. It was not to be. Nevertheless, the New Zealand Polo Association requested, and was granted, permission to hold the competition, which took place at Fielding. Three teams competed: Waikato, East Coast and West Coast. In the final game, the East Coast, Jack Lyons, Jock, Bob and Fred Mackenzie, beat the West Coast's Ken Duncan, Rex McKelvie, Tom Gaddum and Ian Parsons.

When war was declared on 3 September 1939, Harold Elworthy, a polo player from the Pareora Club, rode to Burham Military Camp leading two other horses. Within days, the Canterbury Yeomanry Cavalry had assembled more than one-thousand horses. Years later, Elworthy noted, "They didn't last, of course. It seemed only the Poles and the Canterbury Yeomanry Cavalry were ready to take on Adolf Hitler on horseback!"[37]

South Africa

The evolution of polo in South Africa during the inter-war period was rather slow. The customary conservatism in most, if not all, ruling bodies of the game accounted for much of the creeping process. The question about height of ponies was an example. Measurement was difficult to enforce in the few countries still adhering to the letter of the rules. This issue was discussed for several years within the South African Polo Association at its annual general meetings. In 1919, the motion "that height limit should be done away with" was defeated, while the following year it passed that the height should be 14.2 hands.

In 1922, a long debate took place about the same issue. Hugh Brown, a respected player and administrator, again proposed that the height limit be abolished, and he amplified his motion to include that the ponies must be suitable for polo. Mr. Brown explained that polo in South Africa was under the Hurlingham Rules, and should a team be sent "home" to play in England, the South Africans would be at a great disadvantage. Opponents to the motion pointed out that increasing the height would make the game more dangerous and more expensive. The East Griqualand representative indicated that their ponies were on the small side, and they would not be able to compete against Natal. Some delegates stated that because other countries had abolished height limits, there was no reason why South Africa should follow suit. Like in many other controversial questions everywhere, the matter was postponed, to be reconsidered at the next meeting. After much argument, the decision to abolish height limitation was finally adopted in 1924, South Africa then being in line with all other polo associations.[38]

On the other hand, the issue of individual handicaps had been tackled as early as 1911, when two British Army officers, Capt. the Hon. John D.Y. Bingham, 15th Hussars, and Capt. Maurice N. Kennard, 6th Dragoon Guards, were handicapped at 8 goals in the first list published by the South African Polo Association.[39] At the same time, South Africans Campbell G. Shaw and J.G. "Jo" Shaw were rated at 7 goals. South Africa has never had a 10-goal player; John "Jack" McKenzie and Allan L. Ross, both from the Cotswold Club, were the first 9-goalers, in 1926. George Ian Gibson and E.E.E. "Tommy" Pope, in 1949, were the only other South African players to reach that rarified atmosphere.

The social event of the 1920s in South Africa was the visit of the Prince of Wales, the polo-playing heir to the throne of England. The South African Polo Association went into high gear to assess and solve questions regarding the organization of matches for the prince, the choosing of players, the selection of ponies for the prince and delicate issues of protocol for guests in the Royal Enclosure. There was a very active social set in Durban, the site of the main match, and the 'flappers' of the day, led by the daughters of the affluent society, were in an unseemly competition to be presented to the Prince of Wales. Everything went well. The prince scored a goal during the match at Stamford Hill, which his team duly won by the odd goal in seven. The royal visitor presented a trophy, the Prince of Wales Cup, and acquiesced to be patron of the South African Polo Association. With all the publicity surrounding the visit, it was a high water mark for the game in South Africa.

Polo during this period was dominated by a few clubs. Initially, it was the Cotswold of the Rosses, the Shaws and the McKenzies that held sway, with an occasional hiccup induced by Karkloof. Then, Durban, led by Hugh Brown and completed with Sidney "Algy" Amos, Russell Burdon, Ernest Greene and Dr. Andrew Walbrugh, took over as the top team. Hugh Brown's tragic death in the course of a match at Pietermaritzburg cast a dark spell on South African polo.

The 1930s saw Mooi River and Karkloof divide the spoils of victory. It was a period of growth and improvement for South African players and their ponies. However, writing for the *American Polo* magazine, Leonard Putterill bemoaned the apparent decline of the game in South Africa.

> Climatically the South African sky is usually free from clouds, but from a polo point of view, its azure blue is considerably obscured by a large cloud, which casts something of a shadow on the fair prospect of polo's progress. In its efforts to win recruits, polo is balked by four obstacles. These are rugby, ignorance, motor cars and the press.... Polo in South Africa is generally played in the winter months from March to September. This period clashes, unfortunately, with the football season and as rugby is the South African national game and seems to have an overpowering attraction for all young men athletically inclined; it is obvious that recruits from this source are negligible. Professional and businessmen ... will not entertain the idea of taking up polo on the plea of its overwhelming costliness.
>
> [T]he majority of South African players are anything but well off, and anyone coming to this country with leanings toward polo will be delighted at the small cost at which the game can be played. Misconceptions can perhaps, with time and patience, be removed, but nothing short of a drying up of all petrol supplies will cause polo's chief enemy to succumb. The motor car has removed the horse from the roads, from the farms and, worst of all, from the minds of potential polo players. Horsemanship, in pre-war days, was an universal ambition. Now it is regarded as an accomplishment of very questionable utility.
>
> The South African press (just like the press of other lands) could do much to for the advancement of polo.... Every sport in the country, with the notable exception of polo, owes a debt of gratitude to the press. The majority of South African players are farmers. Professional and commercial men show little interest in the game. The regrettable fact might indicate that South African farmers are in happier financial circumstances than the city men. Such a deduction would be incorrect and in any case polo in South Africa is not necessarily a rich man's game.[40]

The results of the South African tour to Argentina contradicted some of Mr. Putterill's misgivings. It is interesting that one year prior to the polo tour, a Junior Springboks rugby team had traveled to Buenos Aires, and the lessons learned by the locals made a significant contribution to the improvement of rugby football in Argentina. The sporting ties between the two countries have remained alive to this day.

Under Hugh Brown's management, the touring team included Russell Burdon and Ernest Greene from Durban, Ian Gibson from Mooi River, Martin Henderson from Bergville, Tommy Pope from The Levels and Allan Ross from Nottingham Road. The Springboks, as they were called in Argentina, did very well under the circumstances. The circumstances were many and varied. Most important, the pony string was not up to par. Although the Argentine Polo Association had offered to bear the cost of shipping ponies from South Africa, the shipping lines were unable to accommodate the horses. The result was that the South African players had to do with horses that were not to their liking. Bluntly, Ian Gibson said about the ponies: "The only thing they are good at is pulling and by Jove they go and don't stop."[41]

After the touring party had returned home, Hugh Brown stated, "The ponies were on average much bigger than the average South African pony, were schooled in a totally different manner and trained to a different kind of polo from ours. It seems that although the Argentineans hosts had allotted forty ponies for the tourists to choose from few of these were really experienced due to the fact that American and English buyers had snapped up and bought all the best ponies."[42]

In addition to all that, injuries bedeviled the visitors. Ernest Greene was bucked off an overfed pony and was on forced rest for two weeks. Allan Ross was thrown off by a pony and damaged his back, being unable to play for the rest of the tour. Another pony fell on top of

Martin Henderson, who sustained a concussion and was out of commission for two weeks. The Springboks now had only three fit players.

In spite of all those misadventures, the South African team defeated Santa Inés — a three-time Argentine championship team — in the first round, and Coronel Suárez, in a stirring match that went into overtime, in the semifinals, when Henderson played instead of Tommy Pope. Greene, Gibson, Burdon and Pope, who was back and team captain, played in the rest of the Open games, wearing green jerseys with gold springboks. The final game was against the crack team Santa Paula, one of the best teams in the world, as evidenced by past wins in both the United States and Argentine open championships. The South Africans went down to an honorable defeat.

To put the South African team achievement into perspective, only three other foreign teams have reached the final game of the Argentine Open Championship. Meadow Brook took the open in 1932; the American Army team lost to Santa Paula in 1930, and Bostwick Field was defeated by Venado Tuerto in 1950. The Springboks did very well facing adversity and bad luck. Most important, they left behind a sense of sportsmanship and warm friendship within the Argentine polo community that served South African polo well in future years. Argentine and South African teams have always been welcomed in each other's countries, regardless of final scores in polo games.

As a memento of their visit to Buenos Aires, the South African Polo Association presented in 1934 a sculpture of a stylized springbok — South Africa's games image — designed by Durban artist Mary Ann Stainbank. It is played for to this day at Palermo in a series between selected civilian and military teams, which is extremely popular among polo aficionados. The legacy of the 1933 Polo Springboks lives on.

16. The Cup of the Americas

Basically, in the lexicon of American polo there is no situation which does not justify attack. — Herbert Reed[1]

Among the thousands that were present at Meadow Brook for the 1927 Westchester Cup, there was a tall and lean Argentine player, Jack Nelson, who at the time was also the Argentine Polo Association's president. Mr. Nelson was widely respected in the polo world for his role in the celebrated 1922 Argentine team that had taken both the Hurlingham Champion Cup in England and the U.S. Open Championship at Rumson, New Jersey, and his captaincy of the Olympic gold medal team in Paris. His mission was to obtain a place for Argentina in the challenge for the Westchester Cup.

Jack Nelson was a towering figure in Argentine polo. He was born in Buenos Aires into a wealthy Irish family — his mother was a Duggan — that owned extensive estancias such as Salalé and San Marcos and a meat packing plant that exported beef to Britain. Young Juan Diego Nelson was educated at Beaumont College near Windsor, and at Stonyhurst, the Jesuits' school in Lancashire. This accounted for his affinity to all things British: family, education, language and sartorial elegance. The manor house at San Marcos appeared to be a transplant from the English countryside and his ponies always demonstrated superior breeding. Invariably, their turnout was perfect and they were awarded many prizes at international shows, including Best in Show given to his mare Judy at Meadow Brook. As a player, he reached an 8-goal handicap. Nelson was captain on the Argentine team that took the gold Olympic medal in Paris, and non-playing captain of the 1936 team in Berlin. Nelson represented Argentina in the Cup of the Americas and the Coronation Cup, in which he participated intermittently between 1922 and 1953, the last one at an age when most watch polo from the stands. Jack Nelson is one of the few players to have taken the American, Argentine and British Open Championships. Although Nelson invariably played for Hurlingham, he was one of the leaders in the struggle against the Polo Association of the River Plate which culminated with the creation of the Asociación Argentina de Polo. Jack Nelson was a three-time president of the A.A. de Polo. His last term was cut short when he resigned rather than bend to the pressures exerted by the government upon the polo association.

This was the man who met with Mr. Louis E. Stoddard, chairman of the United States Polo Association, and the 2nd Lord Cowdray, his counterpart in the Hurlingham Club Polo Committee. At this meeting, it was made quite clear to him that the terms of deed for the

Jack Nelson was the creator of the Cup of the Americas. Three-time president of the Argentine Polo Association, winner of the Argentine, English and American Open Championships, Olympic gold medalist, and outstanding breeder of polo ponies, Nelson personified high-class polo (Museum of Polo and Hall of Fame).

Westchester Cup stated that competition for the trophy was the absolute preserve of America and the United Kingdom.

Mr. John D. Nelson was convinced that the development of polo in Argentina had reached a level commensurate with those of the United States, and certainly, of Britain. His entreaties being rebuffed, Nelson proposed to Mr. Stoddard the idea of a Championship of the Americas between teams from Argentina and the United States. The seeds fell on fertile ground because since the end of World War I, America had inflicted upon the British team six overwhelming defeats in the series played at Hurlingham and Meadow Brook. Under the terms of the gift of deed, the new series would have to wait until 1930, and America, rising on the crest of the roaring twenties prosperity, was eager for more international contests.

After discussion, the U.S.P.A. Executive Committee accepted the idea and the first series between Argentina and the United States was scheduled for the summer of 1928, to take place at Meadow Brook.

Argentina marshaled their best in men and mounts. Arturo Kenny, a gentleman-rider of repute in the flat and an Olympic polo champion, was the choice to play at number 1. Jack Nelson, another Olympian player, was to fill his usual number 2 position. The team was completed with John Miles and Lewis Lacey; both could play back or number 3 with identical facility. The reserve player was Manuel "Paisano" Andrada, a burly player who always played at back. In essence, it was the 1924 Olympic gold medal team with Lewis Lacey replacing Col. Enrique Padilla. The pony string was truly exceptional; it represented the best of the crop in Argentina. Tommy Nelson, Jack's cousin, was in charge of the horses.

For the well-established American international team it was a time for change. When Devereux Milburn announced his retirement from international polo, the last link with the famous Big Four of 1909 was broken. Harry Payne Whitney had retired from high-goal competition; Monty Waterbury passed away and his brother Larry turned his attention to thoroughbred racing. Out of the successful 1927 team, left-handed Watson Webb retired from high-handicap polo and then Malcolm Stevenson announced he was quitting; however, the thought of abandoning the fray of international challenge was too much for the veteran, and he relented. That left the newly anointed captain, Tommy Hitchcock, solid at number 2, and Stevenson the best choice at number 3. For the number 1 slot, Army Captain Chandler Wilkinson was the early favorite, but he played himself into the ground and lost his form. This left the position to be gained by either Averell Harriman or Stephen Sanford. The latter was selected, but not for long. Being aware that Sanford, although beautifully mounted, was adverse to rough play, Mr. Harriman arranged that in one of the final practice games Manuel Andrada would play at back on the opposing team. During the match, strongman Andrada made mincemeat out of Sanford.[2] Laddie Sanford was out of the international team and Averell Harriman in. The press was not immediately notified of the change; to make matters worse, when the official program was published just before the first match, it listed Stephen Sanford at number 1, and his photograph was included in the program.[3]

At back, Bobby Strawbridge was the initial choice, but his play during the season was not up to his previous standard; therefore, John Cheever Cowdin was chosen over Winston Guest. The rationale was that Cowdin — a sentimental favorite — although not as heavy a hitter as Guest, was a much better defensive player, because up to then Guest had played mostly at number 2. Team captain Thomas Hitchcock, Jr., would have none of that. Tommy Hitchcock proved then, as he was to prove again later, that when it came to assembling the best possible team, he would not allow anything or anyone to stand in his way. Hitchcock felt strongly that Guest was a far better player than Cowdin, and insisted that a change be made. As usual, Tommy got his way and personally told Cowdin he was out of the team. John Cheever Cowdin, his dream of representing America — as his father had done before him — was completely shattered, and abandoned playing polo.

The large number of trial matches proved to be too long, tiring for both ponies and players. It ended with unnecessary public humiliation for two of the best American players, Sanford and Cowdin.

Richard E. Danielson, president and editor of *The Sportsman*, a prestigious magazine, while asserting that the games were intensely exciting and brilliant, felt that the vacillations, shifts, and expediencies surrounding the successive choices of the players to make up the American team were "unedifying and unhappy." "They contrasted rather shabbily with the calm of the gentlemen from Argentina, who faced their difficulties without panic and played what they considered to be their best side without discrimination or dispute."[4]

What were the difficulties experienced by the Argentines? There was only one; however, it was huge. Shortly before the onset of the series, the entire pony string was afflicted with a form of influenza which substantially drained their strength. The indefatigable Tommy Nelson refused all social invitations and lived at the barn, ministering to the horses. The rain that plagued the entire summer and prevented many practice games from taking place allowed some extra time for the ponies to recover. The U.S.P.A. postponed the first game for one week and offered the visitors extra mounts. Nevertheless, the Argentines elected to use their own ponies.

When the first match was played, a slow, persistent rain affected Arturo Kenny's play considerably, because he was wearing spectacles that consistently were fogged. Unable to see well, the usually accurate striker missed many chances at goal and did not keep his forward position, bunching up on his number 2, Jack Nelson. The Americans were indeed lucky to win by the odd goal. Then came the second match. Both teams rode with the wildest sort of chance taking, and in the end, the fierce, concentrated attack of the Argentines finally came through. In Robert F. Kelley's opinion, it was the hardest game played in international competition. For the first time since the American style of polo became the accepted thing, the United States players found themselves facing men willing and able to bump and mix it up in rough play. Argentina took the match easily.

Changes were made in the American team. Malcolm Stevenson, a stalwart defensive player, was sacrificed in a gamble that an all out attack game would break the visitors' tired pony string. Earle Hopping, Jr., at twenty years old the youngest American international, was inserted at number 2, and Hitchcock moved back to number 3.

The third and decisive game was anticlimactic. Lewis Lacey had not fully recovered from a hard fall in the third chukker of the second game, the result of a collision with Tommy Hitchcock. There was talk in the Argentine quarters of replacing Lacey with Andrada; however, it was hard to make changes on a team that had played so well in the second match. Nevertheless, the final result was due to the superior pony power of the Americans. The Argentine ponies, debilitated after the bout of influenza and two hard matches on Saturday and Wednesday, could not handle a third game on Saturday.

In his biography of Tommy Hitchcock, Nelson Aldrich, Jr., writes, "The Argentines for their part were bitterly disappointed. One of them, Miles, blamed the ponies, a strange remark for someone who within a week would sell those same animals for the largest sums ever paid to that time for polo ponies."[5]

Aldrich got it wrong. What John Miles said it was the ponies' health that let them down, not the ponies themselves. Robert Kelley, the highly respected reporter for *The New York Times*, stated, "The United States polo team was lucky to win in the series for the championship of the Americas against Argentina."[6] Kelley adds, "It seems almost an effrontery to criticize the play of anyone in the series of 1928. Giving every credit in the world to the fine fashion in which Mr. Harriman rose to the occasion in that first match, there is still the undeniable fact that the South American ponies were badly out of things for the most part."[7]

It is interesting that no permanent trophy was awarded after the 1928 contest. Photographs taken at the prize-giving ceremony illustrate a large silver bowl that is different from the trophy for the Cup of the Americas presented in 1932. Neither the U.S. Polo Association nor the National Museum of Polo were able to provide information about the cup's whereabouts.[8] What is known is that the association had beforehand decided to only present individual mementos of the series. In the magazine *Polo*, Peter Vischer stated that the U.S. Polo Association carefully avoided setting a precedent by the award of a permanent cup.[9] According to Vischer, the authorities had no desire at the time to tie future generations of polo players to conditions that might prove uncomfortable or undesirable. It was no secret that some of the conditions attached to the Westchester Cup had proved to be a bit irksome. At the time, it had to be challenged every three years, and the holders must accept the challenge, regardless of whether challengers or hosts were ready or not.

Another writer, Robert Kelley, mentioned that the Championship of the Americas, the official title of the series, roused the ire of the Mexican polo authorities, who wanted to know why they had been left out of the competition.[10] Kelley, who also wrote for *The New York Times*, also mentions that a permanent trophy was to have been presented to the winning team of the 1928 contest and the announcement was very nearly made when the conservative fac-

The 1928 United States team, winner of the Cup of the Americas in three hard fought matches. These men won the decisive game at Meadow Brook (from left): Averell Harriman, Earle A.S. Hopping, Thomas Hitchcock, Jr., and Winston Guest (Museum of Polo and Hall of Fame).

tion in American polo carried the day. They held that the Westchester Cup series with the United Kingdom must remain the feature of international polo. Therefore, only the players received individual trophies.

1932 at Palermo, Buenos Aires

Continuing the rather haphazard ways which characterized the initial steps in the Cup of the Americas, the American team's journey to Argentina was remarkable for its conditional participation in the contest. The Americans would defend the Cup of the Americas only if they were successful in the Argentine Open.[11] What would have happened if the American team failed to take the Open Championship? It was a rather unsporting request by the U.S. Polo Association, and the Asociación Argentina de Polo had no choice but to accept the demand. Another request made by the U.S.P.A. was that Tomás Nelson, the celebrated polo pony trainer, would be in charge of the American string.

California player Carleton F. Burke was appointed manager of the American invasion. His selected team, Mike Phipps, Winston Guest, Elmer Boeseke, Jr., and Billy Post, duly won the Open Championship, and, with Guest and Boeseke changing places, took the Cup of the Americas in three hard-contested matches. The American reserve players—Stewart Iglehart,

An aerial view of Palermo grounds in 1937. The Number 1 field is in the foreground and the number 2 field is at a right angle. The Palermo racehorse track is to the right and the River Plate is in the background (private collection).

Seymour Knox, Jimmy Mills, Cocie Rathborne and Laddie Sanford — participated in the Open Championship on different local teams without achieving any success at all.

The visit of the American team was a big event in Buenos Aires; much more so than the previous tour by the U.S. Army team.[12] The final match of the Argentine Open Championship turned out to be a very good game. Santa Paula, on top of the heap at the time, had lost, once more, Alfredo Harrington's services due to a broken leg during the Hurlingham Open. Luis Tomás Nelson, Jack's older brother, replaced Harrington. The rest of the team was the Reynal brothers and Manuel Andrada. Meadow Brook took the open by one goal after trailing until the last chukker. Cocie Rathborne, one of the American alternates, wrote that Meadow Brook had a great deal of luck in winning the Open Championship.[13]

Seymour Knox was showing good form during the practice matches, while Mike Phipps did not play up to his capabilities in the Argentine Open. Team manager Burke decided to keep Phipps in the line-up; however, he changed Winston Guest from the number 2 position to number 3, switching places with Elmer Boeseke. In the event itself, the U.S. team took the first match by three goals, lost the second in sudden death extra time and won the third and decisive game by two goals.

Both the Argentine Open Championship and the Cup of the Americas series stressed the importance of accurate penalty taking. In the Open Championship finals José Reynal and Manuel Andrada missed several penalty conversions, while Winston Guest usually was accurate in his penalty-shooting attempts. The first match for the Cup of the Americas was more of the same. Winston Guest converted three penalties for America, while for Argentina, Reynal missed three and Andrada failed in two attempts. In the second game, José Reynal gave the victory to Argentina when he converted a free hit from 60 yards out.

In his assessment of the series, Cocie Rathborne gives credit to Phipps and Boeseke, the American forwards, for their blocking of Andrada and José Reynal, which allowed Winston Guest to roam free and constantly place the Argentine goal in jeopardy. Billy Post, in the eyes of many observers the best player of the series, played superbly at back. It was also felt that the pony string played by the Americans reached the final stages of the competitions in better condition than the Argentine ponies. The expertise shown by Tommy Nelson in managing the American polo pony string amply confirmed the trust placed on him by the U.S. Polo Association. This well-deserved recognition evoked bittersweet memories in many Argentine sympathizers.

Thus, the brand new trophy for the Cup of the Americas, donated by Argentina's president and manufactured by Mappin & Webb in London, made a journey to America. The trophy itself is copied, like the Grenfell Cup in Canada, from the Warwick Vase. It is decorated with masks and trophies between borders of acanthus and fruiting vines. The rim and pedestal have tongue and dart bead borders and the handles represent entwined vines. The vase features classical bacchal masks and associated emblems such as a pinecone tip staff known as a thyrsus, together with classical leaves and intertwined naturalistic handles, raised on a square plinth.[14]

1936 at Meadow Brook

The Argentines prepared for the 1936 challenge with extreme thoroughness. From a land that prided itself on breeding the best polo ponies came a string of horses that was universally hailed as the best ever to be shipped from Buenos Aires. The team accomplished devastating victories in the Olympic Games, 15–5 versus Mexico and 11–0 against Great Britain. In addition to a superb pony string, fourteen more ponies were sent to New York. The legendary Tommy Nelson was, once more, in charge of the ponies. The team was made up by Luis Duggan, a superior rider who became one of the best ever at number 1; the young giant Roberto Cavanagh, Andrés Gazzotti, and at back, the redoubtable Manuel Andrada. In their prime, they would have been a 38-goal team.

The U.S. Polo Association set aside its long-honored and well-proven selection method in favor of a simple scheme that rewarded the winner of the Open Championship with the responsibility of defending the national colors. Perhaps it was assumed that Templeton, Winston Guest's team, complemented with Mike Phipps and Stewart Iglehart — three members of the victorious American team in London — plus Jimmy Mills, an alternate on the Westchester Cup team, would certainly win the Open and be the best combination to face the mounting threat posed by the South Americans. As it were, Tommy Hitchcock led Jock Whitney's foursome to a sudden death win over Templeton in the Open. The U.S.P.A., having promised the team captains their reward, could not honorably back off. Therefore, it was that the Argentines took the Cup with ease, winning matches, 21–9 and 8–4. At no time was there any indication that the United States team could mount a serious threat to the visitors. At one stage during the first match, the Argentines scored 15 consecutive goals in the most lopsided defeat inflicted upon an international American team since 1886.

The Argentine squad that took the Olympic gold medal in Berlin and the Cup of the Americas at Meadow Brook, a magnificent double, were (left to right) Andrés Gazzotti, Jack Nelson, Roberto Cavanagh, Luis Duggan, Manuel Andrada, Enrique Alberdi and Diego Cavanagh (Museum of Polo and Hall of Fame).

Diego Cavanagh and Stewart Iglehart were the umpires. Diego was Roberto Cavanagh's older brother, so it is probably one of the few instances in international competition when a player's close relative was asked to be an official. Diego Cavanagh was considered the best umpire in Argentina and he had umpired the final game in the Olympic competition in Berlin. The Americans took a different attitude during the East-West series. Earle W. Hopping, Sr., was one of the umpires in the first game; when his son was announced as Mike Phipps' replacement for the second game, Hopping Senior was in turn replaced by James Watson Webb.

Peter Vischer, *Polo* magazine's editor, rushed to defend the U.S. Polo Association's decision in regards to the American international team. "There was no better No. 1 in the Open Championship this year than Pete Bostwick; a superlative horseman, well mounted, quick to strike and a fighting competitor, he would have deserved a place in any international four. There was no stronger No. 2 in the Open than Gerald Balding. Certainly Hitchcock was the outstanding No. 3 and the most successful team leader. And there was only one back in the Open who might fairly be said to have played better than John Hay Whitney, the Greentree back."[15]

Vischer, like many others, felt that the only change that should have been made it was at the number 2 position. "It was obviously absurd to let Gerald Balding play for the United States three months after he had played for Great Britain. The best interests of the game clearly demanded that four Americans represent the United States in an international sporting competition and no consideration, however important it may have seemed at the moment, should have been permitted to set a precedent that may return many times in the future to plague the sport."[16]

With due respect to Mr. Vischer, it is difficult to understand the U.S. Polo Association's rationale in the selection process. If Templeton had won the Open, Tommy Hitchcock, at the time the best player in the world, would have been out of the team. As it was, players of the caliber of Elbridge Gerry, Winston Guest, Earle Hopping, Jr., Stewart Iglehart, Jimmy Mills, Eric Pedley, Michael Phipps and Cecil Smith — two full teams — were left out from the selection process without any consideration. Was it a feeling of *deja vu* on the part of the U.S.P.A. leaders? Alternatively, was it a false sense of security?

There is no question that the U.S. Polo Association leadership bears a great part of responsibility for the debacle of 1936. It is also interesting that the usual white jerseys worn by the American international teams were discarded in this series for the Cup of the Americas. In the first match, the United States team sported red jerseys, while in the second game the players wore Greentree's pink shirts. Perhaps it was a subtle reminder that in the U.S. Polo Association's eyes it was not a real international; therefore, it did not matter too much.

Most certainly, it mattered a lot to the Argentines. When the polo team returned to Buenos Aires, a multitude congregated at the port of Buenos Aires to give the players a heroes' welcome. Two large landowners of Irish descent, a small tenant-farmer son of Italian immigrants and a gaucho with Spanish blood had written a glorious page in Argentine polo: Olympic Gold medalists and champions of the Americas.

1950 at Palermo

The United States delegation that traveled to Buenos Aires was headed by 9-goaler George Oliver at number 3 and young Peter Perkins, an 8-goaler, at number 2. At back, Lewis Smith from Aurora, and George "Pete" Bostwick at number 1, filled out the remaining places on the team. It added up to a 32-goal combination. Reserve players were Delmar Carroll and Jules Romfh, while Robert Strawbridge, Jr., accompanied the team as non-playing captain. Ten ponies were flown to Buenos Aires, to be complemented by sixteen selected ponies loaned by Argentine sportsmen.

The team entered the Argentine Open as Bostwick Field — the reigning U.S. champion — in preparation for the series for the Cup of the Americas. Unexpectedly, Bostwick Field found strong opposition from a 22-goal team, La Espadaña, formed with the Garrahan brothers, Tommy and Louie, Carlos Debaisieux and Héctor Zavalía. It was touch and go until towards the end of the epic contest a few penalties sealed La Espadaña's fate; the dream did not become reality for the local upstarts. In the semifinals, Bostwick Field defeated the military team San Jorge, only to face the mighty Venado Tuerto, which at 37 goals was the top rated team in the world. Cousins Juan and Roberto Cavanagh and brothers Enrique and Juan Carlos Alberdi had survived a monumental scare in their semifinal game versus El Trébol, their ancient adversary. Trailing through most of the match, it was only in the last chukker that they were able to surge ahead by the margin of two goals, in what was called the "match of the century."

Many observers felt that a favorable draw had helped Bostwick Field to reach the finals because the Argentine Polo Association was in need of gate receipts to cover the expenses of bringing over a foreign team. The events of the previous year were very much alive in the authorities' minds, when unheralded La Concepción had eliminated Meadow Brook in the

Open's second round. The expected final encounter between Venado Tuerto and Meadow Brook did not take place and the stands at Palermo were only half full. Nevertheless, Venado Tuerto defeated Bostwick Field to take their sixth Argentine Open.

For the Cup of the Americas series, the Americans made one change: hard-riding Del Carroll, rated at seven goals, replaced eight-goaler Pete Bostwick at number 1. The Argentine Polo Association nominated the full Venado Tuerto team to wear the sky-blue and white national colors. It was a formidable combination, one of the best teams ever. El Trébol's Carlos and Julio Menditeguy were the reserves.

The Argentines, never deficient in patriotism, were full of hope, almost of arrogance, because the Americans had not been very impressive in the Open Championship. This time they were a different team; nevertheless, in spite of a resolute performance, the United States was well and truly beaten after a magnificent match, by 14 goals to ten. In the second match, the Argentine team took off in the first chukker and was never caught. Although the Americans recovered somewhat, the goal differential was the same as in the initial match, 11–7. The men from Venado Tuerto played their usual game, reminiscent of Tommy Hitchcock tactics: two, sometimes three, hard shots placed their number 1, Juan Cavanagh, in a position to take aim at the American goal posts. The rest was pony power and tight man-to-man marking. Simple, yet quite effective.

The American squad acquitted itself well, playing up their aggregate handicap; had the matches been played on handicap, the United States would have won each one by two goals. George Oliver, repeatedly, was the bulwark of the United States team, ably supported by Peter Perkins. Lewis Smith was confined to a purely defensive role, while Carroll's hard riding found more than his match in the strong defense offered by the Alberdi brothers. The Argentine umpires, Hurlingham Club's Anthony Hobson and Daniel Kearney, who had been so lenient in the Bostwick Field game versus La Espadaña, whistled several times penalizing Delmar Carroll in the course of the first match. The second match, delayed several days because of rain, was eventually played on a heavy ground that became quite cut up, especially in front of the goal posts near the pony lines, in those days located in the southwest corner of the grounds. Only three penalties in the entire match were called by the same umpires who had officiated in the first game.[17]

In comparing the four teams representing American polo in Argentina, including Meadow Brook and Bostwick Field in those two years, 1949 and 1950, the consensus was that the 1949 World Championship team — Pete Bostwick, Peter Perkins, Bob Skene and Alan Corey — was the best. The weakest position in the United States team in the Cup of the Americas was at back. The spectators noticed that in the Open Championship, George Oliver took over from Lewis Smith the hit-ins because they lacked both distance and placement. Experienced observers, who ought to know, were of the opinion that the best American team would have been Bostwick, Carroll, Oliver and Perkins, in that order. They remembered the outstanding play shown by Perkins in the previous year during the 30-goal Inter-American series. Perkins played at back, his place at number 2 was taken by Clarence Combs. Like so many theoretical line-ups, it was never put to the test; however, it should be pointed out that it was the foursome originally selected to play in the Argentine Open Championship as Bostwick Field.[18]

1966 at Palermo

After a span of sixteen long years, Northrup Knox brought an American team back to Argentina.[19] Preparation began several months before, when the possible team members traveled to Santa Barbara, California, to compete in the U.S. Open Championship. The U.S. Polo Association changed the dates of the U.S. Open to the spring of 1966, allowing test matches to be played in California and at Oak Brook in Illinois. Alan Corey, George Sherman, Bob Skene and Cecil Smith formed the selection committee, which sent letters to all players rated at seven goals and higher, asking for their participation in trial matches. Pete Bostwick, Del

The American captain in two challenges for the Cup of the Americas, Northrup Knox, is on the bay mare Ragamuffin, one of the top polo ponies of the 1960s (Museum of Polo and Hall of Fame).

Carroll, Alan Corey, Ray Harrington, Bob Skene and Cecil Smith declined to participate in the trials. The final selection consisted of Harold "Chico" and Roy Barry, Robert Beveridge, Dr. William Linfoot, Jack Murphy, Allan Scherer and Lewis Smith, plus Northrup Knox as team captain.

Upon arriving in Argentina, the American players noticed that the Argentine wooden ball was much heavier that the one used in America, which resulted in poor hitting; the suggested solution was changing the mallet heads. The Americans decided not to enter the Argentine Open Championship because their ponies were not ready. In addition to the Cup of the Americas, the Argentine Polo Association had organized a 30-goal tournament in celebration of the 150th anniversary of independence from Spain. England, Argentina and the United States were the entrants.

The Argentine International team was entered in the Tortugas Open Championship, traditionally the initial leg of the Triple Crown. In the finals, the team under the name Selección Tortugas — in which Luis Lalor replaced Juan Carlos Harriott due to an accident suffered by Harriott Senior — defeated Tortugas-Aurora, a 28-goal team, by three goals.

As customary, the Hurlingham Open Championship preceded the Argentine Open. The final match was played between the Argentine 30-goal team — Alfredo and Juan Carlos Harriott, Jr., Gastón Dorignac and Gonzalo Tanoira — versus Windsor Park, who enlisted Alberto Pedro and Horacio Heguy, Daniel González and Prince Philip. Oddly enough, the Argentine team wore Hurlingham's jerseys. The eyes of the spectators were riveted on one of the Windsor Park players, Prince Philip, Duke of Edinburgh. A British prince playing in a Hurlingham Open Championship final was naturally an exciting and romantic event. Prince Philip, a very good back on his own merit, was never out of the picture in the entire match, which was won by the Argentine junior selection by the odd goal. Luck was said to be with the Argentine 30-goal team, but luck generally attends those who can take chances and half chances when they present themselves, and that was what the young team did at every opportunity. Not only that, but also some keen observers of the game felt the 30-goal team was better than the national squad was at 35-goals. The Handicap Committee seemed to agree; after the season was over, Alfredo Harriott was raised from 6 to 7 goals, Gastón Dorignac from 7 to 9 goals and Gonzalo Tanoira from 7 to 8 goals, making the juniors a 34-goal team.

The 30-goal tournament took place next. In a rough match, the British team, Patrick Kemple, Sinclair Hill, Ronald Ferguson and Paul Withers, defeated the Americans, only to be vanquished in turn by the Argentines in a lopsided match: 24–2. The Argentines eventually beat the American team and took the Copa Sesquicentenario.

The matches for the Cup of the Americas provided the best polo since the 1932 series. Two evenly matched teams, at 35 goals each, played two hard fought games, the Argentines emerging the victors, 10–6 and 14–10. The American team was Norty Knox, Dr. Billy Linfoot, Roy Barry and Harold "Chico" Barry. In the first game the Argentine team was Gastón Dorignac, Horacio Heguy, Juan Carlos Harriott, Jr., and Francisco Dorignac. For the second game, the selectors changed Horacio Heguy and Gastón Dorignac's positions.

There were different perceptions regarding the games. The Argentine press was rather restrained in their observations. Juan Carlos Harriott, Jr., was unanimously praised as the best player in the world, while Franky Dorignac drew laudatory comments for his defensive work at back. Horacio Heguy was brilliant at times, interspaced with some errors in front of the goal posts. Gastón Dorignac was not a member of the original squad, not even as an alternate. His outstanding performance on the 30-goal team merited his inclusion as a starter in the Cup of the Americas team when Alberto Pedro Heguy broke his hand in the second chukker of the Argentine Open final. The selectors, Luis Duggan, Juan and Roberto Cavanagh, chose Gastón over the alternates Horacio Baibiene, Daniel González, Luis Lalor and Carlos Torres Zavaleta.

In his diary, Norty Knox wrote: "Looking back at this game in retrospect, it is obvious that we came very close to winning. Although we were never ahead, the game was close throughout, and the score with one minute to go in the sixth chukker was but 11–10 for Argentina. The crowd reaction at this point was fantastic and cries of 'Argentina, Argentina' could be heard all over the field. Unfortunately, Heguy scored on a loose knock in at the end of the period and the U.S. Team could close the gap no further."[20]

What won the Cup of Americas for Argentina was pace. Not the speed of the ponies, which was about equal, but the speed of thinking and anticipation. In the sixteen years from their last series with Argentina, the Americans had been playing 22-goal polo at best, because of handicap restrictions and interchange between the two nations had been limited to individual visits. From America, Bob Skene, by then living in California, took two Open crowns for El Trébol and Pete Bostwick played in the Open for Venado Tuerto, a team that reached the final game. Argentine players participated in the 1957 U.S. Open at Oak Brook: Horacio Castilla on the Knox's Aurora team, Enrique Alberdi on Pete Bostwick's Meadow Brook and Roberto Cavanagh in the Dallas lineup with American ace Alan Corey. The Aurora team lost the final game in overtime.

In the meantime, a changing of the guard gradually took place in Argentina. The old warriors from El Trébol and Venado Tuerto were giving way to the new generation, best exemplified by outstanding men of great character such as Juancarlitos Harriott and Franky Dorignac. The older generations did much more than just move aside and make room for the budding stars. They became mentors to the young players, not only in play making and game strategy, but also in the all-important science of polo pony breeding. Juan Carlos Harriott, Jr., said of his mentor Enrique Alberdi: "The first Open we won, I played at number 2 and he played at number 3. Hell, he was all over me. He could not conceive that you could ever let up. There is going to be a moment in which your opponent is going to be distracted, and then is when you beat him."[21]

Perhaps the weak knock-in by Chico Barry in the second game was the moment of distraction for the American team and the turn-around point in the match, and maybe, in the series. Norty Knox quoted Juan Carlos Harriott, Jr.: "Even Juan Carlitos agreed after the game that if we had won this time, we would also have won the third match."[22]

The Argentine new style of polo, best personified by the Venado Tuerto foursome of the Cavanaghs and the Alberdis, was in many ways reminiscent of Tommy Hitchcock's approach to the game in the late 1920s: hit the ball hard and gallop as fast as your pony will take you in pursuit of the ball. Like those great American teams, Argentina had a superior player and tactician, in their case in the person of Juan Carlos Harriott, Jr. The Americans had to cope with the severe handicap of having a high-goal season lasting only three weeks; it was the only opportunity for the top players to meet each other and benefit for competition at such level. A true sportsman, Northrup Knox also wrote: "The umpiring on the field was very good — under tense conditions for both teams, and we had no excuses of any kind — Argentina was the best team."[23]

Nevertheless, the United States team provided a strong challenge to Argentina's polo supremacy in the South American spring of 1966. Years later, Francisco Dorignac was asked to compare the 1966 series with the 1969 challenge for the Cup of the Americas. His unequivocal answer was that the 1966 competition had been, by far, the most difficult.[24]

1969 at Palermo

In his remarks for the 1969 official program for the Cup of the Americas, Northrup R. Knox stated, "With the conclusion of the 1966 series, the question has never been 'would there be a renewal?' but rather, 'how soon could arrangements be completed?' for another series of matches between the two major polo nations in the world today."[25]

The U.S. Polo Association took the learning experience at the 1966 series to heart. However, something that remained was the burden placed upon one individual, in this case Northrup Knox, to handle both the captaincy of the team and all other matters surrounding the tour. In reading the diaries kept by Seymour Knox and his son Norty, the reader cannot fail to be impressed by the large amount of social events planned for the visiting team members and their wives.[26] Two, sometimes three, daily events, including *asados* (cookouts), cocktails, receptions, dinners and dancing, must have taken its toll upon the players. Perhaps there was no gracious way to send regrets for so many invitations because any visit of a foreign team is a big happening in Buenos Aires, and hosts vie with each other to offer the visitors the best possible hospitality.

Early in 1969, the U.S. Polo Association appointed a selection committee chaired by George Sherman, Jr., with Alan Corey and Cecil Smith as members. Five players were picked to travel: Harold Barry, Bennie Gutierrez, Ray Harrington, Dr. Billy Linfoot and, again as captain, Northrup Knox. Young Joe Barry, Chico's son, later joined the team as reserve. The American team was committed to participating in the Argentine Open following the completion of the Cup of the Americas series.

The Argentine Polo Association trusted the selection and management of the team to Juan Cavanagh, a proven resource and highly respected by the players themselves. No changes were made to the 1966 team; Gonzalo Tanoira, soon to be a 10-goal handicap player, was the alternate. The team experienced a hiccup in the Tortugas Open Championship when Mar del Plata, with Juan José Alberdi, Alfredo Goti, Jorge and Gonzalo Tanoira unexpectedly but deservedly defeated the national team. The "big" team, with Gonzalo Tanoira replacing Gastón Dorignac, easily took the Hurlingham Open.

The story of the Cup of the Americas can be simply told. The American squad arrived in September, allowing plenty of time for ponies and players to become acclimatized. The first match on 25 October did not bode well for the visitors' chances: at the end of four chukkers they were down 1–6. After the interval, Bennie Gutierrez was moved to back, Knox, Linfoot and Barry moving one position forward. The change worked very well, because the score in the last three chukkers was only 6–5 in favor of Argentina. Just like in 1966, the matches lasted seven periods each, as a compromise between the customary six chukkers played in America and the eight chukkers in high-goal Argentine polo.

Norty Knox penned these words in his diary: "We had no excuse after the game. We had all tried our best and had worked hard against a really great team, perhaps the strongest of all time. With Horacio [Heguy] at No. 1 and his extremely fast ponies, we were always on the defensive — always had to cover him, and with the constant aggressiveness of Gaston [Dorignac], our backs were to the game and the flow was in the direction of our goal."[27]

Juan Carlos Harriott's credo, "Force the opponent's number 3 to face his own goal," paid handsome dividends in this match. The pony strength was judged to be about equal between the two strings; however, hitting accuracy and length favored the local team. This time around, the American team found the offered polo balls to their liking; nevertheless, they changed the heads to the R.N.P.A. pattern, without significant improvement.[28]

The second game was more of the same. The Argentines took off from the first throw-in: 4–0 in the first chukker, 7–0 in the second and 9–1 in the third. In this chukker, Chico Barry took a fall when his pony's front legs tangled with Horacio Heguy pony's hind legs. Barry injured his left thumb and had to leave the game. Ray Harrington replaced him, but the die was cast. The final score was 18–6.

A dispirited American team played in the Argentine Open Championship in a round robin format against Coronel Suárez, Mar del Plata and Santa Ana. Victory again eluded the United States team. Following the team's return to America, the U.S. Polo Association adjusted its handicap list, lowering all team members by one goal. The top American players were rated at 8 goals, and the downward spiral affected even low-handicap players.

1979 at Palermo

After a hiatus of one decade, the U.S. Polo Association once more sent a challenge for the Cup of the Americas to its counterpart in Buenos Aires, the Asociación Argentina de Polo. The conditions appeared to be favorable from the American point of view. The 1970s were an epoch of growth and optimism in American polo. They were the best years since the end of World War II. Higher goal-handicap tournaments were staged, most notably the World Cup, started at Oak Brook, near Chicago, and continued with great success at Bill Ylvisaker's concoction, the Palm Beach Polo Club in Florida. The World Cup offered substantial prize money and attracted teams and individual players from Argentina on a scale not seen before.

The 1979 World Cup provided a satisfactory appetizer for the American players. Bart Evans, Tommy Wayman, Lester "Red" Armour and Harold A. "Joe" Barry, playing under the banner Texas–U.S.A., defeated in sudden-death overtime a Coronel Suárez team from Argentina that included the best player in the world, Juan Carlos Harriott, Jr., and was completed with Horacio Araya, Ernesto Trotz and Celestino Garrós.

The selected team, fifty horses, grooms, a veterinarian, farriers, family and helpers departed in early September, as the matches were scheduled for November. Bart Evans declined to travel and the team was completed with Roy Barry, Joel Baker, Corky Linfoot and Charles Smith. Harold L. "Chico" Barry was the coach, while the enterprise was sponsored by Steven Gose to the tune of $600,000. Nothing that could have been planned was left out, for it was the most carefully planned expedition to Argentina ever.

All that was necessary, because the task was daunting. Argentine, barring injuries, was sure to field the best polo team ever, Coronel Suárez, the 40-goal machine of the brothers Alberto Pedro and Horacio Heguy, Juan Carlos Harriott, Jr., and Alfredo Harriott. The reserves were only two: Héctor "Cacho" Merlos, 9 goals, at forward, and yet another 10-goaler, Gonzalo Tanoira, as a defensive replacement.

Rather than select a representative team early, coach Chico Barry decided to try multiple combinations during the weeks of preparation. After much discussion and several changes, the United States foursome in the first match was Charles Smith, Tommy Wayman, Red

Armour and Joe Barry. The high hopes of the large American contingent of supporters that had made the long journey to the southern latitudes were quickly shattered. At the end of the third period, the score was 10–1 in favor of the local team and 12–2 at the break. At the final bell, the scoreboard read Argentina 18, America 6.

Heavy rains forced the postponement of the second match for two weeks, a span of time which the U.S. squad used to obtain some mounts and reflect on how best to face their adversaries. The team was drastically changed. Red Armour was placed at number 1, a position in which he had little experience, Tommy Wayman remained at number 2, Joe Barry was moved up to the pivot position and his cousin Roy played at back. The team played better; however, it was not good enough because the Argentines, although pressed at times, finally won by 16 goals to six.

The recriminations began the morning after and lasted for a while. Ami Shinitzky, the editor of *Polo* magazine, wrote a scathing editorial.[29] The gist of his article was that no one was in charge within the United States organization. According to Shinitzky, the U.S. Polo Association only assumed a supporting role because Steve Gose had provided the financial support and made the arrangements. However, it was the U.S. Polo Association the organization that sent the team to Buenos Aires representing the national colors, not Mr. Gose. The lessons learned in 1966 and 1969, when everything fell upon Northrup Knox's shoulders, were not retained in 1979. Chico Barry was overwhelmed, because he had gone to coach, not to manage. The day of the match, on the way from the Hurlingham club, where the American team was lodged, to Palermo, the players themselves did not know who was going to be on the team.[30]

The Argentine press was critical of the performance put up by the United States team. The matches made the front page of the major newspapers, such was the importance given to polo in Argentina. Attendance surpassed the 20,000 mark in both matches, which also enjoyed live coverage on national television. The sports writers did not spare the rod. *La Prensa*, the oldest daily in Buenos Aires, reported: "There was an incredible difference in strategy, speed and reflexes. In general, the game was a fiasco. North America showed a total lack of experience; there were a few exceptional plays but nothing cohesive. They lacked mobility. Even the horses were heavy. They had a hard time swinging and had the hardest time defending. They left the other team unguarded, especially the Heguys. They were disoriented. Opinions were that the United States performance was very poor, rudimentary."[31]

The morning after the second game, all the newspapers were more complimentary about the United States team's efforts. The reporters were quick to notice the close marking of their opponents and the significant improvement in Armour's play, and commented that Roy Barry should have played at number 3, because his cousin Joe was better at back. As to Juan Carlos Harriott, the comments were brief and accurate: Wise as always, best player in the world, a delight to observe.

1980 at Retama

After the darkest hour, the light comes on. It is a matter of argument whether or not the 1979 Cup of the Americas represented the nadir of American fortunes in the game of international polo. However, there is no question that the 1980 series saw America's return to respectability in polo circles. The core of the American team — Red Armour, Joe Barry and

Tommy Wayman — was kept intact; however, the weakness at the number 1 position was brilliantly filled by young Mexican-born Guillermo "Memo" Gracida, oldest son of Guillermo Gracida Hoffmann, the celebrated international 8-goal player. Memo applied for his American citizenship prior to the series, and the Argentine Polo Association agreed to his inclusion as a member of the American team, thus making him eligible to represent the United States.

Why is there a persistent weakness at number 1 in high-goal American polo? The answer is two fold. First, with very few tournaments above 22-goal handicap, the best players necessarily play at either number 2 or number 3. This practice, therefore, does not allow top players to consistently occupy the number 1 position and become familiar with the nuances of forward play in high-goal polo. The game's pace at the 30-goal and up level is such that it is virtually impossible for even a top player to adjust to the change in position for the occasional match.

Before the start of the series, most observers of the game felt that Argentina, once more represented by the brothers Heguy and Harriott, would be comfortable winners. As it were, win they did, but not in comfort. How this turnaround in America's chances came about?

It was a combination of factors. First, the home field advantage. Some four years before, while playing for Fairfield County Hunt Club at the U.S. Open at Oak Brook, Gonzalo Tanoira was of the opinion that if a 35-goal team series between American and Argentine teams were to be held in the United States, the local team would be the victors.[32] Second, the Argentine polo string was afflicted with a flu and cough epidemic before the start of the series. Shades of the 1928 epidemic at Meadow Brook. Dr. Alvaro Pieres, the team's veterinarian, worked day and night rendering care to the ponies. The string recovered partially; however, the first game had to be postponed for one week. Third, and most important, the American team was stronger than the ones who had played at Palermo six months earlier. The inclusion of Memo Gracida at number 1 made the difference, because it allowed Red Armour to play in his usual position, at number 3. Thus, all four American players were in their customary slots.

The first game was touch and go during the initial four of the seven chukkers, Argentina leading 6–5. The mid-game break was a welcome relief for the visitors, both human and equine. The critical fifth period was all for Argentina, which scored three unanswered goals. The United States recovered in the sixth chukker and started the last one two goals down. The final score was 11–8 in favor of Argentina. To place it into perspective, it was the best result for the Americans since 1932. Nevertheless, it was a close run affair which could easily have gone either way. After the game was over, there was a huge sigh of relief within the confines of the Argentine camp. The feeling was that they had jumped over a high hurdle with sick ponies. However, there was talk that they might concede a walkover for the second game and take their chances in the third match. The ponies recovered enough to play the second match as scheduled. Although *Polo* magazine reported, "The Argentines seemed to make it to the field mounted well,"[33] Juan Carlos Harriott remembers the players' shirts and pants stained with blood from the horses' coughing in the course of the game.[34]

The second game was even for six of the seven chukkers; however, Argentina scored four consecutive goals at the beginning of the match before Memo Gracida found the goalposts. That four-goal difference stood up to the end of the game. Most players and observers were in agreement that the second match was superior to the first; the Argentines played better, and so did the Americans. In the opinion of the Argentine captain, Harriott, it was the best game of all eight he had played for the Cup of the Americas. It was a fitting end to one of the most celebrated careers in the world of polo.

Regrettably, no further meetings have taken place between America and Argentina since the matches at San Antonio. When Gonzalo Tanoira was president of the Argentine Polo Association, negotiations started regarding the possibility of staging a revival of the cup in Palm Beach. It came to naught. The current president of the association, Francisco Dorignac, when queried about the future of the Cup of the Americas, said, "It is safely well-kept in a trophy cabinet at the Asociación Argentina de Polo."[35]

17. The Hallowed Grounds: Hurlingham, Meadow Brook and Palermo

Like all ball games played on turf, polo improves in quality in direct ratio to the quality of the field on which a match is being played. — Sir Terence McLean[1]

Hurlingham

For five years, up to 1879, the Hurlingham polo ground was the only one in London, after play at Lillie Bridge was abandoned. The Hon. Debonnaire Monson, Hurlingham Club's manager, was the individual who saw the future possibilities of the game and recommended to the committee to build a polo field. The famous polo ground occupied the site of the orchard of the old house, which required many trees to be cut down and uprooted. It was at Hurlingham that "guards" or sideboards were first introduced to polo. They replaced the initial white fence, because the ponies developed a tendency to jump over them, perhaps taking it as a hurdle rather than as an enclosure.

The Hurlingham ground was by no means perfect. The rules of the games have always stipulated that a polo field is to be rectangular; however, Hurlingham's ground was egg-shaped. For a while, even the back lines were curved, which made play near the goalposts tricky.[2] In addition, there was a considerable incline towards the north end, popularly known as the chestnuts end. Hurlingham's Number One ground was not the only one with this peculiar characteristic; Myopia, in Hamilton, Massachusetts, features the historic Gibney Field, one of the oldest polo grounds in America still in use, which has a similar incline. Of Gibney Field, Newell Bent wrote, "The dip at the clubhouse end has never been graded, and, after all, to the spectators watching a game, there is always the added interest in the wonder as to whether the players whose bobbing heads can be seen in the distance are making a goal or not. They will still bob after a knock-in, but if they slowly ride towards us, growing in size as first hull down under the horizon, we know that the score has changed and that they are coming back to the center field for play to again begin."[3]

What made up for these oddments at Hurlingham was the turf. It was a luscious, green surface, which provided excellent footing for the ponies and allowed the ball to sit on the grass, giving the striker a perfect target. The field was trodden-in after every game under the direction of Mr. Sutherland, the club's head gardener.

The sports monthly publication *Baily's Magazine* on a few occasions reported about the new game of polo in typical Victorian prose:

> Hurlingham has seen many brilliant gatherings of the noble and the fair, but on Saturday, 26 June, when the Prince and Princess came down and presented a Cup to the victors in a polo match — The Blues v. The 12th Lancers — we think we saw the most brilliant. Generally, Hurlingham has been unlucky in its grand fêtes. About this time last year (1874), when the new polo ground was inaugurated, and royalty and the entire world came to assist, the rain came also, and spoilt the whole thing; and to the tent-pegging day this year came the east wind, pinching the cheek of beauty and unkindly nipping her by the nose. But on this Saturday everything was couleur de rose; it was not too hot and there was a gentle breeze. The King's Road was from soon after 3 P.M. one long procession of coaches and carriages of every description. Very pretty looked the polo ground, gay with a royal marquee, gay with toilets of Ascot beauty, gay with coaches, pretty faces and bright sunshine. The Prince and Princess, with two of their children, arrived about 4 o'clock, and the match immediately commenced. So good was the play on both sides that only one goal was made in the allotted time, and that, thanks to Mr. Brocklehurst, fell to the Blues. It was such an exciting match, and the play was so good, that, though the lawn was at it loveliest, and tea, strawberries and cream, and flirtations awaited society there, society stuck manfully and womanly to polo, and it was only after the Princess had presented the Cup to the victors with some gracious words that the rush on the lawn began.[4]

The first polo pavilion was constructed in 1876 and was enlarged years later. Henry Jamyn Brooks vividly depicted the pavilion, the teams, and, in contemporary Victorian fashion, a considerable number of interested onlookers, suitably dressed. Dated 1890, the original large oil hangs in the club main building; many prints of this famous painting have been struck. Special stands were built for the 1921 Westchester Cup matches in order to accommodate the large number of spectators. In the event, approximately 10,000 people attended the first game and the Number Two field had to be converted to a car park to relieve the traffic congestion.[5] After the series was over, Lt. Col. Arthur Duff, the Hurlingham Club manager, was heartily complimented for his efforts in ensuring that the playing field was in magnificent form.[6]

The large grandstand on Number One polo ground, with seating for 2,600 people, was completed in May 1935, with plenty of time in hand for the summer of 1936 Westchester Cup challenge. The old stand and pavilion on Broomhouse Lane were pulled down and smaller stands erected with seating for 1,200 spectators, to which the public was admitted. For the more important polo matches even the members of the Hurlingham Club had to pay for seats on the large stand.

Both world wars affected the playing grounds. Occasionally, mounted Yeomanry squadrons occupied the clubhouse and grounds. Considerable damage was done to the Number One polo field by a trench mortar firing rounds. Near the war's end, the Royal Air Force built a hangar and used the grounds as a balloon site. On a more happy note, for the first time in the club's history, baseball was played on Number One polo ground on 31 August 1918, between two teams of United States Army officers.[7]

In the Second World War, the Number Two polo ground was used as a site for an antiaircraft battery and the Royal Air Force placed barrage balloons on Number One field. When the ground was no longer needed by the R.A.F., it was handed over to the Fulham Borough Council for use as allotments, a portent of things to come. Number Two ground was used for gun pits, dugouts, ammunition dumps and shelters. Any open space not used for war purposes was ploughed up for growing vegetables. The grandstand was requisitioned for offices and living quarters. For some reason, Hurlingham was a target for the Luftwaffe: twenty-seven bombs and one land mine fell on the grounds.

The Hurlingham Club Number One field was a reflection of some quaint aspects of English character. The organization, whose rules were in force throughout most of the polo world, had a field of play that did not stand up to its own promulgated rules and regulations. The general public was not really welcomed to the grounds and, moreover, the price of admission was considered much too high by the press. However, from the financial point of view, it was a profitable venue. Perhaps the old saying that "Nothing could be called a real success unless a number of people who were dying to 'get in' were kept out," measured success in the Hurlingham Polo Committees' eyes.[8]

In later years, after the compulsory takeover by the Fulham Borough Council, the old Number One ground was converted into a soccer pitch, surrounded by a running track. The grandstand, dilapidated and strewn with graffiti, underwent demolition in 2003. Across Broomhouse Road, apartment buildings, erected on the site of Number Two field, survey the scene where the game of polo grew up in England, achieved maturity in the epic Westchester Cup contests and the Olympic Games, and was the epicenter of world polo for a long time. The Hurlingham polo grounds survived Nazi bombings and River Thames floods only to succumb to the machinations of bureaucrats.

Some years ago, during a visit to the historic club, the late Mr. Nigel Miskin, long-time member and Hurlingham's historian, philosophically told the author: "After all, we could not have afforded to keep polo going on at the club."[9]

Meadow Brook

Meadow Brook has given more than its share to the great names of polo. — Grantland Rice[10]

The Meadow Brook Club, originally a foxhunting organization, was incorporated in 1881 by Francis R. Appleton, Frederick O. Beach, August Belmont, Jr., A. Belmont Purdy and Wendell Goodwin. Polo started on a hastily constructed field located in the middle of a trotting track on the Mineola Fair Grounds on Long Island. It was only three years later when the first polo ground, later known as Number Three field, was built at Meadow Brook in the hollow — being the flattest land available — in the Salisbury Plains. The little brook that gave the name to the club had to be diverted, and another polo field, Number Four, was later built on the opposite side of the brook. Eventually, the club would boast eight polo grounds, of which International Field with its world famous robin's egg blue stands, sufficient to hold 40,000 spectators, was the largest.[11] Yes, there was also golf at Meadow Brook, but it was the "other" game.

With few intervals, the Meadow Brook Club hosted the U.S. Open Championship from 1916 until 1953. The exceptions were the Philadelphia Country Club in Bala in 1919 and 1921, Rumson Country Club in New Jersey in 1922, and Beverly Hills, California, in 1952.[12] As far as international play is concerned, Meadow Brook was the scene of all the Westchester Cup matches played in the United States, with the exception of the inaugural contest in Newport,

Rhode Island, as well as every Cup of the Americas games. Some of the matches against Mexico, for the Avila Camacho Cup, were also played at Meadow Brook.

The Meadow Brook stands were built in 1924 to host the international series for the Westchester Cup. Although located on club property, they belonged to the U.S. Polo Association, and were insured only against loss due to fire. In June 1952, the coverage was extended to include windstorm. The new policy became effective on a Friday, and the following Monday the West Stand was demolished by high winds. The U.S.P.A. *Blue Book* reported, "The Association recovered the value of this stand. In one stroke Dame Fortune made up for many rainy Sundays and disappointing gates."[13]

By 1954, Robert Moses' urbanization plans had reached deep into Long Island and an extension of the Meadowbrook Parkway was planned, its projected north-south path cutting a wide swath through the Meadow Brook Club. The famous blue stands were in a state of disrepair[14] and the struggle against compulsory expropriation was futile. Polo at Meadow Brook Club was gone forever. How prescient was Robert F. Kelley writing in 1939: "Now and again there is a shaking of heads when a particular good flying day brings out the surrounding airplanes like a swarm of wasps. Meadow Brook is doomed. It will have to move, but probably not for many years."[15]

A new entity, named Meadowbrook Polo Club for legal reasons, continued sponsoring polo on Long Island; however, the feeling of history was not the same. It hosted two U.S. Open Championships in the 1990s at Bethpage State Park, an old polo venue more known to the sporting world because of its golf courses, one of which, the Black Course, was the site for the 2002 U.S. Golf Association Open Championship.

The old Meadow Brook Club is gone; however, the glorious players that wore its robin's egg blue colors will remain indelibly in the annals of polo: Bostwick, Corey, Hitchcock, Iglehart, Milburn, Whitney, they are all are surnames intimately associated with the progress and traditions of the game since the dawn of polo in America.

Palermo

"The Cathedral of Polo" is the sobriquet given by Argentine aficionados to the polo complex at Palermo in the heart of Buenos Aires. There are several myths regarding the origin of the name Palermo. The most common is that the area — although already known as Palermo — was so named by dictator Juan Manuel de Rosas to honor a dark Sicilian saint, San Benito de Palermo, whose image was venerated in his residence's chapel, located a few hundred yards from the current polo grounds. Rosas purchased the land and named it San Benito, because the sale's contract was signed on 12 January 1836, San Benito's Day in the Roman Catholic sanctoral cycle. Thus, the property came to be popularly known as Palermo de San Benito, amalgamating both names. The truth is more prosaic.

The name Palermo goes back to the early days of Buenos Aires history, precisely to the second foundation of the City of the Holy Trinity and Port of Santa María of Good Air by conquistador don Juan de Garay on 11 June 1580. In October of that year, Garay allotted tracts of land to the Spanish settlers. Lot number 25, where the polo grounds are now located, was given to Miguel del Corro. Another settler, Juan Domínguez Palermo, had lot number 7, and the area became known as "bañados de Palermo" because it was low-laying terrain, close to the River Plate. The name took roots.[16]

When Rosas was deposed in 1852, all his properties were confiscated. By a law passed in 1874, the parcel of land known as Palermo became a national heritage, a park being created and named Tres de Febrero, the day Rosas' army was defeated. The battle took place in Monte Caseros, very close to Hurlingham in the suburbs of Buenos Aires. There is another link to polo. Within the field of combat, there stood a large circular pigeon-cote, "palomar" in Spanish. The structure, still extant, is on the grounds of the National Military College. A club named Palomar was founded by Col. Samuel Casares on the college's grounds, and one of its teams took the Argentine Open Championship in 1915. The battle of Caseros was one that Rosas never saw, because he had excused himself from duty, prudently seeking refuge on the British frigate HMS *Centaur*, lying at anchor in the River Plate. Nevertheless, the name Tres de Febrero never caught on as the name of Buenos Aires largest green area; it was always referred to as Palermo.[17]

The land where the polo fields are now located was for a while a municipal depot; however, its destiny was to be the site of many sporting endeavors. At the turn of the 19th century, sporting activities in Argentina were a privilege of the few. Baron Antonio de Marchi provided the force behind the establishment of the Sociedad Sportiva Argentina, which occupied the municipal grounds. Balloon ascents were frequent and infant airplanes took off and landed on the Sportiva grounds. The first athletic meetings took place at the grounds. The English football teams Everton and Tottenham Hotspurs played their matches against local teams on the Sportiva's soccer pitch. The game of polo developed an early link to the place when a team representing Sociedad Sportiva — Dr. Pedro Díaz, Eduardo Reynolds, Gastón Peers and Lewis Lacey — took the Copa Anchorena, now the Tortugas Open in 1908.[18] The parcel of land became a polo field that same year when the War Ministry decreed that the military championship was to take place on the old Sportiva grounds.[19]

Two polo grounds were constructed on the Sociedad Sportiva Argentina field, located in the corner of Dorrego Street and Avenida Vértiz, now Libertador, across the main gate of the Argentine Hippodrome. The works involved raising the ground level an average of 1.5 meters because of the risk posed by flooding in the area. The Number One field was build along Dorrego, measuring 327 meters by 140 meters. The Number Two field was constructed at a right angle to the other, in a north-south bearing, along Avenida Vértiz.

The official first match was an encounter on 27 October 1928 between Civilians (Luis Nelson, Ramón Videla Dorna, Carlos Uranga and José Luis Giribone) and Military (Lt. Alberto Paz, Lt. Manuel Molinuevo, Lt. Luis Oddone and Maj. Enrique Padilla), both handicapped at 17 goals. Carlos Uranga scored the first goal in a lackluster match, won by the civilian team by eight goals to six.[20]

The initial wooden stands had capacity for 10,000 spectators. The increased popularity of the game, brought about in no small part by the international matches against teams from the United States, Chile and South Africa, encouraged the Argentine Polo Association to built a cement stand on the Dorrego side of the Number One field, flanked by two wooden stands 85 meters long. On the opposite side of the field, the long and low wooden stands were replaced in 1949 by two cement stands, just in time for the international season. The gap between the high stands was for many years filled in by the smaller official enclosure.

The Number Two field also underwent improvements. A beautiful cement structure with a cantilevered roof that allowed 180 degrees of unobstructed vision was constructed in 1936. The glory of Palermo, its old turf, in place and meticulously cared for since the 1920s, was removed at the end of the 2007 Open Championship and re-seeded with Tifton. Palermo, home of the best polo in the world since the 1940s, is keeping pace with progress brought about by new technology. The new surface was tested in a practice match, behind closed doors, in April 2008.

The Campo Argentino de Polo, Palermo's official name, is the venue of the Argentine Open Championship since 1928 and has hosted the Cup of the Americas in 1932, 1950, 1966, 1969 and 1979, the World Championship in 1949 and the Pan American Games in 1951. It also was the venue for the first 14-Goal World Cup, organized by the Federation of International Polo in 1987.

The three most famous polo grounds in the history of polo have in common modest beginnings. The oldest, Hurlingham, was a tree orchard; Meadow Brook, a hunting field bisected by a narrow stream, and Palermo, a farm and later a multi-purpose ground that arose from a frequently flooded area. In their respective heydays, all three were venues for the best polo ever played on earth. Only Palermo survives, although more than once it has been a target for rapacious land speculators. For the sake of the game, let us hope that they will never succeed in their ambitions.

18. Return from War: The Internationals

The interest of polo will outlive this war, as it has survived many others in its long existence. It will not always be winter or wartime. — The Rev. Thomas Francis Dale[1]

United States

Out of all the Allied nations, the United States was the first to resume polo after the formal surrender of the Japanese armed forces in Tokyo Bay on 2 September 1945. It is nothing short of amazing that an open championship was staged at Meadow Brook in 1946. However, times were a-changing, and out of the eight players who answered the initial bell for the final match, two were Americans and six were Mexicans. The four Gracida Hoffmann brothers, Gabriel, José, Guillermo and Alejandro, defeated a mixed team, Los Amigos, formed with Mike Phipps, Stewart Iglehart, Antonio Nava Castillo and Alberto Ramos Sesma. However, American teams retained the Avila Camacho Cup in that year, both in San Antonio and at Meadow Brook.[2]

In 1949, California hosted Venado Tuerto, a 36-goal team, in the Pacific Open Championship and a special inter–American series at Riviera Country Club in Palisades. Sadly, a portion of that wonderful field was taken over by the city using its right of eminent domain. The rest, with the tax clock ticking, was sold to developers.[3] Polo at Riviera, dating back to 1928 and boasting five polo grounds and stabling for more than 350 horses, went down in spite of heroic efforts by movie producer and 2-goal player Darryl Zanuck, who had leased the last field for the Beverly Hills Polo Club.[4]

The venerable Meadow Brook represented American polo at the international season in Buenos Aires in 1949. This team — Pete Bostwick, Peter Perkins, Alan Corey and Devereux Milburn, Jr.— had an impressive debut at Palermo, overwhelming the Argentine military team. Alas, in the second round the medium-handicap La Concepción gave the shock of the tournament when they defeated the American team 14–12. Many years later, Jorge Torres Zavaleta, who would become president of the Argentine Polo Association, recalled this match as the highlight of his polo career.[5] The magazine *El Gráfico* mentioned that it was the best match of the championship.[6] However, attendance was low, because it was played on a Wednesday afternoon and everyone expected an easy win for Meadow Brook. The biggest shock was reserved for the Argentine Polo Association treasurer, Nicolás Cazón, who had a financial disaster staring him in the face, because a final between Meadow Brook and Venado Tuerto was in the cards. La Concepción, the Cinderella team, made it to the finals, where the mighty Venado Tuerto shattered their hopes, scoring eleven consecutive goals before La Concepción's first tally. At half-time, Venado Tuerto pulled up for a final score of 15–3. As far as attendance, Señor Cazón's fears were unfortunately confirmed. There was still too much good polo to be seen in the season, and ticket prices were high.

The American visitors played in two more tournaments. The first was a 30-goal series between America and Argentina, which won both matches by one goal each. The Argentine team included young Ernesto "Tito" Lalor, Juan Cavanagh, Heriberto Duggan and Juan Carlos Alberdi. On the American team, indoor polo star Clarence Combs replaced Milburn, who had to return home. Peter Perkins moved to back, and Buddy Combs played at number 2. The second tournament was the only World Polo Championship played so far with no handicap limit. The four Gracida Hoffman brothers, Rubén, Gabriel, Guillermo and Alejandro, represented Mexico, while the United States presented George "Pete" Bostwick, Peter Perkins, Bob Skene and Alan Corey. Argentina trusted the Alberdi brothers and the Cavanagh cousins, the full Venado Tuerto team, to wear the sky blue and white national colors. Both Argentina and the United States defeated Mexico, and in the final match, Argentina beat the American team by 11 to 5.

The 1950 edition of the Cup of the Americas was held in Buenos Aires. The story of that series is recounted elsewhere.

The United States declined to participate in the 1951 Pan American Games in Buenos Aires; therefore, the next international appearance was in the Coronation Cup in 1953. Once more, Meadow Brook took the responsibility of representing the U.S.A. The team was Pete Bostwick, Philip Iglehart, Ricardo Santamarina and Devereux Milburn, Jr. Perhaps Dicky Santamarina's marriage to Frances Post qualified him as an American. Cowdray Park defeated Meadow Brook in the first round, but the same teams met in the subsidiary tournament for the Duke of Sutherland Cup. This time Meadow Brook came out the winners by a single goal.

There were no other international appearances for the United States until the 1966 and 1969 Cup of the Americas, but in 1971, the American team took the first of four consecutive wins in the Coronation Cup, now restricted to a single invitational match on International Day.

The Westchester Cup was revived, sort of, in 1988. The negotiations between the U.S. Polo Association and the Hurlingham Polo Association having reached an impasse, the Americans decided to invite a combined Australia–New Zealand team to compete for the trophy. Actually, it was a different cup, not the artistic jewel manufactured by Tiffany and Co. in 1887. The competition was held in Lexington, Kentucky, the site of the U.S. Polo Association headquarters. Two matches were played, the overall winner to be decided on aggregate goals. The American team took the first game 10–3 and lost the second 6–9, thus taking the honors. Scholars of the game will argue about the relative merits of this series to be labeled a true Westchester Cup contest, just as the 1900 single match is being debated to this day. Most certainly, the Hurlingham Polo Association does not recognize the Lexington series as a Westchester event. It is surprising that the U.S. Polo Association chose to ignore the mandate of the deed of gift in inviting a team other than a British representation in staging the competition. The photograph of a trophy in the U.S.P.A. *Year Book* inserted between the results for the 1988 Westchester competition and the Coronation Cup depicts neither trophy. It shows the individual prize given to the winners of the 1927 Westchester Cup.[7]

There is no argument about the next challenge. In 1992, America and England met at Windsor Park, the visitors, having waived their right to defend the cup in their own country, emerged winners by 9–7. John Gobin, Adam Snow, Owen Rinehart and Rob Walton made up the American team. A nostalgic note was the presence at the game of Bob Skene, the last living player from the 1939 English team. It would have been a nice gesture from the U.S.P.A. if it had flown Stewart Iglehart to witness the game, as the Hurlingham Polo Association had done for Bob and Elizabeth Skene.

Five years later, once more at Windsor Park, the English team took the cup for the first time since 1914. Julian Daniels, Henry Brett, William Lucas and Andrew Hine added their names to those of Henry Tomkinson, Leslie Cheape, Fred Barrett and Vivian Lockett as members of the only British teams to recover the Westchester Cup.

England

Thanks to the support of Lord Cowdray, England was able to assemble an international team that did quite well at Palermo in October 1949, when they beat Chile in the inaugural match of a three-nation 24-goal tournament. The British squad was made up of John Lakin, Eric Tyrrell-Martin, Bob Skene and Lt. Col. Humphrey Guinness, with Maj. Peter Dollar as reserve and Lord Cowdray as non-playing captain. Misfortune overtook the team even before they started. Eric Tyrrell-Martin was working for B.O.A.C. (now part of British Airways) in Egypt; sadly, he broke a leg just before departure. His place on the team was taken by John Traill, who was already in Argentina. Upon arrival in Buenos Aires, the Argentine Polo Association arbitrarily assigned a 6-goal handicap to Col. Guinness, John Lakin and Bob Skene. Australian-born Skene's performance was such that, immediately following the tournament, his rating was raised to 8 goals. With Maj. Dollar in Traill's place, the English team, now wearing Cowdray Park's orange colors, entered the Open Championship, only to be narrowly defeated by Los Indios in an early round.

In 1951, a Hurlingham team made up of pre-war players, Lt. Col. Alec Harper, John Lakin, Gerald Balding and Col. Guinness, took the Festival Cup in a series of three matches against La Espadaña, a visiting side from Argentina. By 1953, polo in England was well on its way to recovery when the Coronation Cup was staged as a tournament among six international and local teams. The same 1951 team, with John Lakin at back, reached the finals versus Argentina.

New Zealand

Polo in New Zealand was resumed in 1947 with both the Savile Cup and the Junior Handicap being played. The New Zealand Polo Association sent a representative team to Melbourne to participate in the 1954 Australasian Gold Cup. The team (Gordon Spence, Tommy Mellow, Tim Douglas, Wynn Sherratt) took the prize after a series of matches described as "being rough but there were few fouls."[8] The playing field was far short of what was expected, being uneven and rough. Both Australian and New Zealand polo were handicapped in their endeavors to elevate their level of play by indifferent grounds.

Nineteen-fifty-six was a banner year for New Zealand polo. Led by Hamish Wilson, a team named Aotea, perhaps in remembrance of one of the first canoes that brought the Polynesians to New Zealand, traveled to England with their own ponies and took the Neil Haig Cup. Derrick Glazebrook, A.F. "Sandy" Mackenzie, Tony Kay and Jack Masters joined Hamish Wilson as pioneers in this first venture to the mother country. One notable spectator at one of the games was Lord Glasgow, who as Viscount Kelburn had been one of the Royal Navy players that had been instrumental in bringing the game to New Zealand in the 19th century.

The second big event of that year was the tour of a New Zealand side to Mexico. Tim Douglas, Woodbine and Wynn Sherratt, Gordon Spence and Ron Walker were selected for the tour. It appears that the players were unaware of Mexico City's high altitude — over 7,500 feet — and its deleterious effect upon their stamina. The oxygen debt proved to be too much for the visitors, who went to defeat at the hands of four Gracida brothers in both matches.

A visit by an Australian team led by Sinclair Hill was most influential on Kiwi polo. Hill's penalty shooting was a surprise to the New Zealanders, because he would slowly canter at the ball and hit a shot that would split the uprights 40 or 50 feet high. The custom in New Zealand when taking a penalty shot was to ride back to midfield and then, at full gallop, hit the ball in the general direction of the goal posts. It was an educational experience.

Although the Australians lost in the semi-finals of the Savile Cup, and the Australasian Gold Cup in extra chukker, thanks to an open goal after a penalty, not a word was raised against the umpires, Ken Peake from New Zealand and Peter Roberts of New South Wales.

New Zealand polo had an unpleasant wake-up call when a team from California, led by Bob Skene, visited the island. Aside from the results of the friendly matches, which are inconsequential to the story, Skene was frankly critical of polo in New Zealand: "We are very grateful for the ponies which have been so kindly loaned us wherever we played. They are fine horseflesh, but they are not trained to the game as are horses in other parts of the world, not least California. They are trained by New Zealanders to turn on their forequarters. We turn our ponies on their haunches. As to speed on the turns, swifter reaction and getting inside opponents, there is no comparison."[9]

Bob Skene was equally critical of the polo grounds in New Zealand, which he felt were no more than rough paddocks. In Skene's view, control of the ball and sound positional play were absolute imperatives for first class, spectacular polo. This appeared to be beyond the abilities of most New Zealand players, not because they lacked the ability to learn those skills, but due to the poor quality of the polo grounds. Skene remarked: "Such is the uneven state of most of your fields that the ball bounces in all directions. I defy anyone to hit a ball accurately under those conditions. One is reduced to the hack and the slash. That is not polo."[10]

After the initial shock provided by such constructive criticisms, the New Zealanders took steps to improve their playing surfaces, which, in turn, upgraded their polo. As a prime example, Stuart Mackenzie became a 9-goal player in America, and the New Zealand ponies, now properly trained and bitted, hold their own with the best horseflesh in the world.

South Africa

The game came back to South Africa right after the war, with a handicap tournament scheduled for September. Both the South African Championship and the Prince of Wales Cup were played for in 1946 at the Willow Bridge grounds in Pietermaritzburg. Thirty-six teams participated and nearly 600 horses were stabled.

In 1951, a 26-goal Argentine team led by 8-goaler Heriberto Duggan visited South Africa to play a series of test matches, Argentina taking three out of the four games played. In the following year, South Africa returned the visit to Argentina, under Charles S. "Punch" Barlow's captaincy. The remaining players were Craig Brown, son of Hugh Brown, who had been the non-playing captain of the 1933 tour, Julian W.R. "Buddy" Chaplin, Derek Goodman and Julius Schuld. Bad luck followed this team. Punch Barlow broke a leg in a practice game when his pony collapsed and was forced to follow the rest of the tour from a wheelchair, pushed by a pretty nurse from the British Hospital.[11]

The rest of the players participated in two 26-goal tournaments, the Jockey Club Cup (open) and the Copa Campaña del Desierto (handicap) which traditionally preceded the Argentine Open. The Springboks also entered an international series against civilian and military teams. Although the Springboks did not win any trophies, they exhibited the same congenial attitude shown by their 1933 predecessors. The most impressive players were Chaplin, Schuld and Barlow, until the latter was sidelined by injury. The South Africans had trouble adjusting to the Argentine grounds' heavy turf. Most tried to force the swing, because they were unable to lift the ball, being used to their fast grounds where any shot, including "topping" the ball, goes a long distance. As to the ponies, team members were mounted on fast, manageable horses. Nevertheless, the local observers' opinion was that the 1933 Springboks were a better team than the 1952 tourists were.[12]

Other foreign visitors include another team from Argentina in 1954 and the Hurlingham Rovers with the Beresford brothers and Maj. Ronald Ferguson in 1965. Fittingly, they took the Beresford Cup, emblematic of the South African Open Championship since 1899.

Regrettably, most of the international activity disappeared when, in 1964, South Africa was banned from participating in the Olympic Games in Tokyo. Overseas tours by South African representative teams, especially cricket, tennis and rugby, were marred by demonstrators invading grounds and courts. Foreign players participating in so-called 'rebel tours' saw their sporting careers threatened or damaged upon returning to their homeland. Both the International Cricket Council and the International Rugby Board banned offending players from participating in international competition.

There being no international ruling body in the game of polo before the creation of the Federation of International Polo in 1982, individual players and polo teams ventured into South Africa. Some examples are Los Teros from Uruguay, Coronel Suárez and Pergamino from Argentina, and teams from Peru, United States, Chile, Rhodesia, Australia, the United Kingdom and New Zealand, the latter playing as Kiwis.

The Springboks returned to South America in 1973, visiting Brazil, Uruguay and Argentina. With a graying Buddy Chaplin as manager, the tourists included the best available players in South Africa: Kippy Bryden, Terence Craig, Mike Miller, Mann Oelrich, Pieter Potgeiter and Jim Watson. A few years later, another team visited Guatemala and El Salvador.[13] Tours were undertaken to Rhodesia and Kenya, where there had been an influx of retired army officers after the advent of independence in India and the inevitable partition with Pakistan.[14] Kenya took the series in 1951, the first time it was played; several other visits followed that initial tour.[15]

Polo in South Africa remained the purview of farmers and some businessmen. While the main center of the game remained in Natal, teams based in Griqualand, the Free State and

Transvaal were able to challenge Natal's primacy. Matatiele, also known as The Levels, was the first team to wrestle away the Beresford Cup under the leadership of the legendary Tommy Pope. Ficksburg, Harrismith, Kokstad and Swartberg are the other clubs that managed the same feat.

From the polo point of view, the ban against international competition was a failure. Most of the credit for keeping the game alive goes to Mike Rattray, three-term president of the South African Polo Association, who somehow kept his country in the international picture against heavy odds. The breakthrough came in 1994, when the Hurlingham Polo Association invited a team from South Africa — Murray Rattray, Doug Lund, Simon Armstrong and Clive Hill — to face England in the Coronation Cup on International Day at Windsor Park.

The friendship ties between South Africa and Argentina were cemented by a few test matches. At Shongweni in 2007, Horacio Araya, still playing off a 4-goal handicap at age 66, and his sons Benjamin, Diego and Santiago, defeated Richard Pohl, Russell Watson, Selby Williamson and Gillespie Armstrong. There was also a test match in Buenos Aires, the first South African team in Argentina since the 1952 Springboks.

Australia

The progress of polo in Australia, just as in New Zealand, was hampered by the absence of good polo grounds. The master craftsmen of polo and the select group of other less talented players who have made a life study of the game will tell all and sundry that no game, especially polo, can be any faster than the surface on which it is played.

Hexham was the premier club in Victoria during the immediate period after the war. One of the players was "Uncle Jim" Mann, of who teammate Bill Weatherly said, "He had a fantastic eye and a wonderful ability to run with the ball on a bumpy ground, which Hexham was."[16]

If that was said about one of the better fields, it is not hard to imagine what the playing surfaces were on lesser clubs' grounds. Eventually, Australia would sport some of the world's best polo grounds at Ellerston, but that was a long time ahead.

Hard-riding, strong-hitting Geebung style of polo was the staple of the game in the Antipodes. Nevertheless, good teams and superior players made Australian polo a force to be reckoned with. South Australia got things rolling in 1947, when a Mount Crawford team revived old glories by taking the state championship trophy, the Barr Smith Cup, which the club had first won in 1922, the year of its inception. However, South Australia had to wait until 1969 before taking the Australasian Gold Cup. Traditional clubs such as Adelaide, Hexham, Mount Crawford and Strathalbyn were the winners of the Barr Smith Cup during the following decades. The 1960s saw a resurgence of polo in the state and the beginning of a concentration of players at the Adelaide Polo Club. Better roads and the advent of horse vans meant that players could travel to a larger center and improve their skill in the face of a higher level of competition.

The war's end did not bode well with polo in Western Australia because the Workers Home Board and the State Housing Commission took over the Hurlingham ground in Perth and began subdividing the land to the meet the need for homes for returning servicemen. Nevertheless, William G. Bennett and Bill Carcary started games in 1946 at a paddock near the corner of Kalamunda Road and the Great Western Highway. Sir Ernest Lee-Steere was elected president and the Royal Agricultural Society was asked for permission to use their grounds. Competition for the Joseph Charles Cup was resumed in 1948, allowing Broome-hill to continue its dominance of Western Australian polo; only Kojonup and, later, Walka-way and Minninooka were able to take the state championship trophy.[17]

John Fischer and the late Ian Webster, following Len Hamersley's idea to form teams with local players teamed with higher-handicapped imported players, established the Western Australian Open in 1987. In spite of the long distance involved, Perth hosted the Australasian Gold Cup in 1929, 1956, 1971, 1982 and 1993. Polo in Western Australia, as in the rest of the country, is heavily supported by families. It is a long list, but mention may be made of the Dawkins, Fischer, Haggerty, Hamersley, Hardie, Kiely, Lefroy, Redhead, Reid, Richardson and Swift families, who made significant contributions to the game.

Victoria had its share of glory when representative teams took the Australasian Gold Cup in 1955, 1961 and 1985 with family with names like Kelly and Mann being repeated winners. Berwick, Hexham, Melbourne Hunt, Yarra Glen-Lilydale and, in later years, Yaloak, have engraved their names on the Creswick Cup. The great days of the Western District successes are a distant memory. Melbourne's Werribee Park was the venue for the 14-goal World Cup in 2001, when Australia obtained the silver medal.

Queensland, the last refuge of Geebung polo, remained an important force in post-war Australian polo. Its teams posted victories in the Australasian Gold Cup from the 1950s until the 1990s, with names such as Mervyn Cooke, the Gilmores, Graham Hoey, Jim and Pat MacGinley, Marshall Muller and, more than all, Ken Telford, whose impressive career was cut short by an automobile accident that he was lucky to survive. Ken Telford and Sinclair Hill were the two giants of post-war polo in Australia.

When the New Zealand team toured Queensland in 1964, one of the matches they played was in Cunnamulla, some 400 miles west from the coast. There were three polo fields; as soon as play began, dust rose in a cloud and there being no wind, the next period the game was moved to another field, and so on. In Terry McLean's words, "This was the sort of joy Queensland offered. Magnificent people — they would give you the earth."[18]

The conditions in the south of Queensland were such that the clubs in the Darling Downs area — Allora, Clifton, Pilton, Spring Creek and West Haldon — decided to amalgamate. Players from Darling Downs contributed to Queensland's first and second victories in the Australasian Gold Cup in the 1950s, a feat not to be repeated until 1966.

Within Australia, New South Wales offered the best polo. Wirragulla, of the Mackays, Ken the father and Jaime the son, nicely supported by Mac Alison, Charlie Hooke and Laurie Morgan, held sway until the advent of Quirindi. Then came Scone, sporting historic names such as Ashton, Bragg and Munro from a previous generation of polo players; a resurgent Wirragulla and old-timer Goulburn, which preceded the times of Ellerston.

Nevertheless, polo in New South Wales was dominated by the towering figure of Sinclair Hill. No one spoke of Hill, let alone his full name, John Sinclair Hill. In Australia, it was simply "Sinclair." Everybody knew that.[19] As the scion of a prominent pastoral family, Sinclair was dispatched to England and enrolled at the Royal Agricultural College, near Cirencester. Being near one of the main centers of English polo, his raw talents were quickly spotted by the legendary Rao Rajah Hanut Singh. Not long after, Hill wrote to the college advising his tutors that he was relinquishing his agricultural studies at the royal institution in order to concentrate on his polo studies. It is easy to understand his selection. By most accounts, Hanut Singh was the most charismatic teacher of the game and the lights of Deauville were in stark contrast to the surroundings of the college, no matter how beautiful the panorama is in Gloucestershire.

On his return to Australia, Sinclair Hill led the Quirindi team to years of glory: the Australasian Gold Cup, the Countess of Dudley Cup and the Northern Challenge Cup bear witness to the success of the dominant club of the 1960s. Theo Hill — not related to Sinclair — and Peter Cudmore were the constants with Sinclair Hill, complemented at times with Arthur Carter, John Cobcroft, Hector King, Bruce MacDonald, Rod Murchison and Rob Vickery. At the international series in New Zealand, Oliver "Sandy" Tait from Toompang, Richard Walker from Goulburn and Hugh MacLachlan from Adelaide joined Sinclair in wrestling away the Australasian Gold Cup after a 34-year hiatus.

Sinclair Hill's influence extended beyond playing good polo. His teaching skill matched that of his mentor, Hanut Singh. An enthralling speaker, Sinclair was able to lecture for hours, keeping his audience totally absorbed. As a breeder, he played a significant part in improving the quality of Australian polo ponies. The bloodline from his stallion Deo Juvante became prominent in breeding circles, through sales, leases, and at times, generous lending.[20]

Canada

In spite of a war going on, polo in Western Canada somehow had managed to keep on rolling along, albeit on a very limited scale, at Calgary, High River and Victoria. Late in March 1945, seven members of the Calgary Polo Club gathered for lunch at the Ranchmen's Club. Most likely, they were not aware that Calgary was the only polo club in the whole country. The road back from the war would be long and arduous.

At the beginning, it was a question of survival. The polo field at Chinook Park was beset with problems, mostly molehills and gopher burrows. Instead of mowing the grass, an urgent request was sent for up to thirty sheep. The issue of geographical isolation was partially solved with help from south of the border, when American players from Toppenish and White Swan in the Yakima Valley and the Spokane Polo Club in Washington State started playing matches. Calgary affiliated with the U.S. Polo Association in 1952.

The gas and oil boom in Alberta rejuvenated polo. Many Americans moved to Calgary, among them Charles Hetherington from Oklahoma, Bill Daniels from California and Jake Harp from Louisiana. The city's expansion took over the old Chinook grounds — gophers and molehills included — and new land was bought by the club at De Winton. Polo clubs were again formed in Vancouver and Victoria and old names like Fish Creek and Millarville were revived and went on to make their mark in top American competitions, including a heartbreaking loss in extra time in the U.S. Open.

In 1973, a Canadian team — Tony Yonge, Jonty Parker, Patrick Oswald and Charles Hetherington — embarked on a polo tour to England, finally playing at Guards in Windsor and Cowdray Park. The visit was returned the following year by a British team led by Mervyn Fox-Pitt, one of the hosts in the United Kingdom.

The game in Alberta has benefited greatly from the support given by patrons such as Steve Benediktson, Ron Greene, Morris Palmer, and most of all, Frederick Phillip Mannix. Calgary Polo Club is the keeper of the Calgary Challenge Cup, which dates back to 1892, which surely makes it the oldest polo trophy in the Americas.

To end the story of post-war polo in Western Canada, the Roenisch family must be mentioned. The patriarch was Clinton W. "Kink" Roenisch, born in Minnesota of Swedish and German ancestors.[21] With his brother, they settled in Calgary, and after watching a game, Kink decided polo was his game. Two old ponies were purchased from Lord Strathcona's Horse, and the High River team had recruited a new member. He went on to play the game well into his sixties, and his three sons, Clint, Jr., Davis and Harold, also played. Clint, Jr., made up a team with his own sons, Rich and Rob, and their cousin, Bob Spaith. This third generation of Roenisches took the Calgary Challenge Cup, and when Bob Spaith gave up the polo to become a sculptor, Rob's wife, Julie, joined the team. They won the Calgary Challenge once more. Julie Roenisch made history when she became the first woman to participate in the U.S. Open Championship, in 1992. Their son, Daniel, the fourth generation Roenisch to play polo, is a 5-goal handicap player who represented Canada in the 14-Goal World Championship. Rich Roenisch is a talented sculptor; replicas of one of his many works are presented to the inductees to the United States Polo Hall of Fame.

Polo in Eastern Canada did not match the story of success achieved by the Western clubs. The Montreal Polo Club was not revived after the war, although a club with that name became active in 1981. The Sifton family kept the flame alive in Toronto, and later, also in Winnipeg with the St. Charles Club. Contemporary players such as Brandon Phillips, Fred Mannix, Jr., and David and Todd Offen maintain the high standard of the Canadian game in professional polo.

19. The Rise of Argentina

Two bald men fighting over a comb. — Jorge Luis Borges, on the Falkland (Malvinas) War

The tremendous influence exerted by the British in Argentina was addressed in previous chapters in this book. Just as in the previous conflict, many Anglo-Argentines volunteered to serve in the Commonwealth armed forces. For some unexplained reason, the majority joined the air forces, either in England or in Canada. The polo-playing Traill family suffered the most, because three cousins, Bob, Johnny and Joe, each lost a son while flying in the Royal Air Force.

The times immediately preceding the onset of World War II in Europe witnessed the appearance of the best team in Argentina since the game took root in that South American country in the 19th century. The brothers Heriberto and Luis Duggan, scions of a well-established Irish family from County Longford, joined forces with another set of brothers, Carlos and Julio Mrditeguy, who were of Basque descent. Both families belonged to the exclusive Jockey Club in Buenos Aires. Founded in 1882, the Jockey Club was the governing body of thoroughbred racing in Argentina and keeper of the Stud Book. Together with the Círculo de Armas, they were the symbols of the ruling Conservative Party and the landed aristocracy. In 1953, the palatial social see was set on fire by a Peronist mob, carefully watched by the police. A priceless art collection and an impressive sporting library went up in flames.

Mrditeguy *père* was the owner of Chopp, the winner of thoroughbred racing's triple crown in 1908. Different branches of the prolific Duggan family were the proprietors of several large estancias in Argentina. The Mrditeguy brothers were exceptional athletes and began playing polo at Los Pingüinos, the Braun Menéndez family club in Merlo. The Duggans — there were eight brothers — started the game at their own estancia San José, and were also members of the Hurlingham Club. In 1938, they began playing for El Trébol, a relatively new club close to San José. The foursome took the Hurlingham Open Championship in their first major foray; however, they were beaten in the Argentine Open. Next year, the Mrditeguys temporarily left the team, while the Duggans called upon Manuel Andrada and another sibling, Enrique. They comfortably took the open. Then Julio and Carlos Mrditeguy returned to the fold and El Trébol was unbeaten until 1944, reaching an aggregate 39-goal handicap.

The foundation for the team's unparalleled success was the pony string. The Duggan

191

The Argentine Polo Federation team, winners of the Hurlingham Champion Cup in England and the U.S. Open Championship at Rumson Country Club, 1922. From the left are Lewis Lacey, David Miles, John Nelson and John Miles (Museum of Polo and Hall of Fame).

family carried the reputation of being top breeders; their stallion Morfeo, by Craganour — the unjustly disqualified racehorse in the 1913 English Derby at Epson — out of Sleeping Sickness, was their principal sire. Both brothers were superior gentlemen-riders on the flat; Heriberto was invited as a jockey in England, having ridden at Ascot and Epsom. Heriberto "Pepe" Duggan is considered the best rider in the history of Argentine polo, equal or superior to Lewis Lacey. It was an accolade that he summarily dismissed, pointing out to his older brother, Luis, as the better rider.[1]

For their part, the Menditeguys were also expert equestrians and breeders. When they retired from polo, both became breeders of thoroughbred horses with great success. Three of their racehorses won the Argentine Derby. Charlie Menditeguy was a sports superstar. Ten goals in polo, Formula One race car driver, scratch golfer, nationally ranked in tennis; Charlie excelled in everything he tried his hand at, which he often did.[2]

Older brother Julio was the quiet man. Very tall and thin, he handled very long mallets, mostly 54 inches long. With his uncanny positional instinct, Julio was able to reach impossible balls in play and feed his number 1. He also reached a 10-goal handicap rating, and with his brother, they were ranked in the top five in tennis doubles.[3] His ponies were invariably perfectly schooled. When the great Australian Bob Skene played on El Trébol teams in 1954 and 1956, he was mounted on ponies loaned by the Menditeguy brothers. Skene expressed the view that there was no comparison between the ponies schooled by Julio and those owned by Charlie.[4] Julio Menditeguy had an eye for a horse and his advice was much in

David Miles limps forward to accept the trophy for the 1922 U.S. Open Championship at Rumson C.C., New Jersey. His left leg is bandaged with a polo wrap and he is wearing a tennis shoe. In spite of his injury, Miles was the game's top scorer (Museum of Polo and Hall of Fame).

demand when looking for a suitable animal. The saying was, "If you want a good horse, ask Don Julio."[5]

It was much more than horsepower that propelled El Trébol to absolute supremacy. The players studied Cameron Forbes' *As to Polo* and developed set plays on a billiard table, using four red and four black cards, plus a small chip as the ball. They were four serious students of the game who carefully prepared themselves before each game, spending much time going over the pony list, making sure that in a single chukker two players would not play their weakest mounts. Heriberto Duggan pioneered in Argentina the concept of changing mounts in the middle of the chukker. One of his grooms invariably had a pony behind the back line; when there was a knock in, "Pepe" would change ponies in a few seconds. At the time, it was an ingrained custom to train polo ponies to play seven-and-half minutes plus, and most *petiseros*, who usually schooled the ponies, would be offended if their charges were not able to play the full chukker. The Duggan brothers made and schooled their own ponies, so there was no place for argument. Pepe Duggan also trained the celebrated Paddy, the best pony Charlie Menditeguy ever played.[6]

What made this team so good was the combination of superb ponies, lightning speed, accurate hitting and brilliant team play, with the immeasurable addition of good chemistry among the players. All four players gave credit to Lewis Lacey as their mentor, especially his emphasis on perfect equitation and his belief that the ball always travels faster than any individual player. Extreme pace and medium-range passing to an open man became the staple of El Trébol success.

El Trébol marked a milestone in the development of polo in Argentina. Regrettably, its best years were coincidental with World War II, a fact that prevented such a great team from showing its prowess overseas. The only foreign tour undertaken by the full team was to Mexico in 1945, where they won all the matches. For comparison, the next year the Mexican team of the four Gracida Hoffmann brothers, Cano, Chino, Memo and Pepe, took the United States Open Championship at Meadow Brook. Another El Trébol team, with Julio and Carlos Menditeguy, reached the finals of the U.S. Open in 1949, being handily defeated by a Hurricanes team that counted Cecil Smith and — with great chagrin expressed by many Argentine fans — Roberto Cavanagh, the number 2 from archrival Venado Tuerto. El Trébol's last win in the Hurlingham Open was in 1959 and they took the Argentine Open at Palermo in 1960.

It was precisely the Venado Tuerto team that challenged El Trébol's supreme ways at Palermo and Hurlingham. Roberto and Juan Cavanagh were cousins in that large family whose

Venado Tuerto was one of the best teams in the game's history. From the left are Juan Carlos Alberdi (back), Enrique Alberdi, Roberto Cavanagh and his cousin Juan Luis Cavanagh. The setting is the number 2 ground at Palermo at the north end, near the pony lines (private collection).

ancestors had emigrated from County Wexford and settled near the town of Venado Tuerto in southern Santa Fe Province. They joined with Enrique "Quito" and Juan Carlos "Bebé" Alberdi, whose parents of Basque origins owned an estancia in Coronel Suárez, southwest of Buenos Aires. Both Enrique Alberdi and Roberto Cavanagh had been selected to play in the Berlin Olympics and in the Cup of the Americas; however, a throat infection prevented "Quito" from playing in Berlin and he lost his place on the team. The Venado Tuerto four-some came about with the specific purpose of defeating El Trébol. The Alberdi brothers had taken the Argentine Open before playing on Coronel Suárez teams, but had been notoriously unsuccessful in defeating El Trébol in the open championships at Hurlingham and Palermo, as well as in the handicap tournaments played concurrently, the Joseph Drysdale Cup at Hurlingham and the Copa Provincia de Buenos Aires.[7]

Venado Tuerto was defeated again by El Trébol in 1943; however, the following year Heriberto Duggan developed an infection and was unable to play, his place being taken by Manuel Andrada. Venado Tuerto finally accomplished its goal in an epic match. The team was dissolved after taking the Argentine Open in 1955, although the individual players participated in high-goal polo until the 1960s. The clashes between Venado Tuerto and El Trébol were legendary. Experts could never agree on which one was the better of the teams. Venado Tuerto had a more significant international profile, taking the Inter-American series at Beverly Hills and the World Championship at Palermo in 1949. They added the Cup of the Americas in 1950 and the Pan-American Games gold medal in 1951, the latter against weaker opposition because the United States did not participate. Both teams reached a 39-goal handicap level; there is no question that today both would have been 40-goal teams.

The teams' style of play was very different. El Trébol offered an elegant, classic game, based upon ball control and tremendous pace. Venado Tuerto displayed an unremitting attack; their weapons were speed and hard drives, with long-distance shots at goal. In defense, the Venado Tuerto players were fearless markers, bumping opponents with gusto; El Trébol's style was to place a leg in front of the opponent and use the pony to take him away from the play.

Polo in Argentina thrives on team rivalries. Hurlingham and North Santa Fe in a sort of city versus camp in the early 1900s, Hurlingham again in the 1920s against Santa Inés and Santa Paula in the 1930s preceded one of the most memorable ones: El Trébol and Venado Tuerto. When El Trébol and Venado Tuerto vacated center stage in Argentine polo, their role was taken over by the next super-rivals: Coronel Suárez and Santa Ana. These two teams monopolized the Argentine Open Championship titles from 1961 until 1983. Coronel Suárez's eleven-year winning streak in the Argentine Open Championship is unlikely to be surpassed, just as its twenty-three open wins in a twenty-seven year span. Between 1957 and 1984, the blue and red team took every Argentine Open except in 1960 — won by El Trébol — and 1971, 1973 and 1982, when the champion cup was taken by the Dorignac brothers' Santa Ana. Juan Carlos Harriott, Jr., was on the winning team twenty times and so was his friend Horacio Heguy, if his replacement of Celestino Garrós in the second chukker of the 1980 finals is taken into account. Alberto Pedro Heguy has seventeen open trophies and Alfredo Harriott, thirteen. Juan Carlos Harriott, Sr., won the open seven times.

What made Coronel Suárez, the one of the 40 goals, the best team in the history of the game? First and foremost was the personality and overall playing brilliancy of their captain and undisputed leader, Juancarlitos Harriott. Second, Coronel Suárez made a norm of playing at full speed, constantly. The foursome made a cult of playing throughout the game as if they were trailing by one goal, with only a minute or so to go before the final bell. Their attitude was, "We have to score a goal, if not we'll lose the game. Let's find a way to score one goal."[8]

The third main component was Juan Carlos Harriott's basic polo philosophy: Force the opposing number 3 to play facing his own goal. Obviously, sometimes Juancarlitos himself had to face his own goal, but the intention always was to face the adversary's goalposts. Their thirst for scoring goals was insatiable. Gonzalo Tanoira, who in his day was considered only second to Juancarlitos as the best player worldwide, once said, "If they could win by 100 goals they would never be satisfied with 99. They wanted 100. To me, this is a fundamental attribute for any player. Such desperation to win, such hunger for glory; it was fabulous."[9]

Coronel Suárez's adversaries during more than two decades were teams that included the Dorignac brothers, Francisco, Gastón and Marcelo. Initially playing for Tortugas, and later on for their own Santa Ana, named after their father's estancia in Villa Valeria, in southwest Córdoba Province, both clubs were unlucky to be contemporaries with the 40-goal polo machine, as reporters dubbed the quartette from Coronel Suárez. Francisco, the eldest sibling, was a magnificent striker of the ball as a teenager, though not as great a player of matches as he would become later. Groomed first by his father, Gastón, Sr., then by his 10-goal uncle Enrique Alberdi, his natural skills were polished to brightness when another 10-goaler from Venado Tuerto, Roberto Cavanagh, joined the Tortugas team. The three brothers and the gigantic Roberto took the Hurlingham Open in 1960. From the following year until 1982, Santa Ana and Coronel Suárez collided in the final game of the Argentine Open — or in the decisive match when a round-robin format was in effect — every year except 1978, when Santa Ana did not participate in the high-goal season. Most of the time, each match was decided by one or two goals; it was that close, year in and year out, in the longest rivalry in Argentine polo. Santa Ana did get the spoils of victory on three occasions, by one, two and three goals.

Only one other team came close to challenging these two giants of Argentine polo. The team was Mar del Plata, based upon the brothers Gonzalo and Jorge Tanoira, Alfredo "Negro" Goti and Juan José Alberdi. Mar del Plata also called upon Alfonso and Gonzalo Pieres when they were young, along with Alberto Goti and Englishman Julian Hipwood. Some of these teams were successful, taking the Tortugas and the Hurlingham Open Championships; however, the top prize, the "Abierto de Palermo," was beyond their reach.

Following the retirement of those magnificent teams, Coronel Suárez, Mar del Plata and Santa Ana, a new team formed in 1938 at estancia New Home in Abbott by the brothers Garrahan and Buchanan — talk about Anglo-Irish influence on Argentine polo — ruled the roost. The team's name was La Espadaña. Alfonso and Gonzalo Pieres, Ernesto Trotz and Mexican Carlos Gracida, the latter sometimes spelled by his compatriot Antonio "Chamaco" Herrera and Juan Martín Zavaleta, dominated the high-goal scene. Only the new Indios-Chapaleufú, with the three brothers Marcos, Gonzalo and Horacito Heguy, put a dent in La Espadaña's string of successes. Ironically, the fourth member of the squad was Alex Garrahan, oldest son of Tommy, one of the founding members of La Espadaña.

The 1990s continued the era of absolute supremacy showed by Argentine players. This brought about an element of snobbism because of this newfound dominance in an elite equestrian game. Virginia Carreño, a masterful storyteller of Argentina's society, refers to the game of polo as a vehicle for social climbing because it allowed members of the Argentine high-class society to rub elbows with European and English nobility, and Texas millionaires in the early decades, and, more recently, with rich Australian businessmen and Asiatic princes.[10]

The almost bucolic atmosphere at Tortugas Country Club in Argentina. Here, home team battles Pilarchico (Museum of Polo and Hall of Fame).

The youngsters who had been mere boys in the halcyon days of Coronel Suárez, Mar del Plata and Santa Ana made their presence felt. Gone were the days in which only two, perhaps three, teams could realistically have a winning chance in the Open Championships at Tortugas, Hurlingham and Palermo. The number of serious contenders grew quickly. Indios-Chapaleufú I, that one of the four Heguy brothers, now completed with Bautista, the youngest, took three open championships in a row and four out of five. Ellerstina, Gonzalo Pieres' new concoction that included Adolfito Cambiaso and Mariano Aguerre, won the open three times as well. The other Heguys, Eduardo "Ruso," Alberto, Jr., and Ignacio "Nachi," Alberto Pedro's sons, formed Indios-Chapaleufú II, and so far have taken four titles at Palermo, three with Milo Fernández Araujo and one with Alejandro Díaz Alberdi.[11]

The other Heguys, Bautista, Horacito and Marcos, had an emotional win in the Argentine Open after Gonzalo's tragic death in an automobile accident. With Mariano Aguerre in Gonzalo's slot at Number 2, Indios-Chapaleufú I scored a dramatic victory at Palermo in 2001, defeating Adolfito Cambiaso's La Dolfina by one goal.

La Aguada of the four Novillo Astrada siblings took the Abierto in 2003 and the Triple Crown to boot. The third generation Novillo Astradas — their grandfather Julio took the National Handicap tournament in 1946 and their father Eduardo "Taio" was a 9-goal handicap player who was a finalist in the U.S. Open and a winner of the Hurlingham Open — asked Norberto Fernández Moreno to be the team's coach. They felt they needed someone on the sidelines that could analyze the flow of the game without being involved in the struggle on the field. They also defied convention by playing their best horses in the Tortugas Open, the first leg of the Triple Crown. Common wisdom is that all the best mounts are

Indios-Chapaleufú I, the 2001 Argentine Open Champions, are (from left) Bautista Heguy, Mariano Aguerre, Marcos Heguy and Horacio S. Heguy. They are four 10-goal handicap players of Basque ancestry, so prominent in Argentine polo (Museum of Polo and Hall of Fame).

brought up for the Hurlingham Open and then to Palermo for the Argentine Open. The brothers four took a risk, which paid off. Opinion remains divided as to whether or not it was sound strategy, but the fact stands that no other team has taken all three championships in one year since La Aguada accomplished such exploit.

The Ellerstina team of the brothers Matías and Pablo MacDonough and Facundo and Gonzalito Pieres came close twice, in 2005 and 2007 reaching the final at Palermo after taking the Tortugas and Hurlingham Open Championships, only to be denied by La Dolfina in the finals at Palermo.

The current holders, La Dolfina, have taken the Argentine Open Championship three years in a row; amazingly, all three in sudden death overtime. Adolfito Cambiaso, Lucas Monteverde, Mariano Aguerre and Bartolomé "Lolo" Castagnola are on their way to being considered one of the best teams ever in the history of polo in Argentina, and ergo, in the world.

In addition, clubs such as Centauros, La Martina, La Mariana, El Paraíso, and now a new Ellerstina have had a chance at the championship. In the last few years, no less than six teams were true contenders for the top prize in world polo, the Argentine Open Championship. It is an outstanding achievement. Will it get even better?

20. England's Recovery: Gentlemen Players and Hired Assassins

Cowdray, the man and the club, became synonymous with the revival and subsequent development of the game. — Roger Chatterton-Newman[1]

The United Kingdom was worn out at the end of World War II. With the Labour Party in power, currency restrictions and food rationing were a staple of daily life for years to come. Nevertheless, polo took some feeble steps in the summer of 1947, at both Rugby and Cowdray Park. The Rugby Polo Club's attempt was unsuccessful[2]; however, polo at Cowdray, sometimes with only three-a-side teams and incorporating Lord Cowdray's sisters, slowly took off.[3] Cheshire Polo Club in 1951 and Cirencester Park the following year returned to the fold, as well as Roehampton and Ham, the two remaining London polo clubs, and Woolmers Park in Hertfordshire, Arthur Lucas's creation.

Old silver cups were gradually removed from trophy cabinets, polished with utmost care and offered for competition. The Cowdray Park Challenge Cup was revived as early as 1948; appropriately, it was taken by the host club with a team that included Maj. Colin Davenport, the Hon. Daphne Lakin — Lord Cowdray's sister — her husband John Lakin and Lord Cowdray. Also in that year, the Junior County Cup was taken by the Birkdale team, Dorothy Kidston, Arthur Lucas, Capt. Patrick Butler and Maj. Thomas Hilder. As a sign of changing times, women were on the winning teams of the first two tournaments played after the war. The County Cup was renewed in 1951 and the Inter-Regimental Tournament in 1958, when it was taken by the 7th Hussars. The team captain, Lt. Col. C.T. Llewellen Palmer, was instrumental in reviving this polo tournament, the oldest in the world.

The 1951 Hurlingham Polo Association *Year Book* lists twelve affiliated clubs and fourteen polo-playing regiments, all in the British Army of the Rhine.[4] Of those civilian clubs, only six are active in 2008: Cowdray Park, Ham, Rhinefield, Taunton Vale, Toulston and a revived Woolmers Park. The clubs that now are only memories are Billericay in Essex, Canford Magna in Hantsfordshire, Henley in Middlesex, Orford in Suffolk, Silver Leys in Hertfordshire and Sutton Place in Surrey. Interestingly enough, the Roehampton Club, which offered a busy polo fortnight in London every July until 1956, is not listed in 1951, although quite active.

The Coronation Year loomed large in British polo. As part of the celebrations, a seven-

Top: The Rose of England at Palermo, 1949. Members are, from the left, Jack Traill, John Lakin, Bob Skene and Lt. Col. Humphrey Guinness. England defeated Chile in its first International match after World War II (Museum of Polo and Hall of Fame). *Above:* The Duke of Edinburgh, wearing a dark blue helmet, at Guards Polo Club. Prince Philip founded what is now one of the most prominent polo venues in the world, then known as the Household Brigade Club. Watercolor by Lionel Edwards (private collection, photograph by Alex Pacheco).

Polo at Cirencester Park, oil on canvas, signed T. S. LaFontaine. The painting shows the white and black home team in action against Capt. John Macdonald-Buchanan's Buccaneers on the Ivy Lodge ground, which dates back to the 1890s (private collection).

team, 24-goal tournament was held at Cowdray Park. Argentina, Chile, England and Spain presented national teams, while Meadow Brook carried the United States' banner. Woolmers Park and the host club completed the slate. Argentina (Eduardo Braun Cantilo, Ernesto Lalor, Alex Mihanovich and Juan Carlos Alberdi) faced in the final game an English team, Lt. Col. Alec Harper, Gerald Balding, Lt. Col. Humphrey Guinness and John Lakin, which had defeated La Espadaña two years before in the Festival Cup. However, a much better Argentine team defeated England in a very close match by the odd goal, 7–6. The game was played in the rain and witnessed by the newly crowned Elizabeth II and her consort, the Duke of Edinburgh, already bitten by the polo bug. From the time Prince Philip arrived on the scene, polo had once more become a popular sport in England. Then, and for many years on, until Prince Charles retired from the game, a royal presence at any polo match was a sure indication that the gate would be a substantial one. The attendance of photographers — the sobriquet "paparazzi" was not yet in vogue — and a press willing to provide extensive coverage for a public whose thirst for royalty news and gossip appeared to be insatiable, added considerably to the image of polo as a game for the rich and the powerful.

The style of reporting polo games came under scrutiny. A letter to the editor is worthy of inclusion:

> I was amused to read in a recent issue of Polo the bitter complaint of some outraged critic on the score that the reporting of polo matches in London is in a fearful state of cream-puff, that the comments of the experts in the press are so much butter that would melt in your mouth. This is no discovery.

May I refer you to page 194 of that elegant book on polo written by Mr. T.B. Drybrough, member of Hurlingham, Ranelagh, Roehampton, and so forth.

"Spectators have often most distorted ideas on these subjects. One man will assert that his friends had the best of the game, though they lost by bad luck in goals. 'They ought to have hit a dozen,' he will say. Our notes will probably show clearly that they were never 'in the game,' and that the other side did the goal missing; but we must not tell all the truth about the bad play, especially if we are the guest of the guilty man. Although we should respect men's feelings, there is no need to write flattering nonsense.

"We should remember that players are very touchy about reflections on their ponies. It is dangerous to say that any one was clearly faster than another; for the go-by may have been attributable to other causes than speed, or may for good reasons have intentionally permitted, and the reporter may thus be easily led into flattering the slower pony. Sensible men do not believe all they read, and they always made a liberal allowance for 'gush.' In reporting, it is wise to leave ladies alone, and never to mention their names. If we say nice things, they are apt to consider their expression in print as a liberty, and even if they like the notice, it is just possible that some of their lady friends will not."[5]

The 1950s also saw the start of a new element in British polo: the player, usually from Latin America, commonly known as "the hired assassin." This derogatory term that came into vogue in England after the Second World War was actually mentioned in Burma as far back as 1930. An unsigned article reads, "In spite of this 'hardware' [silver trophies] civilian polo remained moribund, the 'hired assassin' appeared in the land and only the Military Police mantelpieces groaned with silver."[6]

There is no mention of who were the hired hands. A review of the teams participating in the tournaments gives no clue, because no handicaps are indicated. Could he be a Burmese police officer, or a civil servant? Perhaps they were imported players from India, or from neighboring Manipur? The practice of paying players for their skill at polo had started in the 1920s; nevertheless, it was only mentioned in whispers and, most certainly, nothing was written about it. Anyway, the belittling term "hired assassin" commonly applied to Argentine players as generators is unfair treatment, because there were no professional players from that country at the end of World War I, when the term was used in Burma, part of the British Empire. Nevertheless, it remains in common usage, and the fact is that from the inception of the Cowdray Park Gold Cup every winning team but one has had a foreign player in the lineup. The sterling exception is Windsor Park — Lord Patrick Beresford, the Marquis of Waterford, Prince Philip and Paul Withers — in 1969.[7]

A momentous event occurred in 1956 when Lord John Cowdray presented the Cowdray Park Gold Cup,[8] which is emblematic of the British Open Championship, a distinction previously held by the Hurlingham Champion Cup from 1876 to 1939. A visiting team, Los Indios from Argentina, took the honors. The team captain was Antonio Heguy, father of two and grandfather of seven 10-goal handicap players.

In the early 1950s, some enterprising Argentine players started the practice of traveling to Europe, mainly to England, France and Spain, carrying loads of polo ponies. The business was to sell the ponies at good prices at the end of the season. Among those pioneers, Eduardo Rojas Lanusse stands out. Eduardito, as he was called, also taught the game at different clubs and eventually became a kind of icon in British polo circles. Rojas Lanusse was soon followed in his endeavors by other players, such as Miguel Indart, who settled in Cheshire for the season — there is an Indart Cup in the Cheshire polo calendar — and Ernesto "Tito" Lalor (who played at Guards), Wyndham Lacey and Pedro Llorente.

In 1957, an unheralded Argentine 12-goal team made a visit to England, bringing their own ponies and paying their own way. Media Luna, named after the Media Luna Fort, located near two ponds shaped like half moons, is one of the oldest clubs, for polo was played there as far back as 1892. Luis Nelson, Jr., his cousin John P. Nelson, Arturo Reynal and Guillermo Goñi Durañona took the County Cup and the Royal Windsor Cup. Additional rewards came John Nelson's way when he substituted for an injured Windsor Park player in Cowdray Park's Gold Cup. The Windsor Park team that included Prince Philip, Lt. Col. Guinness and Ernesto Lalor went on take the trophy.

The Warwickshire Cup, which dates back to 1894 and is one of the top three English tournaments, was brought back into competition in 1959, initially as the prize in one of quarterfinals for the Gold Cup, and then as a full tournament at Cirencester Park.[9]

A few American teams ventured across the pond to compete in the major British tournaments. A most sporting expedition was that of a team named The Plainsmen, formed by Texan John Armstrong, his son Charles and the Orthwein twins, Peter and Steve. An unheralded team, The Plainsmen reached the semifinals of the 1969 Cowdray Park Gold Cup and were unlucky to lose the final game of the Royal Windsor Cup at Guards in extra time, with widened goals. The most successful American team was Boca Raton, from Florida, sponsored by John Oxley and completed with his son Jack, Roy Barry and Joe Casey. They took Cowdray Park's Gold Cup, defeating Windsor Park in the finals.

The British Commonwealth Team in Argentina, 1966. From the left are the Marquess of Waterford, his brother Lord Patrick Beresford, Patrick Kemple from Rhodesia, Australian Sinclair Hill, Paul Withers and Maj. Ronald Ferguson. The team was lodged at the Hurlingham Club clubhouse, which is seen in the background (private collection, gift of Mr. John P. Nelson).

Eduardo "Gordo" Moore, Argentine-born into a polo family, is the last 10-goaler in England. Moore was a dominant player in the 1970s, mostly within the Vestey organization and aided immensely by the celebrated mares Fabiola and Lass (Museum of Polo and Hall of Fame).

The next year, 1971, Heath Manning's Columbia, from South Carolina, took the Harrison Cup and the Royal Windsor Cup. Dr. William Linfoot, his son Corky and Ronnie Tong were the other players on the team. Billy Linfoot and Ronnie Tong were on the American squad that won the match for the Coronation Cup.

John Reardon "Hap" Sharp brought over his Greenhill team to Europe, playing in Spain and England. With players such as his sons-in-law Robert Graham and Tommy Wayman, Lester "Red' Armour and Maj. Ronald Ferguson, Greenhill was successful at Sotogrande and Cowdray, winning their Gold Cups. Hap Sharp had acquired early fame as a sports car driver, partnering Jim Hall on the Chaparral team that made its mark in American and European racing circuits. This was mostly due to their driving ability, but also for their technical innovations, such as the high-wing spoilers and automatic transmissions in racing cars, at a time when the "heel and toe" technique was the customary mode of changing gears in racing.

Other American teams of note were Bill Ylvisaker's Langham Park, Brook Johnson's C.S. Brooks and John Goodman's Isla Carroll. John Goodman generously gave support to the American team in the 1997 Westchester Cup challenge, the last time the oldest international trophy has been up for competition between America and England.

These American teams contributed significantly to increasing public interest in polo in England because several players represented the United States in four successive matches for the Coronation Cup, which had been dormant since 1953. The success of those matches encouraged the Hurlingham Polo Association after 1974 to continue offering the Coronation Cup to be played for annually against visiting foreign teams. Eventually, International Day at Windsor Park became the largest one-day event in world polo.

Military polo in England took some time to recover. However, in 1951 a dozen regiments in the British Army of the Rhine were playing in Germany. The Inter-Regimental Tournament was resumed in 1958, mainly through the efforts of Lt. Col. Charles "Tim" Llewellen Palmer, 7th Hussars, the son of "Pedlar" Llewellen Palmer of 10th Hussars fame in India. The polo family tradition was continued by Charles and Julian, Pedlar's grandsons. Most appropriately, the tournament was taken by the 7th Hussars.[10]

Maj. Gen. Arthur Denaro gave great impetus to polo in the Army when he was commandant of the Royal Military Academy at Sandhurst.[11] In the best soldier polo tradition, General Denaro was the captain of the R.M.A. team that took the Inter-Regimental Tournament in 1989.[12] The academy has also hosted international teams on its polo grounds to benefit several charities.

Royalty also made an impact on military polo when Cornet Harry Wales was on the Household Cavalry team in 2006, which went on to take the Inter-Regimental. Another team member was Capt. Benjamin J. Vestey, the Hon. Mark Vestey's son, who had cut his teeth in the Pony Club and later on his father's Foxcote team, based in Gloucestershire.

Polo in England went from strength to strength. The twelve affiliated polo clubs of 1951 doubled in the next decade, and again in 2001, when 44 clubs appeared in the *Hurlingham Polo Association Year Book*.[13]

21. Polo in America in the Late Twentieth Century

As long as 26-goal polo is the best we have to offer, we will remain a 26-goal country on the global scale. — Stewart Iglehart[1]

The game of polo in the United States took a long time before it reached a standard of play comparable to the one exhibited in the late 1930s. While it is traditional to blame the mechanization of the U.S. Cavalry as the main cause of the lower quality of play in the immediate post-war period, there were many reasons for the lag in recovery. Military polo was already in decline before the war started — at least for the Americans — in 1941. Many of the stalwart players of the golden years were gone and the others had been away from the game for quite some time. Some top players were dead. Lt. Col. Thomas Hitchcock, Jr., met his fate while testing a Mustang fighter plane that crashed near the cathedral city of Salisbury in Southern England. Lt. Charles Skiddy Von Stade, a most promising young player from a family with deep roots in American polo, was killed in Germany when his jeep ran over a land mine.[2] Peter Perkins, a survivor from the infamous Bataan Death March, languished the rest of the war in a Japanese prisoner of war camp in the Philippines.[3] Polo mounts were scarce and the clubs had — largely — neglected the polo grounds.

The U.S. Polo Association did not publish its annual yearbook until 1949. Forty-six active clubs are listed. Regrettably, only the events held in 1948 are reported; the two previous years remain a black hole in the record of American polo, with only scant coverage in the national newspapers. A visit by the Argentine club Miraflores in 1946 — they took the Monty Waterbury Cup — Venado Tuerto to California in the Spring of 1949 and another by El Trébol to the East Coast served to place the game in front of only moderate audiences, a turn of events that depleted the association's coffers.

The lean years of the 1950s saw Meadow Brook without polo. The U.S. Open moved to Oak Brook in the outskirts of Chicago, where Paul Butler developed a magnificent polo and golf complex. Only four teams entered the 1954 Open Championship in its new home. It was a time of changing of the guard. Stewart Iglehart retired in 1956, his 10-goal handicap still valid. The other American 10-goaler, Cecil Smith, soldiered on until the mid-sixties. In that rarified atmosphere of double-digit handicap, they were joined by Australian-born, later U.S. citizen Bob Skene, who settled as a professional player in Southern California.

The brothers Stewart and Philip Iglehart sit on a 1930s station wagon. Stewart reached a 10-goal handicap, played in two Westchester Cup series and took five U.S. Open Championships. Philip, a 7-goaler, also won one Open title and played in the Coronation Cup. His lasting memorial is the creation of the National Museum of Polo and Hall of Fame (Museum of Polo and Hall of Fame).

International polo was at a low ebb in the United States. Individual visits by Argentine players such as Enrique Alberdi, Horacio Castilla and Gastón Dorignac to participate in the Open Championship added a measure of attraction for spectators. A British Commonwealth squad visited Oak Brook in 1963. Lord Patrick Beresford, Paul Withers, Sinclair Hill and Maj. Ronald Ferguson wearing Cowdray Park's orange colors took the Butler Handicap. This success brought about a spate of frenzy in the British press. The normally staid *Times* reported, "Let the flags fly high at Midhurst tonight and bells ring out at Willow Tree, N.S.W., for this week Australian Sinclair Hill and his team have written the name of Cowdray Park into American history. They have played and defeated two of the best 25-goal teams in the U.S. and in the manner of their victory have earned respect for British polo overseas."[4]

Major Ronald Ferguson tells a story about that journey to America: "During that first tour we stayed at the Drake Hotel. On one occasion our team, being young and high-spirited, behaved rather badly in the swimming pool. As team manager, I was summoned to a breakfast meeting with Jori and Paul [Butler] by Michael, Jorie's brother, where I was given a frightful rocket. Jorie was an absolute dragon. From that day, however, we became good friends and I have affectionately called her 'Dragon' ever since."[5]

An important event for American polo occurred in 1974, when the Argentine team Las Garzas (The Herons) made a seven-week tour in the Northeast. It was the first visit by an Argentine team since 1949, when El Trébol participated in the U.S. Open. Roberto Fernández Llanos, Tommy Garrahan and the brothers Alfredo and Oscar Podestá, with Ernesto Pinto as spare man, played matches at Brandywine, Fairfield County Hunt, Meadowbrook, Potomac and Myopia Hunt. The respective hosts were Fred Fortugno, George Haas and Adie Von Gontard, Jr., Fred Braunstein, Tom Dowd, Don Little and Adam Winthrop.

Las Garzas, a 16-goal team, won all the matches except the first two, against Brandywine and Fairfield. The visitors were provided mounts by their hosts; however, on the game with

Fairfield, Meadowbrook loaned their ponies to the Argentines, and Fairfield then returned the favor, shipping their ponies to Long Island. It is no coincidence that these two games were the best of the entire tour, as both teams were fully mounted.[6]

This almost forgotten tour was significant for American polo because it marked the beginning of a new interchange between Argentine and American players. As a result of this visit, George Haas was invited to play in Argentina, where he was introduced to 10-goaler Gonzalo Tanoira. The following year, Tanoira played on the Fairfield County Hunt team with George Haas and Peter and Steve Orthwein. The U.S. Open Championship at Oak Brook ground was the scene for Gonzalo's magic stick-work and perfect equitation. This started the invasion of Argentine polo players that has remained a feature of polo in the United States to this day.

Although polo had been part of the Florida landscape since the early 1920s, the game really took off thirty years later. The old Gulf Stream Club owned by the Phipps family, with grounds adjacent to the Inter-coastal Waterway, resumed operations. It eventually moved inland to a location close to the Florida Turnpike, developing into a sort of family club, with many owners keeping their ponies next to the polo fields. For many winter seasons, the newly named Gulfstream has been a low-key, fun-loving institution, hosting the national 8-goal Delegate's Cup, the Bronze Trophy and the riotous Alligator Open. Unfortunately, Gulfstream now faces the prospect of developers' greed and the reality of compulsive purchasing of private property by Palm Beach County authorities. Bernard, Binger, Bostwick, Butterworth, Haas, Iglehart, Johnston and Orthwein are some of the family names that will remain associated forever with the Gulfstream Polo Club.

Farther south, in Boca Raton, the Beveridge family started polo after relinquishing their stake in the Gulfstream club. Polo in Boca Raton is indelibly associated with John Thurman Oxley ands his sons Jack and Tom.[7] For many years, the best polo in Florida took place at the Oxleys' club, first on Glades Road and later at its current location on Clint Moore Road. The Boca Raton Polo Club stadium was the best facility to watch a polo match, because if offered unobstructed views of the entire grounds with comfortable seating arrangements. In its heyday, Boca Raton presented the best polo in the United States, including two U.S. Open Championships and the International Challenge Cup, whose trophy is a replica of the famous Westchester Cup. Regrettably, the 2008 season was the last in Boca Raton after 49 years of uninterrupted high-goal polo.

In the late 1970s, the vision of Bill Ylvisaker created the Palm Beach Polo and Country Club in Wellington. Eleven polo fields, a nice stadium with modern equipment, and plenty of land available to construct homes, private polo grounds and stabling facilities converted the small village of Wellington into an equestrian mecca. When the National Horse Show settled for the winter season, more than 11,000 horses were stabled in the area. Southern Florida offered high-goal polo in two excellent clubs and trophies proliferated. The all-professional World Cup started in Chicago in 1976; three years later, it moved to Palm Beach Polo and became its showcase tournament until 1997, when sponsorship dropped off.[8] Notable victories included the U.S.A.–Texas team over a Coronel Suárez squad that included Juancarlitos Harriott and White Birch's seven wins, with five of those during a six-year span.

With a change in ownership, the game at Palm Beach Polo Club went into a progressive decline. A hurricane severely damaged the stadium; because of new regulations, the cost to rebuild the structure up to code standards was prohibitive and the stadium was razed in May 2008. In the meantime, there has been a quantum leap of polo clubs in and around Palm

Beach County. The jewel of the crown is John Goodman's International Polo Club at Palm Beach, located in Wellington almost next to Palm Beach Polo. It is now the home of the U.S. Open Championship, the Gold Cup and the C.V. Whitney Cup, the trophies that really are the triple crown of polo in America, although an argument could be made on behalf of the Monty Waterbury Cup, which was played on handicap by the teams that participated in the U.S. Open since 1922. A "Triple Crown," trademarked by an organization outside the U.S. Polo Association takes place at different venues — California, Florida, South Carolina and Texas — by lower handicap teams. The beautiful trophy manufactured by Tiffany & Co. is matched neither by the quality of the games nor by the tradition and importance of the tournaments.[9]

Polo in California remained vibrant, with old-timer Santa Barbara Polo Club leading the way. It hosted the U.S. Open in 1966, which served as an observation point for the committee charged with the selection of the American team charged with the task of recovering the Cup of the Americas. The Open Championship returned to California in 1987, following Retama Polo Center's departure from high-goal polo, and returned to the same club, Eldorado Polo Club, in Indio, in 1992 and 1993. Glen Holden, Sr., that great supporter of the game, realized his dream of winning the U.S. Open with his own team, Gehache.[10]

The U.S. Open returns to California. From the left, Rubén Gracida, Mike Azzaro, Memo Gracida, Glen Holden Sr., Mrs. Glen (Gloria) Holden and alternate Joe Wayne Barry are on the podium for Gehache (Museum of Polo and Hall of Fame).

The final bell has rung and the 1998 U.S. Open Championship is history. Juan Ignacio "Pite" Merlos drops his crop and runs to embrace his mother in celebration (Museum of Polo and Hall of Fame).

While Santa Barbara, started in 1911, enjoys magnificent views in Carpinteria, Eldorado and neighbor Empire Polo Club thrive in the desert. Santa Barbara was the host club for the fifth World Championship in 1998, a 14-goal handicap tournament played under the umbrella of the Federation of International Polo. It is also the home of the Pacific Coast Open, whose trophy, the Spreckels Cup, is one of the most valuable prizes in the world of polo.[11]

Polo in New England was concentrated in the North Shore of Boston and in Fairfield County in Connecticut. Myopia Hunt, located in Hamilton, is one of the oldest active clubs in America. Started in 1875, polo was added in the summer of 1887 on a pasture at Gibney farm. Now converted into Gibney Field, it has a strong claim to be the oldest polo ground in activity. After World War II, the game was revived by Harvard graduate Forrester "Tim"

Clark, polo captain from the pre-war years, and Crocker Snow, Sr. They were joined by Neil Ayer, Les Crossman, Don Little, his half-brother Crocker "Terry" Snow, Jr., Joseph Poor and Adam Winthrop.[12] The rivalry with Fairfield County Hunt developed soon after and lasted until Fairfield gradually faded away because of attrition, the mantle of polo in Fairfield County being taken over by the Greenwich Polo Club, White Birch's home ground. Myopia also hosted the East Coast Open for the Perry Trophy, which dates back to 1905 when it was presented by Mrs. Marsden Jaseal Perry to the Rumford Polo Club in Rhode Island.

Fairfield County Hunt Club was founded in Westport, Connecticut, in 1924. Polo came into being at the club thanks to the efforts of two ladies, Laura Fraser — the noted sculptress — and Lila Howard.[13] In 1946, the Hunt Club hosted an Argentine team, Miraflores, that went on to capture the Monty Waterbury Cup and repeated the invitation to Las Garzas in 1974 and 1978 to play in the club's International Trophy. This cup was also offered for competition to clubs from Canada, England, the Dominican Republic, Iran, New Zealand and Pakistan. However, the main adversaries were the Myopians from Boston's North Shore, especially regarding the Forbes Cup, emblematic of polo supremacy in the New England states. The old polo ground, donated in perpetuity by the Rudkin family, still host annual polo games; however, horse and carriage shows are the main attractions at the club.[14]

Polo at Saratoga was revived in 1979 by Peter M. Brant, Richard I.G. Jones, Sr., and William S. Farish III, among others. Tommy Glynn rediscovered the old field location and the club secured the old Monty Waterbury Cup, which dated back to 1922, as the centerpiece tournament for the month of August. Eventually, Saratoga passed to a partnership headed by Westporter Jim Rossi, who has re-established the venue to its former balmy days. It is now one of the main centers of summer polo in the Northeast.

The center of polo power in the United States moved westwards when the Meadow Brook Club closed its polo operations and the organization running the Open Championship was taken over by Oak Brook Polo Club. It stayed near Chicago until the accidental demise of Paul Butler sounded the death knell of Oak Brook as we knew it. However, Steve Gose saved the day for American polo when he came forward with his Retama Polo Center near San Antonio, thus providing a new home for the open. The club hosted the Cup of the Americas in 1980, the last time is has been played up to now. Retama Polo Center, since 1979 the home of most of the U.S. Open Championships, fell into financial difficulties in 1986, the last year the open was played on its grounds. The club was taken over by Bossier Bank and Trust in Louisiana, which foreclosed the facilities. Its 700 acres of land were sold to pay off nearly 18 million in debt.[15] Retama, a flashing glory in the annals of American and international polo, finally closed in 1992.

The U.S. Polo Association moved its headquarters from New York City to Chicago, and then to Lexington in Kentucky. A regional office has been created in Wellington, perhaps in response to the fact that Florida is the main hub of polo from January until late April. With the availability of adequate grounds at the Lexington Horse Park, the Open Championship moved to thoroughbred country. It remained in the Bluegrass state for only four years; subsequent venues in California and Long Island were finally replaced in 1996 by Southern Florida, at both Palm Beach and Boca Raton.

In the last 60 years, the game of polo has experienced tremendous growth in America. The 46 active polo clubs in 1946 have increased to 270 in 2007, not counting the universities' clubs.[16] The numbers of players, tournaments and the length of each polo season have also enlarged. The written word has also shown increased publication. However, when you start with only the annual Blue Book, there is only one way to go. *Polo Unlimited* had some vogue in the 1950s, only to fade away. The U.S.P.A. edited *The Polo Newsletter*, which grew into *Polo News*, and then moved forward into *Polo*, under Ami Shinitzky's able although at times acerbic editorial skills. The magazine *Polo*, now under the editorship of Peter and Gwen Rizzo, had to add the wording *Players Edition* to its title because of the legal settlement with the mammoth Ralph Lauren enterprises.

The tactics of polo in America after the war naturally resembled those employed in the late 1930s, which in turn were a slight modification of those brought about by Tommy Hitchcock in 1928. These tactics were modified because the mandatory decrease in the top team handicap allowed in the U.S. Open resulted in lower handicapped players participating in the tournament. Two-goal and 3-goal individual handicaps were then seen participating in the U.S. Open. This trend continued into the 1950s, with playing sponsors in teams such as Dallas and Circle F, both winners of the Open Championship. Three-man polo became the norm on some teams in high-goal competition.

Later on, the game became the province of the big hitters. When Bob Skene — much celebrated by his stick-work — left high-goal polo, players such as William Mayer, Tommy Wayman, Harold "Chico" Barry, his nephew Roy and later on his son Harold "Joe" were the prominent players. Excellent players and good horsemen like William "Doc" Linfoot, "Red" Armour, Ray Harrington, Benny Gutierrez and Tommy Wayman[17] had to work extra hard to carry their teams when facing booming 150-plus-yard strokes from the long-hitters' mallets. Thus, the passing game suffered at the hands of the 'hit long and rush after the ball' approach and the subtle artistry of the game gave way to the force of the long ball. The U.S. Polo Association Handicap Committee saw fit to reward only Tommy Wayman with the accolade of a 10-goal rating. Many impartial observers of polo feel that Armour, the Barrys and Dr. Billy

Linfoot certainly deserved consideration for the top handicap in the United States. Perhaps they suffered when compared to the contemporary 10-goalers in Argentina; however, it must be remembered that all but two games for the Cup of the Americas were held at Palermo and home field advantage is as important in polo as in any other game.

Mexican-born Guillermo "Memo" Gracida appeared on the international scene at Retama in San Antonio.[18] Memo Gracida's rise to the top was meteoric. His keen organizational mind and his painstaking attention to detail were complemented by sound equitation, hitting ability and a sound strategic mind. His incredible record of wins in the U.S.

Bennie Gutierrez, winner of the U.S. Open, international player in the Cup of the Americas, in his Milwaukee days. His high-goal career was cut short at an 8-goal handicap by a serious accident on a Florida polo field. Bennie recovered to lead White Birch in a long string of successes in low- and medium-goal events. Eventually he became one of the best umpires and was appointed chief umpire by the U.S.P.A. (Museum of Polo and Hall of Fame).

Open Championship is testimony of his individual skill as a player and as a leader. A 10-goal rating was his reward; Memo retained that handicap without interruption longer than any other player in history, a tribute to his resilience and competitive hunger.

Four other players were raised to 10 goals since Memo Gracida's heyday. The first was his younger brother Carlos, who was thought by many to be a better individual player than his older sibling; Carlos — a Mexican citizen — is the only one to have taken the United States, British and Argentine Open Championships in the same year, a feat that he accomplished twice, in 1988 and 1989. Owen Rinehart, Michael Azzaro, and in the 21st century, Adam Snow, are the other American players who reached polo's pinnacle after World War II.

In the last ten years, the dominance of Argentine players in American high-goal polo has increased in a vast amount. Since 1997, every winning team in the U.S. Open Championship has had at least one player from Argentina in its lineup.

Nevertheless, for practical purposes, American high-goal polo remains a three-high handicap player game. With the notable exception of White Birch, whose sponsor Peter Brant is a former 7-goal player, all other eleven teams had a patron rated at either one or 0 goals. Even within that narrow margin, significant differences in ability and horsemanship were noticed among the different patrons. While some play above their handicap, others appear to be over-handicapped. In some ways, the handicap committee mimics the match announcers' occasional laudatory comments, a reminder of what Samuel Pepys, that perceptive 17th century writer, recorded in his diary, "4 Jan. [1664] To the Tennis Court, and there saw the King play at tennis and others: but to see the King play was extolled, without any cause at all, was a loathsome sight, though sometimes, indeed, he did play very well and deserved to be commended; but such open flattery is beastly."[19]

22. Bits and Pieces, Strokes and Mallets

The Creation of the Federation of International Polo

The need for an international organization dedicated to promoting and coordinating the game of polo in a worldwide fashion was intermittently discussed among the senior governing bodies for a long time. The main objective was to articulate and publish a single code of rules of the game. Lord Louis Mountbatten was the prime mover in this endeavor, and a meeting of the International Rules Committee was held in London in 1938 to consider the International Rules as drafted by Lord Mountbatten. The project came to naught because of the onset of the Second World War in Europe. In the meantime, the Argentine Polo Association, which up to 1939 had followed the Hurlingham Polo Committee's laws, decided to issue their own code.

The issue remained dormant until 1978 when Marcos Uranga, at the time vice president of the Argentine Polo Association, organized an International Polo Tournament for Clubs, later nicknamed Mundialito, at the Jockey Club grounds in San Isidro, a Buenos Aires suburb. The competition was an unqualified success — it drew 24 teams — and Marcos felt that the time was ripe for expanding the competition into a tournament among countries. In December 1982, the Argentine Polo Association invited all the national associations to a meeting in Buenos Aires to discuss the idea of a world polo federation. The meeting took place at the Jockey Club see in Buenos Aires with representatives from 12 polo-playing countries. Britain and the Commonwealth countries abstained from attending the meeting because of the Falkland Islands conflict. At the end of the meeting it was resolved to create the Federation of International Polo, with Marcos Uranga as president and Luis Valdez y Colón de Carbajal from Spain as vice president.

The Federation of International Polo has organized world championships since 1987, limiting the teams' handicaps to 14 goals total, therefore providing opportunities for many more countries to participate. Buenos Aires, Berlin, Santiago de Chile, St. Moritz, Santa Barbara, Melbourne, Chantilly and Mexico City have been the venues for the competition. Another accomplishment by the F.I.P. is the publication of an international set of rules of the game, which hopefully will become the worldwide code of polo.

A Traditional Ritual

One of the time-honored traditions in polo is that of treading-in or divot stomping by spectators during the half-time break. Where and when it began, it is not exactly known. It probably started in England, where the perennial wet weather made the grounds subject to easily being cut-up. Treading-in was rarely necessary in India because of the hard surfaces. In Argentina, it became prevalent in country polo around the turn of the century, becoming almost compulsory in later years. It was an opportunity to socialize and make new acquaintances. Oddly enough, it was never done at Palermo or San Isidro. In important matches, swarms of Asociación Argentina de Polo employees or army conscripts, many armed with sand buckets, took care of the divots at the end of every chukker.

In American high-goal polo, the half-time ritual is a bit of a carnival. Sky-divers, classic car exhibits, marching bands blaring, balloons, free plastic glasses of champagne dispensed from Hummers, and the occasional scramble for one-dollar bills dropped from the air are part and parcel of the spectacle. The extraneous excess so prevalent in America seems to have percolated to other parts of the world so the polo match appears to be part of the event, not the main reason for the gathering of people. No statistics have been compiled; however, casual observation indicates that the percentage of people stomping divots is very small.

How prescient was Richard Danielson's editorial in 1928: "In the effort to 'sell' polo to the American public, the authorities in the game have gone too far. It is time now to hedge — or the game will belong to the public which has been so successfully 'sold' and will be dominated by people and groups deaf and blind to the spirit of the game, insistently demanding more and better circuses."[1]

In England, halftime is more of a social occasion; sometimes royalty joins the crowd in a rare display of a common effort with the proletariat, flattening divots on behalf of a better game of polo. It is also an opportunity for flirting. The celebrated Julian Hipwood, captain of the English international team for two decades, met his future wife, Patricia, while democratically stomping, not at the Savoy, but on Cowdray Park's polo grounds.[2]

Fancy Strokes

Most textbooks on the game describe four basic strokes in polo, two on the nearside and two on the offside, each with three variations: the straight drive, the pull and the cut shot. There are also out of the ordinary shots, commonly referred to as fancy strokes. Examples are the push shot, now quite in vogue, away from the neck shots and the hook and strike shot. A rare stroke in the early days was the shot in the air, which was a derivative of the stroke allowed in the Silchar rules and copied from the Manipuris. If a player caught the ball with his hands, he could, unimpeded, toss the ball in the air and hit it. A modification of this unusual stroke is well described in *The Maltese Cat*: "It was then that Powell, a quiet and level-headed man as a rule, became inspired and played a stroke that sometimes comes off successfully on a quiet afternoon of long practice. He took his stick in both hands, and standing up in his stirrups, swiped at the ball in the air, Munipore fashion."[3]

The English painter Edward Matthew Hale depicted this action in a small oil painting, and so did the celebrated artist Lionel Edwards. This tiny detail in the narrative caught Edwards's eye and he used the passage as an illustration for a later edition of *The Maltese Cat*.[4]

The "millionaire's stroke," as hitting the ball under the pony's belly has been derisively called, can be a useful shot in close quarters and at slow speed. Dr. Pedro Christophersen emphasizes that all strokes must be executed around the pony and not under it, because such technique is considered bad polo, dangerous to the pony's legs and inefficient.[5] However, Christophersen goes on to say that in exceptional circumstances, hitting under the belly may be an indispensable stroke to score a goal or make a save in a difficult situation. In order not to hit the pony's legs during the follow-through, his advice is to either hit the ground and the ball at the same time, or to cushion the stroke against the player's foot immediately after hitting the ball.

The new tactics in polo have brought into use a variation of the nearside cut shot. In essence, it is a tap or wrist shot as performed on the nearside with the palm of the hand behind the mallet's grip, instead of reversed as in the regular nearside forward stroke.[6]

The Evolution of the Polo Mallet

The game of polo could not possibly be played without a mallet. Interestingly enough, the rules of the game are silent as to the specifications of such tool. Therefore, the field is wide open for designers to ply their craft, and yet there have been very few variations of the shape of the mallet, or stick, as it is also known.

It appears that the initial instrument in Tibet consisted of two broom-like wooden structures held together by an iron contraption. The Manipuris who traveled to Calcutta in the 1860s carried short sticks with a very long cylindrical head, which was placed at an acute angle in relation to the shaft, compared to current practice.

In Britain, the initial walking stick gave way to long hockey sticks. Col. Robert Liddell states that the 9th Lancers developed an improved polo stick, but he fails to describe what the improvement was.[7] The most famous mallet in polo history was a contraption devised by Francis "Tip" Herbert, of Monmouthshire Club fame: "I particularly remember a special stick I had manufactured, so that it would not break. It was of ash, with a head of oak, and shod with iron and square heads. After considerable damage had been done to ponies and men by this stick, it was declared to be undesirable, and was relegated to my barrack rooms."[8]

The length of the mallet became longer along the successive increases in the height of the ponies mandated by the ruling bodies. Currently, length varies between 49 and 54 inches; most players use 51 to 53 inch long mallets.

The mallet's handle has changed little since the game's inception. Round handles were promptly discarded because the player could not "feel" the position of the head in relation to the grip; therefore, an oval or egg shape became the norm. The cover was leather, sheepskin, cotton-cloth or rubber; the last became the most common. A thong or sling was sometimes applied at the handle's end, although for while a finger-loop in the side of the handle was popular. In the 1920s, the Parada sling, based on the same principle, was tried but soon abandoned. The most common handle is the racket type, smooth and with an upper border; the width appropriate to the size of the player's hand.

After the modified hockey stick, the next development was a long cane with a variously shaped head. Canes were made of moonah, also known as rattan (*Calamus manan*) or of malacca (*Calamus ascipionum*). For some time, split canes were popular; the upper half made of the more rigid malacca and the lower of rattan. On the hard and fast Indian grounds, the very flexible rattan with close knots was preferred, while in England the tendency was to use the more rigid variety of rattan, with knots farther apart from each other. In Argentina they played with whatever stick could be found or manufactured. Malacca was either smoked or natural. These canes tended to be very rigid and heavier than the ones made with rattan.

The lower part of any cane is the thinnest and most subject to damage; therefore, three or four rubber rings were placed just above the mallet's head as a form of protection. Experience with fiberglass shafts has shown that, even if practically unbreakable, they may cause a condition similar to tennis elbow. Currently, there are graphite shafts that show promise as an alternative to the traditional canes.

The initial head was called a square head; in practice, it was a rectangular cube. It presented the peculiarity that the cane was not inserted in the center of the head, but near the end closest to the player. The first square head tended to dig into the turf; therefore, the first modifications were to place the shaft at an angle and to make the heads slightly curved. Lt. Col. Jules LeGallais, 8th Hussars[9] and one of the top British players, suggested clipping the head's base near the ends. Thus evolved the LeGallais oval head, one of the most popular designs up to the early 20th century.

Lt. Col. Jules Le Gallais, 8th Hussars, was one of the best players of his time and designer of a mallet that marked a milestone in the evolution of polo (private collection).

In addition, the square head presented some difficulties in lofting the ball. Attempts were made to correct this shortcoming by utilizing trapezoidal heads; however, both the Brunner and the John A. Hayes designs were unsuccessful and promptly abandoned.

A significant development in mallet design was the cylindrical head that had its weight evenly distributed throughout its surface. Lewis Lawrence Lacey further developed the idea when he made a cut in the bottom of a cylindrical head in the heel. Then he further developed the design by making another cut at the far end, the aim being to facilitate shots taken either very close or too far from the pony. Named the 3L head after his initials, it is still in use. After the cylindrical shape had been in general use, better control was then achieved by tapering the ends, cigar-like, which had the effect of concentrating the weight in the center of the head. Now there is a movement to place more weight near the ends, perhaps with the same idea of the perimeter-weighted golf clubs currently in vogue. There was overlapping in the production of heads' characteristics; by the turn of the 19th century, the player had multiple choices.[10]

The quest for longer distance bought about the Jodhpur head in which a strip of wood at the bottom of the head was cut off, thus allowing the ball to be hit well below its equator. The modern Skene head presents the same modification, as the Ashley head in England did during the 1920s. Along those lines, an ingenuous solution was devised by Lord Louis Mount-batten, better known in polo circles as "Marco," who designed an oval head with a vertical diameter five-sixth the length of the horizontal diameter. It became quite popular and is known as the R.N.P.A. head, since Lord Louis assigned the royalties to the Royal Navy Polo Association.

The initial wood in manufacturing mallet heads was bamboo root. In order to prolong the wood's useful life, a vellum cover was used at times. Several other woods were tried, including ash, birch, maple, sycamore and willow. Current fashion is tipa blanca (*Tipuana tipu*), a tree common in parts of Brazil and Northern Argentina. There is a trend towards increasing the angle of the shaft. For a long time, the usual angle was 9 degrees. Nowadays, players are requesting 11-degree angles and, some, up to 12 degrees.

The evolution of the polo mallet has not followed that of the golf club. It makes theoretical sense to apply the concept of a flat surface to a mallet head, rather than the curved surfaces currently in vogue. Tried and tested by Carlos Gracida, the flat surface failed to gain acceptance in spite of its theoretical advantage.

The total weight of the modern mallet is between 450 and 500 grams; the head's weight varies between 175 and 215 grams. The shorter the cane, the heavier the head; for every inch shorter, eight grams can be added to the head without altering the mallet's balance.[11] Some experience is being acquired with laminated and compound materials. How long the age-old wood will withstand the advances of modern technology remains to be seen.

Protective Equipment

Most of the fatal accidents in polo are the consequence of head injury. The pioneers appeared to have been unconcerned about injuries; therefore, they played the game bare-headed or just wearing a forage cap, which offered little or no protection. The earliest depiction of a polo match in Britain is a work by Capt. Ferdinand Hanbury-Williams — a polo player himself, so it is safe to vouch for accuracy — dated 1875. The painting shows nine riders, all wearing forage or pill-box caps; it was illustrated in *PQ International*.[12] In a later painting of a match at Ranelagh Club by George Rowlandson, the central figure is a bareheaded player about to strike the ball.

Following the implementation of an order by Gen. Sir Frederick Roberts, commander-in-chief, that all officers must wear a helmet during play, the pith helmet became a favorite of polo players in India. They provided shade to the eyes, and the thick brim extended the entire circumference of the helmet. The polo helmet or cap was a derivation of the old hunting cap; its design was credited to Gerald Hardy, a player of repute. The protection was provided by layers of pith and cork, with holes provided for ventilation.

The polo cap style became prevalent in America, while that pith helmet remained the staple of British players until after World War II. When Bob Skene participated in the 1954 Argentine Open, he was the only player to wear a pith helmet, with the exception of Jorge O'Farrell, a local player. The pith helmet is known in Argentina as the Australian helmet, although it originated in India.

Polo helmet design underwent few changes until the 1960s, when facemasks attached to the helmet itself made their appearance. They still are a controversial subject. Certainly, they may prevent facial injuries; however, they may also contribute to aggravate cervical injuries because of neck hyperextension at the moment of impact on the ground during a fall. There was no scientific measure of a particular helmet's resistance to stress until the department of neurosurgery at Wayne State University began its testing program. Several models underwent testing in 1979; Boltaron, McHal-Caliente and Oxley, among them. Several others were tested in later years, including the Bond Street, Calcutt, Gratham, Lock, Lodsworth and the NJL Bell and Spectra.[13]

The U.S. Polo Association has devoted significant amounts of time and financial assistance toward the development of a universal helmet.[14] This goal, similar to the one achieved by the National Football League, is in the not too distant future, thanks to the efforts of the safety committee.

The use of knee guards did not become prevalent until the late 1920s and they became customary in the 1940s. Devereux Milburn was one of the first players to wear a knee guard to protect an injured knee. By the mid 1930s many players used knee guards that essentially only protected the patella, or knee cap. Some ten tears later, its use was customary, although some high-goal players such as the Alberdi brothers eschewed its use. By 1960, knee guards were in almost universal usage. Subsequent development saw the knee guards, a protective element in the player's attire, to look more like an offensive implement. They are, however, an indispensable item to protect the knee joint in what, on occasion, becomes rather ferocious bumping, beyond the rules of the game.

Currently, the Hurlingham Polo Association makes knee guards mandatory.[15] On the other hand, goggles for protection of the eyes are only recommended, in spite of a significant number of polo accidents causing the loss of one eye.

Polo is a Family Game

The story of the game is replete with mentions of brothers playing together on polo teams. Many achieved fame and glory. Reggie and Tip Herbert in Britain were one of the earliest examples; like many other Victorians, both were gifted sportsmen. Tip Herbert was hard to beat as an all-around sportsman; as an example, he killed a salmon, shot some grouse and played in the Avergavenny polo tournament all in the same day.[16] The polo exploits of the Peat, Miller, Nickalls, and Grenfell brothers are described elsewhere in this book. In recent times in England, Julian and Howard Hipwood were recognized as the best players in the country. The Tomlinsons, Luke and Mark, are on their way to reaching that standard. At present, Luke and Mark Tomlinson, children of Simon and Claire Tomlinson, are the highest ranked players in England, followed by Malcolm Borwick, Satnam Dhillon and William Lucas, all from polo families. Also at 6-goals is Henry Brett, who is from a non-polo-playing family; however, his mother, Mrs. Hugh (Margie) Brett, is the editor of the magazine *Polo Times*.

Polo is a family game. From the left, Billy and Bill Ylvisaker, Adie Von Gontard, Jr., and young Adie Von Gontard III are pictured before a practice game in the 1970s. A visionary entrepreneur, Bill Ylvisaker's legacy at Palm Beach Polo Club was wasted by greed and mismanagement. The Von Gontards were stalwart players at Fairfield Hunt Club in Connecticut and on their own Pitchfork Ranch team (Museum of Polo and Hall of Fame).

In America, Larry and Monty Waterbury were the first brothers to reach the 10-goal summit. Winston Guest was rated at 10 goals in England, his country of birth, and his younger brother Raymond was an 8-goaler. The four Gerry brothers, Elbridge, Robert, Henry and Edward, made waves with their family Aknusti team; Elbridge achieved a lofty 9-goal handicap.

Sets of high-goal brothers in Argentina are legion. Hugh and Thomas Robson were at their prime well before handicaps were instituted; seasoned observers were of the opinion that Hugh Scott Robson, the first star in Argentine polo, was a true 10-goaler. When the handicap list was finally published in 1911, Hugh was rated at 9 goals and Tom at 8 goals. Two younger brothers, Edward and William, were eight and six goals, respectively. Johnny Traill, the first with a 10-goal handicap in Argentina, had two brothers, Bob and Ned, rated at 8 goals. Lewis Lacey, another 10-goaler, had four polo-playing brothers; however, none went beyond a 5-goal handicap. Both David and John Miles reached the 9-goal plateau. No other than Devereux Milburn expressed the opinion that there was no 10-goal player better than David Miles. In the 1940s, Enrique and Juan Carlos Alberdi reached the 10-goal level; the latter's son Juan José was a 9-handicap player. Carlos and Julio Mewditeguy and their team-

Hero worship is reflected in the boy's stare. Young Miguelito Torres signs a polo ball obliging admirers that are even more youthful (private collection, Dan Burns photograph).

mate Luis Duggan also obtained the top rating, while Heriberto Duggan was a 9-goaler. A sympathetic scribe noted that the failure of the Argentine Polo Association's Handicap Committee to raise Duggan's handicap to the maximum level was one of the greatest crimes since the crucifixion.

The next generation of Argentine poloists featured Juan Carlitos and Alfredo Harriott — whose father Juan Carlos was a 9-goaler — and the brothers Horacio and Alberto Pedro Heguy and Francisco and Gastón Dorignac. Gonzalo Tanoira also joined those superstars at the top of the ranking, while his older brother Jorge reached an 8-goal handicap. Alfonso and Gonzalo Pieres, two of four polo-playing siblings, also achieved a 10-goal rating, while the fourth generation of Piereses, Gonzalo's sons Gonzalito and Facundo, also obtained the same handicap. Facundo Pieres is the youngest player ever to reach 10 goals, breaking the mark previously set by Tommy Hitchcock and later on surpassed by Adolfo Cambiaso. All five sons of Eduardo "Taio" Novillo Astrada — a 9-goaler — are high-handicap players; Miguel, Ignacio and Javier were or are rated at 10 goals, Eduardo nine, and the youngest, Alejandro "Negro," is a 7-goaler on his way to the top. Agustín, Juan Ignacio "Pite" and Sebastián Merlos, the sons of 9-goaler Héctor "Cacho" Merlos, are 10-goalers. The Piereses' cousins Pablo and Matías MacDonough are currently rated at 10 and 9 goals, respectively.

Seven Heguy cousins merit a paragraph of their own. The sons of Horacio Antonio and Alberto Pedro, both 10-goalers, all became 10-goalers on their own. Four sons of Horacio Heguy — Horacio Segundo, Gonzalo, Marcos and Bautista — were or are 10-goal handicap players. Three of Alberto Pedro's children — Eduardo "Ruso," Alberto "Pepe," and Ignacio "Nachi" — also received the same accolade. Their grandfather, Antonio Heguy, was a 6-goal player who took the Argentine Open Championship in 1958 and Cowdray Park's Gold Cup in 1956.

Mexican citizen Carlos and Guillermo "Memo" Gracida also were 10-goal handicap players; their father, Guillermo Gracida Hoffman, reached an 8-goal handicap.[17, 18, 19, 20] Guillermo "Memote" Gracida, the father, and his brothers José "Pepe," Gabriel "Chino" and Alejandro "Cano" wrote polo history as the only four-brother team to take the U.S. Open Championship, an event that took place at Meadow Brook in 1946. It was a Mexican fiesta, because six players from south of the border played in the final match.

Other father-son combinations in American polo are also notable. Thomas Hitchcock and his son Tommy were the first father-son combination to achieve a 10-goal rating, the father in 1894 and the son in 1921. American Earle W. Hopping was a 10-goaler in England, while his son Earle A.S. was handicapped at 8 goals in the United States. Australian Curtis Skene was rated at 8 goals, and his son Bob, a naturalized American citizen, was a 10-goaler everywhere he played. The celebrated Cecil Smith, the cowboy from Llano, was a 10-goaler for a long time, while his son Charles, the American international player, reached a 7-handicap while being a part-time player, commuting from Texas to Chicago at the peak of his career. Finally, David Stirling from Uruguay was a 10-goaler; his grandson, also named David, plays in England and the United States, where he was recently raised to a 9-goal rating.[21, 22]

Based upon this random data, it is safe to assume that in no other game the family connections at the highest level of performance are as prevalent as in polo. Is it a genetic evolution? Is it the fact that a polo-playing scion has more opportunities to start the game at an early age? Is it a combination of both factors?

An examination of a list of 92 players who have reached a 10-goal handicap[23] indicates that 53 players grew up in polo-playing families and 39 in non polo-playing families. The argument can be made that the family environment is a strong influence in the development of high-goal polo players.

The Museum of Polo and Hall of Fame

Every sport and game has its heroes and icons. The parent bodies recognize many individuals while many more languish in relative obscurity because the selection committees demonstrate biases or remain unaware of a player's achievements. The latter situation applies mostly to those players whose days of glory occurred in the formative era of the game. It is a given that a nine-goal player of the 19th century is as worthy of consideration as a contemporary star.

A unique institution exists in America, the National Museum of Polo and Hall of Fame, created by Philip Iglehart, Leverett Miller, George Sherman and Jeremy Chisholm, all polo players. Built on land donated by Mr. Iglehart, and with the financial support of the Beal family, Mr. S.K. Johnston, Jr., the Orthwein family and the late John T. Oxley, the museum opened its doors in 1997.

The holdings include a comprehensive library, a large photographic archive and a respectable collection of polo art. The Philip L.B. Iglehart Library Room was donated by Mr. and Mrs. Carleton Beal. There is a complete run of the U.S.P.A.'s *Year Books*, starting since inception. The *1890 Year Book* is probably the only original in existence.

The Media Room was donated by Adolphus A. Busch IV. It is a state-of-the-art projection facility, which also serves as a conference and meeting room. The movie and video collection numbers hundreds of items, including footage from the 1930 Westchester Cup.

The permanent art collection includes paintings by Paul Brown, Thomas Percy Earl, Kenneth MacIntyre, Larrence McKenna, Sam Savitt and Franklin Voss. There is also a Chinese scroll from the T'ang Dynasty, presented by former chairman of the board and benefactor Leverett Miller, Harry Payne Whitney's grandson. Bronzes by Herbert Haseltine, Rich Roenisch and Charles Cary Rumsey add a singular touch to the exhibits.

The museum is the repository for the U.S. Polo Association's array of trophies, from the U.S. Open Championship prize, a silver 17th century tureen by Sally James Faraham, to the Silver Cup, the oldest trophy awarded by the U.S.P.A., as well as many 19th century polo cups.

Another important part of the museum's mission is the selection of nominated candidates for the Polo Hall of Fame. Categories include the Hall of Fame proper, the Iglehart Award for Lifetime Contributions to the game and the Horses to Remember Award. The different awards are presented at a gala ceremony in the museum every February. The names of all the inductees are displayed on plaques on the Hall of Fame Wall. The honored polo ponies have a wall of their own, each painted by Canadian artist Melinda Brewer.

George DuPont, Jr., the museum's director, and Brenda Lynn, director of development, run the day-to-day operations as well as organizing the temporary exhibits and running the unique traveling exhibit during the summer months, from Newport, Rhode Island, to Santa Barbara in California. The National Museum of Polo also provides something intangible, but nevertheless priceless for lovers of polo: an atmosphere that exudes an exquisite feeling and appreciation for the game's history and timeless traditions.

PART IV: THE PROFESSIONALS

23. Patrons and the Dawn of Professionalism

The powers of British polo have passed a new rule designed to have a far-reaching effect upon the game. The rule reads simply as follows: "No player shall pay or receive payment for playing polo."— Peter Vischer[1]

The issue of who is a professional polo player and who is not has been a matter of debate, mostly *sotto voce*, since the 19th century. Several governing bodies in different games have struggled to define the boundaries between the lily-pure amateur and the full-fledged professional. Racial and social distinctions have at times been used as the reason in discriminatory decisions by governing bodies.

When Richard Ely Danielson started publishing *The Sportsman* in 1927, he candidly expressed the ideals of the amateur code:

> The purposes and aims of *The Sportsman* are — or should be — self-evident. It is addressed to the sportsmen and sportswomen of this country. It is founded on the intention of covering as fully as possible the whole range of their sporting interests. It is dedicated to these convictions:
> That sport is something done for the fun of doing it;
> That is ceases to be sport when it becomes a business, something done for what there is in it;
> That amateurism is something of the heart and spirit — not a matter of exact technical qualifications;
> That the good manners of sport are fundamentally important;
> That the code must be strictly upheld;
> That the whole structure of sport is not only preserved from the absurdity of undue importance, but it is justified by a kind of courage, patience, good temper, and unselfishness which are demanded by the code;
> That the exploitation of sport for profit kills the spirit and retains only the husk and semblance of the thing;
> That the qualities of frankness, courage, and sincerity which mark the good sportsman in private life shall mark all discussions of his interest in this publication.
> And the editors undertake that neither fear nor favor shall temper a straightforward policy of discussing all sporting matters on their merits.[2]

The Sportsman was a publication *Time* magazine referred to as

> unique in its tone, *The Sportsman* is not for the ringside habitué, not for the occasional "hunter" who combs the hills once each year for a legal maximum bag of game, not for the bleacher authority on batting averages. Its rich illustrations depict gentlemen riders taking jumps hand-

somely: "Mr. Lewis Lacey ... leads Mr. Hopping over the boards in the third match at Meadow Brook"; a priest blessing the hounds of Chagrin Valley Hunt Club before the chase.

The Sportsman's contributors are nearly all non-professional writers, mostly men and women of wealth — eager to write of the sports on which they may be authorities. Riding far afield from the game-getters (*Field & Stream*, etc.) and from the magazines for idle gentlefolk (*Town & Country*, *The Spur*, etc.), the gentlemen of the Press who run *The Sportsman* have tried the fence into a field of distinctly sporting aristocracy and cleared it neatly.[3]

Mr. Danielson and his publication's lofty ideals seem to be out of touch with the current reality of sports and games. Professional sports are entertainment, closer to wrestling than to games. As Lt. Col. Alec Harper once said, professionalism came in with spectator sport.

In actuality, the concept of a professional player started in India when the ruling princes enlisted members from their private armies to play polo on their teams. Prowess at polo was a sure way to gain promotion in the armies' ranks. A French polo player, Jean, Comte de Madré, hired Jaswant Singh and Jagindar Singh — both 10-goalers — as professional players to perform on his team, the famous Tigers.

In Argentina, a team formed by Francis Kinchant, a foreman and two peons took the Polo Association of the River Plate Open Championship in 1895 and 1896. The practice of including estancia hands on polo teams remained a common sight in Argentine tournaments. Following John Campbell's Western Camps' second open title in 1909, the P.A. of the River Plate prohibited the participation of peons in official tournaments; however, administrators and managers were allowed to play. In the 1920s, with the democratization of polo under the Asociación Argentina de Polo, estancias' employees were again seen on polo teams and many reached high handicaps.

The intention of the rule against playing for money was to stamp out by decree what was loosely known as professionalism in polo, which the British polo hierarchy believed to be one of the causes of England's decline in polo since the war. Speaking before the British Sportsmen's Club in London at a luncheon given to the Maharaja of Jaipur and the Indian polo team, the Earl of Kimberley, better known in America as Lord Wodehouse, stated,

The standard of what we call first-class polo is lower in this country than it has ever been. The main reason for this is that during the last ten years the canker of professionalism has crept into our game. Our polo today in some cases — I only say in some cases — is almost on a par with professional association football.

Certain players sell themselves and are bought. Certain patrons, rich patrons, bid for these players and the highest bidder gets them. This state of affairs has discouraged many young and promising players from taking up the game seriously, because they felt they had no chance in present-day polo without a hired assassin on their side.

This question was brought up to the notice of the Hurlingham Polo Committee, and in spite of strong opposition from a small section, the stewards have definitely decided to put an end to it after this season. In the future, the stewards will allow any player to have all his expenses paid and get his polo for nothing, but they will not allow any players to make money directly or indirectly out of playing the game.[4]

This new policy put into effect by the English ruling body in handling the perceived problem of professionalism was so different from that of the U.S. Polo Association that Peter Vischer, *Polo* magazine's editor, asked the Hurlingham Polo Committee to clarify the new ruling. In reply, Lord Cowdray, chairman of the Hurlingham Club Polo Committee, and thus the directing head of the game as played in most countries of the world, wrote,

The Hurlingham Club Polo Committee has always recognized that one method by which young players, who are not too well endowed with the world's goods, can be brought on and improved in their polo is that they should be mounted and assisted by individuals who are running teams and can afford to give help of this nature. In passing the new rule, Hurlingham Club Polo Committee has no intention of discouraging this form of assistance, but wishes to discourage a practice that has latterly been growing up whereby certain players have been receiving sums of money largely in excess of their requirements for expenses.

If this practice is allowed to grow, it means that individuals who run teams will be tempted to bid against each other for the high-handicap player and there will be a less likelihood of legitimate assistance being given to the young player. The Hurlingham Club Polo Committee feels that this tendency is contrary to the best interests of the game and the new rule in effect means that payments must be limited to cover genuine expenses.

In order that current arrangements may not be unduly upset and that all concerned may have sufficient time to consider future plans, the stewards do not intend to deal too stringently with the matter this season but in future years the new rule will be enforced in the general interest of the game.[5]

Perhaps the rule was enacted to satisfy the British authorities' conscience, because this is a rule that is practically impossible to enforce. Private dealings between payer and payee seldom leave the confines of the room where the transaction took place. Mr. Vischer was of the opinion that it would be unlikely for America to change its traditional policy about professionalism in polo. "By maintaining a broad-minded attitude, America's polo officials had

Carlos Gracida carries the distinction of winning the Open Championships of America, England and Argentina in the same year, a feat that he accomplished twice. Carlos is wearing patron Lyndon Lea's Zacara team colors (Museum of Polo and Hall of Fame, photograph by Alex Pacheco).

guided the sport clear of those pitfalls which have so hurt the repute of tennis, with its 'tennis bums,' for instance, or college baseball, with its boys playing semi-professionally (whatever that is) under assumed names, or amateur hockey, with its 'shamateurs,' or track athletics, or even golf, with its 'business-man golfers.'

"The policy of the U.S.P.A. as outlined in an article on professionalism in Polo's issue for January 1930, is quite simple as the new British policy. It is that 'if he's an all right person, he's an all right person.' In other words, let the common sense opinion of a man be your guide rather than any set of rules laid down to be evaded."[6]

The issue of professionalism again reared its face in Europe in the 1960s. By that time, it was common practice for Argentine players to travel to England, France and Italy all expenses paid — with their ponies, which they sold at advantageous prices. Gradually, it became a full-season occupation. Wealthy patrons in England like Alfie Boyd-Gibbins, Ronnie Driver, Arthur Lucas, Eric Moller and Sir Evelyn de Rothschild started the trend of hiring Latin American players for their teams. They were followed by the Vesteys, Sam and Mark — perhaps the most

Adam Snow, a third generation player from Myopia, is the latest American 10-goaler. Adam is on Pumbaa, named Best Playing Pony in the 2002 U.S. Open Championship at Royal Palm, Boca Raton (Museum of Polo and Hall of Fame).

successful combination with the Héctor Barrantes and Eduardo Moore duo—Alex Ebeid, John Lucas and Lord Brecknock.

In Italy, patrons such as the Marchese Giacinto Guglielmo di Vulci, whose team La Vulci took the 1963 Gold Cup at Cowdray Park, opened the way for later worthies. Orazio Annunziata with his own Brattas took the Coupe d'Or at Deauville, the Copa de Oro and the Copa de Plata at Sotogrande, and the Open de Paris on five occasions. Another successful Italian patron is Stefano Marsaglia—who emulated La Vulci's success at Cowdray—and later was fined 30,000 pounds, in addition to a 15-month suspension, for insulting and threatening an umpire during the British Open Championship.[7] Then we have Alfio Marchini, Loro Piana's patron, who took the Queen's Cup in England as a one-goal handicap player, while rated 4 goals in Argentina. Diplomatically, David Woodd noted, "Loro Piana was considered to have half lengthened the handicappers."[8] All these Italian patrons have cut an important presence in English and Continental polo.

French sponsors included the late Baron Elie de Rothschild, Edouard Carmignac, Philippe Fatien, Claude Mercier, restaurateur Claude Terrail, and art dealer Guy Wildenstein, whose Diables Bleus were also successful in England and America. M. Patrick Guerrand-Hermès, sponsor of La Palmerai team, is currently the president of the Federation of International

Polo; under his direction the Domaine de Chantilly Polo Club organized the 2004 World Championship.

When the next generation of patrons came on board, the concept of full-fledged professionalism was part of the English landscape. Anthony Embiricos, Brook Johnson, John Manconi, the late Hubert Perrodo, Urs Schwarzenbach and Galen Weston fielded their teams, usually with two foreign players and a lucky young Englishman whose rating met the team's needs in regards to maximum handicap for the tournament in question.

That prescient administrator and keen observer of the game, Lt. Col. Alec Harper, expressed his thoughts on the issue, "Professionalism obviously raises certain problems and wants careful watching as more and more of our best players turn professional. However, it must be admitted that these players generally set an excellent example both of expertise and behavior on the field; they tend to be safe and thoughtful players. The old-fashioned amateur used to play each game as if it were its last. The professional has to think about his important engagement next week."[9]

Perhaps the biggest influence on British polo, extended to most of the world, was the appearance of Kerry Packer on the high-goal panorama.[10] Packer's determination to win, no matter what the cost or the principle, is reflected in his behavior following an incident on the

White Birch's patron Peter Brant led the most successful team in North America since the 1980s (private collection, Dan Burns photograph).

field during the 1993 Queen's Cup. His own Ellerston star player Gonzalo Pieres, upset at some rough play by Sebastián Merlos, rode broadside into his mount. The fracas occurred behind the play but in full view of the spectators and was documented by a *Daily Telegraph* photographer.[11]

The Hurlingham Polo Association suspended Pieres for the rest of the season. Kerry Packer then threatened a lawsuit against the Hurlingham Polo Association, arguing that it was interfering with his contract with an employee. A prominent English polo personality who was to testify on behalf of the H.P.A. withdrew from the case, coincidentally selling a horse to the Ellerston team.[12] The Hurlingham Polo Association gave in to the threatened legal action; Pieres' season suspension was reduced to one game in the Gold Cup. "The stewards felt that they had 'insufficient evidence' to take the matter further; however, they added a sanctimonious rider to their finding that they hoped that international 10-goalers would be a better example to our young players."[13]

Kerry Packer's strong-arm practices extended beyond the polo field. The English base for his polo operation was the Fyning Hill estate near Cowdray Park, with beautiful views of England's southern coast. Packer also purchased Great House Farm adjacent to the village of Steadham. Bulldozers leveled the lush water meadows, untouched for hundreds of years, including an ancient footpath that runs across the property. Permission was not sought from the appropriate authorities on the grounds that it was to be an experimental turf farm. Three polo grounds and a clubhouse took the place of the meadows and the old brick-and-wood barn. Steadham's "Stop the Packer Polo" movement came too late to prevent the changes, although the village council imposed some restrictions.[14]

Kerry Packer's free spending ways changed the economics of polo like no other individual in the game's history. However, a custodian of the game, he was not.

Another distinguished Australian has different views on the issue of patron polo and is quite explicit in his crusade on behalf of the flowing game of polo. John Sinclair Hill, a 10-goal handicap player, had his views on the current state of the game lucidly formulated in *Polo Times* and in *Profiles in Polo*.[15, 16] Patron polo, says Sinclair Hill, has changed the game to such degree that what you see now is a payer and three players. There is no doubt that patrons have improved the quality of the pony strings but they play badly and do not know the rules. Another negative influence is that club loyalty is gone. The game is controlled by hugely wealthy and powerful men around the world. Mr. Hill does not deny that professional players have done a lot for the game; however, they are less prepared to make sacrifices for high success on the field.

Unedited excerpts from a letter written by Sinclair Hill are worth quoting: "The game is suffering from the small time pseudo pros fiddling. The magic spectator value is lost. The excitement is gone or partially destroyed. Sad. The social side has taken over. The patrons don't know enough about the game to control or influence the way the game is played and umpired.... Hanut Singh once told Bob Ashton when asked about dribbling, 'Bob, one fiddle is too many.'"[17]

This is vintage Sinclair. Blunt, honest, direct in his views and opinions in defense of his beloved polo, a game he played so well and with unmatched passion. A much-misunderstood individual, Sinclair Hill has always put the best interests of the game of polo before anything else.

Thoughtful Britishers offered their views to *Polo Times* on the state of English high-goal polo, including this one: "The winning team structure in the 22 goal this year comprising 2 maestros and 2 monkeys, offers nothing to English polo and everything to the Latin Americans. A limit of one foreign sponsored player per 22 goal team would help involve more English players and promote a better team game to the benefit of the viewing public. Perhaps only 26 goal should accommodate the twin maestro line-up."[18]

Not much has changed. In 2008, the British top-rated tournaments, the Warwickshire Cup, the Queen's Cup and Cowdray Park's Gold Cup, still remain at the 22-goal handicap. The top local players are rated at 7 goals; there has been no English 9-goal player since the golden days of the Hipwood brothers.[19]

The question of professionalism in America never reached the level of heated discussion as in England. Perhaps it should be reviewed by the U.S. Polo Association because of the lack of opportunities for up-and-coming young American players to compete in high-goal polo, given the preference shown by most patrons to Argentine professionals.

As to the Argentines, they are amateurs at home and professional players overseas. The professional polo players have not imperiled the traditions of the game, nor threatened the principle of sport for sport's sake. A gentleman, whether amateur or professional, is still a man distinguished for a fine sense of honor, strict regard for his obligations, and consideration for the rights and feelings of others.

24. Women's Polo

Since antiquity, women have played polo and some of them have become quite proficient in a game in which males have been preponderant. For many years after the discovery of the game of *kanjai* in Cachar, any serious consideration of women playing polo faced several obstacles in their attempts to achieve their place under the sun. Among those barriers were the Victorian era unwritten codes of propriety, unwieldy female attire and serious skepticism on the part of men regarding the ability of women to play polo. There was no issue regarding their skill in riding, because their prowess in foxhunting provided ample proof of their talent on horseback. What was under question was their ability to cope with the scrimmages that were such a notorious feature of polo in the early days of the game.

While badminton, croquet, foxhunting, golf and tennis were acceptable pastimes for women in the higher social classes, other athletic endeavors were frowned upon. Baron Pierre de Coubertin, a sports icon because of his role in the revival of the Olympic Games, was of the opinion that athletic endeavors for women were "against the laws of nature."[1] The passage of time did not soften Coubertin's attitude. Thirty-three years after his utterance, writing in 1935, he stated, "I personally am against the participation of women in public competition. At the Olympics their primary role should be like at the ancient tournaments, the crowning of victors with laurels."[2]

The first written reference to women's polo in the modern era appears in Captain George Younghusband's *Polo in India*.[3] A polo match is described between four married ladies and four single ones; each team added one of the opposite gender. Where and when the match took place is not mentioned because the writer — as he states — was bound by a solemn vow not to reveal the pertinent facts. Apparently, the lady-players were riding sidesaddle; the narrator mentions that having the offside of the pony clear, they could get a clean hit on that side. After a break for tea, the game was declared a draw.

America

In America, a 1910 *New York Times* headline read: "Women Play Polo; Miss Eleanor Sears and Sister Players Cause Sensation at Narragansett Pier." The article continued:

> In this resort of sensational happenings, as far as the late season is concerned, at least another event in which women participated took place to-day on the new polo field.
> A polo team comprised of Miss Eleanor Sears, Miss Handy and two other girls opposed a

team of men made up of C.P. Beadleston, C.C. Rumsey, Devereux Milburn and a member of the victorious international team.

About four periods were played, and the young women acquitted themselves very creditably. Two of them rode astride, and because the other two rode side-saddle they were considerably handicapped, but nevertheless played a surprising strong game against their male opponents."[4]

Although not mentioned in the article, the two other members of the women's team were Mrs. Antelo Devereaux and Mrs. Charles Rumsey. It should be noted that the men's team was top-notch. In addition to Milburn, Perry Beadleston and Charles "Pad" Rumsey were 8-goalers and winners of the Open Championship. The unnamed international player must have been either Harry Payne Whitney or one of the Waterbury brothers.

The mercurial Miss Sears was not the only player to make headlines in Rhode Island: "The Point Judith Country Club was an objective point for many of the members of the villa colony this afternoon. There was a lively game of polo on the Point Judith field, in which Miss Emily Randolph of Philadelphia defended the colors of her team and gave a pretty exhibition of horsemanship. Philip Randolph, Jr., Alexander Brown of Philadelphia, and Earl Hooping [sic] were among the other players."[5]

In 1916, another article, under the headline "Society Women Play Polo," mentioned that Miss Eleanor Sears and Mrs. Philip Stevenson were rival team captains, recalling the times when Mrs. Stevenson was Miss Emily Randolph.[6] Once more, the mixed teams included top players. Tommy Hitchcock, only 16 but already a consummate striker, Maurice Heckscher from Meadow Brook, Philadelphian Rodman Wanamaker and the host, Philip Randolph, were all players of repute.

Women's polo owes a debt of gratitude to Eleonora "Eleo" Randolph Sears. A multi-talented sportswoman, she excelled in tennis, taking the U.S. Doubles Championship with Hazel Hotchkiss Wightman, of Wightman Cup fame. True to her pioneering nature, Sears annoyed spectators because she rolled up her sleeves in the course of matches. It is said her membership at a California riding club was put in jeopardy when she rode astride at an arena game. A descendant of Thomas Jefferson, she had the advantage of growing up in a socially prominent Boston family that took their summer holidays in Newport, an early home of tennis and polo in America. Eleanor Sears also won the national title in squash, a game she had learned to play at the all-male Harvard Club. Her determination to compete in many sports and games "paved the way for women's entrance in sports."[7]

Mrs. Thomas (Louise) Hitchcock, Tommy's mother, comes to mind as one who was not only a good player but also an outstanding teacher of polo. For a long time, she had groups of youngsters playing regularly on Long Island and in Aiken, South Carolina, including the wives and children of her polo-playing neighbors. One of her students was Marion Hollins, later to become the national golf champion, the force behind the construction of two outstanding golf courses, Cypress Point and Pasatiempo, and a very good polo player in Aiken, Long Island and California.[8] Mrs. Hitchcock's Meadow Larks girls' teams included Helen Hitchcock, Emily Randolph, Mrs. John S. Phipps, Kitty Penn Smith and Flora Whitney, and, years later, Elizabeth Chase, Eva and Mollie Crawford, Marjorie Le Boutellier (the future Mrs. Stewart Iglehart), Rita Dolan and Paula Murray.[9]

Polo in the West also counted female participation. At the Cheyenne Mountain Country Club in Colorado Springs, a young boys' team played well, but no better than the girls' polo team, which included Hildegarde Neill, Josephine Bogue, Jeanne Sinclaire, Peggy Leonard and Josephine Tutt.[10]

Women's polo was an established game in California by 1926. The first women's polo team was organized at Santa Barbara under the leadership of Mrs. Demming (Dorothy) Wheeler. From stick and ball practice to an occasional participation in men's practice games, polo gradually evolved into a women's team. Out of the dozen women who gathered at the old dirt field, six or seven developed real promise, especially Medora Stedman. In fact, all the neophytes improved to such an extent that the male players occasionally permitted them to use the turf field of the Santa Barbara club. Other players included Mary Chapin, later Mrs. Allen Beemis; Mrs. Grace Terry and Doreen Ashburnham. Substitutes were Mrs. Charles H. Jackson, Jr., and Alice Hanchett. Canadian-born Doreen Ashburnham is the only polo player to have received the George Cross, the United Kingdom's second highest decoration for valor.[11]

Almost simultaneously with Santa Barbara, two teams of women were formed at Will Rogers's Uplifters Club in Rustic Canyon, Santa Monica. There was a tournament match between Santa Barbara and Santa Clara during which Mary Rogers showed great promise as a beginner.

In Boise, Idaho, several mixed teams played exhibition matches at equestrian gymkhanas. Among those helping to develop the sport were Cora Wright, Julia Davis, Bessie Falk and Suzanne D. Taylor. For a welcome change, in Seattle, male members of the Olympic Riding and Driving Club encouraged the formation of a women's team. In Omaha, Nebraska, Daphne Peters organized a polo team.

There are many reports of women's polo activity in other parts of the United States in the twenties and early thirties. In Ohio, the team of Miss Pansey Ireland, Miss M. Allen and Mrs. G. McIntosh played the indoor version of the game in Cleveland. Pansey Elizabeth Ireland became the first woman player to be listed in the U.S.P.A. *Year Book* when she used her initials to obtain a handicap rating in 1925.[12] When this ruse was discovered, her name was promptly erased from the handicap list. In Cincinnati, a group of women was coached by Earle W. Hopping, of international repute as a polo player; the leader was Louise Fleischman, later Mrs. Henry C. Yeiser, Jr., who was the daughter of Julius Fleichsman, one of the prime movers in starting the Sands Point Club on Long Island. Other players included Mrs. Samuel Stephenson, Dorothy Rawson, Miss Resor, Mrs. Lawrence Smith, Mrs. Harold Lion and Mrs. James Benedict.

Similar teams were started in Philadelphia by Mrs. John Hay Whitney, née Altemus, and in Baltimore, where Mrs. Thomas Jefferson Randolph Nicholas led a club of 18 women players. Lydia Archbold, a fabulously wealthy society girl who married U.S. Navy Ensign Elliott Strauss, whose yearly salary was $2,000, organized another polo group in Washington, D.C. As an aside, the marriage ended in divorce. In Asheville, North Carolina, Mrs. Cornelia Vanderbilt Cecil, who lived at the Biltmore mansion, along with Elizabeth Martin, Eliza Cox and Mrs. V. Oldsmith, organized women's polo. Women also played polo in Georgia, where the wives of Army officers gave the game strong support.

The U.S. Polo Women's Polo Association was started in California in 1933 with Dorothy Wheeler as chair. Wheeler wrote to F.S. O'Reilly, secretary-treasurer of the U.S.P.A, asking for recognition of the new entity. O'Reilly haughtily answered, "I think the general opinion among players in the game is that it is not a woman's game." Undaunted, Dorothy Wheeler then wrote to the U.S.P.A. chairman, Robert Earley Strawbridge Jr., whose response was more measured, but still negative. "At the meeting of the Board of Governors, held on October 22, the matter was very thoroughly discussed and it was the final decision that the Polo Association, while it was extremely anxious to foster and encourage polo of every description under its jurisdiction, could not take any official part in the government of women's polo."[13] Thus,

Mr. Strawbridge, a stern Philadelphian who never appears to smile in published photographs, denied recognition to an organized group of women polo players.

The women in California responded by starting a club in Santa Cruz, which drew many members. They named the club Pogonip, after the Native American word for the formation of frost on trees. World War II put an end to women's polo in America for the duration; however, a women's benefit match for the Navy Relief charity at Golden Gate Park in San Francisco drew 8,000 spectators.

Sue Sally Hale was the most prominent figure in American women's polo. Her path to recognition and eventual admiration was difficult. Attempts to obtain a U.S. Polo Association handicap were futile until 1973, when her name appeared in the *Year Book* as a member of Carmel Valley Polo Club.[14] Facing the hostility of many players and encouraged by the support of a few, "Sue Sal" soldiered on, at times disguising herself by hiding her hair under the helmet and sporting a fake moustache. There are reports that she competed under the name A. Jones, her maiden surname.[15] Probably, this happened in local tournaments, because a search of the U.S. Polo Association year books from 1955 to 1972 failed to identify such a name.

However, it was much more than her prowess as a player that endeared Sue Sally Hale to her admirers. Her mentoring, coaching and support of many players on the West Coast was outstanding. Probably her most satisfying achievement was taking the first U.S. Women's Championship with two of her daughters, Stormie and Sunset, better known as "Sunny," and Susan Welker. In 2004, Sue Sally Hale was awarded the Philip Iglehart Award for lifetime contributions to the game of polo, presented by the National Museum of Polo and Hall of Fame.

Sunny Hale continued the legacy of excellence when she became the first woman to take the U.S. Open Championship with Tim Gannon's Outback team. A 5-goal handicap player, the top handicap in the world scene, which she shared with Claire Tomlinson, Sunny Hale was the prime mover in establishing the American Polo Horse Association, an organization that includes a national register for polo ponies.

Many other women have contributed to the growth of polo in America. Gillian Elizabeth Johnston was the first to take the U.S. Open Championship trophy, both as sponsor and player, with her own Coca-Cola team in 2002 at Boca Raton. Gillian now captains her new high-goal team, Bendabout. Vicky Armour, not related to the international player Red Armour, had a promising polo career that she cut short to devote her talent to training polo ponies. Melissa Ganzi has become a respected patron in high-goal polo in Florida and California. Leigh Ann Hall had her moment of glory when her team, Pueblo Viejo, took the Silver Cup, America's oldest polo trophy. Dawn Laurel Jones, actor Tommy Lee Jones' wife, actively participates on the San Saba team.

In the West, Susan Stovall, besides being a good player, managed the Eldorado Club, one of the largest in the country. The Walton sisters, Susan and Mary Alizon, followed a successful inter-collegiate career by managing clubs and winning the U.S. Women's Handicap Championship. In the later endeavor, they were joined by Oatsy Von Gontard.

A lot has evolved during the last fifteen years in women's polo. From the roots level, club polo and inter-scholastic and inter-collegiate polo, to the high-handicap winter and spring tournaments in Florida, the summer feasts in California, Saratoga Springs and Southampton, to the late summer tournaments in Wyoming presented by the fledgling North American Polo League, women players are now a welcome part of the polo scene in the United States.

The Johnston Coca-Cola team, winners of the 2002 U.S. Open at Royal Palm Polo in Boca Raton. From the left are Mrs. S.K. (Gill) Johnston, S.K. Johnston Jr., Gillian Johnston, Adam Snow, Miguel Novillo Astrada, Tommy Biddle and coach Julian Hipwood (Museum of Polo and Hall of Fame).

England

Ladies' polo in England had an early start. The Ranelagh Club in Barnes was the scene of an all-ladies polo match in 1905, with Queen Alexandra being present. Play lasted for half an hour, and although the pace was not particularly fast, the White team easily disposed of the Rainbows by eight goals to nil. The White team was Miss N. Barrow, Mrs. Bampfield and Miss Lilian Arkwright, while the Rainbows were Angela Doris Manners Hume-Spry, Miss K.S. Young and Mrs. Webley. The illustration accompanying the brief report shows some of the ladies riding sidesaddle, while the caption states that Miss Barrow scored most of the goals for her team.[16]

In 1920, Taunton Vale Polo Club in Somerset was reported as unique, because it had the only woman player in England. This was Noëla Whiting, who learned the game in Burma and was handicapped at 2 goals. Noëla Whiting, who later married fellow club player James Brander Dunbar, participated regularly in station games and tournaments, being on winning teams. *Polo Monthly* penned: "There is in this country, for some reason or other, a prejudice against women playing polo, possibly because it is thought that they are not equal to the strenuous happening of the game — the riding-off, etc. But as Miss Whiting is concerned, no such prejudice can exist, as she is a strong horsewoman and can ride out as well as most men. She is very quick on the ball, hits well on both sides of the pony, is a very certain goal hitter, and last, but certainly not least, not only knows the game thoroughly, but plays it. She is well

Sunny Hale, the top American woman player (No. 2), is pursued by Brandon Phillips from Canada at the International Polo Club Palm Beach, the Mecca of winter polo in America (Museum of Polo and Hall of Fame, Alex Pacheco photograph).

mounted on quick, handy ponies. To those who do not believe in a woman being able to play polo all I can say is: come and see her play."[17]

There was more about Noëla. A *Polo Monthly* reader, T.T.M. (probably Col. Thomas Townley Macan, Cameronians Regiment), wrote a letter to the editor in September 1920: "I hardly think full justice has been done to her. Until Miss Whiting arrived in Burma in October 1915 there had been no thought of a 2/5 Somerset polo team. Miss Whiting for several years had ample opportunity of watching good polo and schooling with her stepfather's [Maj. Claude Ward-Jackson] ponies. Within a month, slow chukkers were in full swing, and gradually as the fever developed, polo became the sole topic of conversation. The fact stands that had not been for Miss Whiting's energy and organizing capacity there would have been no team."[18]

The West Somerset Polo Club hosted a two chukker game in 1921, described as a sideshow. Mrs. Maurice Kingscote, Lady Margot Chesham, Miss Waters and Miss Lee played against Mr. R. Corbett, Capt. W.L. Riley, Mr. Gandar Dower and Mr. A.L. Wilson. The ladies did remarkably well, notably Miss Lee, and defeated the males by two goals to one.[19]

Foxbury, Mr. Henry Frederick Tiarks' home, was in 1930 the site of a women's match for a challenge cup, to be played annually, the teams being Foxbury and Invaders. The host team, Foxbury, took the cup defeating the Invaders by four goals to two. Col. Percy Smith, the official umpire for the tournament week, refereed the game. Col. Smith was surprised by the determined play, the pace being fast, the hitting long and the riding-off very business-like.[20] Lady Millicent Tiarks captained the Foxbury team, and the Hon. Yoskill Pearson the Invaders, both women being well-known riders to hounds. The game was of four periods of eight minutes' duration. Miss Cicely Maud Nickalls, Miss P. "Tinker" Nickalls, Lady Milli-cent Tiarks and Miss K. Jackman played for Foxbury, while the Invaders were represented by the Hon. Yoskill Pearson from nearby Midhurst, Mrs. Haley, Miss M. Jackman and Miss E. Jackman. All three Jackman sisters were from Oxfordshire.

During the summer tournament at the Beaufort Club a popular feature was a match between teams mainly composed of women players. Maj. Leonard A. Avery and Maj. Bartlett umpired the match. The Melton Ladies' team was the Hon. Mrs. Edward Greenall, the Hon. Mrs. Gilbert Greenall, Miss Leslie Wilson and Mr. Gerald Balding. The West Country team was Mrs. George Philippi, Mrs. Watts, the Hon. Yoskyl Pearson and Capt. Maurice Kingscote. Both men played at back. The Leicestershire ladies prevailed by four goals to one.[21]

In the 1930s, women's polo in England slowly but surely was making headway. At Nor-ton, in Gloucestershire, on the old Beaufort Polo Club grounds, at the West Somerset Polo Club in Minehead, and in Oxford at Mr. Jackman's place, women played regularly. The first women's polo match played at Beaufort drew a large crowd of onlookers. However, there were difficulties. The Hurlingham Polo Committee decreed that women may not play in tourna-ments, and Hurlingham was the Jockey Club of polo, wielding absolute control over the game in England. However, women players were confident of overcoming the obstacles to their progress. If they could not get permission to play in men's tournaments, some of them pro-posed the intent that a separate women's polo association be established. Since the London clubs would not allow them to play on their grounds, except for an occasional game, they attended the National School of Equitation in Roehampton Vale in southwest London and joined the men in their Saturday afternoon games.

Special mention must be made of Lady Priscilla Willoughby, considered the best female player in the inter-war period. In 1936, Lady Willoughby took two trophies at Harrogate Polo Club as number 2 on men's teams, Boston Spa and Strays Lambs. The male team members were the same; Mr. N. Hardy, Mr. Michael Moseley and Capt. Walter Griffiths. In spite of her achievements as a player, Lady Willoughby was denied a handicap rating by both the County Polo Association and the Hurlingham Polo Committee. While there was no mention of women players in the Hurlingham Committee rules, the County Polo Association stated in its by-laws, "Ladies are not eligible to receive an official handicap or play in Tournaments, but may receive a Local Handicap by the Committee of their Club to enable them to play in a Local Tournament."[22]

By 1938, there was quite a bit of activity in women's polo. The English Women's Open Polo Championship was played at the West Somerset Polo Club in Dunster on 30 July. Lil-borne beat Fontwell Magna by 10 goals to 2 in a match of four chukkers. Lilborne comprised Betty Pacey, "Baby" Balding, Judy Balding and Miss B. Balding. Fontwell Magna was Joan Lanyon, Pat Kelly, Pamela Denison-Pender and Elizabeth Kelly.[23]

Surprisingly, the Hurlingham Club relented a bit and hosted a tournament for the Clan-brassil Challenge Cup, presented by Mr. Hans Rowan-Hamilton. Grimsthorpe, Miss R. Holt, Hon. Mrs. Robert (Yoskyl) Gurdon, Lady Priscilla Willoughby and the Hon. Mrs. George (Angela) Murray beat Rugby, Miss F. Phillips, Miss Judy Forwood, Miss J. Nickalls and Miss B. Balding. The team Oddments — Lady Margaret Drummond-Hay, Hon. Mrs. Gilbert

(Betty) Greenall, Mrs. Philip (Celia) Fleming, and Judith E. Bott—beat Cheetahs, Miss J. Robertson, Nell Campbell, Kitty Meredith Tatham-Warter and Miss R. Giffard. In the final match, Grimsthorpe beat Oddments 5–4.

The Ladies' Inter-Club Invitation Cup at Ranelagh was taken by Rugby, with the same team that had played at Hurlingham, defeating both Grimsthorpe and Oddments. Grimsthorpe, named after the Willoughby de Eresby estate, aligned Miss R. Holt, Hon. Daphne Pearson, Hon. Mrs. Robert (Yoskyl) Gurdon, and Lady Priscilla Willoughby. The Oddments were Mrs. Philip Fleming, Mrs. John Bott, Lady Margaret Drummond-Hay and Kitty Tatham-Warter.[24]

A few matches were played at the obscure Ferne Polo Club in Wiltshire. Probably the club was supported by Lady Margaret Drummond-Hay, who lived nearby. *The Polo Monthly* published a photograph with the caption "Few things in modern polo have been more remarkable than the increasing number of women players, many of whom have taken up the game with great seriousness, and what is more, show no mean skill and no lack of dash. Here is an incident during a ladies' polo match at the Ferne Polo Club, near Shaftesbury Wilts."[25]

The Ladies' Polo Association was started in 1938 after the Clanbrassil Championship Cup had been played at Hurlingham. Among the objectives was to issue a handbook with a ladies' handicap list, the first ever. The publication date was August 1939; the war in Europe began on 1 September. Another initiative was to play indoor polo at the International Horse Show at Olympia. The association had members from Kenya, where there was a ladies' association, along with Brazil and Burma.[26]

When the war was over, women became a common presence as players. It is significant that the teams that took two of the main tournaments included lady players. Mrs. Philip Fleming, also know as Celia Johnson, D.B.E., who enjoyed a long and successful career in the theater and motion pictures, won the 1949 Cowdray Park Challenge Cup. Lord Cowdray's younger sister, Daphne, John Lakin's wife, took the Cowdray Park Challenge Cup on a team that included her husband and her brother. Judy Forwood, another pre-war player from the Rugby Polo Club family, was on the team that took the first Warwickshire Cup played after the war. It would fall to Claire Tomlinson to be the first woman to win the County Cup (1972) and the Queen's Cup (1979). Dorothy Kidston took the Junior County Cup in 1948 with the Birkdale team.

The struggle in England was not for women to be on the handicap list or to be allowed to participate; it was the fight to be permitted to compete in high-goal polo. Two women who came from polo-playing families were the leaders of the pack. Claire Janet Tomlinson was the daughter of Arthur Lucas, the owner of Woolmers Park, who did so much for English polo in the immediate post-war era.[27] The international selectors consistently ignored her brother John, a 6-goal player and winner of the major British championships, who enlisted Claire to find appropriate mounts. After a spell in Argentina and her marriage to Capt. Simon Tomlinson, Claire developed into a most useful number 1.

The second woman was Lavinia Black, whose father, Squadron Leader Alan Roberts, played on his own Maidensgrove team. Just like Claire Lucas, Lavinia Black also honed her polo skill in Argentina. The Hurlingham Polo Association repeatedly denied Lucas the right to play in the high-goal tournaments, although her handicap was higher than that of many men participating in the Gold Cup and the Queen's Cup. Tomlinson's father was one of the Hurlingham Polo Association stewards, which made things a little difficult for her. Acting upon Lord Cowdray's advice, she collected signatures from almost all players who participated in the 1978 Gold Cup. Then she presented the petition to the stewards, who relented in their opposition.[28] Next year, Queen Elizabeth presented the Queen's Cup to Tomlinson, a member of the winning Los Locos team. It was a sort of vindication for all women players in England. Further proof of the ability of women players to participate in high-goal tournaments occurred when Carina "Nina" Vestey (now Clarkin) took the Cowdray Gold Cup in 2003, the first female to do so.

The four Grace sisters, Jane, Katie, Philippa and Victoria, immigrated to England from New Zealand with their parents. Peter Grace, the well-known player, instructor and author, founded the Rangitiki Polo Club in Berkshire, later replaced by the Ascot Park Polo Club.[29] "The Four Graces" playing polo attracted great attention from the public and contributed to the game's expansion by initiating a great number of novices into the mysteries of polo. Victoria "Tor" Grace became one of Britain's top female polo players and Pippa Grace (now Giffard) organized and is the current president of the International Women's Polo Association.

Another all-women team in England that had its moment of glory is Coombe Farm. Lucy Taylor, from the Cheshire polo family, Emma Tomlinson — Simon and Claire's daughter — Nina Clarkin and her sister Tamara Vestey took the 2007 Gerald Balding Cup at Cirencester Park.

This English all-women team took the Gerald Balding Tournament at Cirencester, defeating several good teams. The four ladies are from polo-playing families. From the left, Lucy Taylor, from Cheshire, joined Emma Tomlinson, Nina Clarkin, neé Vestey, and Tamara Vestey, all from Gloucestershire (photograph by Cheryl Miller, ARPS).

Australia

Peggy McComas, from Melbourne, was the prime mover of women's polo in Australia. A show jumping rider at the Melbourne Hunt Club, she started a polo team by recruiting other horsewomen. This was accomplished "despite almost unanimous criticism from the men players, who shook their heads and agreed that this was no game for girls."[30]

In 1934, there were women's teams from Cooronwarnabul, Ranelagh and McComas' own Melbourne Hunt. That same year, the first interstate competition took place in Adelaide, South Australia, and was taken by the visiting team from Victoria. Many years later, Peggy McComas told Chris Ashton that the early misgivings of husbands, brothers, boyfriends and fathers were soon allayed, to the extent that they became the women teams' strongest supporters.[31]

In Tasmania's relative polo isolation, Vera Gwen Cameron, the daughter of polo player Col. Cyril St. Clair Cameron, was a stalwart poloist in her own right during the time between the world wars.

Canada

There is scant mention in polo literature about women's polo in Canada. In 1946, the Calgary Polo Club passed a resolution: "It was decided that the ladies should form its own committee and arrange games to be played either after the regular men's games or on a day that would be suitable to them. It was also decided that the regular Saturday afternoon games should not be mixed."[32]

Whatever the reasons, it was the last mention about women's polo in the club's minutes for many years. It appears that there was no great interest in the game; however, an international series of two matches was played between American and Canadian teams at the Westchester Biltmore Country Club in Rye, New York. Canada was represented by Dorothy Hogan, Bunny Dewdney, May Atkins and Violet May. The American team was Mary Leary, Mrs. James Hewlett, and Sally and Becky Lanier. Dr. Fielding Black was the umpire. The United States team took both matches, 7–1 and 12–3.[33]

In reference to the indoors version of polo, *The Polo Monthly*, in mentioning that it was a regular game in Canada, also states that for some reason, women did not play outdoor polo.[34] As previously mentioned, Julie Roenisch from Calgary, Alberta, was the first woman to enter the U.S. Open Championship playing on the Fish Creek team that was defeated in the final game.[35]

South Africa

On the other hand, women's polo in South Africa was strongly supported in the late 1940s and throughout the 1950s. Women, at the initiative of Cecily FitzPatrick, started the Addo Polo Club in Uitenhage, Cape Province, in 1923. Cecily found many supporters among the British settlers' wives, all keen horsewomen. Dorothy Gibbs, Noel McBean, Margery Merewether, Phyllis Pearce, Iris Rathbone and two Apthorpe girls joined Cecily as players. Cecily FitzPatrick married Jack Niven — there has been a Niven playing at Addo throughout the club's history — and men began to join the fray.

In 1932, the first recorded match was played between ladies' teams from Connington and Durban; the captains were May Woollatt Flower and Maisie McKenzie Brown, respectively.[36] The game ended in a 2-all tie. Flower's husband was D.C. "Jock" Flower, a 5-goal handicap player from Connington, the name of a farm owned by Dr. S.B. Woollatt. The other Connington players were Maureen Taylor, Elizabeth Woollatt, and Barbara Woollatt. Maisie Brown was the wife of Mathew Hugh Brown, the chairman of the South African Polo Association and noted Durban player.

The Natal Ladies Polo Association was formed in 1948, with Barbara McKenzie as president. A Natal Ladies Polo Championship had been instituted a year before; the Lions River team, Moira de Gersigny, Nola Logan Raw, Barbara McKenzie and May Flower, dominated the event until 1951; then the Underberg Rovers won in 1952. Other women players at the time were Mrs. Rodney (Molly) Gold, Mrs. Constance Joan Jackson, Mrs. Gwen Kimber, Mrs. Campbell (Bess) MacNab, Mrs. Michael (Barbara) Pope, Mrs. Tommy (Madalene) Pope, Mrs. Ann Scott-Barnes and Mrs. Maurice (Wilmer) Taylor.[37]

For some unexplained reason, women's polo in South Africa became dormant at the end of the 1950s. When it began to recover some thirty years later, it was a new generation, which also wanted to seek higher standards of play. Tara Bean, Gaye Bryden, Sarah Erskine, Alison Henderson and Fiona Brook Leggatt were some of the new names in South African women's polo, continuing the trail blazed by Cecily FitzPatrick a long time ago.

The River Plate

Women's polo in Argentina has failed to reach prominence. It began in 1927, when a match was held at Los Pingüinos Polo Club in Merlo, near Buenos Aires. Everyone, including the umpires, referee and timekeeper, were women related to the Braun Menéndez family.[38] Women's polo at Tortugas Country Club started in the mid 1930s with a match between Las Gacelas, Sara and Adela Fernández Ocampo, Mabel Aberg Cobo and Rosa M. de Bary, a team that defeated Las Panteras, Susana Inchauspe, Ana Wilson Nevares, Eileen Lacey and Dougall Drysdale. The well-known player Mario Inchauspe umpired the game.[39]

The first woman in Argentina to be included in the official handicap list was Alicia Pamela Greenshields, later Mrs. Harley Storey, who played at the Benitz family's club Los Algarrobos.[40] Women's successes in the Argentine polo calendar have been sporadic at best. María Chavanne, Marcela Cerrutti, María "Mumi" Bellande and Paola Martínez took the Copa Comienzo in 1999, the first time an all-women team had taken an Asociación Argentina de Polo official tournament. A far as individual achievement, Marianela Castagnola took the National Handicap Championship with La Dolfina in 1997.

Across the River Plate, in Uruguay, Marjorie Lancaster played for the Sayago Polo Club, together with her husband Oliver. In 1936, a team from that club that included the Lancasters was the first to tour England.

Social and Legal Issues

Ever since the game started, women have played the part of ornamental spectators. Wives, female relatives and presumed wives of polo players were expected to cheer their exploits on the field, celebrate or commiserate after the match was over, and lend a sympathetic ear to complaints about that dammed umpire, who obviously needed a new set of eyeglasses. Another ritual was that of prize-giving, where the stalwart female was to hand the silver trophies to grinning and sweaty winners of the contest. That has changed. For one, ladies developed trophy-winning ambitions of their own. Also, especially in low-handicap matches, some of the women players were better than a few of the men. The turnaround was completed when a local male worthy was asked to present the trophies to an all-women team. Equality had arrived.

Much more important in the development of women's polo were some of the legal obstacles in the way of female athletes obtaining their rightful place in the sun. The case *Hollander v. Connecticut Inter-Scholastic Athletic Conference, Inc.* (Superior Court Connecticut, New Haven County, 1971) is an important legal document.[41] The court ruled that the plaintiff, a girl, had no right to run cross-country with boys under the Fourteenth Amendment. The wording defies common sense: "Athletic competition builds character in our boys. We do not need that kind of character in our girls — the women of tomorrow."[42]

To end this serious chapter on a comical note, excerpts from an article written by Mrs. Lavinia Roberts Black are worthy of inclusion.

> Everybody always asks me whether the men go easier on the 'weaker sex' when it comes to riding off. The answer is definitely NO. In fact, some men go extra hard, just to try and keep us in our place. When I first played polo in Argentina everybody was so amazed to see a woman playing polo that they wouldn't ride off, only ride alongside without touching. When we came to the ball they would pull up and say, "after you, you hit first!" This very gentlemanly approach soon changed after a couple of goals against them!
>
> The only disadvantage women have against men are language and weight. Ladies are not supposed to swear, although the odd word sometimes slips out. The only disadvantage we have as far as strength is, obviously, in the distance we can hit a ball and possible a little ball control when trying to tap around. With our weaker wrists we will never be able to emulate Howard Hipwood.
>
> When playing at Cirencester some years ago there were, by chance, three ladies on the ground at the same time. Myself, Virginia Bowls and Juliette Worsley. As you can imagine everybody came to have a good laugh and were not disappointed. The only other luckless player I remember was Colonel Alec Harper who was playing with Virginia and myself. In the first chukka he and I somehow got in a tangle and I knocked him off. As he got to his feet, he only glowered at me and muttered under his breath. In the next chukka Juliette crossed him and knocked him for six. Once again, he collected his horse and raising his eyes to heaven (though that didn't help him), he continued. As you can image by this time Virginia and I were nearly helpless with fits of giggles which did not help our polo. Nor it did help Alec, because in the last chukka, with lots of verbal encouragement from the spectators, Virginia, his own teammate, crossed him and for the third time he bit the dust. This time all he could say was, "You bloody women!" It was a long time before Alec could be persuaded to continue. We still claim that he'd had too good a party the night before. Alec still plays as well as ever and against ladies, which just shows how brave he is.[43]

25. The Game's Thinkers

It is axiomatic that a stroke spoiled is equal to a stroke made. — W. Cameron Forbes[1]

Who was the first tactician of the game of polo is a question that cannot be answered with any degree of certainty. This chapter presents a select group of players that made a life-long study of the game and the ponies. By and large, their teachings and opinions are as valid today as they were many years ago.

John Henry Watson

The first strategist of polo was the great Irishman — both in thinking and physical appearance — John Watson, who was a towering figure in British sports. His contributions comprised the tactical invention of the backhander stroke and the organization of the four — or at times five — players as a team, rather than individuals hugging the ball. Proficiency in executing the backstroke immediately made obsolete the contemporary practice of players turning in a wide circle while in possession of the ball. The game of polo became much swifter with the adoption of the backhander, as the American international players found to their chagrin in Newport, Rhode Island, on the event of the inaugural Westchester Cup contest.

As far as combination play, John Watson organized his players as a team, demanding of each to stay in their places, in a situation similar to the tactics known as the straight-line approach, many years later advocated by the American player Cameron Forbes. Under Watson's theory the number 1 player was to take the opposing back, thereby allowing the midfield players gain — or keep — possession of the ball and carry it forward toward the goal. As to back, John Watson's constant position on a team, his role was purely defensive, as well as the one customarily filled by the team's captain. In *The Maltese Cat*—a faithful portrait of 19th century polo as played in the Indian subcontinent — the captain of the Archangels chooses to play forward, "and that is a place from which you cannot easily control your team."[2]

An anonymous biographical sketch written after his death conveys the high regard held towards John Watson by his contemporaries: "His death will be an irreparable loss to the supporters of polo, which, under his guidance, has developed from chaos into scientific play. The

243

name of John Watson is known wherever the British flag flies, and is closely associated with all sports, but more especially identified with polo and foxhunting. In the former his name will always be recorded amongst the fathers of the game, since his prominent influence has done so much to destroy those vulgar brawls from which, in the process of evolution, the game of polo phoenix-like, has arisen."[3]

A search for any writings on polo by John Watson yielded no results; therefore, a request for information was sent to Roger Chatterton-Newman, the authority on the life and times of John Watson. His reply follows: "Sadly, I have never seen John Watson's theories in print. He died just before the old *Polo Monthly* appeared and seems never to have considered writing his memoirs. A pity — they would have been a magnificent read!"[4]

Sir George Younghusband

In 1890, Captain George John Younghusband, Queen's Own Corps of Guides, wrote a little book, *Polo in India*. Further refinements came about in *Tournament Polo*, his second book on the game. *Polo in India*, although published in England, is the first book written about the game of polo as we know it today. The game was only 30 years old; nevertheless, Capt. Younghusband already notes the main elements of evolution that appeared during that period: increase in pace, increase in the size of the ponies and the dimensions of the field of play, and subordination of individual play to the combined operations of a team.[5]

The next to last chapter, "Duties of Different Members of a Team," is the best available description of how polo was played in the 1880s. Capt. Younghusband starts with the back, which should be mounted on the best ponies in the regiment — civilians were apparently of no account — because the team's success depended largely on him. The back's duty in offense was to hit the ball well into the game, to make long shots at goal, and, occasionally, to exchange places with his number 3 and make runs up the field. George Younghusband notes that until a few years before, it was the rule that the back should never go up or make a run. In hitting backhanders, they should be hit hard and on a line diverging to the right or left of the oncoming mob of friends and foes. As to the opposing number 1, his job was to put him offside as often as possible. Number 3 should play with his head, a most useful piece of advice, but one that only first class players appeared to be able to follow. Number 2 was to be the playing man on a team, being able to hit the ball with equal facility on either side of the pony, and be endowed with a nice combination of discretion and dash: discretion in knowing where and when to gallop, and dash in picking up each opportunity of cutting in and scoring.

As to the forward, "Number 1, or flying man, lives only to hustle the opposing back, and to make his existence burdensome to him. From start to finish, he should never relax for a minute his attentions. Ever present, ever in it enemy's way, he is a most invaluable man if he will stick to his business."[6] To encourage the "flying man" to do his job, Capt. Younghusband recommends, "It is a very good education for a No. 1 to play only with a hockey stick, removing thereby the almost irresistible temptation he feels now and then to make runs instead of sticking to his business."[7]

Poor number 1. Not only had he to spend the entire game playing against the best player on the opposing team, stronger and better mounted than himself, but he was also deprived the occasional chance of hitting the ball. It is no wonder that the forward position, the most difficult one to excel at in the game of polo, has been crippled since birth in its development. It is comforting that Adolfo Cambiaso, by most accounts the best individual player ever, has chosen to wear the number 1 shirt on his own team, La Dolfina.

Sir Henry De Lisle

Capt. Henry de Beauvoir De Lisle's contribution to the game started in 1894 with a six-chapter pamphlet printed for regimental circulation only. In 1897, De Lisle expanded this work into *Hints to Polo Players in India*.

Captain De Lisle was of the opinion that an old team will always beat a young team, the reason being the same that, in military terms, gave so much success to Napoleon's veterans of the Imperial Guard: when younger soldiers got excited and their discipline and steadiness were severely tested, that of the older men was as firm as ever.

Instinctively, a team will play better on its own ground, to the extent that some observers thought that two goals should be given to the visiting team to equalize the odds. There are several other reasons why teams playing at home do better. In an even match, De Lisle says, nerves seem to be strained to its utmost and players do not have time to look for the goalposts. In his own field, a man knows instinctively where the flags are, and hits accordingly. The local ponies are also familiar with the footing, and are easier to ride. The ponies are in their normal surroundings and neither tired nor leg-weary from traveling, nor jumping out of their skins from want of work. In the home ground, the encouragement of friends and supporters does much to help a team perform better than usual. Lastly, the playing field may be very different for the visiting team. De Lisle makes the point that prac-

Gen. Sir Henry de Beauvoir De Lisle wears the Magpies jersey and is mounted on Glisten. A captain at the time, De Lisle led the Durham Light Infantry to victory in the Indian P.A. Championship and in the Inter-regimental Tournament, an unusual feat for an infantry unit. Possession, pace and scoring were the basics of De Lisle's polo philosophy (private collection).

ticing at Bombay or Umballa, and then playing at Lahore or Poona is quite difficult, unless adequate time is allowed for the ponies to get used to the new grounds.

De Lisle names as a fact that ponies, especially young ones, tend to pull more in tournament play than in a fast station game. Ponies, like players, sometimes get very excited without apparent cause and the only remedy is time and experience.

An individual's positional play receives thorough attention by Capt. De Lisle. Number 1 should be the position assigned to newcomers to the game or the weakest player on the team, quite often the same man. Those were the days of the offside rule, which distinctly limited the scope of the forwards. De Lisle condemns the practice of fitting number 1 with a hockey stick, instead of a regular polo mallet. Although his advice is that he should never chance a shot at goal, he should never lose the opportunity to score if he gets an easy shot. The minutiae of number 1's role in the throw-in, the knock-in and in taking the corner shot are described in detail, because those are the few occasions in which the tyro can make his presence felt.

Number 2's duties are succinctly described as making the pace, getting hold of the ball when passed forward, and hitting goals. This player should be chosen for his cool head and a straight eye. Number 3 should be a hard driver and able to place the ball in either direction at an angle of 45 degrees to the line he is moving, in order to feed the forwards. De Lisle acknowledges that it is the most difficult position to fill on the team.

Up to that time, back was the position given to the perceived best player on the team. De Lisle takes issue with that practice because it is an easier position to play in than any other on the field. The admonishment to back is that his duty is to feed his forwards, and not make runs himself; if he is so inclined, then he should play at number 3.

Capt. De Lisle's concepts changed little in subsequent years. The abolition of the offside rule, which so dramatically changed the game, was given little notice in his subsequent works. In his own words, written twenty-nine years after *Hints to Polo Players* was published, "I therefore think the duties of No. 1 have in no way changed, but he is now in a far better position to carry them out. These duties are three, all equally important: 1. To prevent the opposite Back getting the ball. 2. To assist his own No. 2 to reach it. 3. To score goals."[8]

The advice rendered in the third edition of *Polo in India* (1924) is identical to the one given in the first, which dates back to 1907. The evolution of polo had left behind Sir Beauvoir De Lisle, as he was later titled. His third book on the game, *Tournament Polo*, came out in 1938. The words of advice were still the same. To give him due credit, De Lisle was the first to categorize the principles of game of polo by enlarging Capt. Younghusband's precepts into a coherent scheme: possession, pace and scoring.

Robert Lumsden Ricketts

The clear-thinking Captain Robert Ricketts then made his appearance with the Alwar team. Years on, by then a brigadier general, Ricketts took the unusual stance that polo is a most inaccurate game; therefore, match strategy must be considered and planned based upon such premise.[9]

Brigadier Ricketts describes the polo ground as the most uneven and imperfect surface in which a game has to be played. Perhaps Ricketts, a very good rackets player, never played a round of golf. As to the polo mallet, he is of the opinion that it compares unfavorably with any bat or racquet or stick, or even the foot, in offering a surface with which to strike a ball. This shortcoming is increased by its length, weight, and general unwieldiness.

As proof of the inaccuracy of polo, Robert Ricketts points out that the number of pure misses of the apparently simple ball is far higher at polo than at any other game. His pertinent question is, if polo players cannot rely on accuracy to develop a first class game, upon what can they rely? Brigadier Ricketts writes,

> There is one factor which affects all moving ball games to an overpowering degree, especially in the higher classes of play, but which is seldom sufficiently recognized. I speak of pace. At polo, the ball can be hit very hard, ponies gallop fast and there is greater scope for increase of pace by taking suitable thought than there is in any other game. Extreme pace singles out the class player at once from amongst his apparent equals (or even superiors) in a game played at ordinary speed. In almost all games, pace, once it has been properly studied, has come out victorious. It must, however, be extreme pace, not merely fast play, to which latter a class performer will almost always react. Pace must not be confused with wild hitting. Wild, hard hitting is not conducive to pace, rather the reverse, because the direction in which the ball is hit, as often as not, gives the opponent plenty of time to reach it, or get into position for the next stroke.[10]

His advice to players was based on the fact that polo grounds in India were hard-surfaced and that sideboards were not in use, forcing the players to keep the ball and most of the line of play towards the center of the field.[11]

Ricketts remained an outstanding thinker in the realm of polo. In 1936, he wrote fifteen chapters — about half the book — in the *Lonsdale Library* volume on polo[12] edited by the Earl of Kimberley, who, when Lord Wodehouse, was an international 10-goal player. Brig. Ricketts delves deep into the subject. His precepts include hard hitting, alertness, speed, and horsemanship. He is a strong advocate of fast practice games, to the limit of horseflesh, and concerted team play. These interesting thoughts, which were successful in tournament play, may perhaps be considered by some theorists to be antiquated and simple. A close study of his teachings in the light of the Coronel Suárez-Santa Ana clashes and the recent Argentine Open Championship in the 1980 to 2000 span — the heyday of polo before the curse of tapping — proves them thoroughly modern, and as vigorous and forceful as ever.

Harry Payne Whitney

Heir to one of the largest personal fortunes in America, Henry (Harry) Payne Whitney made his mark on the development of the game as a meticulous organizer and a great field captain. His comprehensive management of the 1909 challenge for the Westchester Cup is legendary and its story has been written repeatedly.[13] James Calvin Cooley, a veteran polo-player and a perceptive writer on polo, makes the case that Whitney's thoughts about bringing the Westchester Cup to America took root when he acquired the pony Cottontail from Lawrence McCreery in California.[14] Harry P. Whitney realized that in the bay gelding Cottontail he had what was considered the best polo pony in creation. He then proceeded to collect a string of ponies that was unequalled at the time, with the idea of assembling a team in which each player would have entire faith in each other's abilities and would be mounted as no other polo squad hitherto. The Big Four, the polo team that changed the world of polo, was about to be born.

Based upon the premise that the pony was the most important ingredient on the polo menu, Whitney gathered celebrities like the brown mare Balada, the Irish-bred chestnut mare

Ballin a Hone, who had a distinctive blazed face, the chestnut mare Cobnut and that big chestnut mare Ralla. August Belmont loaned his two priceless mares, the black Cinderella and the brown Little Mary, both imported from England.

As to players, Whitney first gathered the Waterbury brothers, Lawrence and James Montgomery, Jr. Although Larry Waterbury had earned his reputation and attendant 10-goal handicap as a back, he joined brother Monty as a forward. They made a big splash on the Hurlingham turf and concomitantly in the evolution of the game. One observer noted, "Every authority on the game had set out his convictions that every attacking shot was a centering shot, and every defensive shot was a wide shot. The Waterburys ruined that conception of the game, and it has apparently remained ruined ever since."[15]

Harry P. Whitney played at number 3, a steady player who always was at the right spot. At back, Whitney picked young Devereux Milburn, already a superb striker of the ball and a man who changed the traditional and time-tested way a defensive player should behave. Early on, Whitney realized Milburn's talent; therefore, his own individual brand of polo was directed to the tactical idea of playing up to Milburn as much as possible, covering the back door. No one ever played a more unselfish part, always in control, never out of place, continuously directing the flow of the game.

Stay back and do not take risks, was the gospel according to John Watson. Devereux Milburn did away with all that. His forays up the field astonished the British, who had never seen anything like that, bordering on recklessness. Although the American team had to cope with two disadvantages; the offside rule that cramped their open style of play, and the second, the slow, thick turf, which also slowed their tempo, "nothing mattered, they attacked all the time at express speed, and though they were all over the place and apparently as wild as hares, there was method and accuracy in every stroke, and always a man in each place. Their hitting was a revelation to us, and the risks they took, and the way they met the ball had never before seen in England. Mr. Whitney kept perfect control of the team and acted as a pivot around which the other three revolved."[16]

A revolution in polo, with compliments from Mr. H.P. Whitney.

Walter Selby Buckmaster

Walter Buckmaster's contributions to the development of the game are condensed in a thin volume that incorporates his articles on tactics, initially published in *The Field*.[17] Walter Buckmaster was the first player in England to achieve a 10-goal handicap, took eleven Hurlingham Champion Cups and played international polo in two Olympiads and in the Westchester Cup. He was eminently qualified to write on a subject that he played so well for a long time. In only 47 pages and six diagrams, Mr. Buckmaster offers advice gained in many years of polo as played at its highest level. His credo is combination, continuous motion, and ball control. Although it is not an exhaustive treatise, most aspects of the game are covered, from "Ball thrown in to commence the game" to "Hitting the ball."

In the throw-in, Buckmaster's advice is that number 1 or number 2, whichever is the most accurate at meeting the ball, should line up first in line. In knock-ins by the opposition, number 1 must have his pony well in hand and on the move, ready to gallop on the line of the ball as soon as he sees at what angle the back is going to hit out. When his own back hits in, number 3 should never forget to have his pony so placed to cover his back.

W.S. Buckmaster, a stockbroker who became the first English 10-goal player, painted by C.J. Long. Walter Buckmaster was the leader of the Old Cantabs team — Cambridge University former students — an international player and the winner of eleven Hurlingham Champion Cups between 1896 and 1921 (private collection, Alex Pacheco photograph).

The secrets of success in being a good number 1 are never to take your eyes off the back, never to let the ball come up to him, and never to be more than a few lengths away from him. In stark contrast to the directive proposed by other writers, Buckmaster tells his number 1 to look out for chances of putting a ball through the goalposts at every opportunity. At last, a refreshing thought for Number 1.

Number 2 should make himself perfect in taking the ball at top speed down the field on both sides of the pony and in shooting at goals. He should be certain of centering the ball when going at racing pace. Number 1 and Number 2 must be interchangeable, and they should practice together as much as possible.

Walter Buckmaster usually played at number 3; therefore, it is not surprising that he considers that position as the pivot of the team. Number 3 should be interchangeable with back and be in support of number 2. Interestingly, Buckmaster voices the opinion that, when number 2 is making a run down the sideboards, it is a better policy for number 3 not to follow him, but to go to the center of the field for the pass, which is almost certain to come. When passing, number 3 should always try to place the ball in front and on the offside of number 2.

Regarding back, Buckmaster repeats the need for interchanging places with number 3. However, once more, he breaks with tradition in suggesting that when hitting-in, it will pay him to hit across his own goalmouth, provided he has indicated his intention to his teammates. The confident player that he was, his thoughts come through in his advice about a play that was anathema to his contemporaries. Walter Buckmaster wrote for advanced players. His ideal that perfect combination is an absolute necessity in playing the correct game was far away from the reach of most polo players in his time.[18]

William Cameron Forbes

When he was the governor general of the Philippine Islands, the Hon. W. Cameron Forbes wrote a short booklet on polo for the use of the government team. Titled *A Manual of Polo,* it

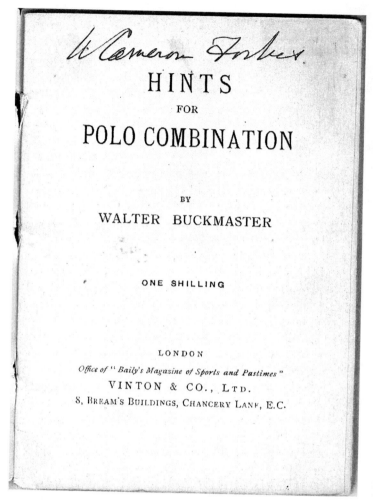

HINTS

FOR

POLO COMBINATION

BY

WALTER BUCKMASTER

ONE SHILLING

LONDON

Office of " Baily's Magazine of Sports and Pastimes "
VINTON & CO., LTD.
8, BREAM'S BUILDINGS, CHANCERY LANE, E.C.

Walter Buckmaster's *Hints for Polo Combination* is a rare book on the game. This is Cameron Forbes' personal copy, an association that makes this volume unique (private collection).

was printed by the press of the 14th United States Cavalry stationed at Fort Stotsenburg, near Manila.[19] In this booklet, Cameron Forbes described his elemental thoughts on the game. His basic premise was that all hitting should be directly up and down the field, except when in front of your own goal. Good players will hit to other players of their own side, not to themselves; any man riding parallel to the ball may be pretty sure that he is playing bad polo; hitting into the offensive corners indicate either bad judgment or bad execution. Those are some of his basic tenets, which hold true today in most play situations. In turning, Forbes' advice is to first pull up the pony and then turn in the shortest possible circle. The reason is that if a player turns in a large circle, he will be out of the line of play, in which case he will foul if he tries to get back, or he will be out of position and, therefore, will lose possession of the ball. In Forbes' teachings, turning in a wide circle is the worst possible polo.

One year later, Cameron Forbes expanded his thoughts in *As to Polo*, the first of six editions of a classic work in polo literature.[20] Together with "Marco's" *Introduction to Polo*, they are the most recognized instructional books on the game.

According to Forbes, there are three cardinal elements in polo. The first is horsemanship, the second is hitting, and the third, the strategy of team play. Three factors control the position of the players. The first is the direction of the play, which in turn is controlled by the position and movement of the ball. The second is the spacing of the players on their own side. The third factor is the position of the opponents, particularly the corresponding one, i.e., number 2 vs. number 3. Taking these three controlling factors, the player should then figure out the location of the "right of way," the basic rule of polo. This is of the essence, because the secret of team play is for a team to get quickly into this right of way the moment it is made possible by the movement of the ball, and then come along with enough speed as to maintain the right of way.

Forbes strongly advises against hitting long strokes around the field, because the only advantage is the case of a brilliant player on a very fast pony. Every stroke should be made with a definite objective in mind.

As far as individual positions, the number 1 requires superior horsemanship, dedication to putting the opposing back out of play and unselfishness in leaving the ball for others behind the play. If the number 2 must be the most active player, number 3 should be the most careful and the most skilled. A defensive stroke by number 3 or back is practically worthless, unless it is followed up by turning it to an offensive play. The back must remember that if he has played well in the defense, he has played his game well, a rather conservative approach at a time when Devereux Milburn dazzled the British with his forays up field.

The main problem with *As to Polo* is that it was not kept up to date. It was, by far, the best instructional book when first published. Editions printed after the first one were essentially reprints, with almost no new material being added. The game of polo played in 1929, the last edition year of publication, was vastly different from the game played twenty years before. Advice given early had become a bit stale in the late 1920s.

Lewis Lawrence Lacey

Most of Lewis Lacey's intellectual contributions to the game of polo are related to the art of equitation.[21] Although he was a brilliant striker of the ball, his horsemanship was superlative.[22] Lacey was convinced that adequate equitation was an essential part in polo; by this, he referred to polo equitation, which encompassed the correct seat, the use of the rider's legs, appropriate use of aids in order to make the pony change leads or to make him stop, and balance. In summary, the rider must be in complete harmony with the pony. Mr. Lacey makes the point that no one ignores the importance of feet position in all sports and games, from golf to target shooting and from boxing to billiards. If this happens in general, it must be fundamental in polo, in which we must think about six feet. It is common to assign the pony's weight distribution as 35 percent on the front legs and 65 percent on the hind legs, an illogical and erroneous conclusion when we look at a standing pony and notice the strength of the hindquarters. Balance is one of the main qualities in the harmony between pony and rider and it must be the main preoccupation in a polo player's mind. It is obtained by teaching the animal to distribute its weight in a balanced way. In Lacey's opinion, it is important that the polo player "make" his own ponies.

Lewis Lacey wrote thoughtfully on the game of polo and was the mentor of three generations of Argentine polo players. His emphasis was on good equitation as the key to reaching a high-goal handicap (Museum of Polo and Hall of Fame).

In order to obtain the best results in making your own ponies, patience and time are of the greatest importance. It is vital to advance slowly, teaching the animal and giving him time to get used to discipline. It is also needed to determine the effect of different bits upon the pony's mouth. Bad examples abound, according to his observations. It is not unusual to watch a pony stopping correctly on his hind legs, but without loosening his jaw, which leads to an incorrect position of the head. It is obvious that the animal has played before he has completed his training, or that he has been poorly schooled.

The rein should be half of the ways used to control the polo pony; the other half is the aids, or directives, to the pony via the rider's legs and the balance of the rider's weight. A well-taught and well-balanced polo pony, who has been trained carefully and methodically to control its speed until he learns to canter as slowly as the rider desires, will immediately respond correctly to the rider's commands.

The bit indicates to the pony to stop; it should never be used to stop the pony because it hurts and hardens the mouth, making the mount unsuitable for polo. Likewise, when hitting the ball there should be no pressure whatsoever on the reins. If there is pressure on the mouth, the pony will instinctively stop at the time of impact.

All these precepts take time, patience and practice, until both mount and rider achieve an instinctive harmony. Lewis Lacey offers the thought that a player cannot expect to progress in his game and reach a high-goal handicap unless his proficiency in the art of equitation is commensurate with his striking ability and tactical thinking.

In his writings, Lewis Lacey mentions two players as examples of superb equitation in polo; one was Capt. Pat Roark, whose riding was so subtle that it gave the impression of effortless skill. The second was David Miles, a born horseman who always seemed to go faster that anyone else. Actually, writes Lacey, his ponies were equal in speed as many others; however, Miles always had his pony collected and ready; invariably, he was first off the mark.

In self-assessment, Lacey tells us how much he learned about riding at a school of equitation in France, even though at the time he was a 10-goal handicap player. Beginners and veterans should take heed of the master's words. Never stop learning.

James Hay Ashton

Jim Ashton was captain of the famous Goulburn team from New South Wales, Australia, that went around the world in 1930. Some eight years later, he put pen to paper and recorded his thoughts on the game in a privately published booklet.[23]

Team play on the field begins with the throw-in. His advice is to get there in plenty of time and position yourself continuously closer to the umpire, ahead of your opposite number. When the ball is thrown by the umpire, number 1 should make a great effort to hit the ball, and hit or miss, he should go up field as quickly as possible. Number 2 should also try to hit the ball, but must remain in the lineout until he finds where the ball is. Number 3 should also try to hit the ball, but otherwise must turn back without looking to see where the ball went. Number 4 should place himself to gallop in if the ball passes number 3.

General hints for all the players include the admonition not to become a spectator of the game, keep the brain alert all the time, and play your position. Play as hard as you can mentally and physically, never let up for a moment, do not check if you think a foul has occurred, and play until the whistle blows.

James Hay Ashton was the undisputed and unquestioned leader of the Goulburn team, a dominant power in Australian polo. Jim Ashton's personality and tactical thoughts left a lasting legacy, continued by Sinclair Hill. He is on favorite pony, Checkers (courtesy James Ashton and Rosemary Foot).

As to individual positions, Jim Ashton states that number 1 should be a great optimist; conversely, back should be a pessimist. Number 2 has to be the hardest worker on the team and have the handiest ponies. Number 3 gets plenty of advice from Ashton, who played in that position, the first being keep your brain alert. Move on the field for positions where you can meet ball; if not possible, take the opposing number 2 and hit a backhander, but never into ponies. When covering your back, cover fast and deep.

These simple directives served Goulburn well. Under Jim Ashton's leadership, the team was practically unbeaten in the 1930s in Australia, and went on to take Hurlingham's Champion Cup.

Rao Rajah Hanut Singh

Hanut, as he was usually called, was the mentor of many great players in India and the United Kingdom, as well of some Argentine players who played the English season at Cowdray Park, Hanut Singh's home base. Unfortunately, his thoughts on the strategy and tactics of game of polo are not recorded, and, certainly, not published.[24] What we know about this remarkable man are his innumerable stories about himself, the game and the horses. There is mention of long sessions at Park House Hotel, his home in Midhurst, with salt and pepper pots and cutlery used as players and ponies in tactical lessons. Sinclair Hill remembers spending hours with Hanut at the dining table with bits of paper describing the diamond formation.[25]

It is a loss for polo that neither Hanut Singh nor any of his followers saw fit to put his teachings in writing. Perhaps Hanut felt that he was bound by the Rajput ethic best expressed in the ancient proverb "A Rajput who reads will never ride a horse."[26]

Hanut Singh was one of the great players in the history of the game. The failure to raise his handicap to 10 goals is a black mark on the handicap committees of both the Hurlingham Polo Association and the Indian Polo Association. What were the qualities that made Hanut Singh, in spite of his egocentric character, the undisputed guru of a polo generation? Maj. John Watson provides the answer.

> First, it was owing to his absolute and immediately recognizable integrity. Hari [Hanut's son] remarks on "his complete respect for the book of rules. This great quality enamoured him to all the players and umpires. If not playing himself in a final he was invariably invited to umpire or referee." Secondly, it was due to the high standards of conduct that he set himself and everyone else. Colonel Harper remembers him once giving a curse and exclaiming "The game is for princes, not grooms!" on witnessing some uncouth behaviour in a match. He was also as famous for saying: "There are men who enjoy the game, there are men who play to shake up their liver and there are men who play for social reasons. I like the men who play for sheer love of the game." How the great man would deplore so much of what is seen in the polo world today — such as disputing umpires decisions, bad horsemanship, scruffy turnout and the departure of classic team play in favour of ball chasing.[27]

26. The Evolution of the Rules

There are additional hazards in the shape of umpires who are supposed to see that the players comply with the rules. — H.R.H. The Duke of Edinburgh[1]

In his influential work *The Meaning of Sport*, Simon Barnes proposes the concept that sports and games started less than 200 years ago with the Victorians' codification of games.[2] The key element is codification, that is, the point at which rules are agreed to be enforced and respected by administrators, players and officials — in the case of polo, umpires and referee — that make it possible to take the game along the path of rational evolution. This organization of the different local codes was the work of British players in India and England in the second half of the 19th century. Silchar Kanjai Club's well-documented claim to primacy in drafting the first rules of polo is hard to contest (see Appendix 1). Both Captain Edward Hartopp and John Watson built upon their foundation, Hartopp on 10th Hussars' mess stationery and the Irishman on more formal official paper.

Doubtful points could be decided by mutual consent or reserved for decision by friendly arbiter. However, as play spread, decisions by mutual agreement or by an umpire specially appointed for the occasion ceased to be a practical solution because local codes became more and more complicated, based upon local traditions and customs. The innumerable variations of home rules only served to emphasize the need for a universal code. Parenthetically, this need is still present. This aim of a single set of rules was achieved in India by adopting the Bombay Code,[3] in England by the regulations promulgated by the Hurlingham Polo Committee, in America by charging one individual, Henry Lloyd Herbert, to draft a set of rules, and in the River Plate by meekly following the English regulations.

Very few games or sports are so static over a period of years that their rules do not need changing. A game of dynamic characteristics, polo has shown over its history numerous developments, with consequent changes in the rules. The path of progress was strewn with many pitfalls; however, the pioneers that drafted the original codes of polo developed the main concepts that still stand. The right of way, the line of the ball, the scoring of goals and the prohibition of both crossing and dangerous riding constitute the foundations of the laws of polo. After these basic precepts had been established, the security of the game rested not so much on the immaculate lawns of the old Hurlingham Club as in the written laws of the game promulgated by the Hurlingham Committee. The code that the founding fathers had fashioned — laws that, although amended from time to time to meet new requirements and new conditions — remain in their fundamental principles in force today.

Henry Lloyd Herbert, a lawyer, was the Polo Association's chairman for some 30 years. Herbert devised and implemented the system of individual handicaps in America and was sole handicapper for several years (Museum of Polo and Hall of Fame).

Even economic pressure seems to have influenced polo's rule-makers, as noted by the increase in the height of ponies, and then finally with doing away with any limitation regarding mounts. These changes were brought about by the increased popularity of the game and by the lack of sufficient ponies of the sizes formerly required. While this change may be attributed to a condition outside of the game itself, this modification has had considerable influence on the character of polo as now played, because it has made possible the training and bringing into the game horseflesh of greater speed, resulting in a faster game.

One only has to glance at old rulebooks to notice the changes that have already taken place, particularly those that have modified the character of the game. For example, the elimination of the off-side rule, which made possible the passing attack so much in vogue among the best British players just prior to the war and particularly among America's famous 'Big Four' of the period from 1909 to 1913.

Compared to other games, the rules of polo are simple. They are burdened neither with the interminable minutiae of the rules governing golf nor with the complexity of the American code of football. The rules of rugby, and even more so than those of association football, are quite simple when measured against the National Football League's regulations.

The cardinal rule of polo is the one pertaining to the right of way, because at all times during a game, a player has the right of way. Crossing that right of way by an opponent is the most common foul in the game of polo. What constitutes a foul is left to the umpire's discretion, who takes into account various factors, such as the relative speed of the mounts, the angle of crossing the line and the distance between the players when the crossing occurs.

Evolution and Comparison of the Rules

A comparison of the rules of game as articulated by the Silchar Club, the rules drafted by Captain Hartopp in longhand, the original and subsequent rules enforced by the Hurlingham Polo Committee, the Indian Polo Association and the Polo Association in America will be described in this section. It should be noted that the Argentine Polo Association played under the Hurlingham rules until 1939.

Number of Players

The Manipuris allowed seven men and two goalkeepers to participate in the game. Teams had two goalkeepers because the entire length of the backline was considered the goal. The Silchar code also specified that no player was to be under the influence of bhang-gouja (hashish) or spirituous liquors.

Lt. Hartopp's rules stated that no more than 12 players could participate in a match, while the first Hurlingham rules (1874) reduced the number of players to six on each side. This modification was needed because the large number of players tended to make the game a succession of mauls and scrimmages, with very few opportunities for a player to gallop hitting the ball.

The Indian Polo Association (1887) further limited the number to four officers. It is to be assumed that civilians and Indian princes were of no consequence. The U.S. Polo Association (1890) allowed teams of two and three players each to compete in special tournaments, such as the Turnure Cup. The 2007 U.S.P.A. rules indicate that no player shall play in a tournament for more than one team. Nevertheless, it is common practice to allow a player from another team to substitute in case of injury.

Substitutes

The Silchar code stated that no rider could use fresh horses, and no horses could have fresh riders. After a fall, no player or horse was allowed a replacement, unless caused by a foul. The Indian Polo Association (I.P.A.) followed suit in allowing no changes, unless needed as the result of an accident.

The U.S.P.A. only specified that each team should have a substitute in readiness. However, in 1998 it went the way of other team games, when unlimited substitutions were permitted at the end of a period, except as provided relating to an injured player. Prior to that year, unlimited substitutions were only allowed in tournaments under a 4-goal handicap. It is difficult to understand the whys and wherefores of different rules for different handicaps.

EQUIPMENT

In Silchar, spurs and whips were freely used. The Hurlingham Polo Committee (H.P.C.) prohibited the use of spurs with rowels, while the Polo Association in America (P.A.A.) specified, "The cruel use of spurs is prohibited." Later, the U.S.P.A. expanded the restrictions, prohibiting sharp spurs and protruding buckles or studs on a player's boots or knee guards.

Both sticks and balls were to be approved by the Committee, faithfully following Capt. Hartopp's wording. The Hurlingham Committee specified, "Members are permitted to play with any description of club."

For the first time, the size of the ball was formulated by the H.P.C., at three inches in diameter. As Kipling wrote, "The Maltese Cat knew that bamboos grew solely in order that polo-balls might be turned from their roots."[4] Following such sage statement, the I.P.A. specified bamboo root for the polo ball, which should be about 10½ inches in circumference and four ounces in weight.

In America, the P.A.A. mandated basswood, with no other covering but paint, the ball to be 3⅛ inches in diameter and not exceeding five ounces in weight. Mallets were to be approved by the committee. It is of note that current rules do not specify the material, size or shape of the polo mallet. Perhaps ruling on a mallet's specification is a hot potato for consideration by the national rules committees.

The U.S.P.A. mandated the use of a helmet or cap with a chin strap. If the two teams' shirts were alike, their use was to be decided by lot. In Argentina, the lower team in the draw was to change shirts.

MOUNTS

The controversies around the issue of ponies' height have been discussed elsewhere in this work. The H.P.C. did not allow any mount showing vice to continue in the game. To that provision, the U.S.P.A. added that a pony out of control was to be removed from the game, therefore putting pressure on the player to maintain his pony under control at all time. Bandages or boots on the front legs were mandatory, but only recommended for the hind legs.

Mount's Equipment

The U.S.P.A. does not allow shoes with an outer rim, toe grab, screws or frost nails. Neither blinkers — frequently and dangerously utilized in polo's early days — nor shallow rolls are allowed.

UMPIRES AND REFEREES

The Silchar code mandated that each team was to nominate an umpire, unless mutually agreed to play with only one umpire. Capt. Hartopp added: "Each team to provide an umpire who, on detecting any irregularity or infringement of the rules, shall be empowered to suspend the game until the irregularity has been corrected." The H.P.C. further added, "[corrected] according to the combined arbitration of both umpires."

The P.A.A. wording was, "Each team to choose an umpire, and, if necessary the two umpires to appoint a referee." In later years, the U.S.P.A. changed the wording to the simple statement, "two mounted umpires and a referee or third man."

FIELD OF PLAY

As mentioned above, in polo as played by the Manipuris, Lt. Sherer and his friends, the entire backline was the goal. The limits of the ground were marked off with a small ditch a few inches in depth.

Edward "Chicken" Hartopp stipulated the goals to be 300 yards apart, exactly the same distance as today. There were boundary flags 150 to 200 yards apart along the sidelines and the goalposts were to be eight yards apart. Hurlingham's first rules maintained the 300 yard separation between goalposts, with the proviso of the ground's length permitting. The width of the ground was from 150 to 200 yards. The I.P.A. rules stated as nearly as possible 300 yards long by 200 yards wide, to be defined by a thinly cut line. Then it exerted its independence by specifying that the goals were to be 22 feet wide, instead of the immemorial 24 feet, thus breaking a long-honored tradition.

The P.A.A. mandated the grounds to be about 750 feet long by 500 feet wide, with a 10 inch guard from end to end, on the sidelines only. The goals were to be 24 feet wide, as ancient custom dictated.

DURATION OF CHUKKERS AND THE GAME

H.P.C.'s rule makers specified that a match should not be longer than one hour. If a large number of playing members were present, the teams must resign the ground at the conclusion of a rubber of three games (goals). The I.P.A. mandated six periods of eight minutes each; the game to last 40 minutes. Six times eight is 48; there was something wrong with the math; perhaps the hot weather....

The P.A.A. time requirements were three periods of 20 minutes each. Time between goals and delays was not counted; two-minutes were taken after a goal and a ten-minute rest occurred between periods. In matches between pairs, there were two periods of 15 minutes each, and between teams of three players, three periods of 15 minutes each.

In the event of a tie at the end of regulation time, the I.P.A. indicated that the match should continue for another eight minutes, the goal flags being widened to 44 feet apart. If there was still a tie, the game was to be continued until one side scored a goal.

The P.A.A. ruled that in the event of a tie, the game was to be continued until one side was credited with a goal or part of a goal. It must be remembered that in America ½ a goal was taken off the offending team in case of a foul and ¼ goal in case of a safety.

Running and Stopping of Clock

The I.P.A. stipulated that a three-minute interval had to be taken after 10 minutes of play and after every goal. Time might be called whenever the ball was out of play, and the game stopped for two minutes.

The H.P.C. changed the duration from less than one hour, and called for matches lasting one-hour and ten-minutes, with a five-minute interval between each 20 minutes of play deducted from the above. It also offered an alternative; four quarters, with three-minute intervals in between.

In America, the 1890 rules mandated three periods of twenty minutes each, time between goals and delays excluded. The rest time between periods was 10 minutes.

Commencement of the Game

The Silchar code mandated the ball to be placed on the center of the ground and one player from each team was to strike it simultaneously, similar to the bully in hockey. Capt. Hartopp modified this procedure, the ball being thrown in the center of the ground, and one player from each team galloping from a point agreed upon by the captains. A dangerous practice at best, this rule was responsible for several accidents.

The I.P.A. approved a safer approach to the start of a game: as in field hockey, the ball was placed in the center of the field and two opposing players crossed their sticks, heads upwards, over the ball, after which any player could strike the ball. On the other hand, the H.P.C. adopted a dangerous system in which each side took up its position behind the goal posts, and on the flag being dropped by the umpire, the game commenced with a mad gallop towards the middle of the field. Perhaps it was an exciting spectacle, but highly dangerous.

The P.A.A. was ambivalent in this matter. The ball was thrown-in between the contestants in the middle of the field, unless the captains agreed to charge. The charge began from a line 30 feet in front of the goal posts. When the signal to charge was given, the first and second players had to keep to the left of the ball until it had been hit. No mention is made of the other players.

This was a dangerous manner to start the game. In the first match held in Massachusetts, on the Myopia grounds in 1888, George von L. Meyer and Percival Lawrence Lowell collided in mid-field and both horses and riders went flying onto the ground. The players had to be taken by ambulance to the clubhouse, where they recovered, perhaps near the bar. Lowell, captain of the visiting Dedham Club, was a famous astronomer; it is quite likely that one of the wags Myopia is well-known for made the comment that Mr. Lowell saw stars. Fifty years later, Mrs. William C. Endicott mentioned to Allan Forbes that she sat next to Percival Lowell at dinner one evening and his face still was black and blue from his fall.[5]

Interruptions and Resumption of Play

When the ball went out of bounds on the Silchar field, it was to be bowled in by the umpire or a bystander, when there were a sufficient numbers of players to receive it. Once more, the H.P.C. followed Hartopp's dictum that the ball was to be put back in play by an impartial person on foot.

The I.P.A. gave a choice of the umpire or someone deputed by them to throw the ball underhand. The ball had to touch the ground before passing the sideline.

GOALS

The Manipuris had the custom of changing sides after every goal. It was adopted in every code ever since, the reason given being the need to even up features such as abnormalities on the ground, the wind and the sun. This archaic rule should be abrogated. It is confusing to the spectators and sometimes to the players. With current improvements in the maintenance of the ground's surfaces, changing goals after each chukker is sufficient.

PERSONAL FOULS

The Silchar code was draconian in this matter: "Any direct or willful act of foul play, when it shall be so declared by the umpire (s), shall at once be declared to have lost the game." It has to be assumed that "game" was meant to be one goal.

Capt. Charles T.I. Roark, the best British player in the inter-war era. "Pat" Roark's tragic death in California, when his exhausted pony collapsed several minutes after the bell had sounded, changed the rules by limiting the time to be played in each chukker. Oil on canvas, signed Kenneth S. MacIntyre (private collection).

The I.P.A. gave the fouled team two choices. The first one was a free hit from where the ball was when the foul occurred, none of the fouling team to be within 10 yards. If the foul occurred near the goal, a free hit was awarded from a spot not within 13 yards of the goal, but as near as possible to where the foul occurred. The second choice was that the side that caused the foul take the ball back and hit it off from behind their goal line. This choice was probably taken by the fouled side when the infraction occurred far away from the adversary's goal posts.

The Polo Association's *1920 Year Book* contains a thorough revision of the rules of the game as played in the United States. At long last, the rule fixing the maximum ponies' height at 15 hands, one inch, was taken off the book. The penalties for a personal foul, half a goal, and a safety, one-quarter goal, to be deducted from the fouling team, were replaced by penalties numbered one to five. Penalty 1 was one goal given to the side fouled. Penalty 2 was a free hit from 50 yards in front of the goal. If a Penalty 3 was awarded, then the hit had to be taken from the spot of the foul. Penalty 4 allowed the sided fouled to hit the ball from the center of their goal line. Penalty 5 was a 60-yard hit after a safety.

Therefore, for the first time, penalties were adjudicated based upon the severity and location of the foul, an important development in the rules of polo. Two years later, the distance in front of the goalposts for a taking a Penalty 2 was reduced to 40 yards, making it a harsher punishment. In 1934, a new penalty 2 was added, a 30-yard free hit to an undefended goal. The other penalties remained the same, only the numbers were changed. The 40-yard free hit became Penalty 3, the 60-yarder Penalty 4, and so on.

In 1997, the U.S.P.A. modified the conditions for taking a Penalty 2, making it the most boring play on the field. The new rule prohibited the fouling side from defending the free hit. Everybody, including the spectators, freeze while the penalty-hitter leisurely approaches the ball and gently taps it through the goalposts — most of the time. It is barely more exciting than watching grass grow. If safety considerations are taken into account, two questions must be answered.

The first one is, why is a 40-yard penalty permitted to be defended? At the speed of the ball, 10 yards makes no difference in the incidence of injuries to mount or man. The second question is, why is a defender allowed to stand still 30 yards in front of a hitter when a 60-yard penalty is taken? The chances of a pony or a player being hit while stationary are much higher than when rushing to intercept a ball hit from the same distance.

Neither the Argentine Polo Association nor the Hurlingham Polo Association adhere to this rule.

Ball Hit Behind Own Line

Also known as safety in America and corner in Argentina, the penalty for hitting the ball behind one's own line has a checkered history. The name "corner" derives from the corner in hockey, a pastime widely practiced in India and applied to that game as well as in soccer. The Silchar code provided a free hit from the nearest corner to be taken by the attacking side (see diagram in Appendix 1). The ball was considered to have been hit off when it traveled more than three yards from the back line.

The H.P.C. was lenient on this issue. If a defending player hit the ball behind his own back line, the defending team was awarded a hit-in from between the goal posts. In reality, it was not a penalty at all, but within the Victorian and Edwardian unwritten codes of conduct, such practice met with disparagement and was considered bad form. During the 1902 Westchester Cup matches, the American players, not bothered with details like that, when hard pressed near their own goal, repeatedly resorted to this legal practice. After the series was over, the H.P.C. promptly changed the rule, allowing the attacking side a free hit from 60 yards, opposite to the place where the ball was hit behind.

In America, when the ball was hit behind its own line by a defender, it was deemed a safety knockout, and one-fourth of a goal was deducted from the player's side. This rule was in effect until 1919.

RIGHT OF WAY

The Silchar rules made no provision regarding the right of way; quite the contrary. The pertinent rule reads: "Any player may interpose his horse before his antagonist so as to prevent his antagonist from reaching the ball, whether in full career or at a slow pace."[6] This is the most perplexing of Silchar's rules because it is the one that addresses the issue of crossing. What must have been the nature of the game's pace? What was meant by "full career?" If it meant full gallop, the tea-planters and English commissioners in Cachar condoned a practice close to manslaughter.

The H.P.C. kept the basic language, with some added softness regarding the possibility of a collision: "A player may interpose his pony before his antagonist, so as to prevent the latter reaching the ball, whether in full career or otherwise, but may not cross another player in possession of the ball unless at such a distance as to avoid all possibility of a collision."

The P.A.A. declared a harsh penalty for a foul: "The referee shall declare a foul when he sees it, without waiting to have it claimed. He may suspend the player for the match, or he may award the opposing side a half goal." This penalty was discontinued in 1919, when there was a general revision of the rules in the United States, in light of recent world developments in the game.

Regarding defending the goal in case of a penalty, as late as 1967, a manual advised that two players should defend the goal from a 30- or 40-yard penalty: "The only hope of saving a straight shot is for No. 3 and Back to cross the back line from opposite sides of the goal, at a gallop and at an acute angle, as the ball is struck."[7]

One can only shudder when contemplating the possible consequences of such practice. For those who saw it happen, the collision between Harold Barry and Norty Knox in the first match for the 1966 Cup of the Americas at Palermo must certainly remain in their minds. Due to a miscommunication, both Barry and Knox went out to defend a 40-yard penalty. The goal was saved, but at the high cost of a nasty fall for Chico Barry, who, visibly shaken, was able to remount among thunderous applause from the spectators.[8]

THE RULE THAT CHANGED THE WAY POLO IS PLAYED

The rule about dangerous riding covers a multitude of sins. Thou shall not ride at an angle or speed dangerous to a player or mount. Thou shall not run into or over the legs of another mount. Thou shall not: pull up on or across the right of way, zigzag in front of another player, run the head of a horse into another player, ride at an opponent in such a manner as to intimidate him, and the all-inclusive "exhibit a lack of consideration for safety."[9]

However, the rule that changed the way polo is played and the main cause of today's delaying tactics in the game was the addition of the wording "deliberately riding one's mount into the stroke of another player." Steve Orthwein, a former chairman of the U.S. Polo Association and a member of the Rules Committee, cogently examines this issue.[10] Mr. Orthwein makes the point that in the final game of the 2007 U.S. Open Championship more than half the fouls whistled down by the umpires were infractions of this rule.

In 1992, the H.P.A. followed suit and changed their own rule to read, "deliberately riding one's mount into the stroke of another player." The result of this rule was to allow the defending player room to change the line to the right and dribble the ball around without committing a foul. This action slows the game and often leads to close quarter play in which ponies are more likely to be hit by the ball or a mallet.[11] Currently, the pertinent rule states, "ride his pony from behind into the forehand or backhand stroke of an opponent.[12]

Many times, the defending player fakes a backhander. How can an opponent be able to react if neither the player's own teammates, his opponent, or for that matter, the umpires, can possibly know if he is going to hit a backhander?

IMPROPER USE OF MALLET

The Silchar code prevented a player from willingly striking or laying his hand on his adversary or his adversary's horse. Hooking a mallet was only allowed when the other player was about to strike the ball. In Captain Hartopp's rules, no player was allowed to hit an adversary's pony. Crooking was permitted, but not over the adversary's pony. The Hurlingham rules were similar. Crooking (hooking) a stick was permitted, but neither over nor under an adversary's pony.

Apparently, players were allowed to hit their own pony with the mallet. *Baily's Magazine* commented in 1895, "Another change in the rules is, I hear, talked of. It is proposed to forbid players to strike the pony with the polo stick when galloping on the ball. The use of the stick, especially over the left shoulder, to hit the animal on the near side has many disadvantages. First, it is dangerous to other players, for many accidents have happened this way; secondly, it is not a skillful way of getting the best out of the pony; thirdly, it is bad for the ponies. If a man wants to rouse a lazy one, the whip is the proper means of waking him up."[13]

DISMOUNTED PLAYER

Silchar Polo Club's rule prohibiting a dismounted player from striking the ball was carried through by all ruling bodies.

GROUND KEPT CLEAR

The Silchar rules stated that no man on foot, or dogs, or cattle were allowed on the playing ground. This sound prohibition regarding animals was vindicated in the 2006 U.S. Open Championship, when, as many eyewitnesses will recall, a runaway terrier brought havoc on the playing field, almost causing an umpire to be unhorsed.

The rule that a player must ride off the field to get a new mallet was also part of the original Silchar code.

THE OFFSIDE RULE

The Manipuris, and their spiritual successors at the Silchar Polo Club, were smart men, for no mention of the offside rule is found in the description of the game as played by the natives or in the Silchar code.

Captain Hartopp included the concept of the offside situation in his rules, possibly adapting it from football's code. The Hurlingham Club Polo Committee, which drew heavily from both Silchar's and Hartopp's ideas, included the offside penalty in its rules and regulations. In essence, this rule retarded the development of a fluid, galloping game for more than three decades. The convoluted wording read, "If a player is 'before his side' i.e., he is in front of the player of his own side who hit the ball, but has no two of the opposite side between him and the hostile goal, and has not come through the bully — he is 'off-side' and sneaking, and out of the game. The player, until he his 'on his side' has no business to impede in any manner one of the opposing side."[14]

The American victory in the 1909 Westchester Cup changed this rule forever.

A LONG-FORGOTTEN RULE

The Silchar code contained a curious provision: "When a player catches the ball in his hands, he can strike it towards his adversaries' goal by tossing it up and hitting it with his stick, and to give him room to do this, he can ride away to clear himself of his enemies but he can carry the ball no nearer to his adversaries' goal than the place where he first caught it."[15]

This practice is derived from the ancient game of hurling, much in vogue in Ireland. It is an interesting sociological question how folk games developed similar characteristics in such different areas as a landlocked Manipur, Cornwall in southwest England, and the Irish isle.

Different Codes: The Need for Unification

The chaotic situation regarding the rules of polo in the 19th century, although much improved, continues to this day. In 1893, the Hurlingham Polo Committee, the Indian Polo Association and the United States Polo Association all had separate codes. Some had significant differences, such as the offside rule and the manner of scoring penalties. In 2008, there are four codes implemented by the Argentine Polo Association, the Hurlingham Polo Association, the Federation of International Polo and the United States Polo Association. They all have different rules of the game. Apparently, at the meetings called to order by the F.I.P., each organization stubbornly rejects compromise. What is needed is a common set of rules for the game, not fine words and exhortations. If soccer is played around the world under one code of rules, why cannot the game of polo do the same?

Seven years ago, Chris Jones, the well-known player from New Zealand, wrote an important letter to the *Polo Times* editor, Margie Brett. Mr. Jones pointed out that there are two challenges to be met in order to achieve one set of rules: "Firstly it requires the political will of the three major associations to achieve that aim and to consider a wider perspective than rules introduced for local conditions or requests. It is going to take strong Presidents and Chairmen to alter local majorities' views in the interest of world polo progress. The second challenge in the process is the mechanics."[16]

As of now, no positive results have emerged from the several meetings held among polo's ruling bodies to reach a compromise and articulate a unified, worldwide, code of the game of polo.

27. On Umpiring

When Lutyens married, his wife did not allow him to play, so he was forced to be an umpire. — Rudyard Kipling[1]

Just like in most games, criticism of the umpires and referees is prevalent in polo. While the time-honored definition of an umpire — an old player who is beginning to lose his eyesight — does not hold sway any longer, it is a rare polo game in which, at the end of the day, someone does not voice a criticism of the officials. Occasionally, even the timekeeper is the recipient of a mouthful from an irate player or team partisan.

One of the characteristics of modern games is that, largely, they are not strictly governed by their rules, but by a vague consensus between players and officials as to what is and what is not acceptable. For example, in ice hockey, a penalty that would probably be whistled in the first period is usually neither invoked by the referee nor expected to be called by the players when the infraction takes place late in the game or in overtime.

The umpire's role in polo has evolved mightily through the years, from a relatively passive attitude to the current overwhelming control of a match's result based upon the huge number of penalties whistled. The Silchar Code mandated that an umpire or umpires be present; however, their duties seem to be to ascertain that both teams were ready to play, to throw-in the ball after it went out of bounds and to penalize a team for committing any direct or willful act of foul play.

The Rev. Thomas Dale's description of an umpire's attitude in 1897 is worth reading:

> The umpire is comparatively a modern institution and any effectiveness he has dates from a few years back. At first, his sole duty was to canter about the ground while a match was going on, and generally, when a question arose he was lighting a cigarette or looking the other way. He them summoned the two Backs and they laid out their case before him, with the result that unable to come to a decision he would ride off to the pavilion to reinforce his own hesitation with other people's doubts. For the most part no one thought of referring to him, and indeed the position of umpire was considered as a sort of sinecure for a person whom it was designed to honor, or as a last tie with the game for a superannuated polo player. At best, the umpire was thus like the children of a generation back, expected to be seen and not heard, and he was not supposed to speak until he was spoken to, or to give an opinion unless he was asked.[2]

The custom was for one team member to apply for a foul to the umpire, who then adjudicated in the matter. This relative peaceful existence for the officials only began to be questioned in the late 1920s, prompting the Hurlingham Polo Committee to address the issue of umpiring from a new angle. The conclusion was that umpiring in England needed some tightening up. The rules, it was suggested, must be interpreted with greater strictness and penalties awarded less sparingly than hitherto been the case. The unknown writer said, "On the other hand, it may be recalled that in writing on the international matches at Meadow Brook last year [1927], Capt. Percy R. Creed said he thought the general opinion at Meadow Brook was that 'the umpires might have exercised a considerable abstemiousness in blowing their whistles without injustice to the players and to the great benefit of the rhythm of the game.' He added, 'continued interruptions by the whistle devitalize the natural buoyancy and pace of the game of polo.'"[3]

However, the 1920s also saw the emergence of a former player who quickly acquired the reputation of being the best umpire in the history of polo. Capt. Wesley J. White, U.S. Army, was a 5-goal handicap player when a polo accident resulted in an injury to his wrist so severe that he had to give up playing polo. Capt. White went on to be an umpire in many international matches, including some in Argentina, where he earned the respect of players and spectators alike because of the evenhanded way in which he officiated. When the U.S. Polo Association decided to publish a booklet on the art of umpiring, they turned to Capt. White to be the author. His *Guide for Polo Umpires* was last reprinted in 1963, some 34 years after

Polo personalities Jack Nelson, Louis Stoddard and Capt. Wesley White, left to right, photographed during the 1927 Westchester Cup series. Nelson was captain of the Argentine Olympic gold medal team in 1924. Louis Stoddard was a 10-goal international player and chairman of the U.S.P.A from 1922 to 1936. Capt. White, his polo-playing career cut short by injury, went on to be the best umpire of his times (Museum of Polo and Hall of Fame).

Umpires Anthony Hobson (left) and Daniel Kearney confer with referee Jack Nelson. The duo was considered the best umpiring crew in the late 1940s and 1950s. Tony Hobson played international rugby for Argentina and Dan Kearney took three Open Championships with the Santa Inés team, named after his wife's estancia. The venue is Hurlingham Club's Number 1 field, now renamed Lewis Lacey Ground, which dates back to 1889 (private collection, gift of Mr. John P. Nelson).

initial publication. Some excerpts will give an idea of Wesley White's thoughts on how to umpire a game of polo.[4]

The question is often asked: Why can't we have our polo games umpired more efficiently? In Captain White's opinion, there are two reasons, the players and the umpires. The players are at fault in any instance when they openly disagree on the field with a decision made by the umpire. After a certain amount of disagreement, which varies with the amount of the umpire's ability to absorb abuse, the umpires say to themselves: Why try to enforce the rules? The result is a loosely played, badly officiated game, with a likelihood of serious accidents and discredit to the game.

The umpires are at fault when they go on the field to judge a polo game not knowing the rules and their practical application. They are not doing their duty to the game if they fail to enforce the rules as they are written.

Umpires who have played a great deal of polo understand quite clearly how a player feels when a foul is called against him after he has made what he thinks is a clever play. It has happened to all polo players. It must be pointed out that what constitutes a foul in many cases is left to the opinion of the umpire. No one can possibly put on paper what constitutes a dangerous bump in all cases, or a dangerous cross, or a dangerous use of the stick, and so forth.

The judgment of the umpire must be relied upon. He must make up his mind and act on the impulse of the moment; it is a foul, in his opinion, or it is not. There can be any number of polo-wise men on the sidelines, watching the play closely, and on any number of decisions given by the umpire there will be disagreement among them as to what happened and as to whether or not the decision of the umpire was correct.[5]

The players have responsibilities as well. In his book *As to Polo*, Cameron Forbes makes the point that "the first care of every player should be to make the game absolutely safe by avoiding committing fouls, which are usually, per se, dangerous riding."[6]

Players must ride onto the field with the preconceived idea that the umpire is always right. This concept places an enormous burden on the officials, who must live up to it. In America, 26-goal polo requires 26-goal umpiring. No excuses are valid. Professional umpires must be up to scratch, with continuing evaluation by independent observers. The umpires must earn the players' respect, not by brandishing a red flag, but by displaying competency, common sense and a lack of arrogance.

Player misbehavior is easy to address. Any player receiving a red flag should face a tribunal within 48 hours of the infraction. If appropriate, the penalty should be suspension rather than a monetary fine. Team captains should be held responsible for the team members' behavior on the field.

Polo is probably one of the most difficult games to umpire. Nevertheless, brilliant players deserve excellence in umpiring. Some umpires would benefit from Dr. William G. Grace's famous words to an umpire on the cricket ground, "They haven't come to see you umpiring, they have come to see me bat."[7] Not that the players themselves are entirely innocent souls. The verbal abuse directed at umpires far exceeds the expected behavior in a challenging and tense environment, let alone basic manners.

Player abuse of an umpire reached its highest point during the 1993 Centennial Cup at Fort Worth, when Miguel Hernandez hit umpire Archie Salinas in the eye with his mallet. When the club's disciplinary ruled on the matter months later, they took no further action, after determining that both parties were partly to blame.[8]

Ed Scanlon, the Southwest Circuit governor, was outraged by the decision. "This sort of incident is not something a club should be responsible for adjudicating. Our procedures were wrong. The argument that the club is closest to the incident and therefore best able to determine punishment holds no water. The club is too close to the situation. Everyone of its members is an interested party and conflict of interest and personal prejudices will always be factors. We need a new procedure because this one does not work."[9]

A statement by Mr. William Ylvisaker, former chairman of the U.S.P.A., is hard to understand: "You just can't have a fast-paced, violent sport like polo and expect that everybody's going to be a gentleman. If somebody gets mad and punches somebody in the mouth, so what? It brings in more people. That's my feeling."[10]

This was a disturbing opinion by a well-known figure in the world of polo. A few letters to the editor, Marty LeGrand, were published in *Polo* magazine criticizing Mr. Ylvisaker's comments. The game of polo is an alluring, exciting and passionate game. It is neither violent nor vicious. There is absolutely no excuse for violence in polo. In the ardor of action, people — players and spectators — sometimes forget how dangerous the game is. There is a long list of casualties dating back to the early days of the modern game proving that point. Regrettably, even practice chukkers have taken their toll on human lives. Does violence in games bring in more spectators? Yes, indeed; however, despite their similarities, ice hockey and polo are different. What attracts people to a polo match is the spectacle of horses running fast and players showing their riding skills and their hitting prowess. Watching a well-struck ball is worth much more than a hard bump, no matter how legal. In a selfish way, the players themselves enjoy playing polo, perhaps more than the audience enjoys watching.

The duo of Lester "Red" Armour III and Benny Gutierrez was the best umpiring crew since Capt. Wesley White's days. Red Armour said of umpiring, "As umpires, Benny Gutierrez and I decided that if were going to have an impact on the game several things had to be done: we would no longer tolerate or communicate with an abusive player, and we would do away with the from-the-spot penalty for minor infractions. Our motto became: If you foul, you will be penalized."[11]

A Day of Shame

The sending-off— the first ever in the tournament's 109-year history — of two players marred the 2002 Argentine Open Championship final match. G.A.D. "Tony" Emerson, a gentleman and a retired Army officer, is an Anglo-Argentine player with polo roots dating back to the 19th century. A keen observer of the game, his report to *Polo Times* is worth reading:

> One of the makings of a good match is when the umpiring appears unremarkable. In this one the umpires were the protagonists, notching up a record of forty one interruptions, one red and eight yellow cards, with the first card being waved at Nachi Heguy after 12 seconds' play. In the fourth chukker Eduardo Heguy found an opponent in his right of way and ran into his horse's rear. There were no falls and Ruso was awarded a 60-yarder in his favor, but he was also yellow-carded for dangerous riding and then harshly given a second yellow card for arguing about the first. In a line-out in the second half, Eduardo Heguy collided with Cambiaso, and he was sent off for a third card offence. Nobody had ever been sent off in the Open and the crowd was stunned. Later in the last chukker, Nachi Heguy lost his cool and was sent off. The umpire, Daniel Boudou, gave five out of the six red cards given by the entire corps of umpires during the season.[12]

The Argentine point of view was described by journalist Carlos Beer, a reporter for *La Nación*, the most prestigious daily newspaper in Buenos Aires:

> While admittedly, the brothers played a rougher game than usual, their expulsions appear to have been a somewhat exaggerated reaction. Nachi was given a yellow card for rough play in the first 12 seconds of the match. Wouldn't it have been better to have given him a stern warning, followed by a yellow card if he repeated the misdemeanor? Something to be kept in mind, regardless of Boudou's abilities as an umpire, is the statistic showing that four of the five cards in the Argentine high-goal season were given by him. Is this balanced umpiring? No. Either the other umpires are too lenient or he is too severe. This is a problem the A.A.P. needs to resolve, so that its umpires use similar criteria for applying sanctions. Similar sanctions were not applied to other games during the entire season. Can players be expected to change the way when in all previous matches the same faults did not merit the punishment meted out on 14 December?
> In unprecedented scenes, the public booed Tanoira when, on his own initiative, he bravely spoke at the awards ceremony supporting the umpires' work.[13]

Mr. Boudou, now a gamekeeper, had forgotten his days as a poacher. An article signed by Gonzalo Tanoira published by the magazine *Centauros* described an incident during a tournament at Coronel Suárez Polo Club, when a penalty whistled by Alfredo Harriott — at the time a 10-goal handicap player and recognized as one of the best umpires in Argentina — was questioned by Daniel Boudou. Mr. Boudou expressed serious doubts as to Mr. Alfredo Harriott's ability to officiate as umpire, in terms that prompted Gonzalo Tanoira to finish his article with the observation, "If we allow our young players to become proficient at the expense of good sportsmanship, which in essence makes our game worthwhile, our legacy will be meager and the future of polo will be very dark."[14]

Unfortunately, problems with umpires remained part of the Argentine polo landscape. Shortly after the start of the game between Indios-Chapaleufú II and El Paraíso at the 2005 Hurlingham Open, the match was out of control, with players from both teams seemingly more intent on fouling each other than anything else. One player, Francisco "Paco" de Narváez, suffered a serious shoulder injury. The Argentine Polo Association issued suspensions and warnings to no less than ten players, as substitutes continued rough play after Paco de Narvaez left the field. For Indios-Chapaleufú II, Ignacio "Nachi" Heguy was suspended for three matches, his brothers Alberto and Eduardo Heguy for one match each. All three Merlos brothers of El Paraíso received a one-match ban. Another four players received warnings. The Argentine Polo Association also suspended the two umpires as a penalty for allowing the game to get out of control to the point of becoming dangerous to players and ponies.[15]

In earlier days, mistakes by umpires in Argentina were taken with gentle understanding. One of the reporters for *Polo & Equitación* wrote that during the Anchorena Cup, now known as the Tortugas Open Championship, one of the umpires consistently awarded a penalty from 40 yards regardless of the location on the field or the severity of the infraction. This quaint practice initially evoked an incredulous response from players and spectators alike, which soon turned to shrugs and condescending smiles.[16]

Issues with umpires have also spread to England. The Hurlingham Polo Association saw fit to censure umpire Andrea Vianini for inappropriate behavior. Mr. Vianini was found guilty of misconduct for riding onto the polo field with a bottle of beer in his ball bag. He threw the glass bottle on the safety zone during the match, causing a hazard to people and horses.[17] Andrea Vianini had previously been suspended for three months and fined 2,000 pounds for playing under the influence of illegal drugs.[18]

The Hurlingham Polo Association was not afraid to ask an outsider to look at the umpire situation. In 2006, England's governing body invited Steve Lane, chief umpire instructor for the Polo Training Foundation of America, to observe and report on the performance of high-goal umpires in England. His conclusions make interesting reading.

Umpires' positioning was the most pressing problem identified by Mr. Lane. "They weren't keeping up and getting behind the play enough and were failing to position themselves so as to get the best view."[19] Other faults noted by Steve Lane were inconsistency in calls and weak field discipline. Regarding accuracy, Mr. Lane admitted that umpires will never get 100 percent of calls right; however, he suggested a suitable level to aim for would be 94–96 percent accuracy. "The [Cowdray Park] Gold Cup was around 80–84 percent. In U.S. high-goal the current percentage is about 94 percent, but we only have six umpires — here in the U.K. you have 13, and the more umpires you have, the more difficult is to improve the percentage."[20]

It would have been interesting to know what his evaluation by British umpires would have been if Mr. Lane had umpired any games in England.

Who Should be an Umpire?

Opinions are varied among polo aficionados as to who is best qualified to be a good polo umpire. In Argentina, for many years high-goal players who were also competing in the tournament umpired the Open Championship. Although in theory this practice may have flaws, in practice it worked fairly well. The advantage was that individuals accustomed to the pace of Open Championship polo controlled the games; it is a world of difference to play and officiate at 20-goal level compared to 30-plus goal level. The biggest disadvantage was that some players were pressured to umpire critical games, the result of which might affect their own team chances in the tournament.

The magazine *Polo en la Argentina* conducted a survey including all players rated at 7 goals and higher as to who were the best umpires in Argentina.[21] The top five were Francisco Dorignac, with 24 votes, followed by Alfredo Harriott, Gonzalo Tanoira, Juan José Alberdi and Eduardo (Taio) Novillo Astrada. The top three were 10-goal players and the other two, 9-goalers. There were no medium or low-goal player-umpires in the top ten. The top medium-goal player was Ricardo Díaz Dale, a 6-goal handicap who was selected to umpire the Cup of the Americas and the finals of the Cowdray Gold Cup in England. Of the top ranked umpires, only Juan José Alberdi pursued a career as a professional umpire when that venue became available in Argentina.

The survey's results suggest that high-handicap players prefer their peers to be umpires. The voters were also asked to explain what they thought were the prime characteristics for an umpire. The overwhelming opinion was that the two most important qualities were absolute knowledge of the rules of polo and the capacity to exude and exercise authority.

There have been examples of excellent umpires who were low-handicap players. José "Pepe" Resano was an icon in Argentina and much sought after as an umpire; his handicap was a modest 2 goals. No player—high handicap or beginner—ever dared to question his judgment. "Don Pepe" was a man of absolute integrity and knew the rulebook to a fault. Santiago "Diego" Cavanagh, Jr., was a 6-goal player in the 1930s who was thought to be the best umpire of his times. Diego Cavanagh officiated in the Olympic Games and at Meadow Brook in the series for the Cup of the Americas.

Australia's Peter Roberts was a non-playing umpire who rose to international status. Initially, Mr. Roberts was viewed with reluctance and had to earn the players' respect, which he did by learning the rules of the game by heart and by officiating games with authority and calm manners. His reputation is such that he is considered the benchmark for all Australian umpires.[22]

Tom Skene, a cousin of the celebrated Bob Skene, was an umpire for more than a quarter of a century. In is own time, like José Resano in Argentine, Tom Skene never faced abuse or defiance. The New South Wales Polo Association requested that he write a report on umpiring: "Players do not necessarily make good umpires, and this includes high-goal players. It is a test of their integrity and an unfair one to put them in the position of umpiring, not least in the semi-finals of tournaments they are contesting against their deadliest rivals."[23]

In his *Introduction to Umpiring*, Lord Mountbatten writes that the first point for an umpire is to know, at every moment of the game, which is the line of the ball.[24] The second point, inseparable from the first, is to know which player is in possession of the ball, because those two considerations determine what is and what is not a cross.

Other opinions voiced by "Marco" are that the umpire should never feel he is blowing the whistle too much, for he feels the bad umpire is the man who blows the whistle too little. He also calls for teamwork if there are two umpires on the field and his view that it is much better to stop the game in error than to allow a foul to slip by. Mountbatten's final point is that strict umpiring does not slow-up the game; quite the contrary.[25]

On Mutual Confidence

None of us has a monopoly on all the virtues, however much we would like to think so. It is no use the players blaming the umpires, the umpires blaming the players, and both blaming the ruling bodies. We are all in this unpleasant soup together. You cannot expect the public to have confidence in the game if players and officials do not have confidence in each other. Brigadier Arthur Douglas-Nugent, former England's Chief Umpire, had these thoughts on engendering confidence: "I have been struck by the importance of umpires getting it right. It is deeply annoying and frustrating for the players if their team is the victim of a bad decision and loses a match thereby. Umpires must be alert at all times and must make every effort to make the right calls. They carry a considerable responsibility. It does not help the confidence of the teams in the umpires if they are constantly and lengthily conferring. That is when the players tend to close in on the umpires making it very difficult for them to come to a rational and correct decision. I am not an advocate of reference to the referee but it is preferable to a long discussion."[26]

Freedom of the Press in Buenos Aires

An example of the seriousness with which Argentines take their polo was in the repercussions following an incident during a hard-fought match between Lanceros General Paz and Santa Inés for the Anchorena Cup. According to the report published in El *Diario*, during the heat of battle, Daniel Kearney, a 6-goal handicap player and number 2 on the Santa Inés team, set sail after Lt. Arturo Saavedra. Lt. Juan Carlos Balbastro, Lanceros' number 2, came thundering up to take out Dan Kearney and did the job so smartly that he sent him smack into Lt. Saavedra, then into a rather distressing but not injurious fall near the boards. The umpires, Dr. Lindsay Holway and Mr. Luis Nelson, both keen players and respected officials, promptly imposed a penalty number 2 from 40 yards on the offending lieutenant.

It sounded just like an incident in a spectacular game, but the polo reporter of El Diario wrote a scathing criticism of the umpires, which promptly had the Argentine Polo Association by the ears.[27]

Mr. Luis Nelson protested at once "against the misguided article, damaging to the interests of polo."[28] Dr. Holway, a bespectacled lawyer — though preferring to let the article pass as unworthy of notice, extremely discourteous, covertly misleading and inaccurate — offered his resignation as vice president of the Polo Association and chair of the Umpires Subcommittee. Dr. Holway pointed out that such articles, permitted to pass unnoticed, would soon sow discord, encourage the intervention of spectators unacquainted with the technique of the game, induce a lack of discipline among players, and lead the vanquished to suspect their referees as unfair or incompetent, "all of which would result in debasing so noble a sport as polo."[29]

A meeting was called of the official umpires residing in Buenos Aires and Capt. Justo J. Galarreta, secretary of the Argentine Polo Association. Dr. Holway and Mr. Nelson appeared before the meeting and gave their version of what had occurred, which proved to be something else again than the account published in the critical El Diario. Captain Galarreta and Mr. Carlos Uranga, who were members of the official list of referees, went at once to the defense of the challenged officials. They said that they considered the match one of the best refereed ever seen. Capt. Galarreta and Mr. Uranga father of Marcos Uranga, the creator of the Federation of International Polo — then made formal protest "against the offensive nature of the criticisms under consideration and the falsity of their statements, trusting that adequately severe measures will be taken to prevent the publication of insidious matter likely to foster a lack of discipline among the players as well as spectators, thereby lowering the moral and social level of polo."

The upshot of the whole affair was that the meeting of umpires instructed Capt. Galarreta to call upon the editor of *El Diario* and request him to prevent the publication of such unjust criticisms in the future, as would lead to unpleasantness among followers of the sport.[30] That was done.

The issue merited spirited coverage in *Polo & Equitación*, the leading polo publication in Argentina, and was reported in America by the magazine *Polo*.[31] It is true that the reporter for *El Diario* committed errors of fact. For instance, the fouling player was not a lieutenant on the military team; it was Kenneth Reynolds, Santa Inés' back. The penalty was called on Santa Inés, not on Lanceros.

Nevertheless, the haughty response from the Argentine Polo Association is reminiscent of the previously mentioned attitude of London's Hurlingham Club in regards to critical remarks about the game made by a London *Times* reporter.

28. The Polo Pony: From Tats to Thoroughbreds

Bernard stared at the horse in silence; not the pregnant and intimidating silence of the connoisseur, but the tongue-tied muteness of helpless ignorance. —"E.Œ. Somerville" [Edith Anna Œnone Somerville] and "Martin Ross" [Violet Florence Martin][1]

The Chinese ponies of the T'ang Dynasty were reported to be fine, upstanding specimens with intelligent heads and high crests. They were big-barrelled, with splendid leg bones, well-formed hooves, small ears and small and prominent eyes. The points of a Chinese pony in those ancient times were 32, of which the eye was considered the most important. The ideal eye should be like a hanging bell and of a fresh, reddish-purple color. The Chinese thought that "there is nothing like pedigree, without reference to which the appraiser is just like a blind man walking at random."[2]

Little has changed in the selection of polo ponies since an unknown Chinese master of the horse enunciated that sage precept. Poring over pedigree charts is as current in the age of embryo transplantation as it was in the Celestial Empire some twelve centuries ago.

When Lt. Joseph Sherer first saw polo in Cachar as played by the Manipuris, the natives were mounted on small ponies, approximately 12 hands in height. Although the small, wiry ponies carried the Manipuris to victory at the proto game in Calcutta, soon enough it was realized that large ponies were needed to sustain the hurly-burly nature of polo at that early stage of development.

The laws of the game mandated that no pony measuring over 13.3 hands be allowed on the grounds. Eventually, the limit was raised to 14.2 hands and remained so in the books but not in practice, especially in regions remote from the august governing bodies and its official measurers.

When deployed to India, the 10th Hussars amply demonstrated the superiority of large ponies in their encounters against other regimental teams. The race for better and faster ponies had started.

Flying low, no feet on the ground: the speed of the game of polo is exemplified by Orphan, ridden by Tommy Wayman (Museum of Polo and Hall of Fame).

Arabs and Indian Country-bred Ponies

Three breeds of ponies were readily available to polo players in India: the Arab, the Australian or Waler — so-called because most came from New South Wales — and the Country-bred. In his seminal work *Hints to Polo Players* in India, Capt. De Lisle advises his readers that Country-breds should not be schooled more than necessary because they become jady.

On the other hand, the more Arabs were schooled with stick and ball, the better they become.[3] De Lisle remarks that the Barb was very much like the Arab, but hardier. The Arab had defects critical in polo; it was slow at starting and at stopping. On the other hand, they could stand a lot of galloping.

The Country-bred, according to De Lisle, was hard to beat during his first two seasons; after that, he tired and tended to bore at the bit, becoming almost unmanageable, or else he shied off other ponies. As to the Walers, he found them very useful, combining the quickness of the Country-bred and the staying power of the Arab.[4]

The English and Irish Ponies

The polo pony as depicted in George Earl's famous painting *Polo Match at Hurlingham, 1877*, is an excellent demonstration of what a polo mount looked like in the last quarter of the 19th century. At the time, when polo in England was in its infancy, the Welsh pony was the first choice of players. As the game evolved from trotting and dribbling to galloping and hitting, the thought that a pony was only a conveyance to the ball quickly became obsolete. The Sussex team of the Peat brothers had unparalleled success in the Hurlingham Champion Cup; even though they were great players, the secret of their success was that they possessed the fastest and best trained ponies.

The writers of the day spent considerable amounts of ink describing the ponies. Many were Arabs, but most were bred in Ireland by thoroughbred horses out of mares with pony blood. The increased speed of the game demanded hot blooded ponies. Needless to say, the increased demand for ponies brought about a rise in prices. Ponies came from all sorts of places; from carts in Ireland, from butchers' yards, farmers' gigs and the occasional vicar's chaise. Nevertheless, the best supply came from the pony races that were so popular in Britain at the time.

Foreign ponies were imported into England; they were valued in proportion as how they resembled the home-bred in shape, speed and handiness. The great qualities of Anglo-Irish ponies were their vitality, their will to gallop and their power to go on even when tired. There was another invaluable asset: their good temper, without which a pony could not make a first-class polo pony.

Rosewater, by Rosicrucian and Lady Day II, a bay stallion bred by A.W. Elphick, the property of Sir Humphrey de Trafford, winner of many races and first prize for polo pony stallions at Hurlingham, was the founder of a long line of polo ponies.[5] Other superior

The grand Irish mare Ralla, sculpted by Herbert Haseltine. Although difficult to handle, Ralla was one of Harry Payne Whitney's best horses. A quarter life-size cast is in the Whitney Museum in New York City (private collection, on loan to the Museum of Polo and Hall of Fame).

Best Playing Pony Menina, a bay mare, with her Irish groom Elie Brien, 10-goaler Mariano Aguerre and presenter Martha Headen Laffaye holding the halter given as a prize (private collection, Dan Burns photograph).

stallions were Othrae, sired by Raeburn by St. Simon, Bold Marco by Marco by Barcaldine, Right For'ard, his sire Mark For'ard by Wrightaway, and Sandiway by Rosewater.[6] Another stallion by Rosewater was Shy Boy, dam Shy Lass by Albert Victor; the exceptional Belsire by Right For'ard, dam Black Bella, and Quiroga, by Davenport by Chippendale, exported to Argentina and considered the best blood in that country.[7]

Sir John Barker was the first breeder to select mares that had made a reputation on the polo grounds and breed good ponies from them at his stud farm, The Grange in Hertfordshire. Other notable breeders were the Earl of Harrington — the Polo and Riding Pony Society's first president — the Earl of Ava, Sir Humphrey de Trafford, Sir Walter and Tresham Gilbey at Whitehall Stud, Sir Gilbert Greenall, Sir Patteson Nickalls, George Norris Midwood and the Rev. D.B. Montefiore.

Ponies from America

The most important breeding operation in America was the Circle V Polo Ranch located in Wyoming's Big Horn Valley, owned by Col. W. Milton McCoy and Mr. Goelet Gallatin. The four principal stallions standing at Circle V were the chestnut Kemano, by Right For'ard and Noteless, from Sir John Barker's Grange stud. Kemano, foaled in 1910, a blue ribbon winner at the first show of the National Polo Pony Society, who was on both the American and British *Stud Books* and in the English *Polo Pony Stud Book.*[8] It was imported by Quincy Shaw II, from Myopia and Greenwood Farm in Virginia. Another Circle V sire was Black Rascal, by Black Tony, a repeated winner for Mrs. Payne Whitney on racetracks. Then there was Kronomo, foaled in 1927, a son of Kemano out of Sophrony Brown, Louis Stoddard's mare, and, finally, Phanthom Prince, by Prince Hall out of Phanthom Maid.[9]

A big time breeder was Edward Q. McVitty at his Bear Valley Ranch in San Miguel, California. Among his stallions were the black Benroe, bred by the brothers Clay, the brown Gargantua, bred by J. Livingston, and Huston, a chestnut with a large blaze on his face. All three were Kentucky-bred. Other McVitty sires were Ibn Canada, J.F. Crowley, Salvortus and Satsuma II, all bred in California.[10]

A celebrated mare was Miss Hobbs, a chestnut with a flaxen tail depicted by Frank Voss in oil and illustrated in the 1923 U.S.P.A. *Year Book* as an fine example of a long, low mare.[11] Miss Hobbs, owned by W. Goadby Loew, was played in the internationals series in 1911 and 1914. No less famous was Louis Stoddard's Belle of All, Champion Polo Pony in 1921–22. Belle of All was bred in Kentucky by E.R. Bradley; her sire was Cunard, dam Black Mary by Star Shoot. Mr. Stoddard also had Flora, a bay mare bred by R.D. Fleming in Colorado. Other great ponies of the 1920s were J. Watson Webb's Naughty Girl, Goadby Loew's Lapwing, Stephen Sanford's Fairy Story, My Girl, None So Pretty — a full sister to the champion Judy —

The famous chestnut mare Judy, champion at the Meadow Brook, Palermo and Ranelagh polo pony shows. Owned and played by Jack Nelson, Julio and Tomás Juárez Celman bred Judy. Top price in the 1926 sale was $13,000, paid by John Sanford (Museum of Polo and Hall of Fame).

The American international Ray Harrington, an 8-goal player, on his pony Ever Ready, a winner of the Hartman Trophy for the Best Playing Pony in the U.S. Open Championship. Both player and mount are enshrined in the Polo Hall of Fame (Museum of Polo and Hall of Fame).

and the gray Lavender. Patchwork, owned by Howard Phipps, took the first prize, mare with foal standing, at the National Polo Pony Society 1921 show.

The depression years had a detrimental effect on polo pony production. Many Argentine ponies were purchased by American buyers; they were made polo ponies, tried, tested and ready to perform in high-goal polo. Florelle, Guatimozin, Chingolo, Pampero, Cometa and Lucky Strike were among the highest prices.

Ponies from Texas were avidly sought after since the early days of polo in the United States. Cecil Smith's Badger, a bay gelding, and Bonnie J, a dun mare, are in the pantheon of polo ponies. After World War II, some celebrated ponies were John T. Oxley's Cat-A-Joy and Woody D, Norty Knox's Ragamuffin and Rotallen, Kaliman, Guillermo Gracida's great pony, Steve Gose's Alabama, played by Joe Barry, Delta Dawn of Roy Barry, Tommy Wayman's Sweet William, Seth Herndon's Electric Charge, Delmar Carroll's Magazin, and Chica Boom, the property of Bart Evans.

Many of the above are enshrined in the Museum of Polo and Hall of Fame Ponies to Remember category, an award started in 2000.

The Western Canadian Pony

In the dawn of polo in the Province of Alberta, stock ponies that earned their keep as working horses in cattle ranches were the mounts for the ranchers and their hands who tried their skill at the galloping game. Many British proprietors hired cowboys and remittance men who took to the game with alacrity. Therefore, the British cattle ranch owners in Southern Alberta and their managers were the ones who started the improvement of the local cow ponies by purchasing thoroughbred mares and stallions from Eastern Canada first, the United States and Britain later. It was from breeding programs initially established to produce racehorses for the local tracks that polo ponies began to develop. A lively trade with England was established and Canadian polo ponies received favorable reviews. The most celebrated Canadian polo pony was Bendigo, played by 10-goaler Walter Buckmaster, who thought he was one of his two top ponies along his long and successful career. Both Tom Drybrough and Ted Miller enthusiastically endorsed Canadian mounts in their writings.[12, 13]

A big step forward in Canadian polo pony breeding occurred in 1919 when T.B. Jenkinson purchased the Virginia Ranch near Cochrane. It was the first operation exclusively devoted to breeding and training of polo ponies.[14] Mr. Jenkinson was able to export ponies to the United States through his connection with McCoy and Gallatin's Circle V Ranch in Big Horn. The pony trail usually went from Sheridan, Wyoming, to Aiken, South Carolina.

Welshman Llewellyn Owen Chambers had arrived to Calgary in 1912 and started a cattle operation in Balzac, just north of the city.[15] "Llew" Chambers played polo at the Calgary club and achieved a well-earned reputation as a breeder and trainer. His lifeline to the United States was to Long Island, where Fred and William Post conducted the largest polo pony operation in the East Coast.

The deteriorating economic situation that began with the Wall Street crash in October 1929 reverberated to Western Canada and essentially decimated both the game of polo and the polo pony business.

The Argentine Ponies

Any horse would do for the pioneers of polo in Argentina. Inevitably, the first mounts for polo were the redoubtable criollos, direct descendants of the Barbs brought over to South America by the Spanish conquistadores. As the game developed, the tireless but slow criollo gradually gave way to faster horses.

The first estancieros to start a breeding program were Frank Bradney and William McNaughten at their estancia La Independencia in Las Rosas, a hotbed of polo in Santa Fe Province. In the early 1890s, they imported Cupid and Meistersinger, both purebred ponies. Gradually, the breeding operation at La Independencia drifted towards racehorses. The mares were purchased by the Drysdales, who continued the breeding at Santa Inés. The bloodline from La Independencia extended well into the 1950s in high-goal polo.

The Traill family imported from England the stallion Springjack, whose progeny was the foundation of a formidable polo pony string that was the best in the country. At a time, the Traills counted more that 2,000 horses in their various estancias. These ponies became a profitable source of income when sold in England by the cousins Joe and Johnny Traill.

Maj. James Porteous and Capt. Charles Knight, co-owners of estancia Las Tres Lagunas, also located in Las Rosas, bred excellent ponies. Lord Harrington gave his stallion Fetterlock to Maj. Porteous; Pride of Fame, one of Fetterlock's offspring out of a thoroughbred mare, was sold to the Comte Jean de Madré and was champion at the Hurlingham Show in London.

Marsden Withington, who owned estancia Santa Rosa in La Colina, was the proprietor of Marechal Neil and Phoenix, the latter one of the best sires imported to Argentina. Both stallions were purchased by Frederick Lomax when the breeding operation ended at Santa Rosa. Mr. Lomax also owned My Boy, by Kennington out of My Girl, who came from Sir John Barker's stud in 1912. In that year, Eduardo Amadeo Artayeta imported for his breeding stud La Providencia the stallion Othrae, by Raeburn out of Othery, from the St. Simon thoroughbred line.

Frank Balfour, long-time secretary of the Polo Association of the River Plate, owned estancia El Colorado in Washington, Cordoba Province. The foundation of his breeding establishment was Shy Boy, by Rosewater out of Shy Lass, purchased from Sir John Barker. The best mares from Shy Boy were bred to Belsire, by Right For'ard out of Black Bella, reputed to be the best British bloodline. Cinders, a grey mare, owned by Robert Strawbridge, Jr., and played by J. Watson Webb in international matches, was one of the first of a long line of Argentine polo ponies played in the United States.

Near Venado Tuerto, Tomás Moore, owner of the celebrated Moore's mares, and Dr. Tomás Kenny, were breeders of high-quality polo ponies. Farther north, in Santa Fe and Córdoba provinces, the Benitz family were successful breeders: Malcolm, Guillermo "Willy" and John Benitz at Los Algarrobos, La California and Monte Guazú.

Plumita, by Collar Stud, one of the top horses from the 1922 Argentine string, ridden by Lewis Lacey (Museum of Polo and Hall of Fame).

In southern Buenos Aires Province, the Martínez de Hoz brothers had the stallion Balcarce at their famous Chapadmalal, the largest thoroughbred establishment in South America. Among the best were Oh Hell!, later Hello, champion at Hurlingham's heavy-weight class and played in the Westchester Cup matches. Córdoba, Anca Mora and Dios Te Ampare were played by the 1924 Olympic team. Chingolo, mounted by Andrés Gazzotti on the gold medal team in Berlin and in the Cup of the Americas at Meadow Brook, carried the top price at Fred Post's sale after the 1936 U.S. Open.

Jack and Luis Nelson had breeding operations at both San Marcos and Salalé, estancias that they inherited from their grandfather Tomás Duggan. There stood Collar Stud, by Collar, also from the St. Simon line. Among those ponies was Gargantilla, played by Devereux Milburn and immortalized on canvas by Sir Alfred Munnings.

In later years, Ricardo Santamarina and his wife, the former Frances Post, bred some of the best ponies from the Mahmoud line, given to the Santamarinas by Pete Bostwick. The famous Santamarina greys were a feature at Palermo for many years.

The Anglo-Argentine breeders spent large amounts of money in purchasing the best available blood. Their efforts are now visible in the large production of top polo ponies, in many cases bred by their direct descendants. The tradition of polo pony breeding in Argentina remains vibrant and profitable some 115 years after Hugh Scott Robson and his band of brothers, Johnny Smyth, Dr. Newman Smith, Frank and Stanley Furber, made the long sea voyage to England and sold their ponies after a successful London season.[16]

Walers

When polo-playing visitors first toured Australia, they failed to convince the locals of the need to import polo ponies. The reason was quite simple. Tough little horses called bush ponies populated the vast grazing areas of New South Wales. The practical Australians took their ponies, grass-fed and unshod, pulled the burrs from their tails and manes, polished them up, gave then a little corn and shod them. Off they went to conquer the world of polo in Australia and India, where they immediately surpassed the local Arabs and Country-bred ponies. By then, they were known as Walers.

The bush pony was a cross between Arab and English breeds; however, it developed its own characteristics. It had been raised for pastoral work, toughened by the climate and the competitive need for forage on its own against millions of sheep. The bush pony developed into a small, hardy breed, intelligent, and endowed with a capacity for great endurance.

The Walers' were acquainted with American polo in 1927, when the Army-in-India team represented Britain in the Westchester Cup at Meadow Brook's International Field, a test of polo if there was one. The Walers did well and commanded good prices at the post-competition sale. Averell Harriman purchased Rufus, an Australian chestnut gelding, for $10,500, only $200 less than the top price in the sale.

The Thoroughbred

The thoroughbred horse has been bred for centuries for only one purpose, to run as fast as possible. The polo horse not only has to run fast, but also has to stop and turn quickly. This is one of the reasons that racehorses, when too slow for the track and purchased as candidates to be good polo ponies, are not as good as those bred specifically for the game.

Thoroughbred blood is essential in modern polo because speed is one of the most sought after characteristics in the polo horse, as it should now be called. Breeders spend considerable time studying the different bloodlines now available by the new technology of embrionary transplantation that allows the inseminated mares to keep on playing matches after the embryo is transplanted to a surrogate mare for completion of pregnancy.

Best Playing Pony Prizes

When the Polo Pony Society was established in London in 1893, under the presidency of the Earl of Harrington, with the purpose of the improvement and encouragement of the breeding of high-class ponies, gold, silver and bronze medals were awarded to different classes in almost every show, from Adlington to Waltham Cross.[17] The practice remained in force until the beginning of World War II.

The oldest prize given to polo ponies in competition is the Lady Susan Townley Cup in Argentina. It was presented in 1908 by the British minister in Argentina, Sir William Townley, to be awarded to the best pony played in the P.A. Association of the River Plate Open Championship. Lady Susan Townley had a particular interest in polo ponies because she was also a breeder; her stallion Don Mike was registered in the Polo Pony Stud Book.

The Lady Townley Cup's first winner was the black mare India, played by Harold Schwind, an estanciero born in Edinburgh who owned estancia El Bagual (wild horse) in the Western Province of San Luis. India was unbeaten in up to 1,000 meter races and was incredibly fast in polo as played in that era. The winner's roster of the Lady Townley Cup is full of hallowed names in Argentine polo. Mano Blanca, owned by Alfredo Peña Unzué, took the honors three years in a row, 1915–1917. The other triple winners were Luis Tomás Nelson's Pampita in 1930, 1932 and 1933, and Marionette, owned by Enrique Alberdi, in 1944–1947 (there was no Open Championship in 1945) otherwise she would have been a quadruple winner, such was her excellence.

Double winners include Sombra, of Daniel Kearney in 1938–37, Luis Duggan's Ruby in 1941–42, Marionette's own descendant Marionette II in 1957 and 1962, and Juan Carlitos Harriott's Burra — his best pony ever — in 1964–65. Northrup Knox, captain of the American team in 1969, made history when his magnificent Ragamuffin won the Townley Cup, the only foreign pony to achieve that distinction. Lechuza, played by Gonzalo Pieres on La Espadaña team, was awarded the trophy in 1986–87. Marsellesa, bred by Luis María "Lucho" Heguy, played by his cousin Marcos in 1988, and by another cousin, Horacio Segundo in 1992, was another multiple winner.

Luna, bred by Héctor and Susie Barrantes at El Pucará and played by Gonzalo Pieres, took the cup in 1989 and 1990. Silverada, owned by the American player Bob Daniels from Myopia, was the second foreign pony to win the Lady Susan Townley Cup, ridden by the late Gonzalo Heguy. Milo Fernández Araujo's mare Paz took the award in 1999 and 2000.

The Cambiaso era began in 1997, when the aging Colibrí took the cup, a success repeated in the following year. Colibrí, a small horse with fantastic speed over short distances, played in his last open in 2001 at age 19. He is now out to pasture at Cambiaso's estancia in Cañuelas. His mare Lili won in 2002 and the stallion Aiken Cura, bred by Santamarina, took the honors in 2005 and 2006. Aiken Cura had a hero's finale, when Cambiaso scored the winning goal in sudden-death overtime. Aiken Cura broke a leg during that chukker, and after desperate attempts to save him, including amputation, there was no other choice than to put him down. All the Santamarina's breeds carry the surname Aiken, because Ricardo met his future wife in that horsy town. Aiken Cura's sire was Alma de Bacán, by Crown Thy Good, his dam was Lady Nun.

In America, the National Polo Pony Society instituted the Prince Friarstown Challenge Cup — named after Mrs. W. Averell Harriman's famous stallion — for the best mare suitable to produce a polo pony. The mare had to play in selected tournaments each year. The National Polo Pony Society's Cup was awarded to the best stallion with three of his get, and finally, the Town and Country Cup for the best pony in the show, which took place at the Meadow Brook Club every year.[18]

The Willis L. Hartman Trophy was presented by Mr. Hartman in 1964 to the U.S. Polo Association, to be awarded to the best pony played in the U.S. Open Championship.[19] The cream of American ponies' names are engraved on the trophy, from Ronnie Tongg's Lovely Sage to the 2008 winner, Pico Blanco, played by Ignacio Novillo Astrada.

Milo Fernández Araujo (right) on his way to the top. Ready to mount, Milo reached a 10-goal handicap and his mare Paz was a two-time winner of the Lady Susan Townley award as the best polo pony in the Argentine Open (Museum of Polo and Hall of Fame).

Polo Pony Societies

The Polo Pony Society was founded in 1893 and kept a stud book for many years. Its importance declined with the abolition of height restrictions in England in 1919. However, the year books were published until the advent of World War Two. Publication was resumed in 1948, under the title *The National Pony Stud Book*.

A similar fate occurred to the National Polo Pony Society in America, started in 1919; only two stud books were published, in 1925 and in 1929. The first stallion registered was Christopher Columbus, by Mark For'ard by Rightaway out of Hall Mark, bred by Sir John Barker. His dam was Little Chris by Bentworth out of Philobelle. Christopher Columbus was a bay with black tail and a white splash on the forehead. It had multiple owners; Horace Havemeyer, William Russell Grace, Allan Pinkerton and Harry T. Peters.

Sunny Hale, one of the top woman players in the world, started in 2006 the American Polo Horse Association, an organization that maintains a registry that collects and records information on polo horses. The A.P.H.A. also organizes breeder's select sales, which includes embryos. Once the owners and breeders register their horses, their complete string can be reviewed online. Still in the developmental stage, the American Polo Horse Association is showing promise as an invaluable tool in researching blood lines and past performances in a growing number of ponies.

In Argentina, the A.A.C.C.P. (Asociación Argentina de Criadores de Caballos de Polo), founded in 1984, is thriving. In 1992, three ponies registered in the A.A.C.C.P. participated in the Argentine Open Championship at Palermo; in 2005, there were 132 registered polo ponies in the same tournament.[20] The association publishes a year book, now numbering 21 annual issues, listing registered stallions, mares and their produce, plus a list of breeders and pertinent articles by recognized authorities. The association presents suitable prizes at different events. The top prize is given to the best playing polo pony in the final game of the Argentine Open Championship at Palermo. It must be a horse registered in the A.A.C.C.P.'s stud book. The last winner was the mare Cuartetera, which adorns the cover of the 2007 *Annual*, painted by the talented Inés Menéndez Behety. Cuartetera was bred, owned and played by Adolfo Cambiaso; her sire is Sportivo, by Lode, and her dam, Lambada, by Sequito. Ever since its inception, the breeders' association has promulgated the rules and standards for the Polo Pony Argentino,[21] a breed now properly recognized by the Argentine Rural Society, that also presents a championship ribbon at its annual cattle show in Buenos Aires.

The Literature of the Polo Pony

Almost every book published about the game of polo contains one or more chapters giving advice about breeding, selection, training, diet, conveyance and stable management of polo ponies. Among this plethora of reading material, two volumes written by U.S. Army officers stand out. The first one is *Polo Ponies* by Lt. Paul G. Kendall, which was published by the famous Derrydale Press, a top of the line literary sports firm owned by Eugene V. Connett.[22] The second is Maj. Ernest Grove Cullum's *Selection and Training of the Polo Pony*.[23] Both were published in the mid–1930s in New York City and offer sound advice on the subject. Both Maj. Cullum and Lt. Kendall were recognized as superb equestrian instructors and their recommendations are borne out of long experience as horsemen and polo players.

Colophon

This is a long chapter about the polo pony, and rightly so. The ponies are the real heroes in the game of polo. They give everything to the game; sometimes even their lives. A large part of polo's attraction as a game and as a spectacle are the ponies — alert, vibrant, graceful and noble. Anyone who has had a mallet in his hand remembers with kind affection, admiration and, why not, enormous pride, those animals that gave all that they could give. It is difficult to recall Devereux Milburn without Tenby, Eduardo Moore without Fabiola, Tommy Hitchcock without Tobiano, H.P. Whitney without Cottontail, Cecil Smith without Bonnie J and Quito Alberdi without Marionette. It is impossible, many would say. The list is endless.

29. The State of the Game in the Twenty-First Century

Polo has contracted a virus, the symptoms being a lot of close contact, changes of direction, and dribbling, a nightmare for the umpires. — Lt. Col. Alec Harper[1]

As polo slides into the final years of the 21st century's opening decade, its evolution appears to be regressing. Lt. Col. Alec Harper's thoughts, articulated in 1995, are as current in 2008 as they were over a decade ago. The game of polo is also beset by a canker, that of match fixing. Only one major ruling body, the Hurlingham Polo Association, has shown the courage of its convictions and addressed in a comprehensive manner the problem of drug usage. Attempts at television viewing are uncoordinated and mostly engendered without clear marketing strategies. International competition has remained at a low level since the 1980s. The rules of the game, although similar in most countries, still differ in many important details. Modifications are haphazard and subject to local changes at the club level. In this era of highly talented professional players, the game is governed by well-motivated amateurs who work hard to perform what is a full-time task.

At the time of writing, the main polo associations have appointed executive officers: Col. David Woodd in Britain, Mr. Peter Rizzo in America and Gen. Mauricio Fernández Funes in Argentina. It is a step forward; nevertheless, there seems to be a collective inability to reach an agreement regarding unified rules of the game, and in certain cases, to effectively address and resolve complicated issues facing the game.

The sad fact is that — with the exception of Argentina — high-goal polo as played at the 22- to 26-goal level in the rest of the world would certainly be in a crisis without the financial support of the patrons. Corporate involvement is usually short-term and subject to change, depending a lot on the personal involvement of a few individuals.

The Tapping Game

Today, the game is controlled by the professional players. Their principal aim — and rightly so — is to win the tournament. When a 10-goal player is paired with a low-goal patron and a brace of medium-handicap players, it is obvious that the superstar will dictate the flow

287

In the 1990s, gaining possession of the ball in the throw-in became a crucial part of a winning strategy. This is Greenwich Polo Club in Connecticut, where some games of the U.S. Open Championship were held in the 1990s (Museum of Polo and Hall of Fame).

and pace of the match. The modern game has evolved into the precepts of possession, rotation, and provoking a foul. More often than not, games are decided by free hits. Masters of the mallet such as Adolfo Cambiaso, Pablo MacDonough and Facundo Pieres have raised ball control to heights undreamed of two decades ago. However, not every player is a Pieres or a Cambiaso who can effectively dribble the ball at great speed. For less adept practitioners, dribbling is reduced to tapping, which, in spite of changes in the rules, has considerably slowed down the pace of play.

Miguel Novillo Astrada, a 10-goal handicap player and self-avowed proponent of the open game, is adamant that the search for the foul is ever-present because penalty conversions win most of the matches in modern polo. It is ugly, but the professionals are paid to win games and tournaments.[2]

Lt. Col. Alec Harper said of tapping the ball:

> This is the result of a player who has an opening, instead of going to the ball as fast as he can and hitting a big one first time, slowing down to take his shot, so as to let his team get into position. But this gives the other team time to get into position too, so no one ever gets clear except by chance. It is terribly frustrating for a forward who has "slipped" his man and gone for a pass and then number 3 takes so long over it that the forward is closely marked by the time the ball arrives. Result, scrimmage after scrimmage.
>
> I think this virus originated a few years ago with the arrival of the low-goal patron. Before that, patrons such as the Vesteys, David Jamison, Geoffrey Kent, Guy Wildenstein, etc., were good enough players to take part in the game. Now many have no influence on the play and their teams are two-man teams who hold the ball and pass to each other, a slow game. This is

not polo as we used to know it, but the result of a 22-goal limit with two super players, one passenger and one boy.

These tactics have been copied for no good reason by teams who do not need them. Even hard riding players can now be seen pulling up when they get the ball instead of wasting no time in banging it up the ground.

Unlike real viruses the doctors, the HPA, know the causes but do not admit that this condition is serious enough for an operation. We are still told that our

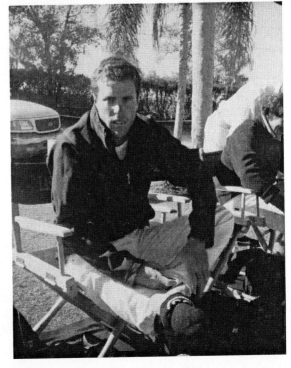

Top: Mariano Aguerre and his chestnut pony Angelina defy the laws of gravity while tapping the ball in the air at Greenwich Polo Club during the finals of the 2007 Tommy Glynn Memorial Tournament (private collection, Dan Burns photograph). *Right:* The latest Argentine 10-goaler, Lucas Monteverde from El Rincón Polo Club, in a candid photograph while preparing for a game. Like many Argentines, Monteverde is a third generation polo player, in his case all christened Lucas (Museum of Polo and Hall of Fame).

Adolfo Cambiaso and Gonzalito Pieres, two of the top players in the world, in action on Florida grounds (Museum of Polo and Hall of Fame, Alex Pacheco photograph).

Left: Superstar Adolfo Cambiaso playing for New Bridge–La Dolfina in Palm Beach (Museum of Polo and Hall of Fame). *Right:* Facundo Pieres, the second of Gonzalo's three sons, was a child polo prodigy, playing in the Argentine Open at Palermo while still a schoolboy. Now he is challenging Adolfo Cambiaso for the title of top player in the world (Museum of Polo and Hall of Fame, Alex Pacheco photograph).

22-goal polo is the best in the world, which it is if you are looking for individual brilliance, but teamwork has gone and the knife will have to be wielded if our polo is not to fall into disrepute.

A welcome sign in 1995 is the appearance of three 4-man teams who are playing attractive polo, and not without success. They are doing a good job showing fans what polo can be.[3]

Regrettably, the welcome sign spotted by Col. Harper failed to gain widespread recognition. The situation got worse with the increase in turning with the ball, a forerunner of tapping.

Turning With the Ball

The new players are impatient of the backhander, which can be a magnificent offensive weapon. In contemporary polo, it has the added benefit of surprise. It appears to be much more pleasurable to turn with the ball — in a way that not too long ago was considered a foul — and then tap the ball down field. Many keen observers of the game feel that something must be done to change this trend. Polo has become much less fun to watch. It is a fine game and should not be turned and tapped into languorous stupor.

It should and can work. A letter to the editor of *Polo Times* lauded the effort:

> In the last tournament of the 1998 season at the Edgeworth Polo Club, the Committee introduced a rule which banned players from turning the ball and, if they did so, a free hit was awarded to the opposition. The success of this ruling was proved when it consistently produced high competitive and flowing games which involved all members from each team; it also highlighted team play and team support.
>
> New Zealand 4-goaler Tim Keyte, who was playing in this tournament, had played under this ruling in Australia and it was his experience of the success of such a condition of play that instigated the change at Edgeworth.
>
> Professionals are more than capable of playing with the entire team instead of just themselves!
>
> The consensus of the spectators was that it increased the speed of the game and made the matches far more enjoyable to watch. From the point of view of the umpires, it reduced the number of fouls, many of which are committed whilst trying to stop a player turning on the ball. The majority of players enjoyed playing under the new rule and as a result of their increased involvement, it will be incorporated in most low-goal tournaments at Edgeworth this year.[4]

Another letter from Mr. Martin Trotter, sometime chief umpire for the Hurlingham Polo Association, recalled words of wisdom from one of the best players ever to grace a polo ground, Hanut Singh, "I well remember Hanut, when in control of the Jersey Lilies, making enough noises to bring down the Taj Mahal, as one of his team started to take it around."[5]

The beauty of polo is based upon the passing game, not on incredibly skillful players going in circles tapping the ball. When the issue of turning on the ball comes up in both formal and informal discussion, somebody inevitably mentions the remembrance of Del Carroll, an 8-goal international American player, who was notorious for his unerring custom of going straight at whatever was in his path, if he believed he had the right of way.

Some governing body has to pave the way and take the leadership in stopping sticky polo. There is plenty of noise regarding the issue of turning with the ball, but the various rules committees are not listening.[6] The rules of polo must be changed to open up the game.

Changing Ponies on the Fly

A relatively recent development is changing ponies in the middle of the chukker. It makes sense. If a pony is expected to play 14 or so minutes during a match, it is far better to split the playing time in quarters of approximately three or four minutes each. The rules of the game mandate that play must be continuous, except when the whistle is blown by an umpire. The rules also allow that the clock shall be stopped when a pony is injured.

Players now take advantage of the latter provision, claiming that the pony is lame or does not feel right. Most other players take the opportunity to change mounts, quite often at the other end of the field, since changing ponies at the sidelines is forbidden. The procedure is repeated time and time again, especially by those teams that do not possess deep pony strings. During the 2008 Palm Beach season the practice reached epidemic proportions and most of the games took well over two hours for the six chukkers to be completed.

In his *Polo Times* column, Brigadier Douglas-Nugent has cogently written about this game-delaying tactic. Another letter, this one from Mr. Doug Brown, puts the practice in perspective:

> The advent of the three minute horse has truly put the mockers on high goal as a spectacle. All that stopping and swapping. Very off putting.
> Of course, we all know that polo exists for the players and that spectators are at low regard. But even the lowly spectator is entitled to expect that the game is played according to the rules.
> And it is not. Rule 15(e) not only requires "that play should be continuous," but goes on to add that play should not be stopped for changing ponies (exceptions being specified).
> This rule is now disregarded. Who is to enforce it? Not the umpires. They have either just flouted the rule themselves or are about to do so.
> Only the patrons, acting in concern, have the clout to wipe out this practice that dires the game.[7]

In reality, the umpires are the ones who must enforce the rules on the field. They are the ones who are empowered, as well as mandated, to apply the rules as written, not the referee, not the team captain nor the patron. It is simply a matter of the umpires exercising their authority.

It is argued that perhaps it is a good rule because it protects the ponies' well-being and it is not up to the umpires to become on the spot veterinarians. In the not too distant past, ponies went an entire chukker without health problems. However, nowadays polo ponies are trained to go only three or four minutes per chukker because the new style of stopping, turning, running and stopping is much harder on the ponies than the old running game. The Hurlingham Polo Association has taken the lead in addressing a tricky situation by the simple expedient of mandating that a pony declared lame by his rider must be tagged and not allowed to play again in the match.

Match Fixing

Since time immemorial, the game of polo has been subject to a culture of excellence. One distinctive feature was the impeccable turnout at all levels. Sinclair Hill more than once said, "Even if you're not a great polo player, try to look like one. Polish yourself up."[8] Casual and formal elegance on the sidelines and faultless turnout of the ponies are part of the polo scene, although sometimes players forget about neat appearance and remove their boots before climbing the podium. However, the biggest embarrassment of all is the certainty that a culture of fixing games runs right through high-goal polo, and that there is a total unwillingness to do much about it. The governing bodies are not even willing to accept that corrupt practices exist, which is the only possible starting point for making things better.

In the first semifinal of the 2007 U.S. Gold Cup, a tournament whose results would determine the seeding for the U.S. Open Championship, organized by the International Polo Club Palm Beach Committee, members of the team La Herradura incurred the committee's displeasure for not trying too hard. The game was considered a sham. That evening, the I.P.C.P.B. Committee held a meeting, which resulted in suspending four of the five La Herradura players from participating in I.P.C.P.B. events for the rest of 2007. La Herradura's captain, Memo Gracida, filed an appeal with the U.S. Polo Association, which declined to review the issue under the excuse that it had no jurisdiction over the matter. Nevertheless, in a letter to Guillermo Gracida, U.S.P.A. Chairman Jack L. Shelton stated that all of the suspended players were in good standing with the U.S.P.A. and could continue to participate in its events.[9] The question must be asked, if the U.S. Open Championship is not an U.S. Polo Association event, then which tournament is?

The conclusion is that the United States Polo Association, the custodian of polo's integrity in North America, elected to wash its hands in a matter involving fundamental issues affecting the well-being of the game. This lack of leadership at the very top was appalling. The game of polo was brought into disrepute.[10]

Once more, the Hurlingham Polo Association has assumed a position of leadership in facing a difficult question. The 2007 *Rules for Polo* explicitly state, "Not trying. Both teams in a match must try to win."[11] It goes on to articulate the correct procedure to follow. Umpires, the referee or the tournament committee are required to warn the team, if the team fails to comply, a report is to be submitted, and the team or individual players may be subject to a disciplinary enquiry, which may take any action, including suspension from the tournament. Just recently, the U.S. Polo Association included in its *Blue Book* a code of conduct that exhorts players to do their best.[12]

Years ago, the matter of fixing games came before the Hurlingham Polo Association stewards, who, after due consideration took no action because there was no evidence proving that matches were fixed. In the stewards' defense, it is very difficult to establish proof; nevertheless, experienced observers of the game can readily note when something is amiss in a polo match.

The root of the problem resides in the league format, which is the usual method to qualify for the eliminatory rounds in most tournaments. It is axiomatic that the fewer the teams in a league, the greater the problem. If the league format is adopted, there should be at least four teams in each league. Then it is quite easy to schedule the final two matches at the same time, in different venues. For some reason, possibly the hope to remain eligible for the straight elimination phase, patrons and players are opposed to the elimination system. A meaning subsidiary eliminatory or league format can be scheduled, offering an almost equal number of games for every team.

According to Gareth Davies, match fixing could become outdated in England, thanks to an innovative system devised for the Gold Cup. In 2004, the fixture was changed with the agreement of players, patrons and Cowdray Park Polo Club officials. That year, the Gold Cup started with a league system encompassing five groups, each made of three teams selected at random. An order of merit was then established, based on the results of the two games played in each group. The order of merit table was based on points, then net goals and, finally, gross goals. There were 15 teams, of which the top one, Dubai, passed directly to the quarterfinals. The other 14 teams played an eliminatory round to qualify the rest of the quarterfinalists. The second team played the 15th placed team, 3rd v. 14th, and so on. The quarterfinalists were then drawn at random.[13]

In spite of Mr. Davies' hopeful words, match fixing continues, at least in America. The vagaries of the draw for the 2008 U.S. Open Championship gave rise to a situation in which six teams were left to compete for the last five slots in the quarterfinal round. Three consecutive matches among the six teams were scheduled one after another in midweek. An examination of the possibilities made clear that in the first match, Audi versus Zacara, if either team won by one goal, both would qualify for the quarterfinals. Zacara won by one goal. In the second match, Pony Express, facing elimination with a loss, needed to win. If they won by one or two goals, both Pony Express and their occasional opponent, Black Watch, would qualify, leaving Isla Carroll and White Birch in a desperate struggle to play for the last open spot. As expected, Pony Express took the match by one goal. Many experienced observers of polo felt that both games had been "arranged," to use the local parlance. In the last event of the day, Isla Carroll was eliminated from the Open Championship after losing a good game to White Birch, 15–14.

After being the most successful team for many years, White Birch's drought in the U.S. Open ended in 2005 when Lucas Criado converted a penalty shot in overtime. From the left are team manager Nick Manifold, Del Carroll Walton, Mariano Aguerre, Lucas Criado, Julio Gracida and alternate Martín Ravina (Museum of Polo and Hall of Fame).

This idea of hardly trying also spread to Argentina. Two meaningless games at Palermo, Ellerstina versus Indios Chapaleufú II and La Dolfina versus Indios Chapaleufú I, elicited comments from the press about saving horses and not taking risks. Adolfo Cambiaso's comment at the game's end, "For us it was a practice match," showed total disregard from a professional player towards the ticket-paying public.[14, 15] These were two matches for the 2001 Argentine Open Championship, the most prestigious polo competition in the world. Who is to blame? The players, for not risking injury to their mounts, or the Asociación Argentina de Polo's authorities, for instituting tournament rules that permit such chicanery?

The issue of fixing games goes far beyond the occasional match. Apart from being a form of cheating, depending upon whose groin is gored, what will the reaction be from the large corporations that act as major sponsors and constitute the future of polo as a game?

Foreign Players in the United Kingdom and in America

The controversy in Britain regarding foreign players goes back a long time. At issue is the progressive role the foreign players, mostly from Argentina, but with sprinklings of Australians, Indians, New Zealanders and the occasional South African, on English grounds. Adding insult to injury, according to some observers, are the new regulations about citizenship laid out by the European Union. The matter has been subject of spirited debate, heated at times, over the last few years.

Harsh language was not spared. In a letter to *Polo Times*, a former polo player and Hurlingham Polo Association steward, who nevertheless hid his identity behind the pseudonym "The Maltese Cat"—an affront to a revered fictional character in the literature of the game—expresses his "dismay at the current situation whereby British polo seems to have been taken over by the South American polo mafia and the Patrons. It is little short of scandalous."[16]

The correspondent goes on to issue a challenge to the Hurlingham Polo Association's chairman—at the time, Mr. John Tinsley—and the stewards to submit themselves to a vote of confidence by all the individual members of the association, if they insist in maintaining the status quo.

The letter prompted a reply from the chief executive of the Hurlingham Polo Association, Col. David Woodd. Colonel Woodd, a former 14th/20th Hussars officer with a reputation as a very able executive, pointed out that over the years, South Americans and other overseas players have done much to improve polo in England. Those who are able to obtain European Union nationality can legitimately play in Britain, taking advantage of a law that many, including the stewards, would prefer that the H.P.A. was not obliged to observe. As to the suggestion that the H.P.A. had done nothing, Col. Woodd noted that the H.P.A. spent 10,000 pounds seeking a legal way around the European Union law.[17]

With the increased latitude regarding nationality requirements in international games, the so named Bosman ruling issued by the European Court of Justice has important implications for international polo. The court ruled that professional players could leave a club after their contracts had expired. It is called the Bosman ruling after Jean Marc Bosman, a player in the Belgian Liege soccer team, who brought up his case before the court. However, in addition to the individual case, the court ruled that clubs could hire unlimited numbers of foreign players. This ruling had important implications for English polo because overseas players, mostly Argentines, could legally obtain European Union passports which gave them equal rights as European citizens.

The most egregious example was observed in the European playoffs for the 2008 F.I.P. World Cup, in which Italy placed three Argentine players with European Union passports in its squad, drawing ire and scorn from other teams and officials. At the time, the highest handicap team Italy could have fielded with native players was eight goals.[18] In the event, the Italian team failed to advance to the final round in Mexico because both Britain and Spain compiled a better record.

The numerical influence of professional players from Argentina is also prevalent in the United States. There were 16 American players participating in the 12 teams that entered the 2008 U.S. Open Championship; however, only four Americans made it to the semifinals. Twenty-eight players were Argentines, of which nine were semifinalists; three were Mexicans, and there was one each from Colombia, England, Uruguay and Venezuela. Out of 12 teams, nine were sponsored by American patrons, and one each was from Britain, Colombia and Venezuela. The inescapable conclusion is that American and foreign patrons prefer to include Argentine professional players on their teams.

At a time when only eight American players are rated above 7 goals, is the solution a compulsory requirement that at least one United States citizen be included in every team? The answer is, probably not. The Hurlingham Polo Association had an identical problem; nevertheless, the H.P.A. has abolished all restrictions for foreign players. It appears that American players who wish to reach high handicaps should compete in tournaments in Argentina. British players such as the Tomlinson brothers have tried such an approach with some success. As an example, they qualified for the final eight round at the Argentine Open Championship, and the Apes Hill team, sponsored by Sir Charles Williams from Barbados, took the 2008 Copa Marcelo Dorignac at the Tortugas Country Club.

The Issue of Drugs: Suspicion and Looking the Other Way

> *The game was never designed to allow players to compete under any other influences but those derived from courage, adrenaline and sober steel.*[19] — Peter J. Rizzo

The issue of drug use by athletes is much discussed throughout the sporting world today. The question of whether or not there is drug usage by polo players is moot. No one knows the answer, for the simple reason that there is no testing for drug usage. To state that there is drug use is wrong, just as it is wrong to say there is no drug use. The only proof will emerge from a randomized drug-testing program approved by the ruling bodies of polo and conducted within strict scientific parameters by federally approved laboratories.

The problem is not new. As far back as 1985, Lester "Red" Armour, an international player who reached a 9-goal handicap and a respected umpire, wrote an article on the issue.[20] Red Armour describes in some detail the requirements placed upon players by the Palm Beach Polo and Country Club, at the time the premier polo club in Florida. The club required that every player intending to compete sign a consent form in which he agreed to submit to a urinalysis at any time between two hours before and two hours after any game in which he was scheduled to play. If any substance defined as illegal in the State of Florida were found, the first offence would result in a written reprimand and warning and the second would be suspension from the club for the remainder of the season. Mr. Armour added,

> Some players may find the implication insulting and some may see it as an infringement on their personal choices. Drugs and alcohol do not belong on a polo field. Even if drug use in our sport is not as widespread as it seems to be in some others, it is a good deal more serious because of the risk factors involved in the high speed and the horses. Even if a player has the right to risk his own neck, he does not have the right to endanger his teammates and opponents. Any restrictions and penalties imposed on players must apply to umpires as well.
>
> I suggest we also start looking into what might be called equine drug abuse — that is, players giving their ponies drugs to enhance their speed and resistance to pain. Perhaps we should look to the racing commission for guidelines and recommendations in this matter. Use of such drugs is not only unfair but creates another potential for danger on the field. I am against anything that compromises the safety of polo.[21]

Implementation of the program took place and one morning all players were tested. No results were ever communicated to the players, and nothing else came out of the club's initiative.[22] Nevertheless, publication of this article raised the awareness of a possible problem. Dr. Tolbert S. Wilkinson, in an article in *Polo*, voiced the opinion that the mere threat of drug testing would probably save more lives and prevent more accidents than anything the actual testing might reveal.[23]

To this day, the U.S. Polo Association has not addressed the potential problem, with the exception of a sanctimonious statement to the effect that the association does not condone the use of drugs.[24]

Conversely, there is a positive attitude in England towards facing this important and difficult issue. As long ago as 1993, John W.M. "Buff" Crisp, at the time Hurlingham Polo Association's secretary, implemented a "Directive on Human Doping," which unequivocally stated at the very beginning: "Doping is strictly forbidden."[25]

In a supporting article, Mr. Crisp added, "Whilst the H.P.A. does not suspect players of use of 'drugs' it does condemn the use of doping substances or doping methods to enhance artificially performance in polo. Doping can be dangerous, it puts the health of the competitor at risk. Doping is cheating, and is contrary to the spirit of that competition. The potential damage that could be done on the polo ground by a player high on drugs is too terrifying to contemplate."[26]

As an aside, it must be pointed out that Mr. John Crisp, besides contributing enormously to the growth of the Pony Club in England, has been a champion of the polo ponies' welfare during all his years in the Hurlingham Polo Association. "Buff" Crisp is one of the unsung heroes of the game of polo.

The matter of individual choices and privacy rights is often mentioned in discussions about drug testing. However, a victim of a polo accident caused by an individual or horse under the influence of drugs, performance-enhancing or otherwise, also has rights. The game is a dangerous one, and polo players should not be subject of additional concern thinking that on the ground are mounts or players under the influence of dangerous substances.

In regards to the disciplinary bodies' authority to investigate and, if deemed appropriate, impose sanctions, *The World Sports Law Report* reported some facts that are relevant to the game of polo. A case was brought to an appeals court by Tom Flaherty because of a failed drug test of a greyhound owned and trained by him. The racing stewards fined and reprimanded Mr. Flaherty. Thereupon, he appealed the ruling. The court ruled against Flaherty.

The legal decision read, "It is the Court's function to control illegality and make sure that a body [i.e. the stewards] does not act outside its powers. Provided they act lawfully and within their powers, the Court should allow them to get on with the job they are required to do."[27]

In his comments on the court of appeals ruling, Brigadier Douglas-Nugent noted that this precedent must give serious food for thought to anyone considering challenging the decision of a sporting disciplinary tribunal. It also acts as a reminder that any disciplinary enquiry must follow to the letter the laid down procedures.[28]

The drug issue in polo will not go away until all ruling bodies take a firm stand against their use in ponies and humans. It is unrealistic to expect the problem to be handled at the club level. Very few polo clubs, if any, have the resources needed to conduct drug testing. Policies, and their implementation, must have the power exercised by the ruling bodies of the game. The Hurlingham Polo Association has taken the lead in this matter in England; it is high time for the rest of the polo associations to follow with their own directives regarding testing procedures and disciplinary measures for the offenders. The integrity and well-being of the game are at stake.

By Way of an Ending

The players learned, very soon, that they were representing the country; and as the first polo wearers of the immortal All Black uniform of black jersey and silver-fern monogram, they were expected to behave, and play, with distinction.— Sir Terence McLean[29]

Currently, the words written by Terry McLean, the New Zealander who was one of the most admired and respected journalists in all of sport, may sound corny in the face of polo players demanding to be paid for representing their country.

The events of the last decade have not bode well for the game. The inexorable pressure leading to the acceptance of professionalism has not resulted in an improvement of polo; quite the contrary. From the point of view of the spectators, the spectacle of polo twenty years ago was much more enjoyable than today. The game has regressed. John Watson, who developed the backhander stroke some 125 years ago, must be turning in his grave. The practices of continuously turning, tapping and looking for a foul are ruining our beloved game. It is up to the governing associations to solve the problem. Mr. Stephen Orthwein's words are apropos: "It is too easy for polo authorities to become complacent and avoid controversy."[30]

The concept of patrons calling the tune in professional polo is still deeply ingrained in the United States and in England. The future of professional polo rests on corporate sponsors marketing their teams. However, there is a long way to go. An all-professional polo tournament was started in 2004 at Coworth Park under the title British Polo Championship, backed by Mr. Nigel à Brassard and British Polo Enterprises. Four commercially sponsored teams entered the tournament, with Williamson Tea taking the honors and the cash. Audi England took the next two championships; after such promising start, the tournament was cancelled due to lack of support. This is difficult to comprehend because the British Polo Championship offered the highest level of polo in Britain in beautiful surroundings and within a short distance from London and Guards Polo Club.

On the other hand, aberrations such as elephant polo, just as automobile polo did in the

1930s, seem to catch on in the popular image. The proliferation of international travel by polo players, their ponies, and their families has not resulted in an increase in the level of international test matches. It seems that the majority of the viewing public prefers to keep on watching a game that, with the exception of polo in Argentina, is basically three-person polo. The current economic situation of the game of polo is absolutely dependent on the good will of the patrons. Without their support, the British and the American open championships most likely would be played at below the 20-goal level.

Polo is not at a crossroads, for the simple reason that at present there is no other alternative. This situation will remain until corporations realize the tremendous marketing potential that the most elegant of games can offer to their products. However, the game's integrity must be preserved at any cost. The big culprit — selling image rather than substance — is to be kept away from the polo grounds. Our beloved game has been mismanaged, a painful situation that has to be corrected. The time to start the rehabilitation process is now.

However, through all the changes of the times, political, social and economic, polo and the spirit of polo have never changed. It will always be the player's, amateur or professional, delightful recreation first and foremost. Spectators' pleasure comes second, and administrators' satisfaction a distant third.

Appendix A:
The Code of Rules for the
Silchar Polo Club, 1863

1. The limits of the ground should be marked off with a small ditch a few inches in depth, as in sketch.

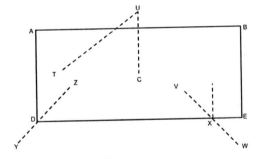

2. The ball should be placed at C, and one of each side endeavor simultaneously to strike it.
3. When the ball is struck off the ground, either across the lines AB or DE, as shown by the dotted line TU, umpires or a bystander should throw it on again in a direction perpendicular to AB, as marked by the dotted line UC.
4. When the ball is struck off the ground, either across the line AB or DE, as shown by the dotted line VW, and goes beyond the goal, it is to be brought back to the point X and thrown perpendicular to the sideline.
5. When the ball is struck over at any of the corners, as shown by the dotted line Z, it is to be brought back to the corner, and struck thence towards C by one of the side whose goal was so nearly invaded, as shown in the line YDZ.
6. No player is willingly to strike either his antagonist or his antagonist's horse.

7. No player is to lay his hand on his antagonist or his antagonist's horse.
8. Any player, when his antagonist is about to strike the ball, may strike at his antagonist's stick or hook it, but only when the ball is about to be struck or in the neighborhood of the ball when there is a rush.
9. Any player may interpose his horse before his antagonist so as to prevent his antagonist from reaching the ball, whether in full career or at a slow pace; and this despite the immediate neighborhood of the ball.
10. When a stick is broken, its owner is to ride out of the ground to replace it, and on no account is anyone to run in with a stick to him.
11. When a stick is dropped, the rider is to dismount and pick it up himself, or one of his side may do it for him, but no outsider is to run in to do so.
12. When any derangement occurs in a player's horse-gear, he is likewise to ride out and have it repaired unless he chooses to play on with it as it is, but on no account is anyone to come on to the ground to repair it.
13. When any player is dismounted he is likewise to catch his own horse to mount again, or one of his own side may catch it for him, as long as the horse runs off the ground it may be caught by an outsider.
14. In regular matches, if a player is disabled by a fall or by a hurt, so long as that fall or hurt is not occasioned by foul play of the opposite party, neither the player nor his horse are to be replaced by a fresh horse. But if the disable-

ment is occasioned by a blow of the adversaries' stick or otherwise, against these rules, a fresh player or a fresh horse may be substituted.

15. As a general rule, therefore, in regular matches no player can use fresh horses, or no horse have fresh riders.

16. The game is to be commenced under a state of full preparation of both parties, so to be declared by the umpire, or, both agreeing.

17. When the ball goes off the ground it is not immediately to be flung on again at the feet of any particular player's horse but, after a time, on to the middle of the ground, when a sufficient number of both sides are there to receive it.

18. When a player catches the ball in his hands, he can strike it towards his adversaries' goal by tossing it up and hitting it with his stick, and to give him room to do this, he can ride away to clear himself of his enemies but he can carry the ball no nearer to his adversaries' goal than the place where he first caught it.

19. No dismounted player can strike the ball while he is on foot.

20. Spurs and whips may be freely used, but only on the rider's own horse; to beat an adversary's horse is foul play.

21. No man on foot (save dismounted riders), or dogs, or cattle, to be allowed on the ground.

22. It is to be understood that no player shall be under the influence of bhang, ganja, or spirituous liquors.

23. Any direct or willful act of foul play, when it shall have been so declared by the umpire or umpires, shall at once be declared to have lost the game in a regular match.

Appendix B:
The Field, 20 March 1869,
Letter to the Editor

Sir,

I am a constant reader of The Field, but I have never seen any account in it of this game, which has been played by Europeans in India for some years. Perhaps the following description may be interesting to your readers; and, as there is a great deal of fun, excitement, and skill in the game, might it not be introduced to this country?

The game was originally played by natives in the district of Munneepoor, from whence it was brought about eight years ago to Calcutta. It was at once taken up by European gentlemen there, who formed a hockey club, and, Government having granted a piece of ground on the Maidan, the club reduced it to good order, and has played there to this day. From Calcutta it found its way to Rangoon, and then to Madras; but it was only in 1868 that it was introduced to Bombay, when a member of the Calcutta Hockey Club brought sticks and balls, and established the game there, where it is now all the rage.

The game is played with sides, as in ordinary hockey or football. There are goals, and the ground is marked out with flags, and all such rules, as "touch," are somewhat similar to our ordinary English game. Each side tries to hit the ball into the adversaries' goal, and thus scores a game. The sticks, made of bamboo (being the lightest and toughest stick we have in India), are about 4½ ft. long, with a headpiece. The ball, which must be very light and hard, is made of the root of the bamboo, and is from twice to three times as large as a new cricket ball. The ground must be a piece of flat grass, kept at level as possible by rolling. In Calcutta, we usually play for an hour and a quarter twice a week, this being as much as the ponies can stand in that climate, which will be better understood by my explaining that all, except the goalkeepers, are galloping throughout the game. The Munneepooree (natives) were the best players as late as 1865–66, when they accepted a challenge from the Calcutta Club, and, headed by an English captain, came down to Calcutta, and carried off the palm. Whether they are so now is an open question, as some of the members of the C.H.C. are remarkably good players. The Munneepooree ponies used by those natives and by the C.H.C. are very small, not averaging, I should think, more than 11½ hands, which is an advantage; they are also very quick, fast, and, as a rule, have the chief requisite for a hockey pony — good mouths. They are, moreover, very plucky (as I known from experience, having taken a first and second spear in a wild boar off one); and this is also most important, as they often get hard hit in the scrummages. The Munneepooree ponies, after a certain amount of training and play, will follow the ball, stop when it is stopped, and will turn with it, with very little persuasion of rein or spur being required. Whereas the Burmese ponies, which are used in Rangoon and Madras, are both clumsier, and pull too hard after a few months' play. I mentioned all this about the ponies, as I wish to state that the chief difficulty would be in getting up the game in any place; and I am sure anyone who knows the game will bear me out in saying the chief difficulty is a good hockey pony. In India we consider the game is the next best fun to pigsticking (or hoghunting, as called by some), and any members of the Calcutta Club would infinitely prefer it to cricket or rackets. Our Calcutta subscription was an entrance fee of one guinea and a half, and six shillings a month, which paid for sticks, balls, pegs, and shandigaff for the members and their friends.

Appendix C:
The Rules of the Game,
as Drafted by Lt. Hartopp
on Mess Paper, 1869

A game of polo is to consist of not more than twelve players, six on each side; a match not more than ten players, viz., five on each side.

The goals to be 300 yards apart, when the ground will admit of such length, and the boundary flags from 150 to 200 yards apart.

The goal posts to be eight yards apart.

All sticks and balls to be approved by the committee.

A ball to be thrown up in the centre of the ground, one player of either side galloping from a point agreed on.

When the ball is hit out of bounds it must be thrown into the playing ground by an impartial person on foot.

No player is allowed to hit an adversary's pony. It is permitted to crook an adversary's stick, but on no account is the player allowed to put his stick over the body of an adversary's pony.

No player going through the bully and lost possession of the ball, and finding himself between the bully and his adversary's goal is permitted to hit the ball until he has at least one player, exclusive of the goalkeeper, between him and the hostile goal.

In all matches, each side shall provide an umpire who, on detecting any irregularity or infringement of the rules, shall be empowered to suspend the game until the irregularity has been corrected.

Chapter Notes

Chapter 1

1. *The Sportsman*, May 1928, 32. Robert F. Kelley was the polo reporter for *The New York Times*.
2. Sir Richard Carew, *Survey of Cornwall* (London: 1602), book i, 75. A modern version was published by Tamar Books in 2000.
3. Eric Dunning and Kenneth Sheard, *Barbarians, Gentlemen and Players* (New York: New York University Press, 1979), 30.
4. *Darab Dastur Peshotan Sanjana, the Kârnâm i Artaakhshir Pâpaknâ* (Bombay: Educational Society's Steam Press, 1876), pp. 6–7, quoted in Houchang E. Chemadi and Allen Guttman, "From Iran to All of Asia: The Origin and Diffusion of Polo," *International Journal of History of Sports*, Vol. 19, September 2001, 384.
5. Anthony Shirley, *The Adventures of the Three Brothers* (London: Hurst, Robinson, 1825), 70.
6. Carl Diem, *Asiatische Reiterspiele* (Berlin: Deutscher Archiv-Verlag, 1941), 121.
7. "Early History of Polo," *Polo* (April 1932), 13. Laufer (1874–1934) was a German anthropologist and orientalist who immigrated to the United States in 1898. He spent most of his career at the Field Museum in Chicago.
8. Take-Eddin-Ahmed-Makrizi, *History of the Mameluke Sultans*, translated by E.M. Quatremère (Paris: 1837), 122. Etienne Marc Quatremère (1782–1857), French Orientalist born in Paris, was professor of Persian in the School of Living Oriental Languages. Quatremère's translation of Makrizi's *History of the Mameluke Sultans* (2 Vols., 1837–41) shows his erudition at its best.
9. L.M. Crump, "The Oldest Polo Goal Posts in India," *The Polo Monthly* (June 1928), 259. Leslie Maurice Crump, C.I.E. (1875–1929), graduated from Oxford University, where he was a halfback on the rugby team that beat Cambridge. He joined the Indian Civil Service and wrote poetry. *The Severing Seas, The Peacock Shari* and *The Lady of the Lotus* are some of his works. At the time of his death, Mr. Crump was the British resident in Gwalior.
10. *Ibid.*, 261.
11. E.H. Parker, "The Origin of Polo: The Game in Ancient China," *Badminton Magazine* (May 1898). Edward Harper Parker (1846–1926) was professor of Chinese at the Victoria University of Manchester.

12. L. Carrington Goodrich, "Polo in Ancient China," *Horse and Horseman* (April 1938), 27. Luther Carrington Goodrich (1894–1986) was the Dean Long professor of Chinese at Columbia University; chairman, Department of East Asian Languages and Cultures; and director of the Ming Biographical History Project. Born in China, Professor Goodrich traveled widely, teaching and writing on Chinese cultural and historical topics.
13. Robert Weir and J. Moray Brown, *Riding-Polo* (London: Longmans, Green and Co., 1891), 244.
14. James T.C. Liu, "Polo and Cultural Change: From Tang to Sung China," *Harvard Journal of Asiatic Studies*, 45, 1 (June 1983), 208.
15. "Bronco," *Polo and Coaching*, "The Sportsman," editor (London: Sports and Sportsmen, no date [1923]), 188.
16. Mika Mori, *Polo: Its History and Spirit* (Tokyo: Asahi Shimbu, 1997).
17. Mika Mori, quoted in *Polo Quarterly International* (London: Winter 1997), 28.
18. Laufer, 16.
19. Weir and Brown, 347.
20. Firdusi was a Persian poet, born near Tús, who flourished at the end of the 10th and the beginning of the 11th century. *Shâhnámah* was composed for the amusement of Sultan Mahmud of Ghazni. This fictional work is replete with the flowery and allegorical language of Oriental rhetoric.
21. Shensi Provincial Museum, *Les Peintures Murales du Tombeau de Li Hsien de la Dynastie des Tangs* (Peking: Editions Wengu, 1974).
22. Mary Ann Wingfield, *Sport and the Artist* (Woodbridge, Suffolk: Antique Collectors' Club, 1988), 262.

Chapter 2

1. T.F. Dale, *Polo at Home and Abroad* (London: London and Counties Press, 1915), 22. The Rev. Thomas Francis Dale (1858–1923) was a prolific author on the game and ponies in general.
2. Report from Col. John George Knowles, 2nd Surma Valley Light Horse, to the chief commissioner of

Assam, April 1919. Quoted by "The Sportsman" in *Polo and Coaching* (London: Sports and Sportsmen, Ltd., no date. [1923]), 7.

3. Although most sources refer to George Stewart as a captain when he took the game to India, he was in fact a lieutenant (perhaps temporary captain). His military record indicates that he was commissioned as ensign in 1856, serving with Havelock's Force during the mutiny; he was promoted to lieutenant in 1857. Later he served in the 1st Sikh Cavalry during the 1860 campaign in China. Stewart was with the 11th Bengal Cavalry in the Umbelya campaign and was promoted to captain in 1868 and major in 1876. Then he joined the Corps of Guides and as a lieutenant colonel and was in command of the Guides Cavalry during the Second Afghan War. He was promoted to colonel in 1883 and retired from the army as a major general in 1887. He received a Companionship of the Order of the Bath.

4. Captain G.J. Younghusband, *Polo in India* (London and Calcutta: W.H. Allen and Co., 1890), 2. Capt. Younghusband quotes an undated note from Maj. Gen. George Stewart. Sir James Hills, later Hills-Johnes, was awarded the Victoria Cross during the Indian Mutiny.

5. Brigadier G. de la Poer Beresford, M.C., in *Polo*, edited by the Earl of Kimberley (Philadelphia: J.B. Lippincott Co., 1936), 19.

6. "H.M.," "On the Origin and Early History of Polo among the English," *Baily's Magazine of Sports and Pastimes* (London: Vinton and Co., 1890), Vol. 53, 415.

7. "The Sportsman," *Polo and Coaching* (London: Sports and Sportsmen, Ltd., no date. [1923]), 8.

8. Lt. Travers Edward Madden, Indian Staff Corps. The J is either a typographical error or a mistake during transcription.

9. Captain John Tessier-Yandell, O.B.E., "The Father of English Polo," *The Polo Magazine*, Vol. 2, No. 2 (May 1978), 17.

10. Knight Commander, Order of the Star of India. Sir George Sherer, Bengal Army, was also honorary aide-de-camp to Queen Victoria.

11. *London Gazette*, 2 December 1862, 23 June 1868, 17 February 1874, 14 March 1879, 11 August 1899.

12. *Baily's Sports and Pastimes*, "The Popularity of Polo" (London: Vinton, July 1875), 133.

13. Robert Weir and J. Moray Brown, *Hunting: Polo* (London: Longmans, Green and Co., 1891), 276.

14. Maj. Gen. Alexander Angus Airlie Kinloch, C.B. (1838–1919) achieved fame as one of the greatest shikaris, or big game hunters, and was the author of *Large Game Shooting in Thibet, the Himalayas, and Northern India*.

15. "H.M.," 416.

16. Col. T.A. St. Quintin, *Chances of Sports of Sorts* (Edinburgh: William Blackwood and Sons, 1912), 230.

17. Younghusband, 5.

18. Rudyard Kipling, "The Maltese Cat," in *The Day's Work* (London: Macmillan and Co., 1898), 247.

19. The winning team was Veterinary Surgeon John Prosser Adams, Lt. Bloomfield Gough, Lt. John James Scott Chisholm, and Capt. Strange Gould Butson. The following year Lts. Charles John William Trower and George Alfred Penrhys Evans took Adams' and Butson's places. Lt. Gough would eventually rise in rank to command the regiment in 1895.

20. Capt. S.G. "Tim" Butson graduated from the

Royal Military Academy, Sandhurst, and was gazetted a cornet, by purchase, into the 9th Lancers in 1870. He was killed at Kabul on 13 December 1879, while leading a charge up a hill, during the Second Afghan War.

21. St. Quintin, 232.

22. The team was Lance Duffadar Hiri Singh, Lt. Howard Goad, Lt. William Allason Simmonds, and Lt. George Ulick Browne.

23. Denzil Holder, *Hindu Horseman* (Chippenham: Picton Publishing, 1986), 161.

24. The K.O.S.B. team was composed of Lt. Reynell H.B. Taylor, Lt. George Nisbet Mayne, Lt. James Henry E. Reid, and Lt. Leonard Gordon.

25. Younghusband, 4.

26. Reprinted in *Polo*, January 1929, 10.

27. E.D. Miller, *Fifty Years of Sport* (New York: E.P. Dutton and Co., no date [1925]), 90.

28. *Baily's*, July 1875, 261.

29. It is rather puzzling that the national governing bodies of cricket and polo in the United Kingdom bear club's names rather than a national one, i.e. British Polo Association.

Chapter 3

1. Roger Chatterton-Newman, "Edward Hartopp: This Must be a Good Game," in *Profiles in Polo*, edited by Horace A. Laffaye (Jefferson, N.C.: McFarland and Co., 2007), 14.

2. *The Polo Monthly* (London: S.B. Vaughn, June 1929), 315. The following information was kindly provided to the author by Roger Chatterton-Newman, 7 November 2007. "Lt. Col. Henry Thompson Russell (1875–1953), of Milford House, Limerick, was commissioned in the Royal Field Artillery in 1894. He married first (1902) Alicia (divorced 1923), daughter of Richard Studdert of Bunratty Castle, Co. Clare; second, Marian, daughter of Patrick Lee of Crumlin, Co. Dublin. His grandson, John, told me that the colonel's second wife was an actress, with whom he ran off. His first wife divorced him and the family never spoke to him again. Milford House was sold (as the colonel's eldest son inherited Bunratty Castle from his maternal grandfather) and is now a nursing home run by the Blue Nuns. John's father (the second son) inherited Dunkathel House, just outside Cork, from a cousin — a beautiful early Georgian house. Two or three years ago John and his widowed mother decided to sell up — they got over £7 million and the place is now a hotel. He looked through his family papers to see if there were any polo albums of his grandfather's but found nothing. I imagine the old man took everything to Dublin with him!"

3. *Stonyhurst Magazine*, December 1927, Vol. 19, No. 272, 388.

4. Norman J. Cinnamond, *El Polo* (Barcelona: Librería Catalonia, no date, [1929]), 27. Norman James Cinnamond y James was a player on the Real Club de Barcelona polo team.

5. T. Levins Moore, "Polo in Ireland," in *Polo and Coaching*, 73.

6. E.D. Miller, *Fifty Years of Sport* (New York: Dutton, no date [1925]), 21.

7. The winning team was Lt. Henry Bingham Morton Mandel-Pleydell, Lt. Lord Percy St. Maur, Lt. Robert Saunders, Lt. George Henry Hayhurst Hayhurst, and Lt. Francis Charles Sartoris.

8. For a biographical portrait of John Watson, see Roger Chatterton-Newman, "John Watson: The Founding Father," in *Profiles in Polo*, 23.

9. "Any two men riding parallel down the field side by side can be certain that they are playing very bad polo, probably inexcusable." *A Manual of Polo* (Camp Stotsenburg, P.I.: Press of the 14th U.S. Cavalry, 1910). 3. The author was Governor General W. Cameron Forbes (1870–1959).

10. William Cameron Forbes, *As to Polo* (Manila Polo and Country Club, private printing, 1911), 66. This book is one of polo's literature classics. It went through six editions, the last one published in 1929, and was translated into Spanish and Japanese.

11. Chatterton-Newman, *Profiles in Polo*, 27.

12. The winning team was Lt. Edward William David Baird, Lt. the Hon. Everard Baring, Lt. Arthur Hughes Onslow, and Lt. Frank Rimington Bowlby.

13. Anthony Maude, Charles C. D'Arcy Irvine, Edward Mervyn Archdale (later Sir Edward Archdale), and John Porter Porter were on the County Fermanagh team.

14. T.A. St. Quintin, *Chances of Sports of Sorts* (Edinburgh: William Blackwood and Sons, 1912), 225.

15. R.S. Liddell, *The Memoirs of the Tenth Royal Hussars* (London: Longmans, Green and Co., 1981), Appendix.

16. The final result was 3–2 in favor of the 10th Hussars. The 9th Lancers were Capt. William Clayton Clayton, Capt. Frank De la Garde Grissell, Capt. Charles Harvey Palairet, Lt. Philip Green, Lt. Richard St. Leger Moore, Lt. Francis Joseph Alphonse Herbert, Lt. Lord William Leslie de la Poer Beresford, and Lt. William Henry Fife-Cookson. The 10th Hussars were Capt. Arthur Barthorp, Capt. Arthur Wellesley Bulkeley, Capt. Thomas Astell St. Quintin, Capt. Uvedale Edward Parry Parry-Okeden, Lt. the Viscount Arthur Valentia, Lt. Thomas Algernon Smith-Dorrien, Lt. Hon. Henry John Lindley Woods, and Lt. Edward Hartopp.

Colonel Robert S. Liddell gives the score as 3–1 in the Hussars' favor. He lists the Hon. Ernest Willoughby as playing for the 9th Lancers, instead of Francis "Tip" Herbert. On the 10th Hussars team, Col. Liddell indicates William Chaine, the Hon. Thomas Fitzwilliam, Hugh Sutlej Gough and Edward Watson, instead of Barthorp, Bulkeley, Parry-Okeden and Woods.

Many of the players went on to achieve fame, or at least recognition. Capt. Clayton died on Christmas Eve 1877 on a polo field in India as the result of an accident. After leaving the service, Capt. Grissell immigrated to America and in 1891 became the original homesteader on a tract of land in Dayton, Wyoming, which he named IXL Ranch, after his regiment, the 9th Lancers. It is now owned by the John P. Ellbogen Foundation. Lt. Green was one of the founders of the Sussex County Polo Club. Lt. Moore transferred to the 5th Lancers and took the first Inter-regimental Tournament in England. Lt. "Tip" Herbert founded the Monmouthshire Club, took Hurlingham's Champion Cup, and was manager of Ranelagh Club and an original member of the Polo Pony Society. Lord William Beresford was awarded the Victoria Cross for gallantry in the Zulu War. Capt. St. Quintin introduced polo to Australia. Lord Valentia was chairman of the Hurlingham Club and of the Polo Pony Society. Lt. "Chicken" Hartopp drafted the first rules of the game in England.

17. St. Quintin, 439.

18. *Ibid.*

19. Terence Tenison Cuneo (1907–1996), a versatile artist, started his career painting motor racing scenes, then moved on to football, aircrafts and equestrian subjects. His best known polo painting is *Pony Lines, Cirencester, 1972*. The central figure, besides the ponies, is Eduardo Rojas Lanusse, an Argentine 6-goal player who made his mark on English polo, not only as one of the earliest visitors after World War II, but also as an instructor. One of the tournaments at the Tomlinson's Beaufort Club in Gloucestershire is the Rojas Lanusse Cup. One of the peculiarities of Cuneo's work is the single tiny mouse unobtrusively present in many of his works. He also painted the official picture of Queen Elizabeth II's coronation at Westminster Abbey. The author is grateful to Mrs. Mary Ann Wingfield for this information.

20. *Baily's Magazine*, May 1875, 59.

21. *Ibid.* The Lords were Lord Arthur Somerset, Lord Cole, Lord Aberdour, Lord Henry Rossmore, and the Marquess of Worcester. The Commons were Hon. Thomas FitzWilliam, Capt. Edward Hartopp, Hon. Charles FitzWilliam, Sir Bache Cunard, and Mr. Adrian de Murrieta.

22. *Baily's*, July 1875, 171. Tent pegging is easily described. A short tent peg of coconut palm is driven about six inches into the ground sloping forward, and the men, taking their position about 150 paces off, ride up at full gallop and endeavor to carry it off on their spears as they pass by.

23. F.A. Herbert, "The Monmouthshire Polo Club and Team," *The Polo Monthly* (June 1909), 251.

24. Chatterton-Newman, 29.

25. Hurlingham Polo Association, 2005 *Year Book*, 80.

26. Capt. Francis Henry's military service recorded in the *London Gazette* is as follows: cornet, by purchase, 30 June 1863; lieutenant, 29 May 1865; retired from the 9th Lancers on 14 September 1866; cornet in the Royal Gloucestershire Regiment of Hussars Yeomanry Cavalry in 1867; promoted to captain in 1875.

27. *The International Gun and Polo Club* [Year Book] (London: T. Brettell and Co., 1876), [5].

28. The Busby Babes was the appellation given to the youthful members of the Manchester United Football Club in the 1950s. Eight of the team perished when their aircraft crashed on take-off from Munich Airport on 6 February 1958. Sir Matt Busby, the Scottish international who nurtured the team, survived the crash and went on to complete a long tenure (1946–1969 and 1970–1971) at the team's helm. He was knighted in 1968.

29. For a concise notice on the club see Roger Chatterton-Newman, "Polo at Cheshire," *The Hurlingham Polo Association Year Book* (Faringdon, Oxfordshire: private printing, 2000), 57.

30. E.D. Miller, *Modern Polo* (London: W. Thacker and Co., 1896), 155.

31. *Ibid.*, 150.

32. Team members were lieutenants William C.

Middleton, William Henry Hippisley, John A.W.O'N. Torrens and Richard Wolfe. The latter won again in 1883, with a County Carlow team that included John Watson.

33. *The International Gun and Polo Club* [Year Book] (London:, T. Brettell and Co., 1879), 13.

34. Brian Gardner, *Allenby of Arabia: Lawrence's General* (New York: Coward-McCann, 1966), 9.

35. Elizabeth Keyes, *Geoffrey Keyes* (London: George Newnes, 1956), 76. Lt. Col. Humphrey Patrick Guinness, Royal Scots Greys (1903–1986), a posthumous son, was a British international from 1930 until 1953. He spent his retirement years at a cottage in Badminton, near the shade of Cirencester Park. The youngest lieutenant colonel in the British Army, Geoffrey C.T. Keyes, V.C., M.C., 11th Scottish Commando (1917–1941), was the leader of the famous "Rommel Raid" in North Africa. He was commissioned into the Royal Scots Greys and was a fellow officer of Lt. Col. Guinness. Geoffrey Keyes played polo at Kirtlington before the war; he was the eldest son of Admiral of the Fleet Sir Roger Keyes (1872–1945), of World War I Zeebrugge fame, an enthusiastic supporter and polo player in Malta, where he was commander-in-chief of the Mediterranean Fleet.

36. Henry Manners Chichester and George Burges-Short, *The Records and Badges of Every Regiment and Corps in the British Army* (London: Gale and Polden, 1990), 85.

37. Philip Mason, *A Matter of Honour* (New York: Holt, Rinehart, 1974), 378.

38. Hurlingham Polo Committee and County Polo Association Handicap List, 1911. Reprinted in E.D. Miller's *Modern Polo* (London: Hurst and Blackett, no date [1911]), 478.

39. J. Moray Brown, "About Some Polo Clubs," *Baily's Magazine* (London: Vinton and Co., June 1894), 371.

40. Robert Browning, *A History of Golf* (London: J.M. Dent and Sons, 1955), 159.

41. F. Caze de Caumont, "Polo," in *Lawn-Tennis, Golf & Croquet, Polo* (Paris: Bibliothèque Larousse, no date [ca. 1895]), 66.

42. Quoted in Pierre Tucoo-Chala, *Histoire de Pau* (Toulouse: Editions Private, 1989), 171.

43. *Ibid.*, 223.

44. *Ibid.*, 222.

45. Perhaps his early observation of the game of polo in Pau led him years later, when ranching in Argentina, to start polo in 25 de Mayo — now a thriving polo community — where families such as Aguerre, Criado, Jaeschke, Monteverde and Tomlinson have polo pony breeding operations. Alberto Laffaye began polo at his estancia, La Agustina, in the 1920s. His wife made the shirts while the recruited players were other family members, neighbors, the foreman and some peons. In 1942, he founded Club de Polo Fortín Mulitas at his mother's estancia La Reforma, which he also managed; its successor club is still active in the town of 25 de Mayo.

46. Jean-Luc A. Chartier, *Cent Ans de Polo en France* (Paris: Polo Club Editions, 1992).

47. *Ibid.*, 32.

48. Miller, *Modern Polo*, 465.

49. *Polo de Paris, Annuaire 2003* (Suresnes: Media Marketing, private printing, 2002), 237.

50. L.V.L. Simmonds and E.D. Miller, editors, *The Polo Annual* (London: Horace Cox, 1913), 157.

51. Cinnamond, 237.

52. *Ibid.*, 67.

53. *Ibid.*, 124. Cristóbal Pascual de Murrieta had purchased Wadhurst Park in Kent. The Murrietas had invested heavily in Latin American countries; when the Baring financial crisis hit London, the firm went into bankruptcy. Wadhurst Park, which served as a frequent host to Edward, Prince of Wales, had to be sold.

54. The founding members were Pedro González, Roderick Creswell, Richard Davis, Francisco Díaz, John Crey Foster, Mr. Gibbett, Juan Murube, Guillermo Ochoteco, and Mr. Smilie.

55. Prince Sergey Belosselski-Belozerski (1867–1951) was a member of the Olympic Games Committee; during World War I he commanded a regiment of Horse Guards. He died, an exile, in London.

56. Simmonds, 218.

57. Keith Neilson, *Britain and the Last Tsar* (London: Oxford University Press, 1995), 52.

58. Simmonds, 220.

59. For a complete history of the club see Heinrich Köler, *Hamburger Polo Club* (Hamburg: Präzi-Druck Höhn GmbH, 1997).

60. E.D. Miller, ed., *Polo Players Guide and Almanack* (Rugby: J.H. Pepperday, 1910), 148.

Chapter 4

1. Andrew Graham-Yooll, *The Forgotten Colony* (Buenos Aires: Literature of Latin America, 1999), 4. Andy Graham-Yooll was for many years editor of *The Buenos Aires Herald*.

2. Letter to the editor, *The Field*, 19 March 1870, 260.

3. *The Standard*, Buenos Aires, 19 September 1872.

4. M.G. Mulhall and E.T. Mulhall, *Handbook of the River Plate* (Buenos Ayres: M. and T. Mulhall, 1885), 702.

5. Víctor Raffo, *El origen británico del deporte argentino* (Buenos Aires: private printing, 2004), 171.

6. *The Standard*, 21 October 1874.

7. Graham-Yooll, 179. There is an almost complete collection of *The Standard* in the Universidad de San Andrés rare books library section. The 20 January 1875 number is missing.

8. Francisco Ceballos, *El polo en la Argentina* (Buenos Aires: Dirección General de Remonta, 1969), 25.

9. Elvira Ocampo de Shaw, *Hurlingham* (Buenos Aires: Casa Impresora Francisco A. Colombo, 1958), 29. Mrs. Shaw grew up and spent most of her life in Hurlingham.

10. Eduardo Olivera, *Orígenes de los deportes brtánicos en el Río de la Plata* (Buenos Aires: Talleres Gráficos Argentinos L.J. Rosso, 1932), 36. Santiago Fitzsimons (1849–1944), a distinguished educator, established sports and physical education in all secondary schools in Argentina.

11. A common practice used by the railroads was to offer to name the stations after landowners' surnames in exchange for the land and right of way. Both railroads and owners benefited from the deal; the railway got free

land and the landowner had transportation for cattle and grain in his back yard. Estancia Chirú, named after a local Indian chieftain, was inherited by the celebrated Joseph Edmund "Joe" Traill, a 9-goal handicap player, and in turn, by his daughter Diana Traill de Harvey. The author is indebted to Dinny Harvey for her help in tracing polo in Santa Fe Province and for information on the Traill family's saga.

12. Three consecutive railroad stations on the Cañada de Gómez to Las Yerbas line were named Las Rosas, after the Houses of Lancaster and York symbols; Los Cardos, after Scotland's national plant; and El Trébol, after Ireland's emblem. All three had polo grounds.

13. Venado Tuerto's story is described in John Macnie, *Work and Play in the Argentine* (London: T. Werner Laurie, no date [1924]), 156–173; Elsa Boglione de Martínez Castro, *100 años de polo en la Argentina* (no place: Edipubli, 1988), and Raúl Ortigüela, *Raíces celtas*. (Córdoba: Alejandro Graziani, 1998).

14. *The Buenos Aires Herald*, August 1884.

15. The winning team was R.W. Isherwood, Percy Talbot, Francis Robinson and Matthew Whish. Isherwood, Robinson and Talbot went on to take the Open Championship. Matt Whish was killed while working cattle, when a steer charged into his horse.

16. Graham-Yooll, 6.

17. Chris Ashton, *Geebung: The Story of Australian Polo* (Sydney: Hamilton Publishing, 1993), 18.

18. For a biographical work on Col. St. Quintin, see Chris Ashton, "Thomas St. Quintin: A Great Polo Pioneer," in *Profiles in Polo*, 17.

19. Ashton, *Geebung*, 30.

20. William Bishop, *History of the Scone Polo Club* (Scone, N.S.W.: private printing, 1982), 11.

21. Lady Rachel Ward, Countess of Dudley (1867–1920), took an interest in making nursing services available in the Outback. During the Great War, she established a hospital in France for wounded Australians. Lady Dudley drowned while bathing off the Irish coast.

22. Ashton, *Geebung*, 36.

23. T.F. Dale, *Polo Past and Present* (London: George Newnes, 1905), 292.

24. Ashton, *Geebung*, 51.

25. F.D.'A.C. De L'Isle, *The Adelaide Polo Club* (Adelaide: Mail Print, 1913), 13.

26. Hans Mincham, "Stirling Sir John Lancelot (1849–1932)," in *Australian Dictionary of Biography* (Melbourne: Melbourne University Press 1976) Vol. 6 200.

27. De L'Isle, 13.

28. *Ibid.*, 13.

29. *Ibid.*, 14.

30. The South Australia team included J.L. Stirling (Capt.), R. Colley, A. Waterhouse, William H. Young, C. Bowman and A.E. Malcom. Western Districts included William W. Hood (Capt.), J. George Ware, Frederick William Palmer, Paroo Hood, Andrew Chirnside and L. Calvert.

31. Ashton, *Geebung*, 224.

32. Gene Makin, *A History of Queensland Polo* (Toowoomba: Harrison Printing, 1999), 8.

33. Ashton, *Geebung*, 40.

34. K.M. Little, *Polo in New Zealand* (Wellington: Whitcombe and Tombs, 1956), 16.

35. Ashton, *Geebung*, 36.

36. H.T. (Reg) Denny, *Polo of Course: A History of Polo in W.A.* (Perth: private printing, 1997), 11.

37. Personal communication from Leonard H. Hamersley, life member of the Western Australia Polo Association, 3 June 2008.

38. Ashton, *Geebung*, 41.

39. *Ibid.*, 121.

40. K.M. Little, *Polo in New Zealand*, 16.

41. *Ibid.*

42. *Ibid.*, 22.

43. Susan Reeve, "Tommy Pope: The Horse Whisperer," in *Profiles in Polo*, 88.

44. Donald C. McKenzie and John R. McKenzie, *A History of Polo in South Africa* (Dargle, KwaZulu-Natal: private printing, 1999), 1.

45. *Ibid.*

46. *Ibid.*, 321.

47. A.G. Parker, *South African Sports* (London: Sampson Low, Marston and Co., 1997), 179.

48. The 5th Lancers team was William Henry Tucker Hill, Harold Hatton Hulse, Robert Browne-Clayton and James Bruce Jardine. Lt. Tucker Hill was killed in the following year at Waggon Hill, Ladysmith, during the Anglo-Boer War. Maj. Browne-Clayton and Capt. Jardine are featured in a nice watercolor by "Snaffles," signed and dated 1907. Captain Jardine had allowed Charlie Johnson Payne, better known as "Snaffles," to sleep in his stables when he was a penniless, unknown artist. The grateful artist presented his benefactor with some paintings. This watercolor is illustrated in Mary Ann Wingfield's *Sport and the Artist*, 281.

49. The winning team was Lt. Charles H. Levenson, Capt. John H.J. McClintock, Lt. John L. Wood and Maj. Charles K. Burnett.

50. The first day of the five-and-a-half month battle of the river Somme in France cost the British 60,000 casualties, the highest in the army's history.

51. The best description of early polo in America is to be found in Newell Bent, *American Polo* (New York: Macmillan, 1929), 1.

52. William Michael Glynn Torquand was commissioned as a lieutenant in the Coldstream Guards in 1866. He retired as a captain on 6 January 1875. In July 1875, Capt. Torquand was living at 18 Denbigh Place, Pilmico. At that time, he was granted a patent for an apparatus to be used in shearing sheep. Was he a sheep farmer in Texas? Capt. Torquand died, age 41, on 14 September 1887, in Green Spring, Ohio, and is buried in Bexar County Cemetery, San Antonio.

53. Quoted in Blair Calvert, *Cecil Smith: Mr. Polo* (Midland, Texas: Prentis Publishing, 1990), 26.

54. C.C. Benham, "Texas Forges to the Front in Polo," *Polo*, December 1929, 15.

55. William S. Freeman, *History of Plymouth County, Iowa* (Indianapolis: B.F. Bowen, 1913), Vol. 1, 430.

56. *The Le Mars Sentinel*, 21 June 1887.

57. Jacob van der Zee, *The British in Iowa* (Iowa City: Historical Society of Iowa, 1922), 203.

58. *Ibid.*, 204.

59. Harry Worcester Smith, *Life and Sport in Aiken* (New York: Derrydale Press, 1935), 84.

60. John H. Daniels, who played polo for Yale University, presented his important book collection the National Sporting Library in Middleburg, Virginia.

61. "Carolina in the Morning," words by Gus Kahn, music by Walter Donaldson, Jerome H. Remick and Co., 1922.

62. Bucky King, *The History of Big Horn Polo* (Sheridan, Wyo.: Still Sailing Publications, 1987), 8.

63. *Ibid.*, 11.

64. *Ibid.*, 2.

65. Dennis Amato, "Early California Polo," *Polo*, April 1996, 35.

66. *Ibid.*

67. Amato, U.S. Polo Association, *1990 Year Book*, 37.

68. *California Polo Annual, 1913–14* (Los Angeles: R.A. Wynne, 1914), 13.

69. Ruth Olson Kahn, "Polo in Colorado in Years Gone By," *Polo Players Edition* (Wellington, Fla., August–June 2007), 62.

70. Marshall Sprague, *The Grizzlies: A History; The Cheyenne Mountain Country Club* (No place: The Club, 1983), 11.

71. "Once upon a Time...," *Sidelines*, Wellington, Fla. (15 December 2001), 8.

72. Tony Rees, *Polo: The Galloping Game* (Cochrane, Alberta: Western Heritage Centre Society, 2000), 7.

73. *Ibid.*, 13.

74. *Ibid.*, 18.

75. Iris Clendenning, *The History of the Montreal Polo Club* (Les Cèdres, Quebec: private printing, 1987), 8.

76. The original vase was 10 feet high and was discovered at the bottom of Lake Tivoli, near the Roman Emperor Hadrian's villa. It was purchased by Sir William Hamilton, British consul to Naples, who was well known for his collection of antiquities. Sir William gave the vase to his nephew, the Earl of Warwick, and it stood at Warwick Castle until 1979, when it was sold to the Burrell Collection in Glasgow.

77. T.P. McLean, *The Savile Cup* (Cambridge: New Zealand Polo Association, 1989), 4.

78. Geoffrey W. Rice, *Heaton Rhodes of Otahuna* (Christchurch: Canterbury University Press, 2001), 62. This book is a full-scale biography of Sir Heaton Rhodes (1861–1956), Arthur's cousin and teammate.

79. *Press*, 9 March 1886, 2d.

80. Three of these officers reached flag rank. Admiral Sir Reginald Yorke Tyrwhitt (1870–1951) was the hero of the battle of Dogger Bank in World War I. Adm. William Oswald Story (1859–1938) retired in 1912 and moved to Canada. In World War I, Admiral Story volunteered to serve and was transferred to the Royal Canadian Navy. The third was Admiral Seymour Elphinstone Erskine (1863–1945), from a family of Navy officers.

81. Maj. Robert Dykes Stewart-Savile (1863–1945) was the son of the Rev. Frederick Alexander Stewart-Savile, of Hollanden Park, Tonbridge, Kent. After Harrow and Cambridge, he was gazetted into the Royal West Kent Yeomanry Cavalry in 1885. His appointment as A.D.C. to Lord Onslow was brief, for he returned to England in 1890 to be the M.F.H. of the West Kent Foxhounds. During the First World War, Savile was in command of the armed yacht *Sea Fay*, and later was a Remount officer.

82. The Christchurch four were Arthur Edward Grovenor Rhodes; A.W. Bennetts; Robert Heaton Rhodes, later Sir Heaton; and Joseph G.F. Palmer.

83. Teddy O'Rorke, who carried the reputation of being an excellent rider, met his death in 1918 while jumping over a water obstacle at a remount depot in England during the Great War.

84. Little, 21.

85. *Ibid.*, 14. Lt. Champion de Crespigny was killed by a broken neck while playing polo in Malta.

86. Rice, 123. The Indian Army team's names are unknown. The Christchurch team was Edward O'Rorke, Dr. Walter Fox, W.H.P. Woodroffe and Heaton Rhodes (captain).

87. Little, 37.

Chapter 5

1. Quoted in Harry Worcester Smith, *A Sporting Tour* (Columbia, S.C.: The State Company, 1925), x. Mr. H.W. Smith was one of the foremost Masters of Fox Hounds.

Lord Roberts was commander-in-chief, India. He wrote *Forty-one Years in India* (London: Macmillan, 1897).

2. H. de B. De Lisle, *Polo in India* (Bombay: Thacker and Co., 1907), ii.

3. "A Lover of the Game," *Letters on Polo in India* (Calcutta: Thacker, Spink and Co., 1918), 4.

4. The 4th Hussars team was Lt. Winston Churchill, Lt. Albert Savory, who was killed in the Anglo-Boer War, Capt. Reginald Hoare and Lt. R.W.R. Barnes, later Sir Reginald Barnes.

5. "A Lover of the Game," 73.

6. Brian Gardner, *Allenby of Arabia: Lawrence's General* (New York: Coward-McCann, 1966), 9.

7. Denzil Holder, *Hindu Horseman* (Chippenham: Picton Publishing, 1986), xiv.

8. For a list of Victoria Crosses awarded to polo players, see Horace A. Laffaye, *The Polo Encyclopedia* (Jefferson, N.C.: McFarland and Co., 2004), 386.

9. H. de B. De Lisle, *Polo in India* (Bombay: Thacker and Co., 1907), 200.

10. Larry Collins and Dominique Lapierre, *Freedom at Midnight* (New York: Simon and Schuster, 1975), 159.

11. Patrick McDevitt, "The King of Sports: Polo in late Victorian and Edwardian India," *International Journal of History of Sports* (London: Routledge, Vol. 20, No. 1, 2003), 23.

12. *Ibid.*, 11.

13. Jaisal Singh, *Polo in India* (London: New Holland, 2007), 72.

14. Byron Farwell, *Armies of the Raj: From the Mutiny to Independence* (New York: W.W. Norton, 1989), 206.

15. Lord Curzon (1859–1925) was India's viceroy from 1900 until 1905. When an undergraduate at Oxford, Curzon was the subject of a doggerel that followed him throughout his life: "My name is George Nathaniel Curzon, I am a most superior person. My cheeks are pink, my hair is sleek, I dine at Blenheim twice a week."

16. The behavior of Brig. Reginald Edward Harry "Rex" Dyer (1864–1927) elicited widespread criticism. The Liberal government in London officially censured his actions. He died, unrepented, in 1927. Memories

were long; in 1940, Sir Michael O'Dwyer was assassinated in London by an Indian fanatic. Both Mahatma Gandhi and Jawaharlal Nehru rejected the assassination as senseless.

17. "A Lover of the Game," 132.

18. Field Marshal Frederick Sleigh Roberts, V.C., later Lord Roberts of Kandahar and Waterford (1832–1914), was commander-in-chief in India and in Ireland. Both Lord Roberts and his son the Hon. Frederick Hugh Sherston Roberts (1872–1899) were one of three father-son recipients of the Victoria Cross, the United Kingdom's highest award for valor.

19. E.D. Miller, *Modern Polo* (London: W. Thacker and Co., 1896), 355.

20. T.F. Dale, *Polo at Home and Abroad* (London: London and Counties Press Assoc., 1915), 14.

21. The 1889 team was E.D. Miller, Alfred Rawlinson, Bertram Portal and Gordon Renton. In 1889, the team was Lord Ava, George Milner, E.D. Miller and the Hon. Herbert A. Lawrence.

22. The 1892 winners were Lt. William Horsley "Atti" Persse, Lt. Valentine George Whitla, Capt. William Kirk, and Lt. Charles Kendal Bushe. In 1893–94, Lt. Herbert William Wilbeforce replaced Lt. Whitla.

23. Sir Henry de Beauvoir De Lisle (1864–1955) expounded about his tactical ideas on several books: *Hints to Polo Players in India*, *Polo in India* and *Tournament Polo*. He also wrote his memoirs under the title *Reminiscences of Sport and War*. His reputation as a polo tactician did not extend to the battlefield — he was not held in great esteem by his commander in Gallipoli, Sir William Birdwood, and was similarly thought of by his junior officers. De Lisle's words referring to the First Newfoundland Regiment during the battle of the Somme are often quoted: "It was a magnificent display of trained and disciplined valour, and its assault only failed of success because dead men can advance no further."

24. Sir Beauvoir De Lisle, *Reminiscences of Sport and War* (London: Eyre and Spottiswoode, 1939), 58.

25. Robert Lumsden Ricketts (b. 1872) wrote *First Class Polo*, first published in 1928. A second edition saw the light of day ten years later. By then Ricketts was a brigadier general. The only additions were some modifications regarding the changes in the duties and characteristics of the number 3 and the back, as well as some observations on the training of individual players.

26. R.L. Ricketts, *First Class Polo* (Aldershot: Gale and Polden, 1928), 4.

27. Foreword by H.R.H. The Prince of Wales, *Profiles in Polo* [xiii].

28. R.L. Ricketts, in *Polo*, edited by the Earl of Kimberley (London: Seeley, Service and Co., 1936), 72.

29. R.S. Liddell, *The Memoirs of the Tenth Royal Hussars* (London: Longmans, Green and Co., 1891), Appendix.

30. David Stanley William Ogilvy (1856–1900) was born in Florence and educated at Eton College and Oxford University. He succeeded to the Earldom of Airlie in 1881. A distinguished military career included the Second Afghan War, the Sudan Expedition, the Nile Expedition and the Anglo-Boer War; he was wounded several times. Lt. Col. the Earl of Airlie was killed while in command of the 12th Lancers, leading a charge that saved the British guns at Diamond Hill, near Pretoria, Transvaal.

31. Kimberley, 72. The other team members were Osman Yar Jung, Abdul Shkoor Khan and Dadir Beg.

32. Brigadier Denis Leonard Ormerod, C.B.E., personal communication, 26 April 2000.

Chapter 6

1. *Polo*, 1927, Vol. 1, No. 4, 29. James Calvin Cooley (1868–1948), a 6-goal player, wrote articles in-depth for *Polo* magazine.

2. Robert Weir and J. Moray Brown, *Hunting: Polo* (London: Longmans, Green and Co., 1891), 259.

3. E.D. Miller, *Polo Players Guide and Almanack*, 167.

4. Reproduced in *Polo*, December 1930, 14. Charles-Fernand de Condamy (1855–1913) was a well-known French artist. Condamy also produced a caricature of James Gordon Bennett in polo garb.

5. John E. Cowdin, "Polo in America," in William Patten, editor, *The Book of Sport* (New York: J.F. Taylor and Co., 1901), 144.

6. *Ibid.*, 151.

7. For a short biography of John Watson, see Roger Chatterton-Newman, in *Profiles in Polo: The Players Who Changed the Game*, Horace Laffaye, ed. (Jefferson, N.C.: McFarland and Co., 2007), 23.

8. There are two known versions of the original painting. One, now in a private collection, was sold at Christie's, London, on 28 May 1999. The hammer price was 245,000 pounds sterling. For a detailed description of the painting, see Christie's catalog, sale 6108, pp. 78–85. Roger Chatterton-Newman, Horace Laffaye and Nigel Miskin were contributors to the entry. There is a "first print" hanging at the Hurlingham Club.

9. F. Gray Griswold, *The International Polo Cup* (New York: Dutton's, 1928), 13.

10. A goal-by-goal description of the match is to be found in Cowdin, 145.

11. The Hurlingham team was Capt. Thomas Hone, Hon. Richard Thompson Lawley, Capt. Malcolm Orme Little and John Henry Watson (captain). The Westchester P.C. players were William Knapp Thorn, Jr., Raymond Rodgers Belmont, Foxhall Parker Keene and Thomas Hitchcock (captain).

12. Nigel à Brassard, *A Glorious Victory, A Glorious Defeat* (Chippenham: private printing, 2001), 21. This book is a comprehensive narrative of the 1921 Westchester Cup.

13. *La Nación*, Buenos Aires, 14 November 1894 (author's translation).

14. The players in the photograph are Percy Louis Grey Bridger, R.E.H. Anderson, Frank Wright Clunie, John Rebbick Garrod, Arthur Lace, Henry Burn Anderson and G.A. Thompson, standing. Seated, Patrick M. Rath, Barrington B. Syer, Henry Meynard Mills, Evans Robert Giffard and Charles W. Thompson.

15. *The Times*, 23 November 1893.

16. "Boots," "Sporting News," *River Plate Sport and Pastime*, 29 November 1893, 8.

17. *Ibid.*, 6 December 1893, 7.

18. Horacio A. Laffaye, *El polo internacional argentino* (Buenos Aires: Edición del Autor, 1988), 61.

19. Francisco Ceballos, *El polo en la Argentina* (Buenos Aires: Dirección General de Remonta, 1968), 60. Francisco "Paco" Ceballos (d. 1948) was president of the Argentine Polo Association from 1929 to 1934 and is credited with the creation of the National Handicap Tournament (0–40 goals).

20. Eduardo Bautista Pondé, letter to the author, 7 March 1987.

21. Jobino Pedro Sierra e Iglesias, *Un tiempo que se fue* (San Salvador de Jujuy: Editorial Universidad de Jujuy, 1998), 223.

22. J. Macnie, *Work and Play in the Argentine* (London: T. Werner Laurie, no date [1924]), 115.

23. "Our Van," in *Baily's Magazine* (London: Vinton and Co., August 1896), 168.

24. Paul H. de Serville, "Manifold, James Chester (1867–1918)," in *Australian Dictionary of Biography*, Vol. 10 (Melbourne: Melbourne University Press, 1986), 391.

25. T.A. St. Quintin, *Chances of Sports of Sorts* (Edinburgh: William Blackwood and Sons, 1912), 237.

26. Ashton, in *Profiles in Polo*, 98.

27. K.M. Little, *Polo in New Zealand* (Wellington: Whitcombe and Tombs, 1956), 35.

28. *The Polo Monthly*, 1909.

29. Alexander Godley, *Life of an Irish Soldier* (London, John Murray, 1939), 131.

30. Harold Schwind (1873–1922), a 7-goal player, was born in Edinburgh, arrived in Argentina at age 21 and was the owner of the 30,000-acre estancia El Bagual in San Luis Province. Schwind won the Junior Championship at Roehampton. In 1912 took his own team, El Bagual (Wild Horse), to England with Johnny and Joe Traill, Leonard Lynch-Staunton and John Campbell. They won the Social Club Cup and the Whitney Cup. His mare India was awarded the Lady Susan Townley Cup for Best Pony in the P.A. of the River Plate Open Championship.

Guards, A.D.C.; Capt. Francis Fawkes, 71st Highland Light Infantry; Count Richard Metaxa, 74th Highlanders; and Lt. Alfred Donald Mackintosh, 71st H.L.I.

10. Asociación Argentina de Polo, *Centauros* (Buenos Aires: Platt Grupo Impresor, 2005), 160.

11. Armando Braun, "El Polo en la Argentina" in *Polo* (Buenos Aires: Asociación Argentina de Polo, 1960), [70].

12. Javier Bustinza, editor, *Polo around the World* (Buenos Aires: Editorial Traful, 2005), 123.

13. *River Plate Sport and Pastime*, 9 March 1892, 3.

14. *Ibid.*, "Boots," "Sporting News," *River Plate Sport and Pastime*, 27 December 1893, 8.

15. *Ibid.*, 28 March 1894.

16. *PoloLine* (*www.pololine.com*), 2006.

17. *Polo & Equitación*, November 1929, 11.

18. Asociación Argentina de Polo, *Centauros*, December 2005, 132.

19. *Polo & Equitación*, November 1929, 11.

20. Asociación Argentina de Polo, *Libro Anual* (Buenos Aires: Tall. Gráf. Damiano, 1933), 60.

21. "La Copa Anchorena," *Polo*, 1960, [28].

22. *U.S.P.A. Year Book* (New York; Oak Brook, Ill.: Lexington, Ky.: 1926–1988).

23. *Polo Players Edition*, January 2002, 27.

24. Letter to the Editor, *Polo Players Edition*, April 2002, 33. "Cecil Smith's record of membership with the USPA, as taken from old Blue Books is as follows: 1925, 0; 1926, 2; 1927, 4; 1928, 5; 1929, 6; 1930, 7; 1931–32, 8; 1933, 9; 1934, 10; 1935, 9; 1936, 8; 1937, 9; 1938–41, 10; 1942, 9; 1949–62, 10; and declining from there until his last listing, at 6 goals, in 1988. [Signed] Sherry T. Browne, USPA Executive Secretary."

25. *Year Book of The Hurlingham Polo Association*, 1957, 2.

26. J.R.C. Gannon, "Polo in 1951," in *The Horseman's Year*, edited by Lt. Col. W.E. Lyon (London: Collins, 1952), 98.

27. Author's collection.

Chapter 7

1. *Webster's Encyclopedic Unabridged Dictionary of the English Language* (San Diego: Thunder Bay Press, 2001), 1272.

2. Henry Manners Chichester and George Burges-Short, *The Records and Badges of Every Regiment and Corps in the British Army* (London: Gale and Polden, 1990), 78.

3. *Ibid.*, 84.

4. T.F. Dale, *The Game of Polo* (Westminster: Archibald Constable and Co., 1897), 4.

5. T.A. St. Quintin, *Chances of Sports of Sorts* (Edinburgh: William Blackwood and Sons, 1912), 225.

6. *The Year Book of The Hurlingham Polo Association* (London: Hurlingham Polo Association, 1957), 22.

7. *Ibid.*, 1962, 25.

8. Horace A. Laffaye, *The Polo Encyclopedia* (Jefferson, N.C.: McFarland and Co., 2004), 240.

9. E.W. Sheppard, *The Ninth Queen's Royal Lancers* (Aldershot, Gale and Polden, 1939), Appendix. The 9th Lancers were Capt. W. Clayton, Capt. F. Grissell, Lord W. Beresford, and Lt. W.H. Fife. The Malta Polo Club team was Capt. Algernon Cecil Dawson, 3rd Dragoon

Chapter 8

1. The Hurlingham Club Annual General Meeting, 14 May 1927, quoted in *Polo*, August 1927, 14. Sir Harold Edward Snagge (1872–1949) was chairman of the committee, the Hurlingham Club.

2. The Hurlingham Club's history was written by Capt. Taprell Dorling, R.N., "Traffail" (1883–1968), in 1953. On its jubilee, the club published in 1924 a booklet, *The Hurlingham Club*, compiled from the club's old records. Nigel Miskin, a long-time member, wrote *Pigeons, Polo and Other Pastimes: A History of the Hurlingham Club*, the most complete and up to date history. The late Mr. Miskin was an expert and gracious guide during our visit to the club in 2001.

3. Nigel Miskin, *Pigeons, Polo and Other Pastimes* (no place: private printing, 2000), 22.

4. T.F. Dale, *Polo at Home and Abroad* (London: London and Counties Press, 1915), 201.

5. Nutting's original oil hangs in a private collection.

6. Miskin, 44.

7. *Ibid.*, 45.

8. For an exhaustive and well-written account of the 1921 challenge, see Nigel à Brassard, *A Glorious Victory, A Glorious Defeat* (Chippenham: Antony Rowe, 2001).

9. Mary Ann Wingfield, *Sport and the Artist* (Woodbridge, Suffolk: Antique Collectors' Club, 1988), Vol. 1, 272. The Duke of Windsor is the second figure from the left, wearing Cowdray Park's orange colors. The caption wrongly identifies the ground as Cowdray Park; it is Hurlingham's Number One Ground.

10. T.F. Dale, *Polo: Past and Present* (London: Country Life, Ltd., 1905), 57.

11. This painting, one of a pair showing Sir Humphrey's polo ponies, is illustrated in color in John Watson's *The World of Polo*, facing page 36. The ponies are Rugby, Sister Grey, Peter, Grey Legs and Rasper.

12. E.D. Miller, *Fifty Years of Sport* (New York: E.P. Dutton and Co., no date [1925]), 149.

13. Lt. George Smith Patton, Jr. (1885–1945) designed the 1913 U.S. Army saber after the British pattern. Patton was a 4-handicap player and a strong advocate of the game's virtues in building character and leadership in young officers.

14. Miller, 152.

15. A color reproduction is in Mary Ann Wingfield, 265.

16. C.P. Nickalls, "The Rugby Polo Club and its Influence on the Modern Game," in "The Sportsman," *Polo and Coaching* (London: Sports and Sportsmen, Ltd., no date. [1923]), 118.

17. *The Polo Monthly*, April 1932, 26.

18. Cirencester Park's story is told in Herbert Spencer's *A Century of Polo* (no place: World Polo Associates, 1994). Quoted in Spencer, 36.

19. The Civilians were Digby Master, John Adamthwaite, W.F. Felton and James Farmer. Gloucester Militia was Maj. Lord Bathurst, Col. Chester Master, Capt. Jesse Gouldsmith and Maj. Arthur Leopold Paget.

20. Dale, *Polo: Past and Present*, 75.

21. In 1917, because of the strong anti–German sentiment in England, George V asked all his relatives who bore German titles to change them to English surnames. Thus, Battenberg became Mountbatten, and Teck took the surname Cambridge, after his uncle, the Duke of Cambridge.

22. There is a short volume about Roehampton: Elizabeth Hennessy, *A History of Roehampton Club 1901 to 1986* (Bury St. Edmunds, Suffolk: Rowland, 1986). She updated the work in 2001.

23. Hennessy, 11.

24. Marqués de Villavieja, *Life has Been Good* (London: Chatto and Windus, 1938), 205.

25. There is a direct link between the Grand Duke Michael and today's polo. George Mountbatten, 4th Marquess of Milford Haven and patron of the Broncos team at Cowdray Park, is his direct descendant.

26. Hennessy, 43.

27. This San Jorge Club, based in that town in Santa Fe Province, is no relation to the current San Jorge, a military club next to Hurlingham Club.

28. Hennessy, 43.

29. The history of Cowdray Park Polo Club told in Derek Russell-Stoneham and Roger Chatterton-Newman, *Polo at Cowdray* (London: Polo Information Bureau, 1992).

30. It would have been nice to find a polo link from the Earl of Southampton to Lord Southampton, winner of the Hurlingham Champion Cup in the 1890s. However, Charles Henry Fitzroy, 4th Baron Southampton, was a direct descendant of Lt. Gen. Charles Fitz-Roy, 1st Baron Southampton (1737–1797). They are different families; the only link is geographical; Lord Southampton was a member of the celebrated Sussex County team that included the brothers Peat.

31. The initial winners were Norman Wilfred Loder, a Cambridge University player; the Hon. Bernard Clive Pearson, who also represented Cambridge; Capt. Hugh C.S. Ashton, Life Guards; and Capt. Eustace Widdrington Morrison-Bell, Rifle Brigade.

32. A Windsor Park team reached the finals of the Hurlingham Open in 1966, but the only English player was Prince Philip, who played with the brothers Alberto Pedro and Horacio Heguy and Daniel González. Another team, composed of members of the Commonwealth squad that entered the 30-goal International Tournament on that year, participated in the Argentine Open. The official program lists the team as "England." The team defeated Tortugas 11–10 and lost in the semifinals to the eventual champions, Coronel Suárez-Indios, 19–6.

33. Peter Webster Dollar (1899–1987), a 6-goal player, was one of the "characters" at Cowdray. Once described as an "unashamed individualist" on the polo field, he gave his German captors a hard time as a prisoner of war during World War II, eventually ending up in Colditz Castle, the prison for repeat offenders.

Chapter 9

1. Dagmar Van Tiel and Wouter Van Tiel, *French Riviera Golf* (Monaco: Edition Van Tiel, 1996), [7]. Dagmar Van Thiel is a professional photographer. Wouter is an author, editor and photographer based on the Côte d'Azur.

2. A Ranelagh team — Godfrey Heseltine, W.C. Harrild, Frederick C.G. Menzies and Edwin T. Hohler — took the cup, mid-May 1912.

3. Nelson Aldrich, Jr., *Tommy Hitchcock: An American Hero* (no place [Gaithersburg, Md.]: Fleet Street Corp., 1984), 150.

4. The first winning team was Franco–Espagnole, with Baron Elie de Rothschild, Juan Antonio Echevarrieta, Rafael Echevarrieta and Henri Couturié.

5. Sarina Singh, *Polo in India* (New Delhi: Lustre Press, 2000), 28.

6. Jaisal Singh, *Polo in India* (London: New Holland Publishers, 2007), 94.

7. Marqués de Villavieja, *Life Has Been Good* (London: Chatto and Windus, 1938), 164.

8. E.D. Miller, *Fifty Years of Sport* (New York: E.P. Dutton and Co., no date [1925]), 205.

9. Villavieja, 183–184.

10. *The New York Times*, 10 May 1908, p. C 3.

11. *The New York Times*, 15 January 1911, p. C 7.

12. *Polo Players Guide and Almanack*, 1910, 55–56. See also Maj. Rouse, "Winter Polo on the Riviera," in *The Sportsman*, 205.

Chapter 10

1. *The Polo Monthly*, June 1910, 273.

2. *Polo Association 1890* [Year Book] (no place: private printing, 1890), 20. This must be one of the most scarce polo books. The only original copy known to the author is at the National Museum of Polo and Hall of Fame. A facsimile edition was published by the U.S.P.A. in 1990.

3. T.F. Dale, *Polo: Past and Present* (London: Country Life, 1905), 342.

4. Examples of *The Meadow Brook Team* are in the Hurlingham Club in Fulham, the New York Racquet Club and in private collections. One cast was on temporary loan at the Museum of Polo in Lake Worth, Florida. There are also individual figures of each player; two of these were models for the mementos given to all eight players in the 1921 and 1924 Westchester Cup matches. The players wear a helmet, while in *The Meadow Brook Team* they are bareheaded. A bronze depicting Ralla in one-third life size is in exhibition at the Whitney Museum in New York City.

5. *Polo*, June 1927, 15.

6. Dennis J. Amato, "Devereux Milburn: A Back for the Ages," in *Profiles in Polo*, 60, note 66.

7. *The Polo Monthly*, September 1931, 427.

8. *Polo & Equitación*, August 1930, 29.

9. The U.S. Army team was Maj. Arthur "Jingle" Wilson (winner of the Congressional Medal of Honor), Maj. Louie A. Beard, Lt. Col. Lewis Brown, Jr., and Maj. William W. "Big Red" Erwin.

10. Wesley J. White, "The Army Four in Argentina," *The Sportsman*, February 1931, 45.

11. Robert Woods Bliss (1875–1962) was an American diplomat whose career was rewarded with ambassadorships to Sweden and Argentina, his last foreign post. Art collectors Ambassador and Mrs. Bliss, who had no children, donated their Washington Georgian mansion, Dumbarton Oaks, with its collection of Byzantine and medieval art and a 50,000-volume library, to Harvard University. In 1944, Dumbarton Oaks, a stately Georgian house, was the site of an international conference that was instrumental in the creation of the Organization of United Nations.

12. *Polo*, July 1927, 24.

Chapter 11

1. *Britain and Argentina in the Nineteenth Century* (Oxford: Clarendon Press, 1960), ix. Canadian-born, Cambridge-educated Professor H.S. Ferns (1913–1992) wrote extensively on the relationship between Argentina and the United Kingdom. Ferns was professor of social science at Birmingham University.

2. Arthur L. Holder, editor, *Activities of the British Community in Argentina During the Great War, 1914–1918* (Buenos Aires: Buenos Aires Herald, 1920), 25.

3. Lieutenant, later captain, John Vincent Holland, Leinster Regiment, was on the staff of the Mechanical Engineer of the Central Argentine Railway in Rosario. Holland volunteered in 1914 and was awarded the V.C. at the storming of Guillemont, during the battle of the Somme, on 3 September 1916.

4. Sir Follett Holt (1865–1944) took the Open Championship in 1894 and 1895 with The Casuals and in 1897 with Hurlingham. He played in England at the Ranelagh Club. After his return to the United Kingdom, where he was knighted in 1934, he became director of several railroads. Holt maintained his commercial attachments with Argentina, being in charge of the British Exposition in Buenos Aires in 1931.

5. Born in Hertfordshire in 1866, Frank John Balfour played polo at the Middlesex Club. Balfour immigrated to Argentina in 1890 and learned the ways of the gauchos while working with Francis Kinchant at estancia Las Petacas. Balfour retired as a polo player when he lost an eye during a match at Hurlingham. He purchased the 12,000-hectare estancia El Colorado, in Washington, Córboba Province, which became an important center for polo pony breeding. His mare Diamond, later exported to the United Kingdom, was awarded the Lady Susan Townley Cup for the best pony in the Open. Upon his return to England in 1912, Balfour left the management of El Colorado to his son-in-law Edgar Carlisle. He settled in Cheltenham and was elected president of the Cheltenham Polo Club and the Polo and Riding Pony Society.

6. Juan Sauro, personal communication, December 2006.

7. *The London Gazette*, 5 March 1918, 3.

8. Eduardo P. Archetti, *Masculinities: Football, Polo and the Tango in Argentina* (Oxford: Berg, 1999), 109.

9. Alastair Hennessy and John King, *The Land That England Lost* (London: British Academic Press, 1992), 4.

10. There are two histories of the Hurlingham Club that yield fascinating reading. Both are written in Spanish — with many quotations in English — by lady members. One is *Hurlingham* (1958) by Elvira Ocampo de Shaw, a charming personal reminiscence by an early Argentine member, and the other, *La historia del Hurlingham Club 1888–1988*, by Isabel Laura Cárdenas de Boadle, whose husband, Alan Boadle, was the club's president in 1942–46 and 1950–53.

11. Andrew Graham-Yooll, *The Forgotten Colony* (Buenos Aires: Literature of Latin America, 1999), 6.

12. Irish-born Father Anthony Dominic Fahy (1805–1871) was a missionary in Kentucky and Ohio before going to Argentina. Fr. Fahy was a supporter of dictator Juan Manuel de Rosas and his role in the Camila O'Gorman affair is a blotch on his record. Camila and Fr. Uladislao Gutiérrez eloped, only to be captured a few months later. Among others, her own father, Adolfo O'Gorman, Dalmacio Vélez Sarsfield — who wrote the Argentine Civil Code — and Fr. Anthony Fahy demanded "an exemplary punishment of the wayward daughter that was also giving the industrious and well-regarded [Irish] community a bad name." María Teresa Julianello, *The Scarlet Trinity: The Doomed Struggle of Camila O'Gorman against Family, Church and State in 19th Century Buenos Aires* (Cork: Irish Centre for Migration Studies, 2000). Without a trial, the lovers were executed by a firing squad on 18 August 1848 in Santos Lugares, near Buenos Aires, on Rosas' orders. Camila O'Gorman was twenty years old and was eight months pregnant.

13. *The Southern Cross*, 16 January 1875. Quoted in Juan Carlos Korol and Hilda Sábato, *Cómo fué la inmi-*

gración irlandesa en Argentina (Buenos Aires: Editorial Plus Ultra, 1981), 7.

14. "Nómina de Socios Fundadores," *Album Jockey Club* (Buenos Aires: Juan F. Tudoni Impresor, no date [1924]), unpaginated.

15. For a short biography of John Arthur Edward Traill, consult Roger Chatterton-Newman, "Johnny Traill: An Irishman from the Pampas," in *Profiles in Polo*, edited by Horace A. Laffaye (Jefferson, N.C.: McFarland and Co., 2007), 54.

16. A detailed description of this evolution is in Archetti, 77–112.

17. J. Traill, *The Long Chukker* (no place: private printing, no date [circa 1955]), 68.

18. Archetti, 108, note 10.

19. *The Standard*, 4 September 1906, 1.

20. The term gaucho derives from *gauche*, literally left, a French word also meaning crude or lacking social graces. In Argentina, this pejorative term was applied to a ragamuffin, invariably a good horseman that peopled the pampas. With the passage of time, the influence of Romanticism on Argentine writing changed the meaning to the opposite; a gaucho became a nice man, and a "gauchada" an act of amity and good will. See Virginia Carreño, *Estancias y estancieros del Río de la Plata* (Buenos Aires: Editorial Claridad, 1994), 20.

21. Robert F. Kelley, "Sportsmen from the Pampas," *The Sportsman*, October 1931, 43.

22. The team was Haakon Haugaard, Nicolás and Bonde Ambrosius, and Ernesto Grant, who had taught the youngsters the game's rudiments. They proved to be good students.

23. *Polo & Equitación*, December 1929, 20.

Chapter 12

1. James Kenneth McManus (1921–2008), known as Jim McKay, was a broadcaster for ABC's *Wide World of Sports* who also reported on twelve Olympic Games.

2. Bill Mallon, *The 1900 Olympic Games* (Jefferson, N.C.: McFarland and Co., 1998), 12.

3. Pierre de Coubertin (1863–1937) took the saying from Fr. Henri Martin Dideon, headmaster of Arcueil College in Paris.

4. Mallon, 142.

5. *Baily's Magazine*, July 1900, 58.

6. Horace A. Laffaye, *The Polo Encyclopedia* (Jefferson, N.C.: McFarland and Co., 2004), 278–279.

7. Bill Mallon and Ian Buchanan, *The 1908 Olympic Games* (Jefferson, N.C.: McFarland and Co., 2000), 206.

8. Norman J. Cinnamond, *El Polo* (Barcelona: Librería Catalonia, no date, [1929]), 183.

9. Bill Mallon, *The 1920 Olympic Games* (Jefferson, N.C.: McFarland and Co., 1998), 221.

10. *The Sportsman*, July 1928, 82.

11. Francisco Ceballos, *El polo en la Argentina* (Buenos Aires: Dirección General de Remonta, 1969), 117.

12. Nelson Aldrich, Jr., *Tommy Hitchcock: An American Hero* (no place [Gaithersburg, Md.]: Fleet Street Corp., 1984), 190.

13. *United States Polo Association Year Book* (New York: private printing, 1925), 50.

14. Eduardo P. Archetti, *Masculinities: Football, Polo and the Tango in Argentina* (Oxford: Berg, 1999), 101.

15. *La Nación*, 7-7-1924: 2.

16. *El Gráfico*, No. 261, 19.

17. Robert Ralph Ashton, quoted in Chris Ashton, *Geebung: The Story of Australian Polo* (Sydney: Hamilton Publishing, 1993), 128.

18. For a personal look at the Berlin Olympics, see Brigadier Jack Gannon, *Before the Colours Fade* (London: J.A. Allen and Co., 1976), 41. Brig. Gannon, longtime secretary of the Hurlingham Polo Association, was in charge of polo at the Olympic Games.

19. *Ibid.*, 51.

20. Michelle Robbins, "Rooted in Memory," in *American Forests*, April 2003.

21. Letter to the Editor, *American Forests*, Winter 2005. From Thomas Robert Lewis (Frank Lewis's son).

22. *The Observer* (London), 19 August 2007.

Chapter 13

1. "The Last of the Grenadiers," *Westchester Cup Program*, U.S.P.A., 1939, 41. Grantland Rice (1880–1954) was the dean of American sportswriters.

2. The story of the 1921 Westchester Cup challenge is painstakingly described by Nigel à Brassard in *A Glorious Victory, A Glorious Defeat* (Chippenham: private printing, 2001).

3. Peter Vischer, "Britain Challenge to American Polo," *Polo*, June 1927, 5.

4. *Ibid.*

5. *Ibid.*, "The International Matches," October 1927, 6.

6. Major A.G. Rudd, "A Discussion of British Polo," *Polo*, December 1927, 7.

7. "Marco," *An Introduction to Polo* (London: Country Life, 1931), 34.

8. à Brassard, 53.

9. Vischer, *Polo*, October 1927, 6.

10. Thomas Hitchcock, Jr., "Rules and Tactics," *Polo*, July 1930, 17.

11. "Chukker," "Summing Up the Polo Season," *The Sportsman*, November 1931, 17.

12. Arthur W. Little, Jr., "Polo from the Near Side," *Country Life*, October 1938, 37.

13. Geoffrey S. Cornish and Ronald E. Whitten, *The Architects of Golf* (New York: Harper Collins, 1981), 579.

14. For short biographical essays on Devereux Milburn and Thomas Hitchcock, Jr., see *Profiles in Polo*, edited by Horace A. Laffaye (Jefferson, N.C.: McFarland, 2007), sections by Dennis Amato, 59, and Nigel à Brassard, 108.

15. Nelson Aldrich, Jr., *Tommy Hitchcock: An American Hero* (no place [Gaithersburg, Md.]: Fleet Street Corp., 1984), 250.

16. *The Spur*, August 15, 1925. See also, Newell Bent, *American Polo* (New York: Macmillan, 1929), 286. An abridged version was included in *Polo* (New York: private printing, 1927), a small booklet published by the haberdashers Brooks Brothers.

17. E.D. Miller, *Modern Polo* (London: W. Thacker and Co., 1896), 14.

18. *Ibid.*, 9.

Chapter 14

1. *Men, Machines, and Sacred Cows* (London: Hamish Hamilton, 1984), 133.

2. *Baily's Magazine*, August 1872, 180.

3. Nigel à Brassard, *A Glorious Victory, A Glorious Defeat* (Chippenham: Antony Rowe, 2001), 45.

4. *British Hunts and Huntsmen: England (North), Scotland and Ireland* (London: Biographical Press, 1911), 511.

5. Geoffrey Bennett, *Charlie B: A Biography of Admiral Lord Beresford of Metennmeh and Curraghmore* (London: Dawnay, 1969).

6. Miller, ed., *Polo Players Guide and Almanack*, 146.

7. Earl of Kimberley, *Polo* (London: Seeley, Service and Co., 1936). An American edition is published by J.B. Lippincott and Co. in Philadelphia.

8. A biography of the Grenfell twins was written by John Buchan, *Francis and Riversdale Grenfell* (London: Nelson, 1920).

9. The Distinguished Service Order was created in 1886 and is second in rank only to the Victoria Cross.

10. The official biography of Lord Mountbatten was written by Philip Ziegler, *Mountbatten* (New York: Alfred A. Knopf, 1985). A shorter essay is Roger Chatterton-Newman's "Earl Mountbatten of Burma: A Tangible Legacy," in *Profiles in Polo*, edited by Horace A. Laffaye (Jefferson, N.C.: McFarland and Co., 2007), 90.

11. Richard Symonds, *The Making of Pakistan* (London: Faber and Faber, 1950), 74.

12. "Marco," *An Introduction to Umpiring* (no place: R.N.P.A., 1934.)

13. The Jaipur team's record included the Hurlingham Champion Cup, the Ranelagh Open Cup, the Roehampton Open Cup, the Coronation Cup and the Indian Empire Shield.

14. "Roehampton Club List of Fixtures for 1930 Season," *The Polo Monthly*, April 1930, 8; "The Hurlingham Club Polo Programme, 1930," *Ibid.*, May 1930, 96; "Ranelagh Club Programme of Principal Events for Season, 1930," *Ibid.*, June 1930, 190.

15. Roy Heron, *The Sporting Art of Cecil Aldin* (London: Sportsman Press, 1990), plate 15.

16. Vincent Haddlesey, "Polo at Dunster," David Findlay Galleries, New York, 1987.

17. Gerald Balding, "Polo as the English Play It," *The Sportsman*, September 1937, 36.

Chapter 15

1. *The Guinness Dictionary of Sports Quotations* (Enfield, Middlesex: Guinness Publishing, 1990), 215. Greek-born Marina Tatiana Lada Sulzberger (1920–

1976) was the wife of *The New York Times* foreign correspondent Cyrus Lee Sulzberger. She wrote *Marina: Letters and Diaries of Marina Sulzberger*.

2. Personal communication from Leonard H. Hamersley, 3 June 2008.

3. H.T. (Reg) Denny, *Polo of Course: A History of Polo in W.A.* (Perth: private printing, 1997), 18.

4. Chris Ashton, *Geebung: The Story of Australian Polo* (Sydney: Hamilton Publishing, 1993), 66.

5. *Ibid.*, 61.

6. The visit to Australia is recounted from the tourists' viewpoint in Lt. Col. Teignmouth P. Melvill's *Ponies and Women* (London: Jarrolds, 1932), 205.

7. T.P. Melvill, "International Polo of a New Sort," *Polo*, December 1928, 31.

8. Chris Ashton, "Jim Ashton of the Brothers Four," in *Profiles in Polo*, edited by Horace A. Laffaye (Jefferson, N.C.: McFarland and Co., 2007), 98.

9. Anthony Hordern (1889–1970) was a scion of the family that owned The Palace Emporium, the largest store in Sydney. Robert T. Melrose was a South Australian landowner.

10. Ashton, *Geebung*, 63.

11. The donors were Jack C. Allen, R.G. Baldock, F.G.C. Couper, Charlie Cooke, Adolph Feez, R.C. Hogarth, Dr. Aeneas McDonnell, Alex McPhie, Ranald Munro, Willie C. Peak, Brig. Gen. C. Robertson, J. Rogerson and the Hon. A.H. Whittington.

12. For a more personal and detailed view, see Ashton, *Geebung*, 85, and *Profiles in Polo*, 98.

13. *The Polo Monthly*, July 1930, 347.

14. Chris Ashton, *Profiles*, 102.

15. *Polo*, August 1930, 50.

16. This regiment was privately raised by Donald Alexander Smith, first Baron Strathcona (1820–1914), for service in the Anglo-Boer War. Many skilled horsemen, such as cowboys and Mounties, enlisted. Apparently, Field Marshal Horatio Kitchener (1850–1916) was surprised at the size of the soldiers from Canada. Their commander, Sir Samuel Benfield Steele (1849–1919), answered, "My apologies, sir. I combed all of Canada and these are the smallest I could find."

17. Charles Llewellen Palmer, Esq., personal communication, 6 April 2008.

18. *The Polo Calendar*, various issues (Meerut: Indian Polo Association, 1912–1914).

19. Miller, *Polo Player's Guide and Almanack*, 141 *et seq.*

20. *Centauros* (Buenos Aires: Asociación Argentina de Polo, 2002), 52.

21. J.N.P. Watson, *Hanut: Prince of Polo Players* (London: Sportsman's Press, 1995), 29.

22. Nigel à Brassard, *A Glorious Victory, A Glorious Defeat* (Chippenham: Antony Rowe, 2001), 36.

23. A.A. de Polo, *Libro Anual*, 1937, 24.

24. Jaisal Singh, *Polo in India* (London: New Holland, 2007), 69.

25. Quentin Crewe, *The Last Maharaja* (London: Michael Joseph Ltd., 1985), 82.

26. Denzil Holder, *Hindu Horseman* (Chippenham: Picton Publishing, 1986), 88.

27. Horace A. Laffaye, *The Polo Encyclopedia* (Jefferson, N.C.: McFarland and Co., 2004), 185.

28. Holder, 209.

29. T.P. McLean, *Polo: The Savile Cup; The First 100*

Years (Cambridge: New Zealand Polo Association, 1990), 46.

30. K.M. Little, *Polo in New Zealand.* (Wellington: Whitcombe and Tombs, 1956), 25.

31. The New Zealand players rated at 10 goals are Derrick W.J. Gould, Jack Lyons, C.F. (Fred) Mackenzie, W.C.A. (Willie) Mackenzie, Charles L. Orbell and Kenneth N. Peake.

32. McLean, 48.

33. Chris Ashton, *Geebung: The Story of Australian Polo* (Sydney: Hamilton Publishing, 1993), 63.

34. Gene Makin, *A History of Queensland Polo* (Toowooma: private printing, 1999), 30.

35. *Ibid.*

36. "Is U.S. Polo Still a Gentleman's Game?" *Polo*, April-May, 1981, 24.

37. McLean, 47.

38. Donald C. McKenzie and John R. McKenzie, *A History of Polo in South Africa* (Dargle, KwaZulu-Natal: private printing, 1999), 6.

39. *The Polo Calendar 1919–1920*, cited in McKenzie, 457.

40. Leonard Putterill, "The Decline of Polo in a Great Land," *Polo*, January 1929, 11.

41. Quoted in McKenzie, 27.

42. *Ibid.*

Chapter 16

1. Herbert Reed, "Brains at Full Gallop," *The Sportsman*, September 1927, 51. Herbert Reed also wrote for *The New Yorker*.

2. Nelson Aldrich, Jr., *Tommy Hitchcock: An American Hero* (no place [Gaithersburg, Md.]: Fleet Street Corp., 1984), 208.

3. U.S. Polo Association, *Argentina vs. United States*, 1928 Official Program, 49.

4. "The Editor takes the Floor," *The Sportsman*, November 1928, 21.

5. Aldrich, 212.

6. Robert F. Kelley, "Prophecy Fails at Meadow Brook," *The Sportsman*, November 1929, 29.

7. *Ibid.*, 88.

8. Personal communications from Mrs. Sherry Browne, at the U.S.P.A., and Mr. George J. DuPont, Jr., executive director of the National Museum of Polo and Hall of Fame.

9. Peter Vischer, "U.S. versus Argentina," *Polo*, October 1928, [5].

10. Robert F. Kelley, "British Done in U.S. Polo?" *Polo*, June 1932, 6.

11. *Year Book of the United States Polo Association*, 1933, 18.

12. The American team's journey to Argentina is recounted by Seymour Knox, Jr., in *To B.A. and Back* (Buffalo: private printing, 1933).

13. J.C. Rathborne, "La Copa de las Américas," *Polo & Campo* (Buenos Aires: February 1933), 9.

14. Philippa Glanville, "Trophy Design," in *Sporting Glory* (London: Sporting Trophies Exhibition, 1992), 151.

15. Peter Vischer, "Argentina's Brilliant Victory," *Polo*, November 1936, 20.

16. Aldrich, 249.

17. Don Juan Manuel, "¡Campeones de América!" *El Gráfico*, 15 December 1950, 54.

18. Asociación Argentina de Polo, *Campeonato Argentino Abierto*, Official Program, 1950, [17].

19. Following in his father's footsteps, Norty Knox recounted from his diary the American experience during the 1966 journey to Buenos Aires. See Northrup Knox, *To B.A. and Back, Again* (Buffalo: private printing, no date. [1967]).

20. *Ibid.*, 49.

21. Interview in *PoloLine*, 21 January 2002.

22. Knox, 49.

23. *Ibid.*, 50.

24. Interview with Francisco Dorignac, 14 July 2006.

25. Northup R. Knox, *Copa de las Americas*, Official Program (Buenos Aires: Asociación Argentina de Polo, 1969), 14.

26. Continuing the Knox's family tradition, the 1969 challenge is described in Northrup R. Knox, *To B.A. and Back, Once More* (no place: private printing, no date. [1970]).

27. *Ibid.*, 29.

28. Royal Navy Polo Association. The mallet's head is oval, the height being 5/6ths of the width.

29. Ami Shinitzky, "Who was Minding the Store?" *Polo*, January-February 1980, 45.

30. Personal communication from Lester "Red" Armour III, 9 March 2008.

31. Shinitzky, *Polo*, January-February 1980, 28.

32. Ami Shinitzky, "Cool Head Latin: Gonzalo Tanoira," *Polo*, January-February 1977, 14.

33. Shinitzky, *Polo*, July-August 1980, 31.

34. Juan Carlos Harriott, Jr., personal communication, December 2005.

35. Interview with Francisco Dorignac, 14 July 2006.

Chapter 17

1. T.P. McLean, *Polo: The Savile Cup; The First 100 Years* (Cambridge: New Zealand Polo Association, 1990). 75. Sir Terence McLean (1913–2004) was a prolific writer on rugby football.

2. T.B. Drybrough, *Polo* (London: Vinton and Co., 1898), 46.

3. Newell Bent, *American Polo* (New York: Macmillan, 1929), 59.

4. "Our Van," *Baily's Magazine*, July 1875, 186.

5. Nigel à Brassard, *A Glorious Victory, A Glorious Defeat* (Chippenham: Antony Rowe, 2001), 38.

6. *Ibid.*, 45.

7. Taprell Dorling, *The Hurlingham Club* (London: private printing, 1953), 61.

8. K.M. Little, *Polo in New Zealand.* (Wellington: Whitcombe and Tombs, 1956), 11.

9. Nigel Miskin, personal communication, June 2001.

10. "I Can Still Remember Distinctly," *Argentina vs. America Program*, U.S.P.A., 1936, 16e.

11. Bent, 25.

12. U.S. Polo Association, *2007 Year Book*, 177.

13. *Ibid.*, *1953*, 1.

14. Russell Corey, personal communication, March 2008. William Russell Grace Corey, a 6-goal international player, is Alan L. Corey, Jr.'s youngest son.

15. Robert F. Kelley, "Meadow Brook," *Westchester Cup Program*, U.S.P.A., 1939, 18.

16. A detailed narrative of the origins of Palermo is in Miguel Sorondo, *Procedencia del nombre de Palermo* (Buenos Aires: Casa Jacobo Peuser, 1939).

17. Horacio Schiavo, *Palermo de San Benito* (Buenos Aires, Municipalidad de la Ciudad de Buenos Aires), 1969.

18. Asociación Argentina de Polo, *Libro Anual* (Buenos Aires: A.A. de Polo, 1933), 60.

19. Enrique Padilla, "El polo en el ejército," in Ceballos, 160.

20. *Polo & Equitación*, October 1928, 11.

Chapter 18

1. T.F. Dale, *Polo at Home and Abroad* (London: London and Counties Press, 1915), 5.

2. The trophy was presented by the U.S.P.A. in 1941 to honor Mexican president Gen. Manuel Avila Camacho (1897–1955), a great polo enthusiast.

3. Geoff Shackleford, *The Riviera Country Club: A Definitive History* (Pacific Palisades: Riviera Country Club, 1995), 44.

4. A Beverly Hills team (Robert Fletcher, Tony Veen, Bob Skene, Carlton Beal) took the U.S. Open in 1952.

5. Interview with Jorge Torres Zavaleta, November 2006. "On that day, everything went our way. We were ahead by one goal, when Milburn hit a knock-in that bounced off my pony's leg, leaving me a sitter in front of the goalposts. We won by two goals." Regrettably, the author was unable to watch the game because of conflict with school attendance.

6. Juan Manuel Puente, "Los polistas norteamericanos eliminados por La Concepción," *El Gráfico*, 18 November 1949, 50.

7. U.S.P.A. *Year Book, 2007*, 172.

8. K.M. Little, *Polo in New Zealand* (Wellington: Whitcombe and Tombs, 1956), 44.

9. T.P. McLean, *Polo: The Savile Cup; The First 100 Years* (Cambridge: New Zealand Polo Association, 1990), 82.

10. *Ibid.*

11. Personal observation, Jockey Club at San Isidro, October 1952.

12. Donald C. McKenzie and John R. McKenzie, *A History of Polo in South Africa* (Dargle, KwaZulu-Natal: private printing, 1999), 55.

13. *Ibid.*, 164.

14. For polo in Rhodesia see Gabriel Ellison and Kim Fraser, *Harmony of Hooves* (no place: Natal Witness, 1999).

15. Susan D. Ellis, "The Horse in Kenya" in *The Horseman's Year*, W.E. Lyon, editor (London: Collins, 1952), 54.

16. Quoted in Chris Ashton, *Geebung: The Story of*

Australian Polo (Sydney: Hamilton Publishing, 1993), 118.

17. H.T. Denny, *Polo of Course: A History of the Game in W.A.* (Perth: private printing, 1997), 57.

18. T.P. McLean, *Polo: The Savile Cup; The First 100 Years* (Cambridge: New Zealand Polo Association, 1990), 97.

19. For the most objective biographical sketch about Sinclair Hill, see Chris Ashton—who knows him better than most—in *Geebung*, 135, and in *Profiles in Polo*, edited by Horace A. Laffaye (Jefferson, N.C.: McFarland and Co., 2007), 148.

20. Ashton, *Geebung*, 112.

21. Tony Rees, *The Galloping Game* (Cochrane, Alberta: Western Heritage, 2000), 273.

Chapter 19

1. Personal communication from Heriberto Duggan, Buenos Aires, October 1979.

2. For a biographical essay on Carlos Alberto Menditeguy, see Horace A. Laffaye, "Carlos Menditeguy: To be the Best was Effortless," in *Profiles in Polo*, 140.

3. Horace Laffaye, "Julio Menditeguy," *Polo Times* (North Leigh, Oxfordshire: July 1993), 14.

4. Personal communication from Bob Skene, Santa Barbara, 1977.

5. Laffaye, "Julio Menditeguy," 14.

6. Luis Ignacio San Román, "El Trébol … 30 años después!" *Centauros*, Buenos Aires, January-February 1968, 27.

7. In those days, and until 1961, the teams defeated in the Open played on handicap the subsidiary tournaments. The Drysdale Cup is presented in memory of Mr. Joseph Norman Drysdale, president of the Hurlingham Club in 1920, and the Copa Provincia de Buenos Aires, from 1937, in memory of 9-goal international player David Benito Miles, who was killed in a plane crash.

8. Interview with Alberto Pedro Heguy, December 2005.

9. Federico Chaine, *Los Heguy* (Buenos Aires: Imprenta de los Buenos Ayres, 2001), 113.

10. For social studies of Argentine rural society, consult Virginia Carreño, *Estancias y estancieros* (Buenos Aires: Editorial Goncourt, 1991), *Estancias y estancieros de Río de La Plata* (Buenos Aires: Editorial Claridad, 1994), Yuyú Guzmán, *El país de las estancias* (Tandil: Tupac Amarú Ediciones, 1985), José Luis de Imaz, *Those Who Rule* (Albany: State University of New York Press, 1970) and María Sáenz Quesada, *Los estancieros* (Buenos Aires: Editorial de Belgrano, 1980).

11. There is no polo club named Indios-Chapaleufú. The name is a combination of Los Indios, the club near Buenos Aires where the Heguy family, starting with the patriarch Antonio Heguy, have boarded their ponies, and Chapaleufú, the family club in Intendente Alvear, La Pampa Province. The shirts, as initially worn by Indios-Chapaleufú I, are also a combination. Los Indios shirt is white with a black hoop; Chapaleufú's is white with a red star and collar. The combined colors are white, with red collar and hoop.

Chapter 20

1. Roger Chatterton-Newman, "Edward Hartopp: This Must be a Good Game," in *Profiles in Polo*, edited by Horace A. Laffaye (Jefferson, N.C.: McFarland and Co., 2007), 180.

2. Mary Ann Wingfield, *Sport and the Artist* (Woodbridge, Suffolk: Antique Collectors' Club, 1988), 347.

3. Derek Russell-Stoneham and Roger Chatterton-Newman, *Polo at Cowdray* (London: Polo Information Bureau, 1992), 36.

4. Hurlingham Polo Association, *Regulations and Rules of Polo* (London: Country Life, no date [1952]), 38.

5. *Polo*, June 1930, 66.

6. "Burma Polo: Past and Present," *The Polo Monthly*, June 1930, 249.

7. Hurlingham Polo Association, *2007 Year Book*, 307.

8. The original trophy was stolen in 1968 and was never recovered.

9. Horace Laffaye, "The Warwickshire Cup," *Polo Times*, June 2002, 18.

10. The winning team was Maj. Hilary Hook, Capt. William H. Richardson, Capt. Michael Quintin Fraser and Lt. Col. Charles Timothy Llewellen Palmer.

11. Maj. Gen. Arthur George Denaro, C.B.E., Queen's Royal Hussars, was the regiment's commanding officer prior to his appointment as commandant, R.M.A Sandhurst. The Queen's Royal Hussars traces its roots to 1688 and Sir Winston Churchill's regiment, the 4th Hussars, is also among the Q.R.H.'s ancestors.

12. O/Ct. Nicholas Harrison, Maj. Gen. Arthur Denaro, Lt. Mark P.F. Dollar and Capt. Alexander D.T. Hawes were on the R.M.A. Sandhurst winning team.

13. The Hurlingham Polo Association, *1961 Year Book*, 14; *2001 Year Book*, 42.

Peter J. Rizzo, "John Oxley: Patron and Benefactor," in *Profiles in Polo*, 185.

8. *Polo*, October-November 1976, 33.

9. *Polo*, August 2005, 55.

10. Ambassador Glen Holden's initials in Spanish — Ge Hache — gave the name to the team.

11. The Spreckels Cup was donated in 1909 by the Coronado Country Club in memory of sugar magnates Adolph and John Spreckels, promoters of polo in California.

12. For further reading, consult Allan Forbes' *Early Myopia* and *Sport in Norfolk County*, and Edward Weeks' *Myopia: A Centennial Chronicle*.

13. Laura Gardin Fraser (1889–1966) designed the Horse Association of America Medal presented to the winners of the best playing polo pony in each club. Another of her works is *Miss Buck*, a polo pony that was property of W. Averell Harriman. She also sculpted a horse that was presented by the U.S.P.A. to those who loaned ponies for the 1928 Cup of the Americas; there is one example in the Museum of Polo. She was married to the artist James Earle Fraser; they resided in Westport, the home of the Fairfield County Hunt Club, all their lives.

14. For a brief history of the Fairfield County Hunt Club see A.M.H. [Mrs. Craig Barry "Penny" Heatley], "An Interview with Tommy Glynn," *Fairfield Polo* (Westport, Conn.: 1973), 24.

15. "The Polo Report," *Polo*, February 1986, 41.

16. U.S.P.A. *Year Book, 2007*, 23 *et seq.*

17. A biographical sketch of Tommy Wayman is in Tex Maule, "No. 1 at Two is Working on Ten," *Classic*, December 1976–January 1977, 130.

18. See Nigel à Brassard, "Guillermo Gracida Jr.: The Field General," *Profiles in Polo*, 253.

19. Henry B. Wheatley, editor, *The Diary of Samuel Pepys* (Boston: C.C. Brainard Publishing Co., 1898), Vol. 7, 4.

Chapter 21

1. *Polo*, May 1985, 22. David Stewart Birrell Iglehart (1910–1993), carried a 10-goal handicap for many years. He retired from polo in 1956.

2. Charles Skiddy Von Stade's posthumous daughter, Frederica, became an acclaimed mezzo-soprano. Based on Von Stade's letters to his wife, Richard Danielpour composed *Elegies* in his memory.

3. At the war's end, Mr. Perkins was rescued by his friend George Oliver, a 9-goal player who was a major in the U.S. Ranger unit that overran the prisoners' camp. When Maj. Oliver greeted Perkins, Peter asked him, "What took you so long?" Personal communication from Mr. Thomas B. Glynn.

4. Quoted in Ashton, "Sinclair Hill," *Profiles in Polo*, edited by Horace A. Laffaye (Jefferson, N.C.: McFarland and Co., 2007), 151.

5. Ronald Ferguson, *The Galloping Major* (London: Macmillan, 1994), 185.

6. Horace A. Laffaye, "Argentine Team Visits the Northeast," *Polo Newsletter*, December 1974, 17.

7. For a biographical sketch of John T. Oxley, see

Chapter 22

1. Richard E. Danielson, "The Editor Takes the Floor," *The Sportsman*, November 1928, 21. Richard Ely Danielson (1885–1957), M.F.H of the Groton Hounds, and a Yale graduate, was also publisher of *The Atlantic Monthly*.

2. Yolanda Carslaw, "Julian Hipwood: A Living Polo Legend," in *Profiles in Polo*, edited by Horace A. Laffaye (Jefferson, N.C.: McFarland and Co., 2007), 233.

3. Rudyard Kipling, "The Maltese Cat," in *The Day's Work* (London: Macmillan, 1898), 250.

4. *Ibid.* (London: Macmillan, 1955), 39.

5. Pedro F. Christophersen, *Teoría y Práctica del Juego de Polo* (Buenos Aires: Asociación Argentina de Polo, 1948), 288. This book was "the polo bible" for generations of Argentine poloists.

6. Jorge MacDonough, personal communication, March 2008.

7. R.S. Liddell, *The Memoirs of the Tenth Royal Hussars* (London: Longmans, Green and Co., 1891), Appendix, not paginated.

8. *The Polo Monthly*, June 1909. Quoted in Roger Chatterton-Newman, "Francis Herbert," *Profiles in Polo*, 28.

9. Lt. Col. Philip Walter Jules LeGallais (1861–1900), one of the best at number 3 in his time, died of wounds near Bothaville during the Anglo-Boer War. His death was a great loss to the British Army and to the game of polo.

10. T.B. Drybrough, *Polo* (London: Longmans and Co., 1906), Fig. 2.

11. The author is grateful to Santiago "Tato" Alvarez, master stick-maker, for sharing his knowledge of the polo mallet.

12. *PQ International*, Spring 2000, 58.

13. See table in *Polo Players Edition*, January 2004, 34.

14. Peter J. Rizzo, "Helmet Science," *Polo Players Edition*, January 2004, 32.

15. Hurlingham Polo Association *2007 Year Book*, 317.

16. E.D. Miller, *Fifty Years of Sport* (New York: E.P. Dutton and Co., no date [1925]), 91.

17. *The Polo Annual*, various editions.

18. Hurlingham P.C. and Hurlingham P.A. *Handicap List*, various editions.

19. Polo Association and U.S. P.A. *Handicap List*, various editions.

20. P.A. of the River Plate and A.A. de Polo *Handicap List*, various editions.

21. Polo Association and U.S. P.A. *Handicap List*, various editions.

22. P.A. of the River Plate and A.A. de Polo *Handicap List*, various editions.

23. Horace A. Laffaye, *The Polo Encyclopedia* (Jefferson, N.C.: McFarland and Co., 2004), 366. Unpublished data, 2008.

Chapter 23

1. Peter Vischer, "Professionalism in Polo," *Polo*, July 1933, 14. Peter Vischer (1898–1967) was editor of *Polo* magazine.

2. *The Sportsman*, January 1927, 3.

3. *Time*, 12 May 1930.

4. Vischer, 14.

5. *Ibid.*

6. Robert F. Kelley, "Sport Without Bickering," *Polo*, January, 1930, 7.

7. Herbert Spencer's "Global View," *Polo Times*, September 2007, 8.

8. "Review of the Season 2007," Hurlingham Polo Association, *Year Book 2008*, 4.

9. A.F. Harper, "The Pros and Cons of Pros," *Polo*, May 1985, 212.

10. For a biographical sketch of Kerry Packer see Chris Ashton, "Kerry Packer: Winning Whatever the Cost," *Profiles in Polo*, edited by Horace A. Laffaye (Jefferson, N.C.: McFarland and Co., 2007), 190.

11. William Loyd, "Postcards from England," *Polo Players Edition*, September 1993, 34.

12. Ashton, *Profiles in Polo*, 192.

13. Loyd, 34.

14. Paul Barry, *The Rise and Rise of Kerry Packer* (Moorebank, N.S.W.: Bantam Books, 1994), 425.

15. *Polo Times*, October 2005, 31.

16. Ashton, "Sinclair Hill: I'll Give You Fancy Pants!" *Profiles in Polo*, 154.

17. Sinclair Hill, O.B.E., personal communication, 15 January 2008.

18. From Mr. Harry Mudd, Letters to the Editor, *Polo Times*, 1 July 1998, 5.

19. Hurlingham Polo Association, *Year Book 2007*, 220.

Chapter 24

1. Allan Lamb, "Team Winners," in *Sporting Glory*, 262.

2. *Ibid.*

3. G.J. Younghusband, *Polo in India* (London and Calcutta: W.H. Allen and Co., 1890), 70.

4. *The New York Times*, 14 August 1910.

5. *Ibid.*, 16 July 1911, 9. The correct name is Earle Hopping, a future 10-goal handicap player.

6. *Ibid.*, 20 August 1916, xxi.

7. A biographical sketch of Eleonora Randolph Sears (1881–1968) is in Joanna Davenport, "Sears, Eleonora — U.S. Sportswoman," in *International Encyclopedia of Women Sports*, edited by Karen Kristensen, Allen Guttmann and Gertrude Pfister (New York: Macmillan Reference, 2001), 980.

8. A biography of Marion Hollins (1892–1944) is *Champion in a Man's World*, by David E. Outerbridge (Chelsea, Mich.: Sleeping Bear Press, 1998).

9. *The Polo Monthly*, May 1928, 110.

10. Marshall Sprague, *The Grizzlies: A History; The Cheyenne Mountain Country Club* (no place: The Club, 1983), 62.

11. Doreen Winifred Ashburnham (1905–1991), later Mrs. Sydney Ashburnham-Ruffner, was an 11-year-old schoolgirl at the time of the award of her Albert Medal. The decoration was exchanged for the George Cross in 1971. While walking to fetch their horses, carrying bridles with snaffle bits, Doreen and her 8-year-old cousin Anthony Farrer were attacked by a mountain lion on Vancouver Island, Canada. The children fended off the animal with their bridles, but sustained severe lacerations and Doreen herself, blood poisoning. Both survived their ordeal. Among the many letters she received, there was one from President Theodore Roosevelt, also a polo player. In the 1930s, Miss Ashburnham moved to California, where she learned flying. During the Second World War, she served as a ferry pilot.

12. U.S. Polo Association *1925 Year Book*, 116.

13. Quoted in *Sidelines*, 6 May 2000, 14.

14. U.S. Polo Association *1973 Year Book*, 153.

15. *The New York Times*, 5 May 2003.

16. "Lady Polo Players at Ranelagh," *The Bystander*, 26 July 1905, 172.

17. *The Polo Monthly*, July 1920, 321. On page 301, there is a photograph of Noëla Whiting in polo garb.

18. *Ibid.*, September 1920.

19. *Ibid.*, September 1921, 442.

20. *Ibid.*, August 1930, 464.

21. *Ibid.*, September 1931, 434.

22. County Polo Association, *Red Book 1937*, 42.

23. *The Polo Monthly*, August 1938, 17.

24. *Ibid.*, August 1938, 30.

25. *Ibid.*, August 1938, 13.

26. *Ibid.*, June 1939, 62.

27. For a biographical essay on Mrs. Tomlinson, see Yolanda Carslaw, "Claire Tomlinson: The Most Influential Lady Player," in *Profiles in Polo*, 206.

28. *Ibid.*, 209.

29. Peter Grace, *Polo* (New York: Howell, 1991), is one of the best instructional manuals ever written. Rangitiki took its name from Mr. Grace's club in Bulls, New Zealand, Rangitikei. It was founded in 1890 and the original field is still used for matches.

30. Chris Ashton, *Geebung: The Story of Australian Polo* (Sydney: Hamilton Publishing, 1993), 66.

31. *Ibid.*

32. Tony Rees, *The Galloping Game* (Cochrane, Alberta: Western Heritage, 2000), 207.

33. Suzanne Dabney Taylor, "Women Who Play Polo," *Polo*, December 1930, 18.

34. *The Polo Monthly*, June 1939, 62.

35. Rees, 275.

36. Donald C. McKenzie and John R. McKenzie, *A History of Polo in South Africa* (Dargle, KwaZulu-Natal: private printing, 1999), 25.

37. *Ibid.*, 407.

38. Norman J. Cinnamond, *El Polo* (Barcelona: Librería Catalonia, no date. [1929]), 177.

39. *Polo & Campo*, No. 53, 10.

40. A.A. de Polo, *Libro Anual 1937*, 204.

41. Annie Clement, "Law," in Karen Christensen, Allen Guttmann and Gertrude Pfister, *International Encyclopedia of Women and Sports* (New York: Macmillan, 2001), 653.

42. Sarah K. Fields, *Female Gladiators* (Champaign: Univ. of Illinois Press, 2005), 169.

43. Mrs. L. Black, "MCP's Beware," *The Polo Magazine*, July 1977, 22. The early career of Lt. Col. Alexander Forrest Harper, D.S.O. (1910–2003), took place in India, where he played for his regiment, the Royal Deccan Horse. In 1951 and 1953, he played for England in the Festival Cup and the Coronation Cup. Alec Harper was a three-time winner of Cowdray Park's Gold Cup, the Queen's Cup and the Gold Cup at Deauville. Lt. Col. Harper was honorary secretary of the Hurlingham Polo Association from 1971 until 1989. His letters to the editors of polo magazines make fascinating reading because of their lucidity and strong support of the game's best interests.

5. G.J. Younghusband, *Polo in India* (London and Calcutta: W.H. Allen, 1890), 23.

6. *Ibid.*, 85.

7. *Ibid.*, 86.

8. Sir Beauvoir de Lisle, *Polo in India* (Bombay: Thacker and Co., 1924, Third Edition), 152.

9. Robert Ricketts, "Strategy for High-Goal Polo," *Polo*, April 1929, 9.

10. *Ibid.*

11. Val ffrench-Blake, "Polo: Past and Present," *Polo Times*, August 2005, 25.

12. Earl of Kimberley, editor, *Polo* (London: Seeley, Service and Co., 1936). An American edition is published by J.B. Lippincott in Philadelphia.

13. For biographical information about Harry P. Whitney, see Nigel à Brassard, "Harry Payne Whitney: Total Polo," *Profiles in Polo*, edited by Horace A. Laffaye (Jefferson, N.C.: McFarland and Co., 2007), 42. The family history is described in Edwin Hoyt, *The Whitneys* (New York: Weybright and Talley, 1976).

14. James C. Cooley, "Whitney Wins!" *Polo*, January 1927, 15.

15. Herbert Reed, "Brains at Full Gallop," *The Sportsman*, September 1927, 51.

16. E.D. Miller, "The Effect of America on Modern Polo," *Polo*, June 1927, 15.

17. Walter Buckmaster, *Hints for Polo Combination* (London: Vinton and Co., no date [1909]).

18. *Ibid.*, 27.

19. Anonymous [W. Cameron Forbes], *A Manual of Polo* (Fort Stotsenburg, P.I.: 14th U.S. Cavalry Press, 1910).

20. William Cameron Forbes, *As to Polo* (Dedham Polo and Country Club, 1911).

21. Luis L. Lacey, "La equitación en el juego de polo," *Los Ranchos*, January 1943, 10.

22. For a biographical essay on Lacey see Horace A. Laffaye, "Lewis Lacey: Master of the Game," in *Profiles in Polo*, 67.

23. Excerpts of Mr. James H. Ashton's writings reprinted in Sinclair Hill, *Advanced Polo* (no place: private printing, no date), 18.

24. There is a biography of Hanut Singh written by Maj. J.N.P. Watson: *Hanut: Prince of Polo Players* (London: Sportsman's Press, 1995). See also, Ashton, "Rao Rajah Hanut Singh," in *Profiles in Polo*, 75.

25. Watson, 38.

26. Quintin Crewe, *The Last Maharaja*. London: Michael Joseph, 1985. 63.

27. Watson, 54.

Chapter 25

1. Allan Forbes, *Sport in Norfolk County* (Boston: Houghton, Mifflin, 1938), 60.

2. Rudyard Kipling, "The Maltese Cat" in *The Day's Work* (London: Macmillan, 1898), 163.

3. *British Hunts and Huntsmen: England (North), Scotland and Ireland)* (London: Biographical Press, 1911), 310.

4. Personal communication from Roger Chatterton-Newman, 25 March 2008.

Chapter 26

1. *Men, Machines and Sacred Cows* (London: Hamish Hamilton, 1984), 135.

2. Simon Barnes, *The Meaning of Sport* (London: Short Books, 2006), 18.

3. Indian Polo Association, *The Polo Calendar* (Meerut: Station Press, 1926), 1.

4. Rudyard Kipling, "The Maltese Cat" in *The Day's Work* (London: Macmillan, 1898), 242.

5. Allan Forbes, *Sport in Norfolk County* (Boston: Houghton Mifflin Co., 1938), 22.

6. "The Sportsman," *Polo and Coaching* (London: Sports and Sportsmen, Ltd., no date [1923]), 9.

7. *Polo: Match Play and Horsemastership in Singapore and Malaya* (Singapore Polo Club, 1967), 19.

8. Northrup R. Knox, *To B.A. and Back, Again* (Buffalo: private printing, no date [1967]), 42.

9. U.S. Polo Association *2007 Year Book*, 96.

10. Stephen Orthwein, "By the [Blue] Book: The Rule that Changed Polo 28 Years Ago," *Polo Players Edition*, July 2007, 42.

11. Alec Harper, "Some Inconsistencies in Field Rules of Polo," *Polo Times*, August 2001, 7.

12. Hurlingham Polo Association *2007 Year Book*, 331, fig. xxi, 364.

13. *Baily's*, August 1895, 107.

14. Robert Weir and J. Moray Brown, *Riding-Polo* (London: Longmans, Green and Co., 1891), 289.

15. "The Sportsman," 10.

16. *Polo Times*, June 2001, 10.

Chapter 27

1. Rudyard Kipling, "The Maltese Cat" in *The Day's Work* (London: Macmillan, 1898), 263.

2. T.F. Dale, *The Game of Polo* (Westminster: Archibald Constable and Co., 1897), 91.

3. "Need for Stricter Umpiring," *The Polo Monthly*, June 1928, 197.

4. Wesley J. White, *Guide for Polo Umpires* (New York: U.S.P.A., 1929).

5. Capt. Wesley J. White, *Polo*, December 1934, 23.

6. Allan Forbes, *Sport in Norfolk County* (Boston: Houghton, Mifflin, 1938), 2.

7. Geoff Tibballs, *Great Sporting Eccentrics* (London: Robson Books, 1990), 8.

8. Marty LeGrand, "A Gentleman's Game?" *Polo*, March 1994, 24.

9. Ed Scanlon, "Anatomy of an Assault," *Polo*, March 1994, 14.

10. LeGrand, *Polo*, March 1994, 35.

11. Red Armour, "Temper, Temper: It's Time to Blow the Whistle on Disrespect," *Polo*, April 1994, 62.

12. Tony Emerson, "The Argentine Open 2002," *Polo Times*, January-February 2003, 24.

13. Carlos Beer, "Umpiring Controversy in Argentina," *Polo Times*, May 2003, 22.

14. Gonzalo Tanoira, "Lo bueno y lo malo" (The Good and the Bad), *Centauros*, No. 131, 11.

15. "Ranelagh," "Umpires Shown the Red Card," *Polo Times*, November-December 2005, 4.

16. "Saltolín," "Entre Chukker y Chukker," *Polo & Equitación*, September 1928, 48.

17. H.P.A. Newsletter No. 262, reprinted in *Polo Times*, August 2004, 11.

18. Hurlingham Polo Association *Year Book 1999*, 143.

19. Yolanda Carslaw, "Stripes Under Scrutiny," *Polo Times*, September 2006, 28.

20. *Ibid.*

21. "Los referees en el banquillo" (The Umpires on Trial), *Polo en la Argentina*, November-December 1981, 24.

22. Chris Ashton: *Geebung: The Story of Australian Polo* (Sydney: Hamilton Publishing, 1993), 116.

23. *Ibid.*, 117.

24. "Marco," *Introduction to Umpiring* (London: R.N.P.A., 1937), 27.

25. *Ibid.*, 29.

26. Arthur Douglas-Nugent, "Keeping Control of the Game," *Polo Times*, September 2003, 8.

27. "A raíz de una crítica" (A Propos of a Criticism), *Polo & Equitación*, October 1928, 43.

28. Letter to the Executive Committee, A.A. de Polo, reprinted in *Polo & Equitación*, October 1928, 43.

29. *Ibid.*

30. *Ibid.*, 44.

31. "Cause Celebre in Argentina," *Polo*, September 1929, 20.

Chapter 28

1. E.Œ. Somerville and Martin Ross, "A Misdeal," in *Some Experiences of an Irish R.M.* (London: Longmans, Green and Co., 1903), 161. The cousins Edith Somerville (1858–1949) and Violet Martin (1862–1915) were novelists who depicted Irish society in their books and short stories.

2. Harry Adsit Bull, "Polo and the Equestrian East," *The Sportsman*, February 1931, 51.

3. H. de B. De Lisle, *Hints to Polo Players in India* (Bombay: Gymkana Printing Press, 1897), 17.

4. *Ibid.*, 30.

5. T.F. Dale, *Polo at Home and Abroad* (London: London and Counties Press, 1915), 120.

6. *Polo Pony Stud Book*, various editions.

7. *Ibid.*

8. *The National Polo Pony Stud Book*, Vol. 2, 1929, 13.

9. *Ibid.*, various editions.

10. Newell Bent, "The Circle V Polo Ranch," *Polo*, January 1928, [5].

11. U.S.P.A. *Year Book 1923*, 153.

12. T.B. Drybrough, *Polo* (London: Vinton and Co., 1898), 2nd edition, 366.

13. E.D. Miller, *Modern Polo* (London: W. Thacker and Co., 1896), 298.

14. Tony Rees, *The Galloping Game* (Cochrane, Alberta: Western Heritage, 2000), 167.

15. *Ibid.*, 169.

16. For additional information on the early development of the polo pony in Argentina, see F. Balfour, "Polo in Argentina," in T.F. Dale (editor), *Polo at Home and Abroad*, 182.

17. *Polo Pony Stud Book*, Vol. 4, London, 1897, xi.

18. *National Polo Pony Stud Book*, Vol. 1, 1925, [3].

19. The trophy was manufactured by Garrard and Co. in London. Willis Hartman, a player from the Fairfield Polo Club in Kansas, was inducted into the Polo Hall of Fame in 2007.

20. Guillermo L. Buchanan, "Evolución de la raza," in Asociación Argentina de Criadores de Caballos de Polo, *Anuario 2005* (Buenos Aires: The Association, 2006), 68.

21. *Ibid.*, 2006, 216.

22. Paul Green Kendall, *Polo Ponies: Their Training*

and Schooling (New York: Derrydale Press, 1933). Eugene V. Connett III (1891–1969) was a Princeton graduate who founded the Derrydale Press in 1927. It was a quality publishing firm dedicated to outdoors books which are much in demand today. The original Derrydale Press closed in 1941.

23. E. Grove Cullum, *Selection and Training of the Polo Pony* (New York: Charles Scribner's Sons, 1934).

Chapter 29

1. Col. Alec Harper, "Polo Virus," *PQ International*, Winter 1995, 52. Lt. Col. Alexander Forrest Harper, D.S.O. (1910–2003), international player and long-time secretary of the Hurlingham Polo Association.

2. Interview with Miguel Novillo Astrada, 19 April 2008.

3. Harper, "Polo Virus," 52.

4. "No Turning on the Ball," from Edgeworth Polo Club, Letter to the Editor, *Polo Times*, 1 April 1999, 7.

5. "Turning on the Ball," from Mr. Martin Trotter, *Polo Times*, 1 May 1999, 7.

6. Stephen Orthwein, *Polo Players Edition*, July 2007, 42.

7. Doug Brown, "The Three-minute Horse," Letters to the Editor, *Polo Times*, April 2005, 10.

8. Chris Ashton, in *Profiles in Polo*, edited by Horace A. Laffaye (Jefferson, N.C.: McFarland and Co., 2007), 153.

9. Letter from Mr. Jack L. Shelton to Mr. Guillermo Gracida, *The Morning Line*, 24 March 2007, 2.

10. Horace Laffaye, "Letter from America," *Polo Times*, June 2007, 12.

11. Hurlingham Polo Association, 2007 *Year Book*, 315.

12. U.S. Polo Association, 2008 *Year Book*, viii.

13. Gareth A. Davies, "Match Fixing," *Polo Times*, August 2004, 9.

14. Matías Dell'Anno, "Chapaleufú: Back on Top," *Polo Players Edition*, February 2002, 29.

15. Tony Emerson, "108° Argentine Open," *Polo Times*, January-February 2002, 17.

16. "The Maltese Cat," "British Polo," Letter to the Editor, *Polo Times*, September 2003, 14.

17. David Woodd, "British Polo," Letter to the Editor, *Polo Times*, October 2003, 13.

18. Herbert Spencer, "Meet Italy: Land of the Asado, Alpargatas, Yerba and Maté," *Polo Times*, June 2007, 46.

19. Peter J. Rizzo, "Drug Testing: Is There a Problem with Drugs in Polo?" *Polo Players Edition*, December 2004, 11. Mr. Rizzo is executive director of the U.S. Polo Association and a 6-goal player.

20. Red Armour, "Cracking Down on Drug Abuse," *Polo*, November 1985, 80.

21. *Ibid.*

22. Personal communication from Lester "Red" Armour, March 2008.

23. Tolbert S. Wilkinson, "Drug Testing in Polo," *Polo*, December 1985–January 1986, 78.

24. U.S.P.A. 2008 *Year Book*, viii.

25. Hurlingham Polo Association, *1994 Year Book*, 154.

26. Buff Crisp, "The H.P.A. on Human Doping," *PQ International*, Autumn 1993, 36.

27. *The World Sports Law Report*, quoted in *Polo Times*, November-December 2005, 13.

28. Arthur Douglas-Nugent, "Checks and Balances in Sport," *Ibid.*

29. T.P. McLean, *Polo: The Savile Cup; The First 100 Years* (Cambridge: New Zealand Polo Association, 1990), 66.

30. Steve Orthwein, *Polo Players Edition*, March 1995, 87.

Bibliography

Books

"Addison Geary" [Addison Geary Smith]. *Mallet and Hounds*. Buffalo: private printing, 1931.

Aflalo, F.G. [Frederick George]. *The Sportsman's Book for India*. London: Horace Marshall and Son, 1904.

Aldrich, Nelson W. [Wilmarth], Jr. *Tommy Hitchcock: An American Hero*. City unknown [Gaithersburg, Md.]: Fleet Street, 1984.

Alles, Jane P. *The History of the Philadelphia Country Club*. Wilmington, Del.: private printing, 1965.

Allison, Benjamin R. *The Rockaway Hunting Club*. Brattleboro, Vt.: private printing, 1952.

Anderson, F. [Fearnley]. *Hints on Polo*. Allahabad: Pioneer Press, 1921.

Archetti, Eduardo P. [Pedro]. *El potrero, la pista y el ring*. Buenos Aires: Fondo de Cultura Económica, 1999.

_____. *Masculinities: Football, Polo and the Tango in Argentina*. Oxford: Berg, 1999.

Arifi. *The Ball and the Polo Stick*. London: Luzac, 1932.

Ashton, Chris. *Geebung: The History of Australian Polo*. Sidney: Hamilton Publishing, 1993.

Asociación Argentina de Polo. *Campeonato Argentino Abierto de Polo*. Buenos Aires: A.A. de Polo, 1993.

Backhouse, Hugo. *Among the Gauchos*. London: Jarrolds, no date.

Barnes, Simon. *The Meaning of Sport*. London: Short Books, 2006.

Barrantes, Susan. *Polo*. Buenos Aires: Larivière, 1997.

Barry, Paul: *The Rise and Rise of Kerry Packer*. Morebank, N.S.W.: Bantam Books, 1994.

Beal, Carl. *Into Polo*. Midland, Texas: Prentis Publishing, 1993.

Bent, Newell. *American Polo*. New York: Macmillan, 1929.

Bishop, W. [William]. A. *History of the Scone Polo Club*. Wooton, Scone: private printing, 1982.

Boadle, Isabel Cárdenas de. *La historia del Hurlingham Club*. Buenos Aires: Ripolli, 1988.

Board, John. *Year with Horses*. London, Hodder and Stoughton, 1954.

_____. *Polo*. Woodstock, Vt.: Countryman Press, no date [1957].

à Brassard, Nigel. *A Glorious Victory, A Glorious Defeat*. Chippenham: Antony Rowe, 2001.

British Hunts and Huntsmen: England (North), Scotland and Ireland. London: Biographical Press, 1911.

Brooks Brothers. *Polo*. New York: private printing, 1927.

Brown, J. [James] Moray. *Polo*. London: Vinton, 1895.

Browning, Robert. *A History of Golf*. London: J.M. Dent and Sons, 1955.

Buchan, John: *Francis and Riversdale Grenfell*. London: Nelson, 1920.

Buckmaster, Walter. *Hints for Polo Combination*. London: Vinton, no date [1909].

Bustinza, Javier, editor. *Polo Around the World*. Buenos Aires: Editorial Traful, 2005.

Caillé, Yves. *Pau Golf Club: Le St. Andrews du Continent*. Pau: J & D Editions, 1990.

Calvert, Blair. *Cecil Smith: Mr. Polo*. Midland, Texas: Prentis Publishing, 1990.

Carreño, Virginia. *Estancias y estancieros*. Buenos Aires: Editorial Goncourt, 1991.

_____. *Estancias y estancieros del Río de la Plata*. Buenos Aires: Editorial Claridad, 1994.

Ceballos, Francisco. *El polo en la Argentina*. Buenos Aires: Dirección General de Remonta, 1968.

Chaine, Federico. *Los Heguy*. Buenos Aires: Imprenta de los Buenos Ayres, 2001.

Champ, Paul, F. de Bellet, A. Després, and F. [Franz] Caze de Caumont. *Lawn-tennis, Golf, Croquet, Polo*. Paris: Bibliothèque Larousse, no date [ca. 1895].

Chartier, Jean-Luc A. *Cent Ans de Polo en France*. Paris: Média France Editions, 1992.

_____. *Cent Ans de Polo en France*. Paris: Polo Club Editions, 1992.

Christensen, Karen, Allen Guttmann, and Gertrude Pfister. *International Encyclopedia of Women and Sports*. New York: Macmillan, 2001.

Christophersen, Pedro Fernando. *Teoría y práctica del juego de polo*. Buenos Aires: A.A. de Polo, 1948.

Cinnamond, Norman J. [James]. *El Polo*. Barcelona: Librería Catalonia, no date. [1929].

Citröen, Jacqueline, Janette Person, Arlette Sadoun and Chantal Bittan. *Les Cent Ans du Polo de Paris*. Paris: Editions Person, 1992.

Clendennig, Iris. *The History of the Montreal Polo Club*. Les Cèdres, Quebec: private printing, 1987.

Coaten, A.W. [Arthur Wells], editor. *International Polo*. London: S.B. Vaughn, 1912.

Coghlan, Eduardo A. [Aquilio]. *Los irlandeses en la Argentina*. Buenos Aires: Abraxas, 1987.

Cornish, Geoffrey S. [St. John], and Ronald E. [Edward] Whitten. *The Architects of Golf*. New York: HarperCollins, 1981.

County Polo Association. *The Training of Mount and Man for Polo*. London: County Polo Association, 1948.

The Courage Exhibition of National Trophies. *Sporting Glory*, London: Sporting Trophies Exhibition, 1992.

Cowley, Guillermo, and Alexandra de Wankowicz. *A Season of Polo*. Palm Beach: Citigroup Private Bank, 2002.

Crewe, Quintin: *The Last Maharaja*. London: Michael Joseph, 1985.

Cullum, Grove. *Selection and Training of the Polo Pony*. New York: Scribner's, 1934.

Dale, T.F. [Thomas Francis]. *The Game of Polo*. Westminster: Archibald Constable, 1897.

_____. *Riding and Polo Ponies*. London: Unwin, 1899.

_____. *Polo: Past and Present*. London: Country Life, 1905.

_____. *Polo at Home and Abroad*. London: London and Counties Press, 1915.

Danckwerts, Brian: *A Century of Polo in Rhodesia/Zimbabwe*. City unknown: private printing, 1995.

Daniels, John H. [Hancock]. *Nothing Could be Finer*. Camden, S.C.: Culler, 1996.

Dawnay, Hugh: *Polo Vision*. London: J.A. Allen, 1984.

_____. *Playmaker Polo*. London: J.A. Allen, 2004.

Deans, Alan: *Garangula's Polo Heritage*. Sydney: Hamilton Publishing, 1991.

De L'Isle, F. D'A.C. [Charles]. *The Adelaide Polo Club*. Adelaide: Mail Print, no date [1913].

De Lisle, H. de B. [Henry deBeauvoir]. *Hints to Polo Players in India*. Bombay: Gymkana Printing Press, 1897.

_____. *Polo in India*. Bombay: Thacker, 1907.

_____. *Tournament Polo*. New York: Scribner's, 1938.

_____. *Reminiscences of Sport and War*. London: Eyre and Spottiswoode, 1939.

Denny, H.T. *Polo of Course: A History of the Game in W.A.* Perth: private printing, 1997.

Devereux, W.B. [Walter Bourchier], Jr. *Position and Team Play in Polo*. New York: Brooks Bros., MCMXIV [sic] [1924].

Dhar, Maharaja of. *With Horses in India*. Bombay: Times Press, 1918.

Dickson, Pat. *The Inanda Club*. Pietermaritzburg, Natal: private printing, no date [1986].

Diem, Carl. *Asiatische Reiterspiele*. Berlin: Deutscher Archiv-Verlag, 1941.

Disston, Harry. *Beginning Polo*. New Brunswick: A.S. Barnes, 1973.

Dorling, Taprell. *The Hurlingham Club*. London: private printing, 1953.

Drybrough, T. [Thomas] B. *Polo*. London: Vinton, 1898.

Dunning, Eric, and Kenneth Sheard. *Barbarians, Gentlemen and Players*. New York: New York University Press, 1979.

Edinburgh, H.H.R. The Duke of. *Men, Machines, and Sacred Cows*. London: Hamish Hamilton, 1984.

Ellison, Gabriel, and Kim Fraser. *Harmony of Hooves*. City unknown: Natal Witness, 1999.

Ferguson, Ronald. *The Galloping Major*. London: Macmillan, 1994.

FitzPatrick, H.L. [Hugh Louis]. *Equestrian Polo*. New York: American Sports, 1904.

Forbes, Allan. *Sport in Norfolk County*. Boston: Houghton Mifflin, 1938.

Forbes, W. [William] Cameron. *As to Polo*. City unknown: Manila Polo Club, 1911.

14th U.S. Cavalry. *A Manual of Polo*. Camp Stotsenburg, Philippines Islands: private printing, 1910.

Freeman, William S. *History of Plymouth County, Iowa*. Indianapolis: B.F. Bowen, 1917.

French, Amos Tuck. *Harvard Polo Club*. New York: Knickerbocker Press, 1930.

Furth, Elizabeth. *Visions of Polo*. Addington, Buckinghamshire: Kenilworth Press, 2005.

Gannon, Jack. *Before the Colours Fade*. London: J.A. Allen, 1976.

Garrahan, María Lía, and Luis Garrahan, editors. *Polo: Abierto Argentino de Palermo*. Buenos Aires: Garrahan Editores, no date [2005].

Godfree, D.W. [Douglas William]. *Some Notes on Polo*. Newport, Isle of Wight: Blake, 1911.

Godley, Alexander. *Life of an Irish Soldier*. London: John Murray, 1939.

Grace, Peter. *Polo*. New York: Howell, 1991.

Graham-Yooll, Andrew. *The Forgotten Colony*. Buenos Aires: Literature of Latin America, 1999.

Griswold, F. [Frank] Gray. *The International Polo Cup*. New York: Dutton's, 1928.

Guest, Capt. Freddie [Reginald E.]. *Indian Cavalryman*. London: Jarrolds, 1959.

Halpin, Warren T. *Hoofbeats*. Philadelphia: Lippincott, 1938.

Harper, Alec. *Horse and Foot*. Petergat: Quack Books, 1995.

Harrington, Isabel H. [Hope] de. *Un criollo irlandés*. Buenos Aires: private printing, 1976.

Hatch, Alden, and Foxhall Keene. *Full Tilt*. New York: Derrydale Press, 1938.

Heguy, Alberto Pedro, and Daniel Martínez Páez. *Biomecánica, estrategia, preparación competitiva y lesions del polo de alto handicap argentino*. Buenos Aires: Fundación de Polo y Entrenamiento Integral, 1994.

Hennessy, Alastair, and John King. *The Land That England Lost*. London: British Academic Press, 1992.

Hennessy, Elizabeth. *A History of the Roehampton Club*. City unknown: private printing, 2001.

Heron, Roy. *The Sporting Art of Cecil Aldin*. London: Sportsman Press, 1990.

Hill, Sinclair. *Polo*. Alexandria, N.S.W.: M.S. Simpson and Sons, no date [1963].

_____. *Advanced Polo*. City unknown: private printing, no date.

Hobson, G.W. [Gerald Walton]. *Ideas on Breaking Ponies*. City unknown: private printing, 1927.

_____. *Some XII Royal Lancers*. Long Compton, Shipston-on Stour: King's Stone Press, 1936.

Hobson, Richard. *Polo and Ponies*. London: J.A. Allen, 1976.

_____. *Riding: The Game of Polo*. London: J.A. Allen, 1993.

Holder, Denzil. *Hindu Horseman*. Chippenham: Picton Publishing, 1986.

Hoyt, Edwin. *The Whitneys*. New York: Weybright and Talley, 1976.

The Hurlingham Club. *The Hurlingham Club: The Ju-*

bilee of Polo, 1874–1924. London: private printing, 1924.

Hutton, Wendy. *The Singapore Polo Club*. Girdwood, 1983.

Ira, Luning Bonifacio. *Manila Polo Club*. City unknown: private printing, 1984.

Jarman, Colin (compiler). *The Guinness Dictionary of Sports Quotations*. Enfield, Middlesex: Guinness Publishing, 1990.

Kelley, Robert F. *The Year Book of the Horse 1934*. New York: Dodd, Mead, 1935.

Kendall, Paul Green. *Polo Ponies*. New York: Derrydale Press, 1933.

Keyes, Elizabeth. *Geoffrey Keyes*. London: George Newnes, 1956.

Kimberley, Earl of (editor). *Polo*. London: Seeley, Service, 1936.

King, Bucky. *Big Horn Polo*. Sheridan, Wyoming: Still Sailing, 1987.

Kipling, Rudyard. "The Maltese Cat" in *The Day's Work*. London: Macmillan, 1898.

Knox, Northrup R. [Rand]: *To B.A. and Back, Again*. Buffalo: private printing, no date [1967].

_____. *To B.A. Once More*. City unknown: private printing, no date [1970].

Knox, Seymour H. [Horace]. *To B.A. and Back*. Buffalo: private printing, 1933.

_____. *Aurora at Oak Brook*. City unknown: private printing, no date [1969].

Korol, Juan Carlos, and Hilda Sábato: *Como fue la inmigración irlandesa en la Argentina*. Buenos Aires: Editorial Plus Ultra, 1981.

Laffaye, Horace A. [Albert]. *El polo internacional argentino*. Buenos Aires: Edición del Autor, 1988.

_____. *The Polo Encyclopedia*. Jefferson, N.C.: McFarland, 2004.

_____, editor. *Profiles in Polo: The Players Who Changed the Game*. Jefferson, N.C.: McFarland, 2007.

Latzina, Francisco. *Diccionario Geográfico Argentino*. Buenos Aires: Editorial Ramón Espasa and Cia., 1891.

Layton, Elizabeth Y. [Yerxa]. *The Golden Mallet*. Kauai, Hawaii: Grey Lady Publishing, 2003.

Levinson, David, and Karen Christensen. *Encyclopedia of World Sport*. Santa Barbara: ABC-Clio, 1996.

Liddell, R.S. [Robert Spencer]. *The Memoirs of the Tenth Royal Hussars*. London: Longmans, Green, 1891.

Little, K.M. [Keith Melvyn]. *Polo in New Zealand*. Wellington: Whitcombe and Tombs, 1956.

Lloyd, John. *The Pimm's Book of Polo*. North Pomfret, Vt.: Trafalgar, 1989.

"A Lover of the Game." [Roland William Wrigley Grimshaw] *Letters on Polo in India*. Calcutta: Thacker, Spink, 1918.

Loyola Brandão, Ignácio de. *Pólo Brasil*. São Paulo: 1992.

Lubash, Robert D. *Polo Wisdom*. City unknown: Jostens, 2003.

"Lucifer" [Hugh Stewart]. *Station Polo*. Calcutta: Thacker, Spink, 1896.

MacMunn, G.F. [George Fletcher]. *The Armies of India*. London: Adam and Charles Black, 1911.

Macnie, J. [John]. *Work and Play in the Argentine*. London: T. Werner Laurie, no date [1924].

Makin, Gene. *A History of Queensland Polo*. Toowooma: private printing, 1999.

Mallon, Bill. *The 1900 Olympic Games*. Jefferson, N.C.: McFarland, 2000.

_____, and Anthony Th. Bijkerk. *The 1920 Olympic Games*. Jefferson, N.C.: McFarland, 2000.

_____, and Ian Buchanan. *The 1908 Olympic Games*. Jefferson, N.C.: McFarland, 2002.

Mangan, J.A. [John] *Pleasure, Profit, Proselitism, British Culture and Sport at Home and Abroad*. London: Frank Cass, 1996.

"Marco" [Earl Mountbatten of Burma]. *An Introduction to Polo*. London: Country Life, 1931.

_____. *An Introduction to Umpiring*. City unknown: R.N.P.A., 1934.

Martínez Castro, Elsa Boglione de. *100 años de polo en la Argentina*. City unknown: Edipubli, 1988.

Mason, Philip [Philip Woodruff]. *A Matter of Honour*. New York: Holt, Rinehart and Winston, 1974.

McKenzie, Donald C., and John R. McKenzie. *A History of Polo in South Africa*. Dargle, KwaZulu-Natal: private printing, 1999.

McLean, T.P. [Sir Terence Power]. *Polo: The Savile Cup; The First 100 Years*. Cambridge: New Zealand Polo Association, 1990.

McMichael, E.H. [Edward Herrick]. *Polo on the China Pony*. Shanghai: Mercantile, 1931.

Melvill, T.P. [Teignmouth Philip]. *Ponies and Women*. London: Jarrolds, 1932.

Mihanovich, Iván: *Polo in Synthesis*. Avellaneda: Gráfico Litteram, 1993.

Milburn, Frank. *The Emperor of Games*. New York: Knopf, 1994.

Miller, B. [Benjamin]. *An American Polo Club: A Study of Leisure Activity as a Process of Production and Consumption, and as a Mechanism for the Maintenance and Enhancement of Elite Status*. Philadelphia: Unpublished thesis, Temple University, 1977.

Miller, E.D. [Edward Darley]. *Modern Polo*. London: W. Thacker, 1896.

_____. *Fifty Years of Sport*. N.Y.: Dutton, no date [1925].

Miskin, Nigel. *History of Hurlingham*. City unknown: private printing, 2000.

Mitchell, Sally. *The Dictionary of British Equestrian Artists*. Woodbridge, Suffolk: Antique Collectors Club, 1985.

Mori, Mika. *Polo: Its History and Spirit*. Tokyo: Asahi Shimbu, 1997.

Olivera, Eduardo A. *Orígenes de los deportes brtánicos en el Río de la Plata*. Buenos Aires: Talleres Gráficos Argentinos L.J. Rosso, 1932.

Ortigüela, Raúl. *Raíces Celtas*. Córdoba: Alejandro Graziani, 1998.

Outerbridge, David E.: *Champion in a Man's World: The Biography of Marion Hollins*. Chelsea, Mich.: Sleeping Bear Press, 1998.

"P.O.V." [Wilmot Gordon Hilton Vickers]. *Practical Polo*. Calcutta: Thacker, Spink, 1931.

Parker, G.A. *South African Sports*. London: Sampson Low, Marston, 1897.

Patten, William. *The Book of Sport*. New York: J.F. Taylor, 1901.

Paterson, A.B. [Andrew Barton] "Banjo." *The Geebung Polo Club*. West Heidelberg, Victoria: Dorr/McLeod Publishing, 1984.

Pearce, J.J. [James Joseph]. *Everybody's Polo*. London: Robert Hale, 1949.

Popham, E.L. [Edward Leyborne]. *Polo Notes*. Poona: Scottish Mission Industries, 1908.

Raffo, Víctor. *El origen británico del deporte argentino*. Buenos Aires: private printing, 2004.

Ramsay, F.W. [Frank William]. *Polo Pony Training with Some Hints on the Game*. Aldershot: Gale and Polden, 1928.

Rees, Tony. *The Galloping Game*. Cochrane, Alberta: Western Heritage, 2000.

Rice, Geoffrey W. *Heaton Rhodes of Otahuna*. Canterbury, N.Z.: University Press, 2001,

Ricketts, R.L. [Robert Lumsden]. *First Class Polo*. Aldershot: Gale and Polden, 1928.

Rodríguez Egaña, Carlos. *Manual de Polo*. Buenos Aires: Bernard Buttafoco, 1923.

Russell-Stoneham, Derek, and Roger Chatterton-Newman. *Polo at Cowdray*. London: Polo Information Bureau, 1992.

St. Quintin, T.A. [Thomas Astell] *Chances of Sports of Sorts*. Edinburgh: William Blackwood and Sons, 1912.

Schiavo, Horacio. *Palermo de San Benito*. Buenos Aires: Municipalidad de la Ciudad de Buenos Aires, 1969.

Secretaría de Turismo de la Argentina. *Argentina: Polo and Golf*. City unknown: Delfos, 1994.

Sessa, Aldo: *Polo Argentino*. Buenos Aires: Sessa Editores, 2001.

Shackleford, Geoff. *The Riviera Country Club*. City unknown: private printing, 1995.

Shaw, Elvira Ocampo de. *Hurlingham*. Buenos Aires: Casa Impresora Francisco A. Colombo, 1958.

Shensi Provincial Museum. *Les Peintures Murales du Tombeau de Li Hsien de la Dynastie des Tangs*. Peking: Editions Wengu, 1974.

Sheppard, E.W. [Eric William]: *The Ninth Queen's Royal Lancers*. Aldershot: Gale and Polden, 1939.

Sherley, Anthony. *The Three Brothers; or, the Travels and Adventures of Sir Anthony, Sir Robert, & Sir Thomas Sherley, in Persia, Russia, Turkey, Spain, etc. With Portraits*. London: Hurst, Robinson, 1825 [Elibron Classics reprint of the original edition].

Shinitzky, Ami, and Don Follmer. *The Endless Chukker*. Gaithersburg, Md.: Polo, 1978.

Singapore Polo Club. *Polo: Match Play and Horsemastership in Singapore and Malaya*. City unknown: private printing, 1967.

Singh, Jaisal. *Polo in India*. London: New Holland Publishers, 2007.

Singh, Sarina. *Polo in India*. New Delhi: Lustre Press, 2000.

"Snaffle-Caveson" and "Standing-Martingale." *How to Make a Polo-Pony*. Allahabad: Pioneer Press, 1922.

Sorondo, Miguel. *Procedencia del nombre de Palermo*. Buenos Aires: Peuser, 1939.

Spencer, Herbert. *Chakkar: Polo Around the World*. New York: Drake, 1971.

_____. *A Century of Polo*. City unknown: World Polo Associates, 1994.

"The Sportsman." *Polo and Coaching*. London: Sports and Sportsmen, no date [1923].

Sprague, Marshall. *The Grizzlies—A History: The Cheyenne Mountain Country Club*. City unknown: The Club, 1983.

Stock, Alphons. *Polo: International Sport*. London: Universal Bridge of Trade, no date [1930].

Strutt, Joseph. *Sports and Pastimes of the People of England*. London, T. Bensley, 1816 (second edition).

Suffolk, Earl of, Hedley Peek, and F.G. [Frederick George] Aflalo. *The Encyclopedia of Sport*. New York: G.P. Putnam, 1897.

Take-Eddin-Ahmed-Makrizi. *History of the Mameluke Sultans*, translated by E.M. Quatremère. Paris: 1837.

Tibballs, Geoff. *Great Sporting Eccentrics*. London: Roboson Books, 1997.

Traill, J. [John]. *The Long Chukker*. City unknown: private printing, no date.

Tucoo-Chala, Pierre, editor. *Histoire de Pau*. Toulouse: Editions Private, 1989.

Tylden-Wright, W.R. [Watterton Royds]. *Notes on Polo*. London: Butterworth, 1927.

Van Der Zee, Jacob. *The British in Iowa*. Iowa City: Historical Society of Iowa, 1922.

Viana, Marqués de. *De la posición y forma de jugar un team en el polo*. Madrid: Imprenta Lacau, 1928.

Villavieja, Marqués de. *Life Has Been Good*. London: Chatto and Windus, 1938.

Wallechinsky, David. *The Complete Book of the Olympics*. New York: Penguin Books, 1988.

Watson, J.N.P. [John Norman Pembroke]. *The World of Polo*. Topsfield: Salem, 1986.

_____. *A Concise Guide to Polo*. North Pomfret, Vt.: Trafalgar, 1989.

_____. *Hanut: Prince of Polo Players*. London: Sportsman's Press, 1995.

_____. *Smith's Lawn: A History of Guards Polo Club 1955–2005*. Wykey, Shrewsbury: Quiller Press, 2005.

Weeks, Edward. *Myopia*. Hamilton, Mass.: private printing, 1976.

Weir, Robert, and J. [James] Moray Brown. *Riding: Polo*. London: Longmans, Green, 1891.

Welcome, John, and Rupert Collens. *Snaffles*. London: Stanley Paul, 1988.

Wheatley, Henry B., editor. *The Diary of Samuel Pepys*. Boston: C.C. Brainard, 1898.

White, Wesley J. *Guide for Polo Umpires*. New York: U.S.P.A., 1929.

Willans, Derek: *The Trails of Argentina*. City unknown: private printing, 1993.

Williams, G. [Glyn]. *The Welsh in Patagonia*. Cardiff: University of Wales Press, 1991.

Wilson, Hamish. *Polo in New Zealand 1956–1976*. Auckland: Viking, 1976.

Wingfield, Mary Ann. *Sport and the Artist*. Woodbridge, Suffolk: Antique Collectors' Club, 1988.

_____. *A Dictionary of Sporting Artists*. Woodbridge, Suffolk: Antiques Collectors' Club, 1992.

Young, H.P. [Henry Pottinger]. *Hints on Sport: Also a Few Practical Suggestions on Polo*. Leamington: private printing, 1907.

Younghusband, G.J. [George John]. *Polo in India*. London and Calcutta: W.H. Allen, 1890.

Annuals and Year Books

Asociación Argentina de Criadores de Caballos de Polo. *Anuario*. Buenos Aires, 1988–2007.

Asociación Argentina de Polo. *Libro Anual*. Buenos Aires, 1924–1980.

_____. *Centauros*. Buenos Aires, 2002–2006.

County Polo Association. *Rules and the Official Handicap*. London: private printing, 1926–1939.

The Horseman's Year. London: Collins, 1952–1960.

Hurlingham Polo Association Year Book. London; Billingshurst, Sussex; Midhurst, Sussex; Kirtlington, Oxfordshire; Little Coxwell, Oxfordshire, 1951–2007.

Malayan Polo Association. *1955 Handbook, 1958 Supplement*. Singapore: Craftsman Press, 1955.

The Polo Association Year Book. New York, 1890–1922.

Polo de Paris. Suresnes, 1956–2004.

The Polo Year Book. London, 1928–1937.

Reisse, Vicente J. *Anuario Argentino de Polo*. Buenos Aires, 1927.

Simmonds, L.V.L., and E.D. Miller. *The Polo Annual*. London, 1913.

Spalding's Polo Guide. New York, 1921–1923.

U.S. Polo Association Year Book. New York, Oak Brook, Ill., and Lexington, Ky., 1923–2008.

Magazines and Newspapers

Badminton Magazine. London, 1898–1905.

Baily's Magazine of Sports and Pastimes. London, 1875–1915.

El Caballo. Buenos Aires, 1949–1989.

Centauros. Buenos Aires, 1955–1983.

The Field. London, 1869.

El Gráfico. Buenos Aires, 1924–2007.

Harvard Journal of Asiatic Studies. Cambridge, Mass., 1983.

Horse and Horseman. New York, 1936–1938

International Journal of Sport. London, 2001–2003.

The Le Mars Sentinel. Le Mars, 1878–1887.

The London Gazette. London, 1845–2007.

Los Ranchos. Buenos Aires, 1942–1943.

Polo. New York, 1927–1936.

Polo. Gaithersburg, Md. and Wellington, Fla., 1972–1996.

The Polo Magazine. Woolhampton, Berkshire, 1977–1979.

The Polo Monthly. London, 1909–1939.

Polo Players Diary. London, 1910.

Polo Players Edition. Wellington, Fla., 1997–2008.

Polo Players Guide and Almanack. London, 1910–1912.

Polo Quarterly International. London, 1992–2008.

Polo Times. North Leigh, Oxfordshire, 1993–2008.

Polo & Campo. Buenos Aires, 1933–1939.

Polo & Equitación. Buenos Aires, 1924–1932.

River Plate Sport and Pastime. Buenos Aires, 1892–1902.

Sidelines. Wellington, Fla., 1974–2007.

The Sportsman. Concord, N.H., 1927–1938.

Index

Numbers in *italics* indicate pages with black and white illustrations.
Numbers in ***bold italics*** indicate pages with color illustrations.